Unfolding Consciousness

Exploring the Living Universe and Intelligent Powers in Nature and Humans

Volume III
Gazing Through the Telescope –
Man is the Measure of All Things

EDI BILIMORIA, DPhil, FIMechE, FEI, FRSA

SHEPHEARD
WALWYN
PUBLISHERS

First published in 2022 by Shepherd-Walwyn (Publishers) Ltd
107 Parkway House, Sheen Lane, London SW14 8LS
www.shepheardwalwyn.com
www.ethicaleconomics.org.uk

British Library Cataloguing in Publication Data
A catalogue record of this book is available from the British Library

ISBN: 978-08-5683-538-4

Copyedit by Elizabeth Medler
Typeset by Ian Wileman

Printed and bound through
s|s|media limited, Rickmansworth, Hertfordshire

Outline Contents for the Four Volumes

Detailed Contents for Volume III

List of Illustrations and Tables for Volume III

Figures

Tables

Abbreviations

CW-'Volume number'	*The Collected Writings* – in Fifteen Volumes by H. P. Blavatsky, compiled by Boris de Zirkoff: Volumes I to VI, The Theosophical Publishing House, Wheaton, Illinois, US, 1988 (Third Edition) to 1975 (Second Edition); Volumes VII to XV, The Theosophical Publishing House, Adyar, Madras, India, 1975 (Second Edition) to 1991.
IU-'Volume number'	*Isis Unveiled* – Two Volume Set by H. P. Blavatsky, edited by Boris de Zirkoff, The Theosophical Publishing House, First Quest Edition, 1994.
KT	*The Key to Theosophy* by H. P. Blavatsky, Theosophical Publishing House, London, 1968.
ML	*The Mahatma Letters to A. P. Sinnett* (in chronological sequence), compiled, numbered, arranged, and annotated by Virginia Hanson, The Theosophical Publishing House, Adyar, First Edition, 1998.
NPB-'Volume number'	*The Notebooks of Paul Brunton* – in Sixteen Volumes by Paul Brunton, Larson Publications, for Paul Brunton Philosophic Foundation, 1984 to 1988.
SD-'Volume number'	*The Secret Doctrine* – Three Volume Set by H. P. Blavatsky, edited by Boris de Zirkoff, The Theosophical Publishing House, First Quest Edition, 1993.
STA	*The Secret Teachings of All Ages* by Manly P. Hall, Diamond Jubilee Edition, Los Angeles, Philosophical Research Society, 1988.
TSGLOSS	Theosophical Glossary by H. P. Blavatsky, Theosophical Publishing Society, 1892.
VS	*The Voice of the Silence* by H. P. Blavatsky, introductory by Boris de Zirkoff, The Theosophical Publishing House, Second Quest Edition, 1992.

For example, *CW*-XII means *The Collected Writings*, Volume XII.
Likewise, for *IU*-, *NPB*-, and *SD*-

What is Life?

The NASA definition of life,
'Life is a self-sustaining chemical system capable of Darwinian evolution'
and considered the specific features of the one life we know—Terran life.

NASA Astrobiology Mailing List, 19 November, 2021

Everything in the Universe, throughout all its kingdoms, is conscious: i.e., endowed with a consciousness of its own kind and on its own plane of perception. We men must remember that because we do not perceive any signs—which we can recognise—of consciousness, say, in stones, we have no right to say that no consciousness exists there. There is no such thing as either 'dead' or 'blind' matter, as there is no 'Blind' or 'Unconscious' Law. These find no place among the conceptions of Occult philosophy. The latter never stops at surface appearances, and for it the noumenal essences have more reality than their objective counterparts … the Universals that were the realities and the particulars which existed only in name and human fancy.

H. P. Blavatsky, The Secret Doctrine

Preamble:
MAN, a Miniature Universe –
a Mirror of Cosmos

ὁ ... ἀνεξέταστος βίος οὐ βιωτὸς ἀνθρώπῳ
(The unexamined life is not worth living)

SOCRATES[1]

– the famous maxim apparently uttered by Socrates at his trial for impiety for which he was subsequently sentenced to death.

Having arrived this far and sustained the journey, it is as well to take stock and reflect over the large tracts of sometimes difficult territory traversed. Few amongst us would argue about the fact that human beings are the most complex creatures on Earth. There are numerous internal and external pressures as well as multiple inner and outer voices constantly demanding attention, along with ingrained habits that continually propel people from one sensation to another, from one thought to the next, and from opinion to judgement. The predominant feature of the conventional world-view of reality seems to be a constant oscillation between the poles of duality, resulting in habitual thoughts and actions.

Self enquiry is of paramount importance

For these reasons, we opened the first Chapter in Volume I of this work by posing that most difficult of all questions: *Who, or What Am I?* Throughout the ages, mystics and poets have captured the essence of this enquiry and sought its resolution with varying degrees of success. Reference was made to John Masefield's acute reflections that man could not be just a 'thing of watery salt' and his equally apposite words, 'Myself unwitting where Their Master dwells [...] the atoning Lord, Here in the flesh, the never yet explored.' However, with rare exceptions, the viewpoint of mainstream science, and therefore of society in general, fuelled by the popular media, is that man is indeed a 'thing of watery salt', or stated differently and more 'scientifically', man is a biological machine topped by another physico-chemical mechanism known as the brain, which is the sole organ responsible for all sentient life and consciousness by a process that science itself admits is still most imperfectly understood. However, there is no question of a 'Master' or 'atoning Lord'.

The main purpose of Volume I was, therefore, to demonstrate the compound nature of man. This was accomplished in two very different ways. First, by explicating the deficiencies in the mainstream scientific paradigm followed by specific areas where the machine-paradigm is coming under increasing criticism from within the scientific camp itself, owing to the inability to explain phenomena like telepathy, near-death experiences, out-of-body experiences, and a host of other veridical experiences, on the basis of the known laws of physics and chemistry. Then, by recourse to the Mystery Teachings of all ages and climes that have affirmed man's terrestrial nature to be essentially immortal spirit expressing and working through mortal bodies, or vestures. The transcendent vision of the great teachers has confirmed the truth of the perennial teachings that there is another way to see and

Mystery Teachings resolve scientific conundrums

experience the world, another vision that exceeds habitual concepts. Awareness of these conditioned responses of establishment science and orthodox religion is the first step in breaking our bondage to them.

In Volume II, our approach was microscopic: an in-depth examination of man's constitution and nature in order to explain the compound nature of his being and detail the immortal and mortal components of his complex makeup. A major objective was to demonstrate that consciousness is not generated by the brain; nor is consciousness solely dependent on the physical body and brain, but subsists after the death of the latter as substantiated in the occult philosophies of widely different cultures from antiquity to the present.

In-depth and
universal
perspectives are
both necessary

In Volume III our approach will be telescopic: seeing the universal picture of man within the grand scheme of Cosmos and Nature. The prime objective is to show that man is indeed a miniature universe and a mirror of cosmos, in that all the forces and powers in nature have their correlate in him. The philosophers of antiquity realized that man himself was the key to the riddle of life, for he was the living image of the Divine Plan. Therefore, as the pre-Socratic Greek philosopher Protagoras (490–420 BC) wrote, *Man is the Measure of All Things*.

But for such an undertaking, we have to be quite clear about the fact that what we experience depends on our state of consciousness. This begs the question: *what is the sensitivity and purity of the instruments of perception; in other words, through which 'eyes' are we looking?*

Instruments of Perception

What is the one central factor that clouds a person's awareness and discernment of the deeper realms of existence? It is not difficult to identify. Materialism is a contributory factor but not the central one, which is, quite simply, worldly weariness. Excessive involvement and engagement with the material world, over and beyond the natural requirements of physical life, induces that inner fatigue of mind that dulls sensitivity and sensibility, and clouds perception. Fuelled by the Internet, we live in an age where it becomes increasingly difficult to discern wisdom from the tsunami of knowledge produced by avalanches of data. As a corollary to this, 'alternative truth' (a virtual reality of truth, perhaps?)—an adulteration of truth in contemporary politics—seems bound to infiltrate other areas of life.

Some three quarters of a century ago, the American-English poet, playwright, and esotericist T. S. Eliot (1888–1965) lamented the drowning of wisdom in a sea of knowledge:

> Knowledge of speech, but not of silence;
> Knowledge of words, and ignorance of the Word.
> All our knowledge brings us nearer to death,
> But nearness to death no nearer to God.
> Where is the Life we have lost in living?
> Where is the wisdom we have lost in knowledge?
> Where is the knowledge we have lost in information?
> The cycles of heaven in twenty centuries
> Brings us farther from God and nearer to the Dust.[2]

The sea of knowledge that Eliot bemoaned would have been a mere garden pond of knowledge in comparison to what it is now. In fact, as far back as the eighteenth century, the

English Romantic poet William Wordsworth (1770–1850) captured this same sense of the human dilemma through excessive worldly cares when he wrote:

> The world is too much with us; late and soon,
> Getting and spending, we lay waste our powers;—
> Little we see in Nature that is ours.[3]

In his time the invasive pressures of 'the world' were of course the burgeoning Industrial Revolution that was transforming the age-old social, economic, and political structures in Britain. But with that remarkable prescience of a mystical poet, Wordsworth foresaw the ongoing pattern whereby excessive technology was slowly, but inexorably, eating into the human spirit and 'roboticizing' the human being of flesh and blood. The world is nowadays awash with data, information, and knowledge. This is the conventional outlook on education in schools and universities. Yet what is needed more urgently than ever are transformational learning processes that empower people to engage in personal transformation leading to wisdom that provides the rudder to navigate skilfully through the current changeable and unsettling times.

Whether it is the overriding concern over making money, then how best to invest it and spend it, or providing for physical needs or the bane of modern life—coping with a daily barrage of e-mails and deleting innumerable frivolous social media texts—attention is absorbed and trapped by needy involvement with the external circumstances of the outer world. What energy and inner space is then left for the demands of the inner world and the inner life? It is but natural that in order to deal with the affairs of the world we need to look through worldly eyes, the eyes of flesh, so to say. But that vision can only show things of flesh. Can sight using the eyes of flesh reveal the things of spirit? Let the *philosophia perennis* speak for itself in this regard.

Clearly, alluding to the fact that what a man understands depends on his state of consciousness, the Christ states: 'Those who live according to the flesh have their minds set on what the flesh desires; but those who live in accordance with the Spirit have their minds set on what the Spirit desires.'[4] The problem with those who ask questions of the spirit, but look through the eyes of flesh is what faced the Pharisee Nicodemus when he tried to fathom the secrets of the Christ's miracles. For that reason, spoke the Christ: 'Though seeing, they do not see; though hearing, they do not hear or understand.'[5] There is a subtle, but enormous, distinction between seeing and looking (observing); between hearing and listening. This confirms the validity of the well-known dictum that blindness is not just an unfortunate loss of physical sight, but also, 'there are none so blind as those who *will not see*.'

Naturally, then, the level of consciousness depends entirely on the sensitivity of the instruments of perception (the inner eyes and ears). In the crisp words of the English poet, painter, and printmaker, William Blake (1757–1827):

> If the doors of perception were
> cleansed everything would appear to
> man as it is, infinite.

> For man has closed himself up, till
> he sees all things through narrow
> chinks of his cavern.[6]

T. S. Eliot and William Wordsworth lament the common human condition

The excessive demands of worldly existence

Discerning outer and inner blindness and deafness

William Blake on sensitivity of the senses

In passing, the current fascination with psychedelic drugs to achieve altered states of consciousness, entirely mistaken for spirituality, is about the best, surest, and quickest way to sully the 'doors of perception'. This will be expanded at length later.

Note the words: 'narrow chinks of his cavern', which echoes the lesson of Plato's Cave (see Endnote III-6, page 378) about not confusing shadows with reality; and 'as it is, Infinite', in other words, not as *māyā*, but reality-in-itself. This means, surely, that there is something which lies beyond the duality and ephemeral nature of everyday life. Though the experience of it may be feeble for the majority of people, yet the dim remembrance still persists on the periphery of awareness, awaiting those moments when the chinks of the cavern widen, whereupon illusory attachment weakens. During those instants it makes its presence known in a brightened perception of the present moment. So different are such momentary experiences from the dreary norm that they become the touchstones of our life's direction. In the words of the French philosophical writer Albert Camus (1913–1960): 'In the depths of winter, I finally learned that within me there lay an invincible summer.'[7] Illusion and reality are the twin strands that weave the fabric of our earthly existence.

The prevailing quality of our forays into reality is a sense of expansion and connection. Just as space seems to divide, but in reality, it connects, defines, and pervades all things, so also, we live, move, and have our being within that consciousness, which not only unites, but is Unity itself. The more profound the experience, the deeper the awareness of an all pervading, undivided consciousness.

A 'Knew' Way of Knowing – A New Way of Looking

Readers are entitled to ask, 'but how are we to know all about the complex, invisible realms of being that no physical instruments can penetrate?' The answer lies in the following factors, considered collectively, drawn from Volume I: in Chapter 6 in relation to the 'geography' of a new continent of thought; and from Chapter 8, especially Table I-2, page 255, which summarized the contrasting, yet complementary, ways of investigating nature and man by science and occult science:

Accordingly, a 'knew' way of knowing is attained—

1. not by a scientific laboratory experiment or an intellectual concept, both of which are useless for this sort of inner enquiry and research;

    …instead by…

2. the accumulated, independent testimony of generations of seers, sages, and occultists of all epochs and religions—from the East and the West—who have divulged the language of the Mysteries and the keys to wisdom through the unfolding of the appropriate instruments of investigation for this purpose, namely, the unfolded faculties and capacities of consciousness;

    …which make evident…

3. consistency and self-consistency with every department of visible–observable and invisible nature;

    …attained through…

4. strenuous personal reflection by dedicated students of the *philosophia perennis* for innumerable decades with no ulterior motive or internal bias;

   …that have shown the…

5. corroboration of the occult tenets with the facts and experience of life, i.e., by experimentation in the 'laboratory of life';

   …by way of…

6. discerning reflections of higher laws in the laws of physical science, for everywhere we find reflections of reflections. The study and experience of these lower reflections helps us to glimpse the nature of the higher realities which they mirror;

   …and above all else through…

7. the 'Voice of the Silence' within (this phrase borrowed from Blavatsky's book of the same name with the significant verses quoted below in a modernized version).[8]

Transcending ordinary consciousness reveals new vistas

Although the voices of religion, philosophy, and the best of modern science in the outer world, are calling out for us to deepen our awareness of the Invisible Higher Power, the only authentic call which we can truly hear, and respond to, is the inner voice of our own Higher Self. In its elusive tones, it continually whispers to us through the intervening layers of our business and worldly involvement to eschew transitory pursuits and look beyond illusion.

Three Halls (States of Consciousness), O weary pilgrim, lead to the end of toils and the conquering of temptation[i] and thence to Rest Eternal.

If you would learn their names, then hearken, and remember.
The name of the first Hall is IGNORANCE.[ii]

It is the Hall in which you first saw the light, in which you shall live and die (the phenomenal World of Senses and of terrestrial consciousness—only).

The name of the second Hall is the Hall of LEARNING. In it your Soul will find the blossoms of life, but under every flower a serpent coiled. (The Hall of Probationary Learning: the astral region, the Psychic World of super-sensuous perceptions and of deceptive states. It is also the realm of drug-induced states.[iii])

The name of the third Hall is WISDOM, beyond which stretch the shoreless waters of the indestructible Fount of Omniscience.

If you would cross the first Hall safely, do not mistake the fires of lust that burn therein for the Sunlight of life.

If you would cross the second Hall safely, stop not to inhale the fragrance of its stupefying blossoms. If you would be freed from Karmic chains, do not seek for your Teacher in those regions of astral illusion.

---

i Temptation: Mārā, The personification of temptation, 'The Great Tempter', 'The Evil One', 'The Devil'. Any demon or obstacle to meditation.

ii IGNORANCE: *Avidyā*, darkness without illumination, the ignorance which mistakes *Māyā*, or illusory phenomena, for reality.

iii No blossom plucked in those regions has ever yet been brought down to earth without its serpent coiled around the stem.

The WISE ONES do not linger in pleasure-grounds of senses [or playgrounds of intellectual concepts].

The WISE ONES do not heed the sweet-tongued voices of illusion.

H. P. BLAVATSKY – THE VOICE OF THE SILENCE[9]

NOTES

1   Plato's *Apology* (38a5–6), which is a recollection of the speech Socrates gave at his trial.
2   T. S. Eliot, 'Choruses from The Rock'
    <http://www.westminster.edu/staff/brennie/wisdoms/eliot1.htm> accessed 17 March 2020.
3   William Wordsworth, 'The World Is Too Much With Us', in *Poems in Two Volumes* (London: Longman, 1807) <https://www.poetryfoundation.org/poems-and-poets/poems/detail/45564> accessed 17 March 2020.
4   Romans 8:5, New International Version.
5   Matthew 13:13, New International Version.
6   William Blake, *The Marriage of Heaven and Hell* (1793; US: Library of Congress, 1906), 26.
7   'Albert Camus', *Goodreads* <http://www.goodreads.com/quotes/2313-in-the-depth-of-winter-i-finally-learned-that-within> accessed 17 March 2020.
8   H. P. Blavatsky, *The Voice of the Silence: Being extracts from the Book of Golden Precepts*, trans. and annotated by H. P. Blavatsky (Wheaton, Illinois: Theosophical Publishing House, 1992).
9   Muriel Daw (ed.), *A Companion to The Voice of the Silence*, 3rd edn, 4, 5 <http://www.blavatskytrust.org.uk/html/md_vos/vos_companion.htm> accessed 12 March 2020.

1 Symbolism – the Language of the Mystery Teachings

A symbol to be properly so called, must be contained in the idea or ideas which it is intended to represent. As a symbol of a house could never be the prow of a boat, or the wing of a bird, but must be contained somewhere in the form of the house itself; that is, it must be an actual part chosen to represent or stand for the whole. It need not be the whole, but may be a lower form or species used as the representative of a higher of the same kind. The word is derived from the Greek words meaning to throw with, *that is to throw together. To be a just and correct symbol, it should be such as that the moment it is seen by one versed in symbolism, its meaning and application become easily apparent.*

W. Q. JUDGE[1]

Every visible object, every abstract thought, every emotional reaction is but the symbol of an eternal principle. Every form is a symbol and every symbol the tomb of an eternal verity. Through education—spiritual, mental, moral, and physical—man will learn to release living truths from their lifeless coverings.

MANLY P. HALL[2]

SYNOPSIS

Chapter 1 concerns symbolism—one of the universal keys to wisdom and the idiom of the Mystery Teachings. As this is a subject that abounds in misconceptions and bewilderment, we commence with a clear statement about the subtle differences of meaning between terms used in figurative language, for example, symbols, allegories, and similes. Thereafter, we show how universal symbols like the labyrinth, the forest, the Philosopher's Stone, and a few others, reveal the inner nature of man and his evolution when the meaning hidden in the symbol is exposed and understood. This Chapter also includes a warning about the serious perils and ghastly rituals (such as animal sacrifice) that ensue when symbols are interpreted literally, or misinterpreted, and therefore misused or plainly abused.

KEY WORDS: symbolism, analogy, labyrinth at Knossos, forest, fish, Tarot cards, chess game, alchemical marriage, Philosopher's Stone, Beethoven's Fidelio, dangers of misuse, animal sacrifice

Why does the literature of religion, esoteric philosophy, and occultism abound in the use of figurative language? For the simple reason that ordinary language wedded to a linear, intellectual mode of thought, which is well suited to conveying precise information, objective facts, and scientific theories, is a poor medium for conveying the subjective realms of experience and deep truths that are, necessarily, beyond words and above ratiocination. Recourse to parables and allegories, metaphors

Figurative language unlocks hidden layers of meaning

1

and similes, and, above all, symbols and analogies, is the only means of unlocking the meaning behind what is in truth, ineffable. Although there is considerable overlap in the nature of these figurative language forms, there are also important distinctions, particularly in the function they perform, which it will be as well to outline, whilst avoiding indulging in dry pedagogy.

Aiming for Clarity of Meaning

A proverb (etymologically, 'words put forth') is a short, pithy saying in common use, held to embody a general truth. By contrast, a parable (from the underlying etymological idea of 'drawing analogies') is a short narrative of imagined events intended to illustrate a moral or spiritual lesson. It differs from a fable in that fables employ animals, plants, inanimate objects, or forces of nature as characters, whereas parables have human characters. An example of a parable from the Bible is, 'for a good tree does not bear bad fruit, nor does a bad tree bear good fruit. For every tree is known by its own fruit. For men do not gather figs from thorns, [...]' to make the point that a man's deeds (rather than his outwardly spoken words) provide the true test of his character.[3] A base character is unlikely to perform noble deeds. The basic danger with interpreting parables—as indeed all figurative language forms—is mistaking their function and context. Too much can be read into the specific details of the story at the expense of the response it is intended to elicit, and the meaning it is intended to convey. Parables, then, are the general means of conveying the esoteric meaning in exoteric parlance—therefore, to be understood and told to the masses. However, that does not mean that so-called common folk do not have 'eyes to see' and 'ears to hear' and therefore that parables cannot be understood at different levels.

An allegory (etymologically, 'speaking otherwise') is a vehicle for conveying truth by representing an abstract or spiritual meaning through concrete or material forms; the subject under question is treated in the guise of the narrative of another, such as in a play, story or poem. For example, the Cretan legend of the Minotaur is an allegorical depiction of the unbridled, carnal passions in man under the guise of a mythological creature with the head of a bull and the body of a man—described by the Roman poet Ovid (43 BC–17/18 AD) as a being 'part man and part bull'.[4]

Regarding similes, the emphasis is to aid the understanding of a subject by using the words 'like' or 'as' to compare the subject to something else. A metaphor is similar to a simile but compares the subject to something else without an illustrative case: the comparison is implied or stated directly. In both cases a descriptive term is applied in the imaginative but not literal sense. An example of a widely accepted simile in mainstream neuroscience nowadays is 'the brain is like a computer'; the equivalent metaphor would be to refer to the brain as a 'wet computer'. A more meaningful simile from classical science comes from the English chemist, physicist, and meteorologist John Dalton FRS (1766–1844) whose model of atoms was solid, indestructible units somewhat like billiard balls. 'Billiard-ball atoms' would be a ludicrous metaphor; but to state that atoms behave like billiard balls is a meaningful simile for explaining such phenomena as the kinetic theory of gases and the law of conservation of mass in the context of nineteenth-century physics and atomic theory.

Proverbs and parables

Allegories

Similes and metaphors

Note, however, that neither similes nor metaphors are models. A model (the original meaning deriving from 'measure') is a re-presentation of the real thing in terms of a theoretical (mathematical) or physical (drawings, plans, structures) replica. A model is constructed, therefore, to represent and predict those characteristics of the performance of real things that interest us. For example, if a computer were used to simulate and study certain aspects of brain functioning, that would constitute a particular model of certain functions of the brain under specified conditions with underlying assumptions. But it is obvious that a model is not an exact replica, hence some dimension, aspect or attribute of the real thing is suppressed. So a model is always limited in one way or another and can never be a complete substitute for the real thing in itself. All this is self-evident, but we are labouring the point because just as a metaphor is sometimes confused with a model, a model is often confused with the reality that it is intended to represent—i.e., the 'map' is frequently confused with the 'territory'. This confusion was highlighted in Chapter 7 of Volume II, regarding the current idea in mainstream science that the brain is essentially a biological ('wet') computer.

Distinguishing models, similes, and metaphors from reality

We now come to, arguably, the most significant forms of figurative languages used in esotericism and occultism—analogies and symbols. In an analogy there is a correspondence, or partial similarity, between two or more things: *they are related by a common principle*. For example, in Chapter 8 of Volume I we showed the correspondences between human birth and the birth of the cosmos, both of which follow similar principles, although obviously worked out through radically different means and forms. Chapter 5 in this Volume concentrates on the power of analogy as the certain guide to grasping recondite teachings.

Analogies, symbols, and icons

A symbol is something (such as a figure or character or picture) regarded as typifying something else, especially in the nature of an idea or quality. Musical notation and the letters standing for the chemical elements are obvious examples. However, there is a deeper aspect to consider. Symbolism is the pictorial representation of an idea or a thought. Archaic or primordial writing initially had no characters, but a symbol generally stood for a whole phrase or sentence. 'A symbol is thus a recorded parable', as Blavatsky explains, 'and a parable a spoken symbol.'[5] The Egyptian hieroglyphic picture writing and the Chinese written language are examples of symbolic writing. For the student of the Mystery Teachings, symbols are a most potent means of unlocking hidden depths of meaning and releasing intuition. The reason for this is that the meaning attaching to a symbol may be taken and understood at many levels—physical, intellectual, spiritual— and what is revealed is entirely dependent on the context and, crucially, the degree of awakened intuition of the seeker.

One such example of a powerful symbol is the ouroboros, or uroboros depicting a snake swallowing or biting its own tail. This ancient symbol can be seen in places like the picture of Śiva Naṭarāja in the Chennai (Madras) Museum, and the seal of the modern Theosophical Society. The basic idea is that of constant regeneration and eternal cyclicity through the renewal of forms. However, there are many hidden layers of meaning. For example in psychology, Carl Jung interpreted the uroboros as having an archetypal significance to the human psyche;[6] and the German Jungian psychologist Erich Neumann (1905–1960) writes of it as a representation of the pre-ego 'dawn state', depicting the undifferentiated infancy experience both of mankind and the individual child.[7] In science,

Uroboros symbol:
its significance

Bernard Carr, the British professor of mathematics and astronomy at Queen Mary University of London, interprets the cosmic uroboros as depicting the hierarchy of scales from the largest (as in cosmology) to the smallest (as in quantum theory), and their interconnection, which are all part and parcel of the triumphant discoveries of modern physics, a triumph involving not only the objects but also the forces in the universe.[8] However, Carr also states candidly that the missing element in the uroboros is Mind. Hence, a complete theory must move from the matter-centric standpoint of current physics towards a more extended form of physics, which includes mind and consciousness and perhaps entails higher dimensions of reality.[9] Note, however, that symbols are not the same as icons. An icon (such as the 'print' image on a word processor) has a fixed meaning; but a symbol applies at many levels and unfolds a multi-layered meaning, as just explained. (Refer to Volume I, Chapter 7, page 190 f. for more insights into the distinction between icons and symbols used in a religious context.)

While the greatest minds of the Jewish and Christian worlds have realized that the Bible is a book of allegories, few seem to have taken the trouble to investigate its symbols and parables. When Moses instituted his Mysteries, he is said to have given to a chosen few initiates certain oral teachings which could never be written but were to be preserved from one generation to the next by word-of-mouth transmission. Those instructions were in the form of philosophical keys, by means of which the allegories were made to reveal their hidden significance. These mystic keys to their sacred writings were called by the Jews the Qabbalah (Cabala, Kaballah).

Justification for
oral transmission
of teachings

The modern world, says Hall, seems to have forgotten the existence of those unwritten teachings which explained satisfactorily the apparent contradictions of the written Scriptures, nor does it remember that the pagans appointed their two-faced Janus as custodian of the key to the Temple of Wisdom.[10] Janus has been metamorphosed into St. Peter, so often symbolized as holding in his hand the key to the gate of heaven. The gold and silver keys of 'God's Vicar on Earth', the Pope, symbolize this 'secret doctrine' which, when properly understood, unlocks the treasure chest of the Christian and Jewish Qabbalah.[10]

The Cone – A Symbol to Clarify Meaning

Esoteric
dimensions are
not geographical
compass points

Readers will soon have discovered that the esoteric literature is full of terms like upper, lower, middle; and similar terms like, up, down, centre or above, below, central. These are not linear distances along the points of a compass. They refer entirely to the distance from, or proximity to, the spiritual source: the spiritual altitudes, so to say. Let us use a cone to illustrate the point. Stand a cone on its base and view it vertically downwards from above. The apex is seen as a point in the exact centre of the circumference formed by the base. Now view the same cone horizontally in elevation. The apex is seen above the base. Now if the apex signifies the source, then *above* indicates degree of proximity to source, and *below* indicates degree of distance from source, source being posited in the actual centre and relative distance being the various locations along the radii from the apex-centre towards the circumference. Hence, in matters pertaining to esoteric philosophy and scripture, *up* should therefore be considered as towards the centre and *down* as towards the circumference: centre being spirit, and circumference being matter. So by this reasoning, *up* is toward spirit along an ascending scale of spirituality; *down* is towards matter along a descending scale of materiality.[11]

Symbolism – One of the Universal Keys to Wisdom

Symbolism then, is the most secret and the most enduring of all mysteries. Why? Because to illustrate a truth through pictures, or epitomize adequately abstract mental verities, is invariably unsatisfactory. This is because the diagrammatic or linguistic representation of one aspect of metaphysical relationships inevitably leaves out other aspects, or, when seen in isolation, may be an actual contradiction of some other aspect. Hence the value of symbols whose primary attribute is that no fixed (dogmatic) interpretation can be fastened to them; rather, they can be understood and impart meaning at several levels ranging from the material to the spiritual. Symbols therefore have an in-built elasticity of meaning in many dimensions.

There is another reason why symbols are so powerful. Chapter 1 of Volume II explained the several reasons for the confusion in terminology amongst the various esoteric and occult systems. One way out of this verbal muddle is to resort to diagrams, as indeed we have done in this work—one diagram is worth a thousand words, as the old saying goes. But diagrams have their limitations as well. They are always plane or flat figures and cannot be otherwise. Hence, diagrams portray a static picture which may give an artificial appearance of clarity, whereas every natural and occult law or phenomenon is a part of the whole organic movement of life that diagrams cannot readily present in terms of a dynamic process of interpenetrating states, processes, conditions, and things. Therefore, no diagram can fully represent esoteric ideas and laws. However, when a diagram is read not as a static picture, but contemplated as a symbol, hidden layers of meaning may dawn, depending on the sensitivity and insight of the aspirant.

Power of symbolism lies in conveying multiple levels of meaning

In addition to visual symbolism, there is also a profound symbolism hidden in theatre and music drama. The various characters in Shakespeare's (Bacon's?) plays, or in the dramatic operas of Mozart, Beethoven, and Wagner, symbolize archetypal forces in nature and aspects of the human psyche, and epitomize the drama and struggle of the human spirit in conquering adversity in its journey towards enlightenment.

A few examples are now provided of powerful symbols that have withstood the test of time and have assumed a virtually archetypal significance in the collective psyche of mankind. Principal sources have been Manly P. Hall's *The Secret Teaching of All Ages*, Greek legends, Druidic mythology, and other sources as referenced. But it cannot be overstressed that the interpretations suggested are necessarily rudimentary, since it is impossible for any author to describe completely the meaning of any particular symbol. Even if such an impossible feat were possible in theory, this would be contrary to the principles of any occult philosophy as the deeper significance of any symbol, and symbolism in general, can be revealed only by profound study and contemplation.

Symbolism is the handmaiden of an awakened intuition.

The Thread and the Dog – Always Finding the Source

The thread is a common symbol of the philosophical quest for truth through the labyrinth, traps, and woes of mortal existence. In the famous Cretan legend, first mentioned in Volume I, Chapter 9, page 271, the hero Theseus unrolls a ball of thread as he winds his way into the labyrinth to encounter and slay the Minotaur, and then follows the thread back out of the maze. The other end of the thread is held firm by Princess Ariadne who falls in love with the handsome youth. (In Middle English, a ball of string, or rolled-up yarn, was called a 'clew'. Eventually, the word took on the metaphorical meaning of something that will lead a person towards a solution and soon, the spelling changed to 'clue'.[12])

In this story there are several symbols and many allegorical meanings. But above all else, it depicts the path of the spiritual hero, that is, each one of us, now or later. Theseus stands for the Human Soul, indissolubly linked and seeking to unite with Ariadne standing for the Spiritual Soul via the 'thread' connection with the Higher Mind that always seeks its Source—see Volume II: Chapter 2, Table II-3, page 21 and Chapter 3, Table II-7, page 44. The Minotaur, of course, stands for the Animal, or Terrestrial soul— man's lower sensual nature—that is lost in the tangled confusions and conflicting demands of the everyday (Lower) mind associated with the trials of earthly existence, and which must be vanquished in order to free the mind and release the spiritual nature from the bondage of earthly desires. The love between Ariadne and Theseus symbolizes the inseparable bond between the Spiritual Soul and its human counterpart. The guiding thread is *Antaḥkaraṇa*, the vehicle of consciousness as bridge between the animal and spiritual natures (see Volume II: Chapter 3, Table II-5, page 40 and the section on Antaḥkaraṇa in Chapter 5, page 86 et seq.). By always following the thread–connection between himself and his Spiritual Soul, a man may wander far into the earthly domain and vanquish all manner of foes—especially his mental demons—without ever losing his way towards reuniting with his Source.

This sacred relationship between the Human Soul and the Spiritual Soul, epitomized by the bond between the disciple and his master, or between the initiate and his god, is also symbolized by the dog, because of its uncanny ability to follow unseen persons for miles. This symbolizes the transcendental power by which the philosopher follows the thread of truth through all psychological struggles or earthly impediments.[13] Moreover, the dog is able to sense when its master is returning home,[14] which shows the bond that exists between the two, symbolizing the union between the Human and Spiritual Soul of each man, as just stated.

A different allegorical significance of the thread is what has been a constant theme throughout this work—the Sanskrit term *Sūtrātman*, meaning the sacred thread that binds, or strings, together. To expand on what was outlined in Chapters 8 and 9 of Volume I, it refers to the secret doctrine (perennial wisdom) which acts as a thread, connecting, like beads on a necklace, all disparate disciplines such as science, religion, and philosophy into an organic unity. Recalling Blavatsky's words, 'the Esoteric Doctrine may well be called the "thread-doctrine", since, like *Sūtrātman*, in the Vedānta philosophy, it passes through and strings together all the ancient philosophical religious systems, and reconciles and explains them all.' As Blavatsky further explains, 'The Ātman or Spirit (the Spiritual SELF) passing like a thread through the five subtle bodies (or principles, *Kośas*) is called "thread-soul," or *Sūtrātman* in Vedāntic philosophy,'[15]—see Volume II: Chapter 8, Tables II-15, II-20, and II-21 on pages 157, 169, and 171.

From the above, the thread has two allegorical meanings for the aspirant: the first, somewhat personal and the second, impersonal and universal: (*a*) to maintain focus and not become lost in the many vicissitudes of changing fortune during life; and (*b*) to unite the disparate elements of the sacred wisdom into an organic whole.

The Labyrinth and the Forest – From Indecision and Confusion to Resolution

The labyrinth and the forest are universal symbols from the West and the East, respectively, for depicting the ordinary mortal existence. The popular meaning, intuitively suggested by both symbols, is the confusions and perplexities of everyday life without illumination to reveal the straight and narrow path ahead.

The Symbol of the Labyrinth

This section is an abridgement of the writer's article, 'Dante – Ptolemaic Cosmology – The Labyrinth'.[16] There are two principal types of labyrinth. In a multi-cursal labyrinth— the traditional *maze*—paths branch out into other paths that branch out further. This makes it difficult, nigh on impossible, for the traveller ever to reach the centre. By contrast, a uni-cursal labyrinth, or meander, has only one path which, however much it may twist and turn, ultimately leads, inexorably and with no dead ends, to the centre. The labyrinth at Chartres Cathedral in France is a meander, whilst the one at Knossos in Crete is definitely a maze—or is it? Let the tale unfold.

There is a double meaning behind the Cretan Labyrinth at Knossos. As just outlined, the Cretan legend and symbolic meaning behind the slaying of the Minotaur by Theseus is well known. Here we only emphasize that mythology demands that the labyrinth at Knossos had to be a maze. There was no doubt that unless we entered the maze with a clew we would soon become lost in its bifurcating passages and get devoured by the Minotaur.

However, the historical labyrinth at Knossos can be seen on early Cretan coins and pottery from an altogether different angle. The design is seen to be not a maze but actually a meander with seven circuits—a-mazing! Why this contradiction between the mythological maze and the historical meander? Why *seven* circuits?

A maze is not a meander

When we enter into terrestrial life we are indeed in a labyrinthine maze of all kinds of experiences. We do not know which of many paths to take and we have to learn to control our personal Minotaur so that its sense-driven appetites do not get the better of our higher nature. When we succeed in disciplining (or 'slaying', to use the traditional term) our lower nature by finding the clew and using the sword of the mind to cut though encumbrances, our path ahead becomes clarified—our personal maze has been transformed into a meander. The labyrinth is thus the symbolic pattern of our coming into birth, and our coming out of birth, as we shall see by 'constructing' and then 'perambulating' the historical labyrinth at Knossos.

Building the Historical Labyrinth at Knossos

Figure III-1 overleaf shows the historical labyrinth, i.e., meander at Knossos. We obtain *seven* circuits which we may label—working from the outermost to the innermost— Saturn, Jupiter, Mars, Sun, Venus, Mercury, Moon, with Earth at the centre—none other than a depiction of Ptolemaic cosmology. The Ptolemaic system is now derided, of course, because of an inability, on the part of our modern astronomers, to understand the distinctions between the heliocentric and Ptolemaic systems. Whereas the former is concerned

Ptolemaic astronomy depicts the incarnation and ex-carnation of man. It has no bearing on physical planetary orbits

Have faith, all ye who enter here

Figure III-1   The Historical Labyrinth

Image Credit: Drawn and annotated from www.doyoumaze.com by Artefact Design

with the physical layout and distances of the planets from the Sun, the latter has nothing to do with physical orbits, but instead with the 'psychological orbits', i.e., spheres of influence of the Sun and planets depicting the incarnation, and ex-carnation of a soul, and its relation with the various planetary influences that constitute its inner, non-physical principles.

Walking Into, and Out Of the Cretan Labyrinth – Entering, and Leaving Incarnation

Let us leave the Fixed Stars and walk into the historical Cretan labyrinth—we intend to be born on Earth. We shall assume that we are old souls and know our path in the life to come. The first circuit we encounter is not Saturn, but Mars, for it is the passion and desire for physical life—the force of *taṇhā* and *tṛṣṇā* (*tṛishnā*), as explained in Chapter 5 of Volume II—symbolized by Mars, that draws us into incarnation. On our way we pass through the circuit of the Moon which symbolizes the model-body (etheric body) upon which the physical body is moulded. The last circuit we encounter before 'falling' on to Earth is Venus, appropriately so, as this planet symbolizes intuitive wisdom and insight, for it is said that just before birth we have an intuitive flash of our life ahead. As we journey into incarnation each planet bestows some of its qualities on the incoming soul. At death, the reverse occurs and we 'hand back' those borrowed qualities to the planets, in turn, as we 'ascend'. So Venus is now the first circuit we encounter as we experience a review of the life we have just lived. And Mars is this time the last planetary circuit we pass through as we must now relinquish (temporarily) the thirst and desire for sentient existence. The planets in the Ptolemaic system, as mirrored in the labyrinth, thus indicate the order in which our life principles are activated as we incarnate and the order in which they must be shed as we excarnate our labyrinth of experience—Earth.

Celestial bearings on incarnation and excarnation

The Symbol of the Forest

In the case of the forest, besides the obvious connotation of mental confusion and so not 'seeing the wood for the trees', there is the added meaning of danger from poisonous serpents, deadly beasts, and wild demons, which all symbolize the untamed passions and ungoverned thoughts which literally, like demons, assail our equanimity and obstruct our life mission. We find the forest mentioned in several Indian legends, most notably the *Rāmāyaṇa*.[17] In this epic, the Lord Rāma is banished with his consort, Sītā, in the Dandaka (*Dandakaranya*) Forest from where Sītā is abducted by the King-Demon Rāvana, which crime precipitates the epic Battle of Lanka. Significantly, *Dandakaranya* translates from Sanskrit approximately to 'The Jungle (*aranya*) of Punishment (*dandakas*)'.[18] Here we can, broadly speaking, draw a parallel with the Cretan legend insofar as Sītā and Ariadne symbolize the Spiritual Soul, and Rāma and Theseus, the Human Soul. But it would not be correct to equate the Minotaur with Rāvana. There is this vital difference. In the former, the carnal and sensual passions are innately ungoverned and so literally have to be slaughtered outright. The latter is more complex. Here we have the case of a god, but a *demon*-god, one who, through great self-effort and sacrifice acquired all the powers of the gods, but who then became so arrogant as to consider himself invincible and therefore *abused the powers conferred on him*. We can clearly discern the same concept applying to totalitarian dictators who acquire virtually unlimited tyrannical power over their people and, considering themselves omnipotent and godlike, abuse their powers. Inevitably, after much bloodshed, their reign of terror is eventually brought to an end by heroic individuals. But whether we talk of the mythological Rāvana or the despotic heads of nations, two clear themes emerge: (*a*) great pride goes with a tremendous fall; and (*b*) supreme power, in the truest sense, is power over oneself. In this sense, Rāvana and his human equivalents were, character-wise, extremely weak. They lacked mastery over their unbridled ambitions and passions—occultly speaking, a perfect example of *Kāma-manas* with kāma heavily dominating.

Why do forests figure strongly in Indian epics?

Deucalion and Pyrrha – The Sequential Unfolding of Consciousness

One of the famous legends of Greek mythology is that of Deucalion and Pyrrha. After the deluge sent by the gods to destroy the iniquities of mankind at the close of the Iron Age, only Deucalion and Pyrrha were left alive. Entering a ruined sanctuary to pray, they were directed by an oracle to depart from the temple and with heads veiled and garments unbound cast behind them the bones of their mother. Construing the cryptic message of the god to mean that Earth was the Great Mother of all creatures, Deucalion picked up loose rocks and, bidding Pyrrha do likewise, cast them behind him. From these rocks there sprang forth a new and stalwart race of human beings, the rocks thrown by Deucalion becoming men and those thrown by Pyrrha becoming women. This legend shows how the Divine Being, through nature, conveys symbolic proofs of imminent momentous events and transitions that are either propitious or ominous.

The evolution of consciousness through forms of increasing complexity

Moreover, this allegory epitomizes the mystery of human evolution: for spirit, by ensouling matter (involution), becomes that indwelling power which gradually but sequentially raises (evolution) the mineral to the status of the plant; the plant to the plane of the animal; the animal to the dignity of man; and man to the estate of the gods.[19] This allegory conveys a similar moral to the proverb quoted in Chapter 8 of Volume I: *I slept in the stone; I stirred in the plant; I dreamt in the animal; and I awoke in the man.*

This is obviously not saying that stones, plants, and animals are all the same as humans. It is affirming that the self-same consciousness seeks newer and subtler forms for evolution and self-expression through vestures ranging from the mineral kingdom to the human kingdom and beyond ... Different versions, from sources in the East and the West, conveying the same essential meaning of the proverb are given in Chapter 10 of this Volume in order to demonstrate our recurrent theme about the fundamental unity of the *philosophia perennis* from disparate sources across the globe.

The Fish and the Pool – Enjoying the World but Seeking its Source

The symbol of the fish is found in the sacred traditions of both East and West. In India, *Matsya* is the avatar of Viṣṇu, the second person of the Hindu Trimūrti (Trinity), in the form of a fish. In one version of the legend Matsya forewarns Manu (primordial Man, or the progenitor of mankind) about an impending flood and orders him to collect all the grains of the world and all living creatures to be preserved in a boat. The remarkable similarity of this legend to that of Noah's Ark and also, in one sense, to that of Deucalion and Pyrrha, outlined above, is another fitting demonstration of the self-consistency and universality of symbolism used to elucidate esoteric knowledge and spiritual truths.

Druidic symbols

In the Druidic traditions of the West, the salmon is a symbol of constant renewal and seeking the Source of all existence.[20, 21] Salmon return to rivers from the ocean and swim upstream to their original hatching place to lay and fertilize their eggs before they die. Swimming upstream is a strenuous activity, so only the strongest fish complete the journey and spawn the next generation of salmon. An inborn sense of smell is believed to guide each species of salmon to its original hatching grounds. This symbolizes the intrepid philosopher who must inevitably face an uphill struggle to seek out, and unite with, the Source of his being which he always intuits within himself, despite all the temptations of earthly life that may deflect his resolve—the survival of the *spiritually* fittest.

Another symbol in the Druidic and other traditions is the Silent Pool fed by four underground streams and flowing out through five streams.[22] Here the five streams symbolize the five senses and the message is that man, since he happens to be born on Earth, should, and must, experience his five senses to the full; but he must also seek out their silent origin. This idea is in contrast to some excessively ascetic practices (especially Indian) that have lost their vitality. These defunct traditions seek to deny or denigrate the life of the senses, instead of understanding their appropriate role and function. Problems do not arise from the experience of the senses, but when sensate experience becomes an end in itself.

Drink from the five streams of the senses. Wisdom comes not from denying the senses but from seeking out their origin.

Druidic streams of wisdom

What do the four underground streams that feed the living origin symbolize? In the Druidic tradition, stated in modern terms they are: (*a*) the narrative of legend and folklore; (*b*) the universality of the perennial tradition, always One in essence but clothed in different forms according to the age and culture; (*c*) an understanding of the transpersonal nature of man; and (*d*) personal gnosis, being the individual insights and teachings to which each person has access. The last stream is the *bête noire* of academia, which is why the gatekeepers of scholarship prefer to bar any entry to personal gnosis: for it is impossible to authenticate, via peer-reviewed references or scientific protocols, the insights that an individual has accessed from within himself. All that can be done is to quote the sources of personal study. But scholarship is not the same as insight; the former engages the intellect, ideally suited to academic circles; however, the latter draws upon intuition and so can be 'nailed down' intellectually most uncomfortably, if at all. On that score, however, Ken Wilber suggests a method of inter-subjective validation. In *The Marriage of Sense and Soul* he reasons that 'the spiritual, subjective world of ancient wisdom' could be allied 'with the objective, empirical world of modern knowledge' by adopting contemplative disciplines related to Spirit, like meditation, and assigning them within a context of what he calls 'broad science', which includes evidence from logic, mathematics, and from the symbolic, hermeneutical, and other realms of consciousness.[23]

The Symbols of the Tarot

We now come to a different form of symbolism, embodied in the Tarot. The Tarot cards represent the elements of life and philosophy, consciousness and its expression. The following three cards are especially germane to this Chapter and the overall theme of this Volume: The Hermit, The Lovers, and The Judgement. Short expositions are provided, taken mainly from Hall,[24] and supplemented from other sources as referenced.

The Hermit – Concealing the Light of Wisdom

The ninth numbered Major Arcana (trump card[i]) shown in Figure III-2 overleaf is called *L'Hermite* (The Hermit), and portrays an aged man, robed in a monkish habit and cowl, leaning on a staff. This card was popularly supposed to represent the Greek philosopher Diogenes(*d. circa* 320 BC) in his quest for an honest man. In his right hand the recluse carries a lamp which he partly conceals within the folds of his cape. The hermit thereby personifies the secret organizations which for countless centuries have carefully concealed the light of the Ancient Wisdom from the profane. The staff of the hermit is knowledge, which is man's enduring support. Sometimes the mystic rod is divided by knobs into seven sections, a subtle reference to the mystery of the seven sacred centres along the human spine (*cākras*, see Chapter 9 later).

The inner light must be carefully guarded

In the pseudo-Egyptian Tarot, the hermit shields the lamp behind a rectangular cape to emphasize the philosophic truth that wisdom, if exposed to the fury of ignorance, would be extinguished like the tiny flame of a lamp unprotected from the storm. Man's bodies form a cloak through which his divine nature is faintly visible like the flame of the partly covered lantern. Through renunciation—the Hermetic life—man attains depth of character and tranquillity of spirit.[25]

Having come this far in the work, readers will have no difficulty in relating the various symbols to the Principles of Man, as expounded in Chapters 2 and 3 of Volume II. The lamp obviously signifies *Ātma*, the Divine Self, indescribably bright in itself, but whose light is dimmed by virtue of refraction through man's intermediate vestures from the

---

i A trump is a playing card which is elevated above its usual rank.

Figure III-2 The Hermit   **Figure III-3** The Lovers   **Figure III-4** The Judgement

Image Credit: Pamela Coleman Smith/https://en.wikipedia.org/wiki/Rider-Waite_tarot_deck

psychic to the physical. The staff denotes the Mind Principle, *Manas*, which, when it becomes man's only permanent support is Higher Manas. The Hermit's cape is a graphic reference to the *Sthūla-śarīra*, which is literally man's physical cape, or final *kośa* (sheath).

The Lovers – The Price of Free Will

The sixth numbered Major Arcana, shown in Figure III-3 above, is called *L'Amoureux* (The Lovers). In one of the two forms of this Tarot card, a youth with a female figure on either side is portrayed. One of these figures wears a golden crown and is winged, while the other is attired in the flowing robes of the bacchante (a Priestess of Bacchus) and on her head is a wreath of vine leaves. The maidens represent the twofold Soul of man (Spiritual and Animal), the first his guardian angel, the second his ever-present demon, *and both love him*—hence the appellation of The Lovers. The youth stands at the beginning of mature life, 'the Parting of the Ways', where he must choose between virtue and vice, the eternal and the temporal. Above, in a halo of light, is the genius of Fate (his star), mistaken for Cupid by the uninformed. If the youth chooses unwisely, the arrow of blindfolded Fate will transfix him.

In the pseudo-Egyptian Tarot the arrow of the genius points directly to the figure of vice, thereby signifying that the end of her path is destruction.

This card reminds man that the price of free will—or, more correctly, the power of choice—is responsibility.[26]

As explained in Chapters 2 and 3 of Volume II, this card illustrates a cardinal teaching of occultism, namely, that the dual nature of the Mind Principle (Human Soul) has the power of two choices: either to 'rise' and align with the guardian angel *Nous* (divine spirit, or substance), whereupon all is well in accordance with divine law; or to 'fall' and attach to the ever-present demon *Anoia* (folly, or the irrational Animal Soul) and create self-imposed trouble. (Refer back to Plato's teaching on the dual choice of the soul in Volume II, Chapter 8, page 175.)

Free will demands responsibility

The Judgement – Liberating the Spiritual Nature from the Material Sepulchre

The twentieth numbered Major Arcana, shown in Figure III-4 opposite, is called *Le Jugement* (The Judgement), and portrays three figures rising apparently from their tombs, though but one coffin is visible. Above them in a blaze of glory is a winged figure (presumably the Angel Gabriel) blowing a trumpet. This Tarot card represents the liberation of man's threefold spiritual nature from the sepulchre of his material constitution. Since but one-third of the spirit actually enters the body (elucidated in Chapter 7), the other two-thirds constituting the Hermetic anthropos, or overman (comparable to Emerson's Oversoul, or Brunton's Overself), only one of the three figures is actually rising from the tomb. In 1781, Antoine Court de Gébelin (1725–1784), a French Protestant pastor, initiated the interpretation of the Tarot as an arcane repository of timeless esoteric wisdom. He maintained that the coffin may have been an afterthought of the card makers and that the scene actually represents creation rather than resurrection.[27] But in philosophy, these two words are practically synonymous. The blast of the trumpet represents the Creative Word, by the intoning of which man is liberated from his terrestrial limitations.

Spiritual nature is temporarily veiled by personality

In the pseudo-Egyptian Tarot it is evident that the three figures signify the parts of a single being, for three mummies are shown emerging from one mummy case.[28]

The threefold spiritual nature liberated from the sepulchre refers to the release of the Upper Triad, *Ātma-Buddhi-Manas* from the mortal personality, upon death for the average person, but in life for the illumined sage (refer to Chapter 5 in Volume II about the post-mortem states of man). Moreover, the three figures signifying the parts of a single being are Spirit, Soul, and Body comprising the tripartite, compound composition of man on Earth.

The Game of Chess – The Drama of Life

In its symbolism, chess is the most significant of all games. It has been called the 'the royal game'—the pastime of kings. Like the Tarot cards, the chessmen represent the elements of life and philosophy, consciousness and its expression. The game was played in India and China long before its introduction into Europe. East Indian princes were wont to sit on the balconies of their palaces and play chess with living men standing upon a checkerboard pavement of black and white marble in the courtyard below. It is popularly believed that the Egyptian Pharaohs played chess, but an examination of their sculpture and illuminations has led to the conclusion that the Egyptian game was a form of draughts. In China, chessmen were often carved to represent warring dynasties, such as the Manchu and the Ming.

The chessboard consists of sixty four squares alternately black and white and symbolizing the floor of the House of the Mysteries. Upon this field of existence, or thought, move a number of strangely carved figures, each according to fixed law. The white king is Ormuzd (the benevolent Power); the black king, Ahriman (the counteracting, so-called evil Power); and upon the plains of Cosmos (the chess board) the great war between Light and Darkness is fought through all the ages. Of the philosophical constitution of man, the king represents the spirit (*Ātma*); the queen the intuitive mind (*Buddhi*); the bishops the emotions (*kāma*); the knights the vitality (*Prāṇa*); the castles, or rooks, the model and physical body (*Liṅga-* and *Sthūla-śarīra*). The pieces upon the king's side are positive;

Chess can be understood at three levels: personal, societal, and cosmic those upon the queen's side, negative. (Note that 'positive' and 'negative' are not 'good' and 'evil' but rather complementary: 'yang' and 'yin', as the Taoists put it well.) The pawns are the perceptive faculties and sensory impulses (*Kāma-manas*)—being the various parts, or aspects of the soul. The white king and his suite symbolize the Self and its vehicles; the black king and his retinue, the not-Self—the false ego and its legion. The game of chess thus sets forth the eternal struggle of each part of man's compound nature against the shadow of itself. The nature of each of the chessmen is revealed by the way in which it moves; geometry is the key to their interpretation. For example: the castle moves on the square; the bishop moves on the slant; but the king, being the spirit, cannot be captured, but loses the battle when so surrounded that it cannot escape.[29]

It is not so far-fetched to mention that the more the governance of nations is organized along the above lines of hierarchy, the more stable and enduring will be its society. For example, in England the hierarchy from monarch (sovereign) to prime minister, to members of Parliament, to Civil Service can easily be correlated in a general sense to the above roles and functions in the game of chess.

The Alchemical Marriage – A Uniting Spiritual Culture

Under the symbolism of an alchemical marriage, the Rosicrucians and mediæval philosophers concealed the secret system of spiritual culture whereby they hoped to co-ordinate the *disjecta membra* (scattered fragments) of both the human and social organisms. Society, they maintained, was (or ought to be) a threefold structure and had its analogy in the triune constitution of man; for as man is a compound of spirit, mind (soul in the generic sense), and body, so they saw society as made up of church, state, and populace. The bigotry of the church, the tyranny of the state, and the fury of the mob are the three murderous agencies of society which seek to destroy Truth as recounted in the Masonic legend of CHiram Abiff. The first six days of *The Chemical Marriage* (also referred to as *The Chemical Wedding*) set forth the processes of philosophical 'creation' through which every organism must pass.[30] The three kings (in the narrative) are the threefold spirit of man (the Upper Triad), and their consorts are the corresponding vehicles of their expression in the lower world (the Lower Quaternary). The mind is the executioner, the higher part of which—symbolized by the head—is necessary to the achievement of the philosophical labour.[31] The sharp edge of the executioner's axe may possibly have an analogous meaning to the sword in Japanese martial arts: both symbolizing the cutting edge of Truth that pares away all that is transitory and delusional in life.

Society modelled on the human constitution

The Philosopher's Stone – Human Regeneration

This is not the place to add to the colossal tracts that have been written for many centuries about alchemy in the West and the meaning of the Philosopher's Stone. We need only state the following as being especially germane to the subject of symbolism in general and as a closing note on the subject.

The true Rosicrucian Brotherhood consisted of a limited number of highly developed initiates or adepts, those of the higher degrees being no longer subject to the laws of mortality, and candidates being accepted into the Order only after long periods of probation. Adepts possessed the secret of the Philosopher's Stone and knew the process of transmuting base metals into gold, but taught that these were only allegorical terms concealing the true mystery of human regeneration through the transmutation of the 'base elements' of man's lower nature into the 'gold' of intellectual and spiritual realization. According to this theory, those who have sought to record the events of importance in connection with the Rosicrucian controversy (or the secrets of the Philosopher's Stone) have invariably failed because they approached their subject from a purely physical or materialistic angle. So for instance, if an alchemist gave directions for the special treatment of Sulphur, Mercury, and Salt, with the assertion that by carrying out these directions properly, one would obtain Aurum (gold), *he really spoke of a method to direct the thinking, feeling, and willing activities of the soul in such a way as to gain true Wisdom.*[32]

True purpose of alchemy

In support of the above assertions, we have only to cite Plato's teaching in the words of one of England's greatest alchemists—Isaac Newton:

> For Alchemy tradeth not wth metals as ignorant vulgars think, which error hath made them distrust that noble science; […] This Philosophy is not of that kind wch tendeth to vanity & deceipt but rather to profit & to edification inducing first ye knowledg of God & secondly ye way to find out true medicines in ye creatures. Plato saith that Philosophy is the imitating God so far forth as man is able. […] so y^t ye scope is to glorify God in his wonderful works, to teach a man how to live well, & to be charitably affected helping or neighbours.[33]

Newton on qualifications for an alchemist

> They who search after the Philosopher's Stone by their own rules obliged to a strict & religious life. That study [is] fruitful of experiments.[34]

Beethoven's Fidelio – The Union of the Spiritual and the Human

Fidelio, originally titled *Leonore, oder Der Triumph der ehelichen Liebe* (Leonore, or The Triumph of Marital Love), is Beethoven's only opera. The German libretto was originally prepared by the Austrian librettist and theatre director Joseph Sonnleithner (1766–1835) from the French of Jean-Nicolas Bouilly (1763–1842), the playwright and politician of the French Revolution. Beethoven laboured on its composition more than any other one work, producing four different overtures, no fewer than sixteen sketches for the opening of the first air by one of the protagonists (Florestan) and 346 pages of sketches for the opera. The noble theme of the two-act opera perfectly suited the lofty thoughts and high moral status of its composer. The story is about the undying love of Leonore for her husband Florestan. Following an attempt to expose the crimes of the corrupt prison governor Pizarro, Florestan finds himself unjustly imprisoned in a dark dungeon and in mortal danger. Amid rumours of his demise, only his wife, Leonore, suspects the truth. Disguised as Fidelio, a male prison guard, her valiant attempt to rescue her husband from certain death triumphs when she acquires the keys to unlock Florestan's chains to set him free, whereupon Florestan and Leonore celebrate their reunion.

Let us now ask some searching questions. Why has this great opera resonated with audiences across the globe for centuries, and still feels disconcertingly relevant today? Like all sublime and timeless expressive forms of art, the answer lies on three levels. On a purely personal level, the obvious answer that a deeply moving story of undying love, courage, personal sacrifice, and heroism that vanquish incarceration, evil, and injustice is bound to make an emotional appeal to audiences. Then on the socio-political front, it can be seen as a political statement about the triumph of freedom over tyranny and evil. In fact, many opera directors have long attempted to cast it in this light. But there is a much deeper reason that could well explain its enduring popularity. The answer lies on the transcendent level. Irrespective of whether or not the librettist or the deaf, sickly composer, single yet yearning for his 'immortal beloved', were consciously aware of it, the story touches a 'spiritual nerve centre' by conveying deep esoteric truths to which all men respond, often (and invariably) without even realizing why. Let us tease out the symbolic meaning concealed in the narrative. There is a considerable body of literature on the symbolism in epic music dramas like Mozart's *The Magic Flute*[35] and Wagner's *Ring* cycle,[36] but there appears to be practically nothing on the esoteric and symbolical import of *Fidelio*; so what follows is the writer's own interpretation.

The unswerving love between the Spiritual Soul and the Human Soul is symbolized by the inseparable bond between Leonore and Florestan. And whether we look to the love of Leonore for Florestan in *Fidelio* or to Ariadne who falls in love with the hero Theseus in the Cretan legend or the love between Sīta and Rāma in the *Rāmāyaṇa* epic or to Beatrice who (after Virgil) guides Dante through *Purgatorio* in the *Divine Comedy*, we find that the Spiritual Soul is always feminine. Florestan imprisoned in a dark cell obviously symbolizes the Human Soul imprisoned in materialism and bereft of spiritual light. The dangers and tribulations facing both Florestan and Leonore symbolize the immense dangers and pitfalls on the path to spiritual enlightenment. Leonore disguised as Fidelio shows the glamourizing power of *māyā* (illusion) casting its spell over the unwary.[37] Finally, the keys to unlock Florestan's chains surely symbolize that the chains that bind man to his lower self can be unlocked only using the philosophic key of esoteric wisdom— an efflorescence of the Spiritual Soul—in order to set him free. The most sublime arias in the opera are Florestan's vision of Leonore come as an angel to rescue him, and the Prisoners' Chorus *O welche Lust* (O what a joy), an exultant ode to freedom sung by a chorus of political prisoners at their joy in breathing the fresh air and seeing the daylight after their long incarceration in the airless and dark dungeon. The symbolism here is obvious.

Dangers of Symbolism Misused and Misinterpreted

The danger of visible symbols in the form of images or statues, is that they can become confused and identified with what they are supposed to be symbolizing, or pointing to. There is an apposite adage, familiar to most, which sums this up well—by focussing exclusively on the finger we fail to notice the moon to which it is pointing. In that case the symbol turns into an idol, which soon degenerates into idol worship. It is for this reason that we are warned in Christianity—and more forcefully in Islam—against idolatry. But there is nothing intrinsically wrong with idols, even for the serious enquirer into the perennial Mysteries. In fact, they can often be of much benefit in providing a focal point for aspiration as, for example, Buddhists have found by placing a small bust of the Lord Buddha in their homes, or Hindus by featuring a painting of the Lord Kṛṣṇa (Krishna) in their temples—with the major proviso, it bears repeating, that the symbol-turned-idol does not become an end in itself, but acts as a messenger and conduit of a higher principle. However, the propensity for misuse is a constant and serious danger. As Manly Hall writes:

> The hopeless confusion of divine principles with the allegorical figures created to represent and personify them to the limited faculties of the uninitiated has resulted in the most atrocious misconceptions of spiritual truths. Concepts well-nigh as preposterous as these, however, still stand as adamantine barriers to a true understanding of Old and New Testament symbolism; for, until man disentangles his reasoning powers from the web of venerated absurdities in which his mind has lain ensnared for centuries, how can Truth ever be discovered?[38]

A few glaring cases of such 'venerated absurdities' are cited below to illustrate the nonsense that follows in the wake of the misunderstanding and subsequent misuse of allegories and symbols.

Biblical Controversies

The modern world seems to have forgotten the existence of those unwritten teachings which explained satisfactorily the apparent contradictions of the written Scriptures. There is, arguably, no finer example of the problems (ranging from acrimony between friends to outright war) caused by a dead-letter, literal interpretation of scriptures than the fate suffered by the Holy Bible. The greatest minds of the Jewish and Christian worlds (and legendary scientists like Newton) have realized that the Bible is entirely a book of allegories, but few others seem to have taken the trouble to investigate its symbols and parables—like Richard Dawkins who is not short of expletives like 'bloodthirsty', 'ethnic cleanser', 'misogynistic', 'megalomaniacal', and 'sadomasochistic' (to name but a few) in his wholesale denunciation of the God of the Old Testament, and religion in general[39]—a perfect example of how small mentalities mangle large truths. Therefore, it has always been the case that the highest teachings were never written down but preserved from one generation to the next by word-of-mouth transmission. As mentioned earlier, these instructions were in the form of philosophic keys, by means of which the allegories were made to reveal their hidden significance as when Moses instituted his Mysteries to elected initiates through oral teachings which could never be written. These mystic keys to their sacred writings were called by the Jews, the Qabbalah. Then, in the East, the sacred Vedas were taught orally and only written down in the form of the Upaniṣads, Brāhmaṇas, and Purāṇas by later generations. Also, the early literature of Buddhism was orally transmitted.[40]

Richard Dawkins takes allegories literally

Why highest teachings were never initially written down

Apostolic and Prophetic Relics as Examples of Ludicrous Associations

A World of Wonders by the French printer and classical scholar Henrie Stephen (1528–1598) was published in 1607.[41] The author mentions a monk of St. Anthony who declared that while in Jerusalem the patriarch of that City had shown him not only one of the ribs of the *Word made flesh* and some rays from the Star of Bethlehem, but also the snout of a seraph, a finger nail of a cherub, the horns of Moses, and a casket containing the breath of the Christ! To a people believing implicitly in a seraph sufficiently tangible to have its proboscis preserved, the more profound issues of Judaistic philosophy must necessarily be incomprehensible. Nor is it difficult to imagine the reaction taking place in the mind of some ancient sage should he hear that a cherub—which, according to St. Augustine, signifies the Evangelists; according to the Hellenistic Jewish philosopher, the Roman Philo of Alexandria, also called Philo Judæus (*circa* 20 BC – *circa* 50 AD), the outermost circumference of the entire heavens; and according to several of the Church Fathers, the wisdom of God—had sprouted a finger nail.[42]

In the East we cite the example of Śrī Dalada Maligawa or the Temple of the Sacred Tooth Relic. Located in the royal palace complex of the former Kingdom of Kandy, Sri Lanka, it is a Buddhist temple in the city of Kandy, which is supposed to house the relic of the tooth of the Buddha. The story goes that after the *parinirvāṇa*[ii] of Gautama Buddha, the tooth relic was preserved in Kalinga and smuggled to the island by Princess Hemamali (Hemamala) and her husband Prince Dantha on the instructions of her father King Guhasiva. They landed in the island at the port of Lankapattana during the reign of Sirimeghavanna of Anuradhapura (301–328) and handed over the tooth relic.[43] Since ancient times, the relic has played an important role in local politics because it is believed that whoever holds the relic holds the governance of the country. Whatever symbolic meaning one wishes to attach to the notion of the Buddha's tooth, it is left to readers whether or not to accept that within the temple there exists an actual physical relic of a tooth that was once in the mouth of the Lord Buddha.

Animal Sacrifice

A common jibe hurled at the pagans and ancient cultures, such as the Incas, Aztecs, Hawaiians, and Egyptians, is that in order to propitiate and appease the gods they sacrificed animals and, in many cases, humans. This accusation is not without some justification, but it displays complete ignorance regarding the status of ancient cultures during their zenith and in their decline. It was only during the later period of degeneration and decay that the eternal truths were progressively, by degrees, corrupted and carnalized. Hence, unable to understand its metaphysical or philosophical import, the symbolic meaning of sacrifice was taken literally and materialized into a physical ritual perpetrated upon hapless animals or humans. A candidate, when first entering the precincts of the sanctuary, must offer upon the brazen altar not a poor unoffending bull or ram *but its correspondence within his own nature.* The bull, being symbolic of earthiness, represented his own gross constitution which must be burned up by the fire of his divinity. The sacrificing of beasts, and in some cases human beings, upon the altars of the pagans was the result of their subsequent ignorance concerning the fundamental principle underlying sacrifice. *They did not realize that their offerings must come from within their own natures in order to be genuine.*[44]

In passing however, we are entitled to point out that those who sneer at such ancient cultures because of their supposedly uncivilized ignorance, resulting in the primitive cruelty of animal and human sacrifice, might wish to reflect on the barbaric brutalities perpetrated by modern, 'civilized' man—all throughout the previous century—such as in Nazi Germany, Communist Russia, and other dictatorial regimes as in Chile and Iraq. Human nature at its vilest is ever the same—in any era, ancient or modern.

---

ii In Buddhism, the term *parinirvāṇa* is commonly used to refer to *nirvāṇa* after death—albeit they own that this transcendent state must have been attained by the Buddha during his lifetime.

Résumé

Symbolism is an indispensable branch of the occult sciences and one of the keys that must be turned to unlock the mysteries of man and Nature. But to reiterate, a complete exposition of the meaning behind symbols and allegories (even if it were possible) is contrary to the principles of any esoteric philosophy. The deeper significance of the symbols is revealed only by profound study and contemplation. Animal sacrifice is a glaring example of what happens when degeneration sets in and the animating vitality of the rarefied esoteric meaning becomes ossified into the dead-letter interpretations of exoteric literalism, with all its ghastly perversions and cruelties. In their zenith, lofty civilizations embodied the noble precepts of the *philosophia perennis*; but when they declined, principles that were once understood as being entirely metaphysical and spiritual were sorely materialized, the esoteric kernel degenerating into the barbaric exoteric rituals of sacrificing beasts and humans. The greater the wisdom upheld, the more it is prone to abomination when fallen and this is what happened regarding the civilizations just mentioned and many others—the degenerate version standing in directly inverse proportion to the noble exposition. But we must keep asking ourselves: what principle is it in man that irresistibly draws him to symbolism, albeit acknowledging its gross perversion in the hands of the ignorant or unawakened?

Spiritual wisdom is inversely proportional to its abuse

This Chapter has shown that figurative language, especially symbolism, is a universal key to wisdom. This is because it unlocks inner truths and subjective realms of experience that are unreachable to understanding through ordinary cerebration. The next Chapter reveals how the unity of Cosmos, Nature, and Man is revealed through symbols.

> *[Symbolism is] the pictorial expression of an idea or a thought. Primordial writing had at first no characters, but a symbol generally stood for a whole phrase or sentence. A symbol is thus a recorded parable, and a parable a spoken symbol.*
>
> H. P. Blavatsky[45]

> *Still, the great spiritual truths are not so deeply concealed as might be supposed. Most of them are exposed to view at all times, but are not recognized because of their concealment in symbol and allegory. When the human race learns to read the language of symbolism, a great veil will fall from the eyes of men. They shall then know truth and, more than that, they shall realize that from the beginning truth has been in the world unrecognized, save by a small but gradually increasing number appointed by the Lords of the Dawn as ministers to the needs of human creatures struggling to regain their consciousness of divinity.*
>
> Manly P. Hall[46]

NOTES

1   W. Q. Judge, 'Theosophical Symbolism', *The Path* (May 1886).
2   *STA*, 'The Hiramic Legend', LXXX. 'Hiramic' pertains to CHiram Abiff, the chief character in an allegorical legend connected with the initiation into the third degree of Freemasonry.
3   Luke 6:43–45, New King James Version.

4   J. S. Rusten, 'Ovid, Empedocles and the Minotaur', *The American Journal of Philology*, 103/3 (Autumn 1982), 332.

5   *TSGLOSS*, 316.

6   Carlos Eire, *A Very Brief History of Eternity* (Princeton: Princeton University Press, 2010).

7   Erich Neumann, *The Origins and History of Consciousness*, trans. R. F. C. Hull, foreword by C. G. Jung (1949; Princeton: Princeton University Press, 2014).

8   Bernard Carr, 'Black Holes, Cosmology and the Passage of Time: Three problems at the limits of science', in Khalil Chamcham, Joseph Silk, John D. Barrow, and Simon Saunders (eds), *The Philosophy of Cosmology* (Cambridge: Cambridge University Press, 2017), 56.

9   B. J. Carr, 'Hyperspatial Models of Matter and Mind', in *Beyond Physicalism: Toward Reconciliation of Science and Spirituality*, ed. E. Kelly, et al. (US and UK: Rowman & Littlefield Publishers, 2015), 227–73.

10 *STA*, 'The Tabernacle in the Wilderness', CXXXIII.

11 *STA*, 'The Human Body in Symbolism', LXXIII–LXXIV.

12 Grant Barrett, 'The Origin of "Clue"', *A Way With Words* (17 November 2012) <https://www.waywordradio.org/clue-theseus-origins> accessed 18 March 2020.

13 *STA*, 'Fishes, Insects, Animals, Reptiles, and Birds – Part Two', XCII.

14 Rupert Sheldrake, *Dogs That Know When Their Owners Are Coming Home: The unexplained powers of animals* (UK: Arrow Books, 2011).

15 *SD*-I, 'Gods, Monads, and Atoms', 610n.

16 Edi D. Bilimoria, 'Dante – Ptolemaic Cosmology – The Labyrinth: Symbolic meanings for the journey of the soul', *The Theosophist*, 133/7 (April 2012), 22-7.

17 *Adhyātma Rāmāyaṇa: The spiritual version of the Rama Saga* (original Sanskrit with English translation by Swami Tapasyananda) (Madras: India, Sri Ramakrishna Math, 1985). A highly readable version of the epic is by Channing Arnold, simplified by Marjorie Sykes, *The Story of the Ramayana* (Calcutta, Bombay, Madras: Orient Longmans, 1951).

18 Abhijit Chandra Chandra, 'In the Footsteps of Rama', *The Pioneer* (4 July 1997) <https://web.archive.org/web/20160507173003/http://www.hindunet.org/hvk/articles/0797/0036.html> accessed 17 March 2020.

19 *STA*, 'Stones, Metals, and Gems', XCVII.

20 Philip Carr-Gomm, *Druid Mysteries: Ancient mysteries for the 21st century* (UK: Rider, 2002).

21 Philip Carr-Gomm and Stephanie Carr-Gomm, *The Druid Craft Tarot: Use the magic of Wicca and Druidry to guide your life*, illus. Will Worthington (UK: Connections Book Publishing, 2004).

22 *ibid.*

23 Ken Wilber, *The Marriage of Sense and Soul: Integrating science and religion* (New York: Broadway Books, 1998), 211.

24 *STA*, 'An Analysis of the Tarot Cards', CXXIX–CXXXII *passim*.

25 *STA, op. cit.,* CXXXI.

26 *STA, op. cit.,* CXXX.

27 Hugh Chisholm (ed.), 'Court de Gebelin, Antoine', in *Encyclopædia Britannica*, vii (11th edn, Cambridge: Cambridge University Press. 1911), 324.

28 *STA*, 'An Analysis of the Tarot Cards', CXXXII.

29 *ibid.*

30 [Johann Valentin Andreæ], *The Chymical Wedding of Christian Rosencreutz*, trans.1690 [Ger. orig., *Chymische Hochzeit Christiani Rosencreutz* (Strasbourg, Germany, 1616)] [online trans.] <http://amra.gr/library-contents/chymical_wedding.pdf> accessed 2 June 2020. See also, John Crowley, *The Chemical Wedding by Christian Rosencreutz: A romance in eight days by Johann Valentin Andreae* (US: Small Beer Press, 2016).

31 *STA*, 'The Chemical Marriage', CLXIV.

32 Ernst Lehrs, *Man or Matter: Introduction to a spiritual understanding of nature on the basis of Goethe's method or training observation and thought*, rev. and enl., Nick Thomas and Peter Bortoft (3rd edn, London: Rudolf Steiner Press, 1958), 243.

33 Newton's own sentiments in the preface to 'Manna', Keynes MS 33, f. 5ᵛ, King's College Library, University of Cambridge. Quoted also in part in Richard S. Westfall, *Never at Rest: A biography of Isaac Newton* (Cambridge: Cambridge University Press, 1995), 298.

34 Newton: Keynes MS 130, a Conduitt Notebook.

35 There is, arguably, no finer analysis of the hidden meaning and symbolism in this legendary opera than by Jocelyn Godwin, 'Layers of Meaning in "The Magic Flute"', *The Musical Quarterly*, 65/4 (October 1979), 471–92.

36 Robert Donington O.B.E., *Wagner's 'Ring' and its Symbols: The music and the myth* (1963; 3rd edn, repr., London: Faber & Faber, 1984).

37 A lucid exposition on *māyā* is by Seymour D. Ballard, 'The Role of Māyā in Man's Evolution', the Blavatsky Lecture 1986 (London: The Theosophical Society).

38 *STA*, 'Qabbalistic Keys to the Creation of Man', CXXV.

39 Richard Dawkins, *The God Delusion* (Boston: Houghton Mifflin, 2006), 51.

40 Alexander Wynne, 'The Oral Transmission of Early Buddhist Literature', *Journal of the International Association of Buddhist Studies*, 27/1 (2004), 97–127.

41 Henrie Estienne Stephen, *A World of Wonders: Or an introduction to a treatise touching the conformitie of ancient and moderne wonders or a preparatiue treatise to the Apologie for Herodotus* (Oxford: Text Creation Partnership, 2005).

42 Reworded from *STA*, 'Qabbalistic Keys to the Creation of Man', CXXV.

43 H. A. P. Abeywardena, *Kandurata Praveniya* (1st edn in Sinhalese; Colombo: Central Bank of Sri Lanka, 2004), 25.

44 *STA*, 'The Tabernacle in the Wilderness', CXXXV.

45 *TSGLOSS*, 316.

46 Manly P. Hall, *Melchizedek and the Mystery of Fire: A treatise in three parts* (Los Angeles, California: The Philosophical Research Society, 1996), 8 <https://www.yumpu.com/xx/document/read/59160828/manly-p-hall-melchizedek-and-the-mystery-of-fire> accessed 19 December 2020.

2 Symbolic Representations of the Unity of Cosmos, Nature, and Man

As God is the pervading principle of three worlds, in each of which He manifests as an active principle, so the spirit of man, partaking of the nature of Divinity, dwells upon three planes of being.

MANLY P. HALL[1]

SYNOPSIS

Chapter 2 concerns the unity of Cosmos, Nature, and Man represented symbolically through the zodiac and the Bembine Table of Isis, which latter displays a system of occult symbols depicting the rites and ceremonies involved in evoking theurgic or (so-called) magical powers. Also described is how the Tablet symbolically depicts the Hermetic Axiom—Cosmos mirrored in man—and how the two great zodiacs—the fixed and the movable—again represented through symbols, are correlated to the physiology of the human body. All this begs the question whether astrology is a pseudoscience. After carefully explaining exactly what is meant by pseudoscience, we justify why astrology (understood and applied in its rightful context) should in fact be regarded as a royal science. This Chapter flows in a natural sense into the next one explaining the basis of the adage: 'Man, the Measure of All Things'.

KEY WORDS: zodiac in astronomy, zodiac in astrology, symbolism of Bembine Tablet, Hermetic Axiom, meaning of pseudoscience

The zodiac, considered in both its physical and esoteric aspects, is the most complete depiction of the unity and correspondences between Cosmos, Nature, and Man. This Chapter focusses on the zodiac from the standpoints of astronomy and astrology and shows how the occult influences of the latter are mirrored in the symbols of one of the finest pictograms of the ancient world—the Bembine Table of Isis. Needless to say, these are enormous subjects so all we can hope for in this short Chapter is to convey a flavour of the majesty of such arcane matters.

The Zodiac – In Astronomy and Astrology

Man has ever gazed heavenwards to contemplate and acknowledge his kinship with the stars (and this is not, as some academic evolutionists claim, because he happened to change from a four-legged to a two-legged animal and so was better able to crick his neck upwards to gaze at the firmament). Even the most hard-nosed astronomers will admit that something inexplicably mysterious moves them to study and map the heavens above. Why then this fascination with the celestial spheres, which they so confidently declare to be just lifeless physical matter in a purposeless universe (the Nobel physicist Steven Weinberg being a prime example—see Chapter 11)? However, the question of extra-terrestrial life has never quite eluded the scientific consciousness, initially on the grounds that given the billions of planets and star systems in the universe, there might be a statistical probability of a solar system or planet with an atmosphere and environmental conditions to support life (in terms of what science regards as life).[2] However, the 'materialistic tune' is always changing as we showed in Volume I with examples of how science has radically altered its verdict on theories it once held as gospel truths. Astrobiology is one case in point: firstly, the possibility of discovering primitive micro-organisms existing on some planets, or in space, was mooted merely as a statistical probability ungrounded in evidence, then as a hypothesis, and now it is a virtual certainty—see of Volume I, Chapter 4, page 106f.

<aside>Why are atheists and hard-nosed materialists fascinated by the heavens above?</aside>

Meanwhile, let us consider the zodiac: astronomical and astrological. There are good reasons for mentioning these two perspectives.

The Astronomical Zodiac and its Signs

In astronomy, the ecliptic is the great circle on the celestial sphere[i] giving the apparent annual path traced out by the Sun against the stellar background, a process that is repeated in a little over 365 days. It is essentially the plane of the Earth's orbit around the Sun. The ecliptic forms the centre of an imaginary band of sky, approximately 18 degrees of arc wide, known as the zodiac, on which the Sun, Moon, and all the solar system planets (except the dwarf planet Pluto, owing to its highly elliptical and inclined orbit) are seen always to move. This band is divided into twelve equal parts, each being a segment of sky 30 arc degrees wide, and each named after a prominent constellation situated in it. These are the signs of the zodiac, the Sun appearing to move through these signs at the approximate rate of one per month. The signs give us a clue about some of the terminology used today. The first point of Aries was named when the vernal equinox was actually in the constellation Aries, when the Greek astronomer and mathematician Hipparchus of Nicaea (190–120 BC) defined it in 130 BC; it has since moved into Pisces. (Hipparchus is considered the founder of trigonometry but is most famous for his incidental discovery of the precession of the equinoxes, explained below.) The zodiacal light is a faint cone of light with its axis on, or close to, the ecliptic extending from the horizon soon after evening twilight and prior to morning twilight. The Italian-born, French astronomer Giovanni Domenico Cassini (1625–1712), also known as Cassini I, correctly interpreted this phenomenon as due to sunlight reflected by interplanetary material in the form of a disc-shaped cloud surrounding the Sun and lying mainly in the plane of the ecliptic.

<aside>The zodiac in its dual meaning</aside>

The word 'zodiac' has a dual meaning. It may refer to the fixed, or intellectual Zodiac containing the fixed stars, or else to the movable, or natural Zodiac containing the movable, or wandering stars. In astronomy, the phrase 'fixed star' (from the Latin *stellae fixae*) is technically incorrect; but nonetheless it is used in an historical context, and in classical mechanics to refer to celestial objects that do not appear to move in relation to the other stars of the night sky. The phrase originated in classical antiquity when astronomers and natural philosophers divided the lights in the sky into two groups comprising the fixed Zodiac containing the band of fixed stars, which appear to rise and set, but keep the same relative arrangement over time; and the other group, comprising the moveable Zodiac, containing the band of wandering stars.

---

i For many purposes, conveniently considered as the sky represented by a sphere of arbitrarily large radius centred on the observer, the celestial objects being projected onto this sphere.

But why is it that so many signs of the zodiac are named after animals—ram, bull, lion, etc.? Is it just because the outline of the constellations can, with a little imagination, be traced to the figures of animals? Or is there a deeper reason? Interestingly and significantly, the word 'zodiac' is derived from the Greek word *zodion*, a diminutive of *zoon*, meaning animal, and here we have our first clue about the subjective influences and correlations concerning the stars and planets. For animals are not dead things; *they typify energies, each according to its nature* (like the resolute endurance of the bull or the noble courage of the lion).

The zodiacal signs given animal names

The Astrological Zodiac and the Ages of Mankind

The zodiac was known in India and Egypt for incalculable ages, and the knowledge of the sages (magi) of these countries with regard to the occult influence of the stars and heavenly bodies on our planet was far greater than profane astronomy ever admits or can ever hope to reach towards. Regarding the 'astrological Zodiac proper', Blavatsky writes that 'it is an imaginary circle passing round the earth in the plane of the equator, its first point being called Aries 0°. It is divided into twelve equal parts called "Signs of the Zodiac", each containing 30° of space, and on it is measured the right ascension of celestial bodies. The movable or natural Zodiac is a succession of constellations forming a belt of 47° in width, lying north and south of the plane of the ecliptic. The precession of the Equinoxes is caused by the "motion" of the s[S]un through space, which makes the constellations appear to move forward against the order of the signs at the rate of 50⅓ seconds per year. A simple calculation will show that at this rate the constellation Taurus (Heb. [Hebrew] *Aleph*) was in the first sign of the Zodiac at the beginning of the Kali Yuga [the Iron Age, or the Black Age], and consequently the Equinoctial point fell therein. At this time, also, Leo was in the summer solstice, Scorpio in the Autumnal Equinox, and Aquarius in the winter solstice; *and these facts form the astronomical key to half the religious mysteries of the world* [writer's emphasis]—the Christian scheme included [as Rudolf Steiner was at pains to emphasize and reclaim].'

Zodiacal correspondences and influences on the Ages of mankind

Blavatsky further elucidates: 'As the nature of the *zodiacal light*—that elongated, luminous, triangular figure which, lying almost in the ecliptic, with its base on the horizon and its apex at greater and smaller altitudes, is to be seen only during the morning and evening twilights—is entirely unknown to science [other than the physical explanation], the origin and real significance and occult meaning of the Zodiac were, and are still, a mystery, to all save the Initiates. The latter preserved their secrets well.'[3]

Indeed, and for good reason did the Initiates preserve their secrets well—but therein lie the keys to the true Royal Science of astrology. Nonetheless, we are able to cast a glimmer of light on the astrological and occult influences of the zodiac mirrored in the universal and occult symbolism of one of the greatest artefacts of antiquity—the Bembine Table of Isis.

The Bembine Table of Isis

In Gallery 2 of the Museo Egizio (Museum of Antiquities) at Turin, rests the *Mensa Isiaca* (Table of Isis) shown in Figure III-5 opposite. It is an elaborate tablet of bronze with enamel and silver inlay, depicting various Egyptian gods and goddesses and is most probably of Roman origin, but emulating the Egyptian style. It was named in the Renaissance

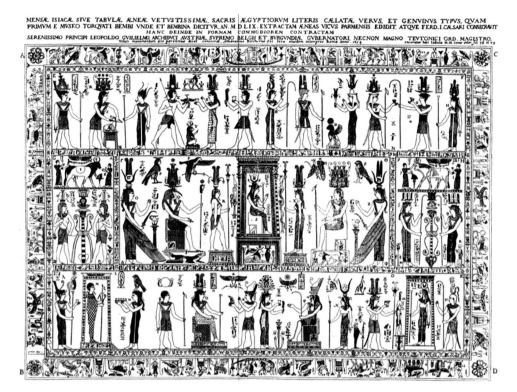

Figure III-5   The Bembine Table of Isis

Image Credit: https://en.wikipedia.org/wiki/Bembine_Tablet#/media/
File:Bembine_Table_of_Isis.png

after Cardinal Bembo (1470–1547), a celebrated antiquarian who acquired it after the 1527 sack of Rome. Later in the seventeenth century, the German Jesuit scholar, polymath, and Renaissance hermeticist Athanasius Kircher (1602–1680) used the Tablet as a primary source for developing his translations of hieroglyphics in his supreme work of Egyptology, *Œdipus Ægyptiacus*[4] published in 1654. The three full folio tomes of ornate illustrations and diagrams were published in Rome over the period 1652–1654 and the work is an example of syncretic and eclectic scholarship in the late Renaissance period.[5] Kircher cited his sources as Chaldean astrology, Hebrew Qabbalah, Greek myth, Pythagorean mathematics, Arabian alchemy, and Latin philology. This work has been dismissed by several scholars, which is not altogether surprising, since the deciphering of symbols and hieroglyphs demands an intuition and understanding of their esoteric meaning and import which goes far beyond the intellectually and historically confined boundaries of pedagogic Egyptology. All the same, it was used as a key to interpreting the 'Book of Thoth', sometimes referred to as the 'Egyptian Tarot' by later occultists, notably by the French occult author and ceremonial magician Eliphas Levi (1810–1875), William Wynn Westcott (1848–1925), the English ceremonial magician, Theosophist, Freemason, and co-founder of the Golden Dawn, and Manly P. Hall. The third volume of *Œdipus Ægyptiacus* deals exclusively with Kircher's translation of Egyptian hieroglyphs.

Genesis and history of Bembine Table

Symbolic Significance of the Bembine Table of Isis

The Table of Isis is directly connected with Egyptian Gnosticism for it concerns the theurgic, or magic, sense in which the Egyptian priests exhibited the philosophy of sacrifice, rites, and ceremonies by a system of occult symbols as exhibited in the images and symbols in the Tablet. In his introduction to the Bembine Table of Isis, as quoted by Hall, Kircher summarizes its symbolism thus: 'It teaches, in the first place, the whole constitution of the threefold world—archetypal, intellectual, and sensible as suggested in the epigraph. The Supreme Divinity is shown moving from the centre to the circumference of a universe made up of both sensible and inanimate things, all of which are animated and agitated by the one supreme power which they call the *Father Mind* and represented by a threefold symbol. Here also are shown three triads from the Supreme One, each manifesting one attribute of the first Trimūrti [see writer's Table III-1 opposite for elucidation on this point and Kircher's terms throughout]. These triads are called the *Foundation*, or the base of all things. In the Tablet is also set forth the arrangement and distribution of those divine creatures that aid the Father Mind, in the control of the universe. Here [in the upper panel] [*sic*] are to be seen the Governors of the worlds [Spiritual Prototypes], each with its fiery, ethereal, and material insignia. Here also [in the lower panel] [*sic*] are the *Fathers of Fountains* [Cosmocreators, or the Demiurge], whose duty it is to care for and preserve the principles of all things and sustain the inviolable laws of Nature. Here are the gods of the spheres and also those who wander from place to place, labouring with all substances and forms (Zonia and Azonia), grouped together as figures of both sexes, with their faces turned to their superior deity.'[6]

'According to the secret doctrine of the Chaldeans', as Hall further explains, 'the universe is divided into four states of being (planes or spheres): archetypal, intellectual, sidereal, and elemental. Each of these reveals the others; the superior controlling the inferior, and the inferior receiving influence from the superior. The archetypal plane was considered synonymous with the intellect of the Triune Divinity. Within this divine, incorporeal, and eternal sphere are included all the lower manifestations of life—all that is, has been, or ever shall be. Within the Kosmic Intellect all things spiritual or material exist as archetypes, or divine thought-forms, which is shown in the Tablet by a chain of secret similes.' Most significantly, the image of Isis is placed in the centre of the Tablet, representing, in Kircher's words, 'the polymorphic [occurring in several different forms] all-containing Universal Idea.'[7] (Refer to the significance of the centre in esoteric philosophy explained in the previous Chapter on page 4.)

Commentary on the Symbolic Significance of the Bembine Table of Isis

Some of the key principles in the above excerpts on the symbolic significance of the Tablet warrant elucidation in the light of the *philosophia perennis*. It is emphasized that the suggestions of the writer, shown in Table III-1 opposite, are by no means exhaustive and readers are invited to supply their own ideas as well.

Readers will have noticed that the Tablet portrays the whole constitution of the world as threefold—archetypal, intellectual, and sensible, whereas the Chaldean universe is classified into four states (planes, or spheres)—archetypal, intellectual, sidereal, and elemental. Does this mean that there is an inconsistency between the two systems?

We need not labour this point since, as explained in Chapter 1 of Volume II, the enumeration of the various aspects of man's composition have perforce to be described, for analytical descriptive purposes, in a serial, sequential fashion, rather like the various layers of a

Table III-1 The Symbolic Significance of the Bembine Table of Isis

Excerpts on the Bembine Tablet	Commentary on the Meaning Concealed in the Symbolism
'The Supreme Divinity is shown moving from the centre to the circumference of a universe'	A treasure trove of meaning is concealed within this simple sentence. It is suggestive of eternal cyclicity: from potentiality to actuality; from the implicate to the explicate; from be-ness to be-ing; from the unmanifest to the manifest. The first in the pair signifies the state that is—the underlying consciousness; the second in the pair denotes the activity born of that state.
'the polymorphic all-containing Universal Idea'	That the figure of Isis is placed in the centre of the Tablet follows directly from the above. The Supreme Divinity, represented here by the Goddess Isis at the centre of a universe, radiates her spherical influence outwards—'moving from the centre to the circumference'.
	This lofty principle has been vouchsafed by modern scientists of metaphysical inclination, for example: Sir James Jeans who declared that 'the universe begins to look more like a great thought than like a great machine' and that Mind is now suspected as being 'a creator and governor of the realm of matter'; and Sir Arthur Eddington for whom 'the universe is of the nature of a thought or sensation in a universal Mind' (see Volume I, Proem, page xlv).
	The explicit references to the primacy of Mind—arguably, 'the polymorphic all-containing Universal Idea'—are undeniable.
various Egyptian gods and goddesses	As we have periodically explained in this work, gods and goddesses are personifications of the various—impersonal—forces and powers in Cosmos and Nature, their dual nature represented in terms of the masculine and feminine aspect of the deity in question.
'Father Mind'	This is Consciousness writ large, the Father term signifying that the Seed (Spirit)—the active, masculine creative principle—must be 'buried' in the Soil (Matter)—the negative and passive feminine principle—for the materialization of its potentiality.
'Fathers of Fountains'	These are spiritual prototypes, variously known as Cosmocreators, or the Demiurge, acting as the agents for transforming Divine Consciousness into the various levels of creation, each with its appropriate grade of Matter. The simile of electrical transformers is apposite here.
'the first Trimūrti'	The Trimūrti is the Brahmā, Viṣṇu, and Śiva of Hinduism, or the Father, Son, and Holy Ghost of Christianity; and similar triune aspects of divinity in all the other great religions.
'the Governors of the worlds'	These are the Dhyan Chohans, the 'Lords of Light' of Hinduism, or the Archangels in Christianity.

Table III-2 The Hermetic Axiom – Cosmos Mirrored in Man

THE MACROCOSM		THE MICROCOSM
Chaldean doctrine	*Egyptian – Bembine Tablet*	*Human Composition*
Archetypal	Archetypal	Spirit
Intellectual	Intellectual	Soul
Sidereal		
	Sensible	Body
Elemental		

cake, or like geological strata, one on top of the other. This has had the unfortunate tendency of conveying a static picture, which loses the wholeness and inter-relationship of parts. Exactly the same is true regarding the classification of the constitution of the universe. Just as man's constitution can be divided into the universal and time-honoured triplicity of spirit–soul–body, or a quadruplicity of *Ātma*–the Causal Body–the Subtle Vehicle–the Physical Vehicle, according to the Tāraka Rāja-Yoga scheme (see Table II-20, page 169 in Chapter 8 of Volume II), so can the constitution of the universe be classified as a threesome, according to Kircher's introduction to the Bembine Table, or a foursome according to the Chaldeans.

Chaldean and Egyptian systems in accord

So there is no inconsistency of 'occult taxonomy' between the two enumerations. As seen in Table III-2 above, the Hermetic Axiom in the classification of Cosmos in the Bembine Tablet and Chaldean scheme (and of course other occult philosophies) is mirrored in man.

The Zodiac, and Man Mirrored through Symbols

Let us further consider the symbolism of the zodiac. With remarkable perspicacity, Hall informs that:

> A more profound interpretation is found in the correspondences between the twelve figures in the upper panel of the Tablet and the twelve in the lower. This furnishes a key to one of the most arcane of ancient secrets—the relationship existing between the two great zodiacs the *fixed* and the *movable*. The *fixed* zodiac is described as an immense dodecahedron, its twelve surfaces representing the outermost walls of abstract space. From each surface of this dodecahedron a great spiritual power, radiating inward, becomes embodied as one of the hierarchies of the movable zodiac, which is a band of circumambulating so-called fixed stars. Within this *movable* zodiac are posited the various planetary and elemental bodies.[8]

Continuing from above, the next quote shows the rationale behind the adage, 'Man, the Measure of All Things' on the basis of the Hermetic Axiom that in man, all the forces and powers in Cosmos find their correlation:

Zodiacal correlations with human respiration

> The relation of these two zodiacs to the subzodiacal spheres has a correlation in the respiratory system of the human body. The great *fixed* zodiac may be said to represent the atmosphere, the *movable* zodiac the lungs, and the subzodiacal worlds the body. The spiritual atmosphere containing the vivifying energies of the twelve divine powers of the

great *fixed* zodiac is inhaled by the cosmic lungs—the *movable* zodiac—and distributed by them through the constitution of the twelve holy animals which are the parts and members of the material universe and signify the inner principles of (archetypal) Man. The functional cycle is completed when the poisonous effluvia of the lower worlds collected by the *movable* zodiac are exhaled into the great *fixed* zodiac, there to be purified by being passed through the divine natures of its twelve eternal hierarchies.[9]

If ever a man were qualified to pronounce on the heavens, the Earth, and their inter-relationship, such a man would surely be that supreme mathematical astronomer, mystic scientist, and alchemist—Isaac Newton. Drawing upon the same wellspring of the *philosophia perennis*, or his preferred term, *prisca sapientia*, upon which the above quotes by Hall are based, Newton has this to say in his letter of 7 December 1675 to Henry Oldenburg FRS (1619–1677), the German theologian, natural philosopher, and First Secretary of the Royal Society:

> For nature is a perpetuall circulatory worker, generating Fluids out of solids, & solids out of Fluids, Fixed things out of volatile & volatile out of fixed, Subtile out of gross and gross out of subtile, Some things to ascend & make the upper terrestriall juices, Rivers and the Atmosphere; & by consequence others to descend for a Requitall of the former. And as the Earth, so perhaps may the Sun imbibe this Spirit copiously to conserve his Shineing, & keep the Planets from recedeing further from him. And they that will, may also suppose, that this Spirit affords or carryes with it thither the solary fewell & materiall Principle of Light; And that the vast aethereall Spaces between us, & the stars are for a sufficient repository for this food of the Sunn & Planets.[10]

Newton regards the whole universe as living

Here we clearly discern the mystic-scientist's thoughts on eternal cyclicity and the spiritual conservation of matter and energy, so to say, between the Earth, Planets, and the Solar system.

But what did Newton make of astrology? There is much evidence that Newton secretly studied astrology.[11,12] But more to the point, the whole issue of planetary influences and forces, and their correspondences and correlations with nature and man was part and parcel of the context and framework of the *prisca sapientia*, and alchemy, as the above brief quote intimates. The following anecdote is often quoted: when the English Astronomer Royal, Edmond Halley FRS (1656–1742), who discovered the comet named after him, once spoke depreciatively on the subject of astrology, Newton is said to have retorted: 'I have studied the matter, you have not!'[13]

Newton never dismissed astrology

Is Astrology a Pseudoscience or a Royal Science?

Accordingly, to round off this section, what are we make of astrology in the context of modern science? Needless to say, virtually without exception, the most prominent and internationally fêted scientists of today regard astrology as a 'pseudoscience', stated politely, or 'utter nonsense', put bluntly. They are not entirely wrong if they base their opinions just on the puerile columns of newspaper astrology without bothering to dig deeper as genuine scientists ought to do. But are these modern pundits missing something?

What is a pseudoscience? In short, it is what appears to be scientific but in fact is not: the mask of science rather than science itself. More technically, according to the Oxford English Dictionary, ninth edition, 1995, pseudoscience is 'a pretended or spurious science;

Standard definition of pseudoscience

a collection of beliefs mistakenly regarded as based on scientific method.' Furthermore, the National Science Foundation, the independent USA federal agency created by Congress in 1950 'to promote the progress of science; to advance the national health, prosperity, and welfare; to secure the national defense …'14 defines what is, and what is not pseudoscience thus: 'Pseudoscience is defined here as "claims presented so that they appear [to be] scientific even though they lack supporting evidence and plausibility" (Shermer 1997, p. 33).[15] In contrast, science is "a set of methods designed to describe and interpret observed and inferred phenomena, past or present, and aimed at building a testable body of knowledge open to rejection or confirmation" (Shermer 1997, p. 17).[16]'

However, the weak link and sticking point in the above definitions are the very words 'science' and 'testable', both restricted to a particular branch of study, namely, physical science underpinned by the prevailing paradigm of scientific materialism. This must be contrasted with science in its widest and fullest sense meaning 'knowledge', etymologically derived from the Latin *scientia*, a noun formed from the present participle of the verb *scīre*, (to) 'know'. (This theme is further developed in Chapter 11.) In other words, there is a knowledge and knowing that can be derived by means not amenable to physical science. And that knowledge, central to the science of astrology, is transcendental metaphysics dealing with the greatest and most abstruse problems concerning the universe and man— a far cry from pure materialism. Reverting, then, to the question of pseudoscience, if astrology endeavoured to explain the dynamics of general relativity—and obviously floun- dered in the attempt—then the charge of pseudoscience would be no exaggeration. Equally, when astronomy, an exact physical science, tries to understand planetary influ- ences and correlations through a materialistic lens, it too flounders and becomes in fact a pseudoscience, since it pretends to know what it does not know and so assumes a mask of science. Paraphrasing Paul Brunton's peerless insights into the works of modern science, he remarks that:

> All those who use the data of science to support their belief in an intellectual materialism and to justify their scorn for astrology or the hermetic sciences deny the very source from which they ultimately draw their intellectual capacity to make their criticisms; and to the extent that it lets them use it in this way, science itself becomes, not just pseudoscience, but faith and ultimately, superstition.17

It is for this very reason that Blavatsky entitled one of the chapters in the Occult Science section of *The Secret Doctrine* 'The Masks of Science'—not to attack science but to point out, as we have just done, that materialistic science is singularly ill-equipped to deal with subjects that lie outside its self-imposed boundaries of investigating objective and physical phenomena; therefore it can only pronounce on the subjective and non-physical realms of existence, as if through a mask. However, Blavatsky is at pains to point out: 'If, even now, when most of the secrets of the Asuramayas [the Atlantean astronomers considered as great magicians] and the Zoroasters are lost, it is still amply shown that horoscopes and judiciary astrology are far from being based on fiction, and if such men as Kepler and even Sir Isaac Newton believed that stars and constellations influenced the destiny of our globe and its humanities, it requires no great stretch of faith to believe that men who were initi- ated into all the mysteries of nature, as well as into astronomy and astrology, knew precisely in what way nations and mankind, whole races as well as individuals, would be affected by the so-called "signs of the Zodiac".'18 What these initiates knew first hand, anyone

Science or pseudoscience depends on context of application

Is scientism (not science) ultimately a faith or superstition?

The magi and legendary scientists acknowledged zodiacal influences on Earth and individuals endowed with a highly sensitive and mystical nature may faintly glean, 'that the entrance of the Sun into each of the twelve zodiacal constellations—or signs—brings with it a new cosmic force into operation, not merely on our earth, but distributively speaking throughout our own individual lives.'[19]

This Chapter has built upon the previous one and shown how symbolism helps to attain a macrocosmic appreciation of the unity and interconnections between man, his world, and the universe he inhabits. The next Chapter deals with insights into the human body—a microcosm of the macrocosm—achieved through the power of symbolism.

But it would seem appropriate to end this Chapter with a rewording of one of Blavatsky's searing insights into the workings of science.

> *Telescopes and spectrometers may solve the mystery of the material parts of the shell of cosmos, i.e., the visible, objective, and physical cosmos: they can never cut a window into its inner principles and secrets to open the smallest vista on any of the wider horizons of being. For life, and everything pertaining to it, including the nature of man, belongs to the lawful domain of the metaphysician and esoteric psychologist,[20] and physical science has no claim upon it.*
>
> THE SCIENCE OF LIFE[21]

NOTES

1   *STA*, 'The Hiramic Legend', LXXX.

2   Institute of Astronomy – University of Cambridge <http://www.ast.cam.ac.uk/public/ask/2856> accessed 19 March 2020.

3   *TSGLOSS*, 387.

4   Athanasius Kircher, *OEdipus Ægyptiacus, Hoc Est Universalis Hieroglyphicae Veterum Doctrinae temporum iniuria abolitae Instauratio* [OEdipus Ægyptiacus, This is a Universal Hieroglyphicae Early Teaching on the Establishment of the Injury of Time, which had been Abolished] (Rome: Vitalis Mascardi, 1652–1654). See also *Oedipus Aegyptiacus*, The Online Books Page (digitized 9 November 2012) <http://onlinebooks.library.upenn.edu/webbin/book/lookupid?key=olbp67641> accessed 19 March 2020.

5   Joscelyn Godwin, *Athanasius Kircher: A Renaissance man in search of lost knowledge* (London: Thames and Hudson, 1979).

6   Athanasius Kircher, quoted in *STA*, 'The Bembine Table of Isis', LVIII.

7   *ibid.*

8   *STA*, 'The Bembine Table of Isis', LX.

9   *ibid.*

10 H. W. Turnbull, J. F. Scott, A. Rupert Hall, and Laura Tilling (eds), *The Correspondences of Isaac Newton*, 7 vols (Cambridge, Cambridge University Press, 1959–77), i, 366.

11 Michel Gauquelin, *The Cosmic Clocks: From astrology to a modern science* (London: Peter Owen, 1969), 49.

12 John Anthony West and Gerhard Toonder, *The Case for Astrology* (UK and Australia: Penguin Books, 1973), 81–3, 97.

13 Sir David Brewster, *The Life of Sir Isaac Newton* (New York: J. & J. Harper, 1831).

14 National Science Foundation <http://www.nsf.gov/sbe/srs/seind02/c7/c7s5.htm#c7s5l2> accessed 19 March 2020.

15 Michael Shermer, *Why People Believe Weird Things: Pseudoscience, superstition, and other confusions of our time*, foreword by Stephen Jay Gould (1997; rev. and enl. edn, Los Angeles: W. H. Freeman & Co, 2000).

16 —— *op. cit.*

17 Paraphrased from *NPB*-5, Part 2: *The Intellect*, 'When Science Stands Alone', ¶45, 121; ¶46, 121.

18 *TSGLOSS*, 387–8.

19 G. de Purucker, *Occult Glossary: A compendium of Oriental and Theosophical terms* (Pasadena, California: Theosophical University Press, 1972), 185.

20 See Alice Bailey, *Esoteric Psychology* (London: Lucis Press, 1972).

21 *CW*-VIII, 'The Science of Life', 241.

3 Man is the Measure of All Things – the Human Body in Symbolism

Are the physicians and surgeons not already worthy to be called dead who know so little of their own selves, and so much of the bodies in which they are lodged?

PAUL BRUNTON[1]

ana'l-haqq *'I am God'.*

MANṢŪR AL-ḤALLĀJ[2]

In him, all things in a most distinct way are also at the same time indistinct. Man in God is God. Man in God is indistinct from everything which is in God.

MEISTER ECKHART[3]

Again, the mystics of many centuries, independently, yet in perfect harmony with each other *[emphasis added] (somewhat like the particles in an ideal gas) have described, each of them, the unique experience of his or her life in terms that can be condensed in the phrase:* DEUS FACTUS SUM *(I have become God).*

ERWIN SCHRÖDINGER[4]

SYNOPSIS

Chapter 3 takes up the theme of the human body in symbolism in much greater detail. We describe the anatomical symbolism of the organs and members of the body. The three main body centres of consciousness are summarized. Then, we show how the current dogma in mainstream neuroscience, which dictates that the brain is the sole organ of consciousness, is slowly being eroded by evidence from science itself—in the form of a budding neurocardiology. This science examines the physiological interplay between the cardiovascular and nervous systems and points to the primacy of the heart, and not the head, as the seat of consciousness in the human body—what occult science has unequivocally affirmed. The Chapter ends with symbolic representations of occult powers in man and discusses how the symbolism of the Great Pyramid unveils the mystery of man.

KEY WORDS: symbolism, macrocosm and microcosm, idols, anatomical analogies, consciousness centres in man, neurocardiology and primacy of the heart, anatomical symbolism of body, occult powers, Meister Eckhart, Manṣūr al-Ḥallāj

The four epigraphs above serve as harbingers of this Chapter for good reason: they convey the same meaning, differently expressed, through philosophy, mystical Islam (Sufism), mystical Christianity, and enlightened science, that the Indweller of that entity known as 'man' is of divine Substance.

The first epigraph was featured in Volume I, Chapter 2 on page 17 and bears repeating. Why? Because it starkly reveals the distinctions between the human state, the human condition, and the human body. The anatomy and physiology of the latter is clearly the supreme achievement of medical science, as is the associated pharmaceutical and surgical treatments resulting from a detailed understanding of the physiological mechanisms of the body. However, it is generally known that, other than with individual practitioners, psychiatry, as a whole, has not achieved the same success rate as physical medicine has using drug therapy and surgery. Why? Because ailments of the mind involve a profound understanding of the human state and condition, not only the neurological processes in the brain. And to the extent that psychiatry divorces itself from spirituality, concentrating on outward behavioural characteristics and treating brain disorders through drugs, its attempts to treat the mind as a whole will be vitiated. As a simile, if an out-of-tune piano were the cause of a poor musical performance, the remedy would be to tune the piano, the physical instrument; but if the pianist be mediocre, no amount of adjustments to the piano would render a polished performance. Here the remedy would be for the pianist to improve his skills—or shut the keyboard lid and eliminate the problem by physical means!

Who, or what is 'man': just his body?

In Psalm 8:5 (King James Version) we read that man is 'a little lower than the angels', and hast been 'crowned with glory and honour.' How, then, do we understand the depth and breadth of what we call 'man' in his entirety?

The previous Chapter explained how symbolism unlocks the mysteries about the inner workings of Cosmos and man. The zodiac was mentioned as one such universal symbol. Starting with some general precepts, this Chapter then focuses on the human body, also one of the oldest, most profound, and universal symbols, and then supplies proofs of universal symbolism concerning the composite nature of man. What is the genesis of the symbol? Why is the human body so venerated? Why did Protagoras (490–420 BC), the pre-Socratic Greek philosopher (numbered as one of the sophists by Plato), open his celebrated work *Truth* with the words: 'Man is the measure of all things'?[5, 6]

General Precepts – Why is Man the 'Measure of All Things'?

As explained in the Proem on page lii f. in Volume I, the esoteric philosophers from antiquity to the present day recognized the futility of attempting to cope intellectually with that which transcends the comprehension of the rational faculties, and so invoked the well known Hermetic Axiom, 'As above, so below'. This was an attempt to understand the inconceivable Divinity by studying Its reflection in man, within the narrow confines of whose nature they found manifested all the mysteries of the external spheres. Deity, or God, was considered as the Grand MAN and, conversely, man as the little god. Continuing this analogy, the universe was regarded as a man and, conversely, man as a miniature universe. Hence the old saying: 'Man is the measure of all things' as per this Chapter title. The greater universe was termed the *Macrocosm*—the Great World, or Body; and the Divine Life, or spiritual entity controlling its functions, was called the *Macroprosophus*. Man's body—the individual human universe, was termed the *Microcosm*; and the Divine Life, or spiritual entity controlling its functions, was called the *Microprosophus*.[7]

Man: a universe in miniature

It must have been this intense realization of the equivalence, rather indistinguishability between the essence of man and deity that prompted the great Persian mystic, poet, and teacher of Sūfīsm Manṣūr al-Ḥallāj to proclaim in the streets and markets of Baghdad his burning love of God, quoted in the second epigraph (also translated as 'I am the Truth'). Words such as 'I am God' or 'I am the Truth' need careful explanation since such exclamatory utterances have been made as often by tyrants and dictators as by saints and martyrs. In the first case it is an assertion of a mammoth ego, where the despot asserts his total power and readiness to annihilate those who oppose him. In the second, as with al-Ḥallāj, there is also an annihilation, but of a radically different kind: the complete annihilation of the ego which therefore allows the divine to speak through the individual—thus, not a boasting of supremacy over others, but a joyous affirmation of union with God. It was this denial of his own self, and of the existence of anything but God that led al-Ḥallāj to proclaim 'that the wise man is, in relation to God, like a Ray of the sun [*Ātma*—see Volume II, Chapter 2, page 20] which proceeds from it and returns to it, and whose light is a flux coming from the sun'.[8] The Azerbaijanian Sohravardi, al-Maqtul (*circa* 1154–1191/2), one of Iran's greatest philosophers, gnostics, and Sūfī masters, explains the meaning as being like 'one who has looked at the sun and then looks at himself, finds he is filled with nothing else but rays of sun, and exclaims, "I am the Sun".'[9]

And it is for this same reason that the German theologian, philosopher, and mystic Meister Eckhart (1260–1328) affirmed the divine status and intrinsic relation between man and God, the former a projection of Archetypal Man (Adam Kadmon—see Chapter 4 later) the Son of God, so to speak, who is not God but his image endowed with all the potentialities of the Father–Mother. The dialectic of indistinction and distinction is presented in Latin Sermon 4 where Eckhart affirms the indistinguishability—not synonymity—between God and man: 'Anything in God is absorbed by God and so a person in God has lost their own identity within the identity of God.' Therefore, as also implied in the third epigraph above, 'Being in God is identified as being God.'[10] It is also implied in the fourth epigraph.

That Eckhart and al-Ḥallāj, coming from widely different cultures and backgrounds, should both espouse the same unequivocal truth about the relation between man and God reinforces a principal strand of our work: that the emissaries of the *philosophia perennis* worldwide promulgate the same essential truths. (Needless to say, the word 'God' used by Eckhart and al-Ḥallāj is meant in the sense of the ABSOLUTE, or Divine Consciousness, as clarified in the Definitions in Volume IV, having nothing to do with the crude anthropomorphic concepts of orthodox theologies. There is no question of proclaiming that the average man = God, so he is Omnipresent, Omnipotent, and Omniscient.)

al-Ḥallāj, Sohravardi, Eckhart, and Schrödinger all proclaim man's intrinsic divinity

So also does Schrödinger, with the aid of a scientific analogy, affirm the indistinguishability between the God-spark (man) and God as we find in the fourth epigraph.

Enough has been said to show that since man is a 'ray' of God, it follows that the latter must also have a twofold constitution, of which the superior part is invisible and the inferior visible. In similar vein, Eckhart affirmed, 'As there is an inner and outer man there is God and the Godhead. The soul or inner man is connected with the Godhead while the flesh and the outer man relate to God.'[11] (This does not mean that Eckhart espoused a dualist philosophy by dividing Unity (God) into two. Rather, as explained in detail in Volume II, Chapter I, page 10 et seq. in reference to man, the two 'parts' are aspects of the One.) In both man and God there is also an intermediary sphere, marking the point where these visible and invisible natures meet. As the spiritual nature of God controls His objective universal form, which is actually a crystallized Idea, i.e., the objective universe is an Idea, or Thought in Divine Consciousness (the 'Mind of God') as scientists like Jeans and Eddington realized (see Volume I, Chapter 3, page 36 et seq.), so the spiritual nature of

Correspondences between constitution of God and man

man is the invisible cause and controlling power of his visible, material body; or in other words, the body is an idea in consciousness. This is the most generic form of expressing the equivalence and interconversion of Spirit and Matter, recognized on the physical plane as energy and matter. It is evident, then, that the spirit of man bears the same relationship to his material body and personality that God bears to the objective universe and its life forms. The Mysteries taught that spirit, or life, was anterior to form and that what is anterior includes all that is posterior to itself. Spirit being anterior to form, form is therefore included within the realm of spirit. It is also a popular belief that man's spirit or soul is within his body. According to philosophy and original theology, however, this belief is erroneous, for spirit first circumscribes an area and then manifests within it. Philosophically speaking, form, being a part of spirit, is within spirit; but spirit is more than the sum of form. So also, brain is a part, or an aspect, of mind and lies within mind (the words 'part' and 'within' understood of course not in a volumetric, but in a metaphysical sense). As the material nature of man is therefore within the sum of spirit, so the Universal Nature, including the entire sidereal system, is within the all-pervading essence of God—the Universal Spirit.

While generally regarded as polytheists, the pagans gained this reputation not because they worshiped more than one God but rather because they personified the attributes of this one nameless God, thereby creating a pantheon of posterior deities each manifesting a part of what the One God manifested as a whole. The various pantheons of ancient religions therefore actually represent the catalogued and personified attributes of Deity. The pagan Mysteries were primarily concerned with instructing neophytes in the true relationship existing between the *Macrocosm* and the *Microcosm*—in other words, between God and man. Accordingly, the key to these analogies between the organs and functions of the *Microcosmic* man and those of the *Macrocosmic* MAN constituted the most prized possession of the early initiates. With the added insights from this Chapter, it is hoped that readers will now appreciate the full force of this seminal passage (quoted at the close of the Proem and Volume II) about the threefold nature of Man inhabiting three worlds:

Why is man key to the riddle of life?

Man is a little world—a microcosm inside the great universe. Like a foetus, he is suspended, by all his *three* spirits, in the matrix of the macrocosmos; and while his terrestrial body is in constant sympathy with its parent earth, his astral soul lives in unison with the sidereal *anima mundi*. He is in it, as it is in him, for the world-pervading element fills all space, and *is* space itself, only shoreless and infinite. As to his third spirit, the divine, what is it but an infinitesimal ray, one of the countless radiations proceeding directly from the Highest Cause—the Spiritual Light of the World. This is the trinity of organic and inorganic nature—the spiritual and the physical, which are three in one, and of which Proclus says that 'the first monad is the Eternal God; the second, eternity; the third, the paradigm, or pattern of the universe'; the three constituting the Intelligible Triad.[12]

This is why the Greeks, Persians, Egyptians, and Hindus, and even the Gnostics (before the orthodox Church suffocated the esoteric dimension of Christianity) considered a philosophical analysis of man's triune nature to be an indispensable part of ethical and religious training. The Mysteries of every nation taught that the Laws, Elements, and Powers of the Universe were epitomized in the human constitution; that everything which existed outside of man had its analogue within man. The writer speculates that what Blavatsky terms 'the world-pervading element [that] fills all space' might correspond, in a general sense, to what Newton designates in the

The World is the Thought of God crystallized

General Scholium of *Principia* as 'a certain most subtle Spirit which pervades [the space] and lies hid in all gross bodies'.[13]

From Exaltation to Idolization

Long before idolatry corrupted religion, the statue of man (possibly even a manikin) was placed in the sanctuary of the temple, the human figure symbolizing the Divine Power in all its intricate manifestations. Thus the hierophants accepted Man as their textbook, and through the study of Him learned to understand the greater and more abstruse mysteries of the celestial scheme of which they were a part. After ages of investigation, the manikin became a mass of intricate hieroglyphs and symbolic figures. Every part had its secret meaning. The measurements formed a basic standard by means of which it was possible to measure all parts of the cosmos. It was an organic and composite emblem of all the knowledge possessed by the sages and hierophants.

In vain did the initiates of old warn their disciples that an image is not a reality but merely the objectification of a subjective idea. The images of the gods were not designed to be objects of worship but were to be regarded merely as emblems, or reminders, of invisible powers and principles. Similarly, the body of man was not to be considered as the individual but only as the house of the individual, in the same manner that the temple was the House of God. In a state of grossness and perversion, man's body is the tomb or prison of a divine inhabitant; but in a state of refinement, the temple of his spirit.

The 'map' is not the 'territory'

Then came the age of idolatry. The Mysteries decayed from within. The secrets were lost and none knew the identity of the mysterious man who stood over the altar. It was remembered only that the figure was a sacred and glorious symbol of the Universal Power, and it finally came to be looked upon as a god—the One in whose image man was made. Having lost the knowledge of the purpose for which the manikin was originally constructed, the priests worshiped this effigy until finally their lack of spiritual understanding brought the temple down in ruins about their heads and the statue crumbled with the civilization that had forgotten its meaning. By progressive stages, the living esoteric meaning was starved in proportion to the increasing adulation of the outward, exoteric form—refer to the section on the misuse of symbols and idolatry in Chapter 1 on page 16 et seq.[14]

The idol is not the living essence

The Anatomical Analogy

Reverting however to the symbol of the human body in its vital, esoteric meaning and proceeding from the assumption of the hierophants that man is actually fashioned in the image of God, the initiated minds of past ages erected the stupendous structure of theology (in its original, uncorrupted form and sense) upon the foundation of the human body. They knew from actual experience that the wisdom and intelligence which have gone into, and are hidden behind, the whole universe have also gone into the 'making' of the human body. The religious world of today is almost totally ignorant of the fact that the science of biology is the fountainhead of its doctrines and tenets. Many of the codes and laws believed by modern divines to have been direct revelations from Divinity are, in reality, the fruitage of ages of patient delving into the intricacies of the human constitution and the infinite wonders revealed by such a study.

Myth and
scripture conceal
anatomical
analogies

In nearly all the sacred books of the world can be traced an anatomical analogy. This is most evident in their creation myths. Anyone familiar with embryology and obstetrics will recognize the basis of the allegory concerning Adam and Eve and the Garden of Eden, the nine degrees of the Eleusinian Mysteries, and the Brahmanic legend of Viṣṇu's incarnations. The story of the Universal Egg, the Scandinavian myth of Ginnungagap (the dark cleft in space in which the seed of the world is sown), and the fish used as an emblem of the paternal generative power—all show the true origin of undogmatized theological speculation. 'The philosophers of antiquity realized that man himself was the key to the riddle of life, for he was the living image of the Divine Plan, and in future ages humanity also will come to realize more fully the solemn import of those ancient words: "The proper study of mankind is man."'15

The Three Grand Centres of Consciousness–Power

Readers will recall what was said earlier, that both God and man have a twofold constitution: the superior part invisible, the inferior part visible, and an intermediary sphere where these two meet; hence, that the spirit of man bears the same relationship to his material body that God bears to the objective universe. The ancient wisdom also teaches that all bodies—whether spiritual or material—have three centres, called by the Greeks the *upper* centre, the *middle* centre, and the *lower* centre. An apparent ambiguity will here be noted. Because, as pointed out in Chapter 1, it is virtually impossible to convey abstract mental verities in their entirety through pictures, or even symbols, for the diagrammatic representation of one aspect of metaphysical relationships may be an actual contradiction of some other aspect. While that which is above is generally considered superior in dignity and power, in reality that which is in the centre is superior and anterior to both that which is said to be above and that which is said to be below. Therefore, it must be said that the first—which is considered as being above—is actually in the centre, while both of the others (which are said to be either above or below) are actually beneath. Here the reader is earnestly requested to refer to Chapter 1, page 4 for clarification on what exactly terms like 'above', 'below', and 'centre' mean *in the esoteric and spiritual context* of their application.

Relative
significance of
three centres in
all bodies

Relative
significance of
heart, brain, and
reproductive
organs in man

Since the superior (or spiritual) centre is in the midst of the other two, its analogue in the physical body is the heart—the most spiritual and mysterious organ in the human body. The second centre (or the link between the superior and inferior worlds) is elevated to the position of greatest physical dignity—the brain. The third (or lower) centre is relegated to the position of least physical dignity but greatest physical importance—the generative system. Thus the heart is symbolically the source of life; the brain the link by which, through rational intelligence, life and form (spirit and matter in the generic sense) are united; and the generative system—or infernal creator—the source of that power by which physical organisms are produced. The ideals and aspirations of the individual depend largely upon which of these three centres of power predominates in scope and activity of expression. In the materialist the lower centre is the strongest, in the intellectualist (namely, the excessive exercise of intellect at the expense of emotions) the higher centre; but in the initiate the middle centre—by bathing the two extremes in a flood of spiritual effulgence—controls wholesomely both the mind and the body.16

These three universal centres: the one above, the one below, and the link uniting them, represent three suns or three aspects of one Sun—centres of effulgence. Says the English Neoplatonist Thomas Taylor (1758–1835):

> The first of these [suns] is analogous to light when viewed subsisting in its fountain the sun; the second to the light [rays] immediately proceeding from the sun; and the third to the splendour communicated to other natures by this light.[17]

The three universal centres have their analogues in the three grand centres of the human body, which, like the physical universe, is a Demiurgic fabrication. Thus, in terms of the anatomical analogy, the writer has restated Taylor's maxim, just mentioned, thus:

Correspondences between man's three centres and three aspects of one Sun

> The first of these suns is analogous to consciousness when viewed subsisting in the heart; the second to the consciousness rays immediately proceeding from the heart to the brain; and the third to the splendour communicated to other human beings by the generative system.

Here we may comprehend the meaning of those immortal words: '*As a man thinketh in his heart, so is he.*' As there are seven hearts in the brain so there are seven brains in the heart, but this is a matter of superphysics of which little can be said at the present time.[18] Nonetheless, this writer maintains that there is no better policy for the modern scientist to follow than '*to think with the heart, and feel with the brain*'.

As light bears witness to life, which is its source, so the mind bears witness to the spirit, and activity in a still lower plane bears witness to intelligence. Thus, in man, the mind bears witness to the heart, while the generative system, in turn, bears witness to the mind. Accordingly, the spiritual nature is most commonly symbolized by a heart; the intellectual power by an opened eye, symbolizing the pineal gland or Cyclopean eye, which is the two-faced Janus of the pagan Mysteries; and the generative system by a flower, a cup, or a hand.

Modern Science is Now Discovering that the Heart Rules the Head

The renowned statement, 'Modern science is our best ally [...]' is no mere wishful thinking on the part of the Adept who stated it.[19] There are numerous signs to show that modern science is slowly, but surely, corroborating the ancient wisdom.[20] The primacy of the heart over the head in the consciousness of the human being is a fine case in point as we illustrate below.

What Occult Science Affirms ...

In a notable paper on occult physiology, Blavatsky explains that the brain, taken as an organ of consciousness, serves as the vehicle on the objective plane of Lower *manas* (the Lower mind), which obviously must work upon its material molecules. The subdivisions of the brain correspond to, and are the organs of, the subdivisions of Lower manas. She explains that there are seven cavities in the brain which, during life are empty in the ordinary sense of the word, but in reality, are filled with *Ākāśa* (*Akasha*), each cavity having its own colour according to the state of consciousness of the individual (such colours being visible, of course, only to purified vision and never the spectroscope). These brain cavities are referred to in Occultism as the 'Seven Harmonies', or the scale of the Divine Harmonies *and it is in these that visions must be reflected, if they are to remain in the brain-memory.*[21] But reflection surely implies a source of light? Where does that light come from? Blavatsky continues by pointing out that the seven cavities are the parts of the brain that receive impressions from the heart, and enable the memory of the heart to be impressed on the memory of the brain.

Brain reflects the
memory of the
heart

In essence, the fountainhead of consciousness in man is the heart and not the brain, whose memory (light) is borrowed from the heart.

... *Western Science Now Confirms*

What is the crux of the recent discoveries in science about the human heart? 'Is God All in Your Head?' is a substantial article by Craig Hamilton, who is a contemporary leader in the emerging field of evolutionary spirituality, a founding member of Ken Wilber's Integral Institute, a member of the Esalen Center for Theory and Research, and formerly a participant in the Synthesis Dialogues, a 35-person interdisciplinary think-tank presided over by His Holiness the Dalai Lama. The article addresses the 'hard problem' of consciousness posed by the philosopher of mind and cognitive scientist David Chalmers, namely, how subjective experience can be the result of physical processes in the brain; as distinguished from the 'easy problem', which involves understanding such things as the neural mechanisms behind perception, how we pay attention, and the differences between waking and sleep (see Volume I, Chapter 3, page 28 et seq. for more details). Hamilton addresses these matters in a comprehensive survey and summary, in three parts, on the whole question of the scientific quest to solve the mystery of consciousness, in the light of the increasing drive in mainstream science to force every aspect of higher human behaviour—from altruism to spiritual seeking—through the mechanistic grid of natural selection. These parts are: towards a science of consciousness, a key element of which is neural correlates of consciousness; then the steps towards a biology of mind; finally, the quest for a new paradigm of mind. Owing to its importance, a key passage from the last part of this article is worth quoting in its entirety:

Softening the
'hard problem' of
consciousness

> The cranium may be home to the smartest organ in town, but when it comes to sheer magnetism, the gray matter in your head may have a little competition on its hands. According to the new science of neurocardiology, we have a *second brain* in the form of a dense cluster of *neurons*, in the *heart*, and its electromagnetic field is five thousand times stronger than the brain upstairs. So, don't be surprised if the next person telling you to 'follow your heart' is your doctor [writer's emphases].[22]

Current research data, some ten years later, from the HeartMath Institute Research Centre (see below) puts the value of the electromagnetic field strength of the heart to around one thousand times stronger than that generated by the brain.

The above is no mere statement of wishy-washy generalities. It is the distillation of what can be gleaned from heavyweight clinical textbooks authored by leading scientists, biochemists, psychologists, and professors of pharmacology.

It is important to distinguish between the 'second brain in the form of a dense cluster of neurons, in the heart,' from what is now commonly referred to as the 'second brain', or 'brain in the gut'. This is the enteric (relating to or occurring in the intestines) nervous system comprising two thin layers of more than one hundred million nerve cells lining the gastrointestinal tract from the esophagus to the rectum.[23]

Neurocardiology and the Primacy of the Human Heart

Owing to its importance regarding the overall theme of this work on the primary and central role of consciousness, an outline (necessarily cursory) of recent discoveries and evidence from clinical medicine about the relationship between heart, brain, and an individual's life experiences now follows.

Basic and Clinical Neurocardiology[24] shows why neurocardiology is becoming increasingly relevant to the management of heart disease. This book presents novel concepts about how neurons, from the level of the heart to the sensorium, exert dynamic control over cardiac electrical and mechanical events over a lifetime. A sequel to this book is a nineteen-page monograph providing ground-breaking research in the field of neurocardiology.[25] This has established that the heart is a sensory organ and a sophisticated information encoding and processing centre, with an extensive intrinsic nervous system sufficiently sophisticated to qualify as a 'heart–brain'. *Brain–Heart Interactions* is another important book dealing with the neurocardiology of arrhythmia and sudden cardiac death.[26] It shows that neuroanatomic connections between the brain and the heart provide links that allow cardiac arrhythmias to occur in response to brain activation. Reviewing possible mechanisms of brain-related arrhythmias, the authors suggest that the nervous system directs the events leading to cardiac damage.

Knowing By Heart: Cellular memory in heart transplants[27] is an impressive book which presents landmark accounts of what occultists have always known: that consciousness is ubiquitous and pervades each and every particle of the universe, as indeed it does the human body and its cells. In the case of the human being, the medical profession uses the safe term 'cellular memory' to define the idea that the cells in our bodies contain information about our personalities, tastes, and histories. Evidence of this phenomenon has been found to be prevalent in heart transplant recipients and cannot readily be explained away by the influence of the drugs used to suppress donor rejection rendering the patient more receptive to the memory of their own forgotten life history. A striking example concerns the heart of a murdered ten year old girl, which was transplanted into an eight year old girl who was subsequently able to provide such accurate details about the crime so as to lead to the arrest and conviction of the murderer.[28] See Endnote III-1 for more details. However, explanations other than cellular memory cannot be ruled out. For example, what is commonly referred to as 'spirit attachment' (see Volume II, especially Chapters 4 and 5 for technical details); or the sudden onset of cases suggestive of reincarnation, as meticulously researched and recorded by the psychiatrist Ian Stevenson, where there is no question of transference of physical cells between bodies of different individuals widely separated in distance and time (see Volume I, Chapter 4).

Possible evidence of cellular memory in heart transplants

HeartMath Institute Research Center (https://www.heartmath.com/institute-of-heart-math/) is an internationally recognized global leader in emotional physiology, optimal function, resilience, and stress-management research. The director of research is the contemporary American psychophysiologist Rollin McCraty, a professor at Florida

Atlantic University whose interests include the physiology of emotion. The centre conducts basic research into psychophysiology, neurocardiology, and biophysics, frequently in collaboration with universities, research centers and health-care-system partners. One of the primary areas of focus is the mechanisms by which emotions influence cognitive processes, behaviour, health, and the global interconnectivity between people and the Earth's energetic systems. What is of great importance to this Chapter is how this research has significantly advanced the understanding of heart–brain interactions.

Effect of heart–brain interaction on emotional wellbeing

A fully referenced technical report, with statistics and author profiles, presents an overview of research conducted on the role of the heart in human performance. Chapter 6 of the report entitled 'Energetic Communication', contains important information about the energetic role of the heart. It is stated that the heart is the most powerful source of electromagnetic energy in the human body, producing the largest rhythmic electromagnetic field of any bodily organ. This field is some one thousand times stronger than the electromagnetic field generated by the brain. The electrical field of the heart is about sixty times greater in amplitude than the electrical activity generated by the brain. This field, measured in the form of an electrocardiogram, can be detected anywhere on the surface of the body. Furthermore, the magnetic field produced by the heart is more than one hundred times greater in strength than the field generated by the brain and can be detected up to three feet away from the body, in all directions, using magnetometers based on SQUID (superconducting quantum interference device). The magnetic field of the heart, which, to reiterate, is the strongest rhythmic field produced by the human body, not only envelopes every cell of the body, but also extends out in all directions into the space around us.[29] It can be measured several feet away from the body by sensitive magnetometers as confirmed in a paper of the *American Heart Journal*.[30] Research conducted suggests that the field of the heart is an important carrier of information.[31]

The reason for mentioning this is to provide further evidence in relation to what has been stated above about the primacy of the heart, and not the brain, as the wellspring of consciousness in the human being. The ramifications are therefore serious and wide ranging. Most immediately, two pieces of evidence spring to mind; these concern the bearing on the consciousness of 'human carnivores', and the impact on the human heart of love unrequited. If each cell is supposed to retain some imprint of the thoughts and feelings (consciousness) of its donor, then what are the implications for meat eaters? Are they not ingesting, at a subliminal level, the element of abject terror that an animal experiences at the moment of death? Concerning our feelings, to die of a broken heart might be more than a sentimental turn of phrase enacted in soap operas. It may be that when the heart, as the seat of love, is bottled up and deprived of its feeling–nourishment, it withers and dies. Perhaps, also, heart attacks may have rather more to do with the *manner* in which we use our heart centre and express (or are unable to express) our feelings and emotions, and less to do with purely physical factors such as diet, exercise, and smoking. Research from HeartMath seems to corroborate this.

Heart as the seat of feelings and consciousness

Indeed our ordinary everyday language and gestures provide us with many clues. We say 'learning by heart' when we have committed something to memory. We do not say 'learning by brain' or even 'learning by mind'. Do we touch our heart or our head when we utter the personal pronoun 'I'? Do we yearn to satisfy out heart's desire or our brain's desire? Are intimate conversations heart-to-heart or brain-to-brain? When alarmed or feeling strongly emotional (about someone or something) do we say, 'My heart was in my mouth' or 'My brain was in my mouth'? Is a thorough examination of our feelings heart-searching or brain-searching? Does overwhelming distress render us broken-hearted or broken-brained? And do lovers refer to one another as 'sweetheart' or 'sweetbrain'?

Hopefully, the case is made that the human heart is more than just a biological pump. But any lingering doubts in the mind of the reader should be dispelled by recent and compelling evidence from a professor of pathology, Asok K. Mukhopadhyay, and a cardiologist, Jay Relan, cited in the academic journal *Annals of Psychiatry and Clinical Neuroscience*. In their paper 'The DeepScience of NeuroCardiology', the authors contend that, 'Contrary to present mainstream science which has accepted [the] heart as a blood-pumping machine working under [the] nervous system, the popular belief system reigns from time antiquity that the heart is the seat of feelings, which participates while making decisions.'[32] The authors argue that the current dichotomy between the brain and the heart could be the principal cause of needless human suffering. Moreover, the heartless pursuance of science, outmoded religious rituals, and politics are the causes of environmental, economic, and human disasters. The remedy lies in a union of the heart and the brain of mankind leading to an integral evolution which embraces the cerebral aspects of brain (and of course the gamut of the mind) as well as the compassion and empathy of the heart. A scientific approach to this issue is however essential, and the disciplines of cardiology, neurology, neurocardiology, psychology, and sociology should be nurtured as, collectively, they represent the science of consciousness. Such a joint endeavour would actuate a meaningful co-existence of neuro-centric with cardio-centric consciousness, rooted in the full realization of the primacy of consciousness.

Clinical evidence that the heart is not merely a pump

Ultimately, however, the brain, heart, gut, proteins, DNA, etc. enable us to express human consciousness whilst on Earth. All these factors play their respective roles in the emergence from the present *Homo sapiens* towards '*Homo spiritualis*' with qualities such as love, trust, and hope, regarded as being centred in the heart. The authors would surely agree with the French philosopher Pierre Teilhard de Chardin that, 'We are not human beings having a spiritual experience. We are spiritual beings having a human experience.'[33] Cardiology and neurology therefore have to look again into their respective disciplines from this point of view so that the hybrid discipline of neurocardiology (or cardioneurology) could develop with the burgeoning of an enlightened science grounded in eternal verities. Such would usher in the fructifying winds of Zephyrus[i] transforming the fields of psychology, psychiatry, neurology, cardiology, social science, economics, and politics whilst hastening a new world-view.

Urgent need for a holistic approach to understanding consciousness

Significantly, we are reminded of how Einstein took serious note of the inadequate development of the *affective* brain (responsible for attitudinal development of personality) in science education, quoting:

> The release of atom power has changed everything except our way of thinking … the solution to this problem lies in the heart of mankind. If only I had known, I should have become a watchmaker (1945).[34]

---

i Zephyrus, a minor god in Greek mythology, is the west wind and bringer of late spring and early-summer breezes.

Uniting Occult Science with Modern Science – Occult Neuroanatomy

Figure III-6 opposite illustrates the salient facts of what we have just presented. The scientific breakthroughs in support of the occult doctrine outlined are summarized in the top half of the diagram. The associated table below the two pictures shows the correspondence between man's Principles and brain function taken from the paper by Blavatsky on occult physiology.[21]

Furthermore, the English Nobel physicist, mathematician, and philosopher of science Sir Roger Penrose OM FRS (*b*.1931) has produced a new mathematics to prove that where dendrites meet at the synapse—of which we have trillions throughout our body and brain—is an electromagnetic aura.[ii] 'And, we find that the electromagnetic field of the heart produces, holographically, the same field as the one produced by the earth and solar system. Now, physicists are beginning to look at the electromagnetic auras as, simply, the organization of energy in the universe. All these are operating holographically—that is, at the smallest, unbelievably tiny level between the dendrites at the synapse, the body, the earth, and on outward [to the solar system, and very likely, beyond]. All are operating holographically and selectively.'[35]

Modern science approaches the Eternal Wisdom

So there is a sacred correspondence between the sun and the heart: something that mystics and occultists have intuited since time immemorial, but which the frontiers of modern science are touching upon. Hence, there are good grounds for claiming that modern science is the ally of occult science for the reason that what occult science affirms, modern science will confirm in the fullness of time.

Anatomical Symbolism of Members of the Human Body

Symbolic significance of left and right sides of the body

From a digest of the relevant parts of Hall's 'The Human Body in Symbolism'[36] we learn that in symbolism the body is divided vertically into halves, the right half being considered as light and the left half as darkness. By those unacquainted with the true meanings of light and darkness, the right half was denominated spiritual and the left half material. Light is the symbol of objectivity; darkness of subjectivity. (By analogous reasoning, sound is the symbol of objectivity; silence of subjectivity.) Light is a manifestation of life and is therefore posterior to life. That which is anterior to light is darkness, in which light exists temporarily but darkness permanently. As life precedes light, its only symbol is darkness, and darkness is considered as the veil which must eternally conceal the true nature of abstract and undifferentiated Being. Moreover, as the Source of Being is in the primal darkness which preceded light, so the spiritual nature of man is in the dark part of his being, for the heart is on the left side of the body.

Among the curious misconceptions arising from the false practice of associating darkness with evil is one by which several early nations used the right hand for all constructive labours and the left hand for only those purposes deemed unclean and unfit for the sight

---

ii Neurons have specialized projections called dendrites which propagate nerve impulses to the cell body, and axons which carry nerve impulses away from the cell body. Electrochemical nerve impulses from one neuron flows to another neuron across a synapse which contains a small gap separating neurons.

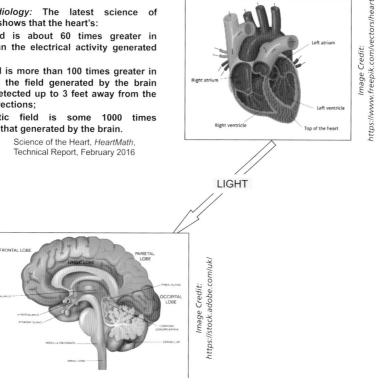

From Neurocardiology: The latest science of neurocardiology shows that the heart's:

o electrical field is about 60 times greater in amplitude than the electrical activity generated by the brain;

o magnetic field is more than 100 times greater in strength than the field generated by the brain and can be detected up to 3 feet away from the body, in all directions;

o electromagnetic field is some 1000 times stronger than that generated by the brain.

Science of the Heart, *HeartMath*, Technical Report, February 2016

LIGHT

Correspondences between –

Man's Principles	Brain Anatomy
Kāma (Desire)	Cerebellum and in the lower part of the body with the Liver and the Stomach
Kāma-manas (Lower mind, Mind driven by Desire)	*Corpora Quadrigemina*
Manas-Antahkaraṇa (Lower mind 'touching' Higher Mind	Pituitary Body (seat of psychic vision)
Manas (Mind *per se*) *Manas-Buddhi* (Mind embraced by Wisdom)	Pineal Gland – conferring spiritual clairvoyance
Auric Egg	Cavity of skull filled with *Ākāśa*

Figure III-6 Neuroanatomy – Scientific and Occult

of the gods. For the same reason, black magic was often referred to as the Left-Hand path, and heaven was said to be upon the right, and hell upon the left. As it happens, the word 'sinister', suggestive of evil, also means left-hand.[iii] Some philosophers further declared that there were two methods of writing: one from left to right, which was considered the exoteric method; the other from right to left, which was considered esoteric. The exoteric writing was that which was done out, or away from the heart, while the esoteric writing was that which, like the ancient Hebrew, was written towards the heart.

---

iii Notwithstanding the above, but to maintain consistency with tradition, the writer has decided to use the term 'Left-Hand path' to denote unclean or immoral practices.

The secret doctrine declares that every part and member of the body is epitomized in the brain and, in turn, *that all that is in the brain is epitomized in the heart*—a fact that is virtually unknown and ignored by modern science, which, with very few exceptions, as cited above, insists on regarding the heart as merely a biological pump. In symbolism the human head is frequently used to represent intelligence and self-knowledge. As the human body in its entirety is the most perfect known product of the Earth's evolution, it was employed to represent Divinity—the highest appreciable state or condition. Artists, attempting to portray Divinity, often show only a hand emerging from an impenetrable cloud. The cloud signifies the Unknowable Divinity concealed from man by human limitation, whereas the hand signifies the Divine activity, the only part of Divinity (God) which is cognizable to the lower senses.

As man's physical body has five distinct and important extremities—two legs, two arms, and a head, of which the last governs the first four—the number 5 has been accepted as the symbol of man (which theme will be developed considerably in the next Chapter). By its four corners the pyramid symbolizes the arms and legs, and by its apex the head, thus indicating that one rational power controls four irrational corners. The hands and feet are used to represent the Four Elements, of which the two feet are Earth and Water, and the two hands Fire and Air. The brain then symbolizes the sacred fifth Element—Æther—which controls and unites the other four. If the feet are placed together and the arms outspread, man then symbolizes the cross with the rational intellect as the head, or upper limb.

Symbolic significance of head and limbs

Let us move 'along' the body. The face consists of a natural trinity: the eyes representing the spiritual power which comprehends; the nostrils representing the preservative and vivifying power; and the mouth and ears representing the material Demiurgic power of the lower world. The first realm is eternally existent and is creative; the second sphere pertains to the mystery of the creative breath; and the third sphere to the creative word. (This will become clearer from the explanation to Figure III-23 later in Chapter 7, page 103.) By the Word of God (*vide* Genesis 1) the material universe was fabricated; and the seven creative powers, or vowel sounds—which had been brought into existence by the speaking of the Word—became the seven Elōhīm, or Deities by whose power and ministration the lower world was organized. Occasionally the Deity is symbolized by an eye, an ear, a nose, or a mouth. By the first, Divine awareness (All-Seeing) is signified; by the second, Divine interest (All-Hearing); by the third, Divine vitality; and by the fourth, Divine command. (As an interesting aside, the iconic Rainbow Portrait of Queen Elizabeth I in Hampton Court Palace depicts the monarch wearing a gown[iv] filled with symbolism, including motifs of eyes and ears, probably denoting that she is All-seeing and All-hearing.[37])

Symbolic significance of facial sensory organs

The fingers and toes also have special significance. The fingers represent the Ten Commandments of the spiritual law, whereas the toes, being in contact with the earth, the Ten Commandments of the physical law. The four fingers of each hand represent the four Elements and the three phalanges of each finger represent the divisions of the Elements, so that in each hand there are twelve parts to the fingers, which are analogous to the signs of the zodiac, whereas the two phalanges and base of each thumb signify the threefold Deity. The first phalange corresponds to the creative aspect, the second to the preservative

Symbolic significance of limb extremeties

---

iv The gown bears a striking resemblance to the Bacton Altar Cloth which once formed part of a dress, embroidered in gold and silver, worn by the Queen herself.

aspect, and the base to the regenerative and so-called destructive aspect. When the hands are brought together, the result is the twenty-four Elders and the six Days of Creation.

The various pantheons of ancient religions therefore actually represent the catalogued and personified attributes of Deity. In this respect they correspond to the hierarchies of the Hebrew Qabbalists. All the gods and goddesses of antiquity consequently have their analogies in the human body, as have also the elements, planets, and constellations which were assigned as proper vehicles for these celestials. Four body centres are assigned to the Elements, the seven vital organs to the planets, the twelve principal parts and members to the zodiac, the invisible parts of man's divine nature to various supramundane deities, while the hidden God was declared to manifest through the marrow in the bones.

Analogues in human body of cosmic powers and celestial bodies

How different would be our sense of relationship and responsibility towards our fellow humans and all of nature if we were to realize that we are, in truth, miniature universes or solar systems. Man's physical and subtle bodies are a visible and objective nature through the structure of which countless waves of evolving life are unfolding their latent potentialities. Not only are the mineral, the plant, and the animal kingdoms evolving, but also unknown classifications and divisions of invisible spiritual life. Just as cells are infinitesimal units in the structure of man, so man is an infinitesimal unit in the structure of the universe. A theology based upon the knowledge and appreciation of these correlations and relationships is as profoundly just as it is profoundly true.

The Occult Powers in Man – Symbolic Representations

Throughout the ages, the hidden, or latent, powers in man have been symbolized in various ways, such as mythological creatures, half human and half beast, or through tales of heroic struggles. The wooden horse of Troy is an excellent example of an exoteric narrative as the outer covering of a hidden, esoteric meaning. It would be instructive first to outline the former in the well-known canonical descriptions drawn from the *Aeneid* of Virgil and Homer's *Iliad*. The narrative depicts how Paris, son of King Priam of Troy, kidnapped and carried away Helene, wife of Menelaus, King of Sparta. When the Trojans refused to return her, the Achaeans (Greeks) formed an army, led by Agamemnon, and including such heroes as Achilles and Odysseus (Ulysses), to wage a war against the City of Troy. However, after an unsuccessful siege of ten years, Odysseus conceived the idea of constructing an enormous wooden horse in order to hide an elite force of the army inside the hollow interior of the construction. The Greeks then pretended to sail away, and the Trojans pulled the horse into their City as a victory trophy. That night the Greek force crept out of the horse and opened the gates for the rest of the Greek army, which had sailed back under cover of night. The Greeks entered and destroyed the city of Troy, and recovered Helene, so ending the war.

Trojan Horse: its mythological context

Ironically, the story itself is in the nature of a Trojan Horse because once the exoteric layers are peeled away, a myriad of meanings bursts forth, both metaphorically and esoterically. There are four key themes. In sequential order they are: transgression, war, subterfuge, and victory. What do they imply?

Metaphorically, the Trojan Horse signifies any trick or subterfuge that causes an innocent victim to invite an enemy into its own protected environment. A computer virus which

Trojan Horse: its
metaphorical and
esoteric
dimension

tricks users into willingly running a malicious software program is a modern example of the malevolent aspect of the Trojan Horse.

Esoterically however, the Trojan Horse symbolizes the latent, or occult, powers in man. The wooden horse of Troy, concealing a force for the capture of Troy, represents the body of man secreting within it those infinite potentialities which will later issue forth and conquer his environment. (The symbolical counterpart of the Trojan Horse is, in one sense, Noah's Ark, which represents the material containment of the spiritual nature of man secreting a host of latent potentialities, symbolized by the various animal characteristics, which subsequently become active.) The siege of Troy (irrespective of whether the war was an historical fact or a mythological tale) is a symbolical account of the abduction of the Spiritual Soul—Helene—by the personality—Paris and its final deliverance, through persevering struggle, and the saving grace of *philosophia perennis*—the Greek army under the command of Agamemnon. Significantly, *Agathon* (*Agathós*) is the Greek word for Plato's Supreme Deity, the equivalent of Divine Self, or *Ātma*—see Table II-23 on page 179 in Chapter 8 of Volume II. Furthermore, it is credible that the name 'Agathon' comes from Agathology, the Science of the Good, *agathós* meaning 'good', which in turn derives from the Ancient Greek *agathòs* (ἀγαθὸς), meaning, 'good', 'brave', 'noble', 'moral'.[v]

In the East we have the legendary epic of the Rāmāyaṇa mirroring the esoteric symbolism of the Trojan War. Here, the Spiritual Soul is symbolized by Sītā (see Chapter 1), her abduction by Rāvana, the giant Demon-King of Lanka, and her eventual rescue after the titanic[vi] Battle of Lanka waged by the army under the command of her husband, the Lord Rāma. The symbolic parallels between the Trojan War and the Battle of Lanka are obvious. Both stories, then, from the West or the East, convey the same message: that final redemption can only occur through the secret doctrine or *philosophia perennis* (of which science is a part)—but never through science and intellect alone and unaided by soul wisdom.

It is no exaggeration to say that establishment, namely, institutionalized science, is the modern Paris of Troy which has imprisoned the Helene of soul–wisdom in a materialistic fortress that can only be breached after untold struggle and travail on the battleground of the Lower mind (the left-brain intellect), under the command of that enlightened science which is so much in evidence nowadays and must, eventually, overpower the old and outworn mechanistic paradigm. The gargantuan expenditure (e.g. €21 billion mooted for another hadron collider involving a 100-kilometre tunnel at CERN, the European Organization for Nuclear Research—see later), the suffering of innumerable innocent animals, the endless laboratory experiments, the acres of academic papers, all trying to discover the nature of consciousness—our very birthright!—and the origins of the universe, are all fitting proof of the fact that when wisdom and intuition are strangled by unbridled materialism, only a titanic effort will release the suffocating grip. And that can only occur through enlightened science wedded to its ally, the secret doctrine (meaning, it bears repeating, the ageless wisdom known by a variety of names as we have periodically emphasized, like perennial

---

v Agathon (*circa* 448–400 BC) was an Athenian tragic poet whose works have been lost. He is best known for his appearance in Plato's Symposium.

vi The word 'titanic' is significant. Titans were giants of divine origin in Greek mythology who made war against the gods—see Volume I, Chapter 9. Prometheus, and the Indian equivalent Rāvana, were two of them.

philosophy, esoteric science, theosophy, occultism, *prisca sapientia*), which alone can dispel that greatest disease of all—*avidyā*, ignorance. But ignorance of what? Ignorance of our true and inner nature—the abiding theme of this work—not our outward bodies, vital as they are for terrestrial existence; such ignorance also known as unconsciousness, or the sleep walking state of common humanity, as Gurdjieff taught (see Chapter 8 on page 178 et seq. in Volume II).38

Of all diseases, ignorance is the worst

The wisest way, then, to use the principle of the Trojan Horse in modern times is for esotericism and spirituality to enter the scientific camp, not to denigrate science, but to open wide the portcullis of the materialistic fortress as the Greeks did the gates of Troy, thereby raising science to a higher metaphysic, a loftier vantage; thus blending physics with metaphysics, showing how physics is honeycombed in metaphysics to ensure that the marvellous discoveries of science will not, like so many of them, be in the nature of headless bodies, but instead be guided by wisdom, love, and intelligence for all humanity.

Other symbols of the composite nature of man, and his latent powers, found in the Mysteries, are the various mythological beasts that abound in the fairy stories of children. Practically all such tales of symbolic monsters are based upon ancient mystic folklore. For example, the Greek Centaur, the Assyrian bull-man, and the Egyptian sphinx have much in common, as all are composite creatures combining animal and human parts that tell-tale their corresponding qualities. Chiron, the Centaur, who teaches the sons of men, symbolizes the intelligences who were the custodians of the secret doctrine. The five-footed Assyrian Lamassu, bearing a human head, bull's body, sometimes with the horns and the ears of a bull, and wings of an eagle, is a reminder that the invisible nature of man has the wings of a god, the head of a man, and the body of a beast. Notice that the Lamassu bears the head of a man on an animal body. Contrast this with the Cretan Minotaur, the monster-creature with the head of a bull on the body of a man, clearly symbolizing that other limitless potentiality of man—the unbridled paroxysms of the sensual nature that wreak havoc when not under control of the mind, or in terms of the Trojan legend, the abduction of the Spiritual Soul by the ungoverned personality. The sphinx expresses the same concept as the Lamassu. As the armed guardian of the Mysteries it crouches motionless at the portal of the temple denying entrance to the profane. Thus placed between man and his divine possibilities, the sphinx also represents the secret doctrine itself.

Mythological symbols conveying man's composite nature and latent powers

Symbols and mythology, then, convey an inexhaustibly rich source of wisdom by stimulating the imagination and appealing to the inner senses rather than the logical mind as Albert Einstein (who almost certainly possessed a copy of Blavatsky's *The Secret Doctrine*—see the Endnote to the Proem in Volume I) must have realized when he said, 'If you want your children to be intelligent, read them fairy tales. If you want them to be more intelligent, read them more fairy tales.'39

Einstein on educational value of fairy tales

But having just touched upon the Sphinx, it would be impossible not to mention the Pyramids. However, a mountain of words has already been written on this ever-popular subject, probably enough books to fill much of the volume of the Great Pyramid itself, and the writer does not wish to add to that bulk! We therefore adhere strictly to the focus of this Chapter on the symbolic representations of man's limitless potentialities and latent powers.

The Mystery of the Great Pyramid – The Mystery of Man

The symbolism of the pyramid operates at many levels, but in general it may be said to represent the totality of man in all realms of his life and being. What does the Great Pyramid teach us about the mind of man? Throughout the ages, explorers, mystics, and scientists have been fascinated with the notion about the existence of secret passages and chambers within its massive interior. Such an enquirer was the legendary sage Paul Brunton who spent a whole night in the inky blackness of the King's Chamber in an attempt to fathom its secrets.[40] There is an occult technique of interiorization of consciousness, and intense inward concentration, that heightens the perceptual faculties to such an abnormal degree that vibrations of force, sound, and light that are beyond the range and reach of normal physical detection can be accessed.[vii] By such means, Brunton was able to contact the spirits of two hierophants[viii] of centuries gone by who were responsible for the initiatory processes bequeathed to worthy candidates in the Great Pyramid—always remembering that the sacred structure was never a burial chamber as mainstream Egyptology would have us believe, but actually a fane (temple) for conducting the rites of passage for the deserving few. In such a sensitized condition, Brunton was shown in what is now known as an out-of-body state, a secret passage leading to a temple-like chamber, containing the ancient records of early humanity. However, upon sensing his intense curiosity to discover the entrance to this chamber the Hierophant instructed:

Hidden meaning of secret passages in the Pyramid

> It matters not whether thou discoverest the door [to the secret chamber] or not. Find but the secret passage within the mind that will lead thee to the hidden chamber within thine own soul, and thou shalt have found something worthy indeed. The mystery of the Great Pyramid is the mystery of thine own self. The secret chambers and ancient records are all contained in thine own nature. The lesson of the Pyramid is that man must turn inward, must venture to the unknown centre of his being to find his soul, even as he must venture to the unknown depths of this fane to find its profoundest secret.[41]

Awakening the Occult Powers in Man's Nature

We have just given a few examples of how the composite nature of man, and his innate potentialities, have been depicted throughout the ages in the symbolism of the East and the West. In Volume I we stated that the Mysteries taught the worthy candidate about the unfolding of his innate nature and *pari passu*, the natural efflorescence of his occult powers as a logical outcome. He was shown how to awaken the forces lying dormant within certain apparently physical organs, channels, and centres in the body, which are in reality the veils, or sheaths, of spiritual centres of forces and powers. What these were, and how they could be awakened to activity, was never revealed to the unregenerate, for the philosophers realized that once he understands the complete working of any system, a man may accomplish a prescribed end without being qualified to manipulate and control the effects which he has produced. For this reason, long periods of probation were imposed, so that the knowledge of how to become as the gods might remain the sole possession of the worthy. Recall

Partial knowledge is dangerous

---

vii Otherwise known as the *siddhis*, or psychic powers, they must never be evoked or tampered with except under strict rules of conduct and the personal, protective guidance from a real Master; otherwise the dangers of derangement and delusion are very real.

viii Arcane priests who interpreted and explained the Mysteries, sacred doctrines and occult processes.

Goethe's tale of 'The Sorcerer's Apprentice', summarized in Volume I, Chapter 7, page 208 about the mayhem resulting from evoking unseen powers with only a fragment of know-how, thus lacking full knowledge about their control. As a simplistic example of how much easier it is to produce a phenomenon than it is to control its effects, or to banish it altogether, a simple, two-step exercise may make the point. Try thinking of something for fifteen seconds, say, for the sake of argument, a monkey. Then, with the monkey picture just in mind, immediately try switching to think of anything else in the whole world— other than a monkey; in other words, erase the mental phenomenon just produced. The second step is virtually guaranteed to be the more arduous!

However, lest knowledge of the Mysteries be lost, it was concealed in allegories and myths, meaningless to the profane, but self-evident to those acquainted with that theory of personal redemption which was the foundation of philosophical theology, esoteric Christianity itself regarded as a case in point. The entire New Testament is, we are told, an ingeniously concealed exposition of the secret processes of human regeneration. The characters, both pleasant and unpleasant, so long considered (especially by literal-minded scientists) as historical men and women are really the personification of certain processes which take place in the human body when man begins the task of consciously liberating himself from the illusion of materialism, its associated bondage to ignorance, and death regarded as the extinguishment of consciousness. In modern times, in step with the enormous discoveries of science that have partially confirmed or alluded to the previously closeted occult secrets, a portion of this knowledge was promulgated (without personifications) through the modern Theosophical movement. A small portion of this is revealed in Chapter 9 in relation to the arousal of latent occult powers associated with certain centres in the human body.

Eternal wisdom can never be lost

Afterword

What sort of man were Manṣūr al-Ḥallāj and Meister Eckhart referring to in the aphorisms quoted in the epigraphs? Did they mean the ordinary man whose mind is full of concepts and beliefs? Stated differently, what quality of mind is required to answer the question? Surely, it can only be answered in a state of deep contemplation, with the mind absolutely quiet. Otherwise, all manner of preconceptions and assumptions will jostle for our attention. Most people have a definition or concept about God, even if it is a hazy one. Even those who deny that there is a Source, must have their own concept of what that Source is in order to deny it. We can be sure though that whatever we think about the Divine, will be very much in our own image, reflecting who we are. The smaller we are, the smaller will be our God. The greatest step we can take is to realize that whilst we can experience great joy exploring our Source, and talking *about* It, we can never define It, since to do so would be to circumscribe It. In fact, as we have repeatedly stressed, to try to define 'God' is a confession of ignorance. It is attempting to define the indefinable which is futile, as declared in the First Fundamental Proposition of *The Secret Doctrine* based on the Stanzas from the Book of Dzyan.[42] To its immense frustration, mainstream science continues to find that the unlimited, the unknown and unknowable are not accessible to the discursive mind operating in the field of logical propositions and processes based on sense observations. But the mind in absolute repose is liberated from all its store of conceptual baggage and so inwardly realizes the nature of that which transcends its ordinary experience. It is

When definitions, however precise, become sterile

only then that it is able to realize the truth of a statement which has the character of universality about it.

This Chapter has shown why the Mystery traditions have revered the human body as a symbol of divinity and the intelligence hidden in the whole universe. The next Chapter delineates how the Principles of Man are beautifully conveyed through symbolism with Nature and the Platonic Solids. Meanwhile, we close with three quotes which are entirely consonant with the pearls of wisdom penned by al-Ḥallāj and Meister Eckhart stated at the opening of this Chapter. The first quote, in regard to an Elegiac Song, was stated in the Postlude to Volume II, Chapter 5, 'Death is Transition'. The second one is from the central religious text of Islam. And the third clearly affirms why Man is the 'Measure of All Things'.

No eyes shall weep for the Divine Spirit hath returned Home.

LUDWIG VAN BEETHOVEN

To God we belong, and to Him do we return.

HOLY QUR'AN[43]

Pythagoras said that the universal Creator had formed two things in His own image: The first was the cosmic system with its myriads of suns, moons, and planets; the second was man, in whose nature the entire universe existed in miniature.

MANLY P. HALL[44]

NOTES

1   *NPB-5, Part 2: The Intellect* ¶62, 123.

2   Quoted in Dr Massoud Homayouni, *The Origins of Persian Gnosis*, trans. F. J. Stone (London: Mawlana Centre, 1992), 13.

3   Meister Eckhart, LW IV, nn. 20–8, Sermon IV/1, quoted also in Ian Richardson, 'The Indistinguishability Between God and Man in the Thoughts of Meister Eckhart', Master of Theology dissertation, University of Wales Trinity Saint David, August 2013, 19 <https://repository.uwtsd.ac.uk/350/1/Ian%20Richardson.pdf> accessed 19 June 2020.

4   Erwin Schrödinger, 'On Determinism and Free Will' from lectures delivered at Trinity College, Dublin, 1943, in *What is Life?* with *Mind and Matter* and *Autobiographical Sketches*, foreword by Roger Penrose (Cambridge: Cambridge University Press, 1993), 87.

5   D. Bostock, *Plato's Theaetetus* 151e (Oxford: Clarendon Press, 1988).

6   C. C. W. Taylor and Mi-Kyoung Lee, 'The Sophists: 1. Protagoras', *The Stanford Encyclopedia of Philosophy* (18 August 2020) <https://plato.stanford.edu/entries/sophists> accessed 17 October 2020.

7   *STA*, 'The Human Body in Symbolism', LXXIII.

8   Dr Massoud Homayouni, *op. cit.*, 14.

9   ——*op. cit.*, 14n.

10 Ian Richardson, *op. cit.*, 19. See also Johannes Eckhart, *Meister Eckhart's Sermons*, trans. Claud Field (London: H. R. Allenson Ltd., n.d.) <http://krishnamurti.abundanthope.org/index_htm_files/Meister-Eckharts-Sermons.pdf> accessed 11 March 2020.

11 ——*op. cit.*, 36.

12 *IU-1*, 'The Elements, Elementals, and Elementaries', 212.

13 Isaac Newton, *Philosophiæ Naturalis Principia Mathematica* [Mathematical Principles of Natural Philosophy], trans. Andrew Motte, rev. Florian Cajori, 2 vols (Berkeley, Los Angeles: University of California Press, 1962), ii, 'The System of the World – General Scholium', 547.

14 This section and the next taken from *STA*, 'The Human Body in Symbolism', LXXIII.

15 *ibid.* The quote is by the English poet Alexander Pope (1688–1744), in 'An Essay on Man', Epistle II (1734).

16 *STA, op. cit.*, LXXIV.

17 Thomas Taylor, *The Six Books of Proclus, the Platonic Successor, on the Theology of Plato* (London: Longman, 1816), ii, xiv.

18 *STA*, 'The Human Body in Symbolism', LXXIV.

19 *ML*, Letter No. 65.

20 Some examples were given in Volume I, Chapter 4. See also Edi D. Bilimoria, *The Snake and the Rope: Problems in Western science resolved by occult science* (Adyar, Madras: Theosophical Publishing House, 2006), 195–242 *passim*.

21 'The Brain: An extract on occult physiology from *The Collected Writings of H. P. Blavatsky*', *Theosophy in New Zealand* (June 2005), from *CW-XII*, 'E. S. Instruction No V', 697–9.

22 Craig Hamilton, 'Is God All in Your Head? Inside science's quest to solve the mystery of consciousness', *What Is Enlightenment?* Magazine Reprint Series, 29 (June–August 2005), 95 <http://consc.net/misc/enlightenment.pdf> accessed 14 March 2020.

23 Jay Pasricha, 'The Gut–Brain Connection', John Hopkins Medicine <https://www.hopkinsmedicine.org/health/wellness-and-prevention/the-brain-gut-connection> accessed 7 July 2020.

24 J. Andrew Armour (Associate Professor of Pharmacology, University of Montréal Faculty of Medicine) and Jeffrey L. Ardell (Professor of Pharmacology, James H. Quillen College of Medicine, East Tennessee State University) (eds), *Basic and Clinical Neurocardiology* (New York: Oxford University Press, 2004).

25 J. Andrew Armour, *Neurocardiology: Anatomical and functional principles* (Institute of HeartMath, 2003).

26 A. M. Davis and B. H. Natelson, 'Brain–Heart Interactions. The neurocardiology of arrhythmia and sudden cardiac death', *Texas Heart Institute Journal*, 20/3 (1993), 158–69.

27 Kate Ruth Linton, 'Knowing By Heart: Cellular memory in heart transplants', *Journal of Science & Mathematics*, 2 (September 2003).

28 Paul Pearsall, *The Heart's Code* (New York: Broadway Books, 1998).

29 Rollin McCraty, *Science of the Heart*, ii: 'Technical Report – Exploring the Role of the Heart in Human Performance: An overview of research conducted by the HeartMath Institute' (Boulder Creek, California: HeartMath Institute, February 2016), 36. See also 'Science of the Heart: Exploring the role of the heart in human performance', HeartMath Institute <https://www.heartmath.org/research/science-of-the-heart/heart-brain-communication> accessed 23 March 2020.

30 Gerhard Baule and Richard McFee, 'Detection of the Magnetic Field of the Heart', *American Heart Journal*, 66/1 (July 1963), 95–6.

31 Rollin McCraty, *Science of the Heart, loc. cit.* See also *BrainCare International* <https://braincare.lu/index.php/en> accessed 23 March 2020.

32 Asok K. Mukhopadhyay and Jay Relan, 'The DeepScience of NeuroCardiology', *Annals of Psychiatry and Clinical Neuroscience*, 3/2 (June 2020), 1.

33 'Teilhard de Chardin', *Xavier University* <https://www.xavier.edu/jesuitresource/online-resources/quote-archive1/spiritual-awareness-quotes> accessed 7 July 2020.

34 Albert Einstein', *reddit* <https://www.reddit.com/r/quotes/comments/clbjne/the_release_of_atomic_power_has_changed> accessed 27 June 2020, quoted in Asok K Mukhopadhyay and Jay Relan, *loc. cit.*

35 Joseph Chilton Pearce and Casey Walker, 'The Holographic Heart', *KVMR* (20 May 1998) <https://cyberspaceorbit.com/holhrt.htm> accessed 2 June 2020.

36 STA, 'The Human Body in Symbolism', LXXIII–LXXVI *passim*.

37 'The Bacton Altar Cloth at Hampton Court Palace', Historic Royal Palaces, <https://www.hrp.org.uk/hampton-court-palace/whats-on/the-lost-dress-of-elizabeth-i/#gs.fuoxvs> accessed 11 September 2020.

38 Peter Demianovich Ouspensky, *Gurdjieffwork*.com
    <http://www.gurdjieffwork.com/site/index.asp?page=110280&DL=243> accessed 4 July 2020.
39 'Albert Einstein', *Goodreads* <http://www.goodreads.com/author/quotes/9810.Albert_Einstein>
    accessed 23 March 2020.
40 Paul Brunton, *A Search in Secret Egypt* (London: Rider and Company, 1954), 57–78.
41 Paul Brunton, *op. cit.*, 77.
42 *SD*-I, 'Proem', 14.
43 Holy Qur'an, 2:156.
44 Manly P. Hall, *Melchizedek and the Mystery of Fire: A treatise in three parts* (Los Angeles, California:
    The Philosophical Research Society, 1996), 23 < https://www.yumpu.com/xx/document/read/
    59160828/manly-p-hall-melchizedek-and-the-mystery-of-fire> accessed 19 December 2020.

4 Symbolic Representations of the Principles of Man

For the soul walks upon all paths.
The soul walks not upon a line, neither does it grow like a reed.
The soul unfolds itself, like a lotus of countless petals.

Kahlil Gibran[1]

Synopsis

Chapter 4 harks back, in one sense, to Volume II, particularly Chapters 2 and 3 regarding the Principles of Man, namely, his occult anatomy and physiology. Here we show the representation of these principles in terms of the universal symbolism found in the sacred literature of the West and the East. We touch upon the symbol of the Mythical Tree and the Rosicrucian Rose and in more detail on Padma, the Lotus, and the Sephirothic Tree of the Qabbalah, both of which beautifully illustrate the unfolding of man's Sevenfold Principles from the spiritual to the physical—something that is also revealed by the unfolding of the cube, one of the Platonic solids.

Key Words: symbolism, Lotus Flower, Rosicruscian Rose, Mythical Tree, Sephirothic Tree, Platonic solids

Whereas the previous Chapters dealt with the various symbolic representations of man in a general sense, the focus is now on the manner in which symbolism portrays the nature of the life-principles and attributes of man's septenary composition. Why is it that throughout the ages, trees, plants, and the Platonic solids have been used by pagans and artists, mystics and occultists as proxies of the universe and man? The universal meaning of the allegory with nature is that the single source of life, and the endless diversity of its expression, has a perfect simile in the structure of a tree or a plant. The single origin of all diversity is beautifully symbolized by the trunk of a tree (or the stem of a plant); its roots embedded in the moist and dark earth symbolize divine nutriment; and its several branches (or flowers) spreading from the central trunk (or stem) represent the infinity of universal effects springing from, and dependent upon, a single cause.

Like all flowers, the lotus represents spiritual unfoldment and attainment. For this reason, the Eastern deities (personifying the evolved powers in nature and man) are often shown seated upon the open petals of lotus blossoms. And, to this day in India, the tradition is preserved by using wreaths of flowers for religious or marital ceremonies, for example in the case of the latter, by garlanding the happy couple with a wreath of roses.

Symbolic significance of trees and plants

Blavatsky provides an interesting account of the striking parallels between the life-principles of plants, animals, and human beings to which we made passing reference in Endnote II-9 from Chapter 7 of Volume II. It bears repeating here as it is key to the next section explaining why man is esoterically ever regarded as the seven-leafed plant:

> The reader who would obtain a clear idea of the commutation of forces and the resemblance between the life-principles of plants, animals, and human beings, may profitably consult a paper on the correlation of nervous and mental forces by Professor Alexander Bain of the University of Aberdeen. The mandragora [a plant whose root has the human form] seems to occupy upon earth the point where the vegetable and animal kingdoms touch, as the zoöphites and polypi do in the sea; the boundary being in each case so indistinct as to make it almost imperceptible where the one ceases and the other begins. It may seem improbable that there should be *homunculi* [representations of small humans], but will any naturalist, in view of the recent expansion of science, dare say it is impossible? 'Who', says Bain, 'is to limit the possibilities of existence?'[2]

Certainly, in view of the recent discovery of the subterranean Galapagos deep within the oceanic crust of the Earth (described in Chapter 10), there seems to be no 'limit [to] the possibilities of existence'.

Saptaparṇa – The Seven-Leafed Man-Plant

In the Esoteric Philosophy, man is called a *Saptaparṇa* which means a seven-leafed (petalled) lotus, or a seven-leafed (petalled) plant, the Sanskrit compound word deriving from *sapta* 'seven' and *parṇa* 'leaf', or 'petal'. The word shows how an esoteric key is concealed by an exoteric description. The latter refers to a plant which gave its name to a famous cave in Râjâgriha, near Buddha Gaya (Bodh Gaya), where the Lord Buddha used to meditate and teach his Arhats. This cave has seven chambers, hence its name, mirroring the seven-petalled lotus.

Why then is man called a Saptaparṇa—a seven-leafed plant? Because, as with the analogy of the tree, the lotus plant symbolizes man's nature and consciousness on the three principal planes of his being: (*a*) the lotus roots in the earth drawing nutrients from the soil symbolize man's bodily dependence on physical matter for sustenance; (*b*) the plant stem in the water connecting the roots at the lower end with the flower on top representing man's soul principle uniting his mortal physical existence with his immortal spiritual nature; and (*c*) the flower turning to face the sun standing for *Ātma*, man's immortal spiritual principle.

It is noteworthy that the stability of the plant is provided by both earth and water, but in different ways. Without any earth for the roots to cling onto, the plant would drift away; and if there were no water for the flower to float upon, the stem would bend over under the weight of the flower atop. *Similarly, man needs to be physically grounded for his material and bodily existence; but he must also be anchored in his soul in order to attain equilibrium at both poles of his being: the physical and the spiritual.*

Lotus: an especially potent symbol

Moreover, as Hall tells us: 'As the lotus exists in three elements (earth, water, and air) so man lives in three worlds—material, intellectual, and spiritual.'[3] As the plant, with its roots in the mud and the slime, grows upward through the water and finally blossoms forth in the light and air, so the spiritual growth of man is upward from the darkness of earthy action and personal desire into the light of truth and understanding. The water also serves as a symbol of the ever-changing world of illusion through which the weary soul must pass in its evolutionary journey to attain the state of spiritual illumination. Thus, the Saptaparṇa also epitomizes: (*a*) that anything that is materialized on Earth has its prior spiritual prototype in the immaterial world; (*b*) that the elements of the life of both kosmos and man are the same; and (*c*) the interdependence on, and interconnection between, spirit, soul, and body required for a terrestrial existence.

But why is a special significance and inner meaning attached to the leaves? It alludes to that principle of unfolding, or unrolling, of innate faculties 'from within without'—that which is hidden and implicate unfurls to become visible and explicate. Whereas the actual plant has seven physical leaves, the 'man-plant' has seven 'metaphysical leaves'—his sevenfold constitution. The form of the leaves for the plant and man is obviously different; but in both cases the essential principle of emanational unfoldment is the same. For just as the seven plant leaves are unfurled from a single originating bud, so also the septenary principles of man are unrolled, or explicated, from an implicate unitary wholeness.

Saptaparṇa and the Constitution of Man

We can draw a simile between the Saptaparṇa and the constitution of man thus:[4]

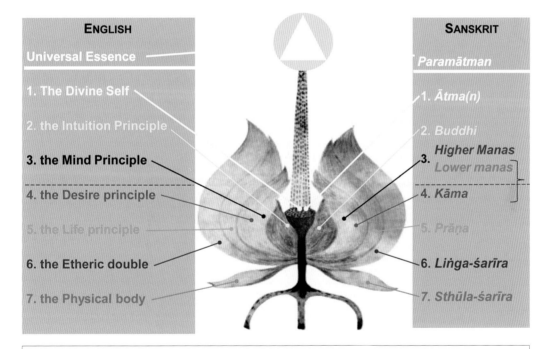

The Lotus, or Padma, is, moreover, a very ancient and favourite simile for the Kosmos itself, and also for man. The popular reasons given are, firstly, the fact [...] that the Lotus seed contains within itself a perfect miniature of the future plant, which typifies the fact that the spiritual prototypes of all things exist in the immaterial world before those things become materialized on Earth. Secondly, the fact that the Lotus plant grows up through the water, having its root in the *ilus*, or mud, and spreading its flower in the air above. The Lotus thus typifies the life of man and also that of the Kosmos; for the Secret Doctrine teaches that the elements of both are the same, and that both are developing in the same direction. The root of the Lotus sunk in the mud represents material life, the stalk passing up through the water typifies existence in the astral world, and the flower floating on the water and opening to the sky is emblematical of spiritual being.[5]

Figure III-7   Saptaparṇa – The Seven-Leafed Man-Plant

Image Credit: See Note 4

The above section encapsulates the essential reasons why man in the Esoteric Philosophy is called a Saptaparṇa. With reference to the accompanying Figure III-7, we now explain why the Lotus plant, or Padma, portrays man's constitution symbolically. We commence from the visible, outside of the blossom, and work inwards (numbering the stages in reverse order from that shown in Figure III-7 because we are starting with the outermost and objective aspect):

1. During the formative stages of a flower, the bud first appears and is fully protected by the sepals on the underside. Then, as the bloom opens, the outer coverings are the first to unfold. They are so represented by the outermost sheath of the seven-leafed man-plant corresponding to the *Sthūla-śarīra* of man, his Physical body. The colour representation is brown, the colour of the earth.

2. The largest petal represents the *Liṅga-śarīra*, or Etheric double, or Model body, the pattern upon which the Physical body is formed. The colour representation of this petal is violet.

3. The next petal is associated with the colour orange and stands for *Prāṇa*, the Life principle, or Life-force.

4. *Kāma*, the motivating Desire principle, is depicted by the petal with a colour representation of red.

5. The next petal, or parṇa, represents *Manas*, the Mind Principle. Figure III-7 shows how this parṇa is almost completely enfolded by Kāma. This depicts the fact that for the vast majority of humanity, the principle of desire generally dominates the mind—desire-driven thoughts largely dominate and control a person's life. The colour representation is green for Lower manas, and indigo for Higher Manas.

6. *Buddhi*, the Intuition Principle is portrayed by the inmost petal of the blossom, with a colour representation of yellow. This petal is most important, for it enwraps the seed-pod lying at the heart of every blossom, and remains—representing man's immortal individuality—when the outer petals drop off—representing man's mortal personality.

7. *Ātma(n)*, the Divine Self is the heart of the Lotus. This is the message of the sublime mantra *Om, mani padme hum!*—'Within every lotus a jewel is enshrined.' It is depicted as the seed-pod, with a colour representation of white. As explained in Volume II, Chapter 2, page 20 et seq., Ātma is a 'partaker' of each one of the principles. And Ātma(n), the universal principle is linked to its Originating Source, *Paramātman*, represented as a white triangle within a golden globe. The rays emanating from Paramātman represent the Monads descending into spheres of manifestation.

The above account should convince readers of the power and meaning behind the beautiful symbolism of the lotus blossom—the Saptaparṇa, representing man as 'the seven-leafed being', the seven-principled entity.

The Flame and the Sparks

Closely related to Saptaparṇa the following *śloka* (verse)[i] conveys the idea of emanational unfoldment of man's sevenfold constitution using the symbolism of the flame and the sparks:

It is the root that never dies; the three-tongued flame of the four wicks. The wicks are the sparks, that draw from the three-tongued flame shot out by the seven—their flame [...].[6]

This beautiful aphorism encapsulates the immortal and the mortal aspects of man's constitution (see Figure III-7, page 57 and also Table II-3 in Volume II, Chapter 2, page 21). The root of Saptaparṇa is likened to the 'three-tongued flame' that never dies—the inextinguishable Upper Triad: Ātma, Buddhi, and Manas. The 'four wicks' are the sparks which burn out—the Lower Quaternary: Kāma, Prāṇa, Liṅga-śarīra, and Sthūla-śarīra.

It is deeply significant that a verse from the Egyptian *Book of the Dead* uses practically the same terms as the Sanskrit śloka:

> 'I am the three-wicked Flame and my wicks are immortal,' says the defunct. 'I enter into the domain of Sekhem [the God whose arm sows the seed of action produced by the disembodied soul], and I enter the region of the Flames who have destroyed their adversaries,' *i.e.*, got rid of the sin-creating 'four wicks.'[7]

The Flame and wicks symbolize man's Immortal and mortal aspects

Again we discern what has periodically been highlighted throughout this work: the unity of the *philosophia perennis*. It is irrational to postulate that the similarity between the Egyptian verse and the Sanskrit śloka is due to a historical transfer of knowledge—as if the ancient Brahmins journeyed by land and sea to the land of the pyramids and divulged their secrets to the Egyptian hierophants—or vice versa. The rational fact, so uncomfortable to academia who yearn for tangible historical evidence, is that the elevated consciousness of the sages of India and Egypt both accessed the One universal fount of Wisdom.

And that Wisdom affirms that Ātma issues from its originating Source first and remains 'unmanifested' throughout the cycle of existence. The other six principles issue forth, or emanate, or unfold, as leaves unfold by means of an interior process. Thus, from Ātma its inseparable *upādhi*,[ii] Buddhi, is emanated. From Ātma-Buddhi unrolls Manas; from Ātma-Buddhi-Manas there arises Kāma; from Ātma-Buddhi-Manas-Kāma springs Prāṇa; from Ātma-Buddhi-Manas-Kāma-Prāṇa unfolds Liṅga-śarīra; from Ātma-Buddhi-Manas-Kāma-Prāṇa-Liṅga-śarīra is finally emanated Sthūla-śarīra. The same emanational unfoldment has brought forth the *Tattvas*, or Elements-Principles (explained in detail in Chapter 8) and the Sephīrōth (explained below)[8].

Thus we clearly see that each principle partakes of Ātma. Stated otherwise, the Divine Self pervades All; the emanational process from the spiritual to the material reflects the title of this work—'Unfolding Consciousness'—Consciousness in increasing concretion of Itself.

The Rosicrucian Rose

The Rosicrucian movement sprouted in the early seventeenth century and still exerts a powerful fascination and influence today. Founded on the legend of the German Christian

---

i Śloka, or shloka (meaning 'song', from the root *śru* 'hear') is 'the Sanskrit epic metre formed of thirty-two syllables: verses in four half-lines of eight, or in two lines of sixteen syllables each'—see *TSGLOSS*, 302.

ii '*Upādhi*', a Sanskrit word meaning basis; the vehicle, carrier, or bearer of something less material than itself—see Volume II, Chapter 3, page 36 f. for a full explanation.

Rosenkreutz (whose life spanned the fourteenth and fifteenth centuries) and the Fraternity of the Rosy (or Rose) Cross,[iii] the rose, like the lotus, its Eastern equivalent, representing spiritual unfoldment and attainment. Their manifestos comprised cryptic texts depicting a pansophy (universal wisdom, or knowledge) and a new philosophy based on alchemy, esoteric wisdom, and religious and spiritual canons. Given their archetypal image of the rose and cross, the recovery of lost knowledge, and the idea of a hidden brotherhood working for the regeneration of mankind, it is easy to understand the widespread wave of enthusiasm from the cognoscenti over much of Europe at the time. The Rosicrucian world-view fired the thoughts of early seventeenth-century occult philosophers such as the German physician and alchemist Michael Maier (1568–1622), the English Paracelsian physician and Rosicrucian apologist Robert Fludd (1574–1637), and the Welsh philosopher and alchemist Thomas Vaughan (1621–1666).

Symbolical equivalence of Rosicrucian Rose and Lotus

Manly Hall has informatively drawn our attention to the esoteric doctrines for which the Eastern lotus stands as having been perpetuated in modern Europe under the form of the rose; hence the identical esoteric symbolism behind the lotus blossom in ancient India and Egypt, and the rose of the Rosicrucians in modern Europe. Moreover, in the 1642 edition of Sir Francis Bacon's *History of the Reign of Henry the Seventh*, the frontispiece shows Lord Bacon with Rosicrucian roses for shoe buckles.[9]

The Sephirothic Tree – The Divine Nature Immanent in Existence

> The Universe is a thought of the Deity. Since this ideal thought-form has overflowed into actuality, and the world born thereof has realized the plan of its creator, it is the calling of all thinking beings to rediscover in this existent whole the original design.
>
> Friedrich von Schiller
> *Theosophie des Julius*, The World and Thinking Being[10]

The Qabbalah (Kabala, or Kabbalah) is the hidden wisdom of the Hebrew Rabbis of the Middle Ages, in turn derived from the older secret doctrines (the archaic Chaldean Secret Doctrine) concerning cosmogony and divine things. The word originates from the root 'QBL', which means 'to receive', or 'to take over', signifying something which is handed down to selected individuals by word of mouth. The Qabbalah, therefore, is essentially the theosophy of the Jews, or rather, the form taken by the universal theosophy of the archaic ages in its transmission through the Jewish mind. It supplies the key without which the spiritual mysteries of both the Old and the New Testament must ever remain unsolved. The *Zohar* is generally regarded as the original and main book of the Qabbalah.[11]

As shown in Figure III-8 on page 62, the Tree of Life, or Sephirothic Tree in the Qabbalah, portrays the ten emanations, or attributes of deity, known in Hebrew as 'Sephīrōth' collectively, and 'Sephīrāh' individually. For this reason, the Sephirothic Tree is sometimes depicted as a human body, thus clearly establishing the true identity of the first, or Archetypal Man as Divine Ideation; in other words, the archetype of man—a microcosm

---

iii Its modern guise is the Fellowship of the Rosy Cross founded in 1915 by the American-born British poet and scholarly mystic Arthur Edward Waite (1857–1942).

of the Universe—an *Idea* in Divine Mind, eloquently expressed by Schiller in the epigram above. This is especially the case with Western Qabbalists who regard Adam Kadmon (Qadmon) as Archetypal Man—the Paradigm of Humanity, or the 'Heavenly Man' not fallen into sin—and apportion the ten Sephīrāh to various parts of the human body. However, a concept more in keeping with the Oriental Qabbalah would be to regard Adam Kadmon in the nature of the Third Logos, which is the idea associated with Brahmā in the Hindu scheme. But in either system it is important to keep in mind the idea that the Sephīrōth are all linked together because of their emanational emergence; hence, there is constant, conscious interaction between them, typifying the interaction present between all grades of beings in the manifested universe.[12] Note, however, that according to Qabbalistic cosmogony (and indeed esoteric cosmogonies of all cultures and epochs), the birth of the physical universe was the last stage, not the first stage, in emanational emergence from Eternity. Creation, strictly speaking emanation, has a much wider *[Tree of Life maps Archetypal Man]* meaning for Qabbalists than it does for materialistic scientists for whom any ideas of after-life or non-physical (i.e., pre-Big Bang) realms never figure (or are never allowed to figure) in their theories about the beginning of the cosmos.

> The Sephīrōthal Tree is the Universe, and Adam-Kadmon represents it in the West as Brahmā represents it in India.[13]

As the Cambridge-trained physicist Stephen Phillips eloquently puts it, and forcefully demonstrates, in his book *The Mathematical Connection Between Religion and Science*: 'As vast, beautiful and mysterious as is the material universe, the superphysical universes [note the plural] outside everyday space–time are still vaster, more beautiful and even more mysterious. The Tree of Life at the heart of Kabbalah is the map of these spiritual and psychological realities. More than that, it is the universal blueprint through which the nature of God manifests in every created thing. For not only is man made in the "Image of God" but everything is designed according to the pattern of the Tree of Life, whether it is a subatomic particle, a human being or the entire cosmos—physical and superphysical. Everything, therefore, is an embodiment of the Tree of Life on its own scale of manifestation and level of unfoldment [an explicit validation of the operation of the Hermetic Axiom on different levels and planes, physical and superphysical].'[14]

Tree of Life also a blueprint of creation

The Image of God in Matter

Continuing with the Western Qabbalah, Figure III-8 overleaf shows how the Sephirothic Tree maps the overflowing of the ideal thought-form into actuality, as per the above quote by Schiller. The diagram illustrates the Unmanifest Worlds and the Manifest Worlds and their respective correspondences in the Macrocosm and the Microcosm. Dealing first with the Unmanifest, the upper triangle in the top centre of the diagram represents the Divine and Formless World of Spirit in the Macrocosm, comprising the triad of: (*a*) Ain, the Hebrew term for the negatively existent, or Deity in repose, and absolutely passive—what occultists refer to as THE ABSOLUTE; (*b*) Ain Soph, Deity awakened, so to say, that is, Deity emanating and extending as the Boundless, or Limitless; and (*c*) Ain Soph Aur, the Boundless Light, which concentrates into Kether, the Crown—the First and highest *[Sephirothic Tree maps Unmanifest and manifest, Macrocosm and microcosm]* Sephīrāh, or emanation of Deity, and synthesis of the ten Sephīrāh standing at the head of the Sephirothic Tree. The Sephīrōth are the ten emanations of Deity (to reiterate, the highest formed by the concentration of Ain Soph Aur, the Limitless Light). Each Sephīrāh

The Universe is a thought of the Deity. Since this ideal thought-form has overflowed into actuality, and the world born thereof has realized the plan of its creator, it is the calling of all thinking beings to rediscover in this existent whole the original design.
Friedrich von Schiller, *Theosophie des Julius, The World of Thinking Being*

The MICROCOSM

The MACROCOSM

ĀTMA
THE DIVINE SELF

THE DIVINE
AND FORMLESS
WORLD OF SPIRIT

AIN   ○ Deity in Repose
AIN SOPH   ○ Deity Emanating
AIN SOPH AUR   ○ The Boundless Light

Kether – The Crown
The Middle Pillar:
Harmony/Balance

The Left Pillar:
The Pillar of Judgement –
Feminine

The Right Pillar:
The Pillar of Mercy –
Masculine

Hokhmāh – Wisdom
Right brain hemisphere

Ōlām Atzilūth
The Archetypal World: the
World of Divine Names

Bināh – Understanding
Left brain hemisphere

Buddhi
the Spiritual Soul

Ḥesed – Mercy
Right arm

Ōlām Berīāh
The Intellectual, or Creative
World: the Archangelic
World of Creations

Geburah – Power
Left arm

Manas
the Human Soul

Beauty
Heart
Tiphereth

Da'at — Doorway

Netzah – Victory
Right leg

Foundation
Generative system
Yesōd

Ōlām Yetzīrah
The Substantial, or
Formative World: the
Hierarchal World of
Formations

Hod – Splendour
Left leg

Kāma
the terrestrial,
or Animal soul

Malkuth – The Kingdom
Two feet

Ōlām Asīah
The Physical Material
World: the Elemental
World of Substances

Liṅga-śarīra
the Etheric double, and
Sthūla-śarīra, or *Rūpa*
the Physical body

The
Unmanifest
Worlds

The
Manifest
Worlds

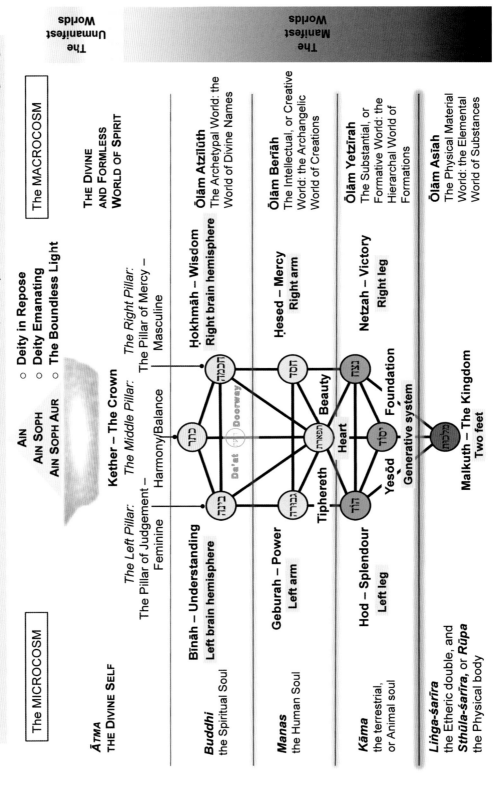

Figure III-8   The Sephirothic Tree of Ten Divine Names

(attribute through which Ain Soph Aur reveals Himself shining through Kether) produces another Sephīrāh by emanation.

The Sephīrōth are thus appositely represented as ten divine globes, or spheres of influence.

Turning now to the Manifest Worlds in the Macrocosm, the right hand side of Figure III-8 shows how the Unmanifest, Divine and Formless World of Spirit has actualized the four Manifest 'World Systems' known as Ōlāms, the three uppermost consisting of three Sephirathic triads: (*a*) Ōlām Atzīlūth, the Archetypal, or Prototypal World; (*b*) Ōlām Berīāh, the Intellectual, or Creative World; (*c*) Ōlām Yetzīrah, the Substantial, or Formative World; and (*d*) the last Ōlām Asīah, the Physical, or Material World—being the lowest, our plane, the visible universe. The vital point to appreciate is that Atzīlūth, being the world of Divine Emanation, is the highest prototype (zure) of other emanated worlds in its image. That is why, '*Atzeelooth* [*Atzīlūth*] is the Great Sacred Seal by means of which all the worlds are copied which have impressed on themselves the image on the Seal.'[15] Thus we see 'The Image of God in Matter', as Phillips so aptly puts it when rephrasing Genesis 1:27, as per the title of the next section.

The trinity of Ain, Ain Soph, and Ain Soph Aur has an unmistakable similarity to Sat-Chit-Ānanda in Hinduism (Sāṁkhya philosophy) and Father-Son-Holy Ghost in Christianity (see Chapter 7 for the Hindu and Christian parallels). The unity of great religious teachings the world over is again evident.

The Image of God in Man

> So God created man in his own image, in the image of God created he him; male and female created he them.
>
> Genesis 1:27 (King James Version)

The left hand side of Figure III-8 opposite shows how the Sephirothic Tree maps the nature of man, the Microcosm, corresponding to the Ōlāms, in the Macrocosm (seen on the right hand side). Thus, the emanations from *Ātma* are: *Buddhi*, the Spiritual Soul; *Manas*, the Human Soul; and *Kāma*, the terrestrial, or Animal soul, each consisting of three Sephirathic triads; finally, the Physical body. (Refer also to Volume II, Chapter 3, especially Table II-7 on page 21.)

The Sephīrōth represented as the ten divine globes are considered as analogous to the ten sacred members and organs of the *Protogonos* (mystic primæval deity of procreation and generation of new life) according to the following arrangement, as seen in Figure III-8:

1. Kether is the crown of the Prototypic Head and perhaps refers to the pineal gland.
2. Ḥokhmāh and Bīnāh are the right and left hemispheres, respectively, of the Great Brain.
3. Ḥesed and Geburah are the right and left arms respectively, signifying the active creative members of the Grand Man.

   Sephirathic correspondences with human body
4. Tiphereth is the heart, or, according to some, the entire viscera.
5. Netzah and Hod are the right and left legs respectively, or the supports of the world.
6. Yesōd is the generative system, or the foundation of form.
7. Malkuth represents the two feet, or the base of being.

Occasionally, Yesōd is considered as the male and Malkuth as the female generative power. The Grand Man thus conceived is the gigantic image of Nebuchadnezzar's dream, with head of gold, arms and chest of silver, body of brass, legs of iron, and feet of clay. The mediæval Qabbalists also assigned one of the Ten Commandments and a tenth part of the Lord's Prayer, in sequential order, to each of the ten Sephīrāh.[16] Furthermore, Figure III-8 shows a mysterious 'doorway', known as 'Da'at', located at the midpoint between Bīnāh, Ḥokhmāh, and Ḥesed. Sometimes referred to, in error, as a Sephīrāh, Da'at (Daath) represents 'the conjunction of Chokmah [Ḥokhmāh] and Bīnāh, Wisdom and Understanding.'[17] In another context, it is called 'The Abyss' in the sense that, 'It is not considered to be a Sephira[h], but one in potential for him who has passed through the door of Supreme Enlightenment into the Divine Life of the Supernal [Uppermost]) Triad.'[18]

The individual Sephīrāh also have correspondences with the various planes of nature. For example, Malkuth which represents the two feet, or the base of being in the human body, would obviously correspond to the dense physical plane; and Yesōd representing the generative system in the human body would correspond to the foundation of form on the physical plane.

Sephīrāh map the planes of nature and symbolize creative potencies

The Sephirothic Tree is sometimes represented as three pillars: the left and right pillars designated 'The Pillar of Judgement' and 'The Pillar of Mercy', respectively. The middle Pillar, also known as *Shekhīnah*, is regarded as the perfect pillar, the mediating factor between light and darkness. Each pillar consists of three Sephirathic triads topped by the first Sephīrāh, the Crown (Kether), as seen in Figure III-8. But what is even more important than the names in themselves or the meanings—which obviously represent lofty qualities—is the fact that they epitomize powers and potencies which are responsible for bringing the universe into manifestation for a period of activity.[19] Thus, as just explained, each of the ten Sephīrāh has its correspondence with a particular plane on which the universe and man—seen and unseen, physical and superphysical—exist and have their being.

The Mythical Tree – The Aswatha or Bodhi Tree

One of Blavatsky's central aims (as is the writer's) was to demonstrate the universality of the Ancient (Ageless) Wisdom by way of verifiable references and evidence drawn from diverse cultures, philosophies, and religions. The ancient theory of evolution is a case in point—this theory is not only embalmed in allegory and legend, but is depicted upon the walls of certain temples in India and, in fragmentary form, has been found in those of Egypt. Moreover, it is recorded on the slabs of Nimroud and Nineveh, excavated by Sir Austen Henry Layard (1817–1894), the English archaeologist whose excavations greatly increased knowledge of the ancient civilizations of Mesopotamia. We find this same evolution–hypothesis of the old Brahmans embodied in the allegory of the mundane tree which they call *Aswatha*. As pictured in Figure III-9 opposite, it is described by them as growing in a reversed position, the branches extending downward and the roots upward; the former typifying the external world of sense, i.e., the visible universe, and the latter the invisible world of spirit, because the roots have their *genesis* in the heavenly regions where, from the creation of the world, humanity has placed its invisible deity. 'The creative energy having originated in the primordial point, the religious symbols of every people are so many illustrations of this metaphysical hypothesis expounded by Pythagoras, Plato, and other philosophers.'[20] 'These Chaldeans', writes the philosopher Philo of Alexandria, 'were of opinion that this Kosmos, *among the things*

Aswatha Tree symbolizes creative origin in invisible spiritual roots

Figure III-9   The Mythical Aswatha Tree
Image Credit: https://www.freepik.com/vectors/tree

that exist [?][iv] is a single point, either being itself God (Theos) or that in it is God, comprehending the soul of all the things.

Chaos-Theos-Kosmos are but the three aspects of their synthesis—SPACE. One can never hope to solve the mystery of this *Tetraktys* by holding to the dead-letter even of the old philosophies, as now extant. But, even in these, CHAOS-THEOS-KOSMOS=SPACE, are identified in all Eternity, as the One Unknown Space, the last word about which will, perhaps, never be known [for aeons]. Nevertheless, the allegories and metaphysical symbols about the primeval and *perfect* CUBE, are remarkable even in the exoteric Purāṇas.'21

Remembering that symbols operate at many levels, it is a fitting demonstration of the universality of symbolism that the Pyramid and Mythical Aswatha, or Bodhi Tree, both reveal the key to the riddle of life and the mystery of man. To compare the two in the physical sense would obviously be meaningless. But esoterically they point to the same idea, for as Blavatsky elucidates: 'The Egyptian Pyramid also symbolically represents this idea of the mundane tree. Its apex is the mystic link between heaven and earth, and stands for the root, while the base represents the spreading branches, extending to the four cardinal points of the universe of matter. It conveys the idea that all things had their origin in spirit—evolution having originally begun from above and proceeded downward, instead of the reverse, as taught in the Darwinian theory. In other words, there has been a gradual materialization of forms until a fixed ultimate of debasement is reached.'22

Man – The Cube Unfolded

The Cube—represented by the *senary* (or number 6), and the Cube unfolded—represented by the septenary, or hebdomad (the number 7)—are both used by occultists as symbols to represent man. Why should this be? The answer lies in the work of Eastern Occultists and their disciples, the great alchemists, who have been privy to the mysteries

---

iv The italicization and question mark are both omitted in the earlier version of this quote—*IU*-I, Chapter V, 'Evolution in Hindu Allegory', 154, quoting from Philo, *On the Migration of Abraham*, xxxii, 179.

of the whole septenate, as opposed to the 'four', or Tetrad—the 'matter' of Western science. In 'The Mysteries of the Hebdomad', Blavatsky says:

> When the Three and the Four kiss each other, the Quaternary joins its middle nature with that of the Triangle [or Triad, *i.e.*, the face of one of its plane surfaces becoming the middle face of the other] [*sic*], and becomes a cube; then only does it [the cube unfolded] [*sic*] become the vehicle and the number of LIFE, the Father-Mother SEVEN.[23]

The symbolism of the above commentary can be elucidated thus: referring to the triangle and the square shown in the lower half of Figure III-10 opposite, 'the Three' represents Ātma-Buddhi-Manas (the Divine Self–Intuition Principle–Mind Principle)—the Higher Triad, or Individuality. The two upright, slanting lines portray the union of Ātma, with its emanation, Buddhi; while the triangle is completed by the base line, Manas. And 'the Four' represents Kāma–Prāṇa–Liṅga-śarīra–Sthūla-śarīra (the Desire principle–Life principle–Etheric double–Physical body)—the Lower Quaternary, or Personality. Now Kāma represents the upper (horizontal) line 4 of the square which, when brought into contact with the lower line 3 of the triangle, 'kisses' the base line of the latter, thus forming the duad, Kāma-manas. This duad, along with the lower vestures, constitutes man's personality.

Regarding the 'cube unfolded': a cube is a three-dimensional solid bounded by six equal squares. If we 'unfold' a cube, the six equal squares can be represented on a plane surface, as shown in the upper part of the figure. The three horizontal squares (representing a Triad) plus the four vertical squares (representing a Quaternary) give seven squares in all (representing man). The overlapping square is counted twice of course, this representing the 'kissing' of the triangle and the square—the 'face of one of its plane surfaces becoming the middle face of the other.' Note that the occult commentary does not declare the Three and the Four touch, but 'kiss each other'. The term 'kiss' is deeply significant. A touch does not signify a relationship; a kiss does—in this case, connoting the loving bond that exists between the Higher Triad and the Lower Quaternary—the Immortal Higher Self of man and his mortal personality.

Again, we see how symbolism provides a powerful way of expounding occult truths. Arguably, the finest demonstration of how numbers symbolize the constitution of the universe and man would be the Pythagorean teachings on the esoteric significance of numbers. For example, in the following extracts from Hall and Blavatsky, we see how the compound nature of man is constituted of the 3 and the 4:

> The 3 (spirit, mind, and soul) descend into the 4 (the world), the sum being the 7, or the mystic nature of man, consisting of a threefold spiritual body and a fourfold material form. These are symbolized by the cube, which has six surfaces and a mysterious seventh point within. The six surfaces are the directions: north, east, south, west, up, and down; or, front, back, right, left, above, and below; or again, earth, fire, air, water, spirit, and matter. In the midst of these stands the 1, which is the upright figure of man, from whose centre in the cube radiate six pyramids. From this comes the great occult axiom: 'The centre is the father of the directions, the dimensions, and the distances.'[24]

'Spirit, mind, and soul' constituting the 'threefold spiritual body' in the above quotation are of course none other than Ātma, Buddhi, and Manas—the Higher Triad; and the 'fourfold material form' is the Lower Quaternary comprising Kāma, Prāṇa, Liṅga-śarīra, and Sthūla-śarīra (refer again to Figure III-10).

△ and □ symbolize the Individuality and personality

Cube unfolded symbolizes union of man's Immortal and mortal aspects

Symbols and numbers both conceal and convey deep occult truths

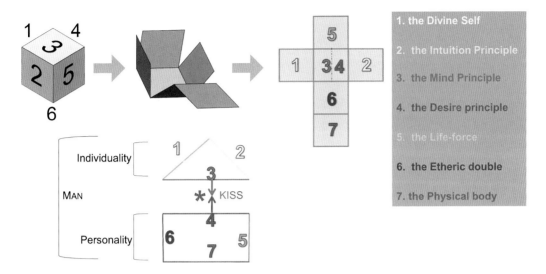

Figure III-10   Man – The Cube Unfolded
Image Credit: Artefact Design

As Blavatsky further declares about the number 7:

> But number *seven*, or the *heptagon*, the Pythagoreans considered to be a *religious and perfect* number. It was called *Telesphoros*, because *by it all in the Universe and mankind is led to its end*, i.e., its culmination.[25]

The following extract both reinforces and summarizes the explanations just given:

> Now, the number *six* has been regarded in the ancient mysteries as an emblem of *physical nature*. For six is the representation of the *six* dimensions of all bodies: the *six* lines which compose their form, namely, the four lines extending to the four cardinal points, North, South, East, and West, and the two lines of height and thickness that answer to the Zenith and the Nadir. Therefore, while the *senary* was applied by the sages to *physical* man, the *septenary* was for them the symbol of that man *plus* his immortal soul.[26]

We are now able to understand why the sages used the cube, 6, to symbolize physical nature, as also physical man; whilst the cube unfolded, 7, was used for physical man plus his immortal soul—Man.

Finally, Hall has this to say about the relationship in symbolism between the body and its informing spirit:

> The *body* of everything was likened [by the ancient philosophers] to a rock, trued either into a cube or more ornately chiselled to form a pedestal, while the *spirit* of everything was likened to the elaborately carved figure surmounting it. Accordingly, altars were erected as a symbol of the lower world, and fires were kept burning upon them to represent that spiritual essence illuminating the body it surmounted. The square is actually one surface of a cube, its corresponding figure in plane geometry, and its proper philosophic symbol. Consequently, when considering the earth as an element and not as a body, the Greeks, Brahmins, and Egyptians always referred to its four corners, although they were fully aware that the planet itself was a sphere.[27]

This Chapter has demonstrated the power of symbolism, drawn from Nature and the Platonic Solids, in order to illuminate the hidden meanings of man's true nature and constitution—meanings that elude descriptions in words. The next Chapter explains how the Hermetic Axiom elucidates the indissoluble link between man and the whole Universe.

> *Flower in the crannied wall*
> *I pluck you out of the crannies*
> *I hold you here, root and all, in my hand,*
> *Little flower—but if I could understand,*
> *What you are, root and all, and all in all,*
> *I should know what God and man is.*
>   ALFRED TENNYSON, FLOWER IN THE CRANNIED WALL[28]

> *Plato saith that Philosophy is the imitating God so far forth as man is able.*
>   ISAAC NEWTON[29]

NOTES

1   Kahlil Gibran, *The Prophet*, introd. John Baldock (London: Arcturus, 2018), 76.

2   *IU*-I, 'Realities and Illusion', 466.

3   *STA*, 'Flowers, Plants, Fruits, and Trees', XCIV.

4   Excerpt, and image adapted by the writer, from Geoffrey Barborka, *The Divine Plan* (2nd edn, rev. and enl., Adyar, Madras: Theosophical Publishing House, 1964; repr. 1980), 182–3.

5   *SD*-I, 'Stanza II: The Idea of Differentiation', 57–8.

6   *SD*-I, 'Stanza VII, śloka 4: Cosmic Evolution', 34; quoted also in *SD*-I, 'Stanza VII: The Parents of Man on Earth', 237.

7   *SD*-I, 'Stanza VII: The Parents of Man on Earth', 237, quoted from: the Egyptian Book of the Dead, Chap. i and vii; *Book of the Mysteries of Rostan* (an occult work on Persian mythology).

8   Geoffrey Barborka, *op. cit.*, 183–4.

9   *STA*, 'Flowers, Plants, Fruits, and Trees', XCIII, XCIV.

10 *Theosophie des Julius* [Theosophy of Julius] © 2015 www.werkvermächtnisse.de <http://www.archiv-swv.de/pdf-bank/Theosophie%20des%20JuliusSchillerOriginal.pdf> accessed 21 February 2020. The first section of the Theosophie entitled, 'The World and Thinking Being' is Schiller's grand cosmology—see Frederick Beiser, *Schiller as Philosopher: A re-examination* (Oxford: Clarendon Press, 2005), 33.

11 See G. de Purucker, *Occult Glossary: A compendium of Oriental and Theosophical Terms* (1933; Pasadena, California: Theosophical University Press, 1972), 137, 138.

12 See Geoffrey Barborka, *The Divine Plan*, 50.

13 *SD*-I, 'On the Hidden Deity, Its Symbols and Glyphs', 352.

14 Stephen Phillips, The Mathematical Connection Between Religion and Science (Eastbourne, UK: Anthony Rowe Publishing, 2009), 18.

15 *TSGLOSS*, 46, quoted from Isaac Myer, Qabbalah (1888) (US: Kessinger Publishing Co, 2003).

16 See *STA*, 'The Tree of the Sephiroth', CXXI.

17 *TSGLOSS*, 93.

18 Stephen Phillips, *The Mathematical Connection Between Religion and Science*, 22.

19 Geoffrey Barborka, *The Divine Plan*, 50.

20 *IU*-I, Chapter V, 'Evolution in Hindu Allegory', 153–4. Gautama Buddha is said to have meditated and attained enlightenment under the Bodhi tree.

21 Philo, *On the Migration of Abraham*, §xxxii, 179, in *SD*-I, 'Chaos—Theos—Kosmos', 344. See also 'On the Migration of Abraham', *Early Christian Writings: The works of Philo* <http://www.earlychristianwritings.com/yonge/book16.html> accessed 25 March 2020.

22 *IU*-I, 'Evolution in Hindu Allegory', 154.

23 *SD*-II, 'The Mysteries of the Hebdomad', 593.

24 *STA*, 'Pythagorean Mathematics', LXXII.

25 *SD*-II, 'The Mysteries of the Hebdomad', 602, quoting from Philo Judaeus, *De opificio mundi*, xxxv.

26 *SD*-II, *op. cit.*, 591, citing Jean Marie Ragon, *Orthodoxie Maçonnique* [Masonic Orthodoxy], etc. pp. 432–3. (*Maçonnerie Occulte* [Occult Masonry] is the second part of this work.)

27 *STA*, 'Stones, Metals, and Gems', XCVIII.

28 Edmund Clarence Stedman, *A Victorian Anthology (1837–1895)* (Cambridge, Massachusetts: The Riverside Press, 1895).

29 Newton's own sentiments in the preface to 'Manna', Keynes MS 33, f. 5ᵛ, King's College Library, University of Cambridge.

5 The Hermetic Axiom and the Law of Analogy

*From **Gods** to **men**, from Worlds to atoms, from a star to a rush-light, from the Sun to the vital heat of the meanest organic being—the world of Form and Existence is an immense chain, whose links are all connected. The law of Analogy is the first key to the world-problem, and these links have to be studied co-ordinately in their occult relations to each other.*

H. P. Blavatsky[1]

Synopsis

Chapter 5 constitutes the pivot point, so to say, of Volume III. It comprises an in-depth treatment of what has been a constant theme throughout this work—the Hermetic Axiom, and closely related matters of analogy, correspondence, and correlation that show how diversity is subsumed in organic unity. The different shades of meaning between the overlapping terms 'analogy', 'correspondence', and 'correlation' are clarified. Thereafter, the fundamental principles behind analogy and correspondence, reduced in all cases to terms of consciousness, are described in three steps. How these abstract precepts are discernible in all life and existence is then shown by three relations: (a) between human principles and corresponding cosmic principles; (b) between human principles and physical nature (the chemical elements); and (c) between human principles with phase states of matter, colours, and sounds. The Chapter ends by explaining why, in Indian classical music, the stringed instrument, known as the Veena, mirrors the divinity within the human body. A summary paves the way for further insights from the *philosophia perennis* on how Divine Consciousness is reflected in human consciousness, and how human principles are the correspondences of analogous principles in Cosmos.

Key Words: Hermetic Axiom, unfolding consciousness, analogy, correspondence, correlation, unity

The philosophic keys that unlock the door to the sacred arcana of truth are generally regarded as seven in number. Symbolism is one of them. Chapter 1 provided a substantial treatise on the meaning hidden in various kinds of symbols; and Chapters 2 to 4 focused on symbolic representations of Cosmos and man.

This Chapter focuses on another principal philosophic key—the Hermetic Axiom—the analogy and correspondence between the macrocosm and the microcosm, which has been a recurrent theme of this work, in order to illustrate a particular aspect of the *philosophia perennis*. Succinctly stated in the Bowen Notes,[i] the Hermetic Axiom underscores a cardinal tenet of occultism that reinforces the epigraph:

---

i The 'Bowen Notes' comprise 'extracts from the notes of personal teachings given by H. P. Blavatsky to private pupils during the years 1888 to 1891, included in a large manuscript volume left to me by my father [Commander Robert Bowen, Royal Navy], who was one of the pupils—P. G. Bowen'—see Reference 2 opposite.

> The Fundamental Unity of All Existence. This unity is a thing altogether different from the common notion of unity—as when we say that a nation or an army is united; or that this planet is united to that by lines of magnetic force or the like. The teaching is not that. It is that existence is One Thing, not any collection of things linked together. Fundamentally there is One Being.[2]

Hermetic Axiom: a major philosophic key

The basics of the Hermetic Axiom were introduced in Chapter 8 of Volume I and three versions of it were shown in Figure I-13 on page 249 including the translation by Isaac Newton. Our purpose now is to explain, in more depth, the reasons for its indispensable importance to esotericism and demonstrate this assertion with examples of its universal application. But first, as is our wont, we strive for clarity by explaining the meaning of terms.

Defining What We Mean by Analogy, Correspondence, and Correlation

Terms like 'correspondence', 'analogy', and 'correlation' are often used loosely or interchangeably, the subtle differences in meaning being overlooked. An analogy implies a similarity, but with differences in proportion and function. A common principle relates two or more things. For instance, the Sephirothic Tree is depicted as a human body because the ten divine globes (Sephīrōth) are considered as *analogous* to the ten sacred members and organs of man (see Chapter 4); but the Tree and man certainly do not correspond, nor do they correlate. Correspondence, or parallelism, means that which is the same in proportion. Thus, the sleeping and dreaming states of man during life correspond to his post-mortem state, but they are not analogous or correlated. A correlation means to have or bring into a mutual relation or connection. The two things so connected must obviously be of the same class or category, otherwise no mutual relation could exist between them. For example, smoking and heart disease are correlated; but there is no analogy or correspondence between them.

Definite words needed for definite things

It must be stressed that correlation is not causation. For example, the physical correlates of altered states of consciousness, like changes in brain rhythms, are not the cause of such states.

The Divine Mandate – The Way of Occult Science

The contrasting methods of science, and occult science, were summarized in broad terms in Chapter 8 of Volume I. Regarding occult science, the following three simple rules, recommended by Blavatsky, are tantamount to a working methodology:

1. Reduce everything to terms of consciousness; which injunction is strongly coupled with –
2. Use the keys of analogy and correspondence. Analogy is the surest guide to the comprehension of the Occult teachings. Everything in the Universe, throughout all its kingdoms, is CONSCIOUS, and follows analogy: as above, so below; but –
3. We must first learn the formula before we can sum up the series.[3]

Consciousness, and its unfolding

We now deal briefly with the above three rules in turn.

Reduce Everything to Terms of Consciousness

In her esoteric instructions, Blavatsky's students were told to 'reduce everything to terms of consciousness'. (This is in stark contrast to the approach of establishment science to reduce consciousness to terms of matter, i.e., matter in motion and its interactions.) It is not difficult to see the truth of this. Consider first man, the microcosm. It is obvious that every *external* motion, act or gesture, whether voluntary or mechanical, organic or mental, is produced and preceded by *internal* thought, feeling, will or volition. Sense experiences are really mental experiences, the movement of consciousness. Now, applying the same principle on a larger scale to the macrocosm, just as no outward motion or change in man's external body can take place unless provoked by an inward impulse, actuated through one of the three functions just named, so with the external, or manifested cosmos. The whole cosmos is guided, controlled, and animated by an almost endless series of Hierarchies of conscious and animate Beings, each having a mission to perform, and who—whatever name we give to them—like Dhyan-Chohans in the East or Archangels in the West—are 'messengers' in the sense only that they are the agents of karmic and cosmic laws. This theme is, arguably, what the Nobel physicist Brian Josephson might well have been alluding to when he stated that 'Physics has things back to front'. He substantiated this insight in his lecture with three more remarkable insights: (*a*) 'Agents are the source of physics – not v/v [*sic*] [vice versa]'; (*b*) 'Physics needs to come to terms with agents'; and (*c*) '[We need to move] Towards a Science of Agents'— see Volume I, Chapter 8, page 243 for more details and references.

Consciousness needs mediators for its unfolding

The Key of Analogy

'*Analogy* is the guiding law in Nature, the only true Ariadne's thread that can lead us, through the inextricable paths of her domain [the labyrinth of confusion, sensuality, and danger], toward her primal and final mysteries.'[4] Analogy, therefore, is the surest guide to the comprehension of the occult teachings because, 'Everything in the Universe follows analogy. "As above, so below"; man is the microcosm of the Universe. That which takes place on the spiritual plane repeats itself on the Cosmic plane. Concretion follows the lines of abstraction; corresponding to the highest must be the lowest; the material to the spiritual.'[5] This idea is illustrated in Figure III-11 opposite using the symbol of the lotus flower as a simile of man's composition (see Chapter 4).

> As above so it is below, as in heaven so on earth.

Following directly from the above quote by Blavatsky is the proposition that 'The Universe is worked and *guided* from *within outwards*. As above so it is below, as in heaven so on earth; and man—the microcosm and miniature copy of the macrocosm—is the living witness to this Universal Law and to the mode of its action.'[6] And this is precisely the reason behind the old saying, 'Man is the Measure of All Things' (see Chapter 3).

Plato stresses the importance of beginning with universals

But it must be remembered, continues Blavatsky, 'that the study of Occultism proceeds [by the Platonic method] from Universals to Particulars, and not the reverse, as [almost universally] accepted by Science' (but refer again to Chapter 8 in Volume I for more details on the different, but complementary, methods of Occult science and Western science). 'As Plato was an Initiate, he very naturally used the former [deductive] method, while Aristotle, never having been initiated, scoffed at his master, and, elaborating a system of his own, left it as an heirloom to be adopted and improved by [Roger] Bacon.'[7]

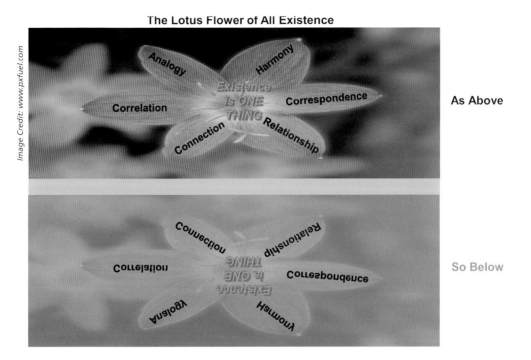

Figure III-11 The Hermetic Axiom and the Law
of Analogy Represented Emblematically

Moreover, Plato was influenced by the pre-Socratic Greek philosopher Parmenides of Elea (late sixth century to mid-fifth century BC) who lived in southern Italy and founded the Eleatic school of philosophy. Nowadays Parmenides is famously known as the founder of Western rationalism in that he introduced logic. But as the British mystic and Cambridge scholar Peter Kingsley (*b.*1953) informs us: 'As for the "logic" that he intro-duced to the western world, this was not some dry intellectual exercise. It was nothing less than a gift from the gods which when understood right, and applied in our daily life, has the mysterious power of taking us back to the gods.'[8] As the first to employ deductive, a priori, arguments to justify his claims,[9] and being one of the earliest philosophers to enquire into the nature of existence itself, Parmenides is justifiably credited as the 'Father of Metaphysics'. So in line with this, Blavatsky further instructs:

> Of a truth the aphorism of the Hermetic Wisdom, 'as above, so below', applies to all esoteric instruction; but we must begin with the *above*; we must learn the formula [relating to the 'above'] before we can sum up the series ['below'].[10]

What this means is as follows.

Parmenides and the spiritual meaning of logic

Learning the Formula Before Summing Up the Series

An elementary mathematical simile might help to explain why it is necessary first to 'learn the formula'. Consider the following entirely arbitrary algebraic equation:

$$(x + y)^2 = x2 + 2xy + y^2$$

The term in brackets to the left of the equals sign is the formula. The summed terms to the right of the equals sign is the series; but this can only be obtained from a prior knowledge of the formula. The series is, in a manner of saying, the explicated, or unfolded version of the implicate, or infolded formula.

The important fact to note, however, is that the formula is a completely general statement: any chosen value of x and y will yield the appropriate series. For example, applying the formula with x equals 2 and y equals 3, we obtain:

$$(2 + 3)^2 = 2^2 + 2 \times 2 \times 3 + 3^2; \text{ i.e.}$$

$$25 \quad = 4 + 12 + 9$$

Thus, in terms of this mathematical simile, the formula represents the statement of Universals as the emanating Source of the vast scheme of creation, which is represented by the series.

It is for this reason of working from the universal to the particular that Occult Science is regarded in the sense of an abstract algebraic formula about creation, cogently demonstrated in this seminal passage by Blavatsky regarding the archaic Stanzas upon which rest the propositions and axioms of the Secret Doctrine:[ii]

The history of cosmic evolution, as traced in the Stanzas, is, so to say, the abstract algebraical formula of that Evolution. Hence the student must not expect to find there an account of all the stages and transformations which intervene between the first beginnings of 'Universal' evolution and our present state. To give such an account would be as impossible as it would be incomprehensible to men who cannot even grasp the nature of the plane of existence next to that to which, for the moment, their consciousness is limited.

The supreme spiritual 'formula'

The Stanzas, therefore, give an *abstract formula* [emphasis added] which can be applied, *mutatis mutandis* [once the necessary changes have been made], to all evolution: to that of our tiny earth, to that of the chain of planets of which that earth forms one, to the solar Universe to which that chain belongs, and so on, in an ascending scale, till the mind reels and is exhausted in the effort.

The seven Stanzas given in this volume [*The Secret Doctrine*] represent the seven terms of this abstract formula. They refer to, and describe the seven great stages of the evolutionary process, which are spoken of in the *Purāṇas* as the 'Seven Creations', and in the Bible as the 'Days' of Creation.[11]

The remainder of this Chapter provides examples to illustrate the general importance of the 'algebraical formula' with the specific objective of showing the universality of its application concerning the analogies between cosmos, nature, matter, and man at different levels. Subsequent chapters will deal with the 'as above, so below' correspondences between Cosmos and man in more depth.

Parallelisms between Human and Cosmic Principles

Figure III-12 opposite shows a comparison of the Human Principles with Cosmic Principles.[12] According to the Hermetic Axiom, it will be apparent how perfect is the analogy between the ever becoming and ever evolving processes of nature in cosmos and in man. Man is born, lives through his allotted life span, and dies; then exists in the

---

ii 'Secret Doctrine' here referring to the Mystery Teachings also known as Eternal Wisdom, Ancient Wisdom, Perennial Philosophy, Secret Knowledge, *Gupta-Vidyā*, and not to be mistaken for Blavatsky's magnum opus, *The Secret Doctrine* (from which the extract which follows is taken), being a representative portion of the Mystery Teachings appropriated to the present stage of humanity—see Figure I-8 in Volume I, Chapter 7, page 185.

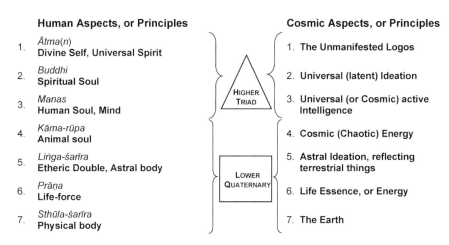

Figure III-12 Parallelisms Between Human and Cosmic Principles

post-mortem realms before a rebirth in a new body (see Table II-10 and Table II-11 in Chapter 5, on pages 66 and 98, respectively, of Volume II). As man's three higher principles (the *Ātma-Buddhi-Manas* Higher Triad) pass into the state of blissful rest (*Devachan*) between terrestrial incarnations, correspondingly, the cycling Monads (Ātma-Buddhi) pass into the transcendent state (*Nirvāṇa*iii) during the state of Cosmic slumber (*Pralaya*iv) intervening between the objective manifestations of cosmos. Continuing the analogy, just as man's four lower principles (the Lower Quaternary of *Kāma, Prāṇa, Liṅga-śarīra,* and *Sthūla-śarīra*) are disintegrated in time and are again reused by nature for the formation of new mortal vestures for the reincarnating entity, the same processes take place in the disintegration and formation of the material of new Worlds. We see here a demonstration of why analogy is the surest guiding law and key to the comprehension of the occult teachings.

As is the Cosmos, so is the human being

Parallelisms between Principles in the Human Being and Physical Nature

Another example along similar lines, but at a lower level, is the correspondence between the principles in man and in physical nature.

It is a triumph of modern astronomy to reveal that 'we are made from star stuff', in the words of the famous American astronomer and astrobiologist Carl Sagan (1934–1996).[13] This is an awesome statement, albeit referring just to the physical plane, for it shows how the chemical elements in the composition of our bodies, and all else in physical nature, were transformed by nucleosynthesis in stars (the nuclear processes that synthesize the heavy chemical elements from the lightest element, hydrogen).

To the occultist who sees the organic unity of cosmos, stars, and man, there is a deeper relation between the human being and 'star dust', as seen in Figure III-13 overleaf, which

---

iii '*Nirvāṇa*', a Sanskrit word meaning, literally, 'out-blow', or 'blown out' is often mistranslated as 'extinction' or 'annihilation'. It is in fact a transcendent state where there is no more thirst for physical existence as all attachments and desires have been extinguished.

iv Literally a period of dissolution: from the compound Sanskrit word *pra,* away; *laya,* from the verb-root *lī,* to dissolve.

	Human Principles		Principles of Physical Nature
1 2 3	**Ātma** **Buddhi** **Manas**	△	There is no correspondence between the principles of physical nature and the higher (non-physical) human principles
4	**Kāma-rūpa**, the principle of animal desire which burns fiercely during life in (physical) matter, resulting in satiety; inseparable from animal existence.	Hydrogen	The lightest of all gases: • burns in oxygen giving off the most intense heat of any substance in combustion and forming water, one of the most stable of compounds; • enters largely into all organic compounds.
5	**Liṅga-śarīra**, the inert vehicle, or form, on which the human body is moulded; the vehicle of Life. Dissipated very shortly after the disintegration of the body.	Nitrogen	An inert gas: • the 'vehicle' with which Oxygen is mixed to dilute the mixture and adapt it for animal respiration; • a major component of several organic substances.
6	**Prāṇa**, Life essence, the active power producing all vital phenomena.	Oxygen	The supporter of combustion: • the life-giving gas; • the active chemical agent in all organic life.
7	**Sthūla-śarīra**, Physical body, the gross matter of which is the substance formed and moulded over the Liṅga-śarīra (Chhāyā) by the action of Prāṇa.	Carbon	The fuel *par excellence*: • the basis of all organic substances; • the chemical element that forms the largest variety of compounds.

Figure III-13   Parallelisms Between Human Principles
and Principles in Physical Nature

As is the human being, so is nature

shows the correspondence between the principles of physical nature and the human principles, namely, the four Elements of physical nature and the Lower Quaternary of man, each principle of which may be regarded as a 'human element', so to speak.[14] The comparison effectively starts from the fourth level downwards—the Lower Quaternary—since there can be no principle in physical nature analogous to the non-physical Upper Triad in man. What exactly is meant by physical nature?

A living organism is composed physically of, very approximately, seventy per cent water and the remainder comprising organic molecules, the keys elements of which are hydrogen, nitrogen, oxygen, and carbon. At the base of all organic molecules is the element carbon, whose versatility enables the formation of all biomolecular structures. In most organic molecules, a linked chain of carbon atoms forms a backbone to which other atoms attach. Covalent bonds (chemical bonds between two non-metal atoms) between carbon and hydrogen atoms form the basis of the simplest organic molecules (such as the gas methane). Other key elements are oxygen and nitrogen—both play crucial roles in life processes by modifying the structure and chemical properties of organic molecules. Other elements, like sulphur and phosphorus, have important roles but the four elements just stated are the crucial ones.

Whether life forms based physically on silicon (instead of carbon) exist somewhere in the galaxy, either now, or at some time in the future, is matter of interesting speculation, but outside the scope of this work.

Figure III-13 shows the importance of the numbers 3 (the Triad) and 4 (the Quaternary), and their union. The numbers 3 and 4 are, respectively, male and female, spirit and matter, in the generic sense, of course; and their union is the emblem of life, eternal in spirit, on its ascending arc, and in matter as the ever resurrecting element, by virtue of procreation and reproduction. The spiritual male line is vertical | ; the differentiated matter-line is horizontal — ; the two forming the cross + . The 3 is invisible; the 4 is on the plane of objective perception. This is why all the organic matter of the universe, when analysed by science to its ultimate, can be reduced to four principal elements only—hydrogen, nitrogen, oxygen, and carbon: and why the three primaries, being the noumenoi of the four, or graduated Spirit (Force), have remained *terra incognita* and mere speculations, to exact science. Science must therefore believe in, and study first, the primary causes (the 'formula') alongside the effects (the 'series'), thereby complementing physics with meta-physics, in order to gain a deeper understanding of the processes of life and creation, *which are not merely the meeting of time, physics, and chemistry as modern mainstream science would maintain and have us believe.*[15]

Physics is imbued with metaphysics

Correspondences between Human Principles with States of Matter, Colours, and Sounds

In expounding the Eastern system of esoteric philosophy, Blavatsky relates the septenary constitution of man to the seven states of matter (using H_2O as an illustration) and the seven colours and sounds, as shown in Table III-3 on page 79.[16] But as Blavatsky warns in studying this tabulation, major confusion would result unless three important factors are borne in mind:

1. Just as objects appear inverted in a mirror, our plane of existence—the terrestrial plane—being a plane of reflection, and therefore illusionary (see Figure III-11, page 73)—*the various notations are reversed and must be counted from below upwards.* Thus, the musical scale begins from below upwards, commencing with the deep *Do* and ending with the far higher *Si*.

2. *Kāma-rūpa* (corresponding to *Do* in the musical scale), containing as it does all potentialities of matter, is necessarily the starting-point on our plane. Further, it commences the notation on every plane, as corresponding to the 'matter' of that plane. Again, it must also be remembered that these notes have to be arranged in a circle, thus showing how *Fa* is the middle note of nature. In short, musical notes, or sounds, colours and numbers, proceed from one to seven, and not from seven to one as erroneously shown in the spectrum of the prismatic colours, in which red

is counted first. The musical scale and colours, according to the scale of vibrations, proceed from the world of gross matter to that of spirit.

3. It is necessary to dismiss from the mind any correspondence between 'principles' and numbers, because the esoteric enumeration cannot be made to correspond with the conventional exoteric equivalent, as found in popular textbooks. The esoteric is the *reality*, the exoteric classified according to illusive/illusory appearances.[17]

As the human principles, so the properties of matter

The final column, on states of matter in the table of correspondences, is in no way meant to suggest a materialistic or matter-centric conception of man. It shows how the critical states of matter marking the transition from one phase state to another (e.g. from water to steam) are in analogous relationship to the equivalent phase transition in the Principles of Man (e.g. from the Spiritual Soul to the Auric Envelope). These different phases may be regarded as different levels of consciousness, namely, consciousness functioning on different planes, each having its own space–time dimensions.

It is always necessary to bear in mind that colour, sound, matter, etc., are, ultimately, different modes of vibration of One Consciousness–Matter. This goes a long way towards explaining one of the energy healing modalities whereby each organ is regarded as having its unique vibratory characteristic; and when the latter is disrupted or blocked for any reason, disease (dis-ease) ensues. Healing is then effected by impressing upon the body the colour or sound of the frequency corresponding to the healthy organ to restore the diseased organ to its normal vibratory state. For instance, cymatics (high-frequency sound waves used for healing)[v] and other applications of sound in medicine and other forms of research, currently in their infancy, could become important healing procedures for the future.[18]

Finally, the table of correspondences opposite has been provided simply as a taster, *and no more*, of the full range of analogies and correspondences that can be enumerated between human principles and various categories, such as: states of consciousness, human senses and organs, metals, days of the week, planets and planetary influences. It provides a graphic demonstration of the fundamental unity of existence and is enumerated in great detail in the Esoteric Instructions given out by Blavatsky to her personal pupils, a small portion of which is presented in Chapter 7. To attempt a simplistic tabulation of such complex relations would be extremely irresponsible. It is not for good reason that Blavatsky expounded this pinnacle of occult science, in guarded fashion, to a few chosen pupils such as Annie Besant, G. R. S. Mead, and Commander Robert Bowen. It underscores the immense gravity of the material and the dangers attendant upon its misuse (like arousing the lower psychic faculties), either deliberately through lack of moral stature or from misguided practices born of superficial understanding. Regarding the latter, to give one example, it is stated in the Instructions that Venus, Manas, and the left eye are set down as correspondences.[19] One can easily imagine the derisory objections from the scientific fraternity that such correspondences are ridiculous, for what possible connection could there be between a planet, the human mind, and a human organ? Exoterically, there is

Esoteric correspondences between planets and human senses

---

v Cymatics is derived from the Greek, κῦμα, meaning 'wave', and is a subset of modal vibrational phenomena. The term was coined by Hans Jenny (1904–1972), a Swiss follower of Rudolf Steiner's Anthroposophy.

Table III-3 Correspondences between Human Principles and Colours, Sounds, Numbers, and Phase Transitions of Matter

Constitution of Man	Colours	Sounds (Notes) Italian Gamut	Sanskrit Gamut	Numbers	States of Matter
Chhāyā **Etheric double, or Shadow**	Violet	Si	Ni	1	Ether
Higher Manas **Spiritual Intelligence**	Indigo	La	Da	2	Critical State, called Air in Occultism
Auric Envelope	Blue	Sol	Pa	3	Steam, or Vapour
Lower manas, or **Animal soul** (see Note)	Green	Fa	Ma	4	Critical State
Buddhi **Spiritual Soul**	Yellow	Mi	Ga	5	Water
Prāṇa **Life principle**	Orange	Re	Ri	6	Critical State
Kāma-rūpa **Seat of Animal Life**	Red	Do	Sa	7	Ice

Note: *Lower manas*, referred to by Blavatsky also as the Animal soul, obviously implies desire-driven thought, or *Kāma-manas*—the orientation of thought towards the desire principle, *kāma*, the Animal soul proper (see Table II-7 in Volume II, Chapter 3, page 44). This is just one example of the absolutely unavoidable ambiguity caused by having to use words that have a precise meaning in Sanskrit, but initially no exact equivalent definition in English. Consequently, the English terminology is bound to change until the meaning 'settles down' into generally accepted usage—see Volume II, Chapter 1, page 3 concerning the problems caused by English terminology.

indeed no such correspondence between a physical planet, the mind, and the physical eye. But *esoterically* there is. For the right eye is the 'Eye of Wisdom', i.e., it corresponds magnetically with that occult centre in the brain which, despite the objections of science, is called the 'Third Eye'; while the left eye corresponds with the intellectual brain, or those cells which are the organ on the physical plane of the thinking faculty. The Qabbalistic triangle of Kether, Ḥokhmāh, and Bīnāh shows this (see Figure III-8, page 62 in the previous Chapter). Ḥokhmāh and Bīnāh, or Wisdom and Intelligence, the Father and the Mother, or, again, the Father and Son, are on the same plane and react mutually on one another. This example shows the dangers of a literal interpretation of correspondences without full cognizance of the level at which they are meaningful and to which they pertain. However, for more detail the earnest reader can always refer to the Esoteric Instructions mentioned above.

The Human Body as a Divine Musical Instrument

An in-depth exposition of the human functioning principles, according to occult science, was given in Chapter 3 of Volume II, where it was stated that the human being

Why is the Veena considered a sacred instrument?

Figure III-14   Goddess Saraswati
depicted playing the Veena
Picture Credit: Raja Ravi Varma/Wikipedia

is in the nature of a divine musical instrument, something that mystics, artists, and musicians since ancient times have sought to mirror in their creations. One of the best examples is the stringed instrument known as the *Veena* belonging to the centuries old Carnatic tradition of music of South India, which is one of the main subgenres of Indian classical music that evolved from ancient Hindu traditions. The Veena has twenty four frets corresponding to the twenty four moveable bones (presacral vertebrae) of the human spine—see https://highonscore.com/anatomical-analogy/. Naturally then, the Indian Veena has always been considered as an instrument of the gods and hence the name 'Divine instrument' has been attributed to it.[20] It is the favourite instrument of several important deities, including Saraswati (Sanskrit: *Sarasvatī*), the goddess of arts and learning—see Figure III-14.

Summing Up

Why exactly is it that we find innumerable instances of the law of analogy operating at all levels in the ever becoming and ever evolving cosmos, nature, and man? It is because Divine Consciousness, ever Unmanifest, is the Source and prototype of everything in the Manifest, which is a repeated projection and reflection of the Unmanifest at different levels. Thus at the three primary levels:

1. The Unmanifest is projected and reflected in the Divine.
2. The Divine is projected and reflected in the Spiritual.
3. The Spiritual is projected and reflected in the temporal and mortal.

Cascading from divinity to materiality

Because the same Reality is projected and reflected at different levels, everything in manifestation is in the nature of a holographic representation of its Source. For this reason, 'the below' corresponds to, and is a diminished reflection of, 'the above', as per the Hermetic Axiom. The natural corollary is that:

1. The appearance of the Manifest from the Unmanifest does not affect, or in any way deplete, the wholeness and perfection of the Unmanifest any more than a mirror would be degraded by virtue of the countless images it reflects.
2. The Manifest is also whole and perfect because it is an emanation of the Unmanifest—such perfection and wholeness pertaining not to the various manifested forms, which are transitory, hence illusory, but to their basic substance—CONSCIOUSNESS.

Taking even the first step towards fathoming the mysteries of existence requires a deep awareness of organic unity and an understanding of the correspondence, at all levels, between the macrocosm and the microcosm. Indeed, this Chapter shows that in order to make sense of the world we inhabit, the universe, and ourselves, we need to recognize the indispensable role of analogy and correspondence and be able to use them wisely. We continue with further insights from the *philosophia perennis* about how Divine Consciousness is projected and reflected in human consciousness and, associated with this, how the human principles are the correspondences of analogous principles in the Cosmos.

For all that happens down here is but the reflection in gross matter of the happenings on higher planes, and we may often find a crutch for our halting imagination in our studies of physical development. 'As above, so below'. The physical is the reflection of the spiritual.

ANNIE BESANT[21]

Extract from Newton's translation of the Hermetic Axiom found among his alchemical papers currently lodged in King's College Library, Cambridge University:

Tis true without lying, certain & most true. That which is below is like that which is above & that which is above is like that which is below to do the miracles of one only thing. And as all things have been & arose from one by the mediation of one: so all things have their birth from this one thing by adaptation.

ISAAC NEWTON[22]

NOTES

1 *SD*-I, 'Forces—Modes of Motion or Intelligences?' 604.

2 Robert Bowen, '*The Secret Doctrine* and Its Study', in Robert Bowen, *Madame Blavatsky on How to Study Theosophy* (London: Theosophical Publishing House, 1960), 8 [online facsimile] <https://www.theosophical.org/component/content/article/23-online-books/1699> accessed 21 December 2020. Known as the 'Bowen Notes', they are reprinted in *Theosophy in Ireland*, II:1 (January–March, 1932) [online] <http://www.blavatskytrust.org.uk/html/booklets/ihoskins_bowen.htm> accessed 21 December 2020.

3 The above three rules are taken from: *SD*-I, 'Explanations Concerning the Globes and the Monads', 173, 177; *SD*-I, 'Stanza VII: The Parents of Man on Earth', 274; *CW*-XII, 'Instruction No. III', 600.

4 *SD*-II, 'Stanza VI: The Evolution of the Sweat Born', 153.

5 *SD*-I, 'Explanations Concerning the Globes and the Monads', 177.

6 *SD*-I, 'Summing Up – The Pith and Marrow of Occultism', 274.

7 See *CW*-XII, 'E. S. Instruction No. III', 599.

8 Peter Kingsley, 'Parmenides & Empedocles' © *2004–2020 Peter Kingsley* <https://peterkingsley.org/parmenides-empedocles> accessed 25 March 2020.

9 Jeremy C. DeLong, 'Parmenides of Elea', *Internet Encyclopedia of Philosophy: A peer-reviewed academic resource* <https://www.iep.utm.edu/parmenid> accessed 25 March 2020.

10 *CW*-XII, 'E. S. Instruction No. III', 599–600. See Volume I, Chapter 8 for more details.

11 *SD*-I, 'Proem', 20–1.

12 Marginally adapted from *SD*-II, 'The Mysteries of the Hebdomad', 596.

13 Carl Sagan, *The Cosmic Connection: An extraterrestrial perspective* (New York: Anchor Press, 1973), 190.

14 Marginally adapted from *SD*-II, 'The Mysteries of the Hebdomad', 593.

15 As an example see Professor Brian Cox and Andrew Cohen, *Human Universe & Forces of Nature* (London: William Collins, 2015).

16 Adapted from *CW*-XII, 'E. S. Instruction No. I', facing p. 532; and *CW*-XII, 'E. S. Instruction No. II', 562.

17 See *CW*-XII, 'E. S. Instruction No. II', 561, 562.

18 Peter Guy Manners, 'Vibrational Therapy', Sound Healers Association <http://www.soundhealersassociation.org/dr-peter-guy-manners-vibrational-therapy> accessed 25 March 2020.

19 See *CW*-XII, 'E. S. Instruction No. II', 545.

20 'About the Veena' <http://www.jayanthikumaresh.com/about-the-veena> accessed 25 March 2020.

21 Annie Besant, *A Study in Consciousness* (Adyar, Madras: Theosophical Publishing House, 1972), 9.

22 'The Chymistry of Isaac Newton', ed. William R. Newman, June 2010 (Keynes MS 28, King's College Library, Cambridge University) <http://purl.dlib.indiana.edu/iudl/newton/ALCH00017> accessed 7 May 2020. The complete version is provided in Volume I, Chapter 8, Figure I-13, page 249.

6 Cosmogenesis: the Unfolding of Consciousness – Kosmic Planes to Terrestrial Planes

*The Universe is worked and **guided** from within outwards.*

H. P. BLAVATSKY[1]

The universe is composed of a part that is material and a part that is incorporeal; and inasmuch as its body is made with soul in it, the universe is a living creature.

HERMES TRISMEGISTUS: HERMETICA, LIB. X.11.

SYNOPSIS

Chapter 6 presents an overview of the principal stages in cosmogenesis: the overall process of kosmic unfoldment on the various planes of manifestation, but here with a specific focus on man as the mirror of kosmos. The Chapter opens with a clear definition of terms to distinguish between their everyday use and their distinctive meaning in an occult context. This particularly applies to the terms 'kosmos' (spelt with a *k*) and 'multiverse', a relatively modern concept to which the former alludes. By invoking the Hermetic Axiom, the correspondences between Divine Consciousness and human consciousness are shown to be equivalent to the correspondences between the different kosmic and human planes (infinitely graded levels of existence, each with its own space–time orders, from the gross material to the most ethereal). The process of kosmic unfoldment on seven principal planes is summarized and followed by a related account of *Ākāśa*, the subtle, all-encompassing primordial Substance that underlies, and becomes all things. This provides a clue about the nature of Universal memory and memory in man. A recapitulation of the principal milestones leads on to the next three Chapters constituting the summit of our enquiry into the unfolding of consciousness in nature and man.

KEY WORDS: Hermetic Axiom, kosmic planes, planetary schemes, planes of manifestation, primordial Substance, Ākāśa, Astral Light, memory, human principles, states of consciousness

A recurrent theme of this work is that man, in his innermost Self, is a miniature universe; so it is impossible to study man without concomitantly involving nature and the universe, for they are essentially one organic Being, ever becoming and perpetually evolving, hence inextricably inter-related. This is why man is said to be the measure of all things (as explained in Chapter 3) because he mirrors Cosmos in that the same principles and laws that govern the unfoldment of the latter apply also to the former. All parts of the cosmos conform to the same law to which cosmos itself conforms (explained in the following section): therefore man also follows the same pattern throughout his life-cycle. This was explained in specific terms in Chapter 5 focusing on the Hermetic Axiom affirming the organic unity and correspondence between the greater and the lesser.

Principles and planes of Cosmos are mirrored in man

Whereas the previous Chapters dealt with such correspondences between Cosmos, Nature, and Man in overall terms, this Chapter provides more substantiation and detail about the unfolding of consciousness regarding two interrelated characteristics that follow directly from the above, namely: how the planes upon which the substance of man's various bodies, or vehicles, is derived are the mirror of the corresponding planes of cosmos; and how the seven principles comprising the constitution of man, the microcosm, are related to corresponding principles in cosmos, the macrocosm. As an understanding of what is meant by 'plane' is absolutely central to this Chapter, the following definition, first given in Volume II, is stated again for convenience:

> [The term 'plane' is derived] from the Latin *planus* (level, flat) an extension of space or of something in it, whether physical or metaphysical, *e.g.*, a 'plane of consciousness'. As used in Occultism, the term denotes the range or extent of some state of consciousness, or of the perceptive power of a particular set of senses, or the action of a particular force, or the state of matter corresponding to any of the above.[2]

The essential meaning conveyed is that of a sphere, or field, of influence. However, the term has a complex meaning, so the reader is urged to recall the further explanations provided in Volume II, Chapter 1, pages 5–7, especially regarding the association of planes with dimensions of space and time, physical and higher.

The Microcosm Mirrors the Macrocosm

Resemblance does not mean just a physical, 'photocopied' appearance or one of structural conformity, but is also to do with function. One of the finest attributes of the Hermetic Axiom is that immense complexity can be concentrated or reduced to elegant simplicity through the law of analogy, or correspondence. Apropos, the reductive methodology of materialistic science may, in one sense, be considered as an application (in a very limited sense, of course) of the Hermetic Axiom, although most scientists would hardly acknowledge this. What we mean is that science attempts to comprehend the universe by reducing physical matter down to elementary *particles*. By contrast, Esoteric Science fathoms the Cosmos through fundamental or elementary *principles* and Occult Science views material particles as the highly attenuated state of '"Spiritual particles", *i.e.*, supersensuous matter existing in a state of primeval differentiation.'[3]

Material particles versus 'Spiritual particles'

Accordingly, the immensely complex inner and outer nature of man is reflectively analogous to that of the total Universal Being. This applies not only to man but also to every other entity. Everything reflects the whole, actually or potentially, to a greater or lesser degree of approximation, dependent on the 'closeness' of each entity to its source. Concerning man, we showed in Chapter 8 of Volume I the resemblance between human birth and cosmic birth as an example of the Hermetic Axiom. We now amplify this by explaining why in the occult literature a human being is said to be a microcosmic representation of Cosmos. As with the cosmic–human birth example, such a comparison makes no sense externally (it is non-sensical) because there is no outward resemblance between the physical body of man and the physical solar system or the cosmos. But if we search behind outer appearances and visible structures and examine the principles, potentialities, and tendencies in the outer forms, it is always possible to discern a remarkable similitude between the function and modes of expression of man the microcosm and Cosmos the Macrocosm.

A slight, but indispensable, digression is now warranted for which the reader's forbearance is pleaded.

Aiming for Clear Definitions – The Distinction between Cosmos, Kosmos, Universe, and World

Given the highly abstruse subject matter of this Chapter, it is necessary to explain the fine distinction of meaning between words that in most other contexts would be practically synonymous. The following is therefore an elaboration of what is provided in the Definitions in Volume IV.

The Meaning of Cosmos

As generally used by H. P. Blavatsky in *The Secret Doctrine* and esoteric literature in general, the term 'cosmos', written with a lower case *c*, is used in the commonly accepted meaning attaching to the word: our solar system comprising the sun and the celestial objects that orbit it, either directly (like the planets) or indirectly (like the planetary moons). Cosmos, written with an upper case *C*, refers to both the objective and subjective aspects of our solar system. The term derives from the Greek *kósmos*, meaning 'order', or 'arrangement', from which is derived the verb *kosmein*, which means 'arrange', or 'adorn'. It appears originally to have been applied by Pythagoras and his School in reference to the *orderliness of creation*.

'Cosmos' and 'cosmos' refer to our solar system

The Meaning of Kosmos

However, 'Kosmos' (written with an upper case *K*) denotes the numberless, infinite Universes, the innumerable Solar systems of the infinite Cosmos. Written with a lower case *k*, kosmos refers to the objective aspect of Kosmos. *The term especially implies the Womb of all Universes to be*: the ever-concealed 'Unknown God' (*Agnostos Theos*) of the Athenians, equivalent to the Vedic *Kalahaṁsā* giving birth to the 'Son', or Universe—Plato's Second God, or the Third Logos, similar to Brahmā. A profound meaning is concealed in the term Kalahaṁsā. *Kāla* in Sanskrit means 'time'. *Haṁsā* means a 'swan', or 'goose' according to the Orientalists; but more accurately in Occultism, it means a mystical bird, analogous to the Pelican of the Rosicrucians. Kalahaṁsā thus means 'the swan *in* and *out* of time'. The image is that of the still body (unmanifest) of a bird given flight (into manifestation) by its two wings (space and time). We find the same idea conveyed in the Zohar and Qabbalah where Ain Soph—the boundless and limitless—is said to 'descend' into the universe, for the purposes of manifestation, using Adam Qadmon (Archetypal Man, or Humanity) as its chariot, or vehicle.

'Kosmos' and 'kosmos' refer to the numberless Solar Systems of infinite Cosmos

All the great philosophies and religions of past times, likewise all the ancient sciences, taught the fact of kosmic life: the existence of inner, invisible, intangible, but *causal realms* as the foundation and background of these innumerable systems. Thus, our physical world (like our physical body) is but the outer shell, or veil, or garment, of other worlds which are inner, vital, alive, and causal and which, *in their aggregate* embody the Kosmic Life. Needless to say, such Kosmic Life is not an individualized entity, being far beyond the range and reach of human conception or similitude, because it is infinite and boundless, beginningless and endless, co-extensive with infinity and with eternity—in truth, the Ultimate Reality behind and within all that is (see Chapter 4, Figure III-8, page 62 on the Qabbalah).

Kosmos and the Multiverse

The relatively new concept of the multiverse, or meta-universe, was completely unknown during the nineteenth century when the Theosophical doctrines were formulated with the main objective of presenting the ageless wisdom and occult sciences through the idiom of the latest science of the day. 'Multiverse' is an umbrella term in physical cosmology for the universe in which we live, *plus the hypothetical set of all other possible universes*. It has resulted from recent developments in cosmology and particle physics, that have led to the remarkable realization that our universe—rather than being unique—could be just one of many universes. Together, these universes comprise everything that exists: the entirety of space, time, matter, energy, and the laws and constants that govern them. The various universes within the overall multiverse are called by names such as 'parallel universes', 'other universes', or 'alternative universes'. Since the physical constants may be different in other universes, the fine-tunings which appear to be necessary for the emergence of life may possibly be explainable. Nevertheless, writing in 2010, Bernard Carr, Professor of Mathematics and Astronomy at Queen Mary University of London, admits that many physicists remain uncomfortable with the multiverse hypothesis, since it is highly speculative and always likely to be unamenable to experimental testing (for obvious reasons).[4] Notwithstanding the above, primordial gravitational waves in the universe, or ripples in space–time, which also appear in Einstein's theory of general relativity, arguably lend support to the recent theory that the universe is constantly giving birth to smaller 'pocket' universes within an ever expanding multiverse. A classic account of gravitational waves comes from a monograph by Carr. It considers the origin and consequences of a cosmological background of gravitational radiation which may be either primordial, in the sense of going back to the beginning of the universe, or produced by quantum processes at the Planck time (a time interval of approximately 5.39×10^{-44} seconds) or generated at some finite time in the past.[5] The existence of gravitational waves was confirmed in 2016 and in recognition of this discovery three American physicists were awarded the Nobel Prize for Physics for 'the observation of gravitational waves'.[6]

Most recently, further support on the parallel universe or multiverse theory was provided in a paper by Stephen Hawking and co-worker Thomas Hertog. Completed a few weeks before Hawking's death in 2018, it reportedly provides mathematical evidence for the theory that there have been multiple 'Big Bangs', of which our own universe is just one such event; hence the possibility of universes existing well beyond our own with completely unknown galaxies, stars, and planets.[7] All things considered, then, given the proviso that the multiverse concept might, in the future, embrace the further notion that the governing laws of the alternative universes could include, but need not be restricted

Multiverse in physical cosmology alludes to kosmos

Stephen Hawking's mathematical multiverse theory

to, physical laws, then the multiverse is the closest approach in contemporary scientific cosmology to Kosmos—the Universe *in toto*, seen and unseen, as defined above, and as implied in the *Second Fundamental Proposition* in *The Secret Doctrine*:

> The Eternity of the Universe *in toto* as a boundless plane; periodically 'the playground of numberless Universes incessantly manifesting and disappearing […]'.[8]

The Meaning of Universe and World

The term 'universe' appears to have been first used by the Roman Cicero. It denotes, etymologically, 'turned into one', hence 'whole', or 'indivisible'. It derives from the Latin *universus*, meaning 'whole', or 'entire'; also, from the Greek *holos*, which also means 'whole'. In a general sense, especially when capitalized, it is virtually interchangeable with Kosmos, apart from this fine distinction of meaning. However, it must be understood that the terms 'Kosmos' and 'Universe', as used in the esoteric philosophy, signify above all else, the indwelling Boundless Life expressing itself through the myriad forms and entities producing the incredible variety—unity in diversity—that we see and experience around us. Nonetheless, the universe (again, like man) may be divided into two general *functional portions*: the 'spirit' side, being the aggregate of consciousness centres, or monads, that the boundless Universe contains; and the 'matter' side, being forms for the aggregate of consciousness-centres passing through that particular phase of their evolutionary journey.

Universe, like man, has its spiritual and material aspects

The Universe is actually and literally, embodied Consciousness.

The term 'world' refers to the Earth, especially during the period of the human race.

The Seven Planes of Kosmos

In essence, Kosmos comprises seven principal planes: six inner, subjective planes and one outer objective plane. Of these, the inner topmost three planes pertain to the Unmanifest Worlds and the remaining four to the Manifest Worlds (noting that the term 'manifest' is not restricted solely to the outermost objective plane but also applies to the three subjective worlds above the latter). Each plane is stratified into seven sub-planes, the characteristics of which correspond in nature to those of the main planes. (These planes are not like geological strata or structured one inside the other like Russian dolls—refer again to Chapter 1 on page 10 of Volume II.) Not only are there sub-planes to each principal plane, but each sub-plane has seven sub-sub-planes and so on, and this accounts for the infinite variety and richness in all departments of manifest nature. This will not seem such a fanciful idea if we bring to mind the beautiful colours of natural scenes like a sunset, a rainbow or the countryside. It requires but three primary colours that can be combined to produce the four secondary colours making up the seven colours of the spectrum, which, in their innumerable combinations, produce the infinite subtlety, shades, and variety of colours in the visible spectrum. Another helpful simile would be the series of overtones associated with a single musical note, each overtone being in a mathematical relationship with all other overtones and the parent note. The infinite nuances and subtleties of polyphonic music are due to the 'sheen' of overtones that are generated by their principal notes. Likewise, the whole compass of every possible experience and the field of Universal Consciousness is

Why is there infinite variety and richness in nature?

due to this heptamerous (in groups of seven) structure of Kosmos constituted of seven principal planes constituting the Unmanifest Worlds and the Manifest Worlds.

Every plane and sub-plane has several correspondences and constitutes a characteristic level, or mode of consciousness, spanning the Unmanifest inner, topmost three planes of the Divine and Formless World of Spirit; and the Manifest outer four planes designated: Archetypal; Intellectual, or Creative; Substantial, or Formative; and Physical or Material. These are 'the four lower planes of Cosmic Consciousness, the three higher planes being inaccessible to human intellect as developed at present. The seven states of human consciousness pertain to quite another question.'[9] It will be realized from this, and the examples just cited of the colour spectrum and musical overtones, that the septenary classification of the spectrum of kosmic planes is anything but arbitrary, since this number is made up of fundamental planes that constitute different levels of Kosmic Consciousness. In order to make a diagrammatic representation of the kosmic planes on paper (a 'plane' surface), it is perforce necessary to depict the former in two different ways.

Characteristics of unmanifest and manifest planes

First, Figure III-15 overleaf represents the seven planes as seven concentric circles with the most exalted plane, i.e., the Divine (Plane I), represented as the innermost circle of the series; and the densest, or most material of the seven planes as the outermost circle (Plane VII), within which our Earth is situated. (Refer to Chapter 1, page 4 where we pointed out that the most exalted and innermost is represented as the heart, or centre of a system.) Each plane has its own 'field of force'. Whereas this diagrammatic representation may not be as clear as the familiar method of representing the seven planes by means of seven horizontal lines, nevertheless, it does convey the notion that each plane is a 'sphere', or 'world' in its own right. Therefore, beings functioning in any one of the seven worlds are quite independent of the other worlds, and are able to function without interference from other worlds. For example, our physical senses are geared to function in the physical world and material plane, and cannot therefore register any contact with finer planes, or planes that are not on the same plane of objectivity as the Earth; however, our subtler senses can aspire to such subtler realms. It is true to say though that we have a different set of senses in dream-life where we see, hear, taste, feel, and function on a different plane of consciousness. This change in our state of consciousness is attested by the extreme rapidity of mental operations as shown by measurement of brain activity during rapid eye movement sleep—a fleeting moment in a dream seems to embrace a series of events and actions covering what seems to us like years. But there is an important fact to note: at any level, relatively speaking, beings of the innermost worlds, because of their loftier status, are able to penetrate to the outermost world; whereas those of the outermost world are unable to contact the inner planes and must therefore function solely in their own world. This is one of the meanings of that mysterious term 'Ring Pass-Not'. As a simplistic illustration of its meaning, recall that a spiritual and refined man can, if he so chooses, behave in a crude and coarse manner; however, a coarse individual can never behave in a refined way, other than through long and arduous self-refinement.

Man is cognizant of different worlds to the degree that he has awakened faculties that correspond to those worlds

Another way of portraying the seven planes of kosmos is to revert to the conventional, because much easier to understand, representation by means of seven horizontal lines superimposed one above the other as in the accompanying diagram on page 89, Figure III-16. The seven horizontal lines represent the seven planes, each group of seven sub-planes represented as a subset of the innermost plane, Kosmic *Ādi*. This diagrammatic

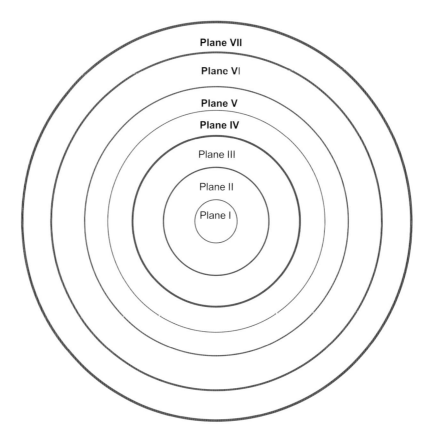

Figure III-15   The Seven Planes of Kosmos – A Diagrammatic
Representation

Adapted from Geoffrey Barborka, The Divine Plan
(Theosophical Publishing House, 1980), 207.

representation highlights three characteristics of the planes: first, the emanational emergence of planes and their associated sub-planes as overtones of the parent, or loftiest plane, as stated above; then the relationship between kosmos and man; finally, that humanity functions on the seventh and lowest plane, the Kosmic Physical plane, which will shortly be explained.[i]

The Process of Cosmic Unfoldment

Let us make a brief excursion into the mysterious territory of Occult Cosmogony. In this arcane subject we sometimes come across the term 'Older Wheels'. It refers to Worlds, or Globes, pertaining to other solar systems as they were during previous epochs of the cosmos. Invoking again the Hermetic Axiom, since human rebirth exists on the smaller scale, there is no reason why this analogous principle should not apply to Cosmos on the grand scale. This is in fact the case. Countless Globes evolve after a periodical *Pralaya* (Cosmic slumber) rebuilt from older material into new forms. The previous Globes disintegrate and reappear transformed and perfected for a new phase of life. In the Eastern *Gupta Vidya* (esoteric, or secret knowledge and science) these Globes are referred to in

---

i 'Macrokosmos' and 'Microkosmos' are used in this diagram (in preference to 'Macrocosm' and 'Microcosm') to make the point that the Hermetic Axiom, 'As above, so below' also pertains to, and applies, on the grand scale of Kosmos.

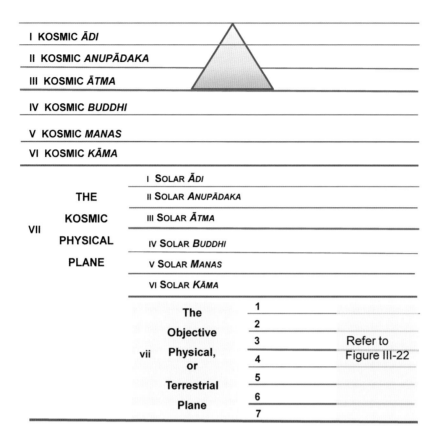

Figure III-16 Macrokosmos and Microkosmos –
The Relation Between Kosmos and Man

*Adapted from J. S. Gordon, Self-Consistent Kosmos
Orpheus Publishing House, 1995) facing p. 23.*

the Stanzas of Dzyan (an ancient work of Tibetan origin) in the quaint phrase, 'THE OLDER WHEELS ROTATED DOWNWARDS AND UPWARDS.'[10]

Exactly the same idea is embodied in the Western *Chaldean Kabala*, where Worlds are compared to the sparks which fly from under the hammer of the great Architect—LAW, for 'Deity is Law, and *vice versa*.'[11] 'Law' understood here, in the broadest sense, as a synonym for Karma, since everything from the highest to the lowest in the scale of consciousness and matter in the universe is living and therefore sentient at its own level, hence, behaving in its characteristic way, fulfilling its unique role in the grand scheme of things. The same meaning in a broad sense could also, conceivably, be attached to the biblical story of Ezekiel's vision of 'wheels within wheels', rather like a celestial gyroscope, indicating God's divine nature and creation of Globes (worlds) within galaxies, within numberless Universes: 'It looked like they were wheels within wheels, like a gyroscope. [...]. When the creatures went, the wheels went; when the creatures stopped, the wheels stopped; when the creatures lifted off, the wheels lifted off, because the spirit of the living creatures was in the wheels.'[12]

It is important to stress here that the universe is self-regulating, by virtue of Divine Law, there being no external 'God' acting as external law-giver or regulator. This is something that the mystical gaze of Newton clearly saw:

Our solar system is one of countless others

> Blind Fate could never make all the Planets move one and the same way in Orbs
> concentrick, some inconsiderable Irregularities excepted, which may have risen from
> the mutual Actions of comets and planets upon one another, and which will be apt to
> increase, till this System wants a Reformation.[13]

Narrow minds diminish large truths by making them in their own image

This sublime extract has been subjected to complete misunderstanding and misinterpre-tation by narrow minds who know no better than to mangle a large truth to suit their metaphysically barren conjectures of an external, capricious God occasionally interfering with his 'creation' and the Laws of Nature to suit His fancy. Given Newton's massive study of the *prisca sapientia*, including alchemy and the original theology, it is obvious that what he was pointing to was the occult law:

> A *law* which acts at its appointed time, and not at all blindly, as science may think, but in
> strict accordance and harmony with *Karmic* law. In Occultism this inexorable law is
> referred to as 'the great ADJUSTER' [or Reformer].[14]

Divine Law mirrored in scientific law

Being a universal law it applies equally 'as above', as it does, 'so below'. Hence, we see evidence of 'the great adjuster' everywhere in nature. Invoking the Hermetic Axiom, then, we apprehend its dim reflection in Newton's Third Law of Motion: *To every action there is always opposed an equal reaction—or, the mutual actions of two bodies upon each other are always equal, and directed to contrary parts.*[15] A clearer example of this universal law mirrored in the laws of science is Le Chatelier's principle, or *The Equilibrium Law*, which

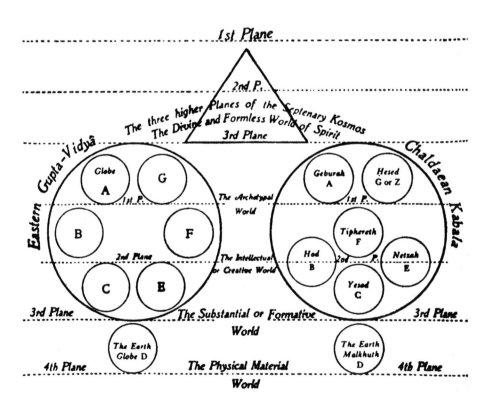

Figure III-17   The Process of Cosmic Unfoldment
Photo Credit: SD-I, 200

states that any change that upsets the equilibrium of a system will result in a predictable shift from within the system itself that will counteract the change and restore equilibrium under a new set of physical conditions. For example, regarding the chemical equilibria of reactions, changes in the temperature, pressure, volume, or concentration of a system will result in predictable and opposing changes within the system in order to achieve a new and *adjusted* equilibrium.

The comparative diagram, Figure III-17 on page 90, shows the identity between these two schools of thought—the *Gupta Vidya* and *Chaldean Kabala* mentioned above—which again reinforces a binding strand of this work: the consistency of doctrine in the ageless wisdom of both East and West. As the diagrammatic orientation of the seven planes in Figure III-17 is rather complex, a simplified version is shown in Figure III-18 alongside.

Examining the diagrams, then, there are seven *planes* that correspond to the seven *states* of consciousness in man. The three higher planes of Cosmic Consciousness, pertaining to the Unmanifest Worlds, are formless (*Arūpā*), where form ceases to exist, on the objective plane. These higher planes, we are informed, are revealed and explained only to the Initiates of both schools (*Gupta Vidya* and *Chaldean Kabala*); whereas the four lower planes in descending order, restated for convenience, are the Archetypal, or Prototypal World; the Intellectual, or Creative World; the Substantial, or Formative World; and the Physical, or Material World—being the lowest, our plane, the visible cosmos.

Is 'Big Bang' or Divine Ideation the origin of all creation?

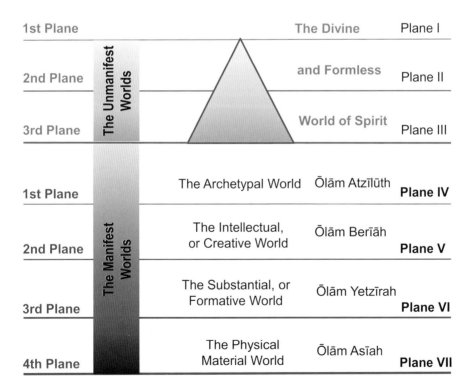

Figure III-18   A Simplified Diagrammatic Representation of the Unfoldment of the Seven Planes of Cosmos

Adapted from Geoffrey Barborka, The Divine Plan,
(Madras: Theosophical Publishing House, 1980), 167 and
Basil Crump of the Middle Temple, London, Barrister at-law (compiled and annotated),
Evolution As Outlined in the Archaic Eastern Records *(Peking: Luzac & Co., 1930), facing p. 64.*

There is a supreme logic to this. In order to build anything on Earth, whether it be the Channel Tunnel or an aeroplane, a chemical plant or a computer, there are four basic stages involved: firstly ideation, then an intellectual (mathematical) or physical model of the proposed idea, followed by the detailed design of the 'nuts and bolts', and finally the finished product in physical matter conforming to the original idea. If that applies on Earth, then why should not the universe conform to the same principles of the Archetypal, Creative, Formative, and Material Worlds as enumerated in the diagrams? Yet, mainstream cosmology tries to fathom the secrets of creation by exclusive emphasis on the last, the material process, and ignores the first three! If a 'Big Bang' is supposed to have occurred, did it not first exist as an Idea in Divine Mind, then as Primordial Thought, followed by Divine Design, and, finally, Divine handiwork—the universe of matter?

The visible universe is the lowest plane of kosmos, which is precisely why it can be investigated by astronomers using physical instruments as extensions to the physical senses. The non-physical, non-visible worlds can be investigated only by means of the instruments of elevated consciousness.

Reverting to Figure III-18, the planes are numbered on the left-hand side according to 'The Unmanifest Worlds' and 'The Manifest Worlds'. In the central portion are represented the four 'Ōlāms', or 'Worlds', as described in the *Chaldean Kabala*, in the nearest English equivalent words to the Chaldean terms alongside. On the right-hand side the planes are numbered in descending order. Also refer back to the fuller exposition on the Qabbalistic system provided in Chapter 4, especially Figure III-8, page 62.

The Four Lower Planes of Manifestation

Because we are dealing with a subject, simple in its self-consistent principles, but highly interconnected and complex in its details, an interim recapitulation of essentials would be useful.

As just explained, kosmos in its totality exhibits a septenary composition, but the occult doctrines have advised that other than for Initiates, the three higher planes are 'inaccessible to human intellect as developed at present.'[16] So other than noting the promising implication that humanity will evolve in the far distant future to a stage where its collective intellect will touch these higher planes of consciousness, there is no point in pursuing this topic any further, since idle speculations, or empty conjectures, would serve no purpose. Reverting then to what human intellect 'as developed at present' can contact, let us confine our attention to the Manifest Worlds, for it is *within* the four lower planes of kosmos that the whole drama of (present) human evolution occurs and the sevenfold stage on which it is enacted. Of these four planes, three are super-physical, or subjective, our Earth alone being on the plane of sensory perception.

Here it is important to interpose a summary of a cardinal occult doctrine. Every celestial body, be it a planet or a sun, comet or nebula; and on the microscale, every particle of matter, be it an atom, electron or quark, is a composite entity comprising, or formed of: (*a*) inner and invisible energies and substances; and (*b*) to us, an outer and generally visible body, or physical vehicle. These elements in totality number seven,[ii] being the seven

---

ii Twelve, in other forms of enumeration—see G. de Purucker, *Occult Glossary* (Pasadena, California: Theosophical University Press, 1972), 51.

principles of every self-contained entity, i.e., individual life-centre. Thus, each of the physical globes we see scattered in the immense reaches of space is accompanied by six invisible
'companion globes', forming what in Theosophy is called a 'Chain of Globes'. This is the
case with every sun or star, planet, and moon of every planet. All are septiform entities;
all have a sevenfold constitution, even as man has, who is a copy, in miniature of what the
universe is in full scale, there being One Life, hence one natural system of laws. As every
entity in the universe is an inseparable part of it, what is in the whole is reflected in every
part, because the part cannot contain anything that the whole does not contain; but it
contains the whole only *in terms of itself* and this is why it cannot supersede or become
greater than the whole.

Bearing all this in mind, then, as shown in Figure III-19 below, six of the seven globes of
our Earth Chain (as other planetary schemes in general) must be envisaged as existing on
the subjective, or inner planes; three on the arc of descent towards increasing materiality,
known as *involution*, and three on the arc of ascent towards an increasingly ethereal condition—otherwise known as *evolution* (but not in the Darwinian sense, of course).

It cannot be stressed sufficiently that there are severe limitations to such diagrammatic
representations, on two-dimensional paper, of subjects that pertain to higher dimensions
of space and time. So this diagram (and indeed all such diagrams in this and other
Chapters) must be understood only in a representational sense. Moreover, the Globes
(like the Principles of man) are not to be regarded as distributed in regions of three-dimensional space, but interpenetrating and occupying the same 'space' (for want of a better
term), six of them being subjective with respect to our Earth. It will therefore be clear that
of the septiform nature of any entity, only one of these, the physical, is perceptible to the
physical senses. This of course applies also to the seven principles of man where only the
body is perceptible to the physical senses since it is the vehicle, or upādhi (see Chapter 3,

*Celestial bodies
are septiform
entities that
display a
septenary nature*

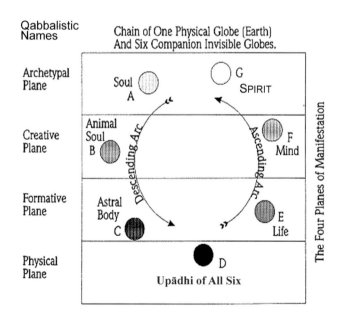

Figure III-19 The Four Lower Planes of Manifestation
Adapted from Geoffrey A. Farthing, Deity, Cosmos and Man: An outline of esoteric science
*(San Diego, California: Point Loma Publications, 1993), 75,
based on SD-I, 'A Few Early Theosophical Misconceptions', 153.*

pages 35–37 of Volume II), of the other six. Thus, using the terms in the diagram, the Astral Body (C) is the vehicle of Life (E), Animal Soul (B) the vehicle of Mind (F), and (Spiritual) Soul (A) the vehicle of Spirit (G).

Ākāśa, the Astral Light, and the Memory of Nature and Man

As there are seven planes of being (six planes of which are non-physical), there are seven corresponding principles in man. Each of these planes is a differentiation of one primordial Root Substance, or Matter, known under a variety of names. Newton used the Latin name *Prima Materia* as seen (underlined for convenience) in Figure III-20 below, which, unsurprisingly, bears a resemblance to Figure III-17 on page 90. Other terms are *Svabhavat* in the East and Æther, or *Ākāśa* (Akasha), in the West. All these terms connote the meaning of 'essential nature', or that which is behind 'world substance', i.e., the spirit and essence of substance.[17] As a general principle, a body is constituted of the material of the plane that it inhabits. So, for example, a motor car made of steel and alloys is fabricated from iron ore and other metallic elements mined from the earth. Likewise, the physical body uses terrestrial material drawn from the terrestrial plane. So also the subtle bodies (like the astral body) draw upon the appropriate grade of subtle material from the non-physical planes composed of finer substance.

Accordingly, the physical body of man is constituted of the physical substance of the lowest, i.e., seventh plane of kosmos—our physical plane of existence. The next lowest, or the first plane above the physical, is the Astral plane constituted of 'astral substance', which has its own vitality, energy, and dynamism. Its functions correspond to the non-physical Astral body of man—see again Figure III-19 on page 93. But just as there are physical processes occurring on the Earth that are not directly related to the Physical body of man, there are also aspects or 'regions' of the Astral plane not directly related to man's Astral body; and these are collectively known as the 'Astral Light'. In both cosmic and human terms this may be regarded as the final interface, or bridge, between the higher subjective planes and the objective physical plane.

[margin note:] How Newton depicts primordial Matter

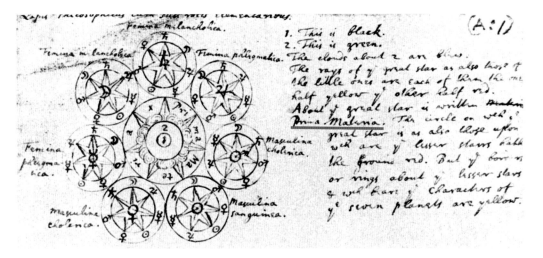

Figure III-20 Newton's Diagrammatic Representation of Primordial Substance as Symbolized by the Philosopher's Stone

Image Credit: Cambridge University Press

The Astral Light is an indispensable element to a study of consciousness, the more so because therein lies the clue to the function and operation of memory. For it is in the Astral Light that the memory of man and nature is 'stored' indelibly and virtually forever—and not, in the case of man, in his fleshly brain, which acts as a retrieving mechanism rather like the heads of a video recorder (see Volume II, Chapter 7). And this explains the ability of highly trained occultists, like Blavatsky, to access nature's memory banks and 'bring down' facts and details long forgotten. (It is a historically verifiable fact that Blavatsky had a library of around thirty books. Yet she was able to quote extensively and accurately from well over twenty thousand books and manuscripts, archaic and modern, providing verifiable page numbers and references.[18])

It is important to note that there is just one Substance, Ākāśa, in progressively lower gradations of tenuousness of *itself*, so that in a broad sense, 'The Astral Light is that which mirrors the three higher planes of consciousness, and is above the lower, or terrestrial plane; therefore it does not extend beyond the fourth plane, where, one may say, the Akâsa [Ākāśa] begins.'[19]

> For AETHER [or ĀKĀŚA], in Esotericism, is the very quintessence of all possible energy, and it is certainly to this universal agent (composed of many *agents* [as intuited, arguably, by Brian Josephson—see page 72]) that all the manifestations of energy in the material, psychic and spiritual worlds are due.[20]

The Septenary Planes of Kosmos Mirror the Septenary Principles of Man

Being the case that the seven states of consciousness in man correspond to seven planes of which the higher are inaccessible to all other than initiates, it remains with man to awaken, and attune to, the three higher states latent in himself in order to contact the three higher planes of kosmos. The actual details of how this is to be done is not known to the writer since, as has been made plain, it is a secret reserved for the very few.[iii] Therefore, suffice it to say that the constitution of man reflects that of kosmos in every particular, in the same sense that a fractal, or a part of a hologram, mirrors the whole of which it forms a part. The whole is obviously not seen in every detail in the parts, but the totality of the overall picture is still maintained. Likewise, the seven principal planes of kosmos constitute a sequence of primary characteristics that are in-built, actually or potentially, into every manifest thing regardless of the plane, or level, on which it functions and has its being. These planes and their sub-planes, etc. constitute a series of vibratory scales that encompass the whole gamut of possible being. The higher the rate of vibration of any manifest being, the closer it is to its source and ultimately, the Source. The lowest rates of vibration are at the physical plane (and lower orders that need not concern us here). This provides a clue to the correspondences that we find in man and all nature since, using the analogy with musical scales, resonance between planes therefore becomes perfectly natural. It also implies that each individual can contact higher planes by means of ever increasing purity of motive and refinement of character.

Accordingly, for ease of understanding, the relation between the seven kosmic planes and the corresponding seven human principles may further be understood by describing

---

iii However, for a theoretical understanding of this awakening process in the best form that words can convey, the reader should consult J. S. Gordon, *The Path of Initiation: Spiritual evolution and the restoration of the Western mystery tradition* (Rochester, Vermont: Inner Traditions, 2013).

[margin note] Astral Light provides the clue to memory

[margin note] Holograms and fractals are useful aids to understanding wholeness and correspondence

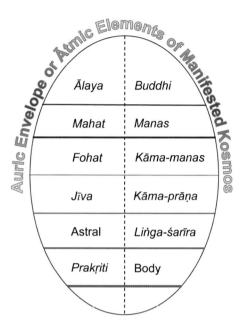

Kosmic planes
mirrored in man's
Principles

Figure III-21   Relating Kosmic Planes to Human Principles

Adapted from Henk J. Spierenburg (compiled and annotated), The Inner Group Teachings of H. P. Blavatsky
(San Diego, California: Point Loma Publications, 1995), 106.

it in two ways: from the spiritual to the material, and then from the material to
the spiritual.

Focussing first from the spiritual to the material, which is the centrifugal movement from
the implicate order to its explication, the ovoid depiction in Figure III-21 above clearly
shows how each of the seven principles in the Macrokosm is related to corresponding
principles in man, the Microkosm.[iv] The first plane is the *Auric* and is depicted as an egg
containing the other six planes, just as man's Auric Egg contains his six principles (refer
to Table II-5 on page 40 in Chapter 3 of Volume II). The second plane is *Alayic* from the
term *Ālaya*, meaning the Universal World-Soul; it corresponds to *Buddhi*, the Intuition
Principle in man. The third plane is *Mahatic*, from *Mahat*, the Universal Mind; it corresponds to *Manas*, the Mind Principle in man. The fourth kosmic plane, the Archetypal, is
Fohatic from the term *Fohat* representing the intelligently directed creative energies; thus
it corresponds in man to *Kāma*, the Desire Principle, strictly, to *Kāma-manas*, the energy
of desire directed by mind. Therefore the word 'Archetypal' must not be taken here in the
sense that the Platonists gave to it, i.e., 'the world as it existed *in the Mind* of the Deity;
but in that of a world made as a first model [or prototype], to be followed and improved
upon by the worlds which succeed it physically—though deteriorating in purity.'[21]

The fifth plane, the Intellectual, or Creative is *Jivaic*, from *Jīva*, the life-energy; it corresponds in man to *Prāṇa*, the Life principle, strictly, to *Kāma-prāṇa*, indicating that the
energy is will-directed and not purposeless brute energy. The sixth kosmic plane, the
Substantial, or Formative, is Astral and acts as the model for the Physical plane of cosmos
just as man's *Liṅga-śarīra* serves as the Model body for his Physical body. The seventh

---

iv As stated earlier, 'Macrokosm' and 'Microkosm' are the kosmic correspondences of the cosmic 'Macrocosm'
and 'Microcosm'.

plane, the Physical and Material is also variously termed the Terrestrial, *Prakritic*, or Objective plane; it corresponds to the *Sthūla-śarīra*, or the Physical body of man.

Working 'upwards' now, centripetally from materiality to spirituality or from the explicate to the implicate, further subtleties are brought to light. The constituent materials of the Physical body are the materials of the physical materials of our world—the plane of objective materiality, the Physical plane. Prāṇa, the vital principle in man is also the animating principle shared by all the kingdoms of nature; for 'Prāṇa, or Life permeates the whole being of the objective Universe.'[22] Next, the subtle, or ethereal counterpart of the Physical body, has its correspondence in the invisible region that surrounds the globe and all objects and creatures in it, namely, the Astral Light, as described above. Similarly, the energy that expresses itself in the instinctive life of an individual and in his desire-nature is drawn from an inner plane of subtle matter that is imperceptible to the physical senses. It has its correspondence with Fohat, the primeval energy sometimes known as cosmic electricity, and, like electricity at the physical level, it is transformable into many forms of energy like heat, light, etc. Furthermore, there is the individual mind, Manas, which is a derivative of the Mind Principle in Nature, Mahat, or Universal Mind. Buddhi is the universal, passive principle that makes possible (by virtue of its being the Spiritual Soul, or spiritual vehicle) any manifestation of *Ātma*—the limitless, active, indefinable, indivisible Reality, the dynamism of the universe. Buddhi has its correspondence with Ālaya, the Anima Mundi, or Soul of the World, as Ātma has with the Auric Envelope.

Relationship Between Kosmic Physical Plane and Septenary Principles of Man

In the earlier section on the seven planes of kosmos, the objective physical plane, with its seven sub-planes, was depicted as constituting the seventh kosmic physical plane as shown at the bottom of Figure III-16 on page 89. This is of crucial importance to our study of man's nature for this is the objective plane in which humanity functions in the objective world. The equivalent diagram, Figure III-22 below, makes this clear by showing the sevenfold subdivision of this seventh kosmic plane, which, to reiterate, is the objective plane in

		1 *Atmic* (Para-Ego)
	The	2 *Buddhic* (Inner-Ego)
	Objective	
	Physical,	3 Higher *Manas* (Ego-Manas)
vii	or	4 Lower *Manas* (Kāma-manas)
	Terrestrial	
	Plane	5 Psychic (*Pranic-kāma*)
		6 Astral
		7 Objective

Figure III-22 The Seventh Kosmic Plane – The Objective Plane of Humanity

which humanity functions in the objective world. In order of emanational sequence, these subdivisions are: Atmic (Para-Ego), Buddhic (Inner-Ego), Higher Manas (Ego-Manas), Lower manas (*Kāma-manas*), Psychic (*Pranic-kāma*), Astral, and Objective.

Recapitulation

This Chapter has been necessarily complex, given the task of describing, unavoidably sequentially, a process that is multi-layered, multi-dimensional, and cyclical rather than linear. A recapitulation of the principal milestones along our journey would be helpful. It is provided in Table III-4 opposite showing in the familiar tabular format, necessarily in rudimentary fashion, the correspondences between the seven kosmic planes and the seven human principles.[23] This Table should be compared with Table II-3, page 21 in Chapter 2 and Table II-5, page 40 in Chapter 3 of Volume II, which provide a detailed taxonomy of the human constitution and nature, respectively.

The human principles are derived from the corresponding sub-principles of the seventh, and lowest, kosmic plane. Hence, as an example, the mental and emotional human principles have their corresponding kosmic sub-principles. The subdivision into sub-principles, corresponding to the sub-planes, is crucial to an understanding of the varieties of experience to which consciousness can respond, as suggested earlier. So, in terms of the constitution of man, these planes (which all have their sevenfold sub-principles and further sub-divisions) correspond to:

1. the Physical body;

2. the non-physical form, or Astral body;

3. the Life principle, Prāṇa;

4. the Desire principle, Kāma;

5. the Mind Principle, Manas functioning as the Higher or the Lower Mind;

6. the Intuition (Wisdom) Principle, Buddhi, being the vehicle in which Ātma, which would otherwise be abstract, can express itself;

7. the highest of the human principles, that of pure Spirit, Ātma.

Therefore, it must again be stressed that all the kosmic and cosmic planes, their sub-planes and further subdivisions, comprise in themselves an almost numberless series of characteristics and qualities which manifest at all levels, and eventually, at the physical level, in sounds, colours, shapes, characteristic qualities, and in faculties and temperaments. The total spectrum, therefore, represents the virtually infinite field of experience, both real and potential, at all levels of being, that is available and accessible to anyone with the necessary and requisite corresponding faculties of consciousness developed and operating at that level. This marks the end of a development stage for any distinct species, mankind included. It is the process of evolution taken to its ultimate end of perfection for its particular stage, but in point of fact, only up to its highest level, relatively speaking. Therefore, it is both arbitrary and illogical to regard the human stage as the final link, or acme, in the evolutionary chain. There are levels of development way above

As the soul's faculties flower so does her field of experience expand

Table III-4 Kosmic Planes and Human Principles shown in the
Familiar Tabular Format

Kosmic Planes	Human Principles and Their Implications	
1 Ākāśa **Spirit Substance**	Ātma **Divine Self (SPIRIT)**	– Seat of Consciousness – SPIRIT (abstract)
2 Ālaya **Universal Soul**	Buddhi **the Intuition (Wisdom) principle**	– Vehicle of SPIRIT, Spiritual Soul – Primal Duality
3 Mahat **Universal Mind**	Manas the Higher Mind **the Mind Principle** the Lower mind	– Orientates towards Buddhi and Ātma – Abstract thought, intuition – Orientates towards Kāma and below – Personal mind, ordinary thoughts
4 Kāma **Universal Energy**	Kāma **the Desire principle**	– Driving energy – The Will at the lower octave
5 **Life Force in** **Everything**	Prāṇa **the Life principle (life-force)**	Vitality without which the body dies
6 **Formative Principle** **Within-Without**	Liṅga-śarīra **the Etheric double (Astral body)**	– Non-physical, material form of body – Collector and reservoir of Prāṇa

7 Prakṛti
Dense Substance
	Sthūla-śarīra
	the Physical body
		– Means of perception and action
		  at physical level
		– Collective vehicle for expression of
		  all human faculties

the human into what is popularly termed the superhuman state, but at non-physical levels. Such advanced Intelligences can, if needed for a specific purpose of service, assume a human *form*. As such, they represent the highest orders of consciousness to be attained and, indeed, such Higher Beings have guided and provided the impulse to nascent humanity in its evolutionary development.[24] This is the basis of ideas like, 'God was an astronaut' or that 'advanced aliens in spacesuits from outer space once visited the Earth', which are not total rubbish, but the dregs of a lofty occult doctrine grossly distorted through the lens of anthropocentric phantasies, unchecked by intellect and reason.

Readers desiring more information on the kosmic planes and their correspondences to man are invited to peruse the references cited in Endnote III-5. Meanwhile, we close this Chapter by reinforcing the occult doctrine that there is a fundamental Unity of kosmos, and therefore, quintessentially, ONE LIFE, which is the origin and root of everything; moreover, this Unity operates through septenary law in man, nature, and cosmos, as succinctly reflected in these words:

> *In nature, then, [as in man] we find seven Forces, or seven Centres of Force, and everything seems to respond to that number, as for instance, the septenary scale in music, or Sounds, and the septenary spectrum in Colours [and the seven Principles in man, as also his seven senses—two as yet latent].*

H. P. BLAVATSKY[25]

NOTES

1   *SD*-I, 'Summing Up – The Pith and Marrow of Occultism', 274.
2   *TSGLOSS*, 255.
3   *SD*-I, 'Stanza VI: Our World, Its Growth and Development – Stanza VI Continued', 200–1.
4   B. J. Carr (ed.), *Universe or Multiverse?* (New York: Cambridge University Press, 2007).
5   B. J. Carr, 'Cosmological Gravitational Waves – Their origin and consequences', *Astronomy and Astrophysics*, 89/1–2 (September 1980), 6–21.
6   'IOP Hails Award of Nobel Prize to Physicists who Worked to Detect Gravitational Waves', *Institute of Physics* (3 October 2017).
7   S. W. Hawking and Thomas Hertog, 'A Smooth Exit from Eternal Inflation?' *Journal of High Energy Physics*, 147 (27 April 2018).
8   *SD*-I, 'Proem', 16.
9   *SD*-I, 'Stanza VI: Our World, Its Growth and Development – Stanza VI Continued', 200.
10 *SD*-I, 'Stanza VI', 199.
11 *SD*-I, 'A Few Early Theosophical Misconceptions', 152.
12 Ezekiel 1, v. 16, 21 <https://www.biblegateway.com/passage/?search=Ezekiel+1-5&version=MSG> accessed 27 April 2020.
13 Isaac Newton, *Opticks, Or, A Treatise of the Reflections, Refractions, Inflections & Colours of Light* (London 1730; 4th edn, New York: Dover Publications, 1979), 402.
14 *SD*-II, 'Stanza XI: The Civilization and Destruction of the Fourth and Fifth Races', 329.
15 Isaac Newton, *Philosophiæ Naturalis Principia Mathematica* [Mathematical Principles of Natural Philosophy], trans. Andrew Motte, rev. Florian Cajori, 2 vols (Berkeley, Los Angeles: University of California Press, 1962), i, 'The Motion of Bodies', 13.
16 *SD*-I, 'Stanza VI', 200.
17 See Ervin László, *Science and the Akashic Field: An integral theory of everything* (Rochester, Vermont: Inner Traditions, 2007).
18 William Kingsland, *The Real H. P. Blavatsky: A study in Theosophy, and a memoir of a great soul* (London: Theosophical Publishing House, 1985), 226–7. See also: Constance Wachtmeister, *Reminiscences of H.P. Blavatsky and 'The Secret Doctrine'* (London: Theosophical Publishing House 1976); Geoffrey Barborka, *H. P. Blavatsky, and Tibetan Tulku* (Adyar, Madras: Theosophical Publishing House, 1986).
19 *CW*-X, 'Transactions of the Blavatsky Lodge, VI', 360.
20 *SD*-I, 'The Masks of Science', 508.
21 *SD*-I, 'Stanza VI', 200.
22 *KT*, 'On the Kama-Loka and Devachan', 176.
23 Adapted from the private correspondence of Geoffrey Farthing to Members of the Esoteric Group of *The Scientific and Medical Network*, 21 January 1997.
24 One of the finest and most accesible books based on a commentary on archaic records in *The Secret Doctrine* is by Geoffrey Barborka, *Peopling of the Earth* (Wheaton, Illinois: Theosophical Publishing House, 1975).
25 *CW*-XII, 'E. S. Instruction No. III, The Tattvic Correlations and Meaning', 610.

7 Anthropogenesis: the Unfolding of Consciousness – Divine Self to Human Body

Fear not for the future, weep not for the past.

PERCY BYSSHE SHELLEY[1]

Spiritual guidance needs guidance. It's like comparing walking on the ground and mountain climbing. Once you learn how to walk, you can walk on the ground by yourself, but if you want to climb Mount Everest, you need a guide.

SEYYED HOSSEIN NASR[2]

SYNOPSIS

Chapter 7 is concerned with the principal stages in anthropogenesis: the coming into being of man from the Divine Self, resulting finally in the human physical body materialized on Earth. How the human senses are derived from the cascading of principles at higher levels is detailed step by step. The exposition is in two major sections. The first is a description of the process from the Sūtras of the Sāṁkhya philosophy of ancient India mirrored by equivalent precepts from the New Testament of Christianity. The second shows the same process according to occult science. The harmony and internal self-consistency between the Eastern and Western scriptures (in their esoteric import) and the occult system are shown to be unmistakable, reinforcing a key premise of this work that however varied its expression may be, the *philosophia perennis* originates from a central universal wisdom-Source.

KEY WORDS: Hermetic Axiom, Divine Consciousness, Sāṁkhya philosophy, New Testament, Causal Body, Astral body, Physical body, Divine Ideas, atom, space, time, illusion, mind, heart, sense organs, sense objects, organs of action, emanation, evolution, esoteric instructions, physical incarnation, H. P. Blavatsky, Śrī Yukteswar Giri, Seyyed Hossein Nasr

Previous Chapters have stressed the indispensable role of the Hermetic Axiom in resolving what would otherwise remain intractable conundrums about the deeper meaning of life and existence. Examples were given of its application to the correspondences between Cosmos, Nature, and man in Chapter 5, and in more detail in Chapter 6 on the sevenfold principles in kosmos, as reflected in the septenary composition of man.

This Chapter concentrates on the Hermetic Axiom in terms of the unfolding of consciousness and associated faculties of the human being. Particular focus is placed on explaining, step by step, how the human senses have developed from the 'flow down' of principles at higher levels. The exposition is in two major sections. The first is a description from religious and philosophical sources, both Eastern and Western, of the progression from Divine Consciousness resulting finally in the human body. The second shows this progression according to occult science. The harmony between the two systems is unmistakable.

The Meeting of East and West – Hinduism and Christianity

One of the finest expositions demonstrating the underlying unity of the great religious and philosophical paths in both the East and the West is *The Holy Science (Kaivalya Darsanam)*3 by the Indian monk and yogi Jnanavatar Swami Śrī Yukteswar Giri (1855–1936) written in 1894, interestingly, during the ascendancy of the Theosophical Society worldwide. The foreword was written by Yukteswar's disciple, the Indian yogi and guru, Paramahansa Yogananda (1893–1952) and the Preface by Walter Evans-Wentz (1878–1965), the American anthropologist and writer who was a pioneer in the study of Tibetan Buddhism, and its dissemination to the Western world. *The Holy Science* demonstrates, cogently, the fundamental harmony between Genesis, the Gospel of John, and the Book of Revelation of the New Testament, and the much earlier Sāṁkhya (Sāṅkhya) philosophy of ancient India regarding the emanational descent of man from the realm of Pure Being, or Divine Consciousness. The Sanskrit term *sāṁkhya* means literally, 'based on calculation', from *samkhyāti*, 'he reckons'.4 One of the six schools of Hindu philosophy, influenced by the Vedas and Upaniṣads, also by Buddhism and Jainism, it teaches that there is an eternal interaction between spirit and matter. Fittingly, this theme of the underlying unity of world religions was taken further and promulgated by Yogananda, one of the pre-eminent spiritual figures of modern times who introduced millions in the West, especially in America, to meditation and the *scientific basis* of yoga through his classic book *Autobiography of a Yogi*.5

Written at the request of his own Master, the Indian monk, yogi, scholar, and astronomer Mahāvatār Bābājī,i Swami Śrī Yukteswar states in the Introduction to *The Holy Science*:

> The purpose of this book is to show as clearly as possible that there is an essential unity in all religions; that there is no difference in the truths inculcated by the various faiths; that there is but one method by which the world, both external and internal, has evolved; and that there is but one Goal admitted by all scriptures.6

Accordingly, 'the book [*The Holy Science*] is divided into four sections according to the four stages in the development of knowledge' which are:

1. The Gospel – 'Seeks to establish the fundamental truth of creation and to describe the evolution and the involution of the world.'

2. The Goal – 'All creatures, from the highest to the lowest in the link of creation, are found eager to realize three things: Existence, Consciousness, and Bliss.'

3. The Procedure – 'Deals with the method of realizing the three purposes of life.'

4. The Revelation – 'Discusses the revelations which come to those who have traveled far to realize the three ideals of life and who are very near their destination.'7

Highly instructive as are the last three sections, they lie outside the scope of this Chapter, which therefore focuses entirely on relevant Sūtras (aphorisms) of the first section, 'The Gospel', concerning the emanational emergence of cosmos and man, tracing the progression and development of key aspects of manifestation. In explanation of the latter, the general pattern henceforth is expounded in the next section.

Sāṁkhya philosophy and biblical texts [margin note]

Outline of The Holy Science [margin note]

---

i According to Yogananda's autobiography, Bābājī has resided for at least hundreds of years in the remote Himalayan regions of India, seen in person by only a small number of disciples and others.

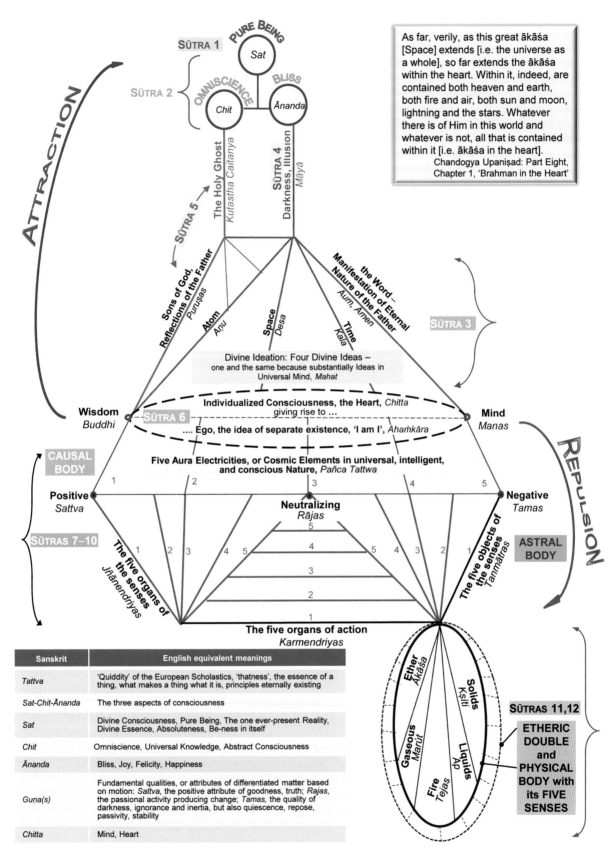

Figure III-23 The Progression of the Main Stages of Emanation –
From Consciousness to Physical Bodily Sensation

Sūtras from *The Holy Science* alongside Verses from The Holy Bible – From the Divine Self to the Human Body

The outline of this section, in three sequential parts, comprises:

1. the Sūtras from *The Holy Science* stated alongside the equivalent precepts from the New Testament as excerpted by Śrī Yukteswar;

2. Śrī Yukteswar's own elucidation of their meaning, but with minimal changes and clarifications by the writer to bring them into line with contemporary English;

3. commentaries by the writer.

Reasons for writing *The Holy Science*

Regarding the importance placed on the harmony between Sāṁkhya and Christianity (point 1. above), Śrī Yukteswar recognized that a synthesis of the spiritual heritage of the East with the science and technology of the West would greatly alleviate suffering in the modern world on all levels of existence—spiritual, psychological, and material. He maintained that East and West must establish a golden Middle Path that harmonized spirituality and activity. Thus, India has much to learn from the West in material development; in return, India can teach the universal methods by which the West will be able to base its religious precepts on the unshakable foundations of yogic science. Albeit well acquainted with the latest scientific discoveries and other advancements of knowledge, Śrī Yukteswar taught that it is not the physicist but the Self-realized master who comprehends the true nature of matter, as also the real science of psychology. Implicit in his understanding was the recognition that hidden behind physical and bodily mechanisms lies a subtle spiritual structure—something that Newton also affirmed at the close of the General Scholium appended to his *Principia* (see Chapter 9, page 179).

Note, carefully, that Śrī Yukteswar stated the Sūtras in Sanskrit only, the English translation being provided by the publishers, Self-Realization Fellowship (founded in 1920). Thus, there are some small differences in meaning attaching to a few Sanskrit terms compared to the meaning given to the same terms used in Theosophy and occultism, as in Volume II of this work. All such differences will be clarified.

Periodic reference should be made to Figure III-23

The progression and development of the various aspects of creation, as enumerated in the Sūtras, are shown on the previous page in Figure III-23, which has been adapted and modified by the writer from the diagram prepared by the publishers of *The Holy Science*. This diagram should be studied alongside the commentaries on the Sūtras.

Sūtra 1: The Gospel *(see top of Figure III-23, page 103)*

This Sūtra deals with the only Real Substance in the Universe, *Sat*, or God, why the man of the material world is unable to comprehend It, and how It may be comprehended. A parallel teaching can be traced to the Gospel of St. John as seen below.

Sāṁkhya philosophy, *The Holy Science*: Sūtra 1	**Gospel of St. John 8:28**
Parabrahma[n] (Spirit, or God) is everlasting, complete, without beginning or end. It is one, indivisible Being.	'Then said Jesus unto them, When ye have lifted up the son of man, then shall ye know that I am he.'

Elucidation by Śrī Yukteswar

Why God is not comprehensible:

1. Man possesses eternal faith and believes intuitively in the existence of a Substance, of which the objects of sense—sound, touch, sight, taste, and smell, the component parts of this visible world, are but properties.

2. Because man identifies himself with his material body, composed of the aforesaid properties, he is able to comprehend by these imperfect sense organs these properties only and not the Substance to which these properties belong.

How God may be comprehended:

3. The Eternal Father, God, or Sat, the only Substance in the universe is therefore not comprehensible by man of this material world, unless he becomes divine by lifting his self [the lower self] above this creation of Darkness, or *Māyā*.

Commentary

1. The teaching on the omnipresence of God, and its impenetrability by the intellect of the ordinary man of the world, is perfectly encapsulated in the First Fundamental Proposition of the Secret Doctrine (*philosophia perennis*), as stated by H. P. Blavatsky:

   > An Omnipresent, Eternal, Boundless, and Immutable PRINCIPLE on which all speculation is impossible, since it transcends the power of human conception and could only be dwarfed by any human expression or similitude. It is beyond the range and reach of thought—in the words of *Māṇḍūkya Upanishad* [*Upaniṣad*], 'unthinkable and unspeakable.'
   > [Verse 7.][8]

   Using the term 'Parabrahman' in the same sense as in Sūtra 1, Blavatsky affirms:

   > Parabrahman (the One Reality, the Absolute) is the field of Absolute Consciousness, *i.e.*, that Essence which is out of all relation to conditioned existence, and of which conscious existence is a conditioned symbol.[9]

   This theme is elaborated in the next Chapter.

2. Likewise, does the profoundly religious Isaac Newton affirm the omnipresence of the divine Substance and Its incomprehensibility to the ordinary man in the General Scholium appended to his *Philosophiæ Naturalis Principia Mathematica*:

   > He [the Supreme God] is eternal and infinite, omnipotent and omniscient; [...] He endures for ever, and is everywhere present; and, by existing always and everywhere, he constitutes duration and space. In him are all things contained and moved. [...]

   > As a blind man has no idea of colours, so have we no idea of the manner by which the all-wise God perceives and understands all things. He is utterly void of all body and bodily figure, and can therefore neither be seen, nor heard, nor touched; nor ought he to be worshipped under the representation of any corporeal thing. We have ideas of his attributes, but what the real substance of anything is we know not. In bodies, we see only their figures and colors, we hear only the sounds, we touch only their outward surfaces, we smell only the smells, and taste the savors; but their inward substances are not to be known either by our senses, or by any reflex act of our minds: much less, then, have we any idea of the substance of God.[10]

Similar message from Śrī Yukteswar, Blavatsky, and Newton on indefinability of God

Continuing in the same vein Newton affirms the image of God in man:

> But, by way of allegory, God is said to see, to speak, to laugh, to love, to hate, to desire, to give, to receive, to rejoice, to be angry, to fight, to frame, to work, to build; for all our notions of God are taken from the ways of mankind by a certain similitude, which, though not perfect, has some likeness, however.[11]

Newton concludes this famous extract by talking about the true business of science:

> And thus much concerning God; to discourse of whom from the appearances of things, does certainly belong to Natural Philosophy.[12]

3. Māyā, or the 'appearances of things', is one of the thorniest issues in philosophy, an appreciation of which, however imperfect, is far preferable to the common error in science of mistaking appearances for reality. The doctrine on Māyā is expounded in depth in the Sāṃkhya Sūtras, relevant extracts from which are presented and explained below.

SŪTRA 2: The Gospel (see top centre of Figure III-23, page 103)

This Sūtra affirms that man is made in the image of God (as also alluded to by Newton—see above). A direct parallel can be traced to Genesis as seen below.

Sāṃkhya philosophy, *The Holy Science*: SŪTRA 2	Genesis 1:27
In It (Parabrahma[n]) is the origin of all knowledge and love, the root of all power and joy.	'So God created man in his own image, in the image of God created he him; male and female created he them.'

Elucidation by Śrī Yukteswar

1. The nature of God, the Father, is demonstrated by the Almighty Force, *Śakti*, or in other words, the Eternal Joy, *Ānanda*, which produces the world; and the Omniscient Feeling, *Chit*, which makes this world conscious.

2. As man is the likeness of God, by directing his attention inward he can comprehend within him the said Force and Feeling, the sole properties of his Self—the Force Almighty as his will, with enjoyment; and the Feeling Omniscient as his Consciousness that so enjoys.

Commentary

1. This Sūtra, and the equivalent verse from Genesis, make it plain why man is the measure of all things, since he embodies, in the lesser, all the forces and powers in the greater. This has been explained in depth in the previous Chapters.

'The kingdom of God is within you.'
Luke 17:21 (KJV)

2. The injunction to direct attention inwards to comprehend within himself the Almighty Force and Feeling is in keeping with the universal counsel of sages and saints since time immemorial, namely that the relative truth needed for provisional use may be learned from books and teachers, etc., but the ultimate truth of the Self (the likeness of God) can be learned only from and within oneself by deep introspection, contemplation, and meditation.

Sūtra 3: The Gospel (see top right side of Figure III-23, page 103)

This Sūtra deals with the dawning of creation, or manifestation, and a direct parallel can be traced to Revelation and the Gospel of St. John as seen below.

Sāṁkhya philosophy, *The Holy Science*: Sūtra 3	Revelation 3:14 and Gospel of St. John 1: 1, 3, 14
Parabrahma[n] causes creation, inert Nature (*Prakṛiti*), to emerge. From *Aum* (*Praṇava*, the Word, the manifestation of the omnipotent Force), come *Kāla*, Time; *Deśā*, Space; and *Aṇu*, the Atom (the vibratory structure of creation).	'These things saith the Amen, the faithful and true witness, the beginning of the creation of God.' 'In the beginning was the Word [Amen], and the Word was with God, and the Word was God …. All things were made by him; and without him was not anything made that was made …. And the Word was made flesh and dwelt among us.'

Elucidation by Śrī Yukteswar

1. The Word, *Amen*, or *Aum*, marks the beginning of Creation. The manifestation of Omnipotent Force (the Repulsion and its complementary expression, the Attraction, or Omniscient Feeling, or Love) is vibration, which appears as a peculiar sound: the Word, Amen, Aum. In its different aspects, Aum presents the idea of change, which is Time, *Kāla*, in the Ever-Unchangeable; and the idea of division, which is Space, *Deśā*, in the Ever-Indivisible.

2. The Four Ideas are the Word, Time, Space, and the Atom. The ensuing effect is the idea of particles—the innumerable atoms, or *aṇu*. However, these four are one and the same, and substantially nothing but mere ideas. The manifestation of the Word (becoming flesh, the external material) created this visible world. So the Word, Amen, Aum, being the manifestation of the Eternal Nature of the Almighty Father, that is, His Own Self, is inseparable from, and nothing but, God Himself, as the burning power is inseparable from and nothing but the fire itself.

Commentary

1. The term 'nothing but mere ideas' needs careful clarification because it can convey the mistaken notion that ideas as such are basically inconsequential. By way of explanation of the power of Ideas and the different species of 'ideas', they comprise the spectrum ranging from: (*a*) idle mental chatter with inconsequential effects; (*b*) factitious ideas which are created by imagination and therefore illusory; (*c*) adventitious ideas derived from personal experience; (*d*) powerful ideas that have been the precursor to works of enduring scientific, artistic, and literary creation on the one hand, and alas, on the other hand, to wars and social upheavals; and (*e*) Ideas in Divine Mind. Needless to say, Sūtra 3 refers to the last. These Ideas are eternal and consubsistent with the Divine, but their *effects* in the corporeal world are the actual unfoldment of the Word and the manifestation of temporal time, space and innumerable atoms, or *aṇu*, as we know them. We have periodically made the point that just as anything that is manifested

Ideas span the range from the trivial to momentous

on Earth starts with an idea, so also the universe is an Idea in Divine Mind, eternally so.

2. The sacred sound *Aum*, or *Om* in Hinduism, Buddhism, Jainism, and Sikhism, is clearly the equivalent of the Word *Amen* in Christianity and indicates its common origin in the Eternal Wisdom.

3. Time and Space are represented as Ideas in Divine Mind—in that which is ever Timeless, Enduring, and Eternal. Walter Russell refers to the idea of change in the Ever-Unchangeable as cosmic 'rhythmic balanced interchange'.[13] (Refer to Volume I, Chapter 9, pages 305–307, for an outline of the philosophy of Russell regarded by many as the Renaissance man for the twentieth century.)

4. The essential Oneness between the Word, the Word made flesh (the external material which created the visible world), and God means that every speck of the universe, including us, is God. This again needs clarification. Obviously, it is not saying that we human beings are God with His omniscient, omnipresent, and omnipotent attributes, but rather that our quintessential being constitutes the God-spark. This is affirmed in the Third Fundamental Proposition of *The Secret Doctrine* about 'the fundamental identity of all Souls with the Universal Over-Soul', like the sparks from a central fire, and the force in each entity impelling it to unite with the parent flame.[14]

The Divine spark is all pervasive

Put otherwise, man is spirit, soul, and body; and spirit is the Light of God, or the spark of God, in man. Thus, in terms of the legendary aphorism in Vedānta: *Tat Tvam Asi*, translated as 'Thou art That', or 'That thou art'; the 'That' referring to the Ultimate Reality, (Para)brahman, and its spark, (Para)Ātman, in every creature.

5. Reference to the Atom as the 'vibratory structure of creation' shows how well the ancient Sūtra is aligned to the discoveries of modern science; stated otherwise, what the sages knew through elevated consciousness, meditation, and acute reflection has been re-discovered in its scientific guise by modern physics through painstaking theory and laborious experiments: that matter, so-called, is concentrated energy, or 'bottled-up waves' as Sir James Jeans puts it (refer to Volume I, Chapter 3, page 37).

6. The Repulsion and Attraction forces, clearly shown in Figure III-23 on page 103, are very similar to the two fundamental polar opposite forces of radiation and gravitation in the cosmogonies of Isaac Newton and Walter Russell, as summarized in Volume I, Chapter 9.

Sūtra 4: The Gospel (see top right of Figure III-23, page 103)

This Sūtra deals with the root cause of *Māyā*, in the sense of the Darkness of perception due to the mistaken identification of illusory appearances with the Real.

Sāṁkhya philosophy, *The Holy Science*: Sūtra 4	Revelation 4:6
The cause of creation is *Aṇu* or the Atoms. *En masse* they are called *Māyā* or the Lord's illusory power; each individual *Aṇu* is called *Avidyā*, Ignorance.	'And in the midst of the throne, and round about the throne, were four beasts full of eyes before and behind.'

Elucidation by Śrī Yukteswar

1. The Atoms, *en masse*, are one of the Four Ideas mentioned in Sūtra 3 above. They are referred to as the throne of Spirit, the Creator, which, shining on them, creates this universe. They are called collectively *Māyā*, the Darkness, as they keep the Spiritual Light out of comprehension; and each of them separately is called *Avidyā*, or Ignorance which makes man ignorant even of his own Self.

2. Hence in the Bible, the aforementioned Four Ideas [the Word, Time, Space, and the Atom], which give rise to all the confusions that beset man, are referred to as so many beasts. This means that so long as man identifies himself with his gross material body, he holds a position far inferior to the primal fourfold Atom and necessarily fails to comprehend this. But when man succeeds in raising himself to that higher level, he not only comprehends this Atom, but also the whole of creation, both manifested and unmanifested, i.e., 'before and behind' in the words of Revelation.

Commentary

1. Pure Ideas in Divine Mind would hardly give rise to ignorance or illusion; rather it would be *man's failure* to see the beauty and import of Them. We naturally tend to make these Ideas in our own image and by doing so we reduce and limit them. Moreover, according to the measure of our own ignorance, we are likely to pervert energies which flow from these Divine Ideas. The reference in the Bible to, 'four beasts', is, as the writer understands it, because the soul can so easily be bound by the illusory snares of the products of *temporal* time and space (as opposed to the Ideas of them), resulting in failure to rise to the Realities of which they are the mere projections. Plato's counsel on the dual choice facing the soul is apposite: to rise to *Nous* or descend to *Anoia*—see Volume I, Recapitulation, on page 324.

2. The common error of identifying the whole of man with the gross material body applies equally, by implication, to that of identifying consciousness with the physical brain. Both errors are actually one and the same and result in an understanding far inferior to the understanding that space, time, and matter are, in the ultimate, Ideas in Divine Consciousness. If nothing manmade can ever be created or produced in the physical world without its prior existence as an idea in the mind of a person, then, by analogy, the universe itself and all its creations are Ideas in Divine Mind (see the section in the previous Chapter describing the process of Cosmic unfoldment from Divine Consciousness). A few celebrated scientists, although not of a religious or mystical bent, may have had vague intimations of the operation of the universal Hermetic Axiom when they use phrases like 'the Mind of God'. One example is Paul Davies in *The Mind of God*;[15] another is Stephen Hawking in his famous book *A Brief History of Time* where he states, 'If we find the answer to that [a complete theory], it would be the ultimate triumph of human reason—for then we would know the Mind of God.'[16] Such statements are not quite as pompous or rhetorical as they may appear at first sight, and certainly not when pronounced with sincerity as, for example, by Einstein, who quite explicitly proclaimed: 'I want to know how God created this world. I am not interested in this or that phenomenon,

Why are scientists so fascinated with the Mind of God?

in the spectrum of this or that element. I want to know His thoughts; the rest are details.'[17] It does not seem unreasonable to suggest that using such words indicates an awareness of the essentially *mental* nature of space, time, and matter (see the Mathematical Codicil on page 349).

This writer takes the view, however, that by confining attention purely to the physical universe and the physical body, such understanding is vitiated, instead of being enriched, by blending physics with metaphysics, by joining physical science with esoteric science—a recurrent theme of this work.

3. On a different note, one wonders how many people realize that nature herself has an unescapably hard lesson to teach the ordinary man about the grave error of identifying himself with his physical body. That lesson is, quite simply, the act and the fact of growing old—with the inevitable onset of wrinkles! There can hardly be a person on the face of the earth who, in advancing years, does not at some time or other yearn for eternal youth. That is quite understandable, but the deeper question that is rarely asked is: 'what exactly is youth, what is so special about it, and why long for it?' For the vast majority of people, especially women, youth denotes the beautiful, supple physical body and velvety skin of teenage years and early adulthood. The cosmetic industry is flooded with all sorts of products, like anti-aging wrinkle creams, that ostensibly claim to restore crinkled skin to its former loveliness. There is also the gamut of dietary advice, BOTOX® applications, and face-lifts. All this clearly shows a total identification of Self with body—again, understandable, but mistaken. The body, being impermanent, must necessarily be subject to the law of birth, growth, maturity, decay, and death. The Buddha's last words, as recorded in the Mahāparinibbāna Sutta (DN 16), were: '*Anda dāni, bhikkhave, āmantayāmi vo, vayadhammā saṅkhārā appamādena sampādethā,*' translated according to Ānandajoti Bhikkhu: 'Come now, monks, for I tell you all conditioned things are subject to decay, strive on with heedfulness.' Another translation is: 'Decay is inherent in all compounded things. Strive on with diligence.' What then is the secret of eternal youth?

4. The secret lies in the enduring quality of consciousness, not the transitory physical texture of the skin. It means living evermore in the present moment, forever jettisoning the burden of time with its weight of memories of past travails, ever seeking the new, striving towards the unknown. In short, living in the Eternal—rather than using facial creams.

Hard lessons from nature on permanence and decay

SŪTRA 5: *The Gospel (see top left of Figure III-23, page 103)*

This Sūtra concerns the state of consciousness that either assimilates or rejects wisdom.

Sāṁkhya philosophy, *The Holy Science*: SŪTRA 5	Gospel of St. John 1:4, 5, 11
The Omniscient Love aspect of Parabrahma[n] is *Kutastha Caitanya* [the Holy Ghost]. The individual Self, being Its manifestation, is one with It.	'In him was life; and the life was the light of men. And the light shineth in darkness; and the darkness comprehended it not.' 'He came unto his own, and his own received him not.'

Elucidation by Śrī Yukteswar

1. The manifestation of Omniscient Love is Life, the Omnipresent Holy Spirit, and is called the Holy Ghost, *Kutastha Caitanya*, which shines on the Darkness, *Māyā*, to attract every portion of it towards Divinity. But the Darkness, or its individual parts, that is, its presence in each man, the Ignorance, or *Avidyā*, being repulsion itself, cannot receive or comprehend the Spiritual Light, but reflects it.

2. The Holy Ghost being the manifestation of the Omniscient Nature of God, the Eternal Father, is no other substance than God Himself; and so these reflections of spiritual rays are called the Sons of God, *Puruṣa*, or *Ābhāsa Caitanya*, as affirmed in the Sūtra and in St. John.

'And the light shineth in darkness; and the darkness comprehended it not.'
John 1:5 (KJV)

Commentary

1. This Sūtra draws the subtle distinction between *Kutastha Caitanya* (*Purushottama*), the Holy Ghost and *Puruṣa* (*Ābhāsa Caitanya*), the Sons of God.

2. It also underlies the teaching that Wisdom 'bounces off', meaning, is reflected, or repulsed, by the state of Darkness, or Ignorance, which cannot absorb and therefore rejects the Light.

SŪTRA 6: *The Gospel (see middle of Figure III-23, page 103)*

This Sūtra concerns the polarization of Chitta and how the illusory idea of separate existence is born.

> **Sāṁkhya philosophy,** *The Holy Science*: SŪTRA 6
> The Atom, under the influence of *Chit* (universal knowledge) forms
> the *Chitta* or the calm state of mind, which when spiritualized is called
> *Buddhi*, Intelligence [Wisdom]. Its opposite is *Manas*, Mind, in which lives the
> *Jīva*: the self with *Ahaṁkāra*, Ego, the idea of separate existence.

Elucidation by Śrī Yukteswar

1. The Atom, *Avidyā*, the Ignorance, being under the influence of Universal Love, *Chit*, becomes spiritualized; and like iron filings in a magnetic field, is possessed of the power of feeling and consciousness, when it is called the Heart, *Chitta*; and being such, the idea of separate existence of self appears in it, called *Ahaṁkāra*, or Ego, the son of man.

2. Being thus magnetized, *Chitta* has two poles, one of which attracts it towards the Real (Eternal, or Primordial) Substance, *Sat*, and the other repels it from the same. The attractive propensity is called *Sattva*, or *Buddhi*, the Intelligence, or Wisdom, which determines the nature of the Real and knows what is Truth; and the repulsive propensity, spiritualized as aforesaid, produces the ideal world for enjoyment (*Ānanda*) and is called *Anandatwa*, or *Manas*, the Mind.

Sāṁkhya teaching on the mind

Commentary

1. This Sūtra is the Sāṁkhya teaching on the double nature of the Mind Principle given in the occult expositions in Volume II in various places, especially in Chapter 2 and associated Table II-3 on page 21. The repulsive propensity towards enjoyment is the equivalent of mind that gravitates towards desire, forming what has been referred to as Kāma-manas, desire-driven mind. The opposing pole of attraction towards Sat is of course the Sāṁkhya version of the occult teaching on Buddhi-manas, or mind drawn to seek union with wisdom. In Plato's teaching, this is the dual choice of the soul considered in the generic sense: whether descending to attach to *Anoia* (folly, or the irrational Animal soul) or ascending to ally to *Nous* (Divine Spirit, or Substance)—see Volume I, Chapter 9, pages 262–264 and Volume II, Chapter 8, pages 175–178 on the Greek teachings.

2. In the Puranic philosophy, *Mahat*, 'The great one' is the first principle of Universal Intelligence and Consciousness. It is the producer of Manas, the thinking principle, in which Ahaṁkāra, egotism, or the feeling of 'I am I' appears in *Lower* manas. Ahaṁkāra, the Ego, or the illusion of the separate existence of self is the interplay or oscillation between Attraction 'upwards' by the light of wisdom (Buddhi) towards SPIRIT (Divine Consciousness) and the downwards Repulsion by the Darkness of Māyā (due to Ignorance, Avidyā) towards Matter (the separate, condensed units of Universal Self).

3. This Sūtra makes abundantly clear what has been stressed in Chapter 3, namely, that man's spiritual core and seat of consciousness resides in the heart and not in the head—see the extract from the Chandogya Upaniṣad shown in the top right hand corner of Figure III-23. Contemporary consciousness research, mainly in the West, is almost exclusively based on brain mechanisms and will never therefore achieve other than a very partial understanding limited entirely to the detailed physical mechanisms of thought production—the Thought *Producer* remaining ever elusive.

SŪTRAS 7–10: *The Gospel (see middle left side of Figure III-23, page 103)*

The following Sūtras are of seminal importance, so they are shown below in contemporary English and in their original version. They explain how potencies in cosmos—the macrocosm (stated in Sūtras 2 to 6 above)—are mirrored in the Causal Body and Astral body of man—the microcosm—and further reflected in his physical body resulting in his *experience* of the five human senses. Hence, they resolve, in a few terse sentences, what is the bane of current consciousness research: to establish a neural correlate of consciousness.

Sāṁkhya philosophy, *The Holy Science*: SŪTRA 7–10

Contemporary English Version	*Original Version*
The spiritualized Atom in which appears the illusory idea of 'I', as being separate from the Universal Self, has five manifestations of the electrical field of the aura (so-called *aura electricities*).	*Chitta*, the spiritualized Atom, in which *Ahaṁkāra* (the idea of separate existence of Self) appears, has five manifestations (aura electricities).
The five aura electricities constitute the Causal Body of Archetypal Man.	They (the five aura electricities) constitute the causal body of *Purusha*.

The five aura electricities, from their three attributes—positive, neutralizing, and negative—produce the organs of sense, organs of action, and objects of sense.

The five electricities, *Pancha Tattva*, from their three attributes, *Guṇas*—*Sattva* (positive), *Rājas* (neutralizing), and *Tamas* (negative)—produce *Jñānendriyas* (organs of sense), *Karmendriyas* (organs of action), and *Tanmātras* (objects of sense).

These fifteen attributes plus Mind and Intelligence (Wisdom) constitute the seventeen 'fine limbs' of the subtle body, the etheric body (double).

These fifteen attributes plus Mind and Intelligence constitute the seventeen 'fine limbs' of the subtle body, the *Liṅgaśarīra* [*Liṅga-śarīra*].

Elucidation by Śrī Yukteswar

1. The Causal Body

    1.1 The spiritualized Atom, *Chitta* (the Heart) being the Repulsion manifested, produces five sorts of aura electricities from its five different parts: one from the middle, two from the two extremities, and the other two from the spaces intervening between the middle and each of the extremities. These five sorts of electricities being attracted under the influence of Universal Love (the Holy Ghost) towards the Real Substance, *Sat*, produce a magnetic field known as the body of *Sattva Buddhi*, the Intelligence, or Wisdom. These five electricities being the causes of all other creations are called the five Root-Causes, *Pancha (Pañca) Tattva*, and are considered the Causal Body of *Purusha (Puruṣa)* the Son of God [Adam Qadmon—see Chapters 4 and 6].

2. Three *Guṇas*, the electric attributes

    2.1 The electricities, being evolved from the polarized *Chitta*, are also in a polarized state and are endowed with its three attributes, or *Guṇas*: *Sattva* the positive, *Tamas* the negative, and *Rājas* the neutralizing (in the sense of the activity needed to effect equilibration or neutralization of polarities).

3. The Astral Body, comprising:

    3.1 The five organs of the senses, *Jñānendriyas*.
    The positive (*Sattvic*) attributes of the five electricities are the five organs of the senses, *Jñānendriyas*: sound, touch, sight, taste, and smell. Being attracted under the influence of Mind, *Manas*, the opposite pole of the spiritualized Atom (*Chitta*, the Heart), these organs are the manifestation of the positive energy of the latter and constitute a body of mind.

    Note: The term *Jñānendriyas* bears a close similarity to sensorium, the seat of sensation involving the whole sensory apparatus and nervous system.

    3.2 The five organs of action, *Karmendriyas*.
    The neutralizing (*Rajasic*) attributes of the five electricities are the five organs of action, *Karmendriyas*: speech, locomotion (feet), dexterity (hands), generation, and excretion. These organs, being the manifestation of the neutralizing (*Rajasic*) energy of the spiritualized Atom (*Chitta*, the Heart), constitute an energetic body, known variously as the body of energy, life force, *Prāṇa*.

Note: The term *Karmendriyas* bears a close similarity to motorium, the part of the nervous system concerned with movement as distinguished from that concerned with sensation.

3.3 The five objects of the senses, *Tanmātras*, or *Vishaya*.
The negative (*Tamasic*) attributes of the five electricities are the five objects of the senses, Tanmātras, pertaining to sound, touch, sight, taste, and smell. Being united with the organs of sense (Jñānendriyas) through the neutralizing power of the organs of action (Karmendriyas), the various desires of the heart are satisfied.

3.4 The fine material body (Etheric double), *Liṅga-śarīra*.

4. These fifteen attributes with the two poles—Wisdom and Mind—of the Spiritualized Atom constitute the *Liṅga-śarīra*, or *Sukshma-śarīra*, the fine material body (Etheric double) of *Puruṣa*, the Son of God.

Commentary

1. The Astral body in the present context is the overarching term for the mortal, but non-physical subtle bodies (comprising the five organs of the senses, five organs of action, five objects of the senses, and fine material body) corresponding in a general sense to what is referred to as the Mental Body, Astral body, and Etheric double in Table II-15 on page 157 in Chapter 8 of Volume II in the column for the Besant classification; and the Causal Body corresponds to the same in the Table.

2. The Physical body, which includes the brain senses (see the bottom right of Figure III-23, page 103) is subordinate to the Mind (*Manas*) and not the cause of Mind (as also explained in Chapter 6 of Volume I); and the body of physical matter, *Sthūla-śarīra*, is moulded on the template of the Etheric double, *Liṅga-śarīra*, being the outcome, or precipitate, of the forces in the latter (see again the bottom right of the figure).

3. The term 'aura electricities' may sound quaint at first but later in Chapter 9 it will be explained that all changes that are of a material nature in the human body are brought about through the agency of electricity and other related forces known to science. So the five aura electricities can best be understood in connection with the nerve properties which are electrical in nature. Each of the five sensory nerves has its unique function to perform. So, for example, the optic nerve 'conducts' light and does not perform the function of the auditory and other nerves, whereas the auditory nerve 'carries' sound only, without performing the function of the other nerves. Thus, invoking the Hermetic Axiom, it is clear that the five properties of cosmic electricity are mirrored in the five aura electricities in the human body.

Nonetheless, for the reasons given later in Chapter 8, the term 'aura electricties' will be replaced by the identical, but more philosophical term, 'Cosmic Elements'.

4. *Tanmātras*, understood as objects of sense, are obviously not meant in the meaning of physical objects, but 'conceptual objects' in the mind.

In recent years, neuroimaging experiments have shown that the brain constantly makes predictions (conceptual objects, so to say) about the external environment in *anticipation* of paltry sensory inputs reaching it from the outside world. Moreover, the brain neural circuits do not remain quiescent until needed for activity, but instead maintain a high level of activity even when nominally 'at rest'. Scientists call this intrinsic activity the 'dark energy of the brain', a subtle reference to the astronomical finding about the unseen energy that represents the mass of the greatest part of the universe.[18] (But is it that unreasonable to postulate that the inhabitants of the universe, including humans and their brains, would be mainly dark energy on the grounds that the universe itself is supposed to be largely dark energy?)

The above discoveries, along with a recent TED talk, 'Your brain hallucinates your conscious reality', could arguably be said to provide a small measure of scientific rationale to the Sāṃkhya doctrine of tanmātras, the five objects of the senses. According to Anil Seth (*b*.1972), the British professor of Cognitive and Computational Neuroscience at the University of Sussex and Co-Director of the Sackler Centre for Consciousness Science: 'The world we experience comes as much from the inside-out, as from the outside-in. We don't passively perceive our worlds. We actively generate them. Right now, billions of neurons in your brain are working together to generate a conscious experience—and not just any conscious experience, your experience of the world around you and of yourself within it.'[19] How does this happen? According to Seth, we are all hallucinating all the time; and when we agree about our hallucinations, we call it 'reality'. (Needless to say, the mainstream view that consciousness is *generated* by billions of neurons working together in the brain resulting in hallucinations is supported neither by a handful of enlightened scientists and psychologists, nor by the united dictum of esotericism the world over since time immemorial.)

Is mainstream neuroscience now alluding to māyā?

Do the above findings about the anticipating and hallucinating propensities of the brain, along with its high level of rest activity, all suggest that we inhabit a self-generated world of illusions—māyā? Yes, and no. This will be taken up shortly.

Sūtra 11: The Gospel (see bottom right side of Figure III-23, page 103)

This Sūtra concerns the idea of the gross material body.

> **Sāṃkhya philosophy,** *The Holy Science*: Sūtra 11
> The aforesaid five objects, which are the negative attributes of the five electricities, being combined produce the idea of gross matter in its five forms: *Kṣíti*, solids; *Ap*, liquids; *Tejas*, fire; *Marút*, gaseous substances; and *Ākāśa*, ether.

Elucidation by Śrī Yukteswar

As stated in the previous Sūtra 10 in paragraph 3.3, the negative attributes of the five electricities are the five objects of the senses, *Tanmātras*, which, being combined together produce the idea of gross matter which appears to us in the five different varieties: *Kṣíti*, the solid; *Ap*, the liquid; *Tejas*, the fiery; *Marút*, the gaseous; and *Vyoma*, or *Ākāśa*, the ethereal. These constitute the outer covering called *Sthūla-śarīra*, the gross material body of *Puruṣa*, the Son of God.

Commentary

1. From this higher standpoint, the physical body may be regarded as the condensate, or precipitate, of the finer, invisible forces in nature, all of which are aspects of consciousness—the forms assumed by ideas in consciousness. We have an inkling of this by noting that any physical discomfort that we may be experiencing in the moment are held in abeyance when our mind becomes deeply absorbed on any subject, only to reappear when our mind reverts to its prior 'body-centric' orientation.

Sūtra 12: The Gospel (see bottom of Figure III-23, page 103)

This overarching Sūtra concerns the twenty-four principles of creation.

Sāṁkhya philosophy, *The Holy Science*: Sūtra 12	Revelation 4:4
These five forms of gross matter and the aforesaid fifteen attributes, together with *Manas*, Mind, sense consciousness; *Buddhi*, discriminative Intelligence; *Chitta*, the Heart or power of feeling; and *Ahaṁkāra*, the Ego, constitute the twenty-four basic principles of creation.	'And round about the throne were four and twenty seats; and upon the seats I saw four and twenty elders.'

Elucidation by Śrī Yukteswar

1. These five gross matters (the solid, liquid, fiery, gaseous, and ethereal, as stated in Sūtra 11) and the aforesaid fifteen attributes (the five organs of the senses, five organs of action, and five objects of the senses, as stated in Sūtras 7–10), together with the Mind (*Manas*), the Intelligence (*Buddhi*), the Heart (*Chitta*), and the Ego (*Ahaṁkāra*) constitute the twenty-four principles, or Elders, as mentioned in the Bible.

2. These twenty-four principles, or Elders, which completed the creation of Darkness, *Māyā*, are nothing more than the development of Ignorance, *Avidyā*; and as this Ignorance is composed only of ideas, as mentioned above (Sūtra 3), creation has in reality no substantial existence, but is a mere play of ideas on the Eternal Substance, God the Father.

Commentary on Māyā and the Difference Between Relative Truth and Real Truth

The epigraph to this Chapter by the English lyric and philosophical poet Percy Bysshe Shelley (mentioned by William James in his lecture 'Human Immortality'—see Volume I, Chapter 6, page 167 et seq.) are his observations on the transitory nature of existence stated with an eloquence out of all proportion to its brevity. We may justifiably ask questions like: 'What is real?', 'Am I dreaming?', 'How do I know if I am awake or dreaming?' Let us set the scene.

Chuang-tzu (*circa* 369 BC – *circa* 286 BC), one of the great Chinese philosophers and Taoist Masters, recounts a vivid and realistic dream he had one night, in which he was a butterfly. The next morning, on recalling how real that dream seemed in his sleep, he remarked, '*Now* I do not know whether it was then I [who] dreamt I was a butterfly, or whether I am now a butterfly dreaming I am a man.'[20] In *Through the Looking-Glass*, Alice in Wonderland dreams that she sees a chess piece King who is asleep, and she is told that she is only a part of his dream. When she wakes up, she sees such a chess piece on the table next to her, and she wonders whether she had been dreaming about the King or the King was even then dreaming about her.[21] We think we are awake, but perhaps our 'waking' is really a sort of sleep as Gurdjieff taught (see Volume II, Chapter 8, page 178). 'A rope in a dream *is not* and yet *is*.'[22]

Chuang-tzu, Alice in Wonderland and Gurdjieff on dreaming and waking

So what is waking, what is dreaming? Are both, ultimately, two faces of the coin of illusion? That is a question that people have often pondered.

What follows, then, are further insights drawn from philosophy, occult science, and modern Western science on that most elusive of doctrines—*māyā*—yet one of utmost importance to grasp (however imperfectly) if we are to discriminate between the Real and the Unreal and make sense of our lives and the world.

1. To be informed by Śrī Yukteswar that creation has in reality no substantial existence (see point 2. opposite) can certainly appear disconcerting, seeming to imply that the created universe is merely a chimera of a person's imagination. However, it is emphatically not affirming that creation *per se* is non-existent, which would be absurd. Nor is it an injunction to reject the body or the world, which would be equally ridiculous. It is underscoring, yet again, that reality is not what it appears to be to the ordinary mind of man—hence, māyā. The reference to no *substantial* existence means that there is nothing in manifested existence that is not *in*substantial, in other words, not subject to change and transition. Hence, that which is substantial, or permanent, is solely the Source of creation, or, as we prefer to put it, the origin of emanation; and that is God the Father, Divine Consciousness, the Absolute, the Real, Parabrahman, or whatever words we may choose to refer to THAT.

Śrī Yukteswar on insubstantiality of creation

2. As Blavatsky enlightens, this universe, and all in it in their mutual relations, is called the great Illusion of manifestation, or *Mahāmāyā*. Expressed in her inimitable words is this tremendous passage from *The Secret Doctrine*:

> Such is the course of Nature under the sway of KARMIC LAW: of the ever present and the ever-becoming Nature. For, in the words of a Sage, known only to a few Occultists:–
>
> 'THE PRESENT IS THE CHILD OF THE PAST; THE FUTURE, THE BEGOTTEN OF THE PRESENT. AND YET, O PRESENT MOMENT! KNOWEST THOU NOT THAT THOU HAST NO PARENT, NOR CANST THOU HAVE A CHILD; THAT THOU ART EVER BEGETTING BUT THYSELF? BEFORE THOU HAST EVEN BEGUN TO SAY "I AM THE PROGENY OF THE DEPARTED MOMENT, THE CHILD OF THE PAST," THOU HAST BECOME THAT PAST ITSELF. BEFORE THOU UTTEREST THE LAST SYLLABLE, BEHOLD! THOU ART NO MORE THE PRESENT BUT VERILY THAT FUTURE. THUS, ARE THE PAST, THE PRESENT, AND THE FUTURE, THE EVER-LIVING TRINITY IN ONE—THE MAHĀMĀYĀ OF THE ABSOLUTE IS.'[23]

Blavatsky on the Grand Illusion

Recalling Shelley's quote in the epigraph, what this means in simple terms and especially in regard to the evolution of human races is:

> There is neither COMING nor PASSING, but eternal BECOMING.[24]

3. Fully consonant with the above quotes, another eloquent depiction of māyā comes from Ramana Maharshi using the familiar metaphor of cinema pictures. This message was telepathically transmitted by the sage to the young Paul Brunton when, in a dejected state, he sought to distract himself at the cinema in Bombay (Mumbai), having decided that his spiritual quest in India had apparently ended in failure:

Ramana Maharshi
on commonplace
illusions in life

> Life itself is nothing more than a cinema play unrolling its episodes from the cradle to the grave. Where now are the past scenes—can you hold them? Where are those yet to come—can you grasp them? Instead of trying to find the Real, the Enduring, the Eternal, you come here and waste time on what is even more deceptive than ordinary existence—a wholly imaginary story, an illusion within the great illusion.²⁵

Those who choose to wallow in the toys of scientific technology or resort to escapism in empty video games, 'Twittering' on their smartphones or watching soppy films—the *Mahāmāyā*, or 'illusion within the great illusion'—may care to take the above reproach in utter seriousness. It is a cutting reminder about what our true priorities and sense of values should be: to seek the real behind the ephemeral and not fritter away time by indulging in the excesses of technology—the popular notion of progress in a scientific age; nor yield to the allurements of the lower psychic worlds, all too frequently mistaken for genuine spirituality by many of the unbalanced, anti-scientific brigade.

4. A profound teaching on māyā also comes from the great Iranian physicist, geologist, linguist, Islamic scholar, and philosopher of religion Seyyed Hossein Nasr, first mentioned in Volume II, Chapter 4. In *Knowledge and the Sacred*, based on his Gifford Lectures, he draws upon the full range of philosophy and the great religious traditions including Islam, Judaism, Christianity, Buddhism, Hinduism, Confucianism, and Zarathuśtrianism to explore how humanity quests for knowledge and for the Divine, and how these quests relate to one another. His essential thesis is that whereas knowledge of the physical and objective universe can be attained through those sciences that are based on physical sense perception, logic, and reason, knowledge of the Ultimate Reality (God) can be attained only through what is known as sacred knowledge—what Nasr calls *scientia sacra* (what Newton referred to as *prisca sapientia*) and what in this work we have referred to by similar terms like *philosophia perennis* and Eternal Wisdom. And the reason for this is that the universe (as perceived by the human mind via the senses) constitutes a veil which conceals the Ultimate Reality of which it is a manifestation. Hence, none of the sciences based on sense perception, reason, and logic alone can pierce this veil. Alongside the quotes by Blavatsky and Maharshi, this extended extract warrants our deepest consideration:

Hossein Nasr on
why ratiocination
spellbound by
māyā cannot
access the Real

> Māyā in its aspect of illusion is also the cause for this impossibility of encompassing Reality in a closed system of thought so characteristic of profane philosophy. The Absolute [Ultimate Reality] is something incomprehensible to those who do not possess the eye or intuition to grasp it conceptually. In any case, ratiocination, belonging to the realm of relativity, cannot be used to prove or perceive the Absolute which remains beyond the reach of all attempts of the relative to comprehend It. But intelligence can know the Absolute and in fact only the Absolute is completely intelligible. Below that level, the activity of māyā enters into play and brings about an element of ambiguity and uncertainty. *The plight of innumerable schools of modern*

philosophy [and we may add, of course, scientific materialism] and their failure to achieve the task of encompassing the Real through the process of purely human thought is caused by the power of māyā which exercises its illusory spell most upon those who would deny her reality [emphasis added].[26]

5. As just stated by Nasr regarding this metaphysical one Absolute Reality, the sheer impossibility of approaching the Absolute through thought, or human conception alone—affirmed as the first fundamental axiom of the Secret Doctrine[ii] (see page 105)—is further avowed in the Tejobindu Upaniṣad:

> And Śiva declared: 'I am of the nature of Parabrahman … I am the I that has given up 'I' … I am beyond the reach of mind and speech … I am Ātman … There is none other than Brahman, and that is I … I alone am the Adiśeṣa [primeval time], without name and form … I am of the nature of the All-Void … I am the unconditioned, the permanent, the Unborn …'[27]

(margin: The Mystery which is beyond telling)

6. Of all scientists, Einstein should know about the distinction between absolute knowledge and the provisional nature of scientific knowledge belonging to the realm of relativity. He succinctly differentiated between the *true* and the *really true*. What may be true belongs to the realm of appearances (in other words, māyā); but what is really true deals with the realities beneath the appearances.

(margin: Einstein on distinction between real Truth and relative truth)

Then comes this seminal observation from the prince of relativity theory:

> We can only know the relative truth; the Real Truth is known only to the Universal Observer.[28]

Who is the Universal Observer of Einstein? The Supreme Consciousness, by whatever name.

Thus it is that the truth investigated by science is always relative and not absolute and its theories are ever liable to change. Would that the majority of scientists today took the trouble to 'draw a distinction between what is *true* and what is *really true*'.[28]

Occultism and the sacred scriptures have precise words to makes this distinction. Just one example: according to Advaita Vedānta, *vyavahāra-satya* refers to knowledge of the world of appearances obtained through the senses and the intellect in contrast with *paramārtha-satya*, supreme, or absolute Truth—direct knowledge of reality, the latter being the faculty of Buddhi-Manas in man (see Volume II, Chapter 3, Table II-5, page 40).

7. Finally, there is no implication that māyā is inherently evil, therefore, something essentially to be shunned (even if that were possible in daily life). The occult injunction is not like that. Like desires that can be used either for self-gratification or philanthropic service, depending entirely on the motive (see Volume II, Chapter 2, page 25 f.), so also, māyā can either lead us astray into the labyrinth of delusion or can be used to enhance creativity and enterprise. There is no shortage of opportunities in modern life to indulge in the former—idle phantasizing, cheap entertainment, vapid social media, psychedelic drugs, etc. Regarding the latter, it is impossible to begin any entirely new artistic or scientific endeavour without the

(margin: Māyā is indispensable: all creativity depends on it)

---

ii *Scientia sacra, theosophia, philosophia perennis*, and other similar terms, are all equivalent appellations for the Secret Doctrine of which H. P. Blavatsky's *The Secret Doctrine* is a representative text.

power of focussed imagination—actively dreaming novel ideas into existence, so to speak; and therein lies the correct use of māyā in the life of man.

Concluding Insights

Three cardinal themes may be gleaned from the above exposition and associated Figure III-23 on page 103. All three point to the primacy of consciousness and its manifestation in the human body.

1. The Sūtras from *The Holy Science* and parallel expositions from the New Testament provide fitting testimony that *the human body is at one and the same time a projection of the divine and a channel for It*, albeit temporarily for the period of a lifetime. Hence, all the powers, latent or active, in divine consciousness—the wisdom and intelligence that have gone into, and are hidden behind, the whole universe—have also gone into and are mirrored in the human body. This is made plain in the closing quote to this Chapter from the Kāṭhaka (Katha) Upaniṣad, which discloses that *the gross matter of the body and brain is the form taken by consciousness at its lowest level of 'descent'; and therefore consciousness is not an epiphenomenon or a product of bodily material interactions, but instead their origin and noumenon.*

The Holy Science and the New Testament attest to the primacy of consciousness

2. A perusal of Figure III-23, and the Sūtras upon which it is based, displays how divine forces 'flow down' from their highest level of emanation to manifest in the human body. Particularly significant is the process of development of the five human senses and their respective and collective experience. Thus a neural correlate of consciousness, the current major research effort in neuroscience, is, strictly speaking, a misnomer because it is based on a false premiss. The neurology is the form and manifestation of consciousness *per se* in the physical body, but which can be traced back directly to its divine fountainhead (Sat-Chit-Ānanda as seen at the top of Figure III-23). Hence, the question of such a material–physical correlation simply does not exist, which is why science has so much difficulty in trying to find what is non-existent in the first place. The enquiry is back-to-front.

3. In the case of the human being, the microcosm, there is nothing that has ever been created in the physical world that did not have its prior existence as a 'mental object', i.e., idea in human consciousness. Just so, the universe, the macrocosm, exists by virtue of Ideation in Divine Consciousness. Whether human or the universe, all manifestations are appearances, māyā, hence impermanent and subject to birth, growth, and decay. That which endures is solely the noumenon behind all manifestation—the Eternal Now, the Ever-Present, the 'Absolute IS'—CONSCIOUSNESS.

The Emanational Emergence of Man – An Esoteric Exposition

An understanding, however imperfect, of the role of *māyā* (for which the popular term 'illusion' is highly unsatisfactory) is still of profound significance in our attempts to fathom the world we inhabit and make sense of our own lives. This is why we have dwelt on this elusive subject at some length, albeit in general terms, supporting the tenets with quotes from occultism, philosophy, and science. The role of māyā, specifically in regard to man's evolution, is a highly recondite teaching of occultism to which justice cannot be done by way of a summary in a few sentences. We therefore revert to the Illusion–Producer—the 'Absolute IS', or Sat—and trace how occult science, through Blavatsky's instruction, has portrayed its emanational descent in a manner remarkably similar to that just described according to Sāṁkhya philosophy and the Bible.

Towards the end of her life, Blavatsky formed the 'Esoteric Section (School) of the Theosophical Society' with the sole aim of bequeathing the deeper aspects of the esoteric and occult sciences to a small number of her most dedicated students. Her instructions were recorded and published in *Some Papers on the Bearing of Occult Philosophy on Life*, also known as *The Esoteric [E. S.] Instructions of H. P. Blavatsky*.[29] They comprise three papers on the bearing of occult philosophy on life, notes on these papers, notes on some oral teachings, and additional notes. Then in the last months of her life, in London in 1890 and 1891, Blavatsky invited selected members of the Esoteric Section (School), including Annie Besant and G. R. S. Mead as Secretaries, to join the newly established *Inner Group* of the Esoteric Section with the objective of teaching practical occultism.[30] The Inner Group instructions have been published completely and, for the first time, from the notebooks of the prominent English Theosophist Alice Leighton Cleather (1846–1938), who was also one of Blavatsky's personal pupils. They contain teachings of even more esoteric weight, comprising three further esoteric instructions, ten transcripts of the Minutes of the Meeting of the Inner Group, variant readings to the Minutes, letters and statements, and what is fondly known as H.P.B.'s Diagram of Meditation. Taken as a whole, these teachings bequeath profound insights into the dynamics and inner structure of a living, spiritualized kosmos and humanity. Subjects include planes and states of consciousness, *lokas* and *talas*, and the correspondences between planetary influences, the elements, colours, sounds, senses, and organs of the human body.

Following the universal code of conduct pertaining to the Mystery Schools (see Volume I, Chapter 7, pages 207, 220), members of the Esoteric Section were bound by a formal pledge of secrecy. What was written, and subsequently publicly disseminated, was therefore in the nature of an approximate enumeration about certain critical aspects of the human principles and not the whole truth, which could not be entrusted to those not pledged. It bears repeating that vital details can only be divulged to those who have qualified themselves to use the knowledge and power thus gained with the utmost responsibility, without any trace of personal motive, and with full control over the effects generated. But whether such vital details were withheld from the published versions of the *Esoteric Instructions* or the (ostensibly complete) *Inner Group Teachings of H. P. Blavatsky to her Personal Pupils (1890–91)* is not known to the writer.

Be that as it may, what now follows is a small selection of these teachings, taken from the instructions of the *Esoteric Section*, to offer the reader a taster of the stupendous depth and range of the esoteric and occult doctrines. Owing to the highly abstruse character of the material, the writer has provided a minimum of commentary. Readers are therefore urged to consult the sources cited and to draw upon their own intuitions to extract the deeper implications of these esoteric teachings.

Highly recondite teachings divulged by the Esoteric Section of the Theosophical Society

Portions from the Esoteric Section Instructions

The evolution of cosmos and man is a central theme of all esoteric philosophies and a mainstay of Theosophical doctrine. Accordingly, a summary of the evolution of man from the spiritual perspective is now presented, followed by a necessarily cursory extract from *E. S. Instruction No. I*, also referred to as *Paper 1*, which deals with the whole subject of the correlation of forces based on the law of correspondences, and provides a particularly illuminating description of the occult teaching on the emanational descent of man from the realm of pure Spirit to the corporeal plane. The subject of human evolution is revisited in Chapter 10 from different standpoints, including suppressed archæological evidence that supports the occult doctrine on the antiquity of man, and the ultimate purpose of human existence.

The Descent of Species

In a fine abridgement of the stupendous doctrine of evolution expounded by Blavatsky, Professor of Esotericism and British historian Nicholas Goodrick-Clarke explains how esotericism could assimilate evolution; but evolution only in the strictly spiritual terms of an emanationist cosmology, which informed and affected all the varied material and physical forms of creation.[31] We have previously stressed the limitations of Darwinian theory and pointed out that the theory has nothing to do with the origin of the human species, but the evolution of the species: (*a*) from a materialistic perspective; and (*b*) from a certain moment in time (see Volume I, Chapter 8, page 242). But as Goodrick-Clarke clarifies: 'By viewing *spiritual* evolution as the underlying purpose and direction of all change in the universe [not restricted just to man], Blavatsky effectively subsumed the material and physical aspects of evolution into a grand, overarching, divine plan. In this respect, it can be seen that Blavatsky restated the Western esoteric tradition in contemporary scientific terms by incorporating the concept of evolution into the celestial and spiritual hierarchies of being from the macrocosm of the whole universe down to the microcosm of man.'[32]

Two points emerge from the above, forcefully and unambiguously:

1. The operative law, so to speak, of the Hermetic Axiom; the logical implication of which is that –

2. Man has evolved by descent from spirit and not by ascent from matter: all things, including man, have their origin in spirit, evolution always beginning from above and proceeding downwards, and not the reverse, 'bottom-up', process taught in Darwinian theory. 'In other words, there has been a gradual materialization of forms until a fixed ultimate of debasement is reached. This point is that at which the modern theory of evolution enters into the arena of *speculative hypothesis* [emphasis added].'[33] It follows, then, that at this point of deepest materiality, man is at the furthest distance from himSELF. (This theme is explained in detail in Chapter 10 later.)

Evolution, including human, commences with spirit, not matter

The above summary of this key doctrine of esotericism is illustrated in Figure III-24 on page 124 taken from *E. S. Instruction No. I*, which shows the macrocosm–microcosm relation regarding the descent of man.[34]

E. S. Instruction No. I

A whole universe of meaning is subsumed in this diagram (but refer to the limitations of diagrams explained in Chapter 6 earlier). We can only but touch on some keynotes.

The first point to highlight is that the emanational process is clearly seen to involve a three staged descent from the spiritual to the physical. Adopting the subtitles in the diagram, these are:

1. *1st–Macrocosm* and Its 3, 7, or 10 Centres of Creative Forces that are mirrored in Heavenly Man (seen in the ovoid just below the uppermost triangle). This is the realm of the ideative—the potency of formative creation.

   Heavenly Man (Adam Qadmon in the Qabbalah, *Puruṣa* in the Sāṁkhya philosophy), otherwise known as Original Man, or Archetypal Man, signifies humanity not fallen into sin, so to say.

2. *2nd–Microcosm (the Inner Man)* and His 3, 7, or 10 Centres of Potential Forces that are the reflections of the forces in the macrocosm.

   This is the realm of the archetypal, or paradigmatic—the potentiality and possibility of formative creation.

3. *3rd–Microcosm (the Physical Man)* and His 10 Orifices, or centres of Action, in turn reflecting the potential forces in the Inner Man.

   This is the plane of action—the activity and actuality of formative creation.

Three stages of man's emanational descent

Readers will note that the three staged descent, just described, corresponds exactly to the explanatory designations of 'MAN', 'Man', and 'man' given in the Definitions in Volume IV.

We clearly see how, 'the upper and highest, and the lower and most animal, stand in mutual relation'[35] (the term 'animal' referring of course to the uncontrolled animal-like propensities of unregenerate man symbolized by the Cretan Minotaur).

The Macrocosm and the Microcosm are the representations of two opposite poles. These are the upright triangle and the inverted triangle shown at the very top and bottom of Figure III-24 overleaf. To elucidate briefly, these two poles are:

(i) the upper pole, mentioned in 1. above, represented by the primordial triangle (shown at the top of the diagram) which has reflected itself in the Heavenly Man;

Relation between higher and lower polarities

(ii) (*a*) and the lower pole as the astral paradigmatic Man mentioned in 2., whose Monad (*Ātman*) is also represented by an upright triangle (as it has to become a ternary in conscious Devachanic interludes—see Volume II, Chapter 5);

(*b*) plus the purely terrestrial man being reflected in the universe of matter mentioned in 3. As any mirror image always appears upside down, so to say, the upper triangle, wherein the creative ideation and potency of the formative faculty resides, is represented in its limited objective realization in the man of clay as an inverted triangle seen at the very bottom of the diagram. This theme is taken up later in this Chapter.

Thus we see how 'the upper and highest, and the lower and most animal, stand in mutual relation' as quoted above.

There is another 'open secret' that was given out in the *Esoteric Instructions* and it concerns the opposite ends of the spiritual pole: *Ātma* and the body. Whereas Ātma was stated as

DIAGRAM I

1ST.—MACROCOSM AND ITS 3, 7, OR 10 CENTERS OF CREATIVE FORCES

A. Sexless, Unmanifested Logos.
B. Potential Wisdom.
C. Universal Ideation.

    a. Creative Logos.
    b. Eternal Substance.
    c. Spirit.

D. The Spiritual Forces acting in Matter.

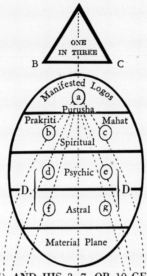

A. B. C. The Unknowable.

a.b.c. This is Pradhāna, undifferentiated matter in Sankhya philosophy, or Good, Evil and Chaotic Darkness (Sattva, Rajas, and Tamas) neutralizing each other. When differentiated, they become the Seven Creative Potencies: Spirit, Substance and Fire stimulating matter to form itself.

2ND.—MICROCOSM (THE INNER MAN) AND HIS 3, 7, OR 10 CENTERS OF POTENTIAL FORCES

(ĀTMAN, although exoterically reckoned as the seventh principle, is no individual principle at all, and belongs to the Universal Soul; is the AURIC EGG, the Magnetic Sphere round every human and animal being.)

1. BUDDHI, the vehicle of ĀTMAN.
2. MANAS, the vehicle of BUDDHI.
3. LOWER MANAS (the Upper and Lower MANAS are two aspects of one and the same principle) and
4. KĀMA-RŪPA, its vehicle.
5. PRĀNA, Life, and
6. LIṄGA-ŚARĪRA, its vehicle.

I, II, III, are the Three Hypostases of ĀTMAN, its contact with Nature and Man being the Fourth, making it a Quaternary, or Tetraktys, the Higher Self.

1, 2, 3, 4, 5, 6. These six principles, acting on four different planes, and having their AURIC ENVELOPE on the seventh (*vide infra*), are those used by the Adepts of the Right-Hand, or White Magicians.

1 The Physical Body is no principle; it is entirely ignored, being used only in Black Magic.

3RD.—MICROCOSM (THE PHYSICAL MAN) AND HIS 10 ORIFICES, OR CENTERS OF ACTION

1. (BUDDHI) Right eye.

3. (LOWER MANAS) Right Ear.

5. (LIFE PRINCIPLE) Right Nostril.

7. The Organ of the CREATIVE LOGOS, the Mouth.

8, 9, 10. As this Lower Ternary has a direct connection with the Higher Atmic Triad and its three aspects (creative, preservative and destructive, or rather regenerative), the abuse of the corresponding functions is the most terrible of Karmic Sins—the Sin against the Holy Ghost with the Christians.

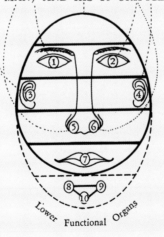

2. (MANAS) Left Eye.

4. (KĀMA-RŪPA) Left Ear.

6. (LIFE VEHICLE) Left Nostril.

7. The Paradigm of the 10th (creative) orifice in the Lower Triad.

These Physical Organs are used only by Dugpas in Black Magic.

Figure III-24   Man the Microcosm – His Descent from the Divine
Photo Credit: CW-XII (see Note 34)

a principle for the purposes of enumerating the occult taxonomy of the human principles for the general public, Blavatsky informed her Esoteric and Inner Group members that Ātman is in fact no individual 'principle' but a radiation *from*, and *one with*, the Unmanifested Logos. Nor can the body, which is the material rind, or shell of the Spiritual man, be, in strict truth, referred to as a 'principle'. In point of fact the chief 'principle' of all, one not even mentioned up until now, is the 'Luminous Egg' (*Hiraṇyagarbha*) or the invisible magnetic sphere in which every man is enveloped (as are the animals, the plants, and even the minerals). 'It *is* the odic,[iii] or rather the auric or magnetic fluid which emanates from man, but it is also something more,'[36] being the direct emanation: (*a*) from the Ātmic Ray in its triple aspect of Creator, Preserver, and Regenerator (Destroyer); and (*b*) from *Buddhi-Manas*, the Higher Mind. The *seventh* aspect of this individual aura is the faculty of assuming the form of its body and becoming the 'Radiant', the Luminous Augoeides. It is this, strictly speaking, which at times becomes the form called *Māyāvi-rūpa*. Apropos, those sensitives and mediums who are gifted with genuine clairvoyance, and claim to see auras, should not automatically assume that what they are 'seeing' is the Luminous Augoeides proper as this appears only to the most purified and spiritually evolved (see Volume II, Chapter 4, page 53).

Man's luminous aura

Continuing with the *E. S. Instruction*, and referring again to Figure III-24, Blavatsky explains:

> The reason why public mention of the Auric Body is not permitted is on account of its being so sacred. It is this Body which at death assimilates the essence of Buddhi and Manas and becomes the vehicle of these spiritual principles, *which are not objective*, and then, with the full radiation of Ātman upon it, ascends as Manas-Taijasa [Taijasi[iv]] [the 'radiant manas', or radiative state of the Higher Ego] into the Devachanic state. Therefore it is called by many names. It is the Sūtrātman, the silver 'thread' which 'incarnates' from the beginning of Manvantara [the period of manifestation of the universe] to the end, stringing upon itself the pearls of human existence—in other words, the spiritual aroma of every personality it *follows* through the pilgrimage of life. It is also the material from which the Adept forms his Astral Bodies, from the Augoeides and the Māyāvi-Rūpa downwards. After the death of man, when its most ethereal particles have drawn into themselves the spiritual principles of Buddhi and the Upper Manas, and are illuminated with the radiance of Ātman, the Auric Body remains either in the Devachanic state of consciousness or, in the case of a full Adept, prefers the state of a Nirmāṇakāya—that is, one who has so purified his whole system that he is above even the divine illusion of a Devachanī. […] In the case of the full Adept the body alone becomes subject to dissolution, while the center of that force which was the seat of desires and passions, disappears with its cause—the animal body. But during the life of the latter all these centres are more or less active and in constant correspondence with their prototypes, the cosmic centres, and their microcosms, the principles. It is only through these cosmic and spiritual centres that the physical centres (the upper seven orifices and the lower triad) can benefit by their occult interaction, for these orifices, or openings, are channels conducting into the body the influences that *the will of man* attracts and uses, *viz.*, the cosmic forces.[37]

Sacred matters revealed partially

---

iii The name given in the mid-nineteenth century to the vital energy, or life force, by Baron Carl von Reichenbach who coined the name, in 1845, from that of the Norse god Odin.

iv *Taijasi* is a Sanskrit term meaning 'radiant', 'flaming', derived from *Tejas* 'fire'.

The above highly shortened and terse exposition should provide at least some measure of the depth and complexity of the subtle forces and processes at work in the human being and why, veiled within the various centres and orifices of the body, there are tremendous forces, that can only be evoked safely under the expert guidance and protection of a genuine master, but must never be artificially aroused by abnormal breathing and other such practices, or the use of psychedelic drugs, with the attendant serious risk of derangement or even death.

The Union of Sāṁkhya Philosophy and Christianity with Theosophy

Readers will not have failed to discern the basic similarities and overlap between *The Holy Science*, based on the Indian Sāṁkhya philosophy, corroborated by Christianity, and the supreme occult teachings bequeathed through modern Theosophy. For ease of comparison, these two systems shown in Figure III-23 and Figure III-24, respectively, are displayed in Figure III-25 on page 128 alongside each other, with much of the detail removed for clarity.

The first and most important point to note is that all three systems enumerate the anthropogenic emanational process in three major stages of descent, from the spiritual to the physical, as summarized below using the same colour scheme for comparison with Table II-3 on page 21 in Volume II.

Sāṁkhya philosophy and Christianity	Theosophy
Stage I: Ideative – MAN as Divine Thought	
Causal Body	Macrocosm
Stage II: Paradigmatic – Archetypal Man	
Astral body	Microcosm (Inner Man)
Stage III: Action – Physical Man	
Physical body	Microcosm (Physical man)

This should come as no surprise if we bear in mind the Hermetic Axiom, for we clearly discern in our everyday world the same three-staged emanational process from the invisible and mental to the visible and physical. For example, to build quite literally anything on earth we need the three-staged process comprising:

1. an idea;

2. a design corresponding to the idea (such as a mathematical model or an engineering drawing) representing the idea;

3. the realization of the design in physical matter.

Three stages of emanational descent

Applying this to building a house, say, the three stages would be: 1. the architect's idea; 2. the plans and drawings on paper; or electronically, by way of computer-aided design; 3. the construction in bricks and mortar.

Reverting to Figure III-25, the following three features are also especially noteworthy:

1. The Upper Triad, Sat–Chit–Ānanda (Pure Being–Universal Knowledge–Bliss) of Sāṁkhya, being in essence the three aspects of Consciousness, corresponds in an obvious way to the Upper Triangle of Theosophy—One In Three: A. Unmanifested Logos–B. Potential Wisdom–C. Universal Ideation.

2. Sāṁkhya and Theosophy both show how Astral, or Paradigmatic Man is the model, or template, of Physical man. Therefore the physical senses have their astral counterpart, which itself is the emanation of forces and powers in Heavenly Man.

3. Related to the above, Sāṁkhya and Theosophy also illustrate how divine forces are 'flowed down' to their end points in the objective physical sense organs, which in turn have their direct correspondences with the constitution of physical man (e.g. the left and right eyes related to Manas and Buddhi, respectively).

Indeed, man and all other creatures are the outcome of Divine Ideation and the body the product of Divine Forces sculpted by Divine Handicraft. This writer maintains that no end of health and social problems that currently beset individuals, societies, and nations would be greatly alleviated were this simple fact realized and acted upon, not from wishful thinking or hearsay, but through study and reflection, contemplation and experience.

Meanwhile, we continue with the implications of the inverted triangle mentioned earlier, seen at the very bottom of Figure III-24, page 124 (and in the same position in the diagram on the right side of Figure III-25 overleaf).

> **REALITY is that which Endures. Permanent and Eternal, It transcends Space–Time. All space and time orders are subsumed within Its limitless potentiality.**

The Incarnation of Physical Man

According to the Mystery teachings, not all the spiritual nature of man incarnates in matter in one lifetime. In daily life we can sense the truth of this in terms of the gulf between our potentiality and our capacity: the common feeling that we could accomplish and create far more, were it not for the limitations of our physical capacities (energy and time). There seems to be a greater part of us that is not able to engage with our physical lives. In popular terms, the spirit is willing, but the flesh is weak.

We also sense this fractional incarnation of our greater Self in the operation of *karma*. Stated briefly, the four types of karma are: (*a*) *sañcita*, the totality of karma from all lifetimes; (*b*) *prārabdha*, the karma for a particular birth, or incarnation; (*c*) *kriyamāṇa*, the immediate karma from present actions; and (*d*) *agami*, the returning karma from this and other lifetimes. We can appreciate that if *sañcita karma* were all packed into a single lifetime, the latter would be totally overwhelmed. It is hard enough to expiate *kriyamāṇa karma* and hopefully, most of *prārabdha karma* over the course of a lifetime! Thus, and stated simplistically, our incarnations are proportioned according to how much karma (both 'good' and 'bad') can productively be processed and expiated in an incarnation. Therefore, according to the spiritual laws of conservation of matter and energy, so to say, not all the spiritual nature of man incarnates in matter in a single incarnation.

Four types of karma

With this insight, referring back to the interpretation of the Tarot card *The Judgement* given in Chapter 1 on page 13, Hall elucidates that, at birth, only a third part of the Divine Nature

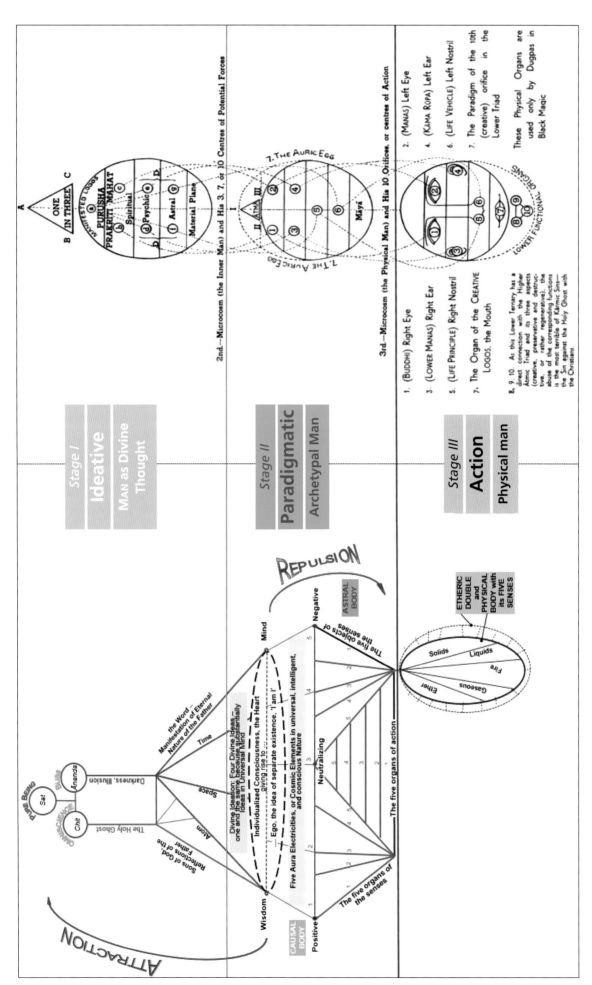

Figure III-25 East Meets West – The Unity of the Perennial Wisdom Tradition on the Three-Staged Emanational Descent of Man

of man temporarily dissociates itself from its own immortality and takes upon itself the dream of physical birth and existence, animating with its own celestial enthusiasm a vehicle composed of material elements part of, and bound, to the material sphere.[38] At death this incarnated part awakens from the dream of physical existence and reunites itself once more with its eternal condition. This periodical descent of spirit into matter is termed the wheel of life and death (see Volume II, Chapter 5). Symbolically therefore, as just stated above, the Spirit of man in earthly incarnation is shown diagrammatically as an equilateral triangle with one point downward. This lower point, which is one-third of the spiritual nature, but in comparison to the dignity of the other two is much less than a third, descends into the illusion of material existence for a brief space of time. That which never clothes itself in the sheath of matter is the Hermetic Anthropos—the Overman—analogous to the Cyclops, or guardian *dæmon* of the Greeks, the *angel* of Jakob Böhme, the Overself of Brunton, the Oversoul of Emerson, 'that Unity, that Oversoul, within which every man's particular being is contained and made one with all other.'[39]

The dream of existence

This, as Blavatsky confirms, is the secret meaning behind the affirmations of virtually all the ancient philosophers, when they declared that the rational part of man's soul never entered wholly into the man, but only overshadowed him, more or less, through the irrational Spiritual Soul (Buddhi, or Nous) not to be confused with Anoia, the irrational, or desire-driven, animal soul.

Man is spirit only partially embodied

Note, particularly, that in its generic sense, the word 'rational' means 'something emanating from the Eternal Wisdom'—the Divine essence; and '*Irrational* in the sense that as a *pure* emanation of the Universal mind it [Buddhi] can have no individual reason of its own on this plane of matter, but like the Moon, who borrows her light from the Sun and her life from the Earth, so *Buddhi*, receiving its light of Wisdom from *Ātma* ["above"], gets its rational qualities from *Manas* ["below"]. *Per se* [however], as something homogeneous, it is devoid of attributes.'[40]

One speculates whether in the case of genius in any field, a greater proportion of the spiritual nature than one-third descends into, and clothes itself in, material existence. Be that as it may, by initiation into the Mysteries and subject to its secret processes, this law of birth and death is transcended, and during the course of physical existence that part of the spirit which is asleep in form is awakened without the intervention of death—the ultimate and inevitable Initiator—and is consciously reunited with the Anthropos, or the overshadowing substance of itself. However, such initiation is always preceded by the most severe testing of the will power and resolve of the aspirant. So for a gripping and factual account of such an initiation process in modern times, we hark back to the earlier description in Chapter 3 on the mystery of the Great Pyramid in connection with the experience of Paul Brunton in the darkness of the King's Chamber, described in 'A Night Inside the Great Pyramid' from *In Search of Secret Egypt*. The awful psychic encounters and horrible spectres that he had to endure and surmount are described in chilling detail before he was given actual proof—as living experience—that:

A possible account for genius

> Man, whose soul was born out of the Undying, can never really die.[41]

This injunction is starkly similar to what the physician Dr Wiltse experienced, also at first hand, during his near-fatal illness (see Volume II, Chapter 5, page 91):

> I have died, as men term death, and yet I am as much a man as ever.[42]

Evidence of man's immortality

This is the great lesson about the state of death, that consciousness also exists apart from the body; hence the immortality of the soul. In other words, the earthly body—the mortal body—has temporarily and cloyingly imprisoned the immortal soul,[v] so eloquently expressed by Brunton's contemporary, Manly Hall, in Volume II, Chapter 5, and worth repeating:

> Man is essentially a permanent and immortal principle; only his bodies pass through the cycle of birth and death. The immortal is the reality; the mortal is the unreality. During each period of earth life, reality thus dwells in unreality, to be liberated from it temporarily by death and permanently by illumination.[43]

Before leaving this subject of esoteric instruction from the highest sources, the writer would like to mention two references that the truly earnest student would find of great value, especially regarding an understanding of consciousness from both the spiritual and physical standpoints. One is of course *The Inner Group Teachings of H. P. Blavatsky to her Personal Pupils (1890–91)* referred to earlier. The other is a large, but eminently accessible book, *Reflections on an Ageless Wisdom* by the American educator and international lecturer Joy Mills (1920–2015), one of the most profound and dedicated students of the Theosophical Society.[44] It contains explanatory comments on the correspondences between Blavatsky's two Adept teachers with two leading Englishmen in British India: Alfred Percy Sinnett (1840–1921); journalist, esoteric author, and Editor of *The Pioneer*, the leading English Daily of India; and Allen Octavian Hume (1829–1912), political reformer, ornithologist, and one of the founders of the Indian National Congress. The Adepts were the inner founders of the Theosophical movement, for whom Blavatsky was their emissary. Their Letters, which may be seen in the British Library, deal with occult science and related matters on a wide front, the main themes being cosmogenesis, anthropogenesis, planes of consciousness, evolution, and the ageless wisdom at the core of all religions. They certainly battered the fortress of materialistic science and orthodox religion (particularly dogmatic Christianity, otherwise known as 'Churchianity') when they were first published in 1923.

Peerless books of wisdom

Résumé

The origin and development of the human species is necessarily a complex affair but, ultimately, it comes down to a three-staged emanational descent, as depicted in Figure III-25 on page 128. To recapitulate, and presage the principal themes in the next Chapter:

Man's divine spiritual, and physical origins

❖ For its moral, psychic, and spiritual nature, mankind is indebted to a group of divine Beings (the names and characteristics of which will be given in Chapter 8).

❖ Mankind, in its first prototypal, shadowy form, is the offspring of the *Dhyāni-Chohans* (the collective hosts of spiritual beings equivalent to the Elōhīm, the Angelic Hosts of Christianity). These are celestial beings charged with the supervision of the Kosmos by way of administering and enacting Divine Laws. They are 'celestial' in the sense of being at a stage on the Ladder of Life superior to the Human Kingdom. This is because they have evolved through the human stage in far past aeons.

❖ In its qualitative and physical aspect, humankind is the direct progeny of the lowest grade of *Dhyānis*, or Spirits of the Earth, also explained in the next Chapter.

---

v The word 'soul' used of course in the generic sense. As explained in Volume II, Chapter 3, there are three principal soul-levels in Man—spiritual, human, and animal.

Collectively, then, men are the handiwork of hosts of various spirits (the hierarchy of active cosmic agents on the various planes); distributively, the tabernacles of those hosts; and occasionally and singly, the vehicles of some of them. Thus, man is not, nor could he ever be, the complete or sole product of the 'Lord God' as some religious fundamentalists would proclaim—any more than a temple can physically materialize from the vision of the architect without a definite plan actuated by builders and craftsmen. But man is the child of the Elōhīm—the minor created gods—so arbitrarily changed into the singular masculine gender. The first Dhyānis, commissioned to 'create' man in their image, could only throw off their shadows, like a delicate model, for the Nature Spirits of matter to work upon. Man is, beyond any doubt, formed physically out of the dust of the Earth, but his creators and fashioners are many. Nor can it be said that the 'Lord God breathed into his nostrils the breath of life', unless that God is identified with the 'ONE LIFE', Omnipresent though invisible.

How man has been 'constructed'

Accordingly, man is composed of countless myriads of lives. Science perceives this truth, at the biological level, being well aware of the countless bacteria and viruses and other infinitesimals in the human body, their role in health and as occasional and abnormal visitors to which diseases are attributed. Occultism—which discerns a life in every atom and molecule, whether in a mineral or human body, in air, fire or water, in bacterium or virus—affirms that our whole body is built of such lives.[45]

This Chapter has outlined the overall emanationist scheme resulting in the coming into being of physical man on Earth from his Divine origins. The next Chapter explains the processes and mechanisms in more detail, such that internal subjective experiences can result from external, quantifiable input to the human physical senses. Meanwhile, we close with three quotes: the first, strangely echoing the first epigraph, from a great statesman who established the Peace Corps in 1961 and who knew a thing or two about *māyā*; the second from one of the greatest modern perennialist philosophers and scholars whose exposition on māyā has figured prominently in this Chapter; and the third, an extract from the Kāṭhaka Upaniṣad which so inspired the American philosopher Ralph Waldo Emerson, quoted in Volume I, Chapter 9, and worth repeating due to its timeless message.

History is a relentless master. It has no [enduring] present, only the past rushing into the future. To try to hold fast is to be swept aside.

JOHN F. KENNEDY[46]

The traditional doctrine of man and not the measurement of skulls and footprints is the key for the understanding of that anthropos who, despite the rebellion of Promethean man against Heaven from the period of Renaissance and its aftermath, is still the inner man of every man, the reality which no human being can deny wherever and whenever he lives, the imprint of a theomorphic nature[vi] which no historical change and transformation can erase completely from the face of that creature called man.

SEYYED HOSSEIN NASR[47]

---

vi 'Theomorphic', is the antithesis of anthropomorphic. It means having divine form, formed in the image of deity, and endued with an unchangeable divine aspect.

Than the powers, the impulses are higher;
Than the impulses, Mind is higher;
Than Mind, Soul is higher; than Soul, the Great Self.
Than the Great Self, the Unmanifest is higher;
Than the Unmanifest, Spirit is higher;
This is the end, the supreme way.

KĀṬHAKA UPANIṢAD[48]

NOTES

1   Percy Bysshe Shelley, *The Revolt of Islam* (London: C. and J. Ollier, 1818), Canto XI, st. 18.
2   Seyyed Hossein Nasr Quotes <https://quotlr.com/author/seyyed-hossein-nasr> accessed 6 November 2020.
3   Jnanavatar Swami Sri Yuteswar Giri, *The Holy Science* (Los Angeles, California: Self-Realization Fellowship), 1990.
4   *Collins English Dictionary – Complete and Unabridged* (12th edn, HarperCollins Publishers, 2014). See also *American Heritage Dictionary of the English Language* (5th edn, Boston, Massachusetts: Houghton Mifflin, 2011).
5   Paramahansa Yogananda, *Autobiography of a Yogi*, preface by W. Y. Evans-Wentz MA, DLitt, DSc (1946; rev. 1951; Bombay, India: Jaico Publishing House with Self-Realization Fellowship, Los Angeles, California, 1972), 248–58.
6   Swami Sri Yuteswar Giri, *The Holy Science*, 3.
7   —— *op. cit.*, 6.
8   *SD*-I, 'Proem', 14. Note: *The Secret Doctrine* by H. P. Blavatsky presents an aspect of the Secret Doctrine—a fragament from the Book of Universal wisdom.
9   *SD*-I, 'Proem', 15.
10 Isaac Newton, *Philosophiæ Naturalis Principia Mathematica* (Mathematical Principles of Natural Philosophy), trans. Andrew Motte, rev. Florian Cajori, 2 vols (Berkeley, Los Angeles: University of California Press, 1962), ii, 'The System of the World – General Scholium', 545–6.
11 —— *op. cit.*, 546.
12 *ibid.*
13 Walter Russell: *Universal Law, Natural Science and Philosophy: Lesson Number 17* (Swannanoa, Virginia, The Walter Russell Foundation, 1951), 310; *The Message of the Divine Iliad*, 2 vols (The University of Science and Philosophy, 1971), i, 33 [online repr.] <https://ia801608.us.archive.org/23/items/THEMESSAGEOFTHEDIVINEILIADVol.11/THE_MESSAGE_OF_THE_DIVINE_ILIAD-Vol.1_1.pdf> accessed 28 April 2020.
14 *SD*-I, 'Proem', 17.
15 Paul Davies, *The Mind of God: The scientific basis for a rational world* (UK: Simon & Schuster, 1993). Davies was awarded the Templeton Prize (1995), an annual award granted to a living person who, in the estimation of the judges, 'has made an exceptional contribution to affirming life's spiritual dimension, whether through insight, discovery, or practical works.'
16 Stephen Hawking, *A Brief History of Time* (London: Bantam Press, 1988), 175.
17 Albert Einstein in Brief, *American Institute of Physics* <https://history.aip.org/exhibits/einstein/inbrief.htm> accessed 28 April 2020.
18 Marcus E. Raichle, 'The Brain's Dark Energy', *Scientific American* (March 2010), 28–33.
19 Anil Seth, 'Your Brain Hallucinates Your Conscious Reality', TED conference, Vancouver, Canada, 2017 <https://www.ted.com/talks/anil_seth_your_brain_hallucinates_your_conscious_reality?language=en> accessed 28 June 2020.
20 William Edward Soothill, *The Three Religions of China: Lectures delivered at Oxford (1913)*, trans. James Legge (Cornell University Library, 25 June 2009), 75. See also John Algeo, 'The Voice of the Silence 2 (Verses 6–32)', *Theosophy Forward* (2 December 2011) <https://

www.theosophyforward.com/theosophy/39-articles/theosophy/510-the-voice-of-the-silence-2-verses-6-32> accessed 28 April 2020.

21 Lewis Carroll, *Through the Looking-Glass, and What Alice Found There* (London: Macmillan and Co., 1872).

22 *CW*-XII, 'E. S. Instruction No. I', 528.

23 *SD*-II, 'Conclusion', 446.

24 '*The Secret Doctrine* and Its Study', in *Madame Blavatsky on How to Study Theosophy* (London: Theosophical Publishing House, 1960), 6, from the Bowen Notes, being extracts from the notes of personal teachings given by H.P. Blavatsky to private pupils during the years 1888 to 1891.

25 Paul Brunton, *In Search of Secret India* (London: Rider, 1934; York Beach, Maine: Samuel Weiser Inc., 1994), 272. A few weeks after this stern admonition, Brunton achieved his glorious spiritual illumination in the presence of Śrī Ramana Maharshi at Arunachala.

26 Seyyed Hossein Nasr, *Knowledge and the Sacred* (New York: State University of New York Press, 1989), 129.

27 Tejobindu Upaniṣad, Chapter 3.

28 Quoted in Prof G. R. Jain, *Cosmology: Old and new* (New Delhi: Bharatiya Jnanpith Publication, 1991), xxvi–xxvii.

29 *CW*-XII, 'E. S. T. Instructions', 477–713.

30 Henk J. Spierenburg (compiled and annotated), *The Inner Group Teachings of H. P. Blavatsky* (San Diego, California: Point Loma Publications, 1995). This work incorporates, in large measure, the Esoteric Instructions.

31 Nicholas Goodrick-Clarke, *Helena Blavatsky* (Berkeley, California: North Atlantic Books, 2004), 175–194.

32 —— *op. cit.*, 176.

33 —— *op. cit.*, 177.

34 —— *op. cit.* 163, extracted from *CW*-XII, 'E. S. Instruction No. I', facing page 524.

35 *CW*-XII, 'E. S. Instruction No. I', 525.

36 *CW*-XII, *op. cit.*, 526.

37 *CW*-XII, *op. cit.*, 526–7.

38 *STA*, 'The Human Body in Symbolism', LXXVI.

39 *STA*, *op. cit.* quoting from Ralph Waldo Emerson, 'Essay IX: The Over-Soul', in *Essays, First Series* (US: BiblioLife, 2009).

40 *KT*, 'The Physical and the Spiritual Man', 102.

41 Paul Brunton, *In Search of Secret Egypt* (London: Rider and Company, 1954), 74.

42 Frederic W. H. Myers, *Human Personality and Its Survival of Bodily Death*, 2 vols (London, New York, Bombay: Longman, Green, and Co., 1903), ii, 316.

43 *STA*, 'The Human Body in Symbolism', LXXV.

44 Joy Mills, *Reflections on an Ageless Wisdom – A Commentary on* The Mahatma Letters to A. P. Sinnett, foreword by Edward Abdill (Wheaton, Illinois: Theosophical Publishing House, 2010).

45 Adapted and rephrased from: *SD*-I, 'Stanza VII—*Continued*: Spirit Falling into Matter', 224, 225; Geoffrey Barborka, *The Divine Plan* (2nd edn, rev. and enl., Adyar, Madras: Theosophical Publishing House, 1964; repr. 1980), 59, 60, 61.

46 John F. Kennedy, *Daily New Quotes* <https://www.dailynewquotes.com/john-f-kennedy.html> accessed 28 April 2020.

47 Seyyed Hossein Nasr, *Knowledge and the Sacred: Revisioning academic accountability* (New York: State University of New York Press, 1989), 162.

48 Kāṭhaka Upaniṣad, I, 3. See also 'Precursors of H.P.B. – The Three Fundamental Concepts of Emerson's Philosophy', *Theosophy*, 24/2 (December 1935), 49–54 <http://blavatsky.net/Wisdomworld/setting/emersontwo.html> accessed 17 December 2019.

8 From External Sensation to Internal Experience – the Subjective Perception of an Objective Universe

The 'Schrödinger Mind–Sensation Problem' can be formulated thus –

It [science] cannot tell us a word about red and blue, bitter and sweet, physical pain and physical delight; it knows nothing of beautiful and ugly, good or bad, God and eternity.

Science cannot tell us a word about why music delights us, of why and how an old song can move us to tears. Science, we believe, can, in principle, describe in full detail all that happens in the latter case in our sensorium and 'motorium' from the moment the waves of compression and dilation reach our ear[s] to the moment when certain glands secrete a salty fluid that emerges from our eyes. But of the feelings of delight and sorrow that accompany the process, science is completely ignorant—and therefore reticent.

SCHRÖDINGER[1]

SYNOPSIS
Chapter 8 addresses the whole issue of the mind–sensation problem and shows how occult science alone is able to resolve the major conundrum that currently plagues neuroscience: to discover a neural correlate of consciousness—how external and objective input to the physical senses of, say, electromagnetic waves on the retina, or air waves on the eardrum, can result in an internal and subjective *experience* of colour or sound. Overriding factors that cause confusion are first considered followed by a stepwise account of the overall process of emanation from Divine Consciousness to the human being on Earth. The approach, therefore, is entirely 'top-down'. As per the Hermetic Axiom, the correspondences and resonances between Universal Mind and individual minds, and how perception results in sensation, are detailed. The clinching issue regarding the 'conversion' of neurology into experience is then laid bare. As this is another complex Chapter, a résumé highlights the chief factors in the resolution of problems in neuroscience by occult science. The resolution of the mind–sensation puzzle is taken a step further in the next Chapter.

KEY WORDS: mind–sensation problem, neural correlate, neural transducer, space, time, illusion, differentiation, consciousness–matter, subject–object, Divine Mind, Archetypal Man, Primoridial Matter, individual mind, mathematics, Cosmic Elements, perception to sensation, vitalism and nervous ether, consciousness and its forms, Isaac Newton, William Shakespeare, Erwin Schrödinger

The emanational process of descent from Divine Consciousness (*Ātma*, the Divine Self, its correspondence in man), to the human body with its five physical sense organs was delineated in broad terms in the previous Chapter. This Chapter deals with the resolution by occult science of what may aptly be called the 'Schrödinger Mind–Sensation Problem'. Succinctly identified by Schrödinger, as evinced in the epigraph to Volume I, Chapter 4 dealing with limitations in the viewpoint of modern science, it is restated, in part, in the epigraph to this Chapter due to its crucial insight. It is one of the thorniest conundrums in contemporary neuroscience, highlighting the whole question of how and why an entirely subjective, internal, and conscious *experience* arises from:

- ❖ external, quantifiable input to the physical senses;
- ❖ moreover, even just the thought about an event or prior experience, without any external input to the five physical senses.

Specifying the Schrödinger Mind–Sensation problem

What follows is a broad treatment about the actual mechanisms of sensation. As stressed earlier, to discover a neural correlate of consciousness and thereby to solve the problem of the experience of sensation are currently white hot topics of scientific debate and neuro-scientific research, both theoretical and experimental. It is associated with the 'hard' problem of consciousness. What exactly does this mean? Let us first clearly state the nature of the problem.

The Schrödinger Mind–Sensation Problem – Identifying Specific Issues

The problem for science is to do with finding a neural mechanism for sensation. In terms of the Schrödinger Mind–Sensation Problem, how do we 'see' colours, for example, the colour red? Stating the case more accurately, how is it that we see red, or experience red, as a visual sensation of colour? It is important, therefore, to be clear about the nature of the conundrum, which may be paraphrased thus: 'I am looking at a red rose. I know that red has a wavelength of 700 nanometres, i.e., 700 billionths of a metre, and a frequency of approximately 428×10^{12} (428 trillion) cycles per second. But my eyes can just about discern to the level of a split hair, around 10 micrometres (one hundred thousandth of a metre), let alone to the finesse of billionths of a metre; nor can I distinguish trillionths of cycles per second with my eyes. So how then do I *experience* the *sensation* of the colour red? Furthermore, I can shut my eyes and still "see" the red rose and experience its beauty, perfume, and symmetry. So what is the neural correlate from the visual perception of the frequency and wavelength of the colour red, to red as a sensation? Moreover, how is it that I have only to think or imagine red with my eyes, either open or closed, in order to "see" red? Likewise, I know from the science of acoustics that music is just sonorous air, so why do vibrations in the air striking my eardrums stir *feelings* of delight or sorrow? But how is it that the mere thought of my favourite tune can also move me to tears when no music is actually playing? What is the neural correlate from external aural perception, or even just the thought of music, to the internal, subjective experience?'

From objective facts to subjective experience

Neuroscience and cognitive science have not, by their own admission (see Volume I, Chapters 2 to 4), come up with a satisfactory answer even after decades of massive research. However much they may have identified specific regions in the brain and associated cerebral mechanisms related to vision and the other senses, the question of how that transforms to sensation, as an experience, has doggedly eluded these scientific disciplines. So let us give occult science a fair hearing. The detail is highly complex and need not concern us here, as there are erudite expositions in the occult literature,[2] but the process can be outlined. Even a hazy understanding is preferable to the cul-de-sac of materialistic hypotheses. One of the sources of confusion is a failure to distinguish between correlates and transducers. This necessarily leads to a blurring of meaning. Some precise definitions of these terms in relation to consciousness would therefore be apposite.

Defining What We Mean – Discerning Neural Correlate from Neural Transducer of Consciousness

In Chapter 5 the distinctions of meaning between the terms analogy, correspondence, and correlate were explained. Regarding a neural correlate of consciousness, this implies that consciousness (although still virtually an unknown phenomenon to science) must somehow be related to neurology, hence of the same type or order as neurology pertaining to the plane of physical substance only. Bearing this in mind, then, a neural correlate of consciousness constitutes the minimal set of neuronal events and mechanisms sufficient for a specific conscious percept. Neuroscientists use empirical approaches to discover neural correlates of subjective phenomena. Accordingly, the neuronal set should be minimal because, under the assumption that the brain is sufficient to give rise to any given conscious experience, the question is, which of its components is only just necessary to produce it? Hence, a neural correlate of the content of experience is any bodily component, such as an electro-neuro-biological state or the state assumed by some biophysical subsystem of the brain, whose presence necessarily and regularly correlates with such a specific content of experience.

How neuroscience understands neural correlates

Conversely, the term 'transducer' means a device that receives a signal in the form of one type of energy and converts it to a signal in another form; for example, a microphone is a transducer that converts acoustic energy into electrical impulses. The transducer therefore acts as the interface, or nexus, to enable the transmission of something that exists at one level, to another level. Here, the two levels are not of the same class or category, even though both may be physical.

Neuroscience barely considers the transducing function

A science of consciousness must explain the exact relationship between subjective mental states and objectively measurable brain states, in other words, the nature of the relationship between the conscious mind and the electro-chemical interactions in the body. Neurobiology focusses on the body and the mind (of course, equating the mind with the brain). In this context and *from the perspective of neuroscience*, consciousness may be thought of as a state-dependent property of some undefined complex, adaptive, and highly interconnected biological system, and the neuronal correlates of consciousness may be viewed as its causes. Because of its practically exclusive focus on neural correlates of consciousness, neuroscience has barely embraced the notion of what we may term 'neural transducers' of consciousness.

The Chief Impediments to Understanding

Why is neuroscience currently experiencing such difficulties and virtually intractable problems in finding a neural correlate of consciousness? There are fundamentally three reasons:

1. The erroneous assumptions, and ensuing perceptions, about the relation between the senses and the mind.
2. The limited outlook on the whole constitution of man.
3. The failure to distinguish consciousness from its vehicles ('bodies') of expression.

Regarding the first, mainstream neuroscience adamantly maintains that the senses are the basic reality and that the mind, being a product of the senses, is therefore subordinate to the sense organs. In fact, it is the other way round in occult psychology, as Chapter 7 showed in detail. The simile of the queen bee and the other bees in the hive is used in Yoga philosophy to illustrate two factors regarding the relation between the senses and the mind: (*a*) that the body, brain, and senses are extensions, or projections, of the mind; and therefore, (*b*) like the bees in the hive, are subordinate to the mind (the 'queen bee'). Stated otherwise, the mind works through the instrumentality of the sense organs via the sensory mechanisms of the physical body.

Is mind the product of the senses?

The second reason above is highlighted by Schrödinger's observations on the realm of sensation, mentioned earlier. To recapitulate, he admits that science understands the detailed mechanisms and processes whereby an external stimulus impinging upon a sense organ, like sound waves upon the ears, are then converted into nervous/nerve impulses, which are transmitted to the corresponding centres in the physical brain; but he laments the complete inability of science to explain how nervous/nerve impulses that are purely electro-physical are transformed into the experience of sensation—sensuous images that are entirely mental. Now this inability of science is due to its viewpoint constrained to the physical domain only, by virtue of its determined resistance to blend physics with metaphysics so as to investigate the whole constitution of man, namely, the physical frame alongside his non-physical counterparts. By contrast, occult science has investigated the whole length and breadth of the constitution and function of man and is therefore qualified to pronounce on this physical-to-mental conundrum for science.

Neuroscience is constrained by its own presuppositions

The third reason stems from the unwarranted assumption that the vehicle, i.e., the brain, is the mechanism considered to produce thought, and consciousness is an epiphenomenon, or emergent property, of material processes in the brain (see William James's lecture on human immortality summarized in Volume I, Chapter 6, page 167 et seq.).

Neuroscience is also constrained by its unsupportable assumptions

So even if, hypothetically, a satisfactory neural correlate were found, it could not in any way explain the nature of sensation or experience. A neural correlate is just that: at best, it can be mapped onto the mental, but it cannot, of itself, account for the transfer from quantifiable data about physical states (like frequencies) to the associated mental sensation. For that to happen we need to invoke a special kind of substance for converting, strictly speaking, transducing, physical nervous impulses into mental sensations.

Steps Towards a Resolution of the Problem of Sensate Experience

What follows is a stepwise account of the process that converts sense perception into sensed experience. The route map presented overleaf in tabular format should assist the reader to navigate what is necessarily a complex subject. Although every endeavour has been made to present the main ideas in the simplest form and, as far as possible, in the sequence and connection in which they originate, we must bear in mind that we are grappling with one of the subtlest mysteries of life.

Major section	Subject matter	Intended purpose
Overriding Considerations	• To introduce three key ideas providing the framework for the ensuing narrative.	• To provide context. • To remove extraneous factors that inhibit or obfuscate clarity of understanding. • To explain key precepts.
Space, Time, and the Role of Māyā in Emanational Manifestation	• The role of space and time in the production of *māyā*, or 'illusion', in existence. • The difference between the absolute and the relative and its exemplification in science and literature.	• To explain the difference between appearance and reality. • To discern the Absolute from the relative.
Consciousness–Matter and Subject–Object Relationships	• The genesis of the Mind Principle.	• To explain how a seemingly objective reality can be perceived as something outside the perceiver.
Distinguishing Consciousness from its Forms	• The discrimination between a principle and its medium of expression.	• To clarify a main source of confusion in neuroscience.
The Overall Process of Emanation	• The principal elements in the mechanism of sense perception.	• To provide a route map through the diverse elements of the emanational process, and their inter-relationships.
Restating the Problem of Sense Perception and Experience	• Setting out the rationale for the two cardinal doctrines to explain the subjective, mental experience of an objective, physical world.	• To re-focus on the exact nature of the mind–sensation problem that is being addressed.
The Interaction of Divine Mind with Individual Mind	• The mental experience of an individual and its source. • The relation between the internal mental world and the external physical world of an individual. • Analogy with a broadcasting station to explain interaction between Divine Mind and individual minds.	• To explain how the mental world of an individual arises.

Section	Content	Aim
From Perception to Sensation and the Role of Cosmic Elements	• The whole process of emanational descent showing all stages from the spiritual to the physical: – The main stages in the descent of functioning principles. – The correspondences between functioning principles. – The correlation between the subjective and objective aspects of mind. • The role of the Cosmic Elements. • The perception of the physical universe.	• To depict the progressive flow-down and correspondence of functioning principles from the spiritual to the physical. • To explain the role of the Cosmic Elements whereby an experience in the mind of the individual is produced by perception of an objective, physical world.
The Perception of the Physical Universe	• The sensory and motoric (active and passive) instruments of perception of the outside world.	• To show how the subjective perception of an objective universe arises.
The Transmutation from Neurology to Experience – Vitalism and the Nervous Ether	• The need for a vital principle. • The role of *prāṇa* as the vehicle of vital force. • The nervous system and its relation to prāṇa.	• To explain the *modus operandi* to resolve the Schrödinger Mind–Sensation Problem.
Non-instrumental Perception and Action	• The meaning of non-instrumental perception and non-instrumental action. • The results ensuing when consciousness is freed from the hindrance of its vehicles of expression. • Insights into near-death experiences.	• To explain the significance of the complexity and simplicity of the vehicles of consciousness.
Résumé	• To summarize the impasse that neuroscience, unaided by occult science, is unable to bridge.	• The implications for neuroscience.
The Interface Between Neuroscience and Consciousness – Its Implications	• How occult science supplies the missing links to resolve the Schrödinger Mind–Sensation Problem.	• To highlight the need to distinguish consciousness from its vehicles of expression.
Problems in Neuroscience Resolved by Occult Science	• The three cardinal inputs of occult science: (a) the role of Space and Time; (b) how the Subject–Object relationship appears; and (c) how internal, subjective experience arises.	• To summarize the resolution by occult science of the Schrödinger Mind–Sensation Problem.

This mystery concerns the relations between consciousness, mind, and matter. Given their strongly interrelated nature, the problem must be treated as a whole; what is organic and undivided cannot be tackled in three isolated parts. Moreover, it is not reasonable to expect a withholding of difficulties that are inherent to a basic understanding of the subject. Such difficulties are of two kinds. First, they are largely of our own making in that they arise from the domination of concepts promulgated in modern society as self-evident truths—but which are, in fact, presuppositions—by mainstream science about a mechanistic paradigm of existence, as explained fully in Chapters 2 and 3 of Volume I. The second difficulty arises from the nature of the problem itself. It is unrealistic to expect cut-and-dried solutions, or precise concepts, as is generally possible in the case of physical phenomena. Hence, a simple, linear, one-to-one relational explanation is not viable on a subject that is multi-dimensional across a wide range of interfaces.

Interrelated problems can only be tackled holistically

Accordingly, in the interests of clarity, it is inevitable that elegance of presentation must occasionally be sacrificed to some measure of reiteration of principal themes—the proverbial moving one step back in order to move three steps forward. Furthermore, any consideration of the detailed and intricate mechanisms at this stage is more likely to cause confusion than lead to an understanding of the subject. Let us, therefore, confine ourselves to the general principles, and what stands in the way of their understanding. It is important to set the scene with a summary of overriding factors before describing the process.

The salient features of this Chapter are a distillation of the relevant sections from the following profoundest sources of occult science and amplified with other material as referenced:

❖ H. P. Blavatsky, *The Secret Doctrine*, The Theosophical Publishing House, 1950.
❖ I. K. Taimni, *Man, God and the Universe*, The Theosophical Publishing House, 1974.
❖ Geoffrey Barborka, *The Divine Plan*, The Theosophical Publishing House, 1980.
❖ Jnanavatar Swami Sri Yuteswar Giri, *The Holy Science*, Self-Realization Fellowship, 1990.

Overriding Considerations

The significance of what was termed *māyā*, or the Lord's illusory power in the whole scheme of emanational emergence, was described in the previous Chapter with comparable aphorisms from Sāṁkhya philosophy and the Bible. The next section of this Chapter elucidates what exactly is meant by such apparently simple terms as 'appearance' and 'illusory power'. The doctrine of māyā is one of the most elusive in occult metaphysics but its importance cannot be overestimated. Its basis was outlined, in broad terms, in the previous Chapter and is taken further in the following section.

Thereafter follows a brief account on the genesis of the subject–object duality, which lies at the basis of the relation between the observer and the observed.

Finally, a clarification about one of the most common sources of confusion in neuroscience and philosophy of mind: a failure to distinguish consciousness from its innumerable forms. Stated otherwise, a blurring of a principle—the active, positive agent—with its vehicle—the passive, negative medium of expression. Warning against this confusion, but to little avail, the great neurologist Sir Francis Walshe explicitly said, 'it would be quite childish to identify the instrument with its user, even though the user be dependent upon the instrument for operating.'[3] (See Chapter 7 in Volume II for a fuller account of Walshe's arguments.)

Space, Time, and the Role of Māyā in Emanational Manifestation

The reader could justifiably take issue with the apparent clumsiness of the above section title. Why not use the simple word 'creation' instead of 'emanational manifestation'? For good reason. The term is used in order to accentuate the point made in the previous Chapter that creation, strictly speaking, is a misnomer. In the truest sense, nothing is ever created. Creation, so-called, is really a process of emanational emergence, which literally means 'to flow out and bring forth'[i]—from Divine Consciousness, or the Unmanifest— to its manifested appearances on various planes of descent culminating in the physical. An outline of how māyā arises in the overall emanational process is now presented. It is an important prelude to an understanding of how internal, subjective experiences of sensation can arise from external, objective input to the five physical senses.

Figure III-26 on page 143 attempts to portray how the limitless diversity of manifestation is subsumed in Divine Consciousness—REALITY, the Ultimate Reality, the Unmanifest are all parallel terms. Shown on the top half of the diagram, Ultimate Space and Eternal Duration (*Mahākāśa* and *Mahākala*) are not a duality, but ultimate principles of Space/Time fully harmonized and integrated in the Unmanifest. What manifests, however, can never be divorced from when such an event happens. Thus, the bottom half of the diagram shows that the '*what*' in space, and its correlate, the '*when*' in time are an inseparable couple in the realm of manifestation at any level.

The Unmanifest and the manifest

Thus, on the left side of Figure III-26, the different orders of space in manifestation on the different planes may be considered to be derived from the root of mental spaces designated as Ultimate Space, *Mahākāśa*. It is from this counterpart in the realm of the Unmanifest that the various mental spaces, *Chidākāśa*, may be considered to be derived by projection and differentiation as coloured lights are derived from the refraction of white light by a prism.[4]

In the manifest, space and time are correlated at all levels

And, as shown on the right side of Figure III-26, a similar relationship exists between the different measures of time in manifestation on the different planes and the ultimate principle of time designated as Eternal Duration, *Mahākala*, from which they may be considered to be derived by projection and differentiation. Therefore, the popular saying, 'time is an illusion', pertains to mental times in manifestation, *Kālas*, which are the products of mind, and not to that Ultimate Time of which they are the shadows derived.

Viewing Figure III-26 as a whole, Space pertains to the *formation* of mental images, whereas Time is the *succession* of these mental images in the Mind of the Logos (the *manifested* deity[ii]) or, by projection, in the mind of the individual. Therefore, both space and time in manifestation depend on the mind and its mental images. So, when the mind is without images,

---

i Etymologically, *emanate* means 'to flow out', from the Latin *emanatus*; and emerge means 'bring forth, bring to light', from the Latin *emergere*.

ii The Greek word *Logos* is a relative term. In its core meaning of the *manifested deity*, it is the outward expression, or the effect of the cause, which is ever concealed. Thus, speech is the Logos of thought. Hence, in its metaphysical sense, Logos is aptly translated by the '*Verbum*' and 'Word (of God)'. (See *TSGLOSS*, 190.)

there can be neither space nor time—only the Real. The various systems of yoga in the East, and meditation systems the world over, have this central aim: to quieten the mind (by whatever techniques) in order that Reality may be glimpsed, however dimly and fleetingly or for longer periods, depending on the depth and period of the mental silence.

In summary, Mahākāśa and Mahākala are the two aspects of REALITY which produce innumerable shadows of mental space and mental time on the different planes of manifestation. It is in the absolute stillness and silence of Mahākāśa/Mahākala that lie the Source and potentiality of the unceasing formation and succession of mental images in space and time which characterize all manifestation, in contradistinction to the changeless and timeless nature of the Unmanifest in which all space and time are subsumed.

The word 'shadows' is highly suggestive of that which is transitory and subject to change. Any manifested event is characterized by its intrinsic changeableness. Whether such change occurs in a fleeting moment, in years, or in aeons (corresponding roughly to the atomic level, human lifetime or planetary schemes) is not the issue, only the fact that it always happens. It is for this reason that the shadows of REALITY, always transitory, are regarded as appearances, or māyā.

Newton and Shakespeare on Space, Time, and Māyā

Newton had his finger on the metaphysical pulse when he avowed that there is nothing absolute in existence—except the Absolute (God). The multi-layered meanings artfully concealed within the legendary General Scholium from Book II of *Principia* (quoted in part in Chapter 5 of Volume II in a different context), one of the most celebrated God-affirming passages of all scientific literature, have been interminably scrutinized by academics and more often than not, twisted to accord with the prejudices of materialistic and atheistic scientists. Newton's statement cannot be understood other than by using the esoteric key to unlock its hidden meaning:

> The true God is a living, intelligent, and powerful Being; […] He is eternal and infinite, omnipotent and omniscient; that is, his duration reaches from eternity to eternity; his presence from infinity to infinity; […] He is not eternity and infinity, but eternal and infinite; he is not duration or space, but he endures and is present. He endures forever, and is everywhere present; and, by existing always and everywhere, he constitutes duration and space.[5]

Note, with every care, the subtle distinction between the words *eternity* and *eternal*, *infinity* and *infinite*, *duration* and *endures*. In terms of the above exposition (see Figure III-26 opposite) they point to: (*a*) the Ultimate Reality; (*b*) the distinction between Ultimate Space (Mahākāśa)/Eternal Duration (Mahākala) subsumed within the bosom of REALITY; and (*c*) Mental Spaces (Chidākāśa) and Mental Times (Kālas) constituting the innumerable space and time orders and dimensions of manifested existence as shadows of 'the true God'— the Ultimate Reality. In passing, the above passage, and others from the General Scholium, make it crystal clear that the true God is everlastingly involved in the universe, His emanation and manifested expression of Himself;[6] the popular idea that God 'created' the 'machine-universe' and then stood apart from it, other than capriciously tinkering with it occasionally, being total nonsense. It is quite deplorable that such 'mechanical universe' ideas are espoused by respected academics and writers from their reading of the General Scholium. For example, in the fine book *The Scientist and the Saint*, appropriately sub-titled *The Limits of Science*

Newton *never* advocated a mechanical, clockwork universe

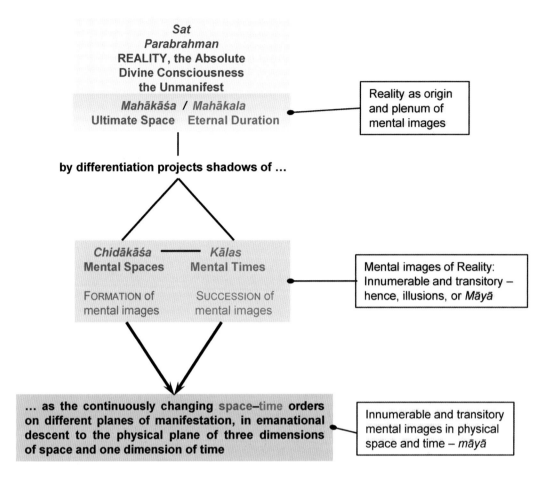

Figure III-26   The Role of Māyā in the Emanational Process

and the Testimony of Sages, it seems that for Newton, 'the universe was a large machine (comparable to a clock) [...].'[7]And in the ever-popular book The Tao of Physics, we are informed that 'such a mechanistic world view was held by Isaac Newton who constructed his mechanics on its basis [...].'[8] Such errors demonstrate the all-too-common error of confusing the description with the described (the 'map' with the 'territory'). What Newton provided was a mathematical map and he explicitly warned that it should not be confused with the reality it represented. At the outset of his Principia, in Definition VIII, Newton took the greatest care to make clear that he did not use the word 'attraction' with regard to the mutual action of bodies in a physical sense. To him it was, he said, a purely mathematical conception involving no consideration of real and primary physical or mechanical causes:

> I use the words attraction, impulse, or propensity of any sort towards a centre, promiscu-
> ously, indifferently, one for another; considering these forces not physically, but mathe-
> matically: wherefore the reader is not to imagine that by those words I anywhere take
> upon me to define the kind, or the manner of any action, the causes or the physical
> reason thereof, or that I attribute forces, in a true and physical sense, to certain centres
> (which are only mathematical points); [...].[9]

Indeed the very title of Newton's book that shook science to its core is Mathematical Principles of Natural Philosophy; it is emphatically not 'Mechanical (or Mechanistic) Principles of Natural Philosophy'.

As Newton, so also did Shakespeare (Francis Bacon?[iii]) affirm space and time as the playground of the *mayavic* nature of existence:

> All the world's a stage [*space*],
> And all the men and women merely players;
> They have their exits and their entrances [*time*],
> And one man [consciousness embodied] in his time plays many parts,
> His acts being seven ages.
>
> *As You Like It*: Act II, Scene 7

Consciousness–Matter and Subject–Object Relationships

As depicted in Figure III-26 on page 143, we may regard manifestation as a differentiation of the Unmanifest, or Ultimate Reality, using the word 'differentiation' in the widest sense of the term.

The primary (horizontal, so to speak) differentiation of the Ultimate Reality is the duality of *Śiva* (Pure, i.e. undifferentiated, Consciousness) and *Śakti* (Matter) its correlate. (*Śakti* is sometimes translated as Energy, or Power, but as modern science has shown, physical matter and energy are fundamentally two aspects of the One.)

Symbolic significance of the Cross

The secondary (vertical, so to speak) differentiation of the Ultimate Reality is the duality of *Sat* (Subject) and *Chit* (Object) its correlate (see the deeper significance of these terms in Chapter 7, Figure III-23 on page 103).

But how does this primary and secondary differentiation arise? What is their cause? What produces them? Two clues may be unearthed from the *The Secret Doctrine*.

The first comes from this maxim:

> That which is motionless cannot be Divine. But then there is nothing in fact and reality absolutely motionless […].[10]

Ceaseless Motion, then, is the basis of phenomenal manifestation, albeit not in a blind, mechanical sense. Blavatsky describes this Absolute Motion as 'the "Great Breath," which is the perpetual motion of the universe, in the sense of limitless, ever-present SPACE.'[11] Further elucidation is provided in *The Snake and the Rope*.[12]

Regarding the second clue, we reaffirm another maxim by Blavatsky, mentioned in the previous Chapter dealing with Sūtra 1, from *The Holy Science*:

> Parabrahman (the One Reality, the Absolute) is the field of Absolute Consciousness, *i.e.*, that Essence which is out of all relation to conditioned existence, and of which conscious existence is a conditioned symbol.[13]

The term 'field' is important. It is not saying that Parabrahman, the Absolute *is* Absolute Consciousness; rather that the former constitutes the playground (i.e., field) of the latter. Blavatsky continues:

---

iii The Shakespeare/Francis Bacon controversy is well documented in: Mark Twain, *Is Shakespeare Dead?* (New York: Harper & Brothers Publishers, 1909); Peter A. Dawkins, *The Shakespeare Enigma: Unravelling the story of the two poets* (UK: Polair Publishing, 2004).

> But once that we pass in thought from this (to us) Absolute Negation, duality supervenes
> in the contrast of Spirit (or consciousness [Consciousness]) and Matter [the primary
> differentiation], Subject and Object [the secondary differentiation].
>
> Spirit (or Consciousness) and Matter are, however, to be regarded, not as independent
> realities, but as the two facets or aspects of the Absolute (Parabrahman), which constitute
> the basis of conditioned Being whether subjective or objective.[14]

These ideas are represented in Figure III-27 below by the Cross, a universal symbol conveying
its meaning at many levels. But for our purposes, the horizontal arm signifies the primary
differentiation of the Absolute, or REALITY, into *Śiva–Śakti* (Consciousness–Matter) and
the vertical arm, the secondary differentiation into the *Sat–Chit* (Subject–Object) relationship. By their action and reaction, and incessant balancing of opposites, these horizontal and
vertical counterparts weave the fabric of the universe. In the Zohar the universe is called 'the
garment of God' woven from His own Substance. This is also eloquently expressed by the
German theosopher, Goethe in his tragic play *Faust*, in which Erdgeist—the Spirit of the
Earth—is depicted as a timeless being who endlessly weaves at the 'Loom of Time', both in
life and in death, and is the means by which the immaterial becomes manifest:

> 'Tis thus at the roaring Loom of Time I ply
> And weave for God the garment thou seest Him by.[15]

The emanation of a universe as an objective Reality, which can be perceived as something
outside the perceiver, is therefore the product of the Subject–Object relationship birthing
two streams, out of itself; one stream on the basis of subjective phenomena and the other
on the basis of objective phenomena—the former relating to the perceiv*er* and the latter
to the perceiv*ed*. These two streams, both deriving from the differentiation of REALITY
(the Ultimate Reality, or Integrated Consciousness), 'descend', in the sense of externalize,
plane by plane, until they reach the physical plane and terminate in the senses and the
agents that stimulate the sense organs, known as *indriyas* and *bhūtas*, respectively. It is at
the junction of the indriyas and bhūtas that the subjective and objective streams meet.

How the
Subject–Object
(Seer–Seen)
relationship arises

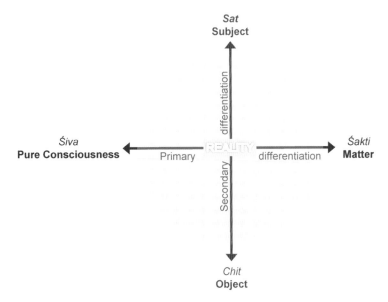

Figure III-27   The Cross Symbolizes the Primary and Secondary
Differentiations of REALITY

The clue to the doctrine that the universe is a phenomenon in and of consciousness lies, therefore, in the nature of the indriya *and* bhūta *streams of consciousness.* This is further explained shortly with the aid of a schematic diagram which shows that, for any mental phenomenon, there has to be a subject, as 'seer' and object of perception as the 'seen', that arises out of the seer and is bound up with it in a polar relationship of some kind.

The appearance, by differentiation, of the Subject–Object relation in Integrated Consciousness is what gives birth to the Mind Principle. In terms of Sāṁkhya philosophy, a mental world appears out of the integrated Sat aspect, due to the functioning of the Chit aspect, and as a result of this, the relation of Self and not-Self is established between the two. This is the root and basis of the Mind Principle *per se* and all mental phenomena and mental operations, from the highest to the lowest (i.e., from the spiritual to the material), that are derived from it. Thus, the whole gamut of Mental phenomena ranges from Cosmic Ideation to Divine Ideation, and thenceforward to individual ideation, all being the expression of the Mind Principle in both its subjective and objective aspects at different levels, or planes, of manifestation. Meanwhile it is important to distinguish the same principle in the realm of the Unmanifest, and in the manifest as shown below in Table III-5 below.

How the Mind Principle arises (margin note)

Distinguishing Consciousness from its Forms

Given that mainstream neuroscience adopts virtually an exclusively 'bottom-up' process from inert matter (regarded as the primary) to consciousness (an epiphenomenon), then how the interactions of matter and physical nervous/nerve impulses can give rise to conscious mental experience must remain a perpetual puzzle for which the only way out would be to seek a supposed neural correlate of consciousness. In this stance, the neural mechanism is conflated with its supposed by-product, consciousness; that is, the physical vehicle of expression is confused with its active governing principle (which error the neurologist Francis Walshe clearly perceived as stated earlier).

The perennial philosophy works from the general to the particular (margin note)

Embracing the 'top-down' approach of the *philosophia perennis* of all cultures since time immemorial, also adopted by enlightened science, the progression is then: consciousness → mind → matter. Ironically (for science), matter could be regarded as an epiphenomenon of consciousness, and not the other way round as science assumes. So on this basis, brain exists in the realm of physical matter: it is the form taken by mind, acting as its vehicle of conscious expression on the physical plane. Mind is the 'form' taken by consciousness, acting as its vehicle of expression on the mental plane. 'Form' and 'vehicle' are thus relative terms,

Table III-5   Correlates of Mind and Matter in the Unmanifest and the Manifest

Unmanifest		
Śiva	— correlate of —	*Śakti*
Manifest		
Puruṣa in its triple aspect of *Sat-Chit-Ānanda* – the root of Mind.	— correlate of —	*Prakṛiti* in its triple aspect of the Guṇas: *Tamas-Rājas-Sattva* – the root of Matter.

Note: See the reference in Chapter 7, page 111 to *Puruṣas* (in the plural) as reflections of spiritual rays, called the Sons of God.

functioning on different levels, and convey the same generic meaning as soul—see Volume II, Chapter 3, page 45.

The difference between consciousness and its forms, or vehicles, is easily illustrated by way of analogy. Let us imagine a beautiful sphere made of gold. The same amount of gold could be melted down and converted into an assortment of cheap-looking trinkets and ornaments or could be fashioned into the form of a dagger to kill someone. So, what was once the perfect form of a sphere can be converted into meaningless ornaments or a weapon of destruction. But in this conversion into articles of different forms and uses, has the basic nature of the underlying substance altered? Obviously not one bit. The different forms and shapes have diverted our attention from the reality of the basic substance— the gold. Or, take another more abstract example—a fountain pen. We can use the pen to sign a peace treaty to end a war or to sign a declaration of war. The first act engenders harmony and reconciliation; the second a declaration of bloodshed. But the ink and the pen are the same. If the results are contrary to our expectations, shall we blame the ink, the pen and the paper—or the writer? This is the sort of thing that happens when consciousness is transformed into the modifications of mind. We get distracted by the innumerable, illusory forms assumed by mind and lose sight of the medium, the consciousness itself, the basic 'substance' from which the modifications of the mind are derived and in which the mental images are formed. It is somewhat like being so engrossed by the fleeting pictures at the cinema that we lose sight of the screen as the permanent backdrop, not to mention the light and projector, film and film script. All these analogies may help to explain the meaning of Verse 6.8.7 of the Chandogya Upaniṣad: *Tat Tvam Asi*,[16] translated variously as 'That art thou', 'That thou art', 'Thou art that', 'You are that', or 'That you are'. Simply stated, all is made out of the basic substance which is Divine Consciousness. The same idea expressed in Verse 3.14.1 is 'Verily this manifested universe is nothing but Brahman'.[iv] It is not merely a speculative philosophical doctrine, but a truth to which modern science inexorably points.[v] It affirms that:

> One substance can have innumerable forms

1. The basis of the universe, or what we call the Ultimate Reality, is Divine (Supreme) Consciousness.
2. The mind itself is a phenomenon in the basic medium of consciousness, being a modification of consciousness presenting as energetic intelligence, or intelligent energy, so to speak.
3. Matter, or crystallized energy, is of the essential nature of mind, which explains why matter is never inert but displays intelligent action at its own level, as shown by chemistry; hence the physical universe of Matter is, in essence, a purely mental phenomenon without any intrinsic physical–material basis at all, which quantum science has conclusively shown (see Max Planck's dictum in the Proem, page xxxiii).

In that case, how do we account for the sensed experience (internal and subjective) of an apparently external and objective material world composed of particles and atoms outside us? This is addressed later in the section entitled 'From Perception to Sensation – The Role of Cosmic Elements'. However, point 3. above provides a clue.

---

iv It is important to distinguish sharply between *Brahman* and *Brahmā*. The former refers to the Unmanifested Logos, or the impersonal and incognizable principle of the Universe; the latter to the spiritual energy–consciousness of the manifested universe or solar systems.

v See Volume II, Chapter 1, page 9 explaining how this legendary maxim has been misused.

The Overall Process of Emanation

At the outset, it is as well to clarify that emanation is not the same as evolution—nor creation, as previously explained. As noted earlier, the word emanation derives from the Latin *emanatus* meaning 'to flow out', namely, 'to pour forth', or 'to pour out of'—the mode by which all things are derived from REALITY, the First Principle. Hence, all derived, or secondary things proceed or flow from the more primary. (Evolution, meaning the unwrapping, or unfolding, of latent powers within the entity itself, is dealt with later in Chapter 10.)

Having then set the scene, we are now in a position to outline the fundamentals in the mechanism of sense perception. First, in order to focus our enquiry, it would be useful to restate the problem that we are addressing in a somewhat different manner to that given earlier in this Chapter.

Restating the Problem of Sense Perception and Experience

As just explained, the appearance of a 'spiritual' universe in the Ultimate (Unmanifest) Reality depends on the secondary (vertical) differentiation resulting in the Subject–Object relationship in Integrated Consciousness (see Figure III-27 on page 145) whereby Divine Mind comes into existence, such that Divine Ideation is made possible. But on the lower planes, we have to take account of the perception and experience of an apparently physical and objective world outside us composed of innumerable material particles, like atoms and molecules, and the interactions between them.

The explanation for this phenomenon rests on two cardinal doctrines: (*a*) that the mental world of an individual is generally the result of the interaction of Divine Mind with the individual mind; and (*b*) the conjunction of the senses with the Cosmic Elements as stimulators of the senses, which is part of Yogic psychology. Both doctrines demand a careful, progressive explanation in order to avoid confusion.

The Interaction of Divine Mind with Individual Mind

Regarding the first doctrine, let us begin with some overriding precepts.

Individual Mind Mirrors Divine Mind

> We might begin by comparing the mind to a mirror. A mirror appears to have objects within it, yet it does not. What we see in the mirror are only images, illusions, reflections. In the same way, the mind knows only the illusive images of the universe, not things themselves.
>
> Annie Besant[17]

It is the impact and mirroring of Universal, Divine Mind on our individual minds that are, in most cases, responsible for our individual mental worlds. It is because the world process has its origin in Divine Ideation that, quite naturally, each individual will receive his own impression of the process according to his position in space and time: hence, those who occupy the same position will receive similar impressions. Such positioning of course means mental positioning—mental co-ordinates, so to speak—which accounts for the similarity (but not sameness) of experiences of different individuals, coloured and conditioned by the development and sensitivity of their own individual minds (receiving apparatus, so to say). Throughout history, there are cases of minds attuned to a common high purpose that will produce works of art or science having a common exalted characteristic. For example, in music the genre of the Nocturne was conceived by both the Irish composer and pianist John Field (1782–1837) and the Polish composer and virtuoso pianist Frederick Chopin (1810–1849). Whereas Chopin may indeed have used the compositions by Field as a model, it is simply not a case of either one copying the other. In science, the calculus was the invention of both Newton and Leibnitz, independently, pondering over similar issues in mathematics. Both were definitely in correspondence which may well have stimulated ideas but not provided the final outcome that could only have occurred for the reason that both individual minds were attuned to a common higher purpose. Newton also corresponded extensively on related issues with the English clergyman Richard Bentley (1662–1742). But, as a result, did Bentley invent the calculus?

Individual mind mirrors Divine Mind

Three Mental Currents

Chapter 4 of Volume I included an overview of the out-of-body (OBE) experience, and related phenomena, concluding with the essential message that there appears to be more than one stream of consciousness operating at one time (see page 89 f.). But we can realize this for ourselves without the privilege of an OBE. Accordingly, let us undertake some strenuous introspection.

Upon a careful mental examination of our own feelings, thoughts, and motives, namely, the contents of our changing world image as a whole, we discover it to be a stream of three currents, intermingling most of the time and flowing singly at certain moments. Generally, these currents are present together in a commingled state and not in equal proportion, so it is difficult to separate them. However, for analytical purposes, we can enumerate them as follows:

The value of introspection

1. The first current arises without any contact with the external world, entirely as a result of the subjective activity of our own mind as in dreams, day-dreams, hallucination, reverie or when we are lost to the world through introspection or engaged in some concentrated and creative mental effort.

2. The second current occurs from the impact, or imposition, of mental images from another mind upon our own mind as in telepathy, thought-transference or hypnotic suggestion.

These two currents are obvious, so warrant no further comment; but the third one is more complex and needs some elaboration.

3. This third current comes from two sources:

   i. First, the familiar case where our mental world can be produced by stimulation from the external world affecting and influencing our mind via our sense organs. This stimulation is provided by the combination of particles and atoms constituting the material world and the vibrations (waves) emanating from them and striking the sense organs through which the stimulation is received. But the sense organs are also nothing but combinations of particles, atoms, and molecules,

Relation between
external world
and internal
world-image

etc. Nonetheless, when the external world acts upon the sense organs it produces the sensation and experience of sound, touch, sight, taste, and smell—all of which qualities are obviously not in the particle and atom combinations in either the external world or the sense organs. Therefore, the world, or mental perception in the individual mind as a result of this external stimulation or contact, really comes internally from within the individual, even though the source of stimulation is apparently outside.

Hence, the important point here is that the stimulation of the senses by the external world, resulting in a world image produced in the mind, has no *literal*, or '*verbatim*' resemblance at all to the external world. This is why the same sound or sight will be interpreted differently by different people (all with normal functioning senses) according to their individual mind-set or mental 'refractive index', so to speak. Any lecturer knows how an apparently crystal-clear exposition on his part will be taken up by his audience in a dozen different ways. But to this there is a rejoinder: sensations are not produced by external stimuli in a random manner but according to definite laws that science has shown to have a mathematical basis. Thus, the message is this: the internal mental world of colour, sound, form, etc. though quite different from the external physical world of aggregates of particles and atoms, etc., is yet naturally and mathematically related to it.

The internal mental world and the external physical world are not the same; but they are mathematically related. As the popular saying has it: 'The map is not the same as the territory', but corresponds to it; otherwise it would not be possible to negotiate the latter without the help of the former. Moreover, many maps are needed to describe different facets of the same territory.

As a simple example of this distinction between the 'map' and the 'territory', consider a flexible strip of rubber or plastic known as a spline used especially by draughtsmen in drawing large curves. Suppose such a device were bent into the shape of a parabola as shown in Figure III-28 below in the picture to the left. A parabola has a precise mathematical equation $y = ax^2 + bx + c$, as depicted in the picture to the right. Several properties of the spline, such as its orange colour and bendable texture are not described by the equation, which depicts only its shape and nothing else. Thus, the physical spline (the 'territory') is not the same as the equation (which 'maps' it) but is mathematically related to it.

Insights from
mathematics
about mind

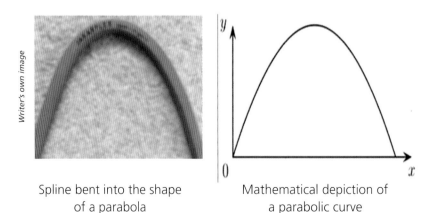

Spline bent into the shape
of a parabola

Mathematical depiction of
a parabolic curve

Figure III-28   A Parabolic Shape and its Mathematical Depiction

The mathematical relation between the mental world and the physical world is exhibited by the very subject of mathematics itself. How can mathematics—a purely mental subject—be used to model the physical world unless the latter were essentially of the nature of mind? This is a matter of enormous significance. It is reserved for the Mathematical Codicil on page 349 which is written for non-scientific readers and amplified with considerable technical details for those who are mathematically minded.

The Nobel prizewinner, Roger Penrose puts it in a nutshell when he says:

> Mathematical truth is not determined arbitrarily by the rules of some man-made formal system, but has an absolute nature, and lies beyond any such system of specifiable rules.[18]

ii. The second source from which the third current derives is the activity of Divine Mind, as for example when the ego is held in abeyance so that we are oblivious to all distractions and totally stilled inwardly by hearing sublime music or witnessing a majestic spectacle of nature, like a glorious sunset, or by an epiphanic experience, as in the case of the American astronaut Edgar Mitchell (1930–2016) when viewing the awe-inspiring beauty of Earth from outer space. And the reason for this is that the whole of the solar system is an expression of the Mind of the Solar Logos unfolding at different levels.

Divine Mind reflected in individual mind

Earlier in Chapter 5 of Volume II we cited the case of the Indian mathematical genius Srinivasa Ramanujan who famously declared that an equation would have no meaning for him unless it represented a thought of God,[19] which can be understood to mean that mental relations (expressed as mathematical equations) mirror Divine 'Thought', itself an Idea in Divine Mind. In the next Chapter we elaborate on how he came to his staggering insights through pure intuition, which provides a vivid demonstration of how a flood of insights occurs when the individual mind is attuned to Divine Mind, such that Divine Ideation and Divine 'Thought', when unencumbered by the ego (*Kāma-manas*) transforms into (in his case) 'mathematical thought'. It would not be labouring the point to clarify that 'normal thought' implies process and of course the Divine would not need to 'think' in the ordinary sense of the term. Being omniscient, the Divine, so to say, Knows Himself (and therefore everything as part of Himself) immediately. This is expounded in depth by H. P. Blavatsky.[vi]

Accordingly, there are just three kinds of mental activity that account for all the activity in the manifested universe and the individual:

1. Cosmic Ideation, which accounts for the appearance and unfoldment (i.e., emanation, or explication) of the entire Cosmos, the latter being a 'Thought' in Cosmic Mind of the Cosmic Logos, so to say.
2. Divine Ideation, which accounts for the appearance and unfoldment of solar systems, including, of course, our own solar system.
3. Individual ideation, which accounts for the mental activity of the innumerable Monads at different stages of development who are evolving in the cosmos.

---

vi See *SD*-I, 'Primordial Substance and Divine Thought', 325–41.

These three mental activities correspond, by reflection, to the three basic realities of the manifested universe:

1. the Cosmic Logos;
2. the Solar Logoi;
3. the Monads which are derived from Divine (Unmanifest) Consciousness and provide its means of expression at these three levels.

Figure III-29 opposite attempts to show these ideas by way of lines radiating from circles.[20] Bearing in mind that Logos means *manifest* deity, the central circle represents the Cosmic Logos. The intermediate circles represent the various Solar Logoi as the radiations of Cosmic Ideation ('Thought'); and the smallest circles represent the Monads as the radiations of Divine Ideation ('Thought').

Perfunctory as the above may seem, yet it presents a small step towards explaining why an idea in the mind of each and every individual is so charged with meaning. For however meaningless or prejudiced the idea might seem to someone else, yet for the individual concerned, it is full of vitality because *it is a mental image, illumined by consciousness, behind which lies the whole of REALITY, the Supreme Consciousness, which underlies the whole universe.* Therefore our mental images (which include our thoughts, imaginings, phantasies) are so animated and tenacious precisely because they can be traced right back to their origin in Divine Ideation. In the extreme, such vibrancy of mental images applies to the lofty ideas that have bequeathed mankind with sublime works of science and culture. Unfortunately, the same also applies to the nefarious beliefs of fanatics and fundamentalist terrorists of *any* religious denomination, and the above exposition may perhaps provide a small clue as to the mind-set of such criminals.

Is this therefore implying that nefarious ideas too can be traced back to Divine Ideation? Sadly, the answer is in the affirmative, but with the major proviso that, clearly, something has gone dreadfully wrong in the 'translation' and 'transducing aspect' from Divine Ideation to individual ideation, such that Ideas essentially pristine and beautiful at Source have been perverted in their 'refraction' through imperfect mind and brain. Readers may recall the following quote from Peter Leggett, who was a Fellow of Trinity College, Cambridge and Vice-Chancellor of Surrey University, first stated in Volume I, Chapter 2:

> By analogy with a pianist and a piano, the mind corresponds to the pianist and the brain to the piano. If either pianist or piano is inadequate, so will be the music.

We have only to substitute 'Divine Ideation' for 'music' and our point is made, and amplified in the next section using an analogy with a broadcasting station.

To reiterate, the mental activity at each level is a projection of the Cosmic Logos reflected at lower levels. Hence, the potency of our mental images (whatever they may be), and why, for each individual, they are full of meaning; for they are ultimately derived from Cosmic Ideation—refer again to Figure III-29. The reflection of Divine Thought in individual thought has been expressed with a rare eloquence by Isaac Newton thus:

> Whence is it that Nature doth nothing in vain; and whence arises all that Order and Beauty which we see in the World? […] And [...] does it not appear from Phænomena that there is a Being incorporeal, living, intelligent, omnipresent, who in infinite Space, as it were in his Sensory, sees the things themselves intimately, and thoroughly perceives

them, and comprehends them wholly by their immediate presence to himself: Of which things the Images only carried through the Organs of Sense into our little Sensoriums, are there seen and beheld by that which in us perceives and thinks.[21]

Newton's insights into Divine Thought

Spiritual Resonances

In order for Divine Mind to act on individual mind there needs to be a mechanism as the actuating interface; and it has obviously got to be a mental mechanism for Mind to affect mind. This will shortly be described. Meanwhile, the interaction between Divine Mind and individual minds is best illustrated by way of an analogy with a central broadcasting station that transmits, say, a music concert to several television receivers via the intermediary of electromagnetic waves. Any television set tuned to those waves, would convert them into sound waves and pictures so that we may hear the music and see the pictures as they are being broadcast in the present moment from the transmitting station. However, each receiver will receive the sound and pictures differently, not in content, but in form and clarity, depending on the fineness of the tuning apparatus. In this simile, Divine Mind may be likened to the broadcasting station, Divine Ideation to the sounds and pictures broadcast, and the several audible and visible reproductions of the *same* music and pictures to the *different* mental images in individual minds. The electromagnetic waves represent the intermediate mental mechanism that enables Ideas in Divine Mind to be reproduced in individual minds.

Broadcasting station as an analogy for Divine Mind

If the receiving apparatus be switched off or tuned to an entirely different frequency, nothing will appear, however powerful the broadcast transmission. If the receiving apparatus be imperfectly tuned, what appears will be distorted by crackle or white noise (random sounds). Just so, individual minds tuned to a common purpose (whatever that purpose happens to be), through the instrumentality of the brain and other consciousness centres, will receive a similar Idea in a form whose clarity will depend on the degree of mental attunement. There are innumerable examples of this in the field of music, science, and literature (two examples from music and science were cited above). On the basis of the Hermetic Axiom, we would like to propose that Divine Mind emanates a 'divine spiritual field'—like the broadcasting station transmits an electromagnetic field—picked up

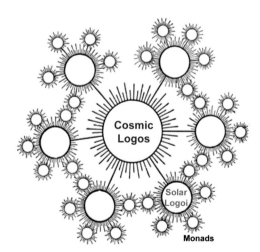

Figure III-29 Individual Ideation derives from Divine Ideation, in turn from Cosmic Ideation

Photo Credit: See Note 20

by individual minds by 'spiritual resonance'—in the same way that animals and humans inherit acquired characteristics by resonance with the morphogenetic field of the species.

The all-important intermediate mental mechanisms are the subject of the next section.

From Perception to Sensation and the Role of Cosmic Elements

Having understood in a general sense the interaction of Divine Mind and individual minds and the basis of the mental currents in individuals, we are now equipped to move on to the second doctrine in occult philosophy about how physical perception produces subjective sensation. It is again best understood as a progressive flow-down from the highest to corresponding lower levels of Cosmic Elements (Element–Principles and Element–Substances), which act as stimulators and receptors of the senses.

In the above exposition on how Divine Mind affects individual mind, it must be made clear that the interaction that we are considering is at the lowest level, namely, the perception of an external world of matter through the instrumentality of the five sense organs in the physical body. This interaction takes place at different levels through the agency of vehicles that have been evolved on the successive planes (see the two depictions alongside in Chapter 7, Figure III-25, page 128 ending with the physical plane). It is here that we face the 'Schrödinger Mind–Sensation Problem'. The physical mechanism of sense perception is well understood by neuroscience. For example in the case of hearing, science knows, in detail, how the contact of the air with the eardrum elicits the appropriate response, the nature of which depends on the vibratory characteristics of the acoustic wave and the cellular composition of the auditory apparatus. Thereafter, the impressions produced in the sense organs are converted into nervous/nerve impulses which are transmitted to the corresponding sensory centres in the physical brain. But how are purely physical nervous/nerve impulses in the brain converted into mental sensuous images? Moreover, how can we experience such sensations without any external sensory input, purely by thought and imagination? This is the thrust of what now follows.

The differentiation into the generic subject–object relationship, stated earlier (pages 144–146), provides only an idea of the general principles underlying the working of the mind at all levels. It does not give us a rational understanding of the mechanism of how, on the physical plane, Divine Mind acts on individual mind through the instrumentality of the sense organs—an apparently material mechanism.

For this further understanding we have to consider another occult doctrine about mental perception. The mind works not only through the subject–object relationship, but in its involution (increasing involvement in matter in its descent and externalization towards the physical) divides into two streams, so to say, one stream serving as the basis of the subjective function and the other stream as the basis of the objective function. This is illustrated in Figure III-30 on page 157, which is a highly simplified version of Figure III-23 on page 103 in the previous Chapter. It is intended to highlight the main stages in the functioning of principles from the highest level, Divine Consciousness, to their correspondences at the lowest level of descent—the material, physical.

At this juncture we need to make an important point before proceeding. At periodic intervals throughout this work, the writer has been at pains to stress that the Eternal Wisdom

The impasse that science is unable to bridge

is universal; that it is neither the prerogative of the West, nor the East. However, there is nothing in the Western teachings (to the best knowledge of the writer) that can touch the authority of the Eastern sages in their understanding of the physio-psycho-spiritual mechanisms of mental perception, as expounded in Yogic philosophy and psychology. Thus, the occasionally liberal use of Sanskrit terms is unavoidable, but as is our policy, they will be explained as clearly as possible, including, for convenience, a few terms used in the previous Chapter.

Supremacy of Eastern wisdom as regards mental perception

The Process of Emanational Descent from the Unmanifest to the Manifest

Viewing Figure III-30, page 157 as a whole: (*a*) the terms in the ovoid at the top show parallel designations from different cultures used to pronounce what is in truth ineffable; (*b*) the left-hand side shows the emanational descent of the subjective aspect—the active, 'spirit-side', or 'force-side'; and (*c*) the right-hand side shows the emanational descent of the objective aspect—the passive, 'matter-side', or 'vehicular-side'. This does not mean that there are two independent streams of descent. There is a singular emanational process eternally in action: the two parallel lines in Figure III-30 are drawn purely for diagrammatic purposes to portray the two *aspects* of ONE REALITY—the active principle ('spirit') and its correlate ('matter') at any level of manifestation. It constantly needs to be borne in mind that anything manifested is a limited expression in form of the limitless potentiality of the Unmanifest, hence manifestation on any level requires a form, or 'matter' as vehicle for the expression of the indwelling 'spirit'. Therefore, as explained earlier, manifestation is an appearance, since all forms will ultimately change and release the indwelling spirit. (The meaning of 'spirit' and 'matter' used in the generic sense was outlined in Chapter 3, page 36 and is further developed in Chapter 10 on the subject of man's evolution. Readers should also refer to the opening of Volume II, Chapter 2, page 16 for the subtle, but important nuances in meaning when lower and upper case letters are used for 'spirit' and 'matter'.)

One emanational descent in its two aspects

The Subject–Object Differentiation
(top of Figure III-30)

DEFINING KEY TERMS

Puruṣa – Heavenly Man, or the Spiritual Self, derived from the Sanskrit verbal root, *pri*, meaning 'to fill', 'to make complete', 'to bestow'.

Key meaning: the Ideal Man, the Qabbalistic Adam Qadmon (Adam Kadmon) as the Archetypal, or Heavenly Man in each individual human being or, indeed, in every self-conscious entity—therefore also a term for the everlasting Divine-Spiritual Self, or Spiritual Monad. Hence, also referred to as 'Sons of God', or 'Reflections of the Father', as stated in the previous Chapter.

In the Vedas, Puruṣa signifies the original Source of the Universe, the Supreme Being. Whereas in Sāṃkhya philosophy, to which this exposition pertains, Puruṣa is used as equivalent to *Buddhi*, the eternal Spiritual Soul in man.

Prakṛti – Originating (not original) substance, originating Source, derived from the Sanskrit compound consisting of the prepositional prefix *pra*, meaning 'before' and *kriti*, a noun form from the verbal root *kri* 'to make', 'to do',[vii] so literally, 'that which makes before'.

Key meaning: Nature in the most primordial sense, generally rendered 'Matter', or 'Substance'. Hence the Source and origin of the 'substance-side', or 'matter-side' of the manifested universe, the great Producer of entities, or things, through which acts the ever-active Puruṣa.

Note: fundamentally and essentially, *Puruṣa* as Spirit and *Prakṛiti* as Matter, its productive veil, or sheath, 'are but the two primeval aspects of the One and Secondless'[22]— the One Unknown Deity. Accordingly, whatever Prakṛiti produces through the influence of Puruṣa is multitudinous and multiform, as clearly evinced by the infinite variety of all entities and nature.

The secondary differentiation in consciousness described earlier, and depicted in Figure III-27on page 145, is indicated at the top of Figure III-30 opposite by ascribing two aspects to REALITY and using two separate phrases for the two aspects, namely:

1. *Brahmā Caitanya*, which is Reality as Consciousness in its subjective aspect. (This is equivalent to *Kutastha Caitanya*, the Holy Ghost, shown in the top left of Figure III-23 in Chapter 7, page 103.)
2. *Śabda-Brahmā*, which is Reality in its vibrational, or wave aspect, the root of the objective phenomenal universe. (This is equivalent to *Māyā* shown in the top right of Figure III-23, page 103 in Chapter 7.) Bearing in mind James Jeans's reference to matter (from a scientific perspective) as 'bottled up waves,' Reality in its wave aspect indicates the role of matter in the most generic sense. Since matter is synonymous with form, and all forms are impermanent and therefore in this sense, an appearance, this objective aspect is therefore referred to as Māyā, or Darkness.

> It is *Puruṣa–Prakṛiti*, the differentiation in consciousness at the highest level, which, projected at a lower level, appears as the bifurcation of the Mind Principle into two streams serving as the basis of the subjective and objective aspects of mind.

It need hardly be stressed that the above references to two streams of consciousness, i.e. two primary aspects of REALITY, pertain solely to monism and in no way imply a fundamental dualism.

The Five Cosmic Elements – Their Active and Passive Aspects in Universal Nature
(grey box, middle of Figure III-30)

The unit of Heavenly Man and Nature (*Puruṣa–Prakṛiti*) just mentioned appears as individualized consciousness, as a 'spiritual atom' in the heart of each person, wherein its lower reflection gives rise to *Ahaṁkāra*, the feeling of 'I am I' (refer back to *The Holy Science*, Sūtra 6 on page 111 and the middle of Figure III-23, page 103 in Chapter 7).

From the earliest stages, the active and passive, subjective and objective functions are abreast and correlated at all levels of emanational descent as will now be explained in stepwise fashion.

---

vii This is the same root from which the term 'karma' is derived.

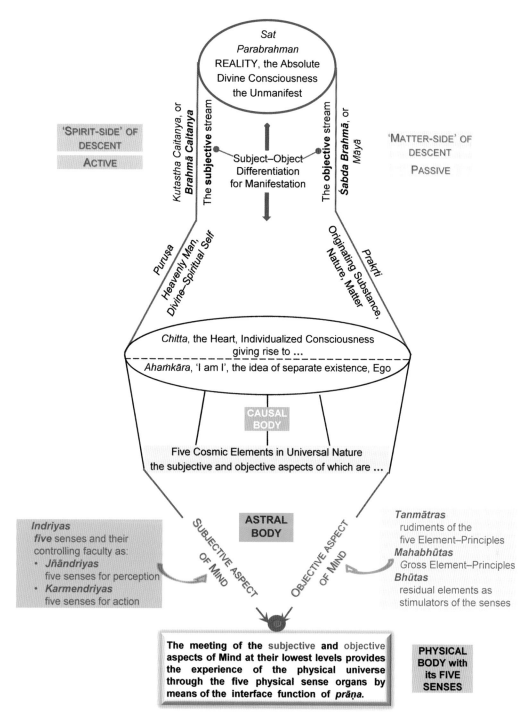

Figure III-30 How Human Experience Arises – Where Subjective Meets Objective
This diagram is a highly simplified version of Figure III-23 in Chapter 7, page 103

DEFINING TERMS

Tattvas, Tanmātras, and *Mahābhūtas* are key terms used in occult metaphysics to convey a specific meaning; however, the overarching ideas associated with this triad are referred to under the simple term 'Elements' for the reason that the word 'Element' is used to translate each one of the Sanskrit words. No single English term can render the subtle meaning of these three Sanskrit words. However, in order to suggest that there is another meaning intended than the one usually associated with the word 'Element', the hyphenated terms (in the plural) 'Element–Principles' and 'Element–Substances' (collectively the 'Cosmic Elements') are used as their common denominator. ('Element', here, is used, of course, in the philosophical sense, not as in physical chemistry.) The human constitution coheres as an organic entity precisely because these Cosmic Elements are represented in it and ever active therein.

The above terms are now carefully defined in two groups.

Five Element–Principles: *Tattvas* – the Spirit-side, or Force-side to the Cosmic Elements

The rudiment active principle

Tattva (also spelled 'Tattwa') – 'That-ness', or eternally existing, derived from the Sanskrit pronominal particle *tat* with suffix *twa*, hence may also be rendered 'Element', reminding one of the 'quiddity' of the European scholastics. Hence, the underlying reality, or essence, behind the outward appearance and physical manifestation.

Key meaning: the Elements of original substance in Nature, existing eternally. Strictly speaking, the different principles, or Elements, in universal, intelligent, and conscious Nature considered from the active force-side, or spirit-side of an element that enables it to 'change', or evolve as the world cycles roll on through the ages; hence referred to as the Element–Principles (in contradistinction to the Element–Substances explained below).

Note here that the five Tattvas correspond to the five human senses, but in fact the Tattvas are seven in number, the remaining two pertaining to the distant future advance and evolution of humanity when two further senses, currently latent, will be brought forth. And so, as stated in Sūtras 7–10 in *The Holy Science* (see Chapter 7, pages 112–113), these five Element–Principles and correlated Element–Substances (see below) are referred to by the Indian monk and yogi Śrī Yukteswar Giri as *Pañca Tattva*, the 'five aura electricities' being the causes of all other creations; therefore called the five Root-Causes, and are considered the Causal Body of *Puruṣa*, the Son of God.[23] (Note that in this Chapter, 'Cosmic Elements', the collective term for 'Element–Principles' and 'Element–Substances' are the preferred philosophical terms used for the identical but rather quaint term 'aura electricities' used by Śrī Yukteswar, as stated in Chapter 7.)

Five Element–Substances: *Tanmātras* and *Mahābhūtas* – the Matter-side, or Vehicular-side to the Cosmic Elements

Tanmātras – the types or rudiments of the five Elements, derived from the compound Sanskrit word *Tat*, meaning 'that' and *matra*, 'a trifle', or 'unit of measure'.

The originant passive medium

Key meaning: the rudiments of an Element, Originant Element, Basic Element devoid of qualities and identical with the properties of the Five Elements—Æther, Air, Fire, Water, and Earth—and correlated to the five senses—sound, touch, sight, taste, and smell. Hence, also referred to as Element–Substances to convey the idea of the Matter-side, or Vehicular-side of the (active) Element–Principles.

Mahābhūtas – Gross Elements derived from the compound Sanskrit word *Mahā*, meaning 'great' and *bhūta*, the past participle of the verbal root, *bhu* 'to be'.

Key meaning: the Gross Element–Principles of matter, as the resultants of the developed, or evolved, Tanmātras (the Rudiment Element–Principles). Note that the Mahābhūtas may be regarded as equivalent to Prakṛiti, when the latter word is used in the plural form to signify the primary essences which evolve the whole visible world.

The evolved passive medium

IN EXPLANATION

Tattva conveys the idea that it is the 'force-side', or 'spirit-side' to the Cosmic Elements, i.e. the Element–Principles, enumerated as five, that enables them to change and develop as they manifest different aspects on the various planes in the course of their evolutionary advancement and unfoldment.

At any level, however, spirit requires matter—its appropriate form, or vehicle in, and through, which to manifest. Thus, *Tanmātras* and *Mahābhūtas* convey the vehicular-side, or 'matter-side' of the Elements, i.e. the Element–Substances. *Tanmātra* is rendered the Rudiment Element, which proceeds, step-by-step, with the changing world condition; this unfoldment and development stage is termed *Mahābhūta*, the Gross Element–Principle. In other words the 'matter-side', or vehicular aspect of the original Element–Principle (Tanmātra), has, by progressive descent and externalizing towards increasing materiality ('densification'), developed into, or become, the Gross Element–Principle (Mahābhūta) that is present on Earth at the present stage of kosmic unfoldment (see Chapter 6, Figure III-16, page 89).

The active principle and passive medium are correlated at all levels

It is most important to appreciate that the Tattvas, Tanmātras, and Mahābhūtas are not mere abstract principles but *conscious* Principles. For this reason they are called *Devatās*, or gods, in Hindu philosophy. On account of the intimate relation of consciousness with sound (vibration) their powers can be invoked, and the corresponding force brought down, through a knowledge of the correspondences and correlations of consciousness with sound and colour, etc. (see for example Chapter 5, Table III-3, page 79). Their powers can be invoked in various ways in order to bring about specific results on different planes, including the physical. This is accomplished in consonance with their respective natures, as they function through various hierarchies of angels and nature spirits of different grades and are related to different types of natural forces.[viii] This is indeed the basis of genuine thaumaturgy (the power of working wonders with the help of the gods), a subject too complex and shrouded in mystery for our purposes. But it would certainly be useful to gain a clear but general understanding of the nature and function of the Cosmic Elements as outlined above. Apropos, the writer speculates whether Brian Josephson's undefined but firmly rooted ideas about 'agents', namely: (*a*) 'Agents are the source of physics'; (*b*) 'Physics needs to come to terms with agents'; and (*c*) 'Towards a Science of Agents', are the great physicist's intuition regarding what occult philosophy refers to as the 'Cosmic Elements' (see Chapter 5, page 72 and Volume I, Chapter 8, page 243).

Consciousness, mind, and intelligence are at the core of all manifestation

---

viii 'Nature-spirits', otherwise known as 'Elementals' (the agents of the Cosmic Elements, so to speak) are incorporeal devic entities concerned with building and maintaining the various forms of the kingdoms of nature as well as helping to control the Elements of Fire, Air, Water, and Earth. They are popularly known, respectively, as the Salamanders, Sylphs, Undines, and at the physical level, Gnomes. The devas are angelic members of the hierarchy of beings parallel to Man.

The Perception of the Physical Universe

(bottom portion of Figure III-30, page 157)

DEFINING TERMS

Indriyas – The generic term for the five senses and their controlling faculty.

Key meaning: the instruments of man's direct perception of the outside world. They are of two kinds: active and passive, i.e., sensory and motoric:

> ***Jñānendriyas*** – the five sense organs by which we know and perceive the material world, i.e., the cognitive functions of consciousness as hearing, touching, seeing, tasting, and smelling.

> ***Karmendriyas*** – the five organs used for action by which we interact with the material world, i.e., the conative functions of consciousness as speaking, grasping, walking, ejaculating, and evacuating.

Both sets of five faculties are correlated with the Five Elements, respectively: Æther, Air, Fire, Water, and Earth. Simultaneous separate impressions of the senses are co-ordinated in 'the mind', the common term for the process shortly described. Thus, we perceive the world through the *jñānendriyas*, and respond via the *karmendriyas*. *Manas* (the Mind) is affected by what it perceives through the indriyas.

Referring to the karmendriyas, namely, the motoric faculty suggestive of mechanized action, or movement, as a passive function may seem surprising at first, for surely, grasping, walking, etc. are all activities? They are indeed, but they are passive in the sense of being the instruments of that which causes such activity to take place. As a simplistic analogy, a horse-drawn chariot (which is often used in ancient Indian scriptures as a symbol for the human body) is entirely passive on its own, and displays its activity only when spurred into action by the charioteer, the active agent using the chariot as his vehicle.

Bhūtas – 'has beens', or 'leftovers' from the past participle of the Sanskrit verb-root 'to be', or 'to become'.

Key meaning: the five Elements as stimulators of the senses, in the sense of the leftovers of the *Mahābhūtas*, as defined above.

Note: *bhūtas*, as used in this context, should never be confused with the other meaning ascribed to this term: ghosts, eidolons, etc., meaning the 'leftovers', or 'shell' of the complete man, from which all that is spiritual and intellectual has fled, leaving behind a decaying astral corpse (see Chapter 5 in Volume II). This is an unfortunate use of the same term applied in different categories; however, the key meaning of bhūta as 'left over' is always the same, whether pertaining to the leftover of a human being, a Cosmic Element–Principle, or any other entity.

IN EXPLANATION

The two subjective and objective streams, i.e., aspects of REALITY in their instrumental aspects are known as the indriyas and bhūtas, respectively. It is easier to understand their essential nature if they are regarded in a general manner without seeking to identify them with their organs on the lowest plane, the physical. Thus, the indriyas should be considered generally as the instruments of the subjective aspects, and the bhūtas as those of the

Active and passive aspects of consciousness

objective aspects of the astral and physical body—see the above definitions with reference to the central portion of Figure III-23, page 103 (in Chapter 7) and Figure III-30 on page 157. Furthermore, indriyas and bhūtas are not the functions in themselves but the instruments (vehicles) of the subjective and objective functions; and it is through them that the two correlated functions of the one REALITY are exercised. Referring again to Figure III-30, the indriyas and bhūtas meet at the lowest level of descent *and it is at their conjunction that mind, in its subjective aspect, conjoins with mind in its objective aspect, such that a subjective perception of an objective universe can take place.*

In summary, it is precisely at the conjunction of the two streams of consciousness— namely, the subjective (indriya) and objective (bhūta) streams of unitary Consciousness—where we find the clue that the universe is a phenomenon in consciousness or of consciousness. For this reason, the perception of the whole manifested universe in its infinite states of subtlety, right down to the physical plane, is the result of the involution of consciousness **as matter** and not **in matter**—thus, to reiterate, a phenomenon of pure Consciousness. (Involution, meaning the progressive involvement in manifestation, is fully explained in Chapter 10.) So when considered from this loftiest of all standpoints the following maxims all make perfect sense since they express in subtly different ways the fundamental insight (which Schrödinger fully realized—see Volume I, Introductory, page lxi) that the individual self (*jīva*) which appears as a separate existence, is in essence (*Ātma*) part and manifestation of the whole (*Brahman*):

Consciousness is primary: Matter its appearance

- ❖ *Sarvam khalvidam brahmā*: 'Verily all this [manifested universe] is nothing but Brahman' (Chandogya Upaniṣad, Verse, 3.14.1).

- ❖ *Tat Tvam Asi*: 'That essence [*tat*, referring to *sat*, 'the Existent'] are you' (Chandogya Upaniṣad, Verse 6.8.7 of the Sama Veda—the Veda of melodies and chants).

- ❖ *Aham Brahmāsmi*: 'I am Brahman' (Brihadaranyaka Upaniṣad, Verse 1.4.10 of the Yajur Veda).

Generally speaking, some atoms, molecules, and cells of the sense organs have special functions serving as the vehicles of the indriyas; other aggregates of atoms, molecules, and cells with specific properties stimulate particular sensations and serve as the vehicles of the bhūtas. The basic material in both cases is the same—the atoms and molecules and their vibratory interactions—but their functions are different.

The perception of the physical universe through the five physical sense organs is thus the product of the meeting of the subjective and objective aspects of mind at their lowest level of descent.

But why should the meeting of indriyas and bhūtas alone necessarily explain the transfer from the objective and physical mechanisms of the five senses, and associated network of the nervous system, to an inner, subjective experience of sensation? There has got to be an interface between the two for this to happen.

The Transmutation from Neurology to Experience – Vitalism and the Nervous Ether

How is the transmutation of physical nervous impulses to mental sensations in the human being brought about?

What Mainstream Neuroscience Proposes

In *Living in a Mindful Universe*, the Harvard neurosurgeon Eben Alexander provides a useful discussion on why materialism is at a loss to explain the above question. Drawing deeply on his practice of decades of neurosurgery and, crucially, on his own near-death experience (see Volume I, Chapter 2, page 15), he states that 'materialist science […] posits that the brain creates consciousness out of purely physical matter—that there is nothing else.' Accordingly, on the basis of this unproven assumption 'it asserts that everything we have ever experienced—every beautiful sunset, every gorgeous symphony, every hug from our child, every experience of falling in love—is merely the electrochemical flickering of around a hundred billion neurons in a three-pound gelatinous mass, sitting in a warm dark bath inside our head.' However, the problem with 'the materialist brain-creates-consciousness model, is that not even the world's top experts on the brain have even the remotest idea *how* [*sic*] the brain could create consciousness,' other than just taking it as read that it does.[24] Just one example out of literally dozens that could be adduced of such unqualified presuppositions (plus confusing metaphors with models)

is an article, appearing in the *RSA Journal*, entitled 'Brain Reactions', where we are explicitly informed that it is in 'our cerebral cortex, where consciousness arises.'[25] As Eben Alexander says, 'mainstream neuroscience just hasn't been doing its homework.'[26] We may add that the bulk of such 'homework' should comprise the metaphysical and philosophical underpinnings of a science of consciousness.

The margin note: Harvard neurosurgeon underlines failings of mainstream neuroscience

A materialistic neuroscience of consciousness is therefore a complete oxymoron.

The Epilogue to this work in Volume III describes a simple thought experiment devised by the writer to demonstrate that consciousness cannot be created by an assembly of neural networks on their own, however vast or complex.

But, for the moment, we may confidently assert that if the brain does not produce, i.e. generate consciousness any more than it actually produces sound waves when we hear music, we need no more convincing that, as Alexander says, 'materialist science as a foundation for comprehending our reality is at a dead end' and 'we are long overdue to rise above this façade.' In fact, 'the inability to identify any physical location of memory [experience, or conscious awareness] in the brain is one of the greatest clues that materialism is a failed world-view'[27]—something that the great neurosurgeon Wilder Penfield demonstrated several decades earlier (refer to Volume I, Chapter 4, page 76). Let us therefore make the case for occult science and outline the role of *prāṇa* in eradicating the false materialist assumption that the brain *generates* consciousness out of physical matter.

The margin note: Why materialism is a 'failed world-view'

What Occult Science Affirms

The transmutation of physical nervous impulses to mental sensations in the human being is brought about through the agency of one of the divine forces appropriated to the human being—*prāṇa*—serving as the vehicle of the vital force. Prāṇa may be thought of as a special kind of transmuting substance—a compound of physical matter and mind. Being on the interface between the two, hence partaking of both matter and mind, it therefore enables mind to affect matter, and matter to affect mind, so to say. The simile with a chemical catalyst is useful. A catalyst is a substance that actuates, or accelerates, a chemical reaction while undergoing no permanent change in itself, nor is it consumed by the reaction; hence can be recovered chemically unchanged at the end of the reaction.

Prāṇa serves as a 'mind/matter catalyst'

This, in essence, is the *modus operandi* to the resolution of what we characterized as the 'Schrödinger Mind–Sensation Problem'. But note that the action goes both ways: matter and mind can affect one another, for example, hunger can be induced by the smell of food; or merely by the thought of a delicious meal.

However, the above reference to prāṇa should not be taken as a literal concept of matter as atoms and molecules, i.e., as physical entities *per se*, since science has explicitly proved that such physical entities are in reality modes of motion or 'bottled-up waves' as Jeans put it. And what we are further suggesting is that there is no logical reason why this *vibrational, or wave nature of matter should not extend from physical matter to the subtlest grades of supra-physical realms*. We make no apology for constantly reiterating this crucial insight of science that has such a strong bearing on esotericism. Paradoxically, then, for the scientist, but quite logically for the occultist, it is waves affecting mind, that is to say, non-physical substance affecting mental substance. Like affects like, and there is no dichotomy between matter and mind *when the essentially mental, or mind-based nature of the former is grasped.*

Matter is quintessentially mental

In her classic textbook *A Study in Consciousness*, Annie Besant addresses the mechanisms of consciousness, informing us that, 'on the physical plane, the life-force, prāṇa builds up (in the sense of an organizing principle) all minerals and is the controlling agent in the chemico-physiological changes in protoplasm, which lead to differentiation and the building of the various tissues in the bodies of plants, animals, and men.' Its presence is shown by the power of responding to stimuli. 'When the currents of prāṇa from the astral plane, with its attribute of sentiency, blend with that of the prāṇa of the physical plane, it begins the building of a new arrangement of matter—the nervous.'[28] This nervous arrangement is fundamentally a cell (details of which can be found in any modern text-book on biology and physiology), whose development consists of internal changes and outgrowths of the matter of the cell, these outgrowths becoming sheathed in medullary matter and then appearing as threads or fibres. The essential point is that every nervous system consists of cells and their outgrowths, the latter proliferating and forming multiple connections between the cells. This takes place *as the expression of consciousness (the active principle) demands an ever more refined and increasingly networked nervous system (the passive medium of expression). Therefore, the degree and sensitivity of response of an organism to external stimuli is directly proportional to the complexity and refinement of its nervous system.*

The nervous system and prāṇa

What Enlightened Science Intimates

The role of prāṇa as the agent of the vital force (first described in Volume II, Chapter 2, page 27) is central to the whole question of how physical neurology can result in an internal experience. This subject is amplified in the next Chapter with regard to what is known as the 'nervous ether'. But, for now, it is worth asking an open question as to whether any quantum processes could explain the 'hard' problem of consciousness. This is now a burgeoning field of enquiry amongst several enlightened scientists of international acclaim, like Roger Penrose and Stuart Hameroff, who have long argued that conscious-ness is the result of quantum gravity effects in microtubules (tubular polymers of tubulin), which they dub 'orchestrated objective reduction' (see Volume I Chapter 4, page 97 f. for more details). *Shadows of the Mind*[29] by Roger Penrose is a sequel to his 1989 book *The Emperor's New Mind: Concerning computers, minds and the laws of physics*. It constitutes a comprehensive account of what modern physics has to tell us about the mind, especially how quantum processes play an essential role in the understanding of human consciousness. Another fine source book is *How Consciousness Became the Universe*[30] comprising a collection of articles from diverse thinkers and scientists to tackle the overriding subject of Consciousness as the basis for the emergence of the universe. This is considered from a variety of disciplines and viewpoints such as quantum physics, cosmology, relativity, evolution, neuroscience, and parallel universes. *Consciousness and the Universe* is also a valuable reference work on the central role of quantum physics in understanding consciousness and the mind.[31] It comprises innovative chapters by a galaxy of radical scientists and philosophers of mind who address interrelated questions such as whether consciousness constitutes the ground of the universe or whether it is a by-product (epiphenomenon) of the universe; whether reality depends on consciousness or whether consciousness simply perceives reality; whether consciousness is primordial or an emergent property of evolution. There is no suggestion, however, that quantum theory, exclusively, can explain consciousness; rather, that consciousness is a key factor in a complete understanding of quantum phenomena.

Does quantum science elucidate the 'hard problem' of consciousness?

All such enquiries would be most profitable in the light of the earlier exposition on prāṇa as the interface transforming agent from neurology to conscious experience.

Non-instrumental Perception and Action

(lower half of Figure III-23, page 103 and Figure III-30, page 157)

Following directly from the above exposition on the vehicles, or instruments of consciousness, there are two important faculties referred to in the Yoga Sūtras of Patanjali which clearly point to the mind *in its essential nature* as independent of the senses and external objects. They are *Pratibha bhava* and *Vikarana bhava*, standing for non-instrumental perception and non-instrumental action, respectively.[32] They pertain to the spiritual planes and correspond, in the astral body, to the *jñānendriyas* and *karmendriyas* as the instruments of the cognitive and connative functions of consciousness, respectively. The general principle is that the translation of will into action is retarded and vitiated in proportion to the complexity and cumbersomeness of the mechanism of its vehicles on the lower planes. This is implied in Figure III-23 (in Chapter 7) and Figure III-30, where the bottom half is more complex than the top half.

So when consciousness is freed from the impediments of the mechanism and vehicle through which it acts—hence, non-instrumental—the perception is free and unrestricted, and the resulting action is direct and unhindered. Obviously, then, the more refined and 'transparent' the vehicle, the less will be its distorting or limiting effect on the freedom of expression of consciousness, so that in the ultimate, when consciousness acts from a centre without the encumbrance of its vehicles, its action is completely unhampered and free. Such non-instrumental perception and action occur through a point centre ('spiritual particle') on the higher planes, whereas on the lower planes the outcome is subject to illusions and limitations. Thus the spiritual will of *Ātma* acting on the spiritual planes is virtually untrammelled, while it can be deflected, hampered, and distorted in its fulfilment on the lower planes, constrained both by ordinary space and time and by the complexity

Vehicles of consciousness condition its degree and freedom of expression

and degree of responsiveness of its vehicles of expression. We may liken this process to a bright light shone through dirty filters or opaque prisms whereby the dimmed or contorted images are entirely due to the refracting medium, and have no bearing on the light, which is always the same. In an uncanny resemblance to the prism, the brain refracts the light of consciousness; hence, derangement or genius has all to do with the quality of the refracting medium and not with consciousness or mind *per se*.

William James's lecture on human immortality (see Volume I, Chapter 6, page 169) propounded essentially the same, but differently worded, Yogic philosophy: that a lowering of the brain threshold permitted a releasing function (rather like the opening of a reducing valve) that enabled a fuller perception of consciousness by virtue of lessened impediment by the brain; and the quality of the transmission depended on the degree of interference by the brain, meaning its degree of 'transparency', like the 'dome of many-coloured glass' that 'stains the white radiance of eternity'[33]—refer to Figure I-7, Volume I, page 171 showing the simile between this sublime canto by Shelley and the refraction of light through a prism.

Terminal Lucidity

In similar vein, this understanding resolves a main bone of contention in neuroscience: how to account for the phenomenon of the near-death experience or 'terminal lucidity' (the clarity and luminous quality shown by subjects in the final stages of dying). Arguments range (and rage) from purely physiological hypotheses (like oxygen deprivation to the brain) to other speculations that refute the latter, but offer no viable alternative (another illustration of the difference between the 'soft' and 'hard' problem of consciousness). But how does oxygen deprivation, or other causes of death, account for the fact that before death, stroke victims, or even raving lunatics, experience a fleeting moment of lucidity? Terminal delusion is a complete misnomer; moreover, it is true to say that some of the deepest insights, or creative peaks, seem to occur to advanced individuals when death approaches—like Heisenberg's profound dying intuitions (see Volume I, Chapter 6, page 172) or the sublime music that Schubert wrote in his last days. The above account on non-instrumental perception, reinforced by James's thesis and Shelley's mystical insight, offers an entirely logical explanation not based on any conjectures, but grounded in the sacred soil of the occult wisdom of the ages, which holds that the consciousness of the individual is gradually freed from the encumbrance and limitations of the brain—its vehicle of expression in normal life—when the sacred hour approaches.

Will mainstream neuroscience ever understand terminal lucidity?

Résumé

What are the implications for neuroscience and how does occult science supply the missing links to resolve the Schrödinger Mind–Sensation Problem? In essence, this involves the interface between neuroscience and consciousness.

The Interface Between Neuroscience and Consciousness – Its Implications

How does neuroscience address the question of why a clear sky looks blue and fresh grass looks green, even though air and water molecules are not blue, and chlorophyll molecules are not green? The methodology, almost always, is to seek a neural correlate of consciousness.

But from all that has been said, it would appear that to seek *just* a *neural correlate* without inquiring further into the *vehicles of consciousness* is simply asking a question that is either wrong (looking for the proverbial black cat in a blackened room) or incomplete (touching one part of an elephant—as in the parable of the blind men and the elephant—and guessing the nature of the beast); hence all the travail and problems generated when science tries to find what does not exist *as science sees it. The correct enquiry involves recognizing the vehicles evolved through which consciousness functions at various levels.* A detailed treatment of the vehicles of consciousness was given in Volume II, especially in Chapters 2 to 4. This was done from the standpoint of explaining the occult composition of man. In the context of this Chapter however, a somewhat different angle on the subject was needed.

Distinguishing neural correlates from 'neural transducers' of consciousness

At the physical level, such vehicles, or instruments of consciousness, may be regarded as neural transducers—using the term 'transducer' in the widest sense of providing both the releasing and transmissive function in connection with the brain as expounded so eloquently by William James, also Ferdinand Schiller from whom many of his ideas were derived (see again Chapter 6 in Volume I). This is related to a general phenomenon in evolution. As soon as the spiritual vehicle starts functioning, the lower vehicles can be dispensed with, although they may still be retained for maintaining contact with, and functioning, on the lower planes. Accordingly, on the lower planes, consciousness has evolved a complicated and unresponsive (relatively speaking) mechanism, and through this mechanism unfolds and perfects the functions of the higher vehicles; and when the higher function is perfected the lower mechanism which helped in the process is discarded or used as an accessory for communication and contact with those on the lower planes. The sense-organs play such a role in relation to the Lower mind, and the vehicles of the personality on the lowest three planes play a similar role in relation to the spiritual vehicles of the individuality. The supposed neural correlates of consciousness are therefore merely the lowest vehicles of consciousness—the senses and neural mechanisms—on the physical plane.

Expression of consciousness conditioned by its vehicles

It is paradoxical that whereas any potentiality for development or growth needs its appropriate vehicle for self-expression, the vehicle also acts as an obstruction to the *full* potential that seeks expression. Hence, the greater the complexity and coarseness of the vehicle, the more will it impede the expression. For example, for a given amount of physical exertion, a heavy body weight would impede an athlete's performance more than a light body. Regarding the expression of consciousness, the simpler, and therefore subtler the vehicle of expression, the finer will be the quality of expression. So the higher spiritual consciousness can dispense with the complex mechanisms of the sense organs needed for the expression of physical consciousness at the lowest level. However, note in passing that the complexity of the vehicle does not apply just to the human body. We may cite the example of the excessive complexity of modern computers and information technology systems that can often obstruct the thought process and thereby complicate judgement and decisions. Sometimes we long for simple pen and paper to capture our innermost thoughts and feelings!

Problems in Neuroscience Resolved by Occult Science

Occult science leads us, step-by-step, by its own inexorable logic and self-consistency, to the inference that behind the apparently physical world, governed by the physical laws known to science, is an underlying mental world containing the noumenal archetypes, principles, modes of motion, and images—all mathematically related and harmonized into an organic whole. This is not to say that there is a physical world and behind it the mental world, but there is only a mental world and the apparently physical world is an appearance of the mental world. This is also the conclusion to which modern science is pointing on the basis of its own theory and rigorous experimental work. (Refer to the quote by Sir Arthur Eddington in Volume I, Chapter 3 that 'the external world of physics has thus become a world of shadows'.)

Whether we consider the progressive unfolding of consciousness towards the spiritual (evolution) or the reverse process (involution), the active and passive functions (spirit and matter) of any principle:

1. have their corresponding functions;
2. and are always juxtaposed and correlated;

at any level of descent (externalization) towards materiality or ascent towards spirituality.

Thus, the resolution by occult science of the mind–sensation problem is underpinned by three cardinal factors:

1. Space and Time constituting the parameters of what is commonly regarded as the objective, physical world, but upon deeper enquiry, is really an appearance, i.e., an illusion (māyā), in the mind of the observer. But in the act of observing the external world, the internal mental world of the observer is not to be regarded as a purely imagined image of the external world, but rather in the nature of a conceptual map of the latter to which it is, in principle, mathematically related.

2. The differentiation of Integrated Consciousness into the Subject–Object relation-ship, and the descent (externalizing) at all levels of these two correlated aspects of consciousness in manifestation.

   Both the above factors are ever present. They cannot be separated out, other than for the unavoidable purpose of an analytical description, as in this Chapter.

3. The crossover from the perception of an apparently objective and physical universe by means of external impulses on the physical senses to an internal, subjective experience of sensuous images is brought about by the dynamic interplay of two influences. The first is of a general nature: that the world image produced in the mind of an individual is predominantly the result of the interaction of Divine Mind on individual mind. The second is the *modus operandi* of how such action of Mind upon mind occurs through the instrumentality of a seemingly material mechanism—the physical sense organs.

   Regarding the first influence, it is possible to discern three qualities of the mental content:

   i. The entirely subjective activity of the mind, as in phantasy, without any contact with the external world.
   ii. The projection of mental images from one mind to another, as in thought transference.
   iii. The activity of Divine Mind on individual mind whether through the instrumen-tality of the senses, the most common, or directly as in profound meditation.

In the second influence, there is a host of extremely complex and subtle mechanisms to consider and these are expounded in Yogic philosophy. However, the three basic ideas are:

i.   The downward flow of the subjective and objective aspects of unitary conscious-ness, and their correspondences and mutual correlations, from the highest levels to the lowest (Divine Consciousness to the physical, or in popular terms, from spirit to matter).

ii.   The fundamental mechanism comprising the conjunction between the senses themselves and the Cosmic Elements, which act as stimulators and receptors of the senses. The Cosmic Elements display two aspects: an active spirit-side, or force-side—the Element–Principles; and a passive matter-side, or vehicular-side—the Element–Substances, which are always correlated at all stages of descent. The Cosmic Elements are not mere abstract principles but conscious Principles related to, and functioning through, various grades of natural forces.

iii. The transmutation from external sensation—the expertise of neurology—to internal, subjective experience—the 'hard' problem of consciousness for neuro-science—occurs at the junction of the subjective and objective aspects of mind and is brought about through Prāṇa, the vital force. In simplistic terms, Prāṇa may be regarded as a compound substance at the subjective–objective interface, hence enabling mind and matter, so-called, to affect one another.

Despite the truly infinite variety and levels of existence in manifestation, there is only one Ultimate Reality from which every variety is derived, and in which all aspects of manifes-tation, without any exception, are contained, or rather, subsumed. The Absolute is the root and fountainhead of the entire Cosmos, seen and unseen, manifest and unmanifest. It is Divine (Supreme) Consciousness. This is all beautifully represented in the symbolism of *Maheśa*, the highest level of manifest Reality. He is represented as both *Pañca-vaktram*—'five-faced'—and *Tri-netram*—'three-eyed'. This clearly symbolizes the fact that the objec-tive universe, cognized through the five sense organs, is nothing but an expression of the same Reality which functions as the cognizer and 'sees' this objective universe through the three eyes: two of the eyes are the normal eyes used for instrumental perception, while the third eye represents non-instrumental perception.[34]

To iterate a crucial insight of occult science mentioned earlier, the perception of the whole manifested universe in its infinite states of subtlety down to the physical plane is thus the result of the involution of consciousness *as matter* and not *in* matter: hence, a phenomenon of pure Consciousness.

This Chapter has built upon the previous one and shown that occult science alone is qual-ified to address, and resolve, what we have termed the 'Schrödinger Mind–Sensation Problem': how external stimuli of the physical senses results in internal experience. We have shown that the resolution of the problem of discovering a neural correlate of consciousness is, simply stated, that the neurology itself is Consciousness manifesting in the lowest aspect (i.e., physical) of *Itself*. The quest in neuroscience to find a neural corre-late of consciousness is therefore, strictly speaking, a *non sequitur*. The correct approach is to identify neural filters and transducers of Consciousness. This theme is developed in the next Chapter. Meanwhile we close with three revelatory verses from the Upaniṣads that clearly show the relation between the perceiver and the sensed objects of perception.

Higher than the senses stand the things (objects of senses),
higher than the objects of senses stands **Manas** *(mind),*
higher than the **Manas** *(mind) stands Buddhi (intellect [intelligence]),*
higher than the latter (Buddhi), the 'great self'.

Higher than that ('the great self') stands Avyaktam, (un-manifest)
higher than that (avyaktam) stands Puruṣa (the highest Being);
higher than this (Puruṣa), there is nothing any more;
he is the final goal and the highest point (of the process).

In all beings, dwells this (Puruṣa)
as Ātman, invisible, concealed from view;
he is only seen by the keenest thought,
by the subtlest (intelligence) of those thinkers who see into the subtle.

KĀṬHAKA UPANIṢAD, III: VERSES 10–12[35]

NOTES

1 Erwin Schrödinger, 'Nature and the Greeks' from the Shearman Lectures delivered at University College, London, 1948, in *Nature and the Greeks* and *Science and Humanism*, foreword by Roger Penrose (Cambridge: Cambridge University Press, 1961), 95, 97. See also Ken Wilber (ed.) *Quantum Questions: Mystical Writings of the World's Great Physicists* (Boston: Shambhala, 1985), 75–97.

2 One of the most comprehensive and readable is I. K. Taimni, *The Science of Yoga: A commentary on the Yoga-sutras of Patanjali in the light of modern thought* (Adyar, Madras: Theosophical Publishing House, 1965). Taimni was Professor of Chemistry at the University of Allahabad in India, an influential scholar in the fields of Yoga and Indian Philosophy, and a leader of the Theosophical Society.

3 Sir Francis Walshe, 'Thoughts Upon the Equation of Mind with Brain', *Brain: A Journal of Neurology*, 76/1 (March 1953), 1–18.

4 What constitutes the 'prism' is explained in detail in Edi D. Bilimoria, *The Snake and the Rope: Problems in Western science resolved by occult science* (Adyar, Madras: Theosophical Publishing House, 2006), 139 et seq.

5 Isaac Newton, *Philosophiæ Naturalis Principia Mathematica* (Mathematical Principles of Natural Philosophy), trans. Andrew Motte, rev. Florian Cajori, 2 vols (Berkeley, Los Angeles: University of California Press, 1962), ii, 'The System of the World – General Scholium', 545.

6 See the striking parallel here with the *Bhagavad Gītā* where the Lord Kṛṣṇa demonstrates to Arjuna, using his spiritual powers, that the Divine Consciousness–Power pervades all existence, but is not in any way depleted by innumerable manifestations of Itself: 'By Me all this world is pervaded in My unmanifested aspect'; 'Having pervaded this whole universe with one fragment of Myself, I remain'— *The Bhagavad Gita*, trans. Annie Besant (Adyar, Madras: Theosophical Publishing House, 1973), Ninth Discourse, Verse 4, 128; Tenth Discourse, Verse 42, 152.

7 Avinash Chandra, *The Scientist and the Saint: The limits of science and the testimony of sages*, (Cambridge, UK: Archetype, 2018), 53.

8 Fritjof Capra, *The Tao of Physics: An exploration of the parallels between modern physics and Eastern mysticism* (1975; 5th edn, Boston, Massachusetts: Shambhala Publications, 2013; quotation from 2nd imp., UK: Fontana, 1977), 21.

9 Isaac Newton, *Philosophiæ Naturalis Principia Mathematica*, i, 'The Motion of Bodies', 5–6.

10 *SD*-I, 'Proem', 2.

11 *ibid.*

12 Edi D. Bilimoria, *The Snake and the Rope*, 118–20, 137, 143.

13 *SD*-I, Proem', 15.

14 *ibid.*

15 Johann Wolfgang von Goethe, *Faust*, trans. Bayard Taylor (published by the Library of Alexandria; n.p., SMK Books, April 2018). This abstruse doctrine is described in detail in Edi D. Bilimoria, *The Snake and the Rope*, 125–77 passim.

16 Edwin Raphael, *The Pathway of Non-Duality, Advaitavada: An approach to some key-points of Gaudapada's Asparśavāda and Śaṁkara's Advaita Vedānta by means of a series of questions answered by an Asparśin* (Delhi, Motilal Banarsidass, 1992).

17 Deanna Goodrich McMain, 'Annie Besant Speaks', *Quest*, 88/5 (September–October, 2000), 184–9.

18 Roger Penrose, *Shadows of the Mind: A search for the missing science of consciousness* (Oxford: Oxford University Press, 1994), 418.

19 Shiyali Ramamrita Ranganathan, *Ramanujan, the Man and the Mathematician* (Bombay, NewYork: Asia Publishing House, 1967), 88.

20 Adapted from I. K. Taimni, *Man, God and the Universe* (Adyar, Madras, 1969; Wheaton, Illinois: Theosophical Publishing House, 1974), 83.

21 Isaac Newton, *Opticks, Or, A Treatise of the Reflections, Refractions, Inflections & Colours of Light* (London, 1730; 4th edn, New York: Dover Publications, 1979), 369, 370.

22 *SD*-I, 'Stanza I: The Night of the Universe', 51

23 Swami Sri Yuteswar Giri, *The Holy Science* (Los Angeles, California: Self-Realization Fellowship, 1990), 29, 30.

24 Eben Alexander and Karen Newell, *Living in a Mindful Universe: A neurosurgeon's journey into the heart of consciousness* (US: Rodale, 2017), 38.

25 R. Douglas Fields, 'Brain Reactions', *RSA Journal*, 4 (2016–2017), 36. This article is based on *Why We Snap: Understanding the rage circuits in your brain* (New York: Dutton, 2016).

26 Eben Alexander and Karen Newell, *Living in a Mindful Universe*, 38.

27 —— *op. cit.*, 49.

28 Annie Besant, *A Study in Consciousness: A contribution to the science of psychology* (Adyar, Madras: Theosophical Publishing House, 1972), 123–4.

29 Roger Penrose, *Shadows of the Mind*.

30 Deepak Chopra, Roger Penrose, Henry P. Stapp, Stuart R. Hameroff, York H. Dobyns, Menas Kafatos, Michael B. Mensky, Gordon Globus, Subhash Kak, and Brandon Carter, *How Consciousness Became the Universe: Quantum physics, cosmology, relativity, evolution, neuroscience, parallel universes* (2nd edn, US: Science Publishers, 2017).

31 Sir Roger Penrose, Stuart Hameroff, Ellen Langer, R. Gabriel Joseph, Chris J. S. Clarke, L. Dossey, Ernest Lawrence Rossi, Giancarlo Ghirardi, Peter Sturrock, Edgar D. Mitchel, Chris King, Walter J. Freeman, Don Page, Henry P. Stapp, Fred Kuttner, Michael B. Mensky, Ian Tattersall, William James, Bruce Rosenblum, and Martin Lockley, *Consciousness and the Universe: Quantum physics, evolution, brain & mind*, ed. Roger Penrose (Canada: Science Publishers, 2017).

32 Georg Feuerstein, *The Yoga-sūtra of Patañjali: A new translation and commentary* (Rocherter, Vermont: Inner Traditions Bear and Company, 1992), Aphorisms III-37 and III-49. See also I. K. Taimni, *Man, God and the Universe*, 429.

33 Percy Bysshe Shelley, *Adonais*, Stanza 52—see Volume I, Chapter 6, page 170.

34 Rephrased from I. K. Taimni, *Man, God and the Universe*, 432–3.

35 Paul Deussen, *Sixty Upaniṣads of the Veda*, trans. from German V. M. Bedekar and G. B. Palsule, 2 vols (Delhi, Varanassi, Patna: Motilal Banarsidass) i, 288 <https://ia801600.us.archive.org/5/items/in.ernet.dli.2015.191073/2015.191073.Sixty-Upanisads-Of-The-Veda--part--Ist_text.pdf> accessed 30 December 2020.

9 Divine Forces in the Human Being – the Awakening of Latent Faculties and Powers of Consciousness

No incident in my scientific career is more widely known than the part I took many years ago in certain psychic researches. Thirty years have passed since I published an account of experiments tending to show that outside our scientific knowledge there exists a Force exercised by intelligence differing from the ordinary intelligence common to mortals. This fact in my life is of course well understood by those who honoured me with the invitation to become your President. Perhaps among my audience some may feel curious as to whether I shall speak out or be silent. I elect to speak, although briefly. To enter at length on a still debatable subject would be unduly to insist on a topic which [...] though not unfitted for discussion at these meetings, does not yet enlist the interest of the majority of my scientific brethren. To ignore the subject would be an act of cowardice—an act of cowardice I feel no temptation to commit.

To stop short in any research that bids fair to widen the gates of knowledge, to recoil from fear of difficulty or adverse criticism, is to bring reproach on Science. There is nothing for the investigator to do [...] but to follow the light wherever it may lead [...]. I have nothing to retract. I adhere to my already published statements. Indeed, I might add much thereto.

SIR WILLIAM CROOKES[1]

SYNOPSIS

Chapter 9 describes the three primary divine forces in the human being and their role in awakening latent faculties of consciousness. The role of one of the divine forces that transmutes external physical sensation into internal experience is described in more detail along with robust scientific corroboration of the occult tenets. This leads on to an explanation of the two chief glands in the human body that act as neural transducers of consciousness. Related to this is the whole question of the means of attaining superphysical powers, like clairvoyance. Three such techniques, and their attendant dangers, for awakening powers normally latent in man are outlined, including the use of psychedelic drugs for such purposes. This exposition is followed by an outline of a simple method to attain higher states of consciousness in safety. Finally, two examples are given of mathematical geniuses who demonstrated, in full measure, the faculty of unerring intuition commensurate with heightened consciousness.

KEY WORDS: divine forces in man, vitalism, ether, neural transducers, polarities, pituitary body, pineal gland, Third Eye, intuition, latent powers, *cākras*, psychedelics, Isaac Newton, Srinivasa Ramanujan, Benjamin Richardson

This Chapter takes further the overall theme of the previous Chapter: the resolution by occult science of what we designated the Schrödinger Mind–Sensation Problem. Accordingly, in this further elaboration we commence by explaining the role of divine forces in the unfolding of consciousness and their particular function in the nature of sensation—that of which, in Schrödinger's frank admission, 'science is completely ignorant' (see the epigraph to Chapter 8). Whereas, in the main, science may indeed be 'completely ignorant', there are exceptional scientists who may not be so unaware. One such scientist was Sir Charles Sherrington, President of the Royal Society, mentioned in Chapter 3, page 42 of Volume I in connection with the influence of Goethean science in relation to the emerging science of qualities. Another glowing example, shown in the epigraph, is the British chemist and physicist Sir William Crookes (1832–1919), President of the Society for Psychical Research in the 1890s, a member of the Theosophical Society, initiated into the Hermetic Order of the Golden Dawn in 1890,[2] and President of the Royal Society (1913–1915): a celebrated scientist who not only realized the nature of the problem, but 'published an account of experiments', not exactly proving, but 'tending to show' the existence of intelligences and forces that lie outside the purview of mainstream science. It is such all-too-rare cases of legendary scientists with integrity who, notwithstanding the condemnation of their peers, had the courage to attempt a blending of physics with metaphysics that provide the beacon light for both science and occult science. No wonder, then, that Crookes's ideas figure so prominently in the occult science portions of *The Secret Doctrine*.[3]

William Crookes shows the courage of his convictions

Central to our thesis, therefore, is to show that the senses are to be regarded as the extended instruments of mind and subordinate to the latter, instead of the conventional scientific view that the senses are the basic reality and mind the product of sensations received through the sense organs. Additionally, whereas 'certain glands [do indeed] secrete a salty fluid that emerges from our eyes', as Schrödinger put it (see again the epigraph to Chapter 8), there are other consciousness-centres and glands in the human body that are particularly connected with the awakening of the latent (occult) forces in man from a state of dormancy to activity. Two such main centres are the pituitary and pineal glands. Their role and function as 'transducers' of consciousness will be outlined.

Divine Forces in the Human Being

The whole human being, but especially the heart, brain, and generative system, as main centres of consciousness, may be regarded as a divine instrument that transforms Universal Consciousness into its physical substrate (see Chapter 5, page 79 f.). Here it would be useful to revisit Chapter 3 on symbolic representations of the human body before perusing what follows on the role of the three principal divine forces in the human being and the manner in which these forces conspire to produce changes, sensations, and development.

The Role of Divine Forces

The Secret Doctrine (as indeed the whole corpus of the *philosophia perennis*) affirms that the conditioned universe is an aspect of the ONE REALITY. Furthermore:

> The Eternity of the Universe *in toto* as a boundless plane; periodically 'the playground of numberless Universes incessantly manifesting and disappearing,' called 'the manifesting

stars,' and the 'sparks of Eternity.' 'The Eternity of the Pilgrim' is like a wink of the Eye of Self-Existence [...]. 'The appearance and disappearance of Worlds is like a regular tidal ebb, flux and reflux.'[4]

'Pilgrim' is the appellation given to the Monad during its cycle of incarnations—indeed, a pilgrimage. It is the only immortal and eternal principle in man, being an indivisible part of the integral whole—the Universal Spirit, from which it emanates, and into which it is absorbed at the end of the cycle.

Simply stated, then, occultism affirms that the entire Universe in its totality, namely, the visible and invisible worlds, is the periodical manifestation of the Unmanifest Reality, which: (*a*) emanates 'numberless Universes'; (*b*) expresses itself through it for a limited period of time (however long that may be); and then (*c*) withdraws it into itself—the whole cycle being repeated numberless times. One of the many popular Hindu myths has it that creation manifests when Brahmā opens his Eye and withdraws when He closes his Eye.

Periodicity is a Universal Law

The universality of that law of periodicity, of flux and reflux, ebb and flow, which physical science has observed and recorded in all departments of nature, is not difficult to perceive. An alternation such as that of day and night, life and death, sleeping and waking, is a fact so common, so perfectly universal and without exception, that it is easy to comprehend that in it we see one of the absolutely fundamental laws of the universe.

However, in order that the Unmanifest Reality may manifest, It must first create, or rather emanate, the raw material which can be worked-up into suitable forms, or vehicles, for Its self-expression through them according to their sensitivity and responsiveness. Thus, there are three well-defined stages involved in manifestation: (*a*) creation of the raw material; (*b*) evolution of the vehicles; and (*c*) expression of REALITY through the vehicles and unfoldment of their infinite potentialities. The Ultimate Reality manifests, whereas on earth we prefer to use terms like 'manufacture' or 'build'. But the above three stages are no different, in principle. For example, we build a home by first gathering the raw materials, the bricks, etc., then developing the shape and structure of the house, and finally living in it, whereupon what was once a material house now becomes our living home. That principle applies equally to man—see the Coda to Volume II, especially Figure II-9, page 201.

Three aspects of Reality related to three functions aligned to three stages of manifestation

Accordingly, as per the Hermetic Axiom, what applies to the universe, applies to its 'child'—man. The clearest and most detailed expositions on the divine forces in the human being are in the occult philosophy of Hinduism. The *trimūrti* (the Trinity as 'three faces', or 'triple form') of *Brahmā*, *Viṣṇu*, and *Maheśa* (an aspect of *Śiva*) represent three aspects of Reality that are related to the three functions corresponding to the three stages of manifestation. This is depicted in Table III-6 on page 175. But it is important to stress that the three functions are performed by the *manifested* Deity known as *Iśvara* in Indian philosophy and *Logos* by the ancient Greeks, as also in Theosophical literature. The Logos works through the agency of the three forces that are derived from, and directly related to, its three aspects, acting as instruments of its respective functions in the body.

Despite its minute and detailed knowledge about the body, of these three divine forces, shown in Table III-6, science knows about, and acknowledges just one—electricity.

In fact, The Royal Institution of Great Britain recently (March 2018) hosted a discussion on 'The Electricity of Life', exploring how our body creates electricity, how it was discovered, and what clues our understanding of electricity can give to help cure disease—although science, as yet, would hardly want to hear about electricity derived from Brahmā, and still less its correspondence with *Fohat*, the creative force of Brahmā. Science has had suspicions about another force referred to vaguely as 'vitalism', but any such notions of vitalism (see Chapter 4, page 69 of Volume I) were effectively anathematized by the principal advocates of molecular biology who dogmatize that life is nothing other than physical chemistry (as explained in the next section on vitalism and the nervous ether). However, vitalism is slowly making a welcome comeback in the modern guise of morphogenesis (see again Volume I, Chapter 4, page 73). The third force is unknown to science. Before proceeding, it is most important to note two facts: first, that Brahmā, Viṣṇu, and Maheśa are not three separate Divine Persons (hypostases), but three Aspects of the *one* Logos in the exercise of His three different functions (in the same sense as in Christianity where Father, Son, and Holy Ghost are the three Persons of one God and not three separate gods, as Newton vehemently maintained[5]); secondly, whereas the three different types of forces are derived from, and related to, the three aspects of the Logos, these forces are not interconvertible (like mechanical energy can be converted to heat), but are three different types of energy poured out from the sun (strictly speaking, the Solar Logos of which the physical sun is its outer 'clothing') and appropriated by the human body for its various functions (see later). For example, is not the vitalizing effect of sunshine a common experience? What is known as 'SAD', the appropriate acronym for Seasonal Affective Disorder, is known to affect many people resulting in feelings of depression because of the reduction of vitalizing prāṇa due to depleted sunlight during long and dark winter nights or overcast skies.

Function of the
three Divine
Forces

All material changes in the human body are brought about by electricity, and other related forces (such as electromagnetism), and their associated organizing fields known to science (as previously touched upon in Chapter 4 of Volume I on pages 79–82 in relation to the thoughts of Gustaf Strömberg). These are related to the form, or material side, of the body and nature, hence derived from Brahmā as Creator. *Prāṇa*, derived from Viṣṇu as Preserver and Pervader, is related to the life side of the body and nature and is responsible for, and underlies, all life processes in the body to make it a living organism, in contradistinction to an insentient aggregate of forces and matter. Most significantly, prāṇa lies at the basis of sensation and without its association with a sense organ, the vibrations received by that organ would remain ineffective and would not be converted into sensation. Hence, the endeavour by neuroscience to discover a neural correlate of consciousness has met with only partial and limited success, and will never attain fruition until due cognizance is taken of vitalism and the role of prāṇa. This was stated frankly in the summary to the previous Chapter with reference to the Schrödinger Mind–Sensation problem: how external stimulus to the physical sense organs produces internal, subjective sensation. Since vitalism and prāṇa are absolutely crucial to our thesis, more details are provided in justification in the following section in order to amplify what was provided in Chapter 8.

Meanwhile, the third divine force, *kuṇḍalinī*, is derived from Maheśa (an aspect of Śiva as regenerator) and is found only in the human being and not in any other living organisms. The reason is complex: in outline, it is because the functioning of the First Logos commences only when the Causal Body is formed, that is, upon individualization. It is

Table III-6 Divine Forces in the Human Being

THE LOGOS – ITS ROLE UNDER THREE ASPECTS		
Third Logos **Brahmā, the Creator**	Second Logos **Viṣṇu, the Preserver**	First Logos **Maheśa, the Regenerator**
STAGES IN MANIFESTATION		
First stage	Second stage	Third stage
ROLE/FUNCTION		
Form-side – Confining/Limiting Creation/Manifestation – Creation of the raw material	Life-side – Immanent/Pervading Preservation/Perception – Evolution of the vehicles	Consciousness-side – Transcendent/Releasing Regeneration/ Renewal – Expression of Reality through the vehicles and unfoldment of their infinite potentialities
PLANE OF OPERATION		
Ātma	*Anupādaka*	*Ādi*
ROLE AND MANIFESTATION OF DIVINE FORCES IN THE HUMAN BEING AND THE CORRESPONDENCES BETWEEN THE TRIPLICITY		
Form	Life	Consciousness
Electricity	Vitalism	Regeneration
Known	Knowing	Knower
Fohat, or *Agni* – the Creative force of *Brahmā*	*Prāṇa*, or *Chi* – the Preserving force of *Viṣṇu*	*Kuṇḍalinī* – the Regenerating force of *Maheśa*
GUṆAS, THE ESSENTIAL ATTRIBUTES OF MATTER		
Rājas	*Sattva*	*Tamas*
ASPECT OF CONSCIOUSNESS		
Chit	*Ānanda*	*Sat*

upon the connection of the monad with the physical body and the associated descent of this eternal element into the Causal Body that man enters the unending and ever progressive cycle of evolution, which literally has no limits and for which the previous evolutionary stages in the animal kingdom serve just as a preparation for this stage. So kuṇḍalinī is intimately connected with the functioning and unfoldment of consciousness in the human body. Again, science has not unlocked, and never will unlock the full mystery of consciousness unless it understands the role and function of kuṇḍalinī, even in cursory fashion.

Finally, on the matter of the three fundamental, Divine Forces, it should never be imagined that during the lifetime of a human being the three Forces act sequentially, with only one force active at any one time. All three Forces are always in action: what varies is the

Three Divine Forces always in action in different degrees

predominance of one force over the others. For example, in a small child an injury to its body (say, a cut to its finger) would heal rapidly because the creative and vital forces of Brahmā and Viṣṇu predominate. Yet, in the background, there is the 'destructive' force of Śiva; otherwise the eventual and inevitable death of the human body would never occur. Around middle age the three forces would be roughly in balance. However, upon reaching old age the Maheśa force in its role as *Śiva Rudra*, the 'Destroyer' would predominate to bring the incarnation to a close, for there has to be a destruction, i.e., break *down* of the outworn form (the physical body) in order for a break *through* into a new phase of consciousness and associated materiality. Nonetheless, the Brahmā and Viṣṇu forces would still operate in the background, so the same finger injury inflicted would take much longer to heal.

> **Even with a modicum of intuition, and provided that our minds are not trammelled by materialistic concepts, we should be convinced that behind such dynamically balanced and finely adjusted forces in the human body lies a supreme Consciousness, a consummate Wisdom, a master Intelligence.**

We move on to a matter of crucial importance: the preserving and vitalizing force of Viṣṇu through the instrumentality of prāṇa, or *chi*. Its role and function were explained in Chapter 8. What follows is more evidence drawn from both science and occultism in support of the vital principle.

Vitalism and the Nervous Ether

Mainstream biology regards life as purely chemistry

The writer once attended a fine talk at Oxford University by the English palæontologist Simon Conway Morris FRS (*b.*1952) popularly known for his theistic views of biological evolution. During question time, Conway Morris remarked, 'of course, we don't now talk about vitalism' in a half-apologetic tone uncharacteristic of the confidence and conviction of his exposition on evolution. A more outspoken statement against vitalism comes from the biologist, science writer, and former editor of *Nature*, Sir John Maddox[i] in his lecture to the British Humanist Society: 'Life is chemistry. And vitalism is dead. That's wisdom in a true sense, and it's invaluable.'[6] These are just two examples of the opinions of the vast majority of world famous scientists who now claim the 'death of vitalism' on the basis of the joint claim by Francis Crick and James Watson that 'the discovery of DNA's double-helix structure was a major blow to the vitalist approach and gave momentum to the reductionist field of molecular biology.'[7] These scientists now see in the phenomenon of life (as in light, heat, and electricity) only properties inherent in physical matter, and deride any notion of a vital principle being independent of, and distinct from, the organism. One wonders how Crick and Watson would have responded some sixty years on to the English physicist Paul Davies (*b.*1946) awarded the Templeton Prize in 1995 who maintains that, 'The secret of life won't be cooked up in a chemistry lab: Life's origins may only be explained through a study of its unique management of information.'[8]

Vitalism is now an anathema to mainstream biology

But if vitalism is now supposed to be 'dead' it must once have been living, in fact is still living. Moreover, scientific opinion is by no means united on this subject and, as in everything else, there are a few men of science whose views veer towards occultism. So

---

i As documented in Volume II, Chapter 7, page 131 f., Maddox is well known for his extreme antipathy towards Rupert Sheldrake's ideas.

despite the outright denial of a vital principle by their peers in biology and physiology, these enlightened scientists have seen through the limitations of the *exclusively* 'reductionist field of molecular biology' towards an insight that, '"We human beings" experiencing our joys and our sorrows, our memories and our ambitions, our sense of personal identity and free will, *cannot possibly* be *just* the behaviour of a vast assembly of nerve cells and their associated molecules.'[9] Therefore, there has to be a distinct principle independent of the organism (of a material nature, just as physical force cannot be divorced from matter), but of a substance existing in a state still unknown to orthodox science and 'the ordinary intelligence common to mortals' as Crookes put it (see again the epigraph). *Life for these few legendary scientists is something more than the mere interaction of molecules and atoms.* They maintain that without a vital principle, no molecular combinations could ever have resulted in a living organism, least of all in the so-called 'inorganic' matter of our physical plane of consciousness. A summary of their views about the vital principle—and especially their justification for its existence—now follows.

Life is More Than Physical Chemistry

That life is more than just chemistry is shown very impressively by Alexis Carrel (1873–1944), the French professor, surgeon, and biologist who was awarded the Nobel Prize in Physiology (or Medicine) for pioneering vascular suturing techniques. In his book *Man, the Unknown* he shows the difference in quantitative ratio in externally similar processes, one of which occurs within the domain of life using the human organism as an example, and the other, outside it. Carrel compares the quantity of liquid necessary to keep artificially alive a piece of living tissue which has been reduced to pulp, with the quantity of blood doing the same within the living organism:

Is human blood just a chemical compound?

> If all the tissues of the human body were treated in this way, it would take 45,000 gallons of circulating fluid to keep them from being poisoned in a few days by their own waste products. Within the living organism [the human body] the blood achieves the same task with 1½ gallons.[10]

Any person who is not so mesmerized by materialistic concepts would draw breath and ask the deeper question: 'what unique properties does the blood possess that cannot be explained by physics and chemistry unaided?'

Amongst modern scientists, Rupert Sheldrake springs to mind with his theory of morphic resonance. This does not mention *prāṇa* specifically, but the whole idea of morphogenetic fields could perhaps be regarded as a restatement of organizing fields, in the context of modern developmental biology, inasmuch as formative causation is not solely the product of molecular interactions and presupposes an independent organizing principle influenced by the past experiences of the species and organisms that it conditions and *in*-forms in the present.[11] Refer to Volume I, Chapter 4, page 69 et seq. about organizing fields, morphic resonance, vitalist theories in general, and the limitations of vitalist theories (e.g. as propounded by Hans Driesch), the chief one being the irresolvable duality between the non-living and the living.

Winding the clock back to the late nineteenth and early twentieth century, there have been many scientists who have postulated organizing fields and vitalism. The explicitly stated views of the eminent British physician, anaesthetist, and physiologist, Sir Benjamin Ward Richardson FRS (1828–1896) on the vital principle which he calls 'nervous ether', its fountainhead in the sun, and the reasons for its existence, are particularly significant. The following extract from Richardson in *Popular Science Review* is also quoted by H. P. Blavatsky due to its relevance to the occult explanation of consciousness:

> The idea attempted to be conveyed by the theory is that between the molecules of the matter, solid or fluid, of which the nervous organisms, and, indeed, of which all the organic parts of the body are composed, there exists a refined subtle medium, vaporous or gaseous, which holds the molecules in a condition for motion upon each other, and for arrangement and rearrangement of form; a medium by and through which all motion is conveyed; by and through which the one organ or part of the body is held in communion with the other parts and by and through which the outer living world communicates with the living man: a medium which, being present, enables the phenomena of life to be demonstrated, and which, being universally absent, leaves the body actually dead....[12]

In referring to the 'refined subtle medium', Richardson continues:

> I use the word *ether* in its general sense, as meaning a very light, vaporous or gaseous matter; I use it, in short, as the astronomer uses it when he speaks of the ether of space, by which he means a subtle but material medium.... When I speak of a *nervous* ether, I do not convey that the ether is existent in nervous structure only: I believe, truly, that it is a special part of the nervous organization; but as nerves pass into all structures that have capacities for movement and sensibilities, so the nervous ether passes into all such parts; and as the nervous ether is, according to my view, a direct product from blood, so we may look upon it as a part of the atmosphere of the blood.[13]

Benjamin Richardson on vitalism, ether, and matter

About the nature of the ether, he says:

> I speak only of a veritable *material agent*, refined, it may be, to the world at large, but *actual and substantial*: an agent having quality of weight and of volume; an agent susceptible of chemical combination, and thereby of change of physical state and condition; an agent passive in its action, moved always, that is to say, by influences apart from itself, obeying other influences; an agent possessing no initiative power, no *vis*, or *energia naturæ*, but still playing a most important, if not a primary part in the production of the phenomena resulting from the action of the *energia* upon visible matter.[14]

Acknowledging the 'wisdom of the elders', Richardson continues:

> The evidence in favour of the existence of an elastic medium pervading the nervous matter and capable of being influenced by simple pressure is all-convincing ... In nervous structure there is, unquestionably, a true nervous fluid, *as our predecessors* taught. Paracelsus for one, who called it *liquor vitæ*, and *Archæus*. [H. P. B.][15]

Then, as a true man of science, Richardson frankly admits that there are still many unknowns, such as the precise chemical composition of this fluid, whether it moves in currents or circulates, whether it is formed in the nerves, the blood or elsewhere, and consequently, its exact uses. But he continues with this passage of major significance:

> It occurs to my mind, however, that the veritable fluid of nervous matter is not of itself sufficient to act as the subtle medium that connects the outer with the inner universe of man and animal. I think—and this is the modification I suggest to the older theory

[of vitalism]—there must be another form of matter present during life; a matter which exists in the condition of vapour or gas, which pervades the whole nervous organism, *surrounds, as an enveloping atmosphere*, each molecule of nervous structure, and is the medium of all motion communicated to and from the nervous centres ... When it is once fairly presented to the mind that during life *there is in the animal body a finely diffused form of matter*, a vapour filling every part—and even stored in some parts; a matter constantly renewed by the vital chemistry; a matter as easily disposed of as the breath, after it has served its purpose—a new flood of light breaks on the Intelligence.[16]

Sun: the reservoir of life-force

A 'new flood of light' is certainly thrown on the wisdom of ancient and mediæval Occultism and its votaries, for, we have an important scientific corroboration for a fundamental tenet of occultism—that (*a*) the Sun is the store-house of life-force, or vital force (see below) and (*b*) that it is from its mysterious depths, that issue those life currents which thrill through Space, as through the organisms of every living thing on Earth, as what occultists refer to as *prāṇa*, our 'life-fluid', and the eminent physician Richardson as 'nervous ether', or 'nerve fluid'. His article amounts to a quasi-occult treatise on life-force, as the above quoted extracts show—'quasi', because there are inaccuracies which Blavatsky points out, and corrects in the light of occultism, for example Sun Force not only flows through Space but fills every point of our solar system (and others that need not concern us here).

However, as Blavatsky again points out, Paracelsus wrote the same thing more than three hundred years ago, namely, in the sixteenth century:

> The whole of the Microcosm is potentially contained in the *Liquor Vitæ*, a nerve fluid.... in which is contained the nature, quality, character, and essence of beings....[17]

Paracelsus on cosmic forces and influences on man

> The Archæus or *Liquor Vitæ* is an essence that is equally distributed in all parts of the human body.... The *Spiritus Vitæ* takes it origin from the *Spiritus Mundi*. Being an *emanation of the latter*, it contains the elements of all cosmic influences, and is therefore the cause by which the action of the stars (cosmic forces) upon the invisible body of man (his *vital liṅga-śarīra*) may be explained.[18]

Moreover, Paracelsus in *Paragranum*, his main work on medical philosophy, states that 'this vital force .... radiates around man like a luminous sphere',[19] which is surely the same as what Richardson regards as 'a matter which exists in the condition of vapour or gas, which pervades the whole nervous organism, *surrounds as an enveloping atmosphere* each molecule of nervous structure.

A century later Newton, who made an exhaustive study of ancient and mediæval alchemy in England and Europe, wrote at the close of the General Scholium of *Principia*:

> And now we might add something concerning a certain most subtle spirit, which pervades and lies hid in all gross bodies; by the force and action of which spirit [...] all sensation is excited, and the members of animal bodies move at the command of the will, namely, by the vibrations of this Spirit, mutually propagated along the solid filaments of the nerves, from the outward organs of sense to the brain, and from the brain into the muscles. But these are things that cannot be explain'd in few words [...].[20]

Newton on all-pervading Spirit. See Volume II, Appendix II-A

Indeed it is so. Recondite matters of such deep import 'are things that cannot be explain'd in few words', and what was revealed by occultists, like Blavatsky, was about the limit of what could lawfully be made public regarding the arcane secrets of life and nature. These, of course, have also been touched upon by enlightened scientists, to their great credit, not afraid to pierce through physical chemistry ring-fenced by a materialistic paradigm and mechanistic ideology in order to look beyond it in their quest for truth.

From all of the above, is it not disappointing for the occultist to hear Nobel laureates in science talking glibly of 'chemical energy', or, to wit, 'life as chemistry', and denouncing the parent vital energy as an exploded superstition?

A brief word now on the Sun Force as the origin of prāṇa, again from Richardson:

Benjamin Richardson and Samuel Metcalfe, on the Sun Force

> At this moment, when the theory of mere motion as the origin of all varieties of force is again becoming the prevailing thought, it were almost heresy to reopen a debate, which for a period appears, by general consent, to be virtually closed; but I accept the risk, and shall state, therefore, what were the precise views of the immortal heretic, whose name [Samuel Metcalfe] [*sic*], I have whispered to the readers respecting sun force. Starting with the argument on which nearly all physicists are agreed, that there exist in nature two agencies, matter which is ponderable, visible, and tangible, and a something which is imponderable, invisible, and appreciable only by its influence on matter, Metcalfe maintains that the imponderable and active agency, which he calls '*caloric*,' is *not a mere form of motion*, not a vibration amongst the particles of ponderable matter, but *itself a material substance flowing from the sun* through space, filling the voids between the particles of solid bodies, and conveying by sensation the property called heat.[21]

The nature of caloric, or Sun Force, is contended for in detail by the American chemist and physician Samuel Metcalfe (1798–1856) in a remarkable work in two volumes, *Caloric: Its mechanical chemical and vital agencies in the phenomena of nature*.[22] It is undeniably the 'immortal heretic' who finds the courage of his convictions to break asunder the prevailing scientific paradigm to reveal new vistas of understanding. This applies in any age. True to type, such heretics, like the modern Rupert Sheldrake, are subject to ridicule by their peers and their ideas and books are 'burnt at the stake of reason and intellect' (refer to Chapter 7, in Volume II on page 131).

Another such heretic is the writer of this work, who does not accept the mandate of mainstream physics that the Michelson-Morley experiment has sounded the final death knell over any question about the existence of an ether. Appendix A to Volume II provided an extensive summary of academic papers and theories in support of an ether and included an extract from Einstein's lecture at Leiden University, where he concluded that, 'according to the general theory of relativity space without ether is unthinkable [...] But this ether may not be thought of as endowed with the quality characteristic of ponderable media,' which is clearly why Newton referred to 'ether' as 'a certain most subtle spirit, which pervades and lies hid in all gross bodies', as quoted above.

Finally on this topic, the importance of *prāṇa*, or *chi*, is recognized world-wide in connection with health and equanimity. *Prāṇāyāma* is one of the ancient Indian yogic disciplines for achieving that purpose. The word is derived from the Sanskrit *prāṇa* and *āyāma* meaning 'control and regulation of the breath'; prāṇa variously translated in yoga systems as the life-force, vital air, vital energy, and life energy. Its health-giving benefits include clearing physical and emotional obstacles in the body, concentration, and mental clarity by freeing the breath and so promoting the unrestricted flow of prāṇa.[23]

The Indian sage Patanjali (dated by Orientalists to 200 BC and by Occultists nearer to 700 than 600 BC) was the founder of the science and philosophy of yoga (the word yoga meaning 'union'); and his classic text on the Yoga Sūtras (aphorisms)[24] mentions *prāṇāyāma* as a means to realize and attain *Samādhi*—the state of consciousness of ecstatic and complete trance, the highest state of Yoga. Such attainment of higher states of consciousness applies, of course, to other yogic techniques when practised with the correct attitude of reverence and under the expert guidance of a qualified teacher.[25] (Trance, in this context, means a proactive spiritual trance in which there is absolute control over all faculties, physical, psychological, and mental, having absolutely nothing whatsoever to do with passive trance states induced by drugs, mediumship or other abnormal breathing practices.)

Prāṇayama and yoga, qigong and t'ai chi ch'uan: their vital role in health

Similar to prāṇayama in its aims, but using quite different techniques, is the ancient Chinese practice of qigong, variously translated as qi gong, chi kung, or chi gung.[26] *Qi*, or *chi* is life energy, with the emphasis on its circulation through the body; though a more general definition, like that of its virtual synonym, prāṇa, is universal life force. All Qigong practices are intended to cultivate and balance chi through co-ordinated body posture and movement, moving meditation, regulated slow flowing movement, deep rhythmic breathing, and a calm state of mind. It is practised variously for exercise and relaxation, preventive medicine and self-healing, alternative medicine, meditation, and self-cultivation. According to Taoist, Buddhist, and Confucian philosophy, Qigong allows access to higher realms of awareness, awakens the true nature of a person, and helps develop human potential.

T'ai Chi Ch'uan (Taijiquan)[27] is a widely practiced Chinese internal martial style exercise based on the theory of *taiji* ('grand ultimate'), closely associated with qigong, and typically involving more complex choreographed movement co-ordinated with the breath, done slowly for health and training, or quickly for self-defence. In modern practice, qigong typically focuses more on health and meditation rather than martial applications. It also plays an important role in training for T'ai Chi Ch'uan and is invariably used to build strength, develop breath control, and increase vitality, or life energy.

Neural Transducers of Consciousness – The Role of the Pituitary Body and Pineal Gland

Latent powers in man partially unveiled

In the section about the unfolding of man's latent (occult) powers in Chapter 3 it was stated that there exist forces lying dormant within certain apparently physical organs, channels, and centres in the body, which are, in reality, the veils, or sheaths of spiritual centres of forces and powers. We stated that a fragment of such secrets on how to awaken these forces, hitherto divulged only to deserving candidates, was made public for the first time through the aegis of the Esoteric Section of the Theosophical Society and the Inner Group Teachings in response to the phenomenal explosion in knowledge in modern times, which has made huge strides in the physical sciences but which has barely touched their occult kernel.

What follows, then, represents a fragment torn from the original fragment regarding the occult forces latent in two principal organs: the pituitary body and the pineal gland, which are psycho-neural transducers of consciousness, so to speak, dormant under normal conditions for the vast majority of people by virtue of the protective veil just mentioned, but which can be aroused under special circumstances. Our objective is certainly not to divulge guarded secrets (even if we knew about them), but to show the limitless—truly unlimited—powers latent in man that are part of his deserving heritage and which can all be accessed in the fullness of time under appropriate circumstances, and given the right qualifications of ethics and character of the aspirant.

We commence with an aphorism of deep significance by Paul Brunton:

> At opposing ends of the spine, the human and the animal oppose each other.[28]

Instead of attempting an outright explanation of its significance, let the meaning dawn gradually into a fuller light as we proceed. First, we outline the physiological functions of these two glands as a precursor to a bare outline of their veiled secrets.

Physiological Role

Of the endocrine organs, the function of the pineal gland was the last to be discovered. About the size of a grain of rice and located deep in the centre of the brain (the vertebrate brain), the pineal gland was once known as the 'third eye' (for reasons that will become apparent). The precise physiological function of the pineal gland is still something of a mystery to medical science. However, it is known that it secretes a single hormone, melatonin, which serves two principal functions: to control the circadian rhythm of the body (24-hour biological cycle characterized by sleep-wake patterns); and to regulate certain reproductive hormones. Melatonin secretion is dependent on light, by virtue of the network of nerve connections between the photosensitive cells in the retina of the eye and the pineal gland, such that secretion is low during daylight hours and high during dark periods.

The pituitary body (gland) is a pea-sized structure located at the base of the brain, just below the hypothalamus, to which it is attached via nerve fibres. It is sometimes known as the 'master gland' of the endocrine system since its physiological function is to produce critical hormones that regulate the functions of other endocrine glands and control various bodily functions.

Latent Powers in Man

Before describing the hidden potentiality in the pineal and pituitary glands for the full flowering of consciousness in man, we first need to touch upon the reason why the pineal gland is referred to under such names as the 'Third Eye', or the 'Eye of Horus' in Egypt, or in Hindu esotericism as the 'Deva Eye', while in the esoteric Buddhism of Tibet and the Trans-Himalayan regions it is referred to as the 'Eye of Dangma'.[29] What are all these various terms pointing to? In order to understand this, it must be borne in mind that every phase of evolution reflects a profound intelligence and wisdom whereby the inner forces of consciousness work through the instrumentality of the outer functions of sense organs and the body, notably the various psycho-physical centres, or *cākras* (chakras), among the highest of which is the pineal gland. These centres continue to develop as man evolves spiritually. However, evolution in the fullest sense also includes previous cycles of involution. Involution means the generation of different forms of increasing concretion as the vehicles for expressing essential types and faculties, as explained fully in Chapter 10. It is concerned with developing self-expression through limitation, hence it has a constraining effect on consciousness—in popular terms, the imprisonment of spirit in matter. Evolution, on the other hand, refers to an expansion of consciousness by transcending the limitations of form—the release of spirit from matter through

> **Evolution is both the divine imperative, and its response in matter creating vehicles of expression.**

conscious knowledge. Science considers just evolution (and only at the physical level), having practically ignored the involutionary cycle; so by restricting itself to less than half of the overall process, can be in no position to pronounce on a complete theory of evolution.

Involutionary and Evolutionary Cycles

The importance of the contrast between the involutionary and evolutionary cycles of development is that both these stages apply to the consciousness and development of humanity. When we think of the 'third eye' several images come to mind. One is an association with animals, such as iguanas or the ancient tuataras of New Zealand, which still have a functional third eye; and scientific evidence today supports the possibility that this organ was the first eye in nature, particularly in the vertebrates and possibly even in man in a rudimentary natural sense. This is because microscopic examination has revealed that it is formed of cells that have the distinct features of the rod-shaped, light-sensitive cells found in the retina, indicating its possible original function as an organ of sight. In higher vertebrates neurons are usually located in the pineal gland.[30] Then there are fertile sources of information about human evolution and the third eye from the universal myths and traditions of the world over, from the West and the East. We may recall stories told in childhood about the one-eyed giant Cyclops, of Greek myth, fought by Ulysses, or the mystical Eye of Śiva, representing intuition, or direct cosmic vision. These mythical traditions also feature early races of one-eyed giants and titans said to have lived long ages ago. The timeless wisdom of this ancient lore provides vital knowledge about how mankind came into existence on Earth, and by blending the interpretations of science with ancient sources in the light of occultism we gain a new perspective and fuller appreciation about the dim past of humanity and the third eye.

> The third eye: antediluvian, mythological, historical, mammalian

What the timeless wisdom has informed us is that in the hoary past, man did not inhabit his present 'coat of skin' but expressed through a body of much more ethereal substance. Not being immersed in physicality at that time, his spiritual and psychic faculties were operative in proportion to the dormancy of his physical faculties. Then over the long course of involution—the progressive burial of spirit in matter—his spiritual and psychic nature diminished in proportion to the ascendency of his physical nature and form. The nadir of this involutionary cycle (deepest immersion in matter) occurred during the latter stages of the Fourth (Atlantean) Root Race (explained on page 187). From then onwards began the slow evolutionary cycle (which science studies exclusively at the physical level) of the release of spirit from bondage in matter. Then as we are told, after aeons, man will arrive at the same point of his original spirituality, but only this time in full self-consciousness as opposed to the instinctive, or reflexive, state of the same condition earlier. Man will cycle backwards to his earlier state of spirituality, by cycling forwards in his evolutionary development.[31]

The Third Eye

The point of all this is that during those early pre-historical epochs, man had one eye, the eye of spiritual sight. Then when he developed two eyes, the Third Eye—the Devā Eye—gradually atrophied and became what is now called the pineal gland. However, this organ can, by specific techniques, be awakened to confer the spiritual insight that was once its role. As Blavatsky avers, the pineal gland is 'the very key to the highest and divinest consciousness in man—his omniscient, spiritual and all-embracing mind'; and moreover: 'This seemingly useless appendage [to allopathic medicine] is the pendulum which, once the clock-work of the *inner* man is wound up, carries the spiritual vision of the Ego [the Higher Self] to the highest planes of perception, where the horizon open before it becomes almost infinite….'[32] We shall return to this theme shortly. Note, however, that it is only for illustra-

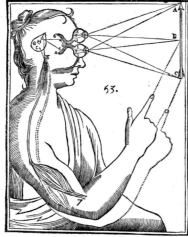

tive purposes, and often out of ignorance, that the third eye has been portrayed as being between the two physical eyes in the forehead. 'The third eye was at the back of the head. The "deva-eye" exists no more for the majority of mankind. The *third eye is dead*, and acts no longer; but it has left behind a witness to its existence. This witness is now the Pineal Gland.'[33]

Figure III-31   The Function
of the Pineal Gland by
Descartes

*Image Credit: Wikimedia Commons/Welcome
Images/ Descartes; A Treatise on the formation of
the foetus Wellcome L0017416.jpg*

The Pineal Gland and the Polarity of Spirituality and Sexuality

But even nowadays the spiritual function of the pineal gland is not entirely defunct. We recognize its activity whenever we have a flash of spontaneous under-standing about a situation, ranging from a hunch to clairvoyant abilities and intuitive awareness. How well it functions in each of us depends on how much we foster our spiritual capacities. A good case in point is none other than Descartes, who suggested (more

wisely than he possibly knew) that the pineal gland, which he correctly located at the back of the head, might be the abode of the spirit of man—see the adjacent Figure III-31. 'Unscientific as this may appear in our day of exact learning, Descartes was yet far nearer the occult truth than is any Hæckel. For the pineal gland, as shown, is far more connected with Soul and Spirit than with the physiological senses of man.'[34] Parenthetically, Ernst Haeckel (1834–1919) was the German biologist, naturalist, philosopher, and physician who promoted and popularised Charles Darwin's work in Germany. He was a contemporary of Blavatsky and his work and ideas have been critically appraised in *The Secret Doctrine*.

At this juncture we need to emphasize the polarity of spirituality and sexuality. As stated earlier, medical science has discovered that sexuality, at the lower pole, is linked to the secretion of the hormone melatonin, at the upper pole, which regulates certain reproductive hormones. However, the connection is not merely physiological, but deeply psycho-spiritual. Occultly, the pineal gland, at the upper pole of the human body, corresponds with the uterus and its analogue in the male at the lower pole; and the peduncles (collection of connecting nerve fibers) of the pineal gland correspond with the fallopian tubes of the uterus. 'Man is androgyne, so far as his head is concerned.'[35]

Practical Occultism founded on the Esoteric Philosophy recognizes the direct and intimate connection subsisting between the pineal gland and the genitalia located at opposite ends of the spine. These two are creative poles, and when one is positive and active, the other is negative and passive in proportion. Thus, when the North Pole of the spine, the pineal gland, is active, it creates, i.e., gives birth to ideas, thoughts, and intuitions; when the South Pole, the generative organ, is active, children of flesh are procreated. In the ordinary individual, the genitalia and pineal gland are both active by turns, and therefore, he is a mixture of lust and love, of passion and compassion. This is the essential meaning behind the earlier quotation by Brunton at the head of this section that the animal and the man oppose each other at opposite ends of the human spine. We see evidence of this strong polarity in highly creative people (especially, musicians, painters, and performing artists) or powerful and influential public figures (like money-and-power-crazed politicians and billionaires) whose personal lives are invariably replete with diverse sexual encounters.

True meaning of chastity

But in no sense whatsoever is there the least implication in this, or for that matter in any of the holy scriptures or occult doctrines, that sexuality, *per se*, is debasing or adverse to spirituality. This entirely mistaken, moralistic idea invariably prevails in religious or spiritual societies when the living message gets mired in dogma and dead ritual. But what is most emphatically inimical to the evolution of spirituality are the sensual, carnal, and lusting appetites of the unbridled lower nature of man—his animal nature, so-called—but not his natural, love-driven desire for procreation. Terms like 'chastity', or the Eastern word *Brahmacarya*, are much misunderstood, having all to do with pure motives and cleanliness of thought, rather than an artificially enforced celibacy of the body—with the mind invariably running amok with sexual phantasies. Is this also not what the Christ meant when He warned that to look upon a woman with lust was tantamount to committing adultery in one's heart?[ii] All this has much to do with the awakening of the occult potentialities within the pineal gland. Meanwhile, what is the occult function of the pituitary gland and its relation to the pineal gland?

The Pituitary Body and its Relation to the Pineal Gland

The occult wisdom affirms that the pituitary gland (body) is connected with pure psychic visions, in contrast to the pineal gland which is linked with spiritual visions. The pituitary gland is therefore the organ *per se* of the psychic plane. Pure psychic vision is caused by its molecular motion (for want of a better term in English), which is directly connected with the optic nerve, and thus affects the sight, hence giving rise to hallucinations. Its motion may readily cause flashes of light, seen within the head, similar to those that may be obtained on pressing the eyeballs, and so causing molecular motion in the optic nerve. When molecular action is set up in the pituitary, these flashes are seen, and further action gives psychic vision, as similar motion in the pineal gland gives spiritual clairvoyance.

Psychic images versus spiritual visions

The pineal gland is the focus of the spiritual, hence inorganic, sensorium. However, the pituitary gland is only the servant of the pineal gland, its torch-bearer, like the servants

---

ii Matthew 5:28, King James Version: 'But I say unto you, That whosoever looketh on a woman to lust after her hath committed adultery with her already in his heart.'

carrying torches that run before the carriage of a princess. In a modern context, the pituitary gland is the emissary of its master, the pineal gland, and it is a matter of considerable speculation by the writer whether these two glands can be correlated with the left and right hemispheres, respectively, of the brain in the context of the groundbreaking book, *The Master and His Emissary* by McGilchrist (see Chapter 7 of Volume II on page 122).

The Opened Third Eye – The Faculty and Fruits of Awakened Consciousness

Earlier we alluded to the faculty intimately connected with the Third Eye, which mythological tradition ascribes to certain antediluvian (in the prehistoric sense) races of man. But terms such as the 'Third Eye', or for that matter, the 'Eye of Śiva', 'Devā Eye', or 'Eye of Dangma' do not convey the full significance of the faculty, which is best expressed in the esoteric phraseology as 'Dangma's open Eye'. What is the significance of the open eye, and what exactly does Dangma mean? 'Dangma' means a purified soul, one who has become a *jīvanmukta*, or the highest adept, or mahātmā. His 'open eye' is therefore the *inner spiritual eye* of the seer, and the faculty which manifests through it is not merely clairvoyance as ordinarily understood, i.e., the power of seeing at a distance, but rather the faculty of spiritual intuition, through which direct and certain knowledge is obtainable. This is the faculty that is intimately connected with the Third Eye.[36]

Insights into intuition

'Intuition' is a word that is commonly and rather loosely used. What exactly does it mean? The stepping stone to an understanding is to perceive more deeply what the phrase 'open eye' means, as hinted above. Physically, an open eye is able to perceive objects that would still be existing were the eye to remain shut, but which are brought into conscious perception when the eye opens. It is the movement from temporary blindness to sight. Spiritually, it is the same process on a higher level. Here the open Third Eye represents spiritual intuition and omniscience. The faculty of *buddhi* exists in man, but in the vast majority of cases it is not so much atrophied, as dormant. However, when there is a conjunction of *buddhi* with *manas*, the dormant faculty of buddhi is awakened and activated, which process is known as the opening of the Third Eye, which also represents the exercise of Spiritual Will. Then the seer destroys, or rather sublimates, things on one plane to bring them to life on a higher plane. For example, at one level, *kāma* is the desire for sensual gratification; but on a higher level, it is the desire for the happiness of all beings. The human principle of manas, when freed from its lower attraction towards kāma, turns toward the luminous faculty of buddhi for illumination, and becomes increasingly receptive. It manifests as intuitive 'flashes', and, at times, as a direct vision—a sort of momentary clairvoyance for an initiate, but for the prophet and seer, what far transcends ordinary clairvoyance—a permanent faculty of spiritual intuition. The Eye of *Dangma* thus enables the initiated one to perceive the essence of things without being influenced by *māyā*, or illusion.

The truths of the ancient rishis of India were not evolved as a result of logical reasoning or systematic philosophy, but were the fruits of *dṛṣṭi*, or spiritual vision. The rishis were not so much the authors of the truths recorded in the Vedas as the seers who were able to discern the eternal truths by raising their consciousness to the plane of universal consciousness, taught by Dr Radhakrishnan.[37] Herein lies the difference between ordinary perception (i.e., brain perception) subject to doubt and illusion, which is located in the aura of the pineal gland, and the pineal gland itself, when illumined, i.e., awakened, which corresponds with Divine Thought and spiritual vision where no uncertainty can exist.

Although the Devā Eye no longer functions for the vast majority of mankind, there was an epoch when all that is now referred to in terms like paranormal, supernatural, weird, or abnormal, once belonged to the *normal* senses and faculties of consciousness common to all humanity of that era, such as thought transference, clairvoyance, clairaudience, and much more—all so puzzling to the few physiologists and parapsychological researchers compelled to admit their existence. At times, the spiritual instructors of humanity have referred to what is known as 'Root Races'. The term has nothing whatsoever to do with racial or ethnic background—least of all, with racial or ethnic superiority or inferiority. On the micro-scale, human development is a predictable process that moves through the principal stages of infancy, childhood, adolescence, and adulthood. Just so, on the macro-scale, Root Races refer to landmark developmental stages in the consciousness of humanity, each Race bringing forth latent aspects of consciousness over the long course of evolution.

True meaning of Root Races

In this regard, Blavatsky informs us that present-day mankind is cycling forwards in order to cycle back on a higher turn of the spiral, as earlier said; for having lost in spirituality that which mankind acquired in physical development until almost the end of the Fourth Root-Race, mankind, now in the Fifth Root-Race, is as gradually and imperceptibly losing now in the physical (i.e., in physicality) in order to regain once more his former faculties in the spiritual *re*-evolution. This process must go on until the period which will bring the Sixth Root-Race on a parallel line with the spirituality of the long extinct epoch of mankind pertaining to the Second Race.[38] Along similar lines, the Bulgarian Master Peter Deunov, otherwise known by his spiritual name Beinsa Douno, spoke of the liminal condition, i.e., the transitional state between two states or conditions. He said in 1944: 'We are crossing the boundary between two epochs […] and entering the new epoch.' The 'new epoch' refers to the transition from Kali Yuga, the fourth and present age of the world cycle of yugas, or 'ages'. It is the end of the four ages that comprise a cycle and is often referred to as the dark age. The Kali Yuga leads to eventual destruction of the world order before the creation of a new cycle of the four yugas. Deunov continues: 'People all over the world, of all nations and races, are now forming the nucleus of a new race, with a new understanding. In the future there will be many more people of the sixth race on the Earth than there are at present. The spiritually wise people throughout the world will form the sixth race. The people of the sixth race will have correct features. They will be beautiful, their beauty having been formed by the high ideal they hold within themselves. They will be far more beautiful than the people of today [i.e., the fifth race].'[39] The last sentence makes it clear that beauty is primarily an internal condition of the human being and not only skin deep. However, the new humanity entailing fellowship between all nations will not emerge without painful birth pangs. This has happened in the past, like the transitions between the Third and Fourth, and the Fourth and Fifth Root-Races and is bound to happen during the transition from the Fifth to the Sixth Race, namely, the large scale geological and environmental disasters entailing immense suffering in order to awaken and purify human consciousness, as Blavatsky and Deunov both forewarn. A recent case in point could well be the warning issued by the United Nations Secretary-General, António Guterres, to negotiators at a major meeting when he said that failing to increase efforts on climate change would be 'not only immoral but suicidal' for the planet. This clearly shows that planetary disasters do not occur out of divine caprice but are largely manmade, being the intelligent

Portends and characteristics of the coming epoch

Peter Deunov on the Sixth Race

response of nature acting as a wake-up call to major portions of humanity still mired in greed and apathy.[40]

The fact that Blavatsky and Deunov, each coming from a different epoch and quite dissimilar spiritual and occult milieus, have espoused the same essential message, is another corroboration of a constant theme of this work—the harmony of the principal tenets of the *philosophia perennis*. These tenets are no fancy, or phantasy, of any alleged teacher or teachers but have been bequeathed to humanity through the instrumentality of appointed emissaries like the two just mentioned, plus others of course.

The subject of Root Races is evidently an enormous one and key to an understanding of evolution. More details are provided in Endnote III-3.

Stories of miracles performed in ancient times by the Christ, and saints and prophets of other religions will always run the risk of being belittled by sceptics on the charge of lack of scientific evidence, other than the hearsay of their gullible believers. But it is not so easy to dismiss in our prosaic, modern days, authentic reports, from both hemispheres of the globe, of individuals with powers and perceptions so extraordinary that no amount of scientific theorizing can ever account for them, explain them away, or disprove their existence.

In India we have the example of the legendary sage Ramana Maharshi who could materialize his presence to his disciples anywhere in the world and then just as soon as the task was accomplished, vanish in 'thin air'.[41] Likewise, in the modern West another such spiritual Master was the Bulgarian Peter Deunov, mentioned above, appropriately referred to as a *Prophet for Our Times* in the book by that name edited by David Lorimer.[42] Reports about his spiritual intuitions and occult faculties are far too numerous and full of specific details to be dismissed as coincidence or the make-belief of supposedly credulous devotees. For instance, regarding the occult faculty of projecting the *Māyāvi-rūpa*, or the 'body of illusion', Deunov was able to appear in different places, and in one instance in a locked room and then disappear without a trace (see Chapter 4, Volume II, page 54 et seq. for explanation and more such examples). On other occasions he was able to sense, remotely, a situation of extreme danger and materialize his presence to save the situation, as when one of his disciples, a train driver, fell asleep at the controls and was suddenly awoken by the train whistle—pressed by the Master standing next to him, who then promptly disappeared just before the driver could address a word of thanks. It is not surprising, then, that Albert Einstein said of Deunov, 'The whole world bows before me: I bow down before the Master Peter Deunov.'[43] Would that there were more scientists like Einstein able to leave a window open to the metaphysical and spiritual dimensions of life and submit to genuflexion in the presence of true Masters. But then, as we have already pointed out, Einstein very likely possessed a copy of Blavatsky's *The Secret Doctrine*; so, presumably, knowing more than a thing or two about matters occult, was able to discern the powers of a true Master, such as Deunov, from the plethora of false gurus masquerading their self-proclaimed messianic powers.

Similarly, in the modern-day West, were the miracles performed by Padre Pio, also known as Saint Pio of Pietrelcina (1887–1968), the Italian friar, priest, stigmatist, and mystic, now venerated as a saint of the Catholic Church. *Padre Pio: The wonder worker*, describes the story of Gemma di Giorgi, a Sicilian girl, born without pupils, whose blindness was believed to have been cured during a visit to Padre Pio.[44] During a trip with her

Authentic cases of modern miracles

Einstein's reverence for Peter Deunov

Padre Pio intercedes to restore a young girl's eyesight

grandmother to see Padre Pio in San Giovanni Rotondo in 1947, the little girl began to see objects, including a steamship and the sea. Padre Pio gave Gemma her first Holy Communion and again made the sign of the cross over each of her eyes. When Gemma returned to Sicily her eyes were again examined by a specialist. To test Gemma, the doctor held up various objects in front of her and she was able to see each one of them. She was able to count the doctor's fingers at a distance of sixteen feet. Even without pupils, Gemma could see. The doctor declared that Gemma's eyes were in no condition to see. There was no medical explanation for it.[45]

From the miracle of physical sight, readers might like to contemplate the miracle of inner sight:

> For now we see through a glass, darkly;
> but then face to face; now I know in part;
> but then shall I know even as also I am known.[46]

The Faculty of Intuition

Intuition, then, is the direct cognition of truth in all things. It is the highest spiritual faculty in man but lies dormant as long as man is overly attached to the senses and the Lower mind. When a poet, a scientist or an artist receives flashes of intuition, his mind has to be silently receptive and 'porous' to the influences from his higher nature—the Higher Mind. Then, in that glimpse, there is a temporary conjunction of *manas* with *buddhi*, as stated earlier. This is because buddhi contains all experiences, right from the monadic stage, so that when manas is conjoined with buddhi it becomes omniscient. In Great Beings like Ramana Maharshi and Peter Deunov in modern times, or Jesus and Buddha long ago, there is a permanent union of buddhi with manas.

Intellect and reason the handmaidens of intuition

In a mundane sense, intuition means that we can know something without knowing how we know it. Just as a doctor can diagnose a physical disease without recourse to an odyssey of clinical tests because of his vast medical experience, so also, an observant psychiatrist learns to judge many things about his patients by intuition. In mathematics, the names of Isaac Newton and Srinivasa Ramanujan immediately spring to mind as examples of geniuses who were mainly autodidactic and came to their staggering discoveries in their twenties largely through intuition. Likewise, intuition may flash through when we are reading the scriptures, depending on our state of mind. When this happens, we sense an inner meaning, which can never be fully conveyed in words. However, if the mind be only partially receptive, then we would experience what is commonly known as a hunch.

By contrast, reason involves observation, experiment, analysis, and the faculty of intellect. It is rather like exploring objects in a darkened and unfamiliar room sequentially; intuition is like turning on the light whereupon everything is revealed in an instant, not one after another, but as a whole. Radhakrishnan said: 'Intuition gives us the idea of the whole and intellect analysis of parts.'[47] Or, as exotically expressed in the Orient, intuition soars far above reason as the eagle soars far above that of the ant crawling on earth. However, both faculties are indispensable and there is never any implication that reason and intellect, in their proper place and rightful context, should ever be jettisoned. As Radhakrishnan further counsels, 'Every intuition has an intellectual content, and by making it more intellectual we deepen the content'[48]—Newton, surely, being the prime example.

From all of the above, what seems to us to be so miraculous is, from the occult standpoint, no miracle at all, for everything happens according to Law; laws on the physical level and laws on planes higher and invisible. It is a matter of unfolding and awakening latent faculties of consciousness. Before we ask how, we need to outline the process. Manly Hall informs us that sufficient similarity exists between CHiram Abiff, as Master of the Builders of Masonic lore, and the *Kuṇḍalinī* of Hindu mysticism to warrant the assumption that CHiram, also known as the Grand Architect of the universe, may be considered a symbol also of the Spirit Fire moving through the sixth ventricle of the spinal column. The exact science of human regeneration is indeed the Lost Key of Masonry, for when the Spirit Fire is *lifted up* through the thirty-three degrees, or segments of the spinal column, and enters into the domed chamber of the human skull, it finally passes into the pituitary body (Isis), where it invokes Ra (the pineal gland) and demands the Sacred Name. Operative Masonry, in the fullest meaning of that term, signifies the process by which the Eye of Horus is opened. The English Egyptologist, Orientalist, and philologist Sir Ernest Alfred Wallis Budge (1857–1934) who worked for the British Museum has noted that in some of the papyri illustrating the entrance of the souls of the dead into the Judgment Hall of Osiris, the deceased person had a pine cone attached to the crown of his head. The Greek mystics also carried a symbolic staff, the upper end being in the form of a pine cone, which was called the *thyrsus* of Bacchus, which, as its name signifies, is the pineal gland, the sacred pine cone in man—the *eye single*, which cannot be opened until CHiram (kuṇḍalinī, the Spirit Fire) is *raised* through the sacred seals, which are called the Seven Churches in Asia. As Hall avers, 'The Christian legends could be related also to the human body by the same method as the Oriental, for the arcane meanings hidden in the teachings of both schools are identical.'[49]

Miracles are only apparent

All 'miracles' happen through Nature's hidden Laws

Awakening the Latent Powers in Man

This section provides a terse description of three commonly regarded means of rapidly awakening, and quickening into activity, powers hitherto latent in man. First, the ancient yogic technique known as *Samyama*. Second, the activation of the *cākras* in the human subtle bodies. Third, the use of psychedelic drugs. In all these, the dangers of premature arousal of powerful forces hitherto latent in the human being cannot be overemphasized.

The next section, however, describes a method which can be practised in safety for attaining higher states of consciousness but with the proviso that this is not a 'quick-fix', and any results would accrue over the course of time.

The Samyama Technique for Directly Accessing Intuitive Knowledge

The following brief exposition is neither comprehensive nor meant to provide any form of instruction into evoking Samyama. The purpose is merely to provide the reader with some details to spur his own study, investigation, and research into this extraordinary power, latent in the vast majority of human beings, but able to be aroused and fully functioning in the case of advanced persons like genuine yogis. *All such powers and capabilities are faculties of consciousness.*

Patanjali's 'Yoga Sūtras'[50] are the most-revered ancient sourcebook on yoga, described in terms of eight components of practice known as *aṣṭāṅga*, a Sanskrit word meaning 'eight-limbed'. The last three limbs are often studied together and are called *antarātma sādhanā*, or the innermost quest. They are:

- ❖ Sixth limb: *Dhāraṇā* – unwavering concentration of attention on an idea or object;
- ❖ Seventh limb: *Dhyāna* – continuous meditation upon the chosen idea or object;
- ❖ Eighth limb: *Samādhi* – complete immersion, or merging of self, in the idea or object. The mind and ego are in complete abeyance and the aspirant literally becomes (in consciousness) the idea or object of his contemplation. There is a graduation from identification with the idea, or object, towards mystical union beyond ordinary space and time—the timeless state of eternity that is quite ineffable and can only be alluded to by way of poetry, allegory, metaphor or, best of all, SILENCE.

When these three practices are collectively applied to an idea or object, driven by the power of the will in order to achieve a loving fusion, the technique is known as *Samyama*, which confers so-called miraculous powers upon the yogi or practitioner. In essence, then, the Samyama technique requires the subject to concentrate completely upon an idea or object until the latter occupies and 'fills' his entire field of consciousness. When concentration is further prolonged, the consciousness of the subject merges with that of the idea or object providing direct knowledge of the latter from the inside, so to speak. As shown by an experiment carried out by Grinberg,[51] the limits of Samyama are unknown and its area of application unlimited.

Yogic faculties and the development of siddhis

For interest, the following eight major *siddhis* (super-physical capabilities and powers), mentioned in Patanjali's Raj Yoga, are enumerated below:

1. *aṇimā* (micro-psi) – to become very small
2. *mahimā*   – to become very big
3. *laghimā*   – to become very light
4. *garimā*   – to become very heavy
5. *prāpti*   – to reach anywhere
6. *prakāmya*   – to attain all desire
7. *īśatva*   – to create anything
8. *vasitvā*   – to command and control anything.

Needless to say, as with all mental disciplines, there are dangers involved and the selfless motives and ethics of the aspirant are of paramount importance. However, it appears that Samyama is not the province of just the few. Apparently, the technique can also be taught to children.[52] This is obviously not to say that young people can (or should) be taught to achieve advanced siddhis, but that they can be encouraged in the meditative practices of Dhāraṇā, Dhyāna, and Samādhi, the more so because at that early age and stage in life, there would be less cerebral baggage to clog the natural flow of the intuitive mind process.

Activation of the Cākras

Cākra (pronounced *Chakra*) primarily means spinning wheel, derived from the Sanskrit *car*, 'to move'. In the technical sense, the word, used in the plural, refers to the psycho-energetic vortices of force that span the levels of man's being from the mental level to the subtle bodies (astral, then etheric), finally manifesting physically as the major ductless glands of the physical body. (The subtle bodies are explained in Chapters 2 and 3 of

Volume II.) These glands that secrete hormones into the bloodstream are the physical precipitation of the activities of the cākras. However, the cākras are not visible to normal physical sight, but they can be seen by anyone possessing a slight degree of clairvoyance as vortices, or saucer-like depressions, in the surface of the etheric double (the subtle counterpart body closest to the physical body—see Table II-3 in Chapter 2 of Volume II on page 21). Besides seven major cākras, there are a number of minor cākras. Thus, some occult systems number the cākras as seven plus two more, others enumerate seven plus three, five or more. Be that as it may, the physical correspondences of the seven well known major cākras are found in the glands, thus:[53]

Cākras correlated with the glands of the body

Head Cākra (*Sahasrāra*) . . . . Pineal Gland
Brow Cākra (*Ājñā*) . . . . Pituitary Body
Throat Cākra (*Viśuddha*) . . . . Thyroid Gland
Heart Cākra (*Anāhata*) . . . . Thymus Gland
Solar Plexus Cākra (*Maṇipūra*) . . . . Pancreas
Sacral Centre Cākra (*Svadhiṣṭhāna*) . . . . . . Gonads
Base of Spine Cākra (*Mūladhāra*) . . . . Adrenals

Physiologically, the endocrine system is the chemical messenger system: the group of glands that produce and secrete hormones that the body uses for a wide range of bodily functions like growth and development, mood, respiration, metabolism, and reproduction. But this is not all. The endocrine system is also the final manifestation and expression of the cākras, or vortices, that whirl into activity the subtle matter of the etheric, astral, and mental levels, thereby acting as force-centres *for the interchange of energy* from one level to another. Leaving technicalities aside, the essential message to take away is as follows.

Each cākra acts as a 'gateway' opening the consciousness to a particular level of being, well expressed by Carl Jung who views the series of cākras in the Hindu systems, as 'a climbing up from gross matter to the subtle, psychical matter. [...]. The transformation of the gross matter into the subtle matter of the mind—the sublimation of man.'[54] Accordingly, the cākras represent an ascent in consciousness blue printed in the being of man: from the gross to the refined; from the physical (corresponding to dense matter or the Earth Element) to the spiritual; from the root cākra to the crown cākra.

As the energy from these various levels finally concretizes and physicalizes into the duct-less glands, it will be appreciated how closely a human being is energetically interlinked at different levels of his being, as seen in Figure III-32 opposite.

Thus, what happens to him at the mental and emotional (astral) levels directly influences the physical level, even in the bloodstream and through the latter linking all parts of the physical body. Here we find the esoteric reasons behind the adage that our thoughts and emotions can affect our physical body and that the causes of dis-eases of the latter (if not purely physical) can invariably be traced to the quality of the mental life of the individual. This fact has emerged, without question, from medical science through epigenetics, which has shown that our thoughts and lifestyle can affect our genes (see Volume I, Chapter 4, page 105). Stated otherwise, the soul can affect and influence both the physiology and the psychology of the personality through the cākras.

The cākras can be activated by specific techniques of concentration, but only under the expert guidance and protection of a true master—refer to Chapter 9 of Volume I on

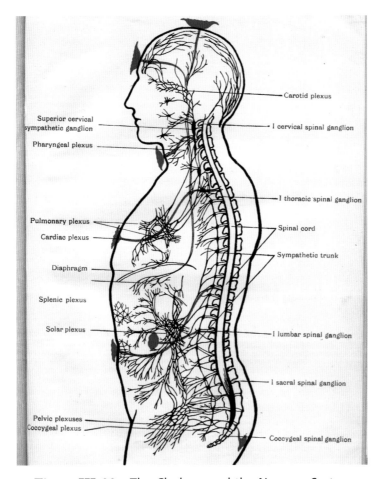

Figure III-32   The Chakras and the Nervous System

From C. W. Leadbeater, The Chakras: A Monograph *(Adyar, Madras: Theosophical Publishing House, 1947), facing p. 38.*

page 271 f. outlining the ten degrees of initiation in the Mystery Schools of India, corresponding, arguably, to the activation of the seven major and three highly esoteric cākras. When that happens, the whole nature is intensified a hundredfold. An obvious result of this is that any base and selfish instincts are tremendously magnified and the individual would no longer be able to restrain undesirable behaviour that he would ordinarily be able to supress in normal life. It is precisely for this reason that any attempt to awaken the cākras is only advisable after they are purified, meaning that the individual in question must be pure in daily life—in thought, word, deed, emotion, and above all, in motive. Therefore, it cannot be emphasized too strongly that any attempt at premature arousal of the cākras would almost certainly produce dire consequences. Death or insanity would be the least of the evils. Far worse (because of the inflammation and intensification of the whole nature, including the base instincts) would be the violation of every moral precept, and a descent into black magic leading the practitioner into touch with a lower order of evolution with which humanity is intended to hold no commerce. It is for this reason that the writer deplores the numerous books and weekend courses now available on so-called cākra development and kuṇḍalinī arousal by self-proclaimed 'masters'. The high initiates, who have attained total and absolute mastery over the mental and emotional nature, having expunged every selfish thought and lower emotion, are alone qualified to use the cākras at will, and for entirely sacred purposes. Endnote III-2 provides a bibliography on the cākras for the serious student.

Perils in arousing the cākras

The Opening of the Third Eye and the Role of Psychedelic Drugs

> You must learn to discriminate between what is psychic and what is spiritual. You will tend to lose power if you yield to that popular hankering after psychic and occult experiences. Those who try to find the kingdom of heaven through drugs, whether plants like Mexican mushrooms or Indian hashish, or chemicals like lysergic acid, [or ayahuasca], may gain glimpses, get signs, and receive hints, but they will not, cannot, escape paying the price of inner deterioration in the end.
>
> Paul Brunton[55]

But by what special techniques or procedures can the Third Eye (the pineal gland) be opened, i.e., awakened into activity? This writer does not know the detailed processes and procedures; still less is he qualified to know. But what he knows (and is qualified to know) for certain, is that no respectable spiritual teacher worthy of the name would ever—under any circumstances—publish any information and techniques on how to 'awaken', 'open', or 'activate' the Third Eye. It is not the right time for this to happen in our present age and the many publications which exist in this regard can at best enable the individual to develop the lower psychic faculties, which are *not* the same as *spiritual* faculties (see the quote above) and, at worst, result in serious physical and psychological harm. The popular idea in so-called spiritual and some (not all) New Age societies that spiritual states can be induced over a weekend course—without careful supervision or any mention of self-discipline, self-surrender, purity, holiness of life, and ultimately, Grace—is utterly pernicious and has led thousands around the world into unholy psychism without their even realising it. There are actually very few individuals in the world who know the safe and true procedures for awakening the many latent potentialities of the pineal gland and they will never say or write anything about this, as they are sworn to secrecy as part of their rules of initiation. It is the selfishness, self-centredness, and sensuality, coupled with mental laziness, impurity, immorality, and above all, the lust for unearned and undeserved extraordinary powers and experiences, which keeps the vast majority of spiritual aspirants these days as far away from the goal as they ever were when they started.

'Let sleeping dogs lie' is sage advice

Latent powers unfold only in propitious circumstances

The writer makes no apology for making this point so starkly. The counsel of saints and prophets since time immemorial (Zarathuśtra, the Buddha, and the Christ to name but three), the writings and numerous first hand reports from the disciples of modern sages, such as Ramana Maharshi and Peter Deunov, and the warnings of modern occultists and philosophers like Blavatsky and Brunton, prove beyond any shadow of doubt that the only sure way to unfold spiritual and occult (not psychic) faculties is through unswerving devotion to the Divine Quartet: Truth and Wisdom, Compassion and Love—supplemented by sincere prayer and deep meditation. Each implies the other and the reason is obvious: when there is no trace of self-interest in the nature, any powers acquired, or bequeathed, would never be misused irresponsibly for selfish gain, and would therefore be directed entirely towards philanthropic service. All other means of forcing the premature development of extraordinary powers, i.e., latent faculties of consciousness, by artificial means, like abnormal breathing practices to activate the cākras or taking psychedelic drugs, may temporarily yield the glamour of lower psychic powers,[iii] but ultimately, they are highways to perdition, delusion, and derangement. One of the few exceptions that may be cited is the mechanically aroused ecstasy trance of the Whirling Dervishes of Sufism—the inner

---

iii There are also the higher psychic power, or the higher *siddhis* (*iddhis*), under the control of a true master.

and mystical dimension of Islam. But this is on a lower plane, and therefore should not be mistaken for the thought-conquering concentration of the true yogi or mystic—of any religion. Notwithstanding this, there are far too many such cases in the world, especially nowadays, of unfortunate spiritual derelicts easily duped by the allure of power and instant renown who attempt to gain powers for personal, selfish motives without possessing the necessary qualifications of purity of character and discipline (see Chapter 7 of Volume I).

Given the current fascination for psychedelic drugs, it would be instructive to outline three of their common uses: controlled, indiscriminate, and medical. We will then give an account of how mind-altering drugs act on the body, the dangers of premature entrance into altered states of consciousness, and how we may evaluate a genuine spiritual experience.

An Example of Controlled Experiments with Psychedelic Drugs

The British psychiatrist Humphry Osmond (1917–2004) is known for inventing the word 'psychedelic' and for his research into the applications of psychedelic drugs.[56] In 1953, the English writer and philosopher Aldous Huxley[iv] participated in an experiment conducted by Osmond. Huxley was administered the psychedelic drug mescaline and Osmond prompted him to comment on the various stimuli around him, such as books and flowers. Huxley recorded aspects of their conversation in *The Doors of Perception*:

Aldous Huxley's drug induced expansion of consciousness

> Each person is at each moment capable of remembering all that has ever happened to him and of perceiving everything that is happening everywhere in the universe. The function of the brain and nervous system is to protect us from being overwhelmed and confused by this mass of largely useless and irrelevant knowledge, by shutting out most of what we should otherwise perceive or remember at any moment, and leaving only that very small and special selection which is likely to be practically useful. According to such a theory, each one of us is potentially Mind at Large.[57]

In the same book, Huxley stated:

Huxley's and William James's theories in broad agreement

> In the final stage of egolessness there is an 'obscure knowledge' that All is in all—that All is actually each. This is as near, I take it, as a finite mind can ever come to 'perceiving everything that is happening everywhere in the universe.'

'Mind at Large', as in the above quote, is the concept proposed by Aldous Huxley to help interpret psychedelic experience. He maintained that the human mind filters reality under normal circumstances and that psychoactive drugs dilate or disable the filter and allow for an enlarged perception of reality whereby everyday objects lose their functionality, and suddenly exist 'as such'; space and dimension therefore become irrelevant, with perceptions seemingly expanded, and, at times, overwhelming. Interestingly, Huxley's 'filter theory' is similar to the releasing and transmissive theories propounded by William James over half a century earlier—see Volume I, Chapter 6, page 168 et seq.

An Example of Mass Havoc Induced by the Indiscriminate Use of Psychedelic Drugs

In 1962, Timothy Leary (1920–1996), the American psychologist from Harvard

---

iv Aldous Huxley is credited with the term 'Perennial Philosophy'—see Volume I, Proem, page xxxviii.

Eventual havoc
wreaked by
indiscriminate
indulgence in
psychedelics

University (whom President Richard Nixon later labelled 'the most dangerous man in America') became fascinated with the sense-enhancing properties of a new drug—lysergic acid diethylamide, or LSD. He believed it to be the portal to a new dimension that would reveal the true nature of ourselves—and the universe. He, and the American writer and countercultural figure Ken Kesey (1935–2001), from Stanford University, became the most enthusiastic LSD evangelists of the hippy era of the 1960s. One member of the so called Californian Family Dog commune[58] claimed: 'With LSD, we experienced what it took Tibetan monks 20 years to obtain, yet we got there in 20 minutes.'[59] However, not all members succumbed to the downward spiral. For example, the former academic and clinical psychologist Ram Dass, born Richard Alpert (1931–2019), known for his personal and professional associations with Timothy Leary at Harvard University in the early 1960s, was a prominent American spiritual teacher.

Nonetheless, all this shows that when people talk about spirituality, they have not the slightest clue about its true meaning. They fatally confuse the mirages of the lower psychic planes—conferring illusion—with the visions of the spiritual realms—bestowing illumination—as we say again. A temporary, artificially induced clairvoyant experience is certainly an altered state of consciousness. But that is no more an indication of spiritual vision than using an elevator to get to the top of a building in order to gain a wider view proves that one has acquired the bird's eye vision. Bursting into a bank to steal a few millions is not the same as acquiring wealth through lawful and deserving means. In fact, resorting to drugs in the hope of attaining spiritual experiences is, arguably, the most insidious form of materialism: using a material agency on a material principle (the brain) in order to transcend materialism—a total nonsense. Unsurprisingly, then, the hippy 'Summer of Love' in 1967 ended with rocketing crime and violence, addiction and malnutrition, bad drug experiences and venereal disease. In fairness however, the argument that the Summer of Love had a transformative effect on mainstream culture is not without substance in that it ushered in a new era of sexual openness and altered music, fashion, and people's perspectives about life. Furthermore, others have used drugs in a sacred indigenous context, but this practice is still a short cut fraught with dangers.

Medical Research Using Psychedelic Drugs

Whereas psychedelic drugs were once the main province of the hippy fraternity and such like, this practice has now appeared under the guise of authentic scientific research into altered brain states and the treatment of psychological problems. For example, the Psychedelic Research Group of the Faculty of Medicine at Imperial College, London focuses on two main research areas: the action of psychedelic drugs in the brain; and their clinical utility, for example, as aids to psychotherapy, with a particular focus on depression.[60] Their website contains an invitation to take part in a survey for their cohort study if a person plans to take a psychedelic in the near future.[61] This is tantamount to encouraging an individual to experiment with drugs for himself and on his own. But given the prevailing mechanistic paradigm, depression is obviously viewed entirely as an atypical brain state to be treated by way of newly researched chemicals (like psilocybin for a randomised control trial at Imperial College in 2018), rather than the 'top down' approach of a spiritual scientist who would maintain that depression, in the vast majority of cases, is primarily a sickness of the soul that manifests, rather than originates, through the brain

Psychedelics
compound the
confusions and
virtual realities of
the modern age

organ. Whereas no one would ever wish to deny anyone the opportunity of resorting to drugs to alleviate suffering—physical or mental—the writer regards this new avenue of research as beset with hidden dangers and prone to immense misuse; in addition to conveying the mistaken idea to the public in general, and especially the youth, that psychedelics are the quick, do-it-yourself fix to a 'maiden's prayer' for spiritual enlightenment—before paying the unavoidable price of inner deterioration. For an earnest, but desperately frustrated aspirant, the only justification to resort to a drug (under strict guidance) would be to kick-start himself out of the rut in which he finds himself hopelessly stuck for long periods, unable to move forward—but this is the rare exception and not the rule. Rather, every earnest neophyte aspiring to function on the higher planes and gain knowledge of the higher worlds swiftly comes to realize the indispensable requirement to undergo an arduous process of self-purification so as not to become ensnared by the allure of the lower nature once the higher powers are activated. The whole purpose is to learn to distinguish the Real from illusions and phantasies, the dividing line between the two becoming ever finer the higher the spiritual ascent. This is of tremendous importance, the more so nowadays when perceptions are blurred by the likes of social media and incessant, highly persuasive, advertising. He will soon come to understand the necessity of crossing the gulf separating the realm of the senses from that of the spirit.

How Mind-Altering Drugs Act on the Human Body

Reverting now to the human body, why are drunkenness and, far worse, hallucinogenic drugs dangerous to mental health and stability, and inimical to spiritual development? It is because, as Blavatsky explains, they cause disorder in the pituitary body, and so produce phantasms and hallucinations. In fact, 'This body is sometimes so affected by drunkenness that it is paralyzed, and the strict forbiddance of alcoholic liquids [and, of course, drugs] to all students of Occultism turns on this effect which alcohol produces on the Pituitary Body and Pineal Gland.'[62] Let us dwell on what is meant by 'phantasms and hallucinations'.

In Place of the Self is a landmark book by Ron Dunselman, General Secretary of the Netherlands branch of the Anthroposophical Society,[63] who also helped pioneer ARTA, a leading Dutch therapeutic community which helps people overcome drug dependency using a holistic, anthroposophical approach. Written in dialogue with former addicts, therapists, and doctors, it is based, as the title indicates, on the premise that a psychedelic drug used over time progressively fragments, displaces, and replaces the user's own sense of self with a sort of virtual reality equivalent of himself. Dunselman places much of the blame for drug use on the modern social world, claiming that drug use in traditional societies, such as ancient Greece or the Incas, was tightly controlled by custom and tradition that not only regulated drug use, but also provided the emotional support structure for the users. To explain how drugs work on the self, Dunselman draws upon Steiner's doctrine of the occult constitution of man. This was described in Chapter 8 of Volume II, where it is seen that the sevenfold constitution can sensibly be grouped into four 'bodies', as per the four strata seen in Table II-26 on page 185: a physical body; a life, or etheric body; an astral body; and a spirit body, which anchors the faculty of self-awareness unique to human beings. The action of drugs is to displace the physical body from its etheric and astral counterparts, thus rendering a person wide open and prey to the

Psychedelic drugs disorder the subtle bodies

multitudinous entities of the unseen worlds, known collectively as elementals. If a benign elemental were drawn into the vortex of a person's thought atmosphere, then such a person is said to have had a 'good trip'. However, and just as much, if not more frequently, a malignant elemental might be invoked, which could play havoc with the mind and attach itself to the aura of the person as a sort of psychic virus; and this is otherwise known as a 'terrifying trip', the outcome of which could be obsessions or what is loosely termed 'spirit possessions'. Given the proviso—and it is a major proviso—that the drug experiment be conducted under the most carefully controlled conditions, under expert supervision and a supportive atmosphere (as with the traditional societies stated above), the person will usually have some control over which elementals he is likely to attract and encounter during his trip. Otherwise, all glib talk of 'rites of passage', etc. using drugs is merely touching the tip of an enormous iceberg with no awareness, let alone understanding, of the immense dangers that lie concealed. Steiner's classic book *Knowledge of the Higher Worlds*[64] contains valuable information on how such super-sensible contact and knowledge may be attained and the attendant trials, not least of which is coming face to face with what is known as the 'Guardian of the Threshold',[65] or 'Dweller on the Threshold', the literary term first used by the English mystic and novelist Edward Bulwer-Lytton (1803–1873) in his romance *Zanoni*.[66] This Dweller on the Threshold is no poetical metaphor or allegory but a real experience. In essence, it is the terrible spectral being epitomizing the abstract of the debit and credit book of the individual, being 'the combined evil influence that is the result of the wicked thoughts and acts of the age in which any one may live, and it assumes to each student a definite shape at each appearance, being always either of one sort or changing each time,'[67] such as 'Cerberus guarding the entrance to Hades; the Dragon which St. Michael (spiritual will-power) is going to kill; the Snake which tempted Eve.'[68] According to Max Heindel (whose teaching on the subtle bodies was summarized in Chapter 8 of Volume II on page 164), the Dweller on the Threshold must be confronted by every aspirant who wishes to progress into, and gain knowledge of, the unseen worlds—and is one of the main causes of obsession.[69]

So in this regard, and in view of the immense trials and dangers facing the earnest spiritual aspirant—let alone a dabbling neophyte hankering after 'other-worldly experiences'—the current, and increasing fascination with psychedelic drugs like ayahuasca, especially amongst young people eager to achieve altered states of consciousness—producing nothing more than psychic experiences on the lower astral plane, entirely mistaken for the spiritual—is deplorable. That such practices now seem to be given the stamp of scientific approval to research brain states is doubly insidious (see below). It is quite incredible that people think that they can achieve enlightenment by using a drug to 'rewire' the brain and therefore to bypass safe meditative and similar such practices.[v] They seem unable to appreciate that a genuine spiritual experience is vouchsafed only to a sincere, spiritual aspirant. Such people would scoff at the idea that an international sportsman could attain his prowess without unremitting work and training or that a concert pianist could perform

There are no short cuts to instant success in life

So should there be shortcuts to genuine spiritual enlightenment?

---

v This is not to deny that certain aboriginal and indigenous races, like those in the Amazon rainforest, have used plant-based psychedelic drugs. However this practice was relevant at a time when the human constitution and nervous system were very different from what they are nowadays. Moreover, the family structures and social setup in these cultures were geared towards such practices by providing the necessary support and counselling. This is a far cry from modern Westerners indulging in a Shamanic course over a weekend or longer, and then being left alone to their own devices in a busy metropolis.

at London's Royal Festival Hall without thousands of hours of disciplined practice and immense self-sacrifice—just by taking a drug. Yet, spiritual enlightenment, the very summit of human attainment and the *finest efflorescence of humanity* can somehow be drug-induced at will! Does not spiritual attainment also have to be earned and deserved through self-effort, by which is not meant the struggle and striving of the ego, but the living of the life conducive to its attainment? There is always the unseen, mysterious hand of Grace and there are numerous reports of so-called ordinary people who have experienced inner illumination like a bolt out of the blue. However, this writer would contend that Grace cannot touch or 'take root' in an unprepared mind and heart any more than the finest corn seed could sprout in barren soil. The task of the human being is, therefore, to prepare the appropriate conditions, the 'soil', for enlightenment—and then leave the rest to the divine handiwork as and when It will. Eloquently put by Christina Feldman, the modern American author and international teacher on mindfulness and meditation: 'If we demand enlightenment, it hides . . . All that we can do is make ourselves enlightenment-prone [through spiritual practice].'70

Warnings from Goethe and Steiner about the Dangers of Premature Entrance into Higher Worlds

In a fine lecture on the meaning veiled in the imagery of Goethe's problem-tale *The Green Snake and the Beautiful Lily*, Rudolf Steiner says:

> Goethe here wished to point out the danger to which a man exposes himself who would force an entrance into the super-sensible region before he has severed himself from his lower self. Only when love has permeated the whole man, only when the lower nature has been sacrificed, can the initiation into the higher truths and powers begin. This sacrifice is expressed by the serpent yielding of its own accord, and forming a bridge of its body across the river—that is to say, the astral plane—between the two kingdoms, of the senses and of the spirit.71

Tempting as it would appear in our present age of wanting a 'quick fix' and instant gratification, it is not possible to leapfrog over intermediate stages in yoga, or any other system of spiritual training, by using psychedelics, any more than a pianist can hope to give a virtuoso performance of a major concerto without passing through all the intermediate stages of arduous technical and musical training. Taking drugs, or any intoxicant, represents the worst kind of illicit and forced entry into super-sensible planes for which dire consequences will assuredly follow, sooner or later, as night follows day. The prayers, fasting, meditations, and rituals of the Mystery Schools all have this central objective of internal cleansing, which any form of drug-taking would completely annihilate and reverse at a stroke.

On this note, those academics and 'consciousness researchers' who confidently claim to access what they refer to as the 'Cosmic Mind' by taking LSD or other psychedelic drugs, would do better to access first their own minds and understand the great dangers to health and sanity of forcing an entry into the higher worlds.72

A drug induced experience is fraught with dangers

To the unwary or gullible, illusion masquerades as illumination; delusion impersonates certainty; glamour is mistaken for reality; an artificially induced ecstasy is mistaken for spirituality; the unreal is confused with the Real. Unhappiness is essentially a *home-sickness* of the soul, as Carl Jung so eloquently elucidates it.73 What is the soul's 'Home'? It is *Ātma*, the Divine Self (see Figure II-9 on page 201 in the Coda to Volume II).

How can a genuine spiritual experience be distinguished from an artificially induced counterfeit?

Hallmarks of a Genuine Spiritual Experience

Altruism and a transformed outlook authenticate genuine spiritual experience

We judge a tree by its fruit: so an obvious way to distinguish a spiritual experience from an artificially aroused ecstasy, whether through drugs or abnormal breathing, is by observing its after effects. The overriding question is whether or not the experience has radically transformed a person for the better—towards less self-centredness and a greater degree of universality of outlook. There are several distinguishing characteristics to be discerned. Firstly, an experience that touches our innermost centre, however fleetingly, leaves an afterglow, the memory of which may, invariably does, fade in time, but is never forgotten and can be summoned up as a feeling in the heart to sustain one during moments of crisis. Although a person may long for a repetition of the former experience, there will not be an addictive hankering after it. Even one such glimpse is enough for a lifetime. But the feeling-memory of artificially induced ecstasy is rapidly lost, which is precisely why the drug-induced experience invariably needs constant renewing.

Moreover, it is difficult to comprehend how a drug-induced experience can provide moral support to a person during difficult times. Crucially, a spiritual experience radically transforms the entire outlook and conduct of a person, who subsequently may, for example, lose all interest in financial acquisitiveness and devote his energies and his wealth towards philanthropic or charitable projects undreamt of beforehand. Quite often, such a person also loses all fear of death, having received intimations of his immortality along with an overwhelming sense of unity. (See the cases of Eben Alexander and Rajiv Parti in Chapter 2 of Volume I.) The drug-induced altered state of consciousness would be unlikely to result in a person inexplicably becoming less selfish and changing the course of his life towards greater acts of benevolence towards others or cause him to lose all fear of death—except in rare circumstances when a genuine near-death experience also results. Finally, anyone who has been blessed with a genuinely spiritual experience is no more likely to talk about it in public than he would discuss the intimate details of his own private and personal relationships. A spiritual experience is a most sacred affair, and what is sacred is perforce silent and private, other than perhaps to one's bosom confidant. However, it is quite noticeable how those who claim to have had 'spiritual' experiences using drugs like to brag about it to all and sundry—and some even like to inform us about their full understanding of the laws of the spiritual world as a result!

But, for the earnest aspirant, there is always a path to be discovered and trodden, however steep and thorny it may be, to acquire higher states of consciousness by safe and legitimate means.

The Eye Made Single – The Broadcasting and Receiving Apparatus of Thought

> Sight is energy leaving the person.
> Leonardo da Vinci[74]

It would be sensible to start from the foundation of what we have, rather than what we eventually hope to acquire. And what we all have are two eyes that have bestowed the marvel of sight. There is a tremendous mystery locked in the eyes (let alone in the Third Eye). First then, let us reflect on the fact that through no other sense-channel may we obtain a truer understanding of the character and mind of a person as through his own eyes. In recorded history, we can think of the quality of the eyes of Cleopatra and Salome, Napoleon and Goethe, to name an arbitrary handful. More to the point, the eyes of the true mystic, saint or yogi, Ramana Maharshi for one, are unmistakable in their steady and flickerless gaze. Why is this? Because he who has held thought in abeyance or in mastery for long periods of time, who is undistracted by fleeting external sensations, who has turned the mind inward upon itself in profound contemplation, cannot but betray it in the abstracted look of his eyes. The reason is the subtle connections between the eyes with the brain, mind, and soul-nature, but for these details readers are referred back to Chapter 3, page 44 et seq. on occult neuroanatomy and the references cited therein.

Scientific evidence of radiation from the eyes

In other words, there is a power *behind* the eyes, and the eyes are emphatically not just passive photographic receivers, but also active organs that radiate the mental and soul nature of the person. This is well known to the yogis of India and the mystics of Islam in Persia and Africa. Hypnotism has provided testimony to the fact that there is a definite radiation from the human eye. The renowned Indian biologist, biophysicist, and botanist Sir Jagadis Chandra Bose FRS (1858–1937) constructed a kind of electroscope sensitive to very fine currents in order to measure the energy in the rays emanating from the human eye. Concentrating the sight on the instrument by mere will-power moved the needle registering the amount of energy in the ray.[75]

More startling scientific confirmation of the radiation from the human eye was reported in the journal *The New York American*, dated 30 March 1933, about a newly invented instrument capable of determining, from a photograph, whether a person had died since their picture was taken. The instrument, which is based on a new application of the laws of science, detects the movement of 'life waves' or 'Z waves' on the photographic plate, and the stillness of these waves (especially from the eyes) after the death of the subject, *no matter how far distant from the photograph*, was reported by E. S. Shrapnell-Smith (1875–1952), one of Britain's noted scientists and an authority on chemistry.[76] Shrapnell-Smith has experimented with more than seven hundred photographs in tests, maintaining that life, or specifically, the human brain, emits a distinct type of wave, rather like a radio station, which can be measured. The instrument enables these life-waves to be amplified and become visible through their movement.[77] Endnote III-4 provides an extract from the journal article, plus other accounts of scientific apparatus to detect the radiation from the human eye. These accounts could, arguably, be a contributory factor in Rupert Sheldrake's researches into the phenomena of the extended mind and the sense of being stared at.[78]

Not for nothing, then, did the American poet and story-writer Edgar Allan Poe (1809–1849) state: 'The eyes are the windows to the soul,'[vi] for no other organ reveals the internal, subtle world of the person better than the eyes. Is there then, a practical and safe technique using our eyes to serve our higher purpose? For good reason did the Master Jesus declare:

> The light of the body is the eye: if therefore thine eye be single, thy whole body shall be full of light (Matthew 6:22, King James Version);

---

vi The saying is also attributed to William Shakespeare (Francis Bacon?).

which is complemented by –

> The fruit of the Light is in all goodness and righteousness and truth (Ephesians 5:9, King James Version).[79]

Note that the current version of the New Testament substitutes 'Spirit' for 'Light', but the fact is that the earliest and most authoritative manuscripts of this scripture, notably the Sinaitic, Alexandrian, and Vatican Codices, as well as the Bezan manuscript in its original form, all agree in reading 'photos' (light) instead of 'pneumatos' (spirit).[80]

Countless numbers have read or quoted this aphorism, but few seem to have understood its occult import. Let us explain. There are two points to consider. Firstly, Light is the first and subtlest manifestation of Divine Consciousness as per the First Biblical Command, 'Let there be Light.' This primal Light is the substance and life-force in all created forms and every microparticle of matter. We need not labour the point about the importance of light (radiation, or waves) in modern science, whereby matter is regarded as 'bottled-up waves' (in the words of James Jeans), and the energy-matter-light interconnection is enshrined in $E = mc^2$. But we do need to stress that Light is the nearest element to Divinity that physically-embodied man can contact, as evinced by ancient cultures which, without exception, based their religion upon homage to Light, and worshipped Light in its supreme expression—the Sun. (That is why, in the writer's view, scientists—even amongst the most hard-headed materialists and atheists—are mysteriously drawn to studying the physical properties of Light.)

The second point to make is the meaning behind the word 'single'. The Greek word 'haplous' which is rendered 'single' in the Matthew quotation means, literally, 'simple', or 'single' in the sense of not being complicated, in other words, in the 'natural' sense.

Combining the above two points, we can amplify the first quotation to educe its full meaning, thus:

> The spiritual light of the body enters through the eye; if therefore the eye be turned away from the complicated multiplicity of the world, and the mind using that eye be withdrawn into its own natural being, thy whole body shall be full of spiritual light.[81]

The technical reason for this is that:

> When the individual consciousness is turned inward a conjunction of Manas and Buddhi takes place[82] [i.e., a conjunction of the mind and intuition, or intellect and wisdom, operating by way of the union of left and right brain hemispheres.[83]]

To state that 'thy whole body shall be full of spiritual light' is not merely a poetical metaphor, but a statement of literal fact. There have been numerous reports from sensitive and spiritually attuned persons who have had the blessing to be in the presence of a true master whilst witnessing a luminous light (aura) encircling the master's body or a disciple rapt in profound meditation (see below). For example, the Italian Catholic friar and deacon Saint Francis of Assisi (1181/1182–1226) and the Spanish mystic and Carmelite nun Saint Theresa of Avila (1515–1582) were both reported to have been enveloped in a cloud of white light. From the world of religious art (e.g. European mediæval artists) there are a number of paintings showing coronae and haloes around the portraits of saints and sages. So the Christ spoke the simple and unvarnished truth when he said that he who has unified his vision and withdrawn his mind into its natural state free from sense impressions and chattering thoughts will be fully illumined psychically and spiritually. And when that happens he can accomplish what we in our ordinary condition call miracles, as exampled above from first-hand accounts about Ramana Maharshi and Peter Deunov.

Scientific Evidence about the Aura during Meditation

Light Changes: Experiences in the presence of transforming light records the widespread nature of light experiences in a scholarly analysis of the history of light experiences in some eight hundred individual accounts gathered from numerous sources, going right back in history.[84] Despite such weighty evidence, accounts of sensitive persons witnessing an aura around the body of saints, sages, and meditators is still open to the charge by sceptics of being anecdotal, historical, subjective or the imagination of gullible devotees. But no longer.

There is now impressive *scientific* evidence that certain individuals can radiate light during deep meditative states that is not only perceived by others, but demonstrated through the quantitative data of neural correlates during such an induced light experience (ILE). 'Neural Correlates of Induced Light Experience during Meditation' is a pioneering study into the light experience induced during meditation. The neural correlates of ILE were investigated by simultaneously recording the EEGs[vii] of an expert meditation teacher, claimed to elicit ILE, and his pupil during joint meditation sessions under various instructions, given separately to the teacher (transmit/do not transmit) and to the pupil (receive/do not receive); and also during transmit/receive instruction but with both wearing goggles, limiting the visual input. A significant increase in the high frequency beta (12–30 Hz) and gamma oscillations (30–70 Hz) was observed in the teacher's brain whenever he was instructed to transmit. Electric field tomography analysis localized these effects over a multitude of brain regions including the fusiform gyrus (part of the temporal lobe and occipital lobe), angular gyrus (a region of the parietal lobe), and the cerebellum (which regulates motor movements). Finally, the teacher's and pupil's brain responses were found to be synchronized especially in the alpha band (8–12 Hz) during the transmit/receive condition, and the information flow was directional, i.e., from the teacher to the pupil.[85]

Scientific evidence on 'auric' light

Altogether, these results provide the first neuroscientific evidence underlying the phenomenological experience of induced light and serve as another piece of evidence in confirmation of the oft quoted occult adage 'Modern science is our best ally.'

The Flowering of Latent Powers in Man – The Fruits of Intuition

There are specific and entirely safe meditation practices for attaining the lofty states described above—by slow degrees. These involve meditations on the mystery of the breath, the heart, and the eye, all underpinned by constant and unremitting self-enquiry, mental discipline, and the cultivation of the utmost refined feelings. A clue is provided in this instruction by Paramahansa Yogananda:

---

vii Electroencephalography (EEG) is an electrophysiological monitoring method to record electrical activity of the brain.

During deep meditation, the single or spiritual eye (variously referred to in scriptures as the third eye, the star of the East, etc.) becomes visible within the central part of the forehead. The will, projected from this point, is the *broadcasting* apparatus of thought. Man's feeling or emotional power, calmly concentrated on the heart, enables it to act as a mental radio that *receives* the messages of other persons, far or near.[86]

Distinguishing trance from stupor

Safe and practical methods are described by Paul Brunton for unfolding latent spiritual faculties through breathing and visualisation exercises as well as mental control through meditation. These were known to the wise men of the East and the illuminati of the West, and have been adapted and simplified by Brunton to suit the modern Western mind.[87]

Accordingly, this final section of the Chapter gives examples of the magnificent spiritual landscape that can be explored by those rare souls who have attained the state of 'the eye made single'.

Taking up the theme of the previous section, there is a further vast gulf between a genuine spiritual state and its drug-induced counterfeit coin. We mentioned earlier the state of *Samādhi*. It is worth exploring this a little further. Samādhi is a compound Sanskrit word formed of *sam*, meaning 'with', 'together'; *a*, meaning 'towards'; and the verbal root *dha* signifying 'to place', 'to bring'. Hence Samādhi, meaning 'to direct towards', which signifies combining the faculties of the mind towards an object; therefore intense contemplation or profound meditation, with the consciousness directed towards the spiritual. For this reason, Samādhi is referred to as the highest form of self-possession in the sense of collecting (or possessing) all the sevenfold faculties of the constitution towards reaching union, or quasi-union (recalling that yoga means 'union'), with the divine–spiritual, whether that sacred contact lasts for a fleeting moment or extended periods. The difference between this state of '*spiritual* trance' and the drug induced stupor is this. The altered consciousness (on the psychic, not spiritual planes) induced by drugs is entirely *passive*, that is, completely drug-dependent. Needless to say, the unfortunate practitioner, who craves to renew his experience periodically, can make no claim (other than self-delusion) to personal command over his psycho-spiritual faculties, nor can he exercise any spiritual faculties *at will*.

Samādhi and its rare votaries

In sharp contrast, he who possesses and has mastered the spiritual–occult power has complete, absolute and *active* control over all his faculties—physical, psychic, and spiritual—and for this reason is said to be completely *Self*-possessed, that is, possessed by the Higher Self. Samādhi is the final, eighth stage of Yoga—a state of consciousness whereby man becomes practically omniscient of the solar universe in which he dwells because his consciousness is functioning at the time in the spiritual-causal worlds.[viii] All knowledge

---

viii The eight stages, or limbs, of yoga are usually enumerated as: (1) *Yāma*, signifying 'restraint', or 'forbearance'; (2) *Niyāma*, religious observances such as fasting, praying, penance; (3) *Āsana*, postures of various kinds (of the school of *Haṭha-Yoga*); (4) *Prāṇāyāma*, various methods of regulating and circulating the breath; (5) *Pratyāhāra*, signifying, 'withdrawal', but technically and esoterically, in the sense of withdrawal of the consciousness from sensuous concerns, or from external objects; (6) *Dhāraṇā*, mental concentration in the sense of firmness, or steadiness, or resolution in holding the mind on an object or a thought; (7) *Dhyāna*, abstract contemplation or meditation when freed from exterior distraction; and finally (8) *Samādhi*, the summit of attainment being the complete absorption of the consciousness and its faculties into oneness or union with the Monadic Essence (*Ātma*) as just described.

is then to him like an open page because he is 'self-consciously conscious' of Nature's inner and spiritual realms—his consciousness has become kosmic in its reaches.[88] This is obviously a rare attainment by the very few like the Christ, the Buddha, Ramana Maharshi, and the Himalayan Adepts who were the inner Founders of the Theosophical movement. Such God–Men are referred to in popular terms as 'super-men' since they have achieved (over innumerable lifetimes) the full flowering of human consciousness and progressed beyond. (Incidentally, this has nothing whatsoever to do with the transhumanist idea of developing 'posthuman beings' with vastly enhanced capabilities, out of all proportion to the natural condition, by means of advanced technologies[89]—see the Epilogue.) Such luminaries are anchored in the Spiritual Soul (such a term, of course, is a total anathema to transhumanists), and other than stating that their consciousness is permanently bathed in Samādhi, attempting a further explanation would be venturing to describe the indescribable. However, we may cite a few examples of the astounding powers and intuitive insights displayed by highly advanced souls who, in their moments of peak creativity, have attained quasi-omniscience in their particular field of endeavour and 'brought through' scientific, artistic or philosophical marvels that have sustained and elevated mankind for centuries.

> **What is intuition? In short, it is that direct perception which *transcends*, not bypasses, the intellectual mind, i.e., the mind functioning in a purely intellectual mode.**

Our first example is that of a genius whose profound thoughts we have encountered several times during the course of this work: a man largely self-taught, born fatherless on Christmas Day, 1642, 'the last wonderchild to whom the Magi could do sincere and appropriate homage' and who, 'until the second phase of his long life, was a wrapt, consecrated solitary, pursuing his studies by intense introspection with a mental endurance perhaps never equalled'[90]—Isaac Newton. Lord Keynes, who bought a large proportion of Newton's alchemical treatises and studied them assiduously declared, 'I fancy his preeminence is due to his muscles of intuition being the strongest and most enduring with which a man has ever been gifted.' The key word is *intuition*, the faculty of direct knowing, perfectly stated in Newton's case, that he 'seem[ed] to know more than he could possibly have any means of proving. The proofs, for what they are worth, were, dressed up afterwards—they were not the instrument of discovery.' As exampled by Keynes, 'there is the story of how he informed Halley of one of his most fundamental discoveries of planetary motion. "Yes", replied Halley, "but how do you know that? Have you proved it?" Newton was taken aback—"Why, I've known it for years", he replied. "If you'll give me a few days, I'll certainly find you a proof of it"—as in due course he did.' A similar note was sounded in modern times by the physicist Richard Feynman who said during his Nobel acceptance speech in 1965: 'A very great deal more truth can become known than can be proven.'[91]

Newton's matchless intuitions

Then, in the opening remarks to his Foreword to Newton's *Opticks* (based on the fourth edition of 1730) Einstein says: 'Nature to him was an open book, whose letters he could read without effort.'[92, ix] Light, in both its physical and transcendent aspects, was of

Newton's discoveries were the fruit of profound contemplation

---

ix In the case of musical genius, when the Czech born Austrian pianist Carl Czerny (1791–1857) first heard his pupil, the eleven-year-old Franz Liszt play to him, he later described the experience in his autobiography: 'It was as if Nature herself had intended him as a pianist'—Alan Walker, *Liszt* (Faber and Faber, 1971), 18.

profound significance to Newton. Whereas Book One, Book Two, and the first section of Book Three of *Opticks* deal with physical light, Book Three ends with thirty-one *Queries* where Newton made tremendous forays into the vast field of alchemy proposing ideas about the nature of light and matter and their properties that presaged the discoveries of Einstein and others centuries later.[93]

Ramanujan's staggering intuitions

As to his method of working, the great French mathematician, Jean Baptiste Biot (1774–1862) records that to one who asked him on some occasion, by what means he had arrived at his discoveries, Newton replied, 'I keep the subject constantly before me, and wait till the first dawnings open slowly by little and little into the full and clear light'[94]—the word 'light' used not in a metaphorical sense, in the writer's understanding, but as a statement of fact (see later). It is the age-old method of prolonged mystic meditation. Thus, it is entirely reasonable to propose that Newton's legendary discoveries, or rather revelations as we would prefer to suggest, were bequeathed to him in a state of profound contemplation akin to Samādhi. Moreover, his highly extended periods of extreme absent-mindedness and introspection could bear resemblance to the condition of spiritual trance mentioned above.

Another striking example is that of a young man who wrote a letter to England's premier mathematician Godfrey Harold 'G. H.' Hardy FRS (1877–1947) at Trinity College, Cambridge, opening with, 'I beg to introduce myself to you as a clerk in the Accounts Department of the Port Trust Office at Madras on a salary of only £20 per annum. I am now about 23 years of age. I have had no University education but I have undergone the ordinary school course.'[95] This was the autodidactic Indian mathematical genius Srinivasa Ramanujan, see Figure III-33 opposite, for whom, like Newton, 'the proofs, for what they are worth, were, dressed up afterwards—they were not the instrument of discovery.' Regarded as the equal of the Swiss mathematical physicist Leonhard Euler (1707–1783) and the German mathematician Carl Jacobi (1804–1851), Srinivasa Ramanujan, mentioned in Volume I, Chapter 5 in the context of scientific revolutionaries, lived during the British Rule in India and died at the tragically young age of thirty-two, but left behind an inspired legacy that is still being plumbed for its secrets today. Born to a humble family, plagued by ill-health and poverty, he once declared, 'when food itself is a problem, how can I find money for paper? I may require four reams of paper every month [for mathematical research].'[96]

Poverty and lack of education are no bars to the flowering of genius

Ramanujan had virtually no formal training in pure mathematics and in fact failed his school examinations in India, only managing to obtain the clerical post mentioned in his letter to Hardy. Yet he made substantial contributions to mathematical analysis, number theory, infinite series, and continued fractions, including solutions to mathematical problems considered to be unsolvable. While on his deathbed in 1920, Ramanujan wrote a letter to Hardy, his mentor at Cambridge, outlining several new mathematical functions never before heard of, along with intimations about how they worked. Scribbled in black ink, about one hundred and thirty unlabelled pages full of mathematical equations that made no sense at first sight were accidentally discovered in 1976 by the American mathematician Professor George Andrews (*b*.1938) of Pennsylvania State University in a box at the library of Trinity College, Cambridge. Once rediscovered, the pages electrified the world of mathematics. They were what the American physicist Freeman Dyson FRS (1923–2020) remarked as, 'flowers that grew from seeds that ripened in Ramanujan's

Figure III-33   Srinivasa Ramanujan

'An equation has no meaning for me
unless it represents a thought of God'

Image Credit: Oberwolfach Photo Collection/Wikimedia
Commons/Srinivasa Ramanujan - OPC - 1.jpg

garden.'[97] Now, well over a century later, American researchers say Ramanujan's formulae could help physicists learn more about black holes—even though such objects were virtually unknown during his lifetime. The Japanese-American Ken Ono (*b*.1968) Professor of Mathematics at Emory University and the Vice President of the American Mathematical Society states, 'We have solved the problems from his last mysterious letters [to Hardy]. For people who work in this area of math, the problem has been open for 90 years.'[98]

Ramanujan's staggering discoveries, *acquired through pure intuition* earned him a Fellowship of the Royal Society (the second Indian to be so elected) and he was also elected Fellow of Trinity College, Cambridge. But in all this, every gratitude and credit is due to Hardy who first recognized the budding genius from their correspondence and invited him to Cambridge, and subsequently nurtured and harnessed the extraordinary, albeit untutored creative effulgence of the mathematical racehorse in his charge.[x] Hardy unhesitatingly confessed that his greatest contribution to mathematics was the discovery of Ramanujan,[99] calling their collaboration 'the one romantic incident in my life.'[100] Furthermore, according to Hardy's personal ratings of mathematicians on the basis of pure talent on a scale from 0 to 100, 'Hardy gave himself a score of 25, [John] Littlewood 30, [David] Hilbert 80 and Ramanujan 100.'[101] But given their diametrically opposed temperaments, the 'father and son' relationship between the atheist Englishman and the devout Hindu could not have been an easy one as, '"the Prince of Intuition", tested his brilliant theories alongside the sophisticated and eccentric Hardy, "the Apostle of Proof".'[102]

---

x   In music we can see a parallel with Carl Czerny (himself a pupil of Beethoven) who was instrumental in taming and disciplining the wild excesses of his eleven-year-old pupil, Franz Liszt, who was to become the undisputed emperor of pianists—see Alan Walker, *Liszt* (London: Faber and Faber), 18–19.

Besides mathematics at Trinity College, Cambridge and the Royal Society, there are further significant parallels between Ramanujan and Newton (whose birth dates in December were just three days apart) that provide insights into the atypical lifestyle and character of geniuses, especially those in mathematics. The following are noteworthy.

Like Newton, Ramanujan initially developed his own mathematical ideas in virtual isolation. Shy and introspective, he lived an ascetic life at Cambridge, was abstemious in diet and a strict vegetarian,[103] a fact that Hardy also remarked upon.[104] Regarding Newton, not much is known about what he ate, except that he cared little for his meals.[105] However, in his book *Vegetable Diet: As sanctioned by medical men, and by experience in all ages*, the American educator and physician Dr William A. Alcott (1798–1859) writes this about Newton:

> This distinguished philosopher and mathematician is said to have abstained rigorously, at times, from all but purely vegetable food, and from all drinks but water; and it is also stated that some of his important labors were performed at these seasons of strict temperance. While writing his treatise on Optics, it is said he confined himself entirely to bread, with a little sack and water; and I have no doubt that his remarkable equanimity of temper, and that government of his animal appetites, throughout, for which he was so distinguished to the last hour of his life, were owing, in no small degree, to his habits of rigid temperance.[106]

The point of mentioning all this is that not only do 'great minds think alike', but apparently, great minds also 'eat alike'! Why? *Because the stratospheric region of thought and intellect demands a human physique of extreme mental sensitivity, which would be severely vitiated by the cloying effects of a carnivorous gourmet diet and, needless to say, by mind-altering drugs.*

Arguably however, the most significant common factor linking both great men is that they were deeply religious, albeit in very different ways, but that is a mere detail. In fact, Hardy has also stated that according to his young protégé, 'all religions seemed to him more or less equally true [obviously, when reduced to their core precepts].'[107] Ramanujan was a devout Brahmin of the Vaishnava sect and credited his creative ability to divinity, maintaining that the mathematical knowledge he displayed was revealed to him by his family goddess, Namagiri Thayar of Namakkal to whom he looked for inspiration in his work.[108] As Ramanujan's biographer relates: 'Scrolls containing the most complicated mathematics used to unfold before his eyes.'[109] One such event was described by him as follows:

> While asleep, I had an unusual experience. There was a red screen formed by flowing blood, as it were. I was observing it. Suddenly a hand began to write on the screen. I became all attention. That hand wrote a number of elliptic integrals. They stuck to my mind. As soon as I woke up, I committed them to writing.[110]

(Furthermore, as the prevailing custom forbade Hindu Brahmins to cross the sea during colonial times, Ramanujan's mother received permission from Namagiri Thayar in a dream for her son to go to England—as stated by none other an authority than Hardy.[111])

This is something of extreme import as it would seem to underpin his oft quoted and celebrated saying, 'An equation has no meaning for me unless it represents a thought of God.'[112] Refer to the section in Chapter 8 on page 150 f. on the mathematical relation between the mental world and its physical counterpart, which theme is developed in the Mathematical Codicil on page 349.

Figure III-34   The Museum in Ramanujan's former home on Sarangapani Sannidhi Street, Kumbakonam

Image Credit: Adiswini/Wikimedia Commons/Wikimedia Commons/Ramanujanhome.jpg

Ramanujan's birthday on 22nd December is now celebrated every year in India as National Mathematics Day with numerous educational events held at Indian schools and universities.[113] Figure III-34 above shows a picture of his simple family home, which is now a museum in Kumbakonam, in the Thanjavur District of Tamil Nadu.

Alluding to the role of intuition as well as pointing to the distinction between the computer and the human mind, the celebrated mathematical physicist Sir Roger Penrose states:

> The inescapable conclusion seems to be: Mathematicians are not using a knowably sound calculation procedure in order to ascertain mathematical truth. We deduce that mathematical understanding—the means whereby mathematicians arrive at their conclusions with respect to mathematical truth—cannot be reduced to blind calculation![114]

In music, the staggering output in the final year of both Mozart's (1756–1791) and Schubert's (1797–1828) lives come to mind. The latter died before the age of thirty-two (practically the same age as Ramanujan). Both are fine examples of souls through whom an unbroken stream of intuition 'flowed through' the 'hardware' of their cerebral mechanisms. How else could such a torrent of works of supernal quality have been materialized in the last few months of these young composers, both plagued with illnesses and financial hardship, other than by receiving visions of scrolls of musical content unfolding before the inner eye?

Our last example of the flowering of latent powers in man gifted to rare individuals, is one whose peerless insights have formed the backbone of Volume II of this work—Helena Petrovna Blavatsky. She also had extraordinarily developed occult powers which, like Ramanujan, it would seem, enabled her to access the 'astral light' as she called it. This is Nature's universal memory which records everything that has ever happened during this cycle of the history of the world. Its Cosmic counterpart, the everlasting Universal Memory, is generally referred to as the '*ākāśic* records' (see Chapter 6 earlier). It was by drawing on

Legendary geniuses who died in their thirties

Blavatsky proves the fact of latent powers in man

this astral light memory that her Adept instructors were able to show her the copious references she needed for her works, such as *Isis Unveiled* and *The Secret Doctrine*, which she wrote down during long and exhausting sessions often involving periods of great mental exertion. There is no other way to explain how a woman generally in serious ill health, working in solitude, with a personal library of some thirty books (see again Chapter 6), could quote extensively from literally several thousands of volumes on every department of human knowledge ranging from archaic manuscripts to modern publications. For example, the writer has checked large portions of the science sections of *The Secret Doctrine* with regard to their source references. Each one has been found to be correct in every detail with regard to citation, reference, and page number. He has also verified each and every one of dozens of references to Newton and found them all to be correct in minute detail.[115] This is why we can affirm, with confidence, that besides displaying the ability to read the indelible scrolls and tablets of Nature, Blavatsky wrote truly as a scientist, providing us with full chapter and verse, with verifiable source references. (But this is not to say that in a work of such gargantuan scale, a few errors may not exist.[xi])

Why are such phenomenal powers gifted to rare individuals as those just cited? For various reasons, but the chief one is something that has repeatedly been stressed in different ways throughout this work: knowledge is power; and the greater the knowledge, the greater the power; and the greater the power, the greater its benefit for the service of humanity or its abuse for the aggrandisement of the ego in its craving for selfish power, control, and sensual gratification at the expense of the untold suffering of humanity. That there are but few people able to use immense power wisely is an understatement (look at the behaviour of most powerful politicians and billionaires, especially nowadays, plus the examples of dictators cited in Chapter 7 of Volume I); and so regarding the dangers from the terrible misuse of powers, let Blavatsky make the point in her own words:

> In occultism, a most solemn vow has to be taken never to use any powers acquired or conferred for the benefit of one's own personal self, for to do so would be to set foot on the steep and treacherous slope that ends in the abyss of Black Magic. I have taken that vow […]. I would rather suffer any tortures than be untrue to my pledge.[116]

Occult powers can, therefore, only be handled safely by a true initiate, or by:

> The adept [who] is the rare efflorescence of a generation of enquirers; and to become one, he must obey the inward impulse of his soul [i.e., the Spiritual, or Supreme Soul] irrespective of the prudential considerations of worldly science or sagacity.[117]

This Chapter has built upon the previous one and, it is hoped, demonstrates that man is not simply the outcome of, but an active channel for, and a nexus with, the three primary divine forces responsible for all manifestation. Details were given regarding the latent powers in man, the circumstances under which they may be aroused, and the fruits of these awakened faculties.

---

xi As a trivial example, Boris de Zirkoff, editor of the 1972 edition of Blavatsky's *Isis Unveiled*, conducted an exhaustive search of the verse attributed by Blavatsky to Ovid in *IU*-I, 'Man's Yearning for Immortality', page 37 and discovered that no such verses have been found either in Lucretius or in Ovid (see *IU*-I, 'Notes by the Editor', 635 n.19). The writer suggests that the verse may in fact be by the Assyrian rhetorician Lucian of Samosat (120–192).

But earnest readers can hardly be blamed if they are left with residue doubts concerning how such powers may be safely and practically awakened. How do we obey the 'inward impulse' spoken of by the Adept in the quote above? Moreover, how are we to distinguish between the false and true in a world that obfuscates the truth by employing a mesmeric range of seemingly attractive escape routes, each taking us further away from reality. In these ways (ranging from psychedelic drugs, mindless entertainment, virtual realities, fake news, and conspiracy theories[118]) we disappear down a long tunnel much like the White Rabbit of Alice in Wonderland fame. But, of course, we can choose not to do these things in the spirit of 'When I was a child, I spake as a child, I understood as a child, I thought as a child: but when I became a man, I put away childish things' (Corinthians 13:11, King James Version).

We close this Chapter with perhaps the best and simplest advice given by the Masters of the Wisdom to the Irish-American esotericist, and co-founder of the Theosophical Society, William Quan Judge (1851–1896). It is advice of peculiar benefit to us all and reads as follows:

But here is advice given by many Adepts: every day and as often as you can, and on going to sleep and as you wake—think, think, think, on the truth that you are not body, brain, or astral man, but that you are that, and 'that' is the Supreme Soul. For by this practice you will gradually kill the false notion which lurks inside that the false is the true, and the true, the false. By persistence in this, by submitting your daily thoughts each night to the judgement of your Higher Self, you will at last gain light.[119]

NOTES

1   'Address by Sir William Crookes FRS, VPCS, President', *Report of the Sixty-Eighth Meeting of the British Association for the Advancement of Science Held at Bristol in September 1898* (London: John Murray, 1899), 29–30 [online facsimile] <https://ia802804.us.archive.org/7/items/reportofbritisha99brit/reportofbritisha99brit.pdf> accessed 16 November 2020. This seminal address is quoted also in: *Nature*, 1506/58 (8 September 1898), 438; *Scientific American* (8 October 1898); and in part by Rebecca Northfield, 'Science of the Supernatural', *The Institution of Engineering and Technology* (October 2016), 71.

2   Alex Owen, *The Place of Enchantment: British occultism and the culture of the modern* (Chicago: University of Chicago Press, 2007), 70.

3   *SD*-I, 'Science and the Secret Doctrine Contrasted: Reasons for these Addenda', 477–676.

4   *SD*-I, 'Proem', 16–17. Further elucidated in Edi D. Bilimoria, *The Snake and the Rope: Problems in Western science resolved by occult science* (Adyar, Madras: Theosophical Publishing House, 2006), 256–7.

5   Edi Bilimoria, 'The Alchemy of Religion', in Ana-Maria Pascal (ed.), *Multiculturalism and the Convergence of Faith and Practical Wisdom in Modern Society* (Hershey, Pennsylvania: IGI Global, 2017), 45.

6   John Maddox, 'The Prevalent Distrust of Science', *Nature*, 378 (1995), 435.

7   J. D. Watson and F. H. C. Crick, 'A Structure for Deoxyribose Nucleic Acid', *Nature* (25 April 1953), 171, 737–8 [repr. online] <https://www.3dmoleculardesigns.com/3DMD-Files/DNA-Discovery/PDFs/AnnotatedWatsonandCrickpaper.pdf> accessed 28 December 2020.

8   Paul Davies, 'The Secret of Life Won't Be Cooked Up in a Chemistry Lab', *The Guardian*, 13 January 2013.

9   A wisecrack by the writer at the Crick Manifesto—see Francis Crick, *The Astonishing Hypothesis: The scientific search for the soul* (New York: Charles Scribner's Sons, 1994), 3.

10 Quoted from Alexis Carrel, *Man, the Unknown* (New York: Harper & Brothers, 1935), in Ernst Lehrs, *Man or Matter: Introduction to a spiritual understanding of nature on the basis of Goethe's method of training observation and thought*, ed. Nick Thomas and Peter Bortoft (3rd edn, rev. and enl., London: Rudolf Steiner Press, 2013), 398.

11 Rupert Sheldrake, *The Presence of the Past* (London: Fontana, 1988).

12 Dr B. W. Richardson, 'Theory of a Nervous Ether', *Popular Science Review* (repr. London: Forgotten Books, 2019; citation from 1st edn 1871), x, 380–3. Quoted also in *SD*-I, 'Life, Force, or Gravity', 531.

13 *SD*-I, *loc. cit.*

14 Dr B. W. Richardson, 'Theory of a Nervous Ether', 379. Quoted also in *SD*-I, 'Forces – Modes of Motion or Intelligences?' 603. See also *CW*-IX, 'The Life Principle', 78–9.

15 Dr. B. W. Richardson, *loc. cit.* Quoted also in *SD*-I, 'Life, Force, or Gravity', 532.

16 *SD*-I, *loc. cit.*

17 *SD*-I, 'Life, Force or Gravity', 532, quoting from Franz Hartmann MD, FTS, *The Life and the Doctrines of Paracelsus* (New York: Theosophical Publishing Company, 1887), 133, quoting in turn from Paracelsus, *De Generatione Hominis* [On the Generation of Man] (Switzerland, Durch Christian Muller, 1577).

18 *SD*-I, *loc. cit.*, quoting from Franz Hartmann, *loc. cit.*, quoting in turn from Paracelsus, *De Viribus Membrorum* [Of Organic Powers] (1572; repr. Generic, ASIN : B07R2MHYLK, 2019).

19 *SD*-I, *loc, cit.*, n. See Paracelsus, *Das Buch Paragranum* [The Book of Paragranum] (1530; repr. Prague, Czech Republic: e-artnow, 2018).

20 Isaac Newton, *Philosophiæ Naturalis Principia Mathematica* [Mathematical Principles of Natural Philosophy], trans. Andrew Motte, rev. Florian Cajori, 2 vols (Berkeley, Los Angeles: University of California Press, 1962), ii, 'The System of the World – General Scholium', 547.

21 Dr B. W. Richardson, 'Sun–Force and Earth–Force', *Popular Science Review* (repr. London: Forgotten Books, 2018; citation from 1st edn 1866), V, 329–34. Quoted also in *SD*-I, 'An Attack on the Scientific Theory of Force by a Man of Science', 524.

22 Samuel Metcalfe, *Caloric: Its mechanical chemical and vital agencies in the phenomena of nature*, 2 vols (1st edn *circa* 1923; repr. US: Arkose Press, 2015).

23 Annie Besant, *An Introduction to Yoga* (Adyar, Madras: Theosophical Publishing House, 1972).

24 Georg Feuerstein, *The Yoga-sūtra of Patañjali: A new translation and commentary* (Rocherter, Vermont: Inner Traditions Bear and Company, 1992). See also: I. K. Taimni, *The Science of Yoga* (Adyar, Madras: Theosophical Publishing House, 1965); note from Sir Yehudi Menuhin, in B. K. S. Iyengar, *Light on the Yoga Sūtras of Patañjali* (UK: Harper Thorsons, 2002).

25 B. K. S. Iyengar, *Light on Pranayama: The definitive guide to the art of breathing* (UK: Harper Thorsons, 2013).

26 K. S. Cohen, *The Way of Qigong: The art and science of Chinese energy healing*, foreword by Larry Dossey, MD (USA and Canada: Random House Publishing, 1997).

27 Jwing-Ming Yang, *Tai Chi Qigong: The internal foundation of Tai Chi Chuan* (US: YMAA Publication Center, 1998).

28 *NPB*-4, Part 2: *The Body*, 'Kundalini', ¶ 1, 141.

29 *SD*-I, 'Stanza I: The Night of the Universe', 45.

30 B. K. Kleinschmidt-DeMasters and R. A. Prayson, 'An Algorithmic Approach to the Brain Biopsy', *Arch Pathol Lab Med*, 130/11 (2006), Part I: 1630–8, Part II: 1639–48.

31 *SD*-I, 'Stanza VII: The Parents of Man on Earth', 224–5.

32 'Constitution of the Inner Man', in H. P. Blavatsky, *Studies in Occultism* (Point Loma, California, The Aryan Theosophical Press, 1910) <https://www.theosociety.org/pasadena/hpb-sio/sio-cons.htm#t1> accessed 21 April 2020.

33 *SD*-II, 'The Races with the "Third Eye"', 294 n., 295.

34 *SD*-II, *op. cit.*, 298.

35 *CW*-XII, 'Instruction No. V', 698.

36 See the fuller explanation in *SD*-I, 'Stanza I: The Night of the Universe', 46 et seq.

37 Michael Hawley, 'Sarvepalli Radhakrishnan (1888–1975)', *Internet Encyclopedia of Philosophy* <http://www.iep.utm.edu/radhakri/#H2> accessed 23 April 2020.

38 Rephrased from *SD*-I, 'Life Force or Gravity', 537.

39 Beinsa Douno, *The Teacher: Volume One – The Dawning Epoch* (London: Shining Word Press, 2016), 119 n.1, 205 n.22, 127 n.11.

40 BBC News – Science & Environment, 'Climate Change – Failure to Tackle Warming "Suicidal"', 13 December 2018 <https://www.bbc.co.uk/news/science-environment-46543704> accessed 24 April 2020.

41 Once such instance is recounted in Paul Brunton, *The Secret Path: A technique of spiritual self-discovery for the modern world*, foreword by Alice A. Bailey (London: Rider & Co., 22nd impression, 1934), 20–1.

42 David Lorimer (ed.), *Prophet for Our Times – The Life and Teachings of Peter Deunov*, foreword by Dr Wayne W. Dyer (UK and worldwide: Hay House, 2015).

43 *ibid.*

44 Bro. Francis Mary Kalvelage, *Padre Pio: The wonder worker* (San Francisco, California: Ignatius Press, 1999), 210.

45 'The Healing of Gemma di Giorgi', Padre Pio Devotions <https://web.archive.org/web/20090608004702/http://www.padrepiodevotions.org/2002april.asp> accessed 26 March 2020. This site includes a photograph of the eyes of Gemma di Giorgi with no pupils.

46 1 Corinthians 13:12, King James Version.

47 S. Radhakrishnan, 'Intellect and Intuition' from The Hibbert Lectures given in the University of Manchester, 1929 and University College, London, 1930, in *An Idealist View of Life* (1931; 2nd edn, London: George Allen & Unwin, 1947), 153.

48 *ibid.*

49 *STA*, 'The Hiramic Legend', LXXIX.

50 *How To Know God: The yoga aphorisms of Patanjali*, trans. Swami Prabhavananda and Christopher Isherwood (US: Vedanta Press, 1983).

51 Jacobo Grinberg-Zylberbaum, *Creation of Experience: The syntergic theory* (Mexico City, Instituto Nacional para el Estudio de la Conciencia, 1988), cited from course notes of the *Centre for the Study of Extended Human Consciousness* by Professor Peter Stewart DSc, FREng.

52 Jacobo Grinberg-Zylberbaum, 'Educacion para la nueva era' ['Education for the new era'], *Conciencia Planetaria*, 1 (1990), 34.

53 Philip S. Harris (ed.), *Theosophical Encyclopedia* (Philippines: Theosophical Publishing House, 2006), 142. There are also several other enumerations of the physical correspondences of the seven major *cākras*.

54 C. G. Jung, *The Psychology of Kundalini Yoga: Notes of the seminar given in 1932 by C. G. Jung*, ed. Sonu Shamdasani (1933; 2nd edn, England: Routledge, and Princeton: Princeton University Press, 1999), 43.

55 Taken from: *NPB-11, The Sensitives: Dynamics and dangers of mysticism*, 'The Lure of Occultism', ¶94, 83; *NPB-7, Part 1: Healing of the Self: Using the forces of life'*, 'Dangers of Drugs and Alcohol' ¶135, 57.

56 Mo Costandi, 'A Brief History of Psychedelic Psychiatry', *The Guardian*, 2 September 2014 <https://www.theguardian.com/science/neurophilosophy/2014/sep/02/psychedelic-psychiatry> accessed 16 November 2020.

57 Aldous Huxley, *The Doors of Perception and Heaven and Hell* (New York: Harper Perennial Modern Classics, 1954), 6.

58 See Timothy Miller, *The 60s Communes: Hippies and beyond* (New York: Syracuse University Press, 1999).

59 'The Summer of Love', *The Week*, 8 July 2017, 11.

60 Faculty of Medicine – Imperial College <http://www.imperial.ac.uk/department-of-medicine/research/brain-sciences/psychiatry/psychedelics> accessed 25 April 2020.

61 Psychedelic Research and Knowledge Sharing <https://psychedelicsurvey.com> accessed 25 April 2020.

62 *CW-XII*, 'E. S. Instruction No. V', 698.

63 Ron Duselman, *In Place of the Self: How drugs work*, trans. Plym Peters and Tony Langham (UK: Hawthorn Press, 1995).

64 Rudolf Steiner, *Knowledge of the Higher Worlds: How is it achieved?* (1923; 8th edn, Forest Row, UK: Rudolf Steiner Press, 2011).

65 'Knowledge of the Higher Worlds X – The Guardian of the Threshold', Rudolf Steiner Archive & e.Lib <https://wn.rsarchive.org/Books/GA010/English/AP1947/GA010_c10.html> accessed 25 April 2020.

66 Edward Bulwer-Lytton, *Zanoni*, 3 vols (London: Saunders and Otley, 1842).

67 Eusebio Urban, 'Dweller on the Threshold', *The Path* (December 1888).

68 Franz Hartmann, 'The Dweller of the Threshold', *The Theosophist*, xi (1889).

69 Max Heindel, *The Web Destiny*, Rosicrucian Fellowship <https://www.rosicrucian.com/wbd/wbdeng01.htm> accessed 25 April 2020.

70 Christina Feldman, *Quotes on Enlightenment – Living Life Fully* <http://www.livinglifefully.com/enlightenment.htm> accessed 8 June 2020.

71 Rudolf Steiner, *The Spiritual–Scientific Basis of Goethe's Work* (Mayotte: St. George Publications, 1982). See also Rudolf Steiner, 'The Spiritual–Scientific Basis of Goethe's Work' [online 5 May 2004] <https://wn.rsarchive.org/Articles/SSBoGW_index.html> accessed 25 April 2020.

72 Christopher Bache, *LSD and the Mind of the Universe: Diamonds from heaven*, foreword by Ervin László (Rochester, Vermont: Inner Traditions, 2019).

73 Carl Jung, *Letters Vol. 2: 1951–1961*, ed. Gerhard Adler, trans. Jeffrey Hulen (Princeton: Princeton University Press, 1976), 503–4, cited in <https://carljungdepthpsychologysite.blog/2019/09/27/carl-jung-on-homesickness/#.XqSwYWhKg5s> accessed 25 April 2020.

74 Brendan D. Murphy, 'How We Sense When We Are Being Stared At', *World-Mysteries* (July 2012) <https://blog.world-mysteries.com/science/how-we-sense-when-we-are-being-stared-at> accessed 11 April 2020.

75 Bernard Hollander, *Methods and Uses of Hypnosis and Self-Hypnosis: A treatise on the powers of the subconscious mind* (1928; London and New York: Routledge, 2015).

76 *The New York American*, 30 March 1933 <http://www.keelynet.com/news/102114d.html> accessed 1 December 2019> See also 'The Mystery of the Eye', in Paul Brunton, *The Quest of the Overself* (1937; London: Rider, 1986), 169–70.

77 *The New York American, art. cit.*

78 Rupert Sheldrake, *The Sense of Being Stared At: And other aspects of the extended mind* (Rochester, Vermont: Inner Traditions, 2013).

79 Paul Brunton, *The Quest of the Overself*, 175.

80 *ibid.*

81 Paul Brunton, *The Quest of the Overself*, 162–76.

82 *CW*-XII, 'E. S. Instruction No. II', 545.

83 This is purely the writer's suggestion based on an extrapolation of the ideas in: Iain McGilchrist, *The Master and His Emissary: The divided brain and the making of the western world* (2010; rev. and enl. 2nd edn, New Haven and London: Yale University Press, 2019); Jill Bolte Taylor, *My Stroke of Insight: A brain scientist's personal journey* (UK: Hodder & Stoughton, 2009).

84 Annekatrin Puhle, *Light Changes: Experiences in the presence of transforming light* (UK: White Crow Books, 2014).

85 Peter Fenwick, Caroline Di Bernardi Luft, Andreas A Ioannides, and Joydeep Bhattacharya, 'Neural Correlates of Induced Light Experience during Meditation: A pilot hyperscanning study', *NeuroQuantology*, 17/01 (January 2019), 31–41.

86 Paramahansa Yogananda, *Metaphysical Meditations* (Los Angeles, California: Self-Realization Fellowship, 1976), 76 quoting from *Autobiography of a Yogi*, preface by W. Y. Evans-Wentz MA, DLitt, DSc (1946; rev. 1951; Bombay, India: Jaico Publishing House with Self-Realization Fellowship Los Angeles, California, 1972).

87 Paul Brunton, *The Quest of the Overself*: Part II – The Practices.

88 The above description is paraphrased and particularized from G de Purucker, *Occult Glossary* (Pasadena, California: Theosophical University Press, 1972), 151.

89 Nick Bostrom. 'A History of Transhumanist Thought', *Journal of Evolution and Technology* (2005).

90 This quotation and the remaining ones in the paragraph are from John Maynard Keynes: 'Newton, the Man', delivered posthumously by Geoffrey Keynes, brother of Lord Keynes at the Royal Society tercentenary celebrations in 1947 <http://www-history.mcs.st-and.ac.uk/Extras/Keynes_Newton.html> accessed 26 April 2020.

91 Richard P. Feynman, 'The Development of the Space–Time View of Quantum Electrodynamics', Nobel Lecture, 11 December 1965 <https://www.nobelprize.org/prizes/physics/1965/feynman/lecture> accessed 26 April 2020.

92 Isaac Newton, *Opticks, Or, A Treatise of the Reflections, Refractions, Inflections & Colours of Light* (London, 1730; 4th edn, New York: Dover Publications, 1979), 1ix.

93 —— *op. cit.*, 30, 374–5.

94 Jean Baptiste Biot, *Life of Sir Isaac Newton*, trans. H. C. Elphinstone, in *Lives of Eminent Persons* (London: 1833), The Newton Project (July 2009) <http://www.newtonproject.ox.ac.uk/view/texts/normalized/OTHE00089> accessed 26 April 2020.

95 Letter to G. H. Hardy (16 January 1913), in 'Ramanujan: Letters and commentary', *American Mathematical Society*, ix (7 September 1995).

96 'Srinivasa Ramanujan, a Mathematician Brilliant Beyond Comparison', San José State University <http://applet-magic.com/ramanujan.htm> accessed 26 April 2020.

97 T. V. Venkateswaran, 'A Lesson from Ramanujan's Elbow', *DownToEarth: Science & Technology* (21 December 2018) <https://www.downtoearth.org.in/news/science-technology/a-lesson-from-ramanujan-s-elbow-62574> accessed 26 April 2020.

98 Jacob Aron, 'Mathematical Proof Reveals Magic of Ramanujan's Genius', *New Scientist* (7 November 2012).

99 'Ramanujan: An estimation', in Alladi K. Krishnaswami, *Ramanujan's Place in the World of Mathematics* (India: Springer, 2013), 3 et seq.

100 Luke Mastin, 'G. H. Hardy: Ramanujan's mentor', The Story of Mathematics (2010) <https://www.storyofmathematics.com/20th_hardy.html> accessed 26 April 2020.

101 K. Srinivasa Rao, 'Srinivasa Ramanujan (Dec. 22, 1887 – April 26, 1920)', *The Institute of Mathematical Sciences*, Madras-600 113 (n.d.) <https://www.imsc.res.in/~rao/ramanujan.html> accessed 26 April 2020.

102 Robert Kanigel, *The Man Who Knew Infinity: A life of the genius Ramanujan* (New York: Washington Square Press, 1991), back cover.

103 —— *op. cit.*, 22.

104 Bruce C. Berndt and Robert Alexander Rankin (eds), *Ramanujan: Essays and surveys* (US: American Mathematical Society, 2001), 47.

105 James Gleick, *Isaac Newton* (New York: Harper Perennial, 2004).

106 William A. Alcott, *Vegetable Diet: As sanctioned by medical men, and by experience in all ages*, introd. Anna Thomas (Boston, 1838; rev. edn, Kansas City, Sydney, London: Andrews McMeel Publishing, 2012), Chapter VI.

107 Robert Kanigel, *The Man Who Knew Infinity*, 283.

108 —— *op. cit.*, 36.

109 —— *op. cit.*, 281.

110 'The Secrets of Ramanujan's Garden', *Science and Nonduality* <https://www.scienceandnonduality.com/article/the-secrets-of-ramanujans-garden> accessed 21 May 2021. See also Michael Katz, *Tibetan Dream Yoga – The Royal Road to Enlightenment* (India: Bodhi Tree, 2011).

111 G. H. Hardy, 'Obituary, S. Ramanujan', *Nature* 105/7 (June 1920), 494–5.

112 Shiyali Ramamrita Ranganathan, *Ramanujan, the Man and the Mathematician* (Bombay, New York: Asia Publishing House, 1967), 88.

113 C. Jaishankar, 'Ramanujan's Birthday will be National Mathematics Day', *The Hindu*, 27 December 2011.

114 Roger Penrose, 'Mathematical Intelligence', in Jean Khalfa (ed.), *What is Intelligence?* (Cambridge: Cambridge University Press, 1994), 107–36.

115 Edi Bilimoria, 'H. P. Blavatsky – A Spiritual Floodlight', *The Blavatsky Trust* <http://www.blavatskytrust.org.uk/html/articles/hpb%20spiritual%20floodlight.htm> accessed 26 April 2020.

116 Constance Wachtmeister, *Reminiscences of H.P. Blavatsky and 'The Secret Doctrine'* (London: Theosophical Publishing Society, 1893), 46. Quoted also in: Geoffrey A Barborka, *H. P. Blavatsky – the Light-Bringer*, the Blavatsky Lecture 1970 (London: Theosophical Publishing House), 41; Edi Bilimoria, *art. cit.*

117 *ML*, Letter No. 2.

118 'An Age of Witch-Hunts – The Victims of Conspiracy Theories Speak Out', *The Week*, 16 February 2019.

119 William Quan Judge, *Letters That Have Helped Me: Volume II* (1905; London: Creative Media Partners, LLC, 2019), Letter 26: On Occult Philosophy. Quoted also in 'Perfecting Human Nature', *The Theosophical Movement*, 77/2 (17 December 2006), 46.

10 Man's Limitless Evolution – Our Unfinished Journey

In this Chapter, we might ask 'What is the task of Man?' Franz Liszt answers:

To strive for the unattainable, towards Truth, Beauty and Goodness—irrespective of how our weaknesses put restrictions on our endeavours—and to try to approach our Maker.

FRANZ LISZT[1]

And by what means? Some two centuries earlier, Francis Bacon counselled:

If we are to achieve things never before accomplished we must employ methods never before attempted.

FRANCIS BACON[2]

SYNOPSIS

Chapter 10 describes the landscapes of our unfinished journey—ever onward and upward. This journey is of course, evolution, limitless and never-ending. But a word that has become common currency tends to attract a fixed meaning; and evolution is taken to be virtually synonymous with Darwinian theory in mainstream science, and therefore in the public eye, propagated by the media. Evolution however, is not as simplistic as the one-sided meaning ascribed to it. Accordingly, as is our policy with complex matters, this Chapter opens with a careful definition of terms. Thereafter, evolution is described from the standpoints of Darwinism and the *philosophia perennis*, followed by the origin of man contrasted with these two perspectives. The subsequent sections provide robust evidence, from meticulous findings in palæontology and archæology, about the enormous antiquity of man that has been ridiculed, or systematically suppressed, by establishment science but is in consonance with the teachings of the Indian Vedas. The related question of intelligent design is then discussed. The final sections of this Chapter elucidate the indispensable complement of occult science on the evolution of man. We propose a simple meditational technique that may help in raising consciousness and show how such an exalted state has a direct bearing on the state of genius.

KEY WORDS: spirit, matter, involution, evolution, devolution, kingdoms of nature, Darwinism, Vedas, antiquity of man, monkeys, intelligent design theories, occult science, elevating consciousness, meditation, genius, Michael Cremo, Richard Thompson

Coming from one of the greatest pianists and composers that ever lived, the epigraph may seem somewhat surprising at first—perhaps less so, when it is remembered that besides his legendary musical gifts, Liszt was devoutly religious and in touch with virtually all the prominent writers, poets, and painters in Europe. Like Beethoven, he was also profoundly philosophical, evincing a knowledge of the philosophy of the West as also the East, the latter through the German Romantic Tradition, which was the dominant intellectual movement in the philosophy, the arts, and the culture of German-speaking countries in the late-eighteenth and early nineteenth centuries. The purpose of mentioning all this is that Liszt's accomplishments provide a fine example of a single man who shouldered the task of undertaking the never-ending voyage of limitless evolution, thus providing a glowing exemplar of the possibilities that lie ahead for mankind. In his last years, Liszt declared that his only remaining ambition as a musician was to 'hurl my lance into the boundless realms of the future.'[3]

What he and a few others of his mettle achieved—in whatever field, whether in music, science, culture or sport, it matters not—each one of us shall also have to do likewise and achieve on our own individual and chosen path in the fullness of time. In fact, there comes a time when we realize that our evolutionary journey is not an option at our bidding, but mandatory. Why? Because there is that essential and unalloyed element within each person that seeks to grow from a bud into a blossom. However, an unfinished journey needs to start, or continue, in the right direction. This means a clear understanding of what is meant by evolution.

But the problem we face nowadays is that, other than with cults like fundamentalist creationists, evolution has become virtually universally accepted currency with the general public, goaded by a simplistic and one-sided rendering by science on the grounds of supposedly proven facts, that 'man came from the apes'. Evolution has therefore become effectively a platitude and a 'catch all' word that in fact encompasses a host of other processes that are not, strictly speaking, to do with it, its true meaning now blurred by overuse and misuse. Accordingly, our policy, as always, is to define our terms carefully when dealing with a complex and multi-layered subject in order to avoid misunderstandings resulting from words commonly used and overused. The rewards in terms of clarity of meaning are entirely commensurate with the demands of patience.

Definite Words for Definite Things

There are five closely interrelated terms that are absolutely central to a complete understanding of cyclic evolution pertaining to all kingdoms of nature, including the human:

- ❖ spirit and matter (defined briefly in Chapter 8 on page 144 f.);
- ❖ evolution and involution, along with devolution applying expressly to humanity (defined in outline in Volume I, Chapter 8 on page 242).

These terms now warrant further elucidation.

1. The term 'spirit' has caused much confusion because of its wide-ranging meaning and lack of agreement between writers as to its definition and use. It is commonly, but erroneously, made synonymous with 'soul' (see Volume II, Chapter 6, page 106 f. for an explanation of the distinction). In the most abstract sense, 'spirit' is a generalizing term for the innate potency that is latent in Cosmos, in man, right down to the minutest particle of matter and smallest unicellular organism. In the occult teachings, the word 'Spirit' is applied wholly to that which belongs directly to Universal Consciousness, and which is its homogeneous and pure emanation on any plane.

Legendary men have shown that evolution is limitless because the soul of man is immortal

Hence to summarize:

- ❖ spirit is the generic term for the active principle, or potency.
- ❖ Spirit (with a capital *S*) is the universal and active principle, or potency, on any plane of manifestation.
- ❖ SPIRIT is, for all intents and purposes, practically synonymous with the spark of Divine, or Universal Consciousness in man, i.e., *Ātma*, the Divine Self (see Table II-3 in Volume II, Chapter 2 on page 21).

2. The term 'matter', or the more abstract term 'substance' is the generalizing term used in occultism for that which provides spirit with its vehicle of expression, i.e., its form, or body of action. In this sense, Matter is the highest expression of *manifested* Spirit in any particular hierarchy of life on any plane of manifestation. The term 'matter' is not therefore restricted to the physical plane as each subtle plane has its appropriate grade of (non-physical) matter for the entities on that plane. On the physical plane, force, energy, and matter are the physicalized expressions of Matter.

It bears repeating that terms like 'spirit' and 'matter' are both abstract and generalizing terms. They are not radically distinct and separate. The two are fundamentally one (like energy and matter on the physical plane), and are eternally co-active and interactive. This was made plain in Chapter 8 in connection with the mind–sensation problem.)

So to summarize:

- ❖ matter is the generic term for the correlate of spirit.
- ❖ Matter (with a capital *M*) is the correlate of Spirit on any plane of manifestation.
- ❖ MATTER is, for all intents and purposes, the correlate of SPIRIT.

3. The term 'evolution' derives from the Latin *evolutio*, a derivative of *evolvere*, a compound formed from the prefix *ex*- 'out' and *volvere*, 'roll'. The etymology is revealing. Hence, evolution means a 'rolling out', 'unwrapping', or 'unfolding' of latent powers and faculties that are intrinsic to, and inherent within, the entity itself—the faculties and powers of its own essential character and associated characteristics. Evolution, however, does not in any way mean adding variation on to other variations, or experience bettered by another experience. Such movement from the rudimentary towards the complex by adding 'building-block upon building-block' would make all entities, including man, a mere aggregate of unconnected parts without an underlying unity or any unifying principle.

Furthermore, the universality of the evolutionary process means that it does not only apply to man, but to all kingdoms of nature, being the emergence of the possibilities inherent in nature from potentiality and latency into ever higher, active expressions of the indwelling consciousness and life. This theme will be taken up shortly.

4. The term 'involution' is the reverse process to evolution: the 'rolling in', or 'infolding' of what previously exists or has been unfolded, deriving from the Latin *involutio*, 'a rolling up', a derivative of *involvere*, 'envelop', 'surround', 'roll into'. Every evolutionary cycle has its corresponding involutionary cycle: every involutionary cycle has its corresponding evolutionary cycle. Thus, what is the evolution of Spirit is

contemporaneously, and at the same rate, the involution of Matter, and *vice versa*. This will be amplified shortly.

5. To the above list must also be added the term 'devolution', which applies essentially to the human species. Deriving from the Latin *devolvere* (*de-* 'down from' and *volvere*, 'roll'), it means to progress gradually from an advanced state to a less advanced state, or to 'rolling down', which is not the same as 'rolling out'. For example, water from a high mountain reservoir flows down (devolves) from a higher state to a lower state. The water does not 'roll out' (evolve) its innate characteristics which remain the same at any level of descent.

> **Involution and evolution never occur, nor can even be conceived of, as operative the one apart from the other, or the one following the other in sequence.**

All this is not splitting hairs or indulging in pedantry. These subtle, but highly significant, differences in meaning are vital to convey and the reader's forbearance is again requested.

Let us see how the processes just described operate. The ensuing narrative is presented in three major sections. First, Darwinian evolution: the objective is not to dwell upon its technicalities or its essential premises, which were summarized in Chapter 3 on page 56 f. of Volume I, but to present its ramifications regarding an understanding of the evolution of physical man. Next follows an explanation of the cyclic process of evolution as a whole according to the *philosophia perennis*, which then, logically, leads to its mirroring in the evolution of man, which is contrasted with the Darwinian scheme. It should be clear by now that the evolution of man, the microcosm, cannot be described in isolation from that of the macrocosm.

Is evolution linear or cyclic?

Evolution in the Darwinian Meaning

> We are just an advanced breed of monkeys on a minor planet of a very average star. But we can understand the Universe. That makes us something very special.
>
> Stephen Hawking[4]

Evolution is naturally an enormous subject with which science has been grappling for over one and a half centuries since Darwin published *On the Origin of Species* which, at the time, was a long overdue scientific acid to corrode the accumulated rust of theological dogma regarding the genesis of man. Nonetheless, such scientific endeavour is limited strictly to the changing physical forms. Why this should be so is best explained by way of a typical example that illustrates the philosophy of science and, correspondingly, its incomplete viewpoint and approach on evolution.

The lotus plant is a universal symbol of the existence of man at all levels of being ranging from the physical (roots in the mud) to the spiritual (flower facing the sun), via the soul (stem in the water)—see Chapter 4, page 56 f. But as science is not interested in metaphysics or universal symbols, preferring to remain with physical and objective reality, let us consider the development of a botanical lotus plant from the bud to the flowers. In order for this to happen, two prime factors are needed: the external environment of sunlight, atmospheric conditions, water, and earth; and the innate potentiality of the lotus seed. Both of these factors are needed and one is not a substitute for the other. Lotus seeds kept in perpetual darkness would not blossom; nor would, say, buttercup seeds produce lotus blossom even if exposed to just the right external environment for the lotus plant.

Growth depends on both nurture and nature

This much is obvious, but it needs to be stressed because science and Darwinism, as exemplified in the quote above, look purely to the change in outer form to the virtual exclusion of the innate potentiality of the entity—its purpose, hence its plan, corresponding to its design. Recall the meaning of 'entelechy' explained on page 70 in Chapter 4 of Volume I: that which realizes, or makes actual, what is otherwise merely potential. The concept is intimately connected with Aristotle's distinction between matter and form, or the potential and the actual. He analysed each thing into the 'stuff', or elements, of which it is composed and the form which makes it what it is. The mere stuff, or matter, is not yet the real thing; it needs a certain form, essence, and function to complete it. Matter and form, however, are never separated; they can only be distinguished. However, as pointed out in the same Chapter, concepts such as entelechy and teleology (goal-orientation) are an anathema to science because they beg the question of intelligent design.

Darwinism focuses exclusively on change of form. Purpose and plan do not figure

Nonetheless that is no bar to our purpose, so let us first consider evolution in general before considering man's role in the overall scheme of nature.

Evolution of the Kingdoms of Nature according to the Perennial Philosophy

Scientific enquiry into evolution, limited strictly to the changing physical forms, as just stated, continues to be a mammoth undertaking as the innumerable books, academic papers, and conference proceedings bear ample witness even though, as Richard Dawkins would have it: 'Our own existence once presented the greatest of all mysteries, but that [*sic*] it is a mystery no longer because it is solved.' 'Darwin and Wallace solved it,' continues Dawkins, 'though we shall continue to add footnotes to their solution for a while yet.'[5] Certainly, the surfeit of Dawkins's own books on evolution seems to add up to an immense number of 'footnotes' to a problem supposedly solved.

To reduce complex things to their simplest building blocks, as in science, tends to blur an understanding of the whole system or organism. By contrast, concentration of complexity into simple precepts maintains the whole picture, so in this sense, could be likened to an algebraic equation that provides a solution to any input variable within its field of application (see Chapter 5, page 73 f.).

Notwithstanding all this bluster, how much more gruelling would be the task to study evolution on other planes of nature! Indeed it would be, in one sense, but to undertake such a challenge is not our purpose. On the other hand, the task is made easier by the fact that immense though the details may be, they can all be reduced to precepts whose simplicity lies in direct proportion to their complexity. This concentration of the complex in terms of the simple is a feature of the *philosophia perennis*. It has similar overtones to reductionism in science, but is not the same thing.

Correspondingly, these precepts are shown in the following three quotes. They are entirely comparable and, as with eternal truths, they find their echo in the West and the East.

> A stone becomes a plant, a plant an animal, an animal a man, a man a spirit, and a spirit a god.
>
> Qabbalistic axiom

> God sleeps in stone, breathes in plants, dreams in animals, and awakens in man.
>   Manu's Mânava Dharma-Shâstra and featured in other Brahmanical books

> I slept in the stone; I stirred in the plant; I dreamt in the animal; and I awoke in the man.
>
> Occult catechism

Elaborating on these quotes, the evolutionary impulse in the fullest sense pertains to the various planes of existence whereupon all life exists in different stages of *being* and *becoming*, so that:

> Grains of sand are in the process of *becoming* human in consciousness but not necessarily in form; that human creatures are in the process of *becoming* planets; that planets are in the process of *becoming* solar systems; and that solar systems are in the process of *becoming* cosmic chains; and so on *ad infinitum*.
>
> *The Secret Teaching of the Ages*[6]

Evolution pertains to all kingdoms of nature—not just man

This same theme is beautifully expressed by the Persian Sufi and mystic Jalāl ad-Dīn Muhammad Rūmi (1207–1273) in one of the most influential works of Sufism, commonly called 'the Qur'an in Persian'[7]:

> I died as mineral and became a plant,
> I died as plant and rose to animal,
> I died as animal and was man.
> Why should I fear? When was I less by dying?
> Yet once more I shall die as man, to soar with angels blest;
> But even from angelhood I must pass on …
> 'To Him we shall return[i]'
>
> *Masnavi*[8]

This is the real principle of evolution—understood best as occult science affirms—*all* life (not merely biological life) is in various stages of *becoming*. As beautifully expressed in *Masnavi*, 'the whole course of evolution bears witness to the principle of dying for the sake of life.'[9] This is obviously not saying that by virtue of some incredible futuristic materials technology or genetic engineering, a mineral, like a grain of sand, is going to 'die' in order to 'grow up' to become a human being or get converted into a robot possessing human-like qualities of 'soul' and 'spirit'. It is saying that there is an evolution of *kingdoms of nature* from the mineral kingdom (exemplified by the 'grains of sand' in the quote from *The Secret Teachings*), to the human kingdom, and far beyond. Hence, the 'I', referred to in the Occult catechism above, is none other than the universal and divine Consciousness that seeks ever newer and more complex vehicles and forms—kingdoms of nature—in order to express, to ever greater degrees, its limitless potentiality. The death of the form therefore does not mean the extinguishing of consciousness; on the contrary, it means that consciousness 'sheds' outworn forms that no longer serve its ongoing evolutionary march. The following analogy might help to clarify this principle.

Unitary consciousness evolves through ever more complex forms

Recasting the above quotes in terms of the phase states of H_2O:

- melting ice is in the process of becoming liquid H_2O (water) but not necessarily in the square form of ice cubes as in a domestic freezer;
- boiling water is in the process of becoming vapourized H_2O (steam) but not in the form taken by the water in a kettle;
- ice, water, and steam are, therefore, phase states, or forms, taken by H_2O. So by analogy, humanity is a phase state of consciousness in its evolutionary impulse.

---

i Qur'an, Sura 28:88.

And if that sounds too far-fetched, let us see its correspondence in the human body. The American biologist and evolutionary theorist Lynn Margulis (1938–2011) was the primary modern proponent for the significance of symbiosis (any type of a close and long-term biological interaction between two different biological organisms) as a source of evolutionary innovation.[10] What this means is that any physical association between individuals of different species for significant portions of their life history is a symbiosis. All participants in the symbiosis are 'bionts' (microbes, or discrete organisms living in a specific environment), and therefore the resulting assemblage is a 'holobiont', the term coined by Margulis to refer to an assemblage of a host and the many other species living in or around it, which together form a discrete ecological unit.[11] This means that countless lesser lives are all living and evolving within the field of the host parent human body. Some 100 trillion microbial symbionts (symbiotic microbes) live in the body and are fundamental to nearly all aspects of our lives, including our form and function. Thus, we can detect a gradual, but unmistakable change in the scientific outlook on life, away from living creatures (humans, animals, and plants) regarded as autonomous biological entities, towards holobionts, composed of the host plus its countless bionts. Needless to say, Margulis's ideas, like virtually all innovative ideas in science, were initially reviled and her research papers repeatedly rejected. Being a strong critic of neo-Darwinism served to attract further vituperation. Eventually her contribution to evolution theory was vindicated when President William (Bill) Clinton presented her with the National Medal of Science in 1999 and the Linnean Society of London awarded her the Darwin–Wallace Medal in 2008.

As is man, so is the Earth on which he dwells. The following section is significant in showing how recent scientific discoveries are finding an inexhaustible richness, interconnectedness, and diversity of life previously undreamt of.

As the Human Body, So is Earth

The oceanic crust, extending five to ten kilometers (three to six miles) beneath the ocean floor is mostly composed of different types of basalts (a dark, igneous rock formed from the rapid cooling of magnesium- and iron-rich lava exposed at, or very near, the surface of the earth).[12] Scientists have now discovered new life forms deep within the oceanic crust that appear to be sustained by energy released from chemical reactions of rocks with water. On the eve of the annual meeting of the American Geophysical Union in 2018, nearing the end of a ten-year international collaboration to reveal the innermost secrets of planet Earth, scientists with the Deep Carbon Observatory[ii] reported several transformational discoveries, including the amount and variety of life existing in the deep subsurface under the greatest extremes of pressure, temperature, and low nutrient availability.[13] Drilling 2.5 kilometres into the seafloor, and sampling microbes from continental mines and boreholes more than five kilometres deep, scientists have approximated the size of the deep biosphere as 2 to 2.3 billion cubic kilometres (almost twice the volume of all oceans); and estimated the carbon mass of deep life as 15 to 23 billion tonnes (an average of at least 7.5 tonnes of carbon per cubic kilometre subsurface). Key discoveries and insights were

Countless lesser lives are living and evolving through the human body

Countless lesser entities are living and evolving through the earth's oceanic crust

---

ii Deep Carbon Observatory is a global community of more than 1000 scientists on a ten-year quest to understand the quantities, movements, forms, and origins of carbon inside the Earth.

that the deep biosphere constitutes a world that can be viewed as a sort of 'subterranean Galapagos' and includes members of all three domains of life: bacteria, archaea (microbes with no membrane-bound nucleus), and eukarya (microbes, or multicellular organisms, with cells that contain a nucleus as well as membrane-bound organelles, which are specialized structures within a living cell). Moreover, about seventy per cent of the earth's bacteria and archaea live in the subsurface. Apparently, deep microbes are often very different from the surface variety, with life cycles on near-geologic timescales, and, in some cases, living on nothing more than energy released from chemical reactions of rocks with water as said above. Most significantly, these bacteria and other forms of life constitute an immense amount of carbon deep within the earth's subsurface—245 to 385 times greater than the carbon mass of all humans on the surface; and the genetic diversity of life below the surface is comparable to, or exceeds that above, the surface.[14]

Further stark evidence about the radical unity and interconnectedness of life is provided by fungi. Recent research and discoveries have revealed how fungi, airborne but largely underground, make up a massively diverse kingdom of organisms that supports and sustains nearly all living systems. *Entangled Life* shows how fungi provide a key to understanding the planet on which we live. Some fungi can range for miles underground and are apparently the largest organisms on the planet, while others link plants together in complex networks known as the 'Wood Wide Web'. Fungi have no brain but they can manipulate animal behaviour with precision, play a crucial part in metabolism and are key players in most processes of life, thereby stretching traditional definitions of 'intelligence'.[15]

> Fungi are extensive and form the 'Wood Wide Web'

Implications for an All-embracing Understanding of Evolution

The purpose of mentioning this is to underscore (as we have done periodically throughout this work) how the progressive aspect of modern science, the ally of occult science, is slowly corroborating a fundamental tenet of the latter as exampled above and reflected in the quote below. This is in its discovery of the ascending grades, or stages, of embodied consciousness, or manifested existence in the ladder of life, such that at any level in the universe from the lowest to the highest, a parent body—whether that be minerals or primitive life forms; or the cells in plants, animals, and humans; or plants, animal, and human bodies; or Earth; or higher life forms—is host to lesser lives that are existing and evolving through it.

> The radical unity of the ultimate essence of each constituent part of compounds in Nature—from Star to mineral Atom, from the highest Dhyāni-Chohan [Archangel] to the smallest infusoria,[iii] in the fullest acceptation [sic] of the term, and whether applied to the spiritual, intellectual, or physical worlds—this is the one fundamental law in Occult Science.[16]

> Cardinal dictate of occult science is unity of life at all levels

Hence, as occultism teaches, whether we consider kingdoms of life that are subhuman, human or superhuman, each unit of life lives within the field of the greater life, its host, evolving towards the next stage. Thus, the human being, at all levels, is host to countless lesser lives all evolving towards the next higher stage in the evolutionary ladder, as Margulis discovered. Just so, human beings live within, and evolve towards, the overriding solar consciousness and so on (see Figure III-29 in Chapter 8, page 153).

---

iii Infusoria are single-celled organisms which consist mainly of ciliate protozoans.

What, therefore, especially stands out is that *human evolution cannot be split off from the evolution of other kingdoms of nature*; it is part and parcel of the total process since, as previously affirmed in Chapter 8 of Volume I:

The whole order of nature evinces a progressive march towards *a higher life*. […] The whole process of evolution with its endless adaptations is a proof of this.[17] [Occultists] antedated Darwin, embraced more or less all his theories on natural selection and the evolution of species, and largely extended the chain at both ends. They never turned aside from the double parallel path traced for them by their great master Hermes. 'As above, so below,' was ever their axiom; and their physical evolution was traced out simultaneously with the spiritual one.[18]

From the above, it should become clear that the general notion of evolution was not born with Darwin and his peers but is, along with involution, one of the hoariest tenets of the *philosophia perennis*, except that, in this context, it is preferable to use the more accurate word 'emanation', as defined at the beginning of Chapter 8 (which included a description of the overall emanational process). Strictly speaking, therefore, emanation is not the same as evolution and such subtle differences of meaning are significant. However, given that the word 'evolution' is now universally accepted currency, it will be used henceforth in the strict sense as defined earlier in this Chapter.

The clear implication is that man, like all other evolving entities has everything in him that the cosmos has because he is an inseparable part of it, its child—the microcosm of the macrocosm. Everything that is in the cosmos is in him, active or latent, and evolution is the awakening, and bringing out, of what lies dormant within. It is a truism that any evolving entity can become only what it is in its essential nature, hence, to reiterate, evolution is an unfolding, or opening out of what already pre-exists, active or latent, from within. So from the standpoint of the *philosophia perennis*, the core meaning of evolution is that the nucleus, or core, of every entity is a Spirit (technically, a Monad) that expresses its powers and faculties through the ages in Matter—the various bodies, or vehicles, which change and improve in refinement and complexity as the ages pass—enabling Spirit, progressively, to express a greater proportion of its innate potentiality on any plane of manifestation. For man, these vehicles comprise not just the physical body, but the subtle bodies, or interior sheaths of consciousness, which collectively form man's entire composition extending from: (*a*) the divine monad; (*b*) through the intermediate stages of consciousness, i.e., man's soul in generic terms; (*c*) to the physical body (see Volume II, Chapters 2 and 3). Hence, the *philosophia perennis*, whilst not opposed to Darwin's limited theory (incidentally, adopted and adapted from the ideas of Wallace and Lamarck), regards it only in a perfunctory and subordinate sense.

In essence, then, it is consciousness, strictly speaking, the centres of consciousness, or the divine monads (each monad known as the 'Pilgrim'—see Chapter 9, page 173) that undergo their journey of unceasing growth. Growth is the key to the meaning of evolution, being the expression, in detail, of the general process of the unfolding faculty and its associated organ of action, which the conventional terms 'evolution' and 'involution' include. Walter Russell alludes to this in his unfolding–refolding principle. According to him, 'The two opposite electric expressions of desire of Mind unfold all idea of Mind from its pattern in the seed [idea] into merged forms to simulate the idea of Mind and refold it back into its recorded pattern in the seed, for again unfolding. Each one unbalances the other in order that each may seek balance in the other to disappear and reappear as the other.'[19]

The theory of evolution did not originate with Darwin and Wallace.

Evolution is a central tenet of the perennial philosophy

Evolution activates potentiality into actuality

This has echoes of the principle of Yin and Yang. However, Russell's unfolding–refolding principle may correspond to, but is not the same as, David Bohm's explicate and implicate order which pertains to higher dimensions of universal order.

Cyclic Evolution and Involution Involving Spirit and Matter

One of the difficulties faced in the understanding of consciousness is our failure to recognize that man is an aggregate of many lives, or units of consciousness, all functioning at different levels. Man is linked with, and embodies the consciousness of, all the kingdoms of nature.

Given the above explanations, the process of evolution and involution may be summarized thus. First, we clearly have to discern the coming into being on two fronts: the 'form-side', or 'matter-side' and the 'spirit-side', or 'consciousness-side'—these precepts were explained earlier in Chapter 8. The former is the sole interest of science on the physical plane. To the occultist, it concerns the matter and bodies evolved to act as vehicles to express the latter which, in contrast, is that potency that seeks ever finer material for its innate self-expression. In popular terms: *spirit without matter is impotent: matter without spirit is barren; spirit and matter are productive when conjoined.*

The process of coming into being on the form-side (contradistinctive to the spirit-side) is achieved through the gradual and progressive descent from spheres and planes of spirituality into spheres and planes of materiality, or concretion. This is the evolution of matter: representing the rolling out of the material potencies serving to express the form-side of life. Concurrently with the process of development on the matter-side (i.e., the bodies and vehicles of the indwelling spirit, or consciousness), there is the involution of spirit: the gradual and progressive limitation of the expression of the spirit-side, because the potencies of spirit are progressively being enwrapped, or involved (turned inwards), while matter is progressively being evolved (opened outwards). At the lowest point of cyclical descent, the greatest involvement in concretion, or materiality, is attained; whereupon a return cycle is commenced towards a greater expression of the spirit-side as a progressively greater development of spirituality is being achieved. This is the evolution of spirit occurring concurrently with a gradual and progressive recession of materiality: the involution of matter.

Evolution and involution are cyclical involving spirit and matter

From this it should be clear that the terms 'evolution' and 'involution' apply to *both* spirit and matter on opposite sides of the cycle. But as science is only concerned with developmental changes in form, it deals with just one-quarter of the overall process. This is our justification for saying, earlier, that the *philosophia perennis* views Darwinism as a secondary issue.

Thus as I. K. Taimni explains, we see that involution and evolution are two opposite forces working in the realm of manifestation.[20] The first is centrifugal in character, i.e., from the centre to the circumference. The second is centripetal, from the circumference to the centre. This is a prime example of the separation of the One Reality into two opposite forces which seek to balance each other and to maintain the harmony and balance of the whole. (On the physical plane we see this as Le Chatelier's principle, or *The Equilibrium Law*—see Chapter 6, page 90 f.) A further consideration of the two processes shows that involution is accompanied by increasing differentiation and evolution by increasing integration. When spirit (consciousness) moves from the centre to the circumference it undergoes increasing fragmentation *as matter—not in matter*. The sense of separateness becomes increasingly marked, reaching its upper limit at the level of the physical. In the reverse movement from the circumference to the centre the process of integration begins, the sense of separateness decreasing progressively and finally disappearing on reaching the centre. Refer to Chapter 1, page 4 on symbolism explaining the significance of the terms 'centre' and 'circumference'.

Summary of Overriding Precepts on Evolution

> Evolution is the process whereby the types in nature become more and more like their parent archetypes.
>
> Anon.

The above section has drawn together several strands, from diverse sources, to provide a comprehensive account of evolution. It would be helpful, therefore, to provide a summary of all-embracing precepts explaining, in particular, why, 'The whole order of nature evinces a progressive march towards *a higher life*', as quoted on page 224.

Earlier in Chapter 4 of this Volume (with the aid of Figure III-8, page 62) we explained the 'overflowing' of Divine Thought into actuality—the emanation from the Divine and Formless spiritual realms, Ain Soph Aur, the Boundless and Absolute Light, into the manifest worlds of form.

The emanational imperative from the unmanifest to the manifest worlds is beautifully condensed in *The Origins of Persian Gnosis* from a lecture given in 1992 by the Islamic and Sūfī scholar Dr Massoud Homayouni of the Islamic Azad University, Tehran.[21] What follows is a slight rewording of the exposition by that able author.

As we have noted above, the first emanation of God[iv] is Light (Ain Soph Aur), which manifests: as external light, the Sun, which illumines the material world awakening everything to life; and as internal light, Love, which inspires all creation with the desire to aspire upwards, towards self-perfection, in search of the true Beloved, God, thus bringing about the evolution of all creation. Light thus shines down upon all that exists, and all the atoms of the world, in desire for this light, are impelled to strive upwards, towards self-perfection, in search of their Beloved. Thus everything in the world is kept in perpetual movement by Love.

The higher forms of life which receive most light have the duty of transmitting light and grace to those beneath them, and the lower, the duty of accepting and using these gifts, not only on their own path towards progress and evolution, but on that of others, both human and other forms of life. Thus all creation and evolution is based upon the eternal law of downward links of sacrifice and upward links of obedience. Homayouni draws our attention to how the Iranian Sūfī and Islamic philosopher and theologian Mullā Ṣadrā (*circa* 1571–1640) in *Temple of the Pagan Idols*[22] explains the philosophy of the Azerbaijanian Sohravardi, al-Maqtul, one of Iran's greatest philosophers and Sūfī masters, executed (unsurprisingly) because he alienated the powerful religious elite of Aleppo in Syria:

---

iv We need not labour the point that the term 'God' means the Absolute, Divine Consciousness, or the 'Beloved' as beautifully phrased by the Sūfīs—all these terms having nothing whatsoever to do with the crude anthropomorphic concepts of religious orthodoxy. We prefer to avoid using this term but have retained it in this section for consistency with Dr Homayouni's exposition and subsequent cited quotation.

Love of God, the most Holy, and the desire to witness Him is inherent in all creation, even in minerals and vegetables. And this desire compels all creation, high and low, exalted and humble, to evolve in the next highest being [kingdom of nature], and so on upwards until it finally reaches the culmination of its desires. For example, although the mineral world is in search of Almighty God, its Path towards Him is through the vegetable world, thence towards the animal world and on into man. From there it moves from imperfect to perfect man, until finally reaching the highest object of desire.

In this way, the Mineral Soul seeks its Beloved the Vegetable Soul, which in turn seeks the Animal Soul [*Kāma*], which seeks the Reasonable Soul (human soul) [*Manas*], which aspires to the Universal Soul or Spirit [*Buddhi-Manas*]. Each, on the path to its Beloved [*Ātma*], is transformed at every step into a higher form of life, until finally it attains that highest form, the Beloved of all Beloveds, the fulfilment of all desire, which is incomparable, unique, wise and all powerful.[23]

Love, light, and self-sacrifice at the heart of the evolutionary impulse

Each world (kingdom of nature) thus serves the world above it and finds its evolutionary Path 'to it's Beloved' through the world above.

Readers will not fail to discern how closely this quote from a Sūfī Master resonates with similar quotes given earlier in this Chapter from the Qabbalah, the Brahmanical books, and the occult Catechism: widely different sources conveying the same message of truth which, as we insist in repeating throughout these Volumes, is a hallmark of the *philosophia perennis*. It is important to bear in mind that evolution, and for that matter all the multifaceted aspects of this perennial wisdom, can oft-times be illumined more brightly through *bhaktī* (devotion, or the heart) than through *jñāna* (the intellect) and the above quote is surely a fine example of the Way of the Heart.

At the centre of your being You have the answer. You know who you are, and You know what you want.[24]

The Origin of Man

Having just outlined the cyclical processes of evolution and involution as pertaining in general to spirit and matter, we now focus on the origins, appearance, and evolution of man on the world stage. The express purpose is to provide solid scientific evidence, corroborated by the great wisdom traditions of the world, showing that humans (along with other living things) are not just complex forms and arrangements of ordinary physical matter, but combinations of spirit (pure consciousness), mind (soul in the generic sense), and matter. Specifically, regarding humanity in its present physical form, this process did not happen by evolution 'up' from matter, but rather by devolution 'down' from the realm of pure consciousness, or spirit, as will shortly become clear.

First though, what does Darwinism teach about the origin of man?

Darwinism

We thus learn that man is descended from a hairy quadruped, furnished with a tail and pointed ears, probably arboreal in its habits, and an inhabitant of the Old World.

Charles Darwin, *The Descent of Man* (1871), Vol. 2, p. 389.

Neo-Darwinism is adamant that man is 'just an animal'

With a few exceptions, neo-Darwinism is virtually the sole dictum of the scientific establishment on the theory of evolution. How that descent occurred through genetic mutation and natural selection (as summarized in Volume I, Chapter 3, page 56) is a side issue, in the context of this Chapter, to the virtually unequivocal assertion by Darwin, enthusiastically taken up by mainstream biologists, that man descended (devolved?) from a hairy quadruped (four-footed mammal); the inescapable upshot being that man, with all his joys and sorrows, inhumanity and benevolence, stupidity and genius is, in the final analysis, merely an animal, or 'an advanced breed of monkeys' as Hawking proclaimed (see his quote on page 219).

The phrase used by Darwin 'descended from' is highly significant and revealing as we shall see shortly.

But the neo-Darwinian theory is not without its critics amongst an increasing number of eminent scientists professing no religious views or having any other axe to grind, other than finding the theory incompatible with mounting evidence from biology, palæontology, and consciousness studies in general. Even during Darwin's lifetime (1809–1882) there have been dissenters, like the German embryologist-philosopher August Weismann FRS (1834–1914), at one time a fervent Darwinist, who then developed a hypothesis very much in line with the occult doctrine of reincarnation, as we shall see shortly. Moreover, Darwin's erstwhile collaborator, Alfred Russel Wallace, fully realized the limitations of the theory of natural selection, as will also be explained in addition to what was stated towards the close of Volume I, Chapter 3, page 58.

Neo-Darwinism is under mounting criticism

In modern times, the radical views of Thomas Nagel were described in Chapter 7 on page 131 of Volume II. Another dissenter from the orthodox neo-Darwinian paradigm is the Indian born quantum physicist Amit Goswami (b.1936), a radical amongst a growing body of eminent renegade scientists who have questioned the exclusively materialistic theories about life and consciousness. Drawing upon the philosophical and metaphysical insights from quantum physics, he has invoked a spiritual dimension in an attempt to resolve intractable conundrums in evolutionary science.[25] Another valuable source is the research of William Roger Corliss (1926–2011), the American physicist and writer whose books provide a compendium of numerous anomalous phenomena in a variety of fields extracted from peer reviewed journals, academic books, and scholarly articles. Other than adding his evaluation of both the reliability of the claims, and their ranking as anomalies, Corliss generally provides little in the way of his own opinions or editorial comments, preferring to let the articles and their source references speak for themselves. Of particular value for our purposes is the *Biological Anomalies* series in six volumes: three for mammals and birds, and a further three for humans.[26]

However, the research and publications of the American author and researcher in the history and philosophy of science, Michael Cremo (b.1948), are in a class of their own as regards exposing the weaknesses in Darwinian theory. He is an associate in the history of archæology, member of the World Archæological Congress, and a member of the European Association of Archæologists. Cremo has lectured at universities throughout the world, and has given invited lectures on his work at many prestigious scientific institutions, such as the Anthropology Department of the Russian Academy of Sciences in Moscow, the Archæology Department of the Ukrainian Academy of Sciences, and the Royal Institution in London (which lecture the writer attended). His work is a glorious illustration of the joint contribution of science and spirituality, whereby outworn scientific concepts have been eroded by the process of science itself, thus preparing the ground and providing substantial evidence for spiritual and esoteric teachings in line with the oft quoted occult maxim, 'Modern science is our best ally.' The following exposition, therefore, is based largely on Cremo's work, supplemented, as appropriate, from other sources which are referenced.

The True Origin of Species

In consequence, the ensuing narrative is logically in three parts. First, to present the scientific data and weight of evidence deduced from human artefacts regarding the antiquity of man that has been systematically filtered out and suppressed because it contradicts Darwinian theory about the stage when *homo sapiens* first made its appearance. This process of knowledge filtration was described earlier, on a wide range of subjects, at the end of Chapter 4 of Volume I on page 115 et seq. Here we deal with the data and discoveries pertaining specifically to evolution and the antiquity of man. Next, to show how such data on human antiquity appears to be compatible with the time cycles given in a principal mainstay of the Ageless Wisdom—the Vedas. Finally, with a measure of confidence established in the latter by virtue of such corroboration with scientific data, to explain the Vedic account of human devolution—the true and real 'origin of the species'.

The above begs the question of intelligent design, which will also be addressed.

The Antiquity of Man – The Evidence from Archæology

As a prelude to the focus of this section upon the antiquity of man, it must be stated that this subject cannot be divorced from that of lost continents of immense pre-historical antiquity on which the early races of man flourished. Whereas most geologists deny the existence of ancient continents such as Gondwanaland, Lemuria, and Atlantis, or relegate them to the realm of folklore, their existence is not without evidence from geology—and in abundance from the ancient records of the Mystery Teachings. Regarding the former, 'Long-Lost Continent Found Submerged Deep Under Indian Ocean' was the heading of an article in the 31 January 2017 edition of *New Scientist*. Traces of the continent were found in the volcanic island of Mauritius, five hundred miles east of Madagascar. Whereas the location, duration, and formative forces behind lost continents continue to be matters of lively scientific debate, the fact of their existence is becoming increasingly problematic to deny. Our purpose, however, is not to delve into this fascinating subject but to point to scientific evidence for the enormous antiquity of the early human races that inhabited these prehistoric continents. For example, the German biologist, naturalist, philosopher, physician, and marine biologist Ernst Haeckel was a staunch defender of Darwinian evolution. Yet, he went so far as to propose that the disappearance of Lemuria may have accounted for the absence of 'missing link' fossils, locating the original human species on this lost continent. In *Pedigree of Man*, he wrote: 'Probably Southern Asia itself was not the earliest cradle of the human race; but LEMURIA, *a continent that lay to the south of Asia, and sank later on beneath the surface of the Indian Ocean.*'[27]

> Evolution, geology, and archæology are intertwined

But the definitive modern scientific evidence comes from Michael Cremo's books, *Forbidden Archeology*[28] (952 pages) and its condensed edition, *The Hidden History of the*

Human Race.[29] Co-authored with the American mathematician and evolutionary biologist Richard L. Thompson (1947–2008), these books contain a massive amount of detailed facts and figures assembled with meticulous scholarship. The following account can therefore make no claims as to its comprehensiveness, being an arbitrary selection provided as a foretaste culled primarily from the above books, plus a few complementary details from other referenced sources.

Michael Cremo's
books are
definitive on
human antiquity

When the American commercial broadcasting television network NBC (National Broadcasting Company) featured *Forbidden Archeology* in its 1996 program *The Mysterious Origins of Man* hosted by the American actor Charlton Heston (1923–2008), establishment scientists lobbied the Federal Communications Commission (the government agency responsible for regulating domestic and international communication) to fine NBC for airing this opposing view. We may be sure that when new discoveries that undermine well established theories in science are met with vituperation instead of reasoned argument, the issue has nothing to do with the scientific evidence presented, but because the status quo of the mainstream scientists (and everything that depends on it, like position and authority) is threatened by such anomalous findings. Unfortunately, this proved to be the case for physicist, Robert Jahn and biologist, Rupert Sheldrake—see Volumes I and II. And this applies equally to Cremo's work. Notwithstanding the worldwide acclaim it attracted from physicists, biologists, geologists, sociologists, philosophers, and complementary medical practitioners, establishment scientists have predictably denounced it as 'goofy, popular anthropology; it is a veritable cornucopia of dreck' and 'pure humbug and does not deserve to be taken seriously by anyone but a fool'—not on the basis of data and discoveries but because 'to have modern human beings … appearing a great deal earlier, in fact at a time when even simple primates did not exist as possible ancestors, would be devastating not only to the accepted pattern. It would be devastating to the whole theory of evolution.'[30]

These adverse criticisms further reinforce two points that have been made throughout this work regarding the typical attitude of establishment scientists (in any field) when faced with anomalous evidence:

1. The 'map' must always take precedence over the 'territory'; in this case, the theory of evolution must be preserved at the expense of all evidence (even a 952 page book of data) that challenges it.

2. Cheap language (using words like 'goofy', 'humbug', 'dreck') reveals the weakness and vulnerability of the criticizer who, having no recourse to scientific rebuttal, desperately seeks refuge in emotionally-charged expletives to denounce solid evidence that challenges his prejudices and entrenched concepts (see Volume II, Chapter 7 for more such examples).

On this score, and given the radical nature of what is proposed, readers are urged to consult for themselves the source references cited above before deciding upon their significance. For example, in addition to numerous tables and diagrams dispersed throughout the text and the detailed bibliography, *The Hidden History of the Human Race* provides a wide-ranging summary of anomalous evidence related to human antiquity categorized into: Part 1—General, and Part 2—North and South America only.[31]

From these works, it appears that the oldest human artefacts can be dated back to some 2.8 billion years. They are metallic spheres, one or two inches in diameter, recovered a few

Figure III-35 Grooved Metallic Sphere from South Africa Found in Precambrian Deposits dated to 2.8 Billion Years

from Michael Cremo and Richard Thompson, The Hidden History of the Human Race *(Los Angeles: Bhaktivedanta Book Publishing, 1999), 121.*

decades ago from a mine in South Africa near Ottosdal in the West Transvaal region. Metallurgical analysis shows them to be made of hematite, a naturally occurring iron ore. However, what is certainly not naturally occurring are the parallel grooves around the centres of these spheres. Some spheres have four grooves, some two, some only one groove, and others have three grooves, as seen in the adjacent Figure III-35, all indicating some specific, but unknown purpose. The metallurgists who examined them said they were not produced naturally. Therefore, the objects must have been manufactured by someone with humanlike intelligence. Yet they were found solidly embedded in mineral deposits over 2½ billion years old.

Another discovery demonstrating human antiquity going back, in this case, to over 500 million years is the shoe print found by an American draftsman and amateur fossil collector William J. Meister Sr (1904–1987) in 1968 during a fossil hunting expedition near Antelope Springs, Utah.[32] The print appears to have been made by a human wearing some type of primitive shoe or sandal 10¼ inches long and 3½ inches wide.[33] When Meister split open a two foot slab of rock, the footprint impression was revealed within the slab. It appears that the human that left the imprint stepped on a living trilobite (now a fossil group of extinct marine arthropods) as seen within the foot impression shown in Figure III-36 below, the print itself seen to the left, and the impression of the print to the right. The trilobite that was stepped on can clearly be seen around the heel of the print. A comparison of the Meister shoe print with a modern shoe print is shown in the adjacent Figure III-37. On the left is the Meister shoe print; and alongside it, outlined in white, is the same print which barely deviates from the shape and heel of a modern shoe. (The Meister shoe print would correspond to a modern shoe size of 7.5 according to the Adidas Footwear Sizing in the UK.[34])

Metallic spheres bear out antiquity of man

Fossil shoe print alludes to antiquity of man

Figure III-36 Human Shoe Print Considered to be 500 Million Years Old

Image Credit: GenesisPark.com

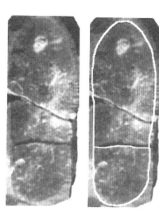

Figure III-37 Modern Shoe Print

from Michael Cremo and Richard Thompson, The Hidden History of the Human Race *(Los Angeles: Bhaktivedanta Book Publishing, 1999), 119.*

Meister claimed that when he had the print examined by a geologist, he was offered $250,000 for it. But when Meister asked him, 'What are you going to do with it if I sell it to you?' the geologist replied, 'I'm going to destroy it; it destroys my entire life work as a geologist.'[35] If this report is accurate, it clearly illustrates the tendency on the part of the scientific establishment to filter out, or destroy, findings which they find anomalous and threatening to their established world-view—see the section on knowledge filtration in science in Volume I, Chapter 4, page 115 et seq.

There have of course been criticisms of Meister's findings under the general title of 'bad archæology' which readers are strongly encouraged to consult in the spirit of impartial scientific enquiry.[36] Furthermore, Cremo and Thompson also state candidly that 'the Meister print, as evidence for a human presence in the distant past, is ambiguous', but that 'it should be evaluated on its own merits, rather than on the basis of inflexible preconceptions.'[37]

In 1979, footprints were also found in Tanzania by the British palæoanthropologist Mary Leakey (1913–1996). Known as the Laetoli footprints, they were found in layers of solid volcanic ash and dated to 3.6 to 3.8 million years by the potassium-argon method.[38] Although relatively recent in comparison to the above findings, this date is much older than what most scientists believe to be the date when human beings capable of making such footprints came into existence, which is around 100,000 years ago. Significantly, however, whilst admitting the existence and the date of these footprints, Mary Leakey and other scientists did not believe that humans of our type existed around 3.7 million years ago in Africa; so they proposed that some kind of ape-man or hominid with feet exactly like anatomically modern humans must somehow have existed at that time. Unfortunately, there is no physical evidence to support this idea, as the numerous hominid skeletons from that period show ape-like feet and none of the characteristics of the modern human foot.

<aside>Footprints suggest antiquity of man</aside>

In this case, knowledge filtration would not have succeeded in hiding the discoveries, since the footprints were discovered, and then publicized, by a major international scientist. So the next recourse by the establishment, when faced with anomalous evidence, was to invent an unproven and hypothetical scenario about hominids with feet like modern humans. This is a classic case of 'the map dictating the territory' (i.e., the Darwinian paradigm dictating what should be regarded as evidence), or even worse, inventing a territory (hominids with human-like feet) to square with the map.[39]

One could argue that, other than from shoeprints or footprints, more substantial evidence about humans existing 3.7 million years ago would come from discovering anatomically modern human skeletons of that age. That is indeed the case. For example, the Italian Giuseppe Ragazzoni (1824–1898), a prominent geologist and professor from the Istituto Techniche di Brescia, discovered anatomically modern human skeletal remains of a woman, a man, and two children from a Middle Pliocene formation in Castenedolo in northern Italy—and the Pliocene dates from about 2 million to 5 million years back. The woman's cranial capacity was 1340 cubic centimetres, which is well within the range of modern humans. He carefully inspected the overlying layers of sediment and found them to be undisturbed, thereby ruling out recent burial. A skeleton of similar age was found by other researchers at Savona, Italy. In 1883, the Italian anatomist Giuseppe Sergi (1841–1936) examined the human remains and the site, fully confirming Ragazzoni's findings. He absolutely ruled out intrusive burial, noting that 'clay from the upper surface

<aside>Skeletons denote antiquity of man</aside>

layers, recognizable by its intense red colour, would have been mixed in.' There are other such discoveries from other parts of the world.[40]

The evidence for the antiquity of man comes not only from human shoe prints and human skeletal remains but also from the age of implements used by man. A case in point is the bola, which is a type of throwing weapon made of weights, typically stones, on the ends of interconnected cords used to capture animals or birds by entangling their legs. Bola stones have been artificially rounded, and several also have a groove carved around the middle, as shown in Figure III-38 below. According to archæologists, bolas are a weapon made and used only by anatomically modern humans, namely, humans of our kind. However, the British palæoanthropologist and archæologist Louis Leakey (1903–1972) found bola stones in the lower levels of Olduvai Gorge in Tanzania, which dates to the Pliocene period (2 to 5 million years). Leakey also found there a bone needle, which he believed was used for sewing leather. Then at Miramar, in Argentina, the Argentine archæologist, palæontologist, and explorer, Carlos Ameghino (1865–1936) reported finding bola stones in undisturbed Pliocene formations about 3 million years old. In the same layer, he also discovered the bone of an extinct South American mammal with a flint arrowhead embedded in it. Still later, another researcher found a partial human jaw in the same formation.[41] But according to the current Darwinian theory of human evolution, humans capable of making bola stones, arrowheads or bone needles did not exist until between 100,000 and 150,000 years ago.

Implements indicate antiquity of man

In summary, Cremo and Thompson have found that over the past 150 years, archæologists have discovered huge amounts of evidence, in the form of human footprints, human skeletal remains, and human artefacts that are tens of millions, even hundreds of millions of years old, going all the way back to over 2½ billion years. By contrast, current textbooks on archæology, based on the Darwinian paradigm that modern humans appeared between 100,000 and 150,000 years ago, mention no such findings or evidence. Nevertheless, the latest pronouncement from mainstream science pushes the origin of anatomically modern humans further back. This is supported by a series of recent findings, including radioactive analysis of a prehistoric jawbone found at the Misliya cave site in North Israel, which suggests an earlier timeframe from between 177,000 and 195,000 years ago. According to the Jewish archæologist and anthropologist Professor Israel Hershkovitz (*b.*1950) who led the research, this finding is a 'revolution in the way

Evidence from massive weight of data support antiquity of man well beyond mainstream scientific dictates

Figure III-38   Stone Bolas Extracted from the Late Pliocene formation at Miramar, Argentina

from Michael Cremo and Richard Thompson, The Hidden History of the Human Race *(Los Angeles: Bhaktivedanta Book Publishing, 1999), 82.*

we understand the evolution of our own species.'[42] Michael Cremo himself states that mainstream science currently places the origin of anatomically modern humans at between 200,000 and 300,000 years.[43]

Many such revolutions in mainstream science will be required before the enormous antiquity of the human race is finally realized as being completely in accord with literally all the great esoteric and occult traditions the world over, but which finds its clearest exposition in the Vedas.

Comparison of Suppressed Archæological Evidence with Vedic Doctrine

The Vedas, means 'divine knowledge'. Deriving from the verbal root *vid* signifying 'to know', the Vedas are the most ancient literary and religious works of India. Written in the sacred Sanskrit tongue, they mention a human presence that goes back over 2 billion years on Earth. Before developing the implications of this, we need to make a short detour to explain the Vedic concept of time.

The modern scientific concept of time is linear, commencing with the supposed origin of the universe at the moment of the 'Big Bang', until the present time and into the future. By contrast, the Vedic (Hindu) concept of time is not linear, but cyclical with minor cycles within major cycles within megacycles. As the Hermetic Axiom teaches, just as human life is divided between cyclic periods of waking and sleeping, so also the universe has its cyclic periods of activity, known as *manvantara* followed by slumber, known as *pralaya*. Also known as the 'Day of Brahmā' and the 'Night of Brahmā', each period lasts 4.32 billion years, which is the basic unit of cyclical time.[44] Furthermore, as with the period of a human life, the Days follow the Nights in endless succession: during the Day, life is manifested in the universe, and during the Night, it is dormant. This cyclicity is not without its faint echo in modern cosmology where the idea of a Big Bang followed by a 'big crunch', or a 'big bounce' (the latest hypothesis), is taken seriously.[45]

Scientific time is linear; Vedic time is cyclical

The current Day of Brahmā, pertaining to life now, began about 2 billion years ago, which figure must not be confused with the current age of the universe of 13.8 billion years, according to physical cosmology.[46] So by this account, we should expect to see signs of life, including human life, going back about 2 billion years on Earth. This is in fact the case as documented in *Forbidden Archeology* and *The Hidden History of the Human Race*— see also Figure III-35 on page 231. Moreover, the oldest undisputed fossil evidence for life on Earth recognized by palæontologists is also about 2 billion years old, referring here to the fossils of single-celled life forms. From this, a parallel between the Vedic cosmological calendar and the findings of modern palæontology seems plausible, since both indicate the first presence of terrestrial life about 2 billion years ago, although the latter does not of course include human life, as does the former.

Antiquity of man borne out in esoteric doctrines of all world cultures

To round off this section, Manly Hall's book *Invisible Records of Thought and Action* refers to the ability of the human mind to access universal memory, stating that, 'it's reasonable to assume that the end of all knowledge in terms of history and time will be in this restoration of world memory' and that 'only by such restoration will it ever be possible to establish ethical content in history.' He states that history is in a 'lamentable condition' since humankind has probably been here more like 'a hundred million years' and less than 5,000 years is being documented by mainstream science for the modern human.[47]

Accordingly, it bears repeating that teachings on the antiquity of the human race, its origins, and devolution are at the core of all esoteric and spiritual instruction. It is to be found in the Qabbalah, Gnostic Christianity, and the doctrines of the ancient Egyptians, American Indians, and Scandinavians. However, it finds its most forceful, clear and detailed account in the Vedas, which is presumably why Cremo has chosen this particular great stream of spiritual learning for his narrative on devolution which now follows.

Devolution – The Actual Origin of Species

Before we ask the question, 'Where did human beings come from?' we again need to contemplate, 'Who, or what exactly is a human being?' As we have seen in Volume I, most scientists of course maintain, in no uncertain terms, that a human being is simply a biological machine comprising: (*a*) a complex combination of physical matter consisting of the ordinary chemical elements; such that (*b*) mind is the product of these material interactions; hence (*c*) consciousness is an epiphenomenon; and therefore (*d*) intelligence emerges from complexity only after aeons of evolution and is not an intrinsic characteristic of the entire process.[48] However, as we have periodically asserted, humans are quintessentially divine consciousness presenting as combinations of mind and matter. Hence, Cremo affirms in *Human Devolution*[49] that humans have not evolved 'up' from matter (or 'descended from a hairy quadruped'); but instead have devolved, or descended, from the realm of pure consciousness, or spirit, its emanation (refer to the definitions given earlier in this Chapter). He bases his response on the *joint findings* of modern science and one of the world's greatest wisdom traditions—the Vedas.

Is man a compound of biological matter or Divine Consciousness physically embodied?

It is important always to bear in mind that humanity is one of the kingdoms of nature, one stage on the Ladder of Life, representing a phase state of consciousness so to speak, as steam is a phase state of H_2O, as explained earlier (but see also the correspondences shown in Table III-3 of Chapter 5, page 79). Our present humanity is not the only humanity. The terrestrial human body is both a vesture and a vehicle for a conscious self, the 'temple of the spirit', in popular terms—and the rightful use of the vehicle is to awaken the conscious self to an awareness of its original state in a realm of pure consciousness, where spiritual human forms (archetypes) have always existed beyond time. That is man's original Home. (Recall the Zen koan: 'what was your original face before you were born?') The human devolution process is, then, the process by which conscious selves enter or take on a material form, i.e., in human bodies on Earth, a process that has been going on for vast periods of cyclic time, not only in this universe, but in countless other universes where the *state* of humanity, that is, consciousness expressing through the human kingdom, has been manifest also for aeons, but not necessarily in the human *form* as on Earth. If this sounds too far-fetched it is only because of an unduly anthropocentric outlook inculcated by modern science which seems to regard the human species as one of those inexplicable accidents that happened to occur on a supposedly 'minor planet of a very average star'— planet Earth (see Stephen Hawking's quote on page 219). But the evidence for the antiquity of humanity on Earth, and that the human state exists in other domains of the kosmos, can all be found in sources like: the archaic stanzas of occultism; the *Mahābhārata* and the *Rāmāyaṇa*, the chief Sanskrit epics of ancient India; the collection of symbolical and allegorical writings known as the Purāṇas, the sacred literature of Hinduism; plus the sources given in Endnote III-3 and Endnote III-5.

For example, as Cremo explains, 'the Vedic writings speak of some 400,000 humanlike species scattered throughout the universe.' Moreover, he continues, 'anatomically modern humans and the various hominids, such as the australopithecines, could be placed among those 400,000 species. All of these species, and all of the other plant and animal species, were designed as vehicles for conscious selves. Today we see that auto manufacturers design and build many different kinds of vehicles of different types and sizes and prices for people of different tastes, needs, and purchasing power. So the "intelligent designer" does the same thing: designs and builds various kinds of bodies for conscious selves with different desires and karmas;'[50] except that, as previously stressed, 'intelligent designer' means Divine Thought and not the handiwork of an extrinsic 'God-as-Intelligent-Designer', a point that warrants further elucidation shortly.

Distinguishing apes and ape-like men in Darwinism and the Vedas.

But what about apes and ape-like men? Do they figure at all in the devolutionary lineage of man according to the Vedic process as they do, critically, in the Darwinian paradigm? Most certainly. But the 'Darwinian ape' is not the same thing at all as the 'Vedic ape'. Therefore, the role of apes and ape-men needs careful explanation. As just proposed, the idea of ape-men is not something that was first mooted by Darwin and his proponents of the nineteenth century. The ancient Sanskrit writings mention creatures with ape-like bodies, human-like intelligence (but of a low order), and a low level of material culture, but not without psychic abilities and instinctive spirituality.[v] For example, the *Rāmāyaṇa* mentions the *Vānara*, a species of ape-like men that existed millions of years ago.[51] *But alongside these ape-like men existed humans of our type. The relationship was one of coexistence rather than evolution.* It is stressed that these ape-like men bear no relation to the simian or anthropoid primates from which, according to Darwinism, present humanity is supposed to have evolved. It has to be borne in mind that humanity of those early times (as indeed now) displayed an incalculably vast range of intelligence and the reference to 'ape-like men' in the Vedas and Purāṇas is to the Vānara, the men of the Third Root Race (the Lemurian race) in the majority of whom the mind principle existed, but was unawakened—hence ape-*like* in mentality. How the mind principle was awakened from dormancy to activity during the course of the evolution of the Root Races is one of the most fascinating and convoluted subjects of occult science. It cannot be explained here in a few words without doing grave injustice to the profoundness of these complex teachings and the floodlight thrown upon the whole question of mind and consciousness that science is currently grappling with to little avail. Those who are not afraid to dive into deep waters should consult the authentic references provided in Endnote III-3. However, in essence:

Man has not evolved from apes or monkeys as Darwinism teaches

> According to the Mysteries, the monkey [or ape] represents the condition of man before the rational soul entered into his constitution. Therefore it typifies the irrational man. By some the monkey is looked upon as a species not ensouled by the spiritual hierarchies; by others as a fallen state wherein man has been deprived of his divine nature through degeneracy. The ancients, though evolutionists, did not trace man's ascent through the monkey; the monkey they considered as having separated itself from the main stem of progress.[52]

Reverting to the devolutionary process, a fundamental principle of consciousness is the Source of the monads, or individual units of consciousness within the all-encompassing

---

v 'Instinctive spirituality' is meant in the sense of the involuntary, or unthinking, characteristic of the innate nature, with or without a very limited degree of conscious awareness.

field of consciousness, rather like individual water droplets within the raincloud by way of a simplistic simile. When the fractional conscious selves give up their connection with their Source, they 'drop', or 'rain down' into lower regions on rungs of the cosmic hierarchy, predominated by subtle material substance (mind) and then gross material substance (ordinary matter). When Archetypal Man (*Puruṣa*, or Adam Kadmon) gives up his willing connection with that supreme Conscious being, He 'descends' to regions of the cosmos dominated by the subtle and gross material elements, mind, and matter (see Chapter 7, Figure III-25 on page 128). Forgetful of His original position, He attempts to dominate and enjoy the subtle and gross material elements. For this purpose, He acquires bodies made of the subtle and gross material elements. The subtle material body is made up not only of mind, but of the even finer material elements as explained fully in Volume II, Chapters 2 to 4 and summarized in the Coda.

Paradoxically, then, Darwin's book *The Descent of Man* has a perfectly correct title, but is completely mistaken in its meaning: man has descended (devolved) from Divine Consciousness. In popular terms, man is a Fallen Angel; he has not descended from a hairy quadruped (or a barbarian—see later). It is illogical even to suggest that a higher entity—man—can evolve from a lower entity, a hairy quadruped—by *descent*. Descent from such a lowly creature can only result in even cruder versions of the same type, that is, a lower entity, not an ascent to a higher entity—man. Stated otherwise, rolling out (evolving) the potencies of a quadruped can only produce a similar, or lower entity— which is not man. In fairness, the counter-argument lies in theories of emergent properties that have been called 'emergentism' (see Volume I, Chapter 3, page 30). To recapitulate, emergence is the condition of an entity having properties that its parts do not have, due to interactions among the parts. Emergence plays a central role in theories of integrative levels and of complex systems. So in terms of emergentism, the phenomenon of life as studied in biology is an emergent property of chemistry; and psychological phenomena emerge from the neurobiological phenomena of living things, which in turn emerge from chemistry, itself underpinned by physics. The deep flaw in attempting to use this argument to explain the emergence of man from a barbarian is that emergentism, which is a subset of non-reductive physicalism, cannot completely uphold the concept that all substances are physical, or are exhaustively composed of physical substance, and are therefore explainable by physics. And the reason is that non-reductive physicalism faces the intractable problem of mind and the subjective experience of self because of its commitment to the view that all particulars are ultimately physical—see Volume I, Chapter 3, pages 29–32. This argument is clinched by the co-discoverer of the theory of natural selection, Wallace, who was able to see its limitations and therefore, as per the title of his essay, *The Limits of Natural Selection as Applied to Man*:

> To say that mind is a product or function of protoplasm, or of its molecular changes, is to use words to which we can attach no clear conception. You cannot have, in the whole, what does not exist in any of the parts; and those who argue thus should put forth a definite conception of matter, with clearly enunciated properties, and show, that the necessary result of a certain complex arrangement of the elements or atoms of that matter, will be the production of self-consciousness. There is no escape from this dilemma—either all matter is conscious, or consciousness is something distinct from matter, and in the latter case, its presence in material forms is a proof of the existence of conscious beings, outside of, and independent of, what we term matter.[53]

Emergent properties of matter cannot explain the 'descent' of man from matter or monkey

Alfred Russel Wallace clearly saw deficiencies in natural selection

Here Wallace is clearly recognizing the limitations of the theory of natural selection pertaining to the evolution of man as postulated by Darwinism. If we cannot have 'in the whole, what does not exist in any of the parts', then it is not possible to argue that mind is an emergent property of matter since mind has then to be an inherent property of so-called matter. Furthermore, and crucially, Wallace does not seem to regard consciousness or mind as a product of material processes in the brain since he asks those who argue that the brain is the producer of consciousness or mind to provide the evidence by way of clearly defined properties of matter, such that 'a certain complex arrangement of the elements or atoms of that matter, will be the production of self-consciousness.'

In which case, it is logical to consider that if the human organism is composed of consciousness (spirit), mind, and gross matter, then, as Cremo postulates, it is natural to suppose that these elements come from reservoirs of such elements. This suggests that the kosmos is divided into regions, or levels of gross matter, mind, and consciousness, each inhabited by beings adapted to life there. This is absolutely so, as described in Chapters 5 and 6 earlier, regarding the correspondences between the macrokosm and the microkosm: the kosmic planes and human principles. There is first a region of pure consciousness, *Brahman*, with its correspondence in the human—*Ātma(n)*. Consciousness, as we experience it, is individual and personal. This suggests that the original Source of conscious selves may also be experienced as individual and personal (which is not to suggest that such original Source is individual or personal). As the Indian-born writer and philosopher P. D. Mehta elegantly put it, 'If Brahman were to utter the word "I", that "I" is the meaning of Ātman'[54]—see Volume II, Chapter 2 for further elucidation.

Three principal regions of kosmos and correspondences in man

There is thus a kosmic hierarchy of conscious beings. Accounts of this can be found not only in the Eastern Purāṇas, but also in the cosmologies of Western cultures like the Qabbalah of Judaism. All these esoteric cosmologies postulate: (*a*) a realm of pure Consciousness; (*b*) a subordinate creative principle, or demiurge, actuated by many varieties of demigods and demigoddesses inhabiting a subtle material region of the cosmos; and (*c*) an earthly realm, dominated by gross matter and inhabited by humans like us. The gross material body is made of the philosophical Elements Earth, Water, Fire, Air, and Æther. Bodies made of these gross and subtle material Elements are vehicles for conscious selves. They are designed for existence within the realms of the subtle and gross material Elements.

All this suggests that the universe of our experience should show signs that it was designed by higher Intelligences for accommodating human and other forms of life.

The Question of Intelligent Design

Modern cosmology does provide support for an enquiry into the notion of intelligent design, the striking factor being the discovery that numbers representing the fundamental physical constants and ratios of natural forces appear to be finely tuned for the existence of the universe and for life on Earth. The British astrophysicist and cosmologist Lord Martin Rees (*b*.1942), former Astronomer Royal and a past President of the Royal Society, considers six of these numbers to be especially significant. In his book *Just Six Numbers* he says: 'These six numbers constitute a "recipe" for a universe. Moreover, the outcome is sensitive to their values: if any one of them were to be "untuned", there would be no stars and no life.'[55]

Does the 'fine tuning' of six fundamental numbers beg the question of intelligent design?

There is no argument in science about the 'fine tuning' of the physical constants and laws of nature to produce an exquisitely orchestrated universe; but plenty of debates regarding an explanation about how this is so. What follows is a terse account of four theories put forward, all in vogue. These have a bearing on evolution and on the whole question of consciousness: either as an emerging property of matter; or eternally so, and therefore an intrinsic characteristic of the vast cosmic scheme, since its inception and subsequent evolving life.

Blind Chance

To avoid the uncomfortable question of the fine-tuning of the universal constants by virtue of intelligent design, and therefore the necessity of invoking an intelligent designer, some scientists resort to blind chance—the futile example is often cited that a monkey seated at a typewriter could, by pure chance, faultlessly reproduce a Shakespeare sonnet. The chance of a monkey typing merely the word 'Monkey' on a standard typewriter is, however, calculated to be 1 in 1.5×10^{17}—a figure which, incidentally, is of the same order as the approximate age of the universe in seconds.[56] The reader can estimate the chance and time taken to type out a sonnet by such inane means, and then move on to consider the chance of all necessary factors conspiring to manifest a cosmos. Other scientists recognize that although random behaviour *could* produce the works of Shakespeare or explain the manifestation of the universe, in fact it does not, because such behaviour contravenes the Second Law of Thermodynamics, which, simplistically paraphrased in the present context, is that monkeys will always behave like monkeys, leaving lofty literature to Shakespeare.

Is blind chance the last refuge for the desperate materialist?

So the odds are not exactly in favour of this argument, nor a satisfactory explanation—other than blind chance, again—of how an entire universe that manifested according to pure chance could, in its ongoing evolution, display such beauty, dynamism, structure, and organization; and human beings in it displaying characteristics ranging from unspeakable cruelty to ineffable genius. Does chance beget chance? Are the advocates of the chance hypothesis the product of chance (by virtue of their own premise)? Can order come from chance at a future date, by chance? We need not dwell on this topic further.

Intelligent Design by a Creator God

Here we experience the head-on collision with creationists and fundamentalists who maintain that since chance cannot account for the fine-tuning of the universe and all life in it, this shows the handiwork of intelligent design by God, the Intelligent Designer. It is no surprise that the most vociferous amongst the intelligent design fundamentalists are Christian, as in the Intelligent Design movement in the USA. But design by a designer begs the question who designed the designer, and so on, to an infinite regress, for which the intelligent design protagonists offer not even a partially satisfactory answer. Merely stating that the Bible literally says so, or resorting to terrestrial visitations by UFO aliens in spacesuits (God was an astronaut), does not cut even shallow water with thoughtful people.

Is a Creator God the final resort for the religious fundamentalist?

Like the Darwinists, the intelligent design advocates accept that humans, and other living entities, are merely complex forms of matter. The only difference between the Darwinists and the intelligent design theorists is how the complexity came to be. The Darwinists attribute the complexity to evolution by genetic mutation and natural selection, whereas the intelligent design proponents attribute it to intelligent design by an extrinsic 'Creator God' who, presumably, somehow managed to design Himself, by Himself. As with blind chance, we need not labour the futility of such arguments.

The Multiverse

The multiverse hypothesis was introduced in Chapter 6 to cite an example of a partial approach by contemporary scientific cosmology to *kosmos* (the womb of cosmos) as understood in occultism. Many cosmologists admit that the odds against the fine tuning are too extreme for simple chance to be offered as a credible scientific explanation. But to avoid having to invoke the question of a providential designer, they have proposed the multiverse, being the existence of a practically unlimited number of universes, in each of which the value of the fundamental constants and laws of nature are adjusted in a different way—and we just happen to live in the one universe with everything adjusted correctly for the existence of human life. Indeed, the Australian physicist Neil Manson (*b.* 1940) of the Australian National University has said, 'The multiverse hypothesis is alleged to be the last resort for the desperate atheist.'[57]

As also stated in Chapter 6, these other parallel universes have, as yet, only a theoretical existence, albeit the theory is most impressive as in Stephen Hawking's last paper referenced therein, which reportedly provides mathematical evidence for the multiverse. But even if their existence could be physically demonstrated, one would further have to show that in these other universes the value of the fundamental constants and laws of nature is in fact different from those in our universe.[58]

Occult cosmology (including the Vedic of course) also speaks of 'numberless Universes',[vi] but all of them are designed for life *at their level* and through the appropriate substance for the expression of life at that level. But beyond all of these material universes, or globes, with their levels of gross and subtle matter, is the level of pure Consciousness, i.e. Divine Consciousness, or REALITY (SPIRIT). This is a vast and deeply abstruse teaching of occult science under the general title of 'Planetary Rounds'. Interested readers should consult the sources listed in Endnote III-5.

The Anthropic Principle

There are good reasons to suppose that humans, and other living things, are combinations of three things: ordinary matter, a subtle mind element, and an element of pure Consciousness. The anthropic principle is the philosophical consideration that observations of the universe must be compatible with the conscious and sapient life that observes it, or put slightly differently, the cosmological principle that theories of the universe are constrained by the necessity of allowing human existence. This is posited as a necessity,

Is the multiverse the final recourse for the despairing atheist?

The multiverse is the closest scientific approach to occult cosmology

---

vi 'Numberless', meaning strictly 'beyond number' conveys an important, subtly different meaning to words like 'many' or 'innumerable' or 'infinite'.

because if life were impossible, no living entity would be there to observe it, and thus it would not be known. One of the first papers on this topic is by Bernard Carr co-authored with Martin Rees.[59] The later book *Universe or Multiverse?* contains several important chapters on the anthropic principle, including one by Carr.[60]

Some proponents of the anthropic principle reason that it explains why this universe has the age and the fundamental physical constants necessary to accommodate conscious life. As a result, it is unremarkable that this universe has fundamental constants that happen to fall within the narrow range thought to be compatible with life, as propounded by the English cosmologist John Barrow FRS (*b.* 1952) and the American cosmologist Frank Tipler (*b.*1947) who jointly propose the 'strong anthropic principle', which maintains that such is the case because the universe is in some sense compelled eventually to have conscious and sapient life emerge within it.[61] Some critics of the strong principle argue in favour of a 'weak anthropic principle' similar to the one defined by the Australian theoretical physicist Brandon Carter FRS (*b.* 1942).[62] This posits that the ostensible fine tuning of the universe is the result of selection bias, i.e., only in a universe capable of eventually, after billions of years, supporting life will there be living beings in it capable of observing and reflecting upon fine tuning. Such arguments invariably draw upon some notion of the multiverse for there to be a statistical population of universes to select from, and from which selection bias (our observance of only this universe, compatible with our life) could occur. Since no mention is made of how the universe is so compelled eventually to have conscious life, or who, or what, does the compelling, one is entitled to ask whether it all happened because our universe, being the fittest to survive, evolved by 'natural cosmological selection' from a star pool of countless other universes. This begs a more philosophical treatment of the subject which Carr has provided in his book, *Mathematical Structures of the Universe.*[63]

Strong anthropic principle and weak anthropic principle both invoke multiverse concept

In summary then, the anthropic principle was formulated as a response to a series of observations that the laws of nature and parameters of the universe take on values that are consistent with conditions for life as we know it, rather than a set of values that would not be consistent with life on Earth. That much is not in doubt. But whether we invoke the strong or the weak anthropic principle, it is still, like the concept of the multiverse, a circular argument and a tautology. As observed by the English ecologist, philosopher, and co-ordinator of *Faith-in-Scholarship* Richard Gunton (*b. circa* 1981),[vii] in this form it corresponds closely to Descartes' famous *Cogito ergo sum* (I think, therefore I am); and indeed Carter paraphrased the strong anthropic principle analogously as '*Cogito ergo mudus talis est*'—'I think, therefore the world is such [as it is]'—because it is taken as the conclusion to a premise derived from an act of *reflexive* reference.[64] It is like saying that but for life, we would not be living, so observation of living beings shows that life exists. Hence, life must be compatible with the living beings who observe and experience it. It is the circular argument of the materialist mind-set that intelligence would have to emerge after

Is the anthropic principle (strong or weak) ultimately a circular argument?

If the universe could be heard whispering 'I think, therefore I exist' this would be a true statement because it would confirm a profound tenet of the perennial philosophy that mind and not matter is the root and basis of existence. For man, the microkosm, the body is an idea in consciousness, so also, the Universe, the Macrokosm, is the World-Idea in Divine Consciousness.

---

vii 'Faith-in-Scholarship' is a network of fellowship and support for Christian thinkers.

billions of years of evolution to produce creatures displaying such intelligence, namely, humans, who are, somehow, capable of reflecting on intelligence.

In passing, the multiverse (just described) is often used to circumvent the implications of the anthropic principle and not very parsimonious as Rupert Sheldrake once remarked to Martin Rees![65]

Afterword – Darwinism and Materialism Through the Looking-Glass

Earlier on we stated candidly that the onset of Darwinism was good medicine to counter the lack of intellectual rigour of Christian dogma about creation. But does Darwinism have any value now? Should it be modified or supplanted? Should we still uphold the rigid concept that:

> The main conclusion arrived at in this work, namely that man is descended from some lowly-organised form, will, I regret to think, be highly distasteful to many persons. But there can hardly be a doubt that we are descended from barbarians.
>
> Charles Darwin, *The Descent of Man* (1871), Vol. 2, p. 404

We commented earlier that Darwin's book *The Descent of Man* is, ironically, an accurate title, but is mistaken in its concept. Let us further develop this idea. If a refined substance is produced from something crude, this cannot happen by itself. There has to be some sort of external input. For example, high octane petrol is produced from crude oil by a chemical process involving heat and pressure. Gold is refined in a chemical smelter at high temperatures, around 1600 degrees Celsius, in order to separate the pure metal from the impurities (slag). Left on its own to the external environment, gold does not refine itself from crude ore to a purity of say, 24 carat. There has to be a refining principle at work. Thinking along analogous principles, in the case of man it is the Higher Self seeking ever more refined and complex bodies (personalities) through which to manifest, via the pressure of evolution, across innumerable incarnations (see Volume II, Chapter 5). So if barbarians are to evolve towards cultured people, there has to be a refining principle at work. Natural selection and genetic mutation are supposed to ensure the survival of the fittest. But that could apply to ensuring the survival of just the fitted amongst the barbarians or 'some lowly-organised form'. Why do they evolve (refine, in terms of the mineral simile) towards a higher order of life and complexity? What then, is the ever active refining principle in man (the equivalent of heat and pressure in the mineral kingdom)? It is the evolution of Consciousness. Man has descended (devolved) from Divine Consciousness (SPIRIT); so also has cosmos. Therefore, man has in him everything that cosmos has because he is an inseparable part of it. Man is the child of cosmos: man cannot be separated from his parent. Every principle that is in cosmos is in him, latent or active; and evolution is the bringing forth of what is within; hence, the growth and refinement of man is quite literally, limitless. Therefore, man cannot possibly be 'descended from some lowly-organised form', or 'descended from barbarians.' Nor indeed can the unfoldment of consciousness in man be merely a passive process, i.e. automatic or mechanical. It also requires aspiration and directed effort.

It is fashionable these days for intellectualists to scoff at the supposed ignorance of so-called primitive cultures—'the barbarians'—who ostensibly believed in a flat Earth. But

Evolution needs an active refining principle and goal-directed effort. Natural selection and mutation are not enough

our modern biological and evolutionary savants are terribly proud of their reputed simian or anthropoid origins and choose to turn a blind eye to the evidence and experience of all the great spiritual teachers, sages, and mystics who have unequivocally proclaimed our divine origin. Small wonder then, that such glorification of animal propensities has had the natural consequence of exonerating and tolerating the expression of the animalistic behaviour that characterizes much of our modern civilization. We prefer to use the term 'animalistic' rather than 'animal' since no animals are known to behave in the manner of the unspeakable felony and brutality of large swathes of the human population; therefore to ascribe animal characteristics to the base behaviour of some humans is an affront to the animal kingdom. Of course, 'animals predators kill to survive, but animal aggression is not even remotely equivalent to the violence of mankind. Humans are the most violent animals to our own kind in existence.'[66] It is more likely that humans project their own aggression and cruelty on to animal behaviour—a convenient dodge. *So the dream of the hubristic materialist to have the proud privilege and proof of being descended from the apes will therefore ever remain unfulfilled and short-lived as the wedge of solid, new scientific evidence widens the cracks in neo-Darwinian theory.*

Why are mainstream scientists so bent on proclaiming man's supposedly animal descent?

A similar fate also awaits those who fancy themselves as the scientific debunkers of all things spiritual;[viii] they will find their cherished phantasy that the brain-equals-mind is nothing more than a 'wet' computer, soon turned into a nightmare as solid evidence from impeccable scientists mounts apace about consciousness beyond the material brain, as we have shown in Volumes I and II. Here we cannot resist quoting a cutting remark by the Master KH, one of Blavatsky's Adept instructors:

> And to show you how exact a science is occultism let me tell you that the means we avail ourselves of are all laid down for us in a code as old as humanity to the minutest detail, but everyone of us has to begin from the beginning, not from the end. Our laws are as immutable as those of Nature, and they were known to man an eternity before this strutting game-cock, modern science, was hatched.[67]

Occult Science, not physical science, is the true exact science

This comment makes three important points: (*a*) that it is occultism that is the true exact science; (*b*) that there are innumerable questions and conundrums that modern science cannot answer unless and until the latter prepares itself to understand the answers by virtue of learning the hidden laws of Nature and educating its perceptions; and (*c*) that a large dose of humility is needed by modern science in order to fathom the secrets of Nature (occultism) that have been known throughout the ages to the custodians of such wisdom by those generally known as Adepts, Masters, or Mahātmās.

But how different would our civilization be—morally and ethically, that is—if scientists would logically trace human ancestry to the two Divine Positive and Negative Principles, *Śiva* and *Śakti*, as our true spiritual Father and Mother, instead of insisting on a lineage to lowly-organized forms like quadrupeds, barbarians or monkeys. Yet they like to regard themselves as rational and examining all the evidence with scientific rigour!

We should also keep in mind that most people in the world are not qualified scientists, but they still have common sense and intuitions. Although they may accept at face value the theory of evolution as propounded by mainstream science and the media, many are

---

viii Refer to the many examples of such debunkers cited in Volumes I and II.

troubled by its implications. The supporters of exclusive Darwinism are now facing a mounting crisis, as can be judged from the howls of protest from scientists who denounced Thomas Nagel's reservations about Darwinian theory (see Chapter 7, Volume II on page 131). It behoves one, therefore, not to relent in the endeavour to produce more evidence and discoveries to overturn the undue dominance of the Darwinists.

And such evidence must be complemented by a clear explanation that the problem has been caused, as previously stated, by confusing and conflating the outer form with the inner function and content. Outwardly, physical man is like an ape (and vice versa), in the sense that he sometimes behaves like, or worse than apes or other animals, and his appearance to some extent resembles an ape, and vice versa; but inwardly, he is fundamentally different from all the animals, including apes, and evolved in every aspect, because in him resides the divine element derived from *Maheśa* (an aspect of *Śiva* as regenerator—see Chapter 9, page 174) which is absent in the case of the animals (or only potentially present, so to say, especially in the higher animals). This divine element is the *Śiva Tattva*, the highest principle in existence. But why do scientists (other than transhumanists—see the Epilogue) never talk of evolution beyond the human kingdom? Do they consider humans as the acme and culmination of evolution?

> It is not against zoological and anthropological discoveries, based on the fossils of man and animal, that every mystic and believer in a divine soul inwardly revolts, but only against the uncalled-for conclusions built on preconceived theories and made to fit in with certain prejudices. Their premises may or may not be always true; and as some of these theories live but a short life, the deductions therefrom must ever be one-sided with materialistic evolutionists. Yet it is on the strength of such very ephemeral authority, that most of the men of science frequently receive undue honours where they deserve them the least.
>
> H. P. Blavatsky[68]

In defence of Darwin: what he said in addition

But we must close this section with a few words in Darwin's defence. It is no fault of Darwin that his followers have converted his theories into what virtually amounts to a dogmatic theology of evolutionary scientism. The 'survival of the fittest' has virtually become a Darwinian motto for those who seek to justify their self-centred behaviour and disregard for the common good. But is this what Darwin exclusively proposed?

Rediscovering Darwin is an important book by David Elliot Loye (*b.*1925), an American psychologist and evolutionary systems scientist.[69] He used a word search program for Darwin's *The Descent of Man* and discovered that Darwin had written about the survival of the fittest only twice, but ninety-five times about love and ninety-two times about the moral sense, especially in relation to love and community: 'those communities, which included the greatest number of the most sympathetic members, would flourish best, and rear the greatest number of offspring.'[70] Darwin also highlighted the love between animals and the development of the moral sense in human society. Here he was influenced by two of his contemporaries: the Scottish moral philosopher Alexander Bain (1818–1903) and the Englishman Henry Sidgwick (1838–1900) who was one of the most influential ethical philosophers of the Victorian era.

Darwin clearly acknowledges love, the moral sense, and spiritual agencies

One wonders what the concept of the 'selfish gene' would have meant to Darwin given that he repudiated the notion of selfishness in evolution, distinguishing between higher and lower forms of motivation, the former related to philanthropy since,

'Prudence, […] which does not concern the welfare of others, though a very useful virtue, has never been highly esteemed.'[71] Apropos, invincible atheists would not derive much comfort in justifying their stance by appealing to Darwin's theories; for although Darwin maintained that 'the ennobling belief in God is not universal with man,' however, 'the belief in active spiritual agencies naturally follows from his other mental powers'[72]—thus clearly showing the influence of his theological studies at Cambridge where he most likely gained a First being classified 10 out of 178 candidates.

One further speculates how Darwin would have responded to Richard Dawkins, one of the most vociferous defenders of the neo-Darwinian faith. In the intervening gap of three decades between the first edition (in 1976) and the thirtieth anniversary edition (with a new introduction by the author) of his 'million copy international bestseller' *The Selfish Gene*, Dawkins seems not to have changed his original dictum: 'Much as we might wish to believe otherwise, universal love and the welfare of the species as a whole are concepts which simply do not make evolutionary sense.'[73] Are we entitled to conclude that Dawkins (given his penchant for extolling selfishness to the status of scientific credibility) has either not read or, more likely, not understood the import of the ninety-five references to 'love', and the evolutionary sense of 'the welfare of others' in *The Descent of Man*?

But for those of us who appreciate that Darwin was a product of his times and are therefore able to situate his theories in the scientific, religious, and cultural milieu of his era, the underlying message is that Darwin was advocating cultural evolution and not just the biological evolution with which he is mainly associated by mainstream biologists. As Loye maintains, Darwin's insistence on the *moral sense* as the primary drive in human evolution is the pressing message for our times. The survival of the fittest refers to the 'morally fittest'.

We have no quarrel with Darwin, only with his 'disciples' who have proselytized his theories with the zeal of religious fundamentalists. This dogmatic stance has seriously haemorrhaged evolutionary science and biology.

The Evolution of Man – The Indispensable Complement of Occult Science

The above narrative on the antiquity of man, his origins, and devolutionary descent from Divine Consciousness are clear indications that by limiting its purview to the physical plane and either ignoring or denying the higher and subtler dimensions of existence, science must necessarily have a partial and inaccurate understanding of evolution as a whole.

One of the most puzzling problems that still continues to dog scientists is the sudden break in the evolutionary sequence of bodies on Earth. Despite their strenuous attempts to find such a 'missing link', they have not succeeded so far. Nor are they ever likely to succeed in the future for two main reasons: (*a*) that our bodies are not in a continuation of the series of bodies evolved from the animal kingdom, including the apes, as said earlier; and (*b*) inter-species transitions occur at the subjective level with no objective or outward signs—see the further explanation and example given in Chapter 5, page 138 of Volume I.

Finding the 'missing link' still beleaguers evolutionary biology

Occult science complements and corrects errors in the scientific picture by virtue of taking in the wide sweep of evolution on all kingdoms of nature, *especially the inner worlds and their causative influence on the outer*. Regarding man, this includes evolution on the mental and psychic planes in addition to the physical. By contrast, biology and evolutionary theory are concerned entirely with the outer forms constituted of physical atoms and molecules, and the physical and electro-chemical forces acting between them. Whereas a few biologists will uneasily and privately admit the notion of vitality which is present in all living forms, nonetheless, conventional biology misses three things:

1. Even with its exclusive emphasis on the outer form, it cannot account for the actual physical form, shape, and structure of things, living and non-living. Theories about vitalism and teleology are a step in the right direction and Sheldrake's theory of morphic resonance is a splendid account of morphogenesis (see Volume I, Chapter 4, page 74 et seq.). These ideas are slowly gaining ground, but still not accepted currency in the mainstream (as of the second decade of the twenty-first century).

Mainstream biology overlooks three points

2. Related to the above, there is *prāṇa*, the vital force, which is invisible, but associated with the visible form. (See Chapters 8 and 9 on the close relation between prāṇa and vitalism.)

3. Visible forms are evolving primarily in order to provide and serve as increasingly sensitive vehicles for the evolving mind and unfolding consciousness. Earlier, we explained that the degree of the potentiality unfolded is directly related to, and limited by, the degree of refinement of the vehicles of expression: the more cumbersome the vehicles and mechanisms, the more is the translation of the will-interaction retarded. However, biology and evolutionary theory have no time for such ideas and regard the change or refinement of form purely according to Darwinian theories. However, it does not seem to occur to science that the mineral kingdom (regarded by science as non-living) and the plant kingdom are also evolving in form, and this neglect and ignorance is mainly due to orthodox science turning a blind eye to anything invisible that cannot be comprehended by other than mechanistic theories or physical means.

Every faculty must have a vehicle through which it can be expressed. We know of any principle only what we have evolved of it so far.

Thus it is that by revealing the missing link and supplying the missing gaps in knowledge, occult science thereby enables a much richer and deeper understanding of evolution and elucidates the purpose and planned progression of the whole evolutionary process, without which the evolution of forms would be a futile, chance endeavour by nature.

Reincarnation is a key occult doctrine and central to the evolution of man. The process was outlined in Volume II, Chapter 5 in the overall context of the ubiquity of consciousness that expresses through the constant renewal of temporal forms for the finer development of its potentialities, which is why Chapter 5 of Volume II was entitled 'Death is Transition'. In all this, however, we face two major hurdles. First, the doctrine of reincarnation is so completely misunderstood, especially in the West. Secondly, the role, function, and imperative of reincarnation cannot be appreciated in its fullness without invoking other doctrines that are not synonymous, but to which it is strongly related, principally, *Karma and reincarnation are indispensable components of evolution* the *Doctrine of Essential Identity and Rebirth*, or the *Doctrine of Constant Renewal*, aspects of which are the doctrines of *Transmigration*, and of *Metempsychosis*, which, incidentally, have nothing whatsoever to do with a human being born again as an animal (or stone, etc.) in the next life, which is a grotesque distortion of sublime doctrines. This clearly illustrates the close interrelation of the diverse teachings of the *philosophia perennis*. The great advantage is that each doctrine: (*a*) explains a specific aspect of the teaching; (*b*) assists in the understanding of another related teaching; and (*c*) elucidates, holographically, the whole body of teachings. The potential drawback of such strong interrelations is a misunderstanding of terms and ideas—refer to Volume II, Chapter 1, page 3ff. about the principal reasons for the misperceptions caused by confusing terminology in the numerous expositions of the perennial philosophy.

The evolutionary process being the transmission of not just the physical but, more significantly, the psychic and mental characteristics from one life to the succeeding ones along any given series of lives, this means, for man, from one personality to the next personality in a series of terrestrial incarnations. What is the causative link between lives? It cannot be just a physical hereditary connection. The answer is the Auric Envelope, or Egg (or its equivalent for every living thing). In it are stored: (*a*) the karmic residues of each man's successive lives; and (*b*) the *skandhas*, which are the aggregate of those elementals that are conditioned by all man's activities, both objective and subjective, during life. An army is a good illustration of the distinction between *karma*, *skandhas*, and *elementals*: the general (karma) issues the commands; and the body of soldiers (skandhas) execute them under his orders. In this simile, elementals are the individual soldiers whose actions, in aggregate, comprise the skandhas. Karma and reincarnation comprise the core teaching of esoteric science and it would be out of place to present an outline in just a few words (but refer back to Volume II, Chapter 5, and the source references cited therein, regarding reincarnation). However, the discoveries of August Weismann, mentioned earlier in this Chapter, are particularly relevant to this section on the bearing of reincarnation (rebirth) on the evolution of man.

Role of the Auric Egg, karma and skandhas

Science in Borderless Touch with Occult Science

August Weismann's theory is telling because even Darwin's contemporaries were not unanimously in accord with the materialistic ideas of the transmission of characteristics then in vogue. In *Beiträge zur Descendenzlehre* (Articles in the Theory of Descent),[74] Professor Weismann veers towards the teachings of the Vedas on reincarnation, showing how one infinitesimal cell, out of millions of others at work in the formation of an organism, determining alone and unaided, by means of constant segmentation and multiplication, the correct image of the future man (or animal) in its physical, mental, and psychic characteristics. It is that cell which impresses on the face and form of the new individual the features of the parents or of some distant ancestor; it is that cell again which transmits to him the intellectual and mental idiosyncrasies of his sires, and so on. The term 'germ plasm' was first used by Weismann to refer to the *immortal* portion of our bodies—simply through the process of successive assimilations. Darwin's theory, viewing the embryological cell as an essence, or the extract, from all other cells, is set aside by Weismann because it is incapable of accounting for hereditary transmission. 'There are but two ways of explaining the mystery of heredity; either the substance of the germinal cell is endowed with the faculty of crossing the whole cycle of transformations that lead to the construction of a separate organism and then to the reproduction of identical germinal cells; or, *those germinal cells do not have their genesis at all in the body of the individual, but proceed directly from the ancestral germinal cell passed from father to son through long generations*. It is the latter hypothesis that Weismann accepted and worked upon; and it is to this cell that he traces the *immortal* [emphasis added] portion of man.'[75]

August Weismann's theory of 'germ plasma'

Esoteric import of August Weismann's theory

According to the germ plasm theory, inheritance in a multicellular organism only takes place by means of the germ cells: the organism's reproductive cells, or gametes, such as egg cells and sperm cells. Other cells of the body do not function as agents of heredity. One has only to complete the 'germinal cell', or 'physical plasm' of man, as Blavatsky asserts, with the 'spiritual plasm', so to say, that contains the overshadowing spiritual and psychic principles, and there is a complete account of the occult teaching on the mysteries of embryology.[76]

When science understands, accepts, and extends to higher dimensions this concept from a contemporary of Darwin, and at one time himself an ardent Darwinist, then science will have crossed the Rubicon into the domain of occult science, having blended biology with meta-biology, and stepped for ever out of the realm of mechanistic transformation, as Darwin taught.

In closing this section, it must always be remembered that evolution applies as much to the individual man as to the whole of humanity—the human kingdom—of which each man is a living part—a *conscious* 'human cell' in the Body of Humanity. Thus an organism becomes a vibrant ecology of relations and interrelationships.

How do we Raise our Consciousness to Supernal Heights?

This Chapter, as indeed this entire work, has affirmed in various ways that the origin of physical man is Divine Consciousness—SPIRIT, in popular terms. When Man (here meaning *Puruṣa*, or Adam Qadmon, the Archetypal Man, or Humanity—see Chapter 8, page 155) descends from His true spiritual abode, the conscious Self takes on forms in appropriate bodies, or coverings, acting as its vehicles of expression and action on the lower planes of being. This 'covering process' is what Michael Cremo has referred to by the apt word 'devolution'. That man has not only devolved from, but been demoted, so to say, from his spiritual Source provides the clue to the universal instinct, rather, aspiration (albeit sometimes unconscious) in all mankind to reclaim the Promised Land, his empyrean birthright. How men have set about this task of reclamation, or 're-evolution', as Cremo puts it, ranges from the ridiculous to the sublime, but what is in no doubt is that all men, without exception, want to better themselves, to gain contact, however fleetingly with their original and uncorrupted Self. Therefore, every genuine wisdom tradition has developed, through its own particular religious and cultural milieu, some ways and methods of accomplishing that ultimate contact through such means as meditation, yoga, prayer or selfless service. But whatever ways are adopted, the aim is always the same: raising consciousness to the highest possible level to approach its own Source.

Raising Consciousness – Explaining what it Means

What exactly is meant by that familiar phrase 'raising consciousness'? The meaning of phrases in common usage gets progressively adulterated until it turns into a mere cliché. Since raising consciousness is the central plank of all spiritual and genuinely religious practices, it is worth elucidating exactly what is meant by this. With such understanding the final section of this Chapter will become much clearer, being a simple and safe meditation technique suggested for moving towards attaining such a purpose.

An analogy with physical sight would be helpful to illustrate what is meant by raising consciousness. Suppose we want to explore the layout of a city. There are two principal ways to do this, and neither one is right or wrong: both are entirely context-dependent. We could adopt a 'horizontal' approach and explore the city street by street. This would give considerable details about the layout and specific features of the streets, but it would be hard to get an overall appreciation of the main routes through the city. Alternatively, we could ascend in a helicopter and view the city as a whole. The primary motorways and overall layout would soon come into view, but the detailed layout of streets would be less discernible. We could easily find our way, say, from east to west, but would have difficulty in locating a particular street address. The important point here is that the city has not changed to suit our vantage point: it is exactly the same, but we have attained a new vista by virtue of ascending rather than being confined to the horizontal plane. The same principle applies to raising consciousness.

Raising consciousness entails higher and subtler dimsensions of space and time, and a holistic outlook

Let us now take this a step further and discover several ways in which we can perceive a spiritual book, for example, the *Bhagavad Gītā*, from ascending levels of consciousness. First, supposing our consciousness were linear, i.e., confined to a line. In this case we could only (like a bug, say) crawl from side to side along one edge. We would see neither the other edges, nor the surface, still less the solid aspect of the book. Next, supposing our consciousness were two dimensional. We would immediately perceive a new world, now being able to explore the surface of the book, though not able to leave that surface and see another adjacent surface. Moreover, if we ventured beyond any edge we would simply fall off, as into a chasm. Raising our consciousness to three dimensions would enable us to perceive the solidity of the book. We would discover that entirely new aspects of the book, which were completely hidden from our view and which we could not even imagine, suddenly emerge into our consciousness: *they were there all the time, but hidden from our perspective.* Next, we can raise our consciousness to the fourth dimension, so to say, and read the book in a dead-letter, literal, and exoteric sense—and there are many books for which this is all that is needed. But for a book of timeless spiritual instruction, like the *Gītā*, there is no limit to raising our consciousness to ever higher dimensions to eke out the esoteric and spiritual import of what in the book is necessarily confined to words in Sanskrit and many translations.

The message here is that the same thing—be it the same book, or the same science, or the same religion, or ultimately, the same truth—does not change according to our level of consciousness; but it will reveal more of itself, to the higher dimensions of consciousness that are invoked in attempting to access it. It bears repeating, *exactly the same thing reveals more of itself the higher we ascend in consciousness.* The occultist is one who is able to perceive truths concealed in the world religions, sciences, and philosophies from this higher dimensional standpoint. Similarly, the individual, great (but not necessarily famous) scientist, often working alone, comes to his ground-breaking discoveries by virtue of not being hidebound by orthodox concepts; therefore, better able to see further into the nature of things than establishment scientists. As stated by the French novelist and essayist Marcel Proust (1871–1922) in *La Prisonnière*, the fifth volume of *In Search of Lost Time* (also known as *Remembrance of Things Past*):

> The real voyage of discovery consists, not in seeking new landscapes, but in having new eyes.[77]

The understanding that comes from such a higher dimensional standpoint is organic and holistic instead of linear and sequential. Therefore, the occultist can perceive relations and underlying causes before their appearance in the ordinary space-time world of four dimensions. The phenomena of clairvoyance and remote viewing have all to do with such altered states of consciousness. (Although remote viewing is sometimes used as a modern equivalent term for clairvoyance, the two are not the same as they use different psychic faculties. The point however is that they both require consciousness to function in higher dimensions.)

Higher orders of space and time may provide scientific clues to *psi* phenomena

It is the writer's strong conviction that the explanation of paranormal phenomena, *psi*, apparitions, and a host of psychic phenomena, lie in higher dimensions above the familiar four-dimensional world of space-time we normally inhabit. Here, physics has much to offer in terms of superstring theory and M-theory that invoke higher dimensions (see the definitions of these theories given in footnotes i and ii to Chapter 1, Volume II, on page 7). An extremely comprehensive, albeit technical exposition on this subject is in *The Mathematical Connection Between Religion and Science*.[78]

Let us give a concrete example to illustrate how in science the same thing can be described in ordinary terms and then from a higher level of consciousness: it is the difference between intellect, and intelligence born of intuition. Earlier we cited James Jeans's mature insights—deduced from the proven facts of modern science—that what we regard as visible and ponderable physical matter is, in its essence, 'a vibration', or 'bottled-up waves' to use his terms (see Chapter 7 for example). Yet there are scientists aplenty, of enormous intellectual brilliance, who spend their lives in fundamental particle research trying to discover the 'ultimate particle' of matter, but seem completely unaware that they are in truth dealing with a mode of vibration (see the Epilogue for a graphic illustration of this). These same scientists are fully capable of being struck by the beauty of a sunset, the symmetry of a flower or the emotional power of great music, but with rare exceptions, like Schrödinger (see Volume I, the epigraph to Chapter 4), will not stop and ask the further question: if science can only explain the physical mechanisms, but not the subjective experience of sensation, surely, there must be a deeper principle at work? And that deeper principle is, of course, mind; but science has self-limited itself severely by excluding mind as an independent principle from its scope of enquiry, other than attempting to explain (away) mind in physical terms, hence science continues on its own treadmill of constantly seeking answers to questions (such as the nature of consciousness, or the origin of the universe) without regard to the subtler realms of nature and the superphysical, or subtle bodies of man.

A Diagram of Meditation

Having explained what is meant by raising consciousness and the higher internal vision so attained, it is obligatory to describe a simple process to aspire towards this goal. The process has its roots in the wisdom of both the West and the East. Dealing first with the former, we touch upon the account of the Tabernacle of Moses in the Wilderness in the biblical Book of Exodus: Chapters 35–40 which largely detail the construction of the Tabernacle whose blueprints and furnishings were revealed in Exodus 25–31. We first describe the exoteric version as taught in practically every Sunday School Bible Class, and then the rarely understood esoteric symbolical meaning hidden within the historical

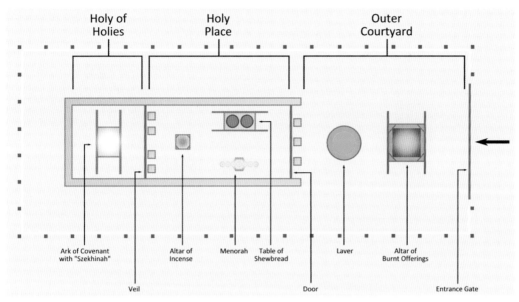

Figure III-39 The Tabernacle of Moses (Exodus 35–40)

Image Credit: Wikimedia Commons/Adik86/Tabernacle.png

narrative. This description will provide the basis for each person to 'construct' his own Tabernacle within his own mind.

The Tabernacle of Moses in the Wilderness

From a digest of the relevant portions of Hall's 'The Tabernacle in the Wilderness',[79] we learn that the well-known exoteric reading in the Old Testament states that the Tabernacle (meaning a sanctuary in the form of a tent) was a sacred place where God chose to meet His people, the Israelites, during the forty years of their wanderings in the desert under the guidance of Moses. It was the place where the leaders and people came together to worship and offer sacrifices. The Tabernacle was first erected in the wilderness one year after the Passover when the Israelites were freed from their Egyptian slavery (*circa* 1450 BC). It comprised a mobile tent with portable furniture with which the nomadic tribe travelled and set up wherever they pitched camp. The Tabernacle would be in the centre of the camp, and the Twelve Tribes of Israel would set up their tents around it according to tribe. The instructions on how to build the Tabernacle were first communicated by God to Moses in the wilderness, who then gave the orders to the Israelites. The specifications of the Tabernacle are described in the Book of Exodus, twenty-fifth chapter, verses 2 and 9:

Exoteric narrative of the Tabernacle of Moses

> And the LORD spake unto Moses, saying,
> [2] Speak unto the children of Israel, that they bring me an offering: of every man that giveth it willingly with his heart ye shall take my offering.
> And let them make me a sanctuary; that I may dwell among them.
> [9] According to all that I shew thee, after the pattern of the tabernacle, and the pattern of all the instruments thereof, even so shall ye make it.[80]

And so God dwelled among His people in the Tabernacle in the wilderness. He appeared as a pillar of cloud over the Tabernacle by day, and a pillar of fire by night in the sight of all Israel. The people would not set out on their journey unless the cloud lifted. It was an unmistakably powerful signal indicating God's presence among them.

What is the esoteric allegory behind the exoteric form of this story? As the Tabernacle was the dwelling place of God among men, likewise the soul and body in man are the dwelling place of his divine nature. 'There is no doubt that the Tabernacle, its furnishings and ceremonials, *when considered esoterically* [writer's emphasis], are analogous to the structure, organs, and functions of the human body.'[81] Referring to Figure III-39 on the previous page, the picture to the left shows the Altar of Burnt Offerings, five cubits long and five cubits wide, but only three cubits high, standing at the entrance to the outer court of the Tabernacle.[ix] The upper surface of the Altar was a brazen grill upon which the sacrifice was placed, while beneath was a space for the fire. This Altar signified that a candidate, when first entering the precincts of the sanctuary, must offer upon the brazen altar not a poor unoffending bull or ram but its correspondence within his own nature. The bull, being symbolic of earthiness, represented his own gross constitution which must be burned up by the fire of his Divinity. (The sacrificing of beasts, and in some cases human beings, upon the altars of the pagans was the result of their ignorance concerning the fundamental principle underlying sacrifice. They did not realize that their offerings must come from within their own natures in order to be acceptable. Refer to the section on animal sacrifice at the close of Chapter 1 on page 18.)

Esoteric meaning of the Tabernacle of Moses

Farther westward, in line with the Brazen Altar, was the Laver of Purification. It signified to the priest that he should cleanse not only his body but also his soul from all stains of impurity, for none who is not clean in both body and mind can enter into the presence of Divinity and live. In the centre of the room, almost against the partition leading into the Holy of Holies, stood the Altar of Burnt Incense, made of wood overlaid with golden plates. Its width and length were each a cubit and its height was two cubits. This altar was symbolic of the human larynx—see the central and right hand pictures of Figure III-39— from which the words issuing from the mouth of man ascend as an acceptable offering unto the Lord, *for the larynx occupies the position in the constitution of man between the Holy Place, which is the trunk of his body, and the Holy of Holies, which is the head with its contents.* (Refer also to the exposition on the anatomical symbolism of members of the human body in Chapter 3 page 44 et seq.)

It is very likely that the Jews in those early times would have been versed in the esotericism of their religion, hence would have realized that their Tabernacle was not only a physical erection, but a symbolic edifice. The Tabernacle of yore is long gone, but its meaning lives on forever in the hearts and minds of all those who are drawn to the life spiritual. Let us then update this archaic symbol using a homely example—our own home—to illustrate how we may progress through the veils of consciousness towards ultimate union—rather, conscious re-union—with Divine Consciousness.

The Tabernacle – Our Own Home

> 'The God in the sun is the "I" in me'—this, put tersely, is the essence of man's relationship to divinity. A whole book may be needed to explain it, a whole lifetime to get direct experience of its truth as insight.
>
> Paul Brunton[82]

---

ix The cubit is an ancient standard of measurement of approximately eighteen inches, being the length between the elbow and the extreme end of the index finger.

Figure III-40 overleaf shows a natural scene of a sunset and, alongside it, an imaginative simile of a lamp in a house—As above, so below. Both represent, in a remarkable way, the *inner* nature of both cosmos and man, showing how pure Light as the *radiance* of Consciousness shines through and illuminates manifold, differentiated layers of Itself.

The sunset scene shows how the invisible (to us) Central Spiritual Sun irradiates its power upon our visible sun (its garment, or vesture), whose own radiated light is diffused by the intervening clouds and hazy atmosphere before reaching the surface of the sea, where the ripples cause multiple images of the one light, which in turn casts shadowy images for all the marine creatures on the sea bottom. For these creatures, the flitting underwater images constitute the reality of their world. They think that these dancing images are caused entirely by the motion of the water—their environment; but they are unaware of the sun as the hidden source of all this play of light and shadows in the water and on the seabed. (This allegory is none other than a recasting of Plato's legendary allegory of the cave. The ravages of sectarianism and, even worse, dogmatism leading to fundamentalism can all be alleviated through an understanding of the allegory—see Endnote III-6.)

How the glow of sunlight is dimmed

We can appreciate that at the seabed, the bright sunlight has been diffused and coruscated by three factors: (*a*) the intervening clouds and hazy atmosphere; (*b*) the choppy sea; and (*c*) refraction through the water. These are all to do with the various properties of water, which, since time immemorial, has symbolized the emotional nature.

The above scene from nature can be recast as a diagram for meditation on the inner human constitution as shown in Figure III-40 in the diagram to the right. It was originally proposed by the sage Ramana Maharshi and later adapted by his principal disciple Paul Brunton[83] (whose unique gift was to render the abstruse Eastern teachings intelligible to the Western psyche); and to which the writer has combined and added his own ideas. All the same, it is quite remarkable that this diagram, as originally proposed by Maharshi, should bear such a close resemblance to the Tabernacle of Moses shown in Figure III-39, page 251. But this should not surprise us at all. For it is yet another demonstration of the universality of symbolism in conveying what has been a constant theme of this work: the unity and self-consistency of the Eternal and Ageless Wisdom—from all quarters of the globe. It is therefore the writer's wish that such a powerful diagram finding its corroboration in sacred sources, both in the West and in the East, may constitute a useful diagram of meditation.

Let us imagine that electricity from a remote, invisible, generator powers a bright lamp, the light from which is transmitted to the four walls of an inner chamber. In one wall there is a partially open door through which only a fraction of the full and bright light passes into an adjacent antechamber to fall upon a dusty mirror affixed to a wall. This mirror then reflects the light outwards onto five dirty windows through which the rays are refracted towards an external veranda. Let us further suppose that the rays pass onwards through the narrow entrance of an adjoining shed (not shown in the diagram) and cast shadows on the wall of the shed. The inhabitants of the shed, rather like the inmates of Plato's cave (and the marine creatures in our sunset simile above), never having left the confines of their own world, mistake what they see for the objective reality of the world outside.

How the brilliance of physical light is reduced

The important point to note is that the original power and brilliance of the light has again been diminished by three factors, in this case by: (*a*) the partially open door; (*b*) dusty mirror; and (*c*) dirty windows.

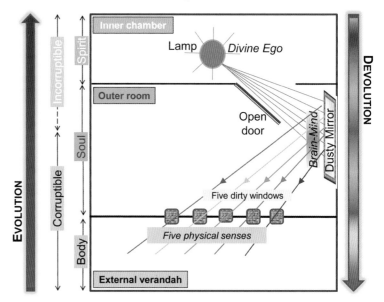

Figure III-40   Man, Know THYSELF – 'The God in the sun is the "I" in me'

Image Credit: https://all-free-download.com/free-photos/download/
sun_sunset_rays_236347_download.html

How the Divine Ego is clouded by the personality

How does this evoke from within us the super-physical truths about ourselves? Reading Figure III-40 as a whole in its symbolic sense of a map of our occult anatomy and referring to Table II-8 on page 46 in Volume II for the technical meaning of terms, we appreciate how the power and pristine luminosity of the Divine Ego (sun/lamp) has been thrice diminished and diffused by three factors: (*a*) the Lower mind, or brain-intellect (atmospheric haze/partly open door) identified with, therefore gravitating to (*b*) the emotions (rippling water/dusty mirror); and (*c*) the five gross physical senses (refraction in water/five dirty windows). The simile also shows how man's constitution can be considered as dual, triple, or septenary. The *Monad* (i.e., *Ātma-Buddhi* together with *Higher Manas*) is our immortal Individuality. Of the brilliant radiation from the Individuality, only a fraction is mirrored and reflected by the personality, i.e., a fraction of the radiation of the Divine Ego, its Spiritual light, is caught by *Kāma-manas*; and the physical body, animal in nature, with its five senses causes further obstruction to the original light. This movement outwards from the Source thus represents the process of devolution: the light of the Divine Ego is being progressively dimmed at each stage of descent to the physical plane. Hence, waking consciousness, which science almost without exception regards to be the highest state of consciousness, is in fact the lowest, for the light has been thrice removed from its Source. In this wise, it cannot be too strongly emphasized that the heart, and not the head (brain) is the seat of consciousness, as we realized in Chapter 3, page 41 et seq. The intellect lives by a borrowed light. Only in deep meditation when we close the shutters on the windows of senses, dispense with the mirror of the intellectual/emotional mind and close the door behind us to enter

How the radiance of spiritual light is darkened

the inner chamber do we become one with the pure light of the lamp itself—the state of undifferentiated Consciousness when Light as pure Consciousness is virtually the same as Consciousness as pure Light. Then it is directly realized that the Sun (Deity) cannot possibly be separated out from Its Rays (individual human beings)—that ultimately our inner nature, as indeed that of every creature and all creation, is of the Sun. This movement towards the Source—towards our true Home—therefore represents the process of evolution: the light of the Divine Ego being progressively uncovered at each stage of ascent from the physical plane. (Refer back to the brief exposition on Sun Force in Chapter 9 and its relation to *prāṇa*.)

The simile of the Tabernacle—whether in the desert or in our home—also shows why nature must always appear to Western science *in abscondito*, that is, as a kaleidoscopic mirage of largely inconsistent theories, because science chooses to restrict its scope to the outer room (i.e., the physical world) and so is conditioned by Kāma-manas (the union of the Lower mind and emotion[x]), and the five physical senses, which cause the pure and single ray of intuition from the Divine Ego, its Spiritual Light, to be split into multiple images (appearances) because of reflection and refraction by the personality. Conversely, in the inner sanctum (the inner chamber of our home in the symbolism of Figure III-40), nature is always seen, or rather experienced, *in actu* that is, in reality—the high ground of Occult Science.

Let us summarize this section by reverting to the quotation in the title to Figure III-40: 'The God in the sun is the "I" in me.' Without resorting to superficial mental concepts, it establishes the indissoluble relationship and connection between Cosmos, Nature, and man. The Individuality is the Higher Triad of man, his divine-spiritual-mental part; therefore immortal and deathless. The Individuality is the very essence of man, his inner god, the Spiritual Sun within. As the physical sun, mortal and temporal, is the outer, visible garb of the eternal God within—the Central Spiritual Sun, or 'the God in the sun'—so also, man's immortal inner essence—'the "I" '—dwells during the course of a lifetime 'in me'—its psycho-physical cloak, or the personality.

The State of Enlightenment and the Quality of Genius

How does the above provide a clue regarding enlightenment and genius? There is the old saying that we only use a fraction of our brains. In a popular sense it is true enough but strictly speaking, it is inaccurate. The true meaning is that we are overusing our brains! In the case of the ordinary man, the brain threshold is at such a (high) level so as to permit only a fraction of the Spiritual Light to penetrate into physical existence (the door being partly open and the windows dirty, referring to the simile depicted in Figure III-40). Paradoxically, then, as so carefully explained by William James (see Volume I, Chapter 6, page 170), the state of high creativity requires a lowering of the threshold of brain activity in order to minimize its obstruction to the light, i.e., minimize the impediment of the ego. However by appropriate self-effort (which does not mean egoistic striving), the brain can be made to reflect an increasing proportion of the light from its divine Source.

Let us invoke the Hermetic Axiom in order to understand this point. Of particular significance is the fact that moonlight, being light reflected from the sun, is greatly reduced

---

x Alas, the perfect ingredients for potential prejudice and bigotry.

Moonlight and 'brain-light' are both reflected lights, tremendously reduced in power compared to their source.

in brilliance. Just so, the light of the brain (intellect) is a reflected light borrowed from the Divine Ego—again much diminished in luminosity.

In astrology, the Moon, by it position and aspects to other planets in the horoscope, is an indicator of a man's brain quality, i.e., his intellectual–emotional nature. By contrast, the Sun in a horoscope indicates man's level of consciousness (his inner nature and heart quality)—a fraction of which Light is caught by the brain and thrown outwards into his physical nature. *It is not far-fetched , then, to suggest that the difference between the average man and the sage or genius is in direct proportion to the difference in brightness between moonlight and sunlight.*

Psychological insights from astrology

Broadly speaking, then, the Sun signifies Spirit (Being) and the Moon Soul (Life). Together with Mercury (Lower mind) and Jupiter (Higher Mind), they form a trinity of Being, Life, and Mind. The difference between the average man and the sage, or genius, is in direct proportion to the degree to which the soul has opened to the Light (Sun) of Ideas (Mercury-Jupiter) within and above himself and is able to manifest those in his life (Moon) through a form of service he chooses for himself. In Jungian terms, wholeness is individuation, the complete actualisation of potential, and the marriage of not only the Sun and Moon, but of all the planets into one glorious whole.

Hence, the entry into the inner sanctum, i.e., the unific ground of being and state of complete repose has everything to do with the *awakening* of genius. Why? Because in the inner sanctum, with the personality utterly quiescent (door shut), our consciousness is that of profound meditation, akin to the condition of deep, dreamless sleep. This is a state of Eternity, or timelessness, when we are closest to the light of the Divine Ego, the fountainhead of true genius. The intrusive sense of personality has been stilled so that the Divine Ego is now self-engrossed in Itself, in what the Bible poetically describes as 'God brooding on His face in the waters of the deep.'[84]

Genius conditioned by clarity and transmissivity of the personality

But we cannot dispense with the terrestrial personality if we are to express the Spiritual Light of the Divine Ego in the physical world. So, for this to happen, the timeless must be carried on the wings of time—the door has to open. This brings the reflective mirror into operation, whereupon the Light has come into contact with the Human Ego. *For the ordinary man, the brain intellect greatly diminishes the power that it now reflects, but for the sage and the adept whose vehicles are purified, the divine radiation passes through unhindered.*

To summarize, the outward movement from the inner chamber towards the external balcony (Figure III-40, page 254) comprises the devolutionary process whereby the radiance of man's essential nature—unalloyed consciousness—is progressively dimmed by virtue of being layered in coats of subtle bodies and, finally, his coat of skin. Conversely, by prayer and meditation, study and philanthropic service, man slowly sheds his outer layers of encumbrance as he evolves and hence unites with, and becomes one with, his own essential nature—consciousness. In such an exalted state he realizes, not through books or the mediation of intellect, but through direct experience—by reading the 'Book of Life', which each man writes for himself from moment to moment—the truth of the Vedic maxim, which is concerned with the highest principle in existence:

Saṃkaraḥ puruṣāḥ sarve striyāḥ sarvā Maheśvari

which, translated literally from Sanskrit into English means:

All men [expressions of] *Saṃkaraḥ* [Śiva] and all women [expressions of] *Maheśvari* [Śakti];[xi]

thus unequivocally asserting the Divine origin of mankind and indicating the essentially divine nature of the relation between the sexes.[86]

✢ ✢ ✢

Having reached the end of this admittedly complex Chapter on the contrasting viewpoints of science and occult science on evolution, and before opening the next Chapter comprising a summing up of the three Volumes of this work, readers are asked to decide for themselves which of the following quotes better portrays the splendour of man and his infinite evolution, growth, and refinement.

The first one is:

> *Our ancestor was an animal which breathed water, had a swim-bladder, a great swimming tail, an imperfect skull & undoubtedly was an hermaphrodite! Here is a pleasant genealogy for mankind.*
>
> Charles Darwin, Letter to C. Lyell, 10 January 1860[87]

The second quote, strongly echoing the quote by Franz Liszt[xii] in the epigraph, is a glowing example of personal evolution by one whose indomitable spirit triumphed over all constraints of matter, namely, his wretched health, dire physical circumstances, and the limitations of the piano stretched to new possibilities of expression:

> *There is no loftier mission than to approach the Godhead more nearly than other mortals and by means of that contact to spread the rays of the Godhead through the human race.*
>
> Ludwig van Beethoven, in a Letter of 1823[88]

But with what attitude of mind and heart shall this be done? As every saviour the world over has ever declared, for example in the words of the Christ:

> *Verily, verily, I say unto you, He that believeth on me, the works that I do shall he do also; and greater works than these shall he do; because I go unto my Father.*
>
> John 14:12, King James Version

And how shall this be done? Again, as all sages have counselled, for example in the words of Paul Brunton:

> *The truth needed for immediate and provisional use may be learned from books and teachers but the truth of the ultimate revelation can be learned only from and within oneself by meditation.*
>
> *In the end, as in the beginning, we have nothing else to do except obey the ancient command to LOOK WITHIN.*[89]

---

xi Śiva is pure, undifferentiated Divine Consciousness, the correlate of Śakti, Divine Power. See *The Snake and the Rope* for a full explanation of the meaning and significance of these terms.[85]

xii Liszt was an ardent admirer of Beethoven and did much to promulgate his music. It is a moving story of how the twelve year old Liszt played to Beethoven whereupon the Master planted a kiss on the forehead of the young boy—see Alan Walker, *Liszt* (London: Faber and Faber, 1971), 20.

NOTES

1 Liszt's response in writing to the first question put to him by Wilhelm Voigt, Master of the Lodge *Zur Einigkeit* [To Unity] in Frankfurt am Main in order to be initiated as an Apprentice Freemason (Masonic First Degree), 18 September 1841. See Anders Gabriel Sundström, 'Franz Liszt as Freemason', *The Liszt Society Journal*, 37 (2012), 3.

2 'Francis Bacon', *goodreads* <https://www.goodreads.com/quotes/218422> accessed 22 July 2020.

3 Alan Walker, *Franz Liszt: Volume Three – The Final Years, (1861–1886)* (Ithaca, New York: Cornell University Press, 1997), 455.

4 Stephen Hawking, 'Questioning the Universe', *TED Talk* (April 2008) <https://www.ted.com/speakers/stephen_hawking> accessed 2 April 2020.

5 Richard Dawkins, *The Blind Watchmaker* (UK: Norton & Company, 1986), ix–x.

6 *STA*, 'The Zodiac and its Signs', LVI.

7 Jalal al-Din Rumi, *The Masnavi, Book One*, trans. and introd. Jawid Mojaddedi (Kindle edn: Oxford University Press, 2004), xix.

8 Reynold A. Nicholson (trans. and ed.), *The Mathnawi* [*Masnavi*] *of Jalaluddin Rumi* (Lahore, Pakistan: Suhail Academy, 2011), in Dr Massoud Homayouni, *The Origins of Persian Gnosis*, trans. F. J. Stone (London: Mawlana Centre, 1992), 24.

9 *ibid.*

10 Lynn Margulis and René Fester (eds), *Symbiosis as a Source of Evolutionary Innovation Speciation and Morphogenesis* (Cambridge, Massachusetts: MIT Press, 1991).

11 *ibid.*

12 'Crust', *National Geographic Society* <https://www.nationalgeographic.org/encyclopedia/crust> accessed 2 April 2020.

13 'Deep Carbon Science', *Deep Carbon Observatory* <https://deepcarbon.net/index.php/dco/deep-carbon-science> accessed 8 June 2020.

14 'Life in Deep Earth Totals 15 to 23 Billion Tons of Carbon – Hundreds of Times More Than Humans', *Deep Carbon Observatory* (10 December 2018) <https://phys.org/news/2018-12-life-deep-earth-totals-billion.html> accessed 2 April 2020.

15 Merlin Sheldrake, *Entangled Life: How fungi make our worlds, change our minds & shape our future* (New York: Random House; Illustrated Edition, 2020).

16 *SD*-I, 'Stanza V: Fohat – The Child of the Septenary Hierarchies', 120.

17 *SD*-I, 'Summing Up', 277.

18 *IU*-I, 'The "Impassable Chasm"', 427.

19 Walter Russell, *The Secret of Light* (3rd edn, Swannanoa, Virginia: University of Science & Philosophy,1974), 148.

20 I. K. Taimni, *Man, God and the Universe* (Adyar, Madras, 1969; Wheaton, Illinois: Theosophical Publishing House, 1974), 186.

21 Dr Massoud Homayouni, *The Origins of Persian Gnosis*, 3, 16.

22 For a comphrehensive list of Mullā Ṣadrā's writings, see James Winston Morris, *The Wisdom of the Throne: An introduction to the philosophy of Mulla Sadra*, Princeton Library of Asian Translations (Princeton: Princeton University Press, 1981), 261 [Persistent Link http://hdl.handle.net/2345/4256] <https://dlib.bc.edu/islandora/object/bc-ir%3A100493/datastream/PDF/view> accessed 15 June 2020.

23 Dr Massoud Homayouni, *The Origins of Persian Gnosis*, 17.

24 Attributed to Jalāl ad-Dīn Muhammad Rūmī (1207–1273) or Lao Tzu (604BC–531BC).

25 Amit Goswami, *Creative Evolution: A physicist's resolution between Darwinism and intelligent design* (Wheaton, Illinois: Theosophical Publishing House, 2008).

26 William R. Corliss (compiler), *Biological Anomalies: Humans I, Humans II, Humans III – A Catalog of Biological Anomalies* (US: Sourcebook Project, 1992).

27 Ernst Haeckel, *The Pedigree of Man* (1874; London: Freethought Publishing Company, 1883), 73. Quoted also in *SD*-II, 'The Fossil Relics of Man and the Anthropoid Ape', 679.

28 Michael A. Cremo and Richard L. Thompson, *Forbidden Archeology: The hidden history of the human race* (Los Angeles, California: Bhaktivedanta Book Publishing, 1993).

29 Michael A. Cremo and Richard L. Thompson, *The Hidden History of the Human Race*: The condensed edition of *Forbidden Archeology* (Los Angeles, California: Bhaktivedanta Book Publishing, 1999).

30 —— *op. cit.*, 'Adverse Criticism from Establishment Scientists', opposite page i.

31 —— *op. cit.*, 267–80.

32 —— *op. cit.*, 118–20.

33 'The Meister Print', *Footprints in Stone* <http://www.footprintsinstone.com/the-footprints/meister-print> accessed 2 April 2020.

34 'Men's and Women's Adidas Footwear Sizing', *adidas* <http://www.adidas.co.uk/size-chart-size-shoes.html?> accessed 2 April 2020.

35 'The Meister Print'.

36 'The "Meister Print" – An Alleged Human Sandal Print from Utah', © *Glen J. Kuban*, 1998–2011, <http://paleo.cc/paluxy/meister.htm> accessed 2 April 2020. See also: <https://onlinelibrary.wiley.com/doi/10.1002/gea.3340090408> <http://www.ramtops.co.uk/> <http://www.badarchaeology.com/other-chronologies/forbidden-archeology/> accessed 13 December 2021.

37 Michael A. Cremo and Richard L. Thompson, *op. cit.*, 119.

38 —— *op. cit.*, 261–4.

39 Michael A. Cremo and Richard L. Thompson, *Forbidden Archeology*, 422–32.

40 *ibid.*

41 Michael A. Cremo and Richard L. Thompson, *The Hidden History of the Human Race*, 80-6.

42 *The Week*, 10 February 2018, 21.

43 E-mail correspondence from Michael Cremo, 18 January 2018.

44 Geoffrey Barborka, *The Divine Plan* (2nd edn, rev. and enl., Adyar, Madras: Theosophical Publishing House, 1964; repr. 1980), 6.

45 Edi D. Bilimoria, *The Snake and the Rope: Problems in Western science resolved by occult science* (Adyar, Madras: Theosophical Publishing House, 2006), 204.

46 'How Old is the Universe?', National Aeronautics and Space Administration (2012) <https://wmap.gsfc.nasa.gov/universe/uni_age.html> accessed 2 April 2020. See also 'Planck 2015 Results. XIII: Cosmological Parameters', Cornell University Library, 3 (17 June 2016) <https://arxiv.org/abs/1502.01589> accessed 2 April 2020.

47 Manly P. Hall, *Invisible Records of Thought and Action – A Practical Guide to Subtle Vibrations, their Causes & Effects* (Los Angeles: Philosophical Research Society, 1990).

48 John Barrow and Frank Tipler, *The Anthropic Cosmological Principle* (Oxford: Clarendon Press, 1986).

49 Michael A. Cremo, *Human Devolution: A Vedic alternative to Darwin's theory* (Los Angeles, California: Bhaktivedanta Book Trust, 2003).

50 Michael Cremo, 'Human Devolution: A Interview with Michael Cremo' (16 February 2012) <https://openrevolt.info/2012/02/16/devolution> accessed 2 April 2020.

51 *Adhyātma Rāmāyaṇa: The spiritual version of the Rama Saga* (original Sanskrit with English translation by Swami Tapasyananda) (Madras: India, Sri Ramakrishna Math, 1985). A highly readable version of the epic is by Channing Arnold, simplified by Marjorie Sykes, *The Story of the Ramayana* (Calcutta, Bombay, Madras: Orient Longmans, 1951).

52 *STA*, 'Fishes, Insects, Animals, Reptiles, and Birds – Part Two', XCII.

53 Alfred Russel Wallace, 'The Limits of Natural Selection as Applied to Man', final essay in *Contributions to the Theory of Natural Selection* (Cambridge: Cambridge University Press 1871), 365–6.

54 P. D. Mehta, *The Heart of Religion* (UK: Element Books, 1976), 106.

55 Martin J. Rees, *Just Six Number: The deep forces that shape the universe* (UK: Basic Books, 2000), 3–4.

56 See Edi D. Bilimoria, *The Snake and the Rope*, 210.

57 Neil A. Manson, 'Introduction to *God and Design*' <http://home.olemiss.edu/~namanson/G&Dintro.pdf> accessed 3 April 2020.

58 See Edi Bilimoria, 'The Scientific and Medical Network: GOD or MULTIVERSE – Review of Open Dialogue at Downing College, Cambridge on 24th November 2007', *Journal of the Scientific and Medical Network*, 97 (2008), 27–30.

59 B. J. Carr and M. J. Rees, 'The Anthropic Principle and the Structure of the Physical World', *Nature*, 278 (1979), 230.

60 B. J. Carr (ed.), *Universe or Multiverse?* (New York: Cambridge University Press, 2007).

61 John Barrow and Frank Tipler, *The Anthropic Cosmological Principle* (Oxford: Clarendon Press, 1986).

62 Brandon Carter , 'Large Number Coincidences and the Anthropic Principle in Cosmology', in *IAU Symposium 63: Confrontation of Cosmological Theories with Observational Data* (Dordrecht, Holland: Reidel), 291–8; republished, 'General Relativity and Gravitation', introd. George Ellis, *Springer Verlag*, 43/11 (November 2011), 3225–33.

63 B. J. Carr, 'Metacosmology and the Limits of Science', in M. Eckstein, M. Heller, and S. Szybka (eds), *Mathematical Structures of the Universe* (Kraków, Poland: Copernicus Center Press, 2014), 407–32.

64 Richard Gunton, 'Fine-tuning Arguments for the Existence of God: A shot in the foot?' in Neil Spurway (ed.), *Laws of Nature: Laws of God*, Proceedings of the Science and Religion Forum Conference, 2014 (UK: Cambridge Scholars Publishing, 2015), 185.

65 E-mail correspondence from David Lorimer, 7 March 2018.

66 Jeffrey Masson, *Beasts: What animals can teach us about the origins of good and evil* (New York: Bloomsbury, 2015), 48.

67 *ML*, Letter No. 90.

68 *SD*-I, 'Cyclic Evolution and Karma', 636–7.

69 David Loye, *Rediscovering Darwin: The rest of Darwin's theory and why we need it* (n.p., Romanes Press, 2018).

70 Charles Darwin, *The Descent of Man, and Selection in Relation to Sex* (London: John Murray, 1871), 82; [Darwin Online] <http://darwin-online.org.uk/content/frameset?itemID=F937.1&viewtype=text&pageseq=1> accessed 1 April 2020.

71 —— *op. cit.*, 95.

72 —— *op. cit.*, 106.

73 Richard Dawkins, *The Selfish Gene* (Oxford: Oxford University Press, 2006), 2.

74 August Weismann, *Studies in the Theory of Descent*, 2 vols (London: Forgotten Books, 2015).

75 *SD*-I, 'Stanza VII: The Parents of Man on Earth', 223 n.

76 *SD*-I, *op. cit.*, 224.

77 Marcel Proust, *In Search of Lost Time*, trans. C. K. Scott Moncrieff, ed. Richard Howard (New York: The Modern Library, Slp edn 2003), cited in <https://bhma.org/wp-content/uploads/2017/03/The-real-voyage-of-discovery-origin-of-Proust-Quote.pdf> accessed 3 April 2020.

78 Stephen Phillips, *The Mathematical Connection Between Religion and Science* (Eastbourne, UK: Anthony Rowe Publishing, 2009), 45–59.

79 *STA*, 'The Tabernacle in the Wilderness', CXXXIV–CXXXV.

80 Exodus 25, King James Version.

81 *STA*, 'The Tabernacle in the Wilderness', CXXXIV. See also: *The Works of Flavius Josephus*, trans. William Whiston (London: Routledge, 1892); 'Ten Books of the Antiquities of the Jews', in Flavius Josephus, *History of the Jews*, trans. William Whiston, ed. Alex. Murray, 20 vols (1544; London: Virtue, Spalding, and Company, 1874), ii, 497 et seq. [online facsimile] <https://www.google.co.uk/books/edition/History_of_the_Jews/iRR6kLnJG3gC?hl=en&gbpv=1&pg=PA479&printsec=frontcover> accessed 29 December 2020.

82 *NPB*-16, Part 1: *World-Mind in Individual Mind*, 'God is in Man', ¶1, 3.

83 Paul Brunton, *The Quest of the Overself* (1937; London: Rider, repr. 1986), 196–8.

84 Genesis, 1:2.

85 Edi D. Bilimoria, *The Snake and the Rope*, xvii, 123, 132–6.

86 I. K. Taimni, *Man, God and the Universe*, 245.

87 Frederick Burkhardt, Janet Browne, Duncan M. Porter, and Marsha Richmond (eds), *The Correspondence of Charles Darwin: Volume 8, 1860* (Cambridge University Press, 1993), cited in 'Darwin Correspondence Project' (University of Cambridge) <https://www.darwinproject.ac.uk/letter/DCP-LETT-2647.xml> accessed 3 April 2020.

88 Emily Anderson (ed.), *The Letters Of Beethoven*, 3 vols (London: Macmillan, 1961), Letter no. 1248.

89 *NPB*-4, Part 1: *Elementary Meditation*, 'Preparatory', ¶14, ¶7, 5.

11 Summary of the Theme – Consciousness is an ELEMENT

Between degrading superstition, and still more degrading brutal materialism, the white dove of truth has hardly room where to rest her weary unwelcome foot.

THE MAHÂ-CHOHAN'S LETTER[1]

Scepticism alone is a cheap and barren affair. Scepticism in a man who has come nearer to the truth than anyone before, and yet clearly recognises the narrow limits of his own mental construction, is great and fruitful, and does not reduce but doubles the value of the discoveries.

ERWIN SCHRÖDINGER[2]

You must first actually become wholly god-like and wholly beautiful if you intend to see god and Beauty.

PLOTINUS[3]

I much prefer the empire of the mind, and I regard it as the highest of all spiritual and worldly monarchies.

LUDWIG VAN BEETHOVEN[4]

SYNOPSIS

Chapter 11 comprises a summing up of the entire work in three sections. Referring to the epigraph, the whole purpose of the three volumes is to show where 'the white dove of truth' can 'rest her weary unwelcome foot'.

Starting with science, its role is highlighted in terms of its two sharply divergent facets: the first being its inestimable contribution in alleviating immense personal suffering and adding immeasurably to our physical life and existence, plus our understanding of the universe, nature, and the miraculous workings of the human body; the second concerning the hidden side of the universe, nature, and man that mainstream science struggles to understand, but provides no satisfactory answers. Sadly, this latter facet has contributed to progressive dehumanization through barren intellectual concepts and excessive technology, leaving modern man in search of a soul. This section closes with an exposition on the business of science, qualifying the reasons why the true scientific spirit is deemed a rare quality. Turning to the *philosophia perennis*—the binding thread of all science, religion, and philosophy in their origins—the principal attributes are highlighted, leading on to general precepts and fundamental propositions, the latter expressed in three ways: through the idiom of occult science, Western science, and esoteric philosophy. The Chapter closes with the resounding message of this work that answers the riddle of life: CONSCIOUSNESS is the primal ELEMENT. By now, the reader will be clear that all the manifestations of Consciousness are energetic forms on different planes of existence, and so all our joys and sorrows, dreams and attainments are experienced, by, in, and through CONSCIOUSNESS. This understanding leads naturally to a brief mention of destiny and purpose.

KEY WORDS: enlightened science, mainstream science, benefits and transgressions of science, value and drawback of scepticism, limitations of intellect, the scientific spirit of enquiry, true role of science, hallmarks of the true scientist, masks on truth, promissory materialism, attributes and precepts of the *philosophia perennis* as universal solvent, Hermetic Axiom, paradigm transformation, Consciousness an Element, mental health, spiritual crises, spiritual blessings, spiritual façades, destiny and purpose of man, David Bohm, Albert Einstein, Kahlil Gibran, J. Krishnamurti, Isaac Newton, Erwin Schrödinger, John Arthur Thomson, Steven Weinberg

M arc Kamionkowski (*b.*1965), the American Professor of Physics and Astronomy at Johns Hopkins University gleefully announces: 'It's not every day that you wake up and learn something new about the first trillionth of a trillionth of a trillionth of a second after the Big Bang. I don't think you need to be a cosmologist to think that's cool [in fact, unimaginably hot if we were allowed to replace a cliché with a cosmological theory].'5 But then, if we were, quite naturally, to ask: 'What came before the Big Bang?' 'No one from our collaboration is allowed to answer that,' says John Kovak (*b.*1970), the American Associate Professor of Astronomy and Physics at Harvard University and principal investigator of the BICEP2 telescope,6 measurements from which, announced on 17 March 2014, were thought to give support to the idea of primordial gravitational waves.7

Mainstream science conveniently side-steps deeper questions

It is completely beside the point that this supposed discovery of gravitational waves was seriously doubted by other scientists who maintained that the findings were in error due to the scattering effect of cosmic dust (and in fact gravitational waves were subsequently confirmed in 2016—see Chapter 6, page 85). What is of note is that remarks coming from the likes of Kamionkowski and Kovak are typical of the fascination of ideas as intellectual playthings amongst the majority of academic scientists, and the tremendous resistance they show about addressing deeper questions about the origins of life and the universe that could run the risk of veering from the strictly defined boundaries of physics into the forbidden domain of metaphysics. In fact, it would be hard to find a finer justification of H. P. Blavatsky's comment about the need:

> To enlarge the domain of physical science by trespassing on the forbidden grounds of metaphysics, so distasteful to some materialists. [...] For all their wonderful discoveries would go for nothing, and remain for ever *headless* bodies, unless they lift the veil of matter and strain their eyes to see *beyond* [...] and search within the unknown depths for the living and real entity, for its SUB-*stance*—the noumenon of evanescent matter.8

It is the writer's judgement that our understanding of the universe would be even more 'cool' for being better served if scientists crossed the Rubicon of micro-trillionths of a second and speculated constructively over metaphysical issues of origins and purpose, than by all the hubris and bravado over phenomena thought to occur at hair-splitting intervals after the supposed 'Big Bang' when matter is most certainly evanescent. We pointed out in Chapter 6 (in the section 'The Process of Cosmic Unfoldment') that everything we build on the Earth commences with thought, after which relevant details are worked out resulting in a finished product that conforms to the original idea. However, mainstream scientists, and cosmologists in particular, seem to be convinced that they can discover our cosmic origins by concentrating exclusively on physical processes—the final

Science virtually ignores profound insights from its own brightest lights

stage—but actively disdain any notion of Primordial Thought as the precursor to the manifestation of the universe. And this in the face of such legendary scientists as Sir James Jeans and Sir Arthur Eddington who have openly pronounced that the universe is of the nature of a Thought in a universal Mind rather than a great machine (see Volume I, Chapter 3, page 36).

It is precisely for these sorts of reasons that throughout this work we have made the point that the *philosophia perennis* (by whatever other similar names we may choose to call it, such as esotericism, or theosophy) concerns itself primarily with the evolution of consciousness; and only secondarily with the substance and objective forms derived from, and constituting, the vehicles of consciousness. That is why we opened this work by posing that most difficult of all questions—'Who, or What Am I?'—the answer to which—'Man, Know Thyself'—is worth each person's finest efforts, however unsatisfactory or perfunctory the actual enquiry may be. There can be few people at some stage in their lives, invariably in moments of distress or crisis, boredom or world-weariness, who do not ask questions like: 'What makes my life worth living; what happens after I die; why am I in such pain; what is the meaning behind all the cruelty and sorrow in the world; what place has love and joy in a world full of evil and injustice; what goals should I choose; do I have a place in the overall scheme of things, if indeed there be such a scheme; how can I discern what is true from what is false; what is knowledge; is everything I experience just a matter of luck, chance or coincidence; if there is supposed to be a loving God, then why am I unloved and suffering in loneliness?'

> *Can physical science, unaided, point man to 'know himself'?*

The above list of doleful self-questioning could be extended indefinitely but all questions are part and parcel of one big question, and they all coalesce towards a single, central problem: that there are times when a person feels either pinned down to a hard rock or like a feather blown around in the wind. We need not labour the point that the better we know ourselves—and thereby, our fellow beings and the world we live in—the more will our lives have purposeful energy and direction during adverse circumstances, and the more intelligently will we navigate the reefs and rocks of doubts and difficulties exemplified by the sorts of issues just raised. For that reason, the more important but less common question that few bother to ask of themselves is: '*Who* is asking the question?' Pondering over this issue may reveal the difference between who we truly are and who we think we are; in other words, the difference between our Self and our Self-image. And thereafter to the realization that the answers lie within each of us. Nonetheless, we have constantly emphasized that such Self-knowledge must be multi-levelled and integrated to involve all planes (dimensions) on which man lives and has his being. It is evident that a knowledge of physical man, obtained through science, is as indispensable to the understanding of man as the insights into his soul and spiritual nature revealed by the perennial philosophy: 'between the shores of the ego and the ocean of the soul there are many planes of consciousness.'9

> *Self enquiry must be on many levels*

Chapter 8 of Volume I presented in general terms the paradigms of science and the *philosophia perennis* in its particularized concentration as occult science. Their contrasting world-views, methodologies, and resultant strengths and drawbacks were summarized in Table I-2 on page 255. Having come this far in the work, it would be appropriate to focus on the implications of these two world-views *vis-à-vis* our central, interrelated themes of life, consciousness, and above all, self enquiry.

The Janus Faces of Science

The above heading has been chosen for good reason since, in ancient Rome, Janus was the god of beginnings, endings, and transitions. Janus is depicted with two heads, one looking forwards into the future, and the other looking backwards into the past. In order for science to unfold its full potential, it needs to look to both the future and the past, drawing upon all that has gone before in order to build a new and better informed world. In his book *Tertius Interveniens*,[10] the German astrologer, mathematician, and astronomer Johannes Kepler (1571–1630) exhorts us not to 'throw out the baby with the bath water'.[11] Although, it is undoubtedly true that mainstream science has become tainted by a nihilistic paradigm wholly foreign to its true nature, we need to peel back those accretions to reveal true science, simultaneously learning from our past mistakes and precluding the time and effort of reinventing the proverbial wheel. It is notable that Janus in himself combines both future and past and, therefore, in a sense, transcends both in the ever present Now. Enlightened science is in that same Now as it is able to unfold timeless truths applying them to the zeitgeist of the Age to the lasting benefit of mankind.

Learning from the past to embrace the future

Without this understanding of the 'dual embrace' in the unity of the Now, the Janus face turned to the past becomes enmeshed in outmoded thoughts and actions, a fearful submission to establishment authority and an inability to be receptive to new evidence. The face turned to the future becomes equally handicapped by failing to profit from the wisdom of the past resulting in past errors being repeated due to the same mindset that led to them.

The 'enlightened' Janus, outlined above, and the 'dark', pseudo Janus in which major areas of modern science have become immured, are best illustrated by way of two quotations, both from modern Nobel physicists: Albert Einstein and Steven Weinberg.

The Enlightened Janus Face of Science Embracing both Past and Future – The Indispensable Role of Science

> One thing I have learned in a long life was that all our Sciences, measured against Reality, are primitive and child-like—and yet it is the most precious thing we have.
>
> Albert Einstein[12]

By some supreme irony, it is science that has bestowed upon mankind a recognition of the need of what mystics have realized, but individually: unity, interconnection, and interdependence. It is science that, by its own discoveries, is now slowly transcending the materialistic philosophy of its own past (see the pronouncements by James Jeans, Arthur Eddington, and Karl Popper in Volume I, Chapter 3) and alluding to a world in the nature of a Universal Mind. Long ago, in 1705, Newton likened Earth to a *living* organism. The reader might like to recall to mind the quotation mentioned in Chapter 8, page 237 of Volume I:

> Thus this Earth resembles a great animall [...] draws in aethereall breath for its dayly refreshment & vitall ferment & transpires again wth gross exhalations;

which continues with

> This [aether] is the subtil spirit, this is Natures universall agent, her secret fire [...].
> The material soul of matter [...] being constantly inspired from above [...].[13]

This is gradually being borne out by enlightened science, again by its own methods and theories. The 'heat death' of a non-living universe[i] once confidently predicted is no longer a firm possibility since the universe is not regarded nowadays by many scientists as 'just a machine', subject to the laws of classical mechanics and thermodynamics, but as a living, breathing, and vital organism—a 'cosmic Gaia.' This paradigm transformation has come about through three broad avenues of science: (*a*) relativity theory; (*b*) quantum theory; and, recently, (*c*) the science of qualities. These three pillars of modern science have forced metaphysics into the domain of physics. As previously stated, despite being limited to the physical plane only, relativity in its essential idea of relations, rather than absolutes, has introduced the idea of the world as what, in the East, Gandhi called 'appearance', and the Hindus generally call *māyā* (mistranslated as merely 'illusion'); and what in the West was called by the German philosophers Johann Gottlieb Fichte (1762–1814) 'idea' and Arthur Schopenhauer (1788–1860) 'representation'. As described in Chapter 4 of Volume I, page 95 et seq., quantum physics has broken down, not only the entrenched concepts of classical (materialistic) physics, but the philosophical implications of the latter: that an intrinsic unity exists at a deep level of the universe, that what we call 'matter' is but a conglomeration of forces, and the interconnection of all parts of the universe. This has been shown by rigorous theory and punctilious, repeated experiments. Whereas the philosophical implications of the rarefied ideas of the latest physics have still to pervade the collective consciousness of mainstream science (especially in biology), which is firmly wedded to the classical paradigm, it can only be a matter of time before this happens. We can then be in no doubt that when the paradigm adopted by mainstream science changes from materialism toward holism, from objects and matter towards consciousness and mind, the media will (hopefully) swiftly report this radical change in outlook and the public understanding of science will be much elevated.

Modern science is gradually embracing metaphysics

This is already happening, albeit slowly. By its own methods, research, and discoveries, avant-garde science is now slowly transcending the materialist philosophy, presaging the threshold of a major spiritual revival and pointing towards a new meaning of a living world. Scientific studies of a range of spiritual practices reveal that they have remarkable benefits for health of mind and body, and give a greater sense of connection with a transcendent Reality (called the Universal One by Walter Russell), which goes above and beyond the confines of the ordinary human personality. Such practices include meditation and prayer, service and gratitude, rituals and pilgrimage that are now widely available to people of all religions, and to those who uphold no orthodox religion. This theme of spiritual practices relevant to a scientific age is in *Science and Spiritual Practices*[14] and *Ways to Go Beyond*,[15] two of the latest books by Rupert Sheldrake, an all-too-rare individual who effortlessly integrates cutting edge science with spiritual sensitivity and has the courage to promulgate his ideas dispassionately in stark contrast to the rhetoric and intemperate attacks upon him by his detractors (see Volume II, Chapter 7, pages 131–2).

Modern science is showing the interrelationship and unity of the universe and life

Science has also widened and elevated the consciousness of humanity by forcing a shift from the 'village mentality' to a global outlook. This has come through such factors as

---

i This is a condition postulated in which the universe will have attained a state such that temperature differences, or other processes, can no longer be exploited to perform work. Technically stated, this happens in the event that the universe eventually reaches thermodynamic equilibrium (maximum entropy) when there is no thermodynamic free energy available and hence there can be no processes that increase entropy.

international trading agreements, globalization of world markets, and high speed travel. Near instant communication between people, news reporting, and the ubiquitous Internet has 'shrunk' the world onto our computer screens. Such incredible facilities are the products of advanced technology—in turn the fruit of scientific materialism! Obviously, these science-driven opportunities have created massive problems in their wake—like damage to the ecosystem and electronic hacking—which science itself will have to sort out. Nonetheless, it is suggested that the recognition (if not yet the realization) of global brotherhood which currently exists primarily at the economic and material level, i.e., the physical level, is an unstoppable trend which will gradually flower in the fullness of time towards an understanding and a realization of the spiritual affinity amongst mankind and nations, and between man and nature.

Modern science has widened and elevated man's outlook and mentality

In essence, science has not only enlarged the sphere of its own disciplines, but assimilated the experiences of mystics. Scientism (in fact, a pseudoscience for the reasons given at the end of Volume I, Chapter 4, page 119 et seq.), which still has its head in the proverbial sand, may not be prepared to recognise this, but real Science recognized these experiences long ago because they validate the truth upon which they stand. This sea change in modern science has been possible because of the tremendous advances in neuroscience and brain mapping techniques that have clearly demonstrated the changes that occur in both brain state and brain structure during profound states of meditation (see Chapter 9, page 203). Hence, there is now concrete evidence demonstrating their enlightening and beneficial effects upon the practitioner. Indeed, Oneness, the deep interrelationship of life, and the dynamic nature of reality are factors that have *always* been the experience of advanced mystics, but they are now being confirmed by science, especially through the life sciences and ecology.

Mystically inclined scientists and scientifically trained mystics are our brightest hope for disseminating the Eternal Wisdom through a scientific idiom which will be a lasting boon to mankind.

So for all the above reasons and much else, science has in our era earned its respect, besides, in almost all cases, having gained the upper hand over other ways of knowing. It has rightfully earned its status by the great value and utility of its practical applications, as well as its methods, leading to results that are generally factual, repeatable and accurate. Let us think of a concrete example to illustrate the immense practical contribution of science (and scientific materialism, to wit) to humanity in contemporary society.

Serious industrial accidents are a fact of modern life, so let us consider a hypothetical case of a person who has suffered a head injury, or loss of limb, in such a mishap. Naturally, he and his family would do literally anything to restore at least some measure of his former health and mobility. Whereas religion might offer him solace in his darkest moments, and philosophy a measure of forbearance, would he turn to occult science to learn about the divine forces in the human body or follow someone claiming to have acquired 'secret powers' by revelation to restore life and limb? Or would he turn to science for medical assistance?

Man's indebtedness to modern science and medicine

Assuming the obvious, the next question is, why would he look to science for help? It would be because of the great merit of science that after decades of meticulous research, trials, and testing, its methods and procedures produce results that are reliable, definite, independently verifiable, under the same or similar set of conditions, and therefore predictable. Our unfortunate victim is not likely to turn away from science on the grounds that it is not spiritual, but only materialistic. In fact he would justifiably consider that many scientists, say his own doctor and surgeon, who espouse materialism have been driven to it by their sincere allegiance to truth (as they see it) and by their unimpeachable intellectual honesty—not because they are basically 'anti-spiritual', whatever that may mean. It is science that has poured cold water on past eras of superstition and mystery-mongering. Science has shown us that unless statements and knowledge can be verified, they may be true, but they cannot be regarded with certitude; therefore, there is security and safety in the methodical cultivation of theories based on observed facts, or independently verified experiments, as a guide to action. The evidence from industry, business, engineering, and technology speaks for itself. Accordingly, we round off this section by describing one of the most exciting developments from neuroscience and brain research: how thought can be used to control prosthesis. This topic is especially germane to the theme of this work.

For decades, neuroscientists have been working to develop prosthetic devices that are driven by brain signals. Most of this work has been focused on brain activity related to hand trajectory signals recorded from the motor cortex area of the brain, which governs movement. However, because so many movement-related areas of the cortex converge into this one pathway, a prosthetic device based on motor cortical signals might only be able to perform one task at a time. Moreover, this approach would not work if motor cortical pathways were damaged by injury or disease.

How cutting edge science and medicine have alleviated suffering

Scientists at the California Institute of Technology (Caltech) have taken an important step in the development of a strategy to use the higher level neural activity of the brain to drive a prosthetic device. Such a strategy would allow paralysed individuals to use their thoughts to move a device when unable to move their limbs. A new, innovative approach by the Caltech team relies on brain signals that initiate movement based on sensory input. This breakthrough was first conceived in the mid-1990s when the researchers discovered a visual area of the brain, known as the parietal reach region (PRR), in the parietal cortex of monkeys which was found to be involved in planning motor movements based on preferences and goals. The abstract, high level nature of the PRR precedes the lower level brain activity related to motor cortical control of hand movements. The PRR was then discovered in humans in 2003 by researchers from the University of Western Ontario. This discovery, and its cognitive function, led scientists to consider creating a neural interface that could decode signals from PRR brain waves, allowing people with paralysis to manipulate prosthetic limbs or robotic devices through their thoughts. For this to happen, an implantable, multi-electrode device, to connect a brain signal decoder to a computer cursor, was specially designed and manufactured.[16]

In 2015, engineers at the Johns Hopkins University Applied Physics Laboratory developed a next-generation prosthetic: a robotic arm that has twenty-six joints, and is controlled by thought, just like a regular arm. Intricate neurosurgery was needed to remap the remaining nerves from the missing arm, allowing brain signals to be sent to the prosthetic. The customized socket can pick up brain signals to control the arms, known as Modular Prosthetic Limbs, just by *thinking* about the movements. The device has successfully been used by a man aged fifty-nine years who lost both arms at his shoulders following an electrical accident decades earlier as a teenager.[17]

Notwithstanding any understandable reservations about experimenting on animals, none of these marvellous and inspiring discoveries, and associated technologies, could have accrued from any amount of understanding of the perennial philosophy or occult science. It is the painstaking and meticulous researches in neuroscience, with its understanding of brain functions and neural pathways, combined with cutting edge electronic and computer technology, that has offered immense hope to severely injured people and amputees. Apropos, this new avenue of thought-to-action research, and development using brain wave-sensing technology, is now being applied to emails actuated by thought alone—which would be a real boon if all thinking were concise and benign![18, 19]

All this and much more, far too numerous to mention, represent the triumph and altruistic application of materialistic science, its bright, upward looking face. Would that all of science progressed in this vein! However, we must also take a balanced and objective view of the dark, downward looking Face.

The Dark Face of Science – What Science Pretends to Know and Answer

> The more the universe seems comprehensible, the more it also seems pointless.
>
> Steven Weinberg[20]

Given that the purpose and point of the universe is an enormous question that has perplexed the finest minds since time immemorial and can hardly be answered adequately merely by an appeal to ratiocination, Weinberg's forthright assertion would surely have elicited this rejoinder from Erwin Schrödinger, quoted in Volume I, Introductory and which bears repeating:

> Science sometimes pretends to answer questions in these domains, but the answers are very often so silly that we are not inclined to take them seriously.[21]

Moreover, what would Schrödinger have to say about his peer Nobel physicist whose message to us on the final page of the Epilogue to his famous book on cosmology, *The First Three Minutes*, is the pointlessness of the universe as quoted above? And especially after Weinberg clarified his remark in his later book, *Dreams of a Final Theory* that he, 'did not mean that science teaches us that the universe is pointless, but rather that the universe itself suggests no point.'[22] In that ilk, gone are the days when we should proclaim with King David: 'The heavens declare the glory of God; and the firmament showeth His handiwork'[23] or rise to our feet upon hearing the majestic 'Hallelujah Chorus' from Handel's Messiah and sing, 'For the Lord God omnipotent reigneth [...]. The kingdom of this world; is become the kingdom of our Lord [...].'[ii] And why not? 'Since David's day', Weinberg informs us, ' the sun and other stars have lost their special status; we understand that they are spheres of glowing gas, held together by gravitation, and supported against collapse by pressure that is maintained by the heat rising up from thermonuclear reactions in the stars' cores. The stars tell us nothing more or less about the glory of God then do the stones on the ground around us.' Thus, the celestial orbs, like human bodies, and all

Establishment science continues to rob the universe, nature, and man of divinity

---

ii When he completed the Hallelujah Chorus, Handel reportedly told his servant, 'I did think I did see all Heaven before me, and the great God Himself seated on His throne, with His company of Angels'—see 'History of "Hallelujah" Chorus', The Tabernacle Choir (22 February 2016) <https://www.thetabernaclechoir.org/articles/history-of-handels-hallelujah-chorus.html> accessed 12 June 2020.

else, are supposed to be nothing more or less than matter and its interactions, ultimately explainable by physics and chemistry. Furthermore, 'If there were anything we could discover in nature that *would* [*sic*] give us some special insight into the handiwork of God, it would have to be the final laws of nature' because 'Knowing these laws, we would have in our possession the book of rules that governs stars and stones and everything else.' So for this reason Weinberg considers it natural that some physicists, like Stephen Hawking, refer to the laws of nature as the 'mind of God'. [24]

Are the stars, then, imbued with divinity, or they are just glowing fireballs? Both, as it depends on the eyes we are looking through. Like is only seen by like—beautifully encapsulated by Saint Paul:

Saint Paul discerns between the carnal eye and the eye of Spirit

> For they that are after the flesh do mind the things of the flesh; but they that are after the Spirit the things of the Spirit. [25]

> As it is written: 'God gave them a spirit of stupor, eyes that could not see and ears that could not hear, to this very day.' [26]

Whether we see matter or divinity depends on whether we look through the eyes of flesh or spirit.

Note, carefully, that we are not singling out Weinberg for special censure. We cite him, arbitrarily, as a typical example of the majority of celebrity scientists who uphold this unequivocal viewpoint, claiming to know the purposelessness of the universe and all existence. Another case in point is the Oxford professor of chemistry Peter Atkins who plainly informs us:

> We shall have gone the journey of all purposeless stardust, driven unwittingly by chaos, gloriously but aimlessly evolved into sentience, born unchoosingly into the world, unwillingly taken from it and inescapably returned to nothing. Such is life. [27]

Readers are reminded of Whitehead's nihilistic wisecrack, featured in the Proem in Volume I, page 1, about 'scientists animated by the purpose of proving that they [and the universe] are purposeless'. How has this cynical attitude come about? As so cogently expressed by Vasileios Basios (*b.*1962), the Greek physicist specializing in chaos and complexity, and the physics of complex systems, working within the team of the Russian Nobel physicist Ilya Prigogine at the University of Brussels, this stance is 'greatly aided by the idea of matter as a machine, a prevailing worldview of meaningless atoms in the void, mechanically and haphazardly evolving to become brains excreting consciousness as a by-product, an epiphenomenon of blind evolution.' [28] In that case, as Basios further remarks:

> Are we just useful parts of a purposeless machine operating in the midst of randomness? [29]

Does mainstream science recognize its own boundaries?

Indeed we are, according to many internationally famous scientists as just cited. It appears, then, that science has created its own prison—but science has also created the key to unlock it. So it boils down, then, to science appreciating its legitimate playing field, which necessarily means working within its boundaries and context. In this wise, science reigns supreme in its understanding of physical mechanisms and behaviour, whether of the body of man, or the body (shell) of the universe, i.e., the visible and objective universe; but any attempt to understand the destiny of man, or the purpose of cosmos, will invariably prove unsatisfactory without a concomitant understanding of the nature of Mind. This is because the universe of so-called matter is of the essential nature of Mind, as we have explained at length in Chapter 8 and elsewhere in this work. (See the Mathematical Codicil on page 349.)

How do these celebrity scientists view religion and philosophy? Again citing Weinberg arbitrarily as a representative example, in an address at the Conference on Cosmic Design, he claimed that, 'Religion is an insult to human dignity' justified on the grounds that, 'With or without it you would have good people doing good things and evil people doing evil things. But for good people to do evil things, that takes religion.'[30] In a subsequent article, based on his address, he upheld his opinion in which the same words by citing arguments from the scriptures that were used in the English Parliament to defend the slave trade: 'With or without religion, good people can behave well and bad people can do evil; but for good people to do evil—that takes religion.'[31] And regarding religious experience, whereas this can be 'deeply satisfying' and 'can suggest a meaning for our lives' as well as holding out 'a promise of some continuation after death', in contrast to the 'abstract and impersonal worldview gained from scientific investigation', yet, 'For just these reasons, the lessons of religious experience seem to me [Weinberg] indelibly marked with the stamp of wishful thinking.'[32] Apart from a few notable exceptions, 'Most physicists today', so Weinberg informs us, 'are not sufficiently interested in religion even to qualify as practicing atheists.'[33] It may be impolite to point out to a great scientist that what may also be 'indelibly marked with the stamp of wishful thinking' is the olive branch of promissory materialism with its 'abstract and impersonal worldview' that provides a materialistic bunker to protect the scientific status quo against the uncomfortable need to face up to the deeper questions of life and 'continuation after death', unanswerable by science, so swept aside and explained away *en masse* using thoroughly subjective terms like 'wishful thinking'.

In a substantial Chapter, ironically entitled 'Against Philosophy', Weinberg's treatment of the subject seems to be ambivalent.[34] He does acknowledge that, 'Physicists do of course carry around with them a working philosophy. For most of us, it is a rough-and-ready realism, a belief in the objective reality of the ingredients of our scientific theories. But this has been learned through the experience of scientific research and rarely from the teachings of philosophers.'[35] He addresses a phenomenon he decides to call 'the unreasonable ineffectiveness of philosophy' that 'even where philosophical doctrines have in the past been useful to scientists, they have generally lingered on too long, becoming of more harm than ever they were of use.'[36] He quite correctly cites the example of 'mechanism'; that in the history of human thought the mechanical world-view has played a heroic role (see Volume I, Chapter 3, page 51 et seq. for a précis on the historical basis of materialism). But mechanism has now 'propagated beyond the boundaries of science' and 'although after Einstein there was no place in serious physics research for the old and naïve mechanical worldview, some elements of this view were retained in the physics of the first half of the twentieth century [and well beyond],' despite the fact that 'in 1929 physics began to turn towards a more unified worldview.'[37] So it seems that whereas Weinberg (quite rightly) does not uphold a 'mechanical world-view' he certainly espouses a mechanistic paradigm—the universe and its contents are physical matter so best understood through physics and chemistry.

He does not eschew the need to examine metaphysical presuppositions. However, he sees the service of philosophy as invariably a negative one in that 'it helped only to free science from the constraints of philosophy itself'; for example, the influence of philosophers like Voltaire and Kant who upheld the old Cartesian (mechanical) philosophy that all phenomena could be reduced to the impact of material bodies or fluids on one another

The conventional scientific opinion on religion

The established scientific regard for philosophy

(and who are therefore unable to explain the gravitational force between bodies separated by 'empty' space).

Ultimately, though, we must honour and accept a world without a divine principle and, on the basis of the best ideas in physics, that the universe 'seems pointless', as quoted and referenced above. Given that Weinberg has ignored the best ideas in philosophy and religion, arbitrarily confined his enquiry entirely to materialistic concepts which *do not represent the best ideas in modern physics*, and disregarded the metaphysical dimension of that subject for which he was awarded the Nobel Prize—quantum physics, which points to the primacy of consciousness—his message of bleak despair should hardly surprise us. It is a perfect example of the airless cul-de-sac of materialistic science grappling with concepts completely beyond its ken. Never more so than over questions of Divinity where Weinberg complains that, 'The more we refine our understanding of God to make the concept plausible, the more it seems pointless.'[38] This is a clear example of a lack of appreciation of the worth of philosophy. Scattered throughout the pages of these Volumes, the writer has adduced much evidence from the *philosophia perennis* that all intellectual speculation on Deity is impossible since it is beyond the range and reach of thought and therefore transcends the power of human conception and could only be dwarfed by any human expression or similitude.[39] Perhaps Weinberg has not heeded the wise words of his fellow American Ralph Waldo Emerson who eloquently argued, in his classic essay 'The Over-Soul', that such matters as deity and soul can never, ultimately, be understood through language and definitions, but known, rather experienced, only by following the path of moral actions—see Volume I, Chapter 9, page 293 f. Stated otherwise, man does not know deity by logic or by reason but rather by realizing the divine presence within himself. The founders of the world's great religions did not work to a set plan or timetable. Responding spontaneously to humanity's needs, their message, however voiced in many tongues, was always the same—to lead man from the conditioned towards the unconditioned state—from bondage towards freedom from the burden of conformity to the past. Clearly, atheists, like Weinberg and his peers, who purport to have no belief or knowledge of God and His Aspects, the gods, are ill equipped to comment on such subjects—after all, is not like only knowable to like? That said, anyone who purports to be an atheist is hoisted by their own petard, as in order to deny anything one has to have recognised it, on some level.

The laws of nature are impersonal but not cold or heartless

How science is constrained by its underlying metaphysic

By contrast, however, we affirm, on the collective basis of the finest science wedded to sacred scripture, esoteric philosophy, and occult science, that the more the universe becomes comprehensible, and the more we apprehend the inner nature of man, the more does the majestic cosmic drama and all of its creations and creatures, including man, display teleology, godliness, and Consciousness—and become supremely meaningful. Let another celebrated atheist physicist have the last word on this matter:

The White Light of Truth cannot be perceived through the lens of science alone: only through the convergence of science, religion, and philosophy. High intellect is no guarantee of elevated spirituality.

> I think I would say that the universe has a purpose, it's not somehow just there by chance.
>
> Roger Penrose[40]

The Black Arts Dissembling under the Guise of Scientific Progress

As Manly Hall so astutely points out, scientists conveniently forget that although the demonism of the Middle Ages, which they take such delight in scorning, seems to have disappeared, there is abundant evidence that the black arts, or *'black magic has merely passed through a metamorphosis, and although its name be changed its nature remains the same* [emphasis added].' Witness the many forms of so-called 'prosperity thought', 'will-power building', high-pressure salesmanship.[41] (Bearing in mind that Hall penned his remarks in the 1920s, one shudders to think of what he would have said about much of the contemporary scene in science as in the remainder of this paragraph.) Add to that, the abuse of nuclear energy. Then, the ghastly experiments on animals and the abuse and wholesale slaughter of animals to fuel human greed by boosting food production, especially during national holidays like Christmas and Thanksgiving in the United States. Apropos, turkeys are a favourite dish during festive seasons. Thanksgiving (founded, incidentally, as a religious observance for all the members of the community to give thanks to God for a common purpose) is also colloquially known as 'Turkey Day'—and for good reason. The National Turkey Federation, estimates that of the more than 200 million turkeys consumed in the US in 2015, nearly 50 million of them were eaten on Thanksgiving;[42] and in 2016 an estimated 276 million Americans spent around $1.05 billion on the festive poultry.[43] The 'Broad Breasted White' is commercially the most widely used breed of domesticated turkey but as the males are incapable of mating, the factory-farmed female turkeys are forcibly inseminated in a revolting manner that we prefer not to describe.[44]

'Mediæval
demonism'
aplenty
nowadays—
the spectre
underlying
technologies
without ethics

Next, abnormal genetic engineering like producing a mouse from two female parents;[45] xenotransplantation (the process of grafting, or transplanting organs or tissues, between members of different species) such as baboons recently given transplanted, gene-edited hearts from pigs and the eventual hope to transplant similar genetically modified pig organs into humans;[46] a human head transplant on a corpse with an operation on a live human allegedly set to take place imminently;[47] the transhumanism and cryonics movements (see the Epilogue), and the latest exemplar—internet radicalization by religious fanatics (the faith is irrelevant) … and the repellent list of black arts in the guise of modern science and using modern scientific technology *unethically* seems depressingly endless.

Still on the question of vivisection, arguably for genuine medical research, is there any moral justification in experimenting on animals to appease human vanity? Earlier we cited the wonderful work done at Johns Hopkins University where a man who lost both his arms in an accident was able to control a prosthetic robotic arm simply by thinking about the movements. But without strict ethical controls this line of research can all too easily transform into dark practices. A good case in point is Elon Musk, who said in an interview that a monkey has been wired up to play video games with its mind using technology devised by Neuralink, a company he founded, headquartered in San Francisco. A computer chip was inserted into the monkey's skull and 'tiny wires' were used to connect it to its brain. 'It's not an unhappy monkey,' said Musk during a talk on Clubhouse, a new social media app.

Neuralink is now trying to figure out if it can use its chips to get monkeys to play 'mind Pong' with each other. The next step for Neuralink's team of around one hundred people is trying to develop an implementable computer-brain interface, the avowed aim being *to increase the rate at which information can flow from the human brain to a machine.*[48]

We are entitled to ask, however: who granted Elon Musk the 'divine' right to use a monkey as his 'scientific plaything'; besides, what is his yardstick for evaluating the happiness of a monkey?

The Spiritual Crisis of Modern Man in Search and Reclamation of a Soul

Modern science has bequeathed humanity with precious gems—for which humanity has had to pay a terrible price. On the one hand science has been instrumental in alleviating untold poverty and physical suffering and has given us living conditions, medicines, hygiene, and transport undreamt of a few centuries ago. Anyone who visits his dentist for a tooth extraction—let alone undergoes major surgery—should fall on his knees in gratitude for the discovery and skilful use of anaesthetics. So also do we owe an enormous debt of gratitude to neuroscience and brain surgery, as described above. What better additional example to cite than the novel surgery performed on a violinist diagnosed with a brain tumour located in the right frontal lobe of her brain, close to an area that controls the fine movement of her left hand? Understandably concerned over losing the ability to perform, she played the violin during the operation so that surgeons could ensure parts of the brain which control hand movements and co-ordination were not damaged during the millimetre-precise procedure.[49]

Indebtedness of modern society to science

But on the other hand the price extracted has been, arguably, even worse than the legacy of modern weapons of mass destruction, man-made ecological disasters, or the assault upon nature and the countryside—under the guise of civilization. And that price is the *spiritual* crisis of modern man; the suffering and poverty of his soul; his impersonalized and dehumanized (if not quite yet, 'inhumanized') existence aided and abetted by the alarming increase in artificial intelligence devices; his feeling of social isolation and dislocation (greatly exacerbated by the COVID-19 pandemic in 2020); his feeling that he is merely a utilitarian cog in a giant economic power machine; the treadmill and drudgery of his daily existence. All this, and more, through the dead hand of entrenched materialism feeding him with the numbing idea that we human beings are *merely* animals, and that both humans and animals are, in the final analysis, *just* complex biological machines and nothing else. In this wise, the English philosopher Nicholas Maxwell (*b*. 1937) has devoted much of his working life to arguing that there is an urgent need to bring about a revolution in academia so as to promote wisdom and not just acquire and accumulate knowledge.[50] This revolution in education is also a principal theme of *Harmony: A new way of looking at our world* by Charles, HRH The Prince of Wales.[51] The whole issue is compounded by the problems caused by excessive use, and misuse, of the Internet—short attention span, hyper-consumerism, and spectacularly, shallow or lewd entertainment.

Price paid by modern society for gifts of scientific and medical technology

According to the *National Review (New York)*, some 27% of Americans live alone nowadays, compared to 13% in 1960; and a 2010 survey showed that a third of adults were chronically lonely, compared to 20% in 2000. The same article states that white Americans are dying not just of heart disease or cancer, but of diseases that imply a *'sickness of spirit as much as of body—suicide, drug overdoses, and cirrhosis of the liver* [emphasis added].'[52]

In Britain, the statistics are equally depressing. This is what the contemporary British award-winning physician and consultant in integrated medicine Dr Kim Jobst calls 'diseases of meaning', in other words, that disease ought to be seen as a meaningful state that can inform

How our age of
scientific
technology
divorces man
from his soul

health workers how to help patients to heal themselves. In this way, instead of being regarded as meaningless, individual problems become *diseases of meaning*, enabling people to move away from a victim mentality towards a state of empowerment by seeing that things are not necessarily 'going wrong' but are, in fact, helping them become stronger, to live more fully and with more understanding.[53] Data compiled for the BBC by NHS Digital showed that between 2011–12 and 2015–16 the number of patients with psychiatric problems who attended accident and emergency units rose by nearly 50% to 165,000. Young people are especially vulnerable; for example, for the under eighteens alone, the numbers almost doubled to nearly 22,000.[54] Then, at the Tory Conference in 2017, Sir Paul Coleridge (*b.*1949), the retired English High Court judge and Chairman of the Marriage Foundation, spoke about the 'river of human misery' that he had seen during his career. He was not referring to such matters as economic privation or drug abuse, but to the high rate of family breakdown in Britain. Across the Developed World, only America fares worse than Britain. In 2014, 70% of British children were living with two parents, compared with the Organization for Economic Co-operation and Development average of 82%. The Marriage Foundation estimates that, on the basis of such trends, nearly half of all children born in Britain in 2017 will have experienced a family break up by the age of fifteen.[55]

The plight of young people is now a matter of increasing concern. A recent survey found that a quarter of girls and one in ten boys were self-harming. Furthermore, a report in the British Medical Journal found that self-harm among adolescent girls in the UK has risen disproportionately by 68% in just over three years; moreover, that those young people who self-harmed were at significantly increased risk of committing suicide.[56] *Yet these distressed teenagers are not exactly poverty-stricken and seem fully capable of indulging their every technological and electronic whim via their smartphones, iPads, and such like.* But under the strain of coping in the excessively pressurized times now prevailing (driven largely by social media), life for many of them (but by no means all) has become meaningless. Science policy-makers need to act to counteract the increasing dehumanization and spiritual starvation in society through excessive materialism.

There are obviously many complex factors involved. However, two points need to be made. First, all external factors, such as social and economic problems, job prospects, and family breakdowns, are underpinned by the prevailing paradigm. *Materialism at the expense of spirituality has been the cause of the majority of these problems; however, materialistic solutions are sought in order to resolve them when, in fact, they should be employed the least.* Einstein perspicaciously observed that problems cannot be solved at the level at which they are generated. Hence, debates on never-ending problems in science and society tend to generate much heat but little light. But they are effectively resolved and dissolved through the Eternal Wisdom Tradition—their universal solvent.

Distinguish
communication
from communion

Secondly, the marvels of science and technology that have enabled practically instant communication through social media, e-mails, Twitter, etc., have not cured but, in some cases, exacerbated the problem of loneliness; nor enabled man to be at peace with himself, and therefore with others. It seems that increasing access to the technology of communication has resulted in a proportionate decline in true communication, or rather, communion—from heart to heart.

One can, of course, argue about the accuracy of the above statistics, but not about the fact of an alarming, general increase in mental illness or 'sickness of soul' over the long term, especially during the loneliness induced by the lockdowns imposed during the COVID-19 pandemic. There seems to be no shortage of psychologists and psychiatrists in the West, especially in America pronouncing on mental wellbeing and happiness. But, in the opinion of this writer, they have not achieved other than limited success in general, with notable exceptions,[iii] because their focus is almost exclusively based on the brain. Latest in the line of such experts pontificating in a cure for unhappiness is, as a typical example, the Welsh neuroscientist, author and comedian Dean Burnett (*b. circa* 1986) who expounded his views in a lecture at the Royal Institution of Great Britain focusing on why the modern world affects the human *brain*, leading to so many mental health issues.[57] Recall the observations of the great psychiatrist and reincarnation researcher Ian Stevenson quoted in Volume I, Chapter 4, page 102, that developments in neuroscience have greatly advanced with the infusion of funds it received during the current 'decade of the brain'. However, he remains sceptical that the reductionist approach of nearly all neuroscientists will contribute to understanding the mind-body problem. Thus, he looks forward eagerly to the 'decade of the mind'.

> Can socio-economic palliatives alleviate spiritual malaise?

Given that the predominant model of the mind is materialistic, no wonder, then, that it is ill-equipped to understand, or heal, sickness and yearnings of soul, what, as we have previously stated, Carl Jung so aptly referred to as 'homesickness'.[58] Is it surprising then that the words and the melody of the song 'Home, Sweet Home' have exerted such a powerful appeal to millions for virtually two centuries—an irresistible musical evocation even when at home, to return HOME?[iv] Small wonder, also, that two seminal books by visionaries of the last century were aptly titled *Modern Man in Search of a Soul*[59] and in similar vein, *The Spiritual Crisis of Man*,[60] the first by Carl Jung and the second by Paul Brunton.

Although man expresses outwardly through a physical body that displays the characteristics of mechanical behaviour, he is spiritual in his inner nature; so it is a grave mistake to conclude, as mainstream science and psychology do, that man is therefore nothing more than a higher form of animal or just a bio-physical machine.

This is why we have headed this overall section as 'The Janus Faces of Science'. Thus, there is an inevitable tension caused by the two opposing Faces of science: the one gazing ever onwards and upwards seeking a loftier standpoint; and the other staring backwards and downwards steeped in materialism. This tension is not caused by errors in methodology but is inherent within the contrasting world-views of the opposing Janus Faces themselves.

The main diagnosis of this problem is that the 'emissary' has usurped the role rightfully belonging to his 'master'. It has been assumed that cold intellect represents the zenith of human mental capacity, whereas spirituality has been allowed to fall and wither by the wayside. Accordingly, intellect, or rather 'intellectualism', has been artificially elevated to a position of ultimate authority and is supposed to be able to deal with problems and phenomena that actually lie completely outside and beyond its legitimate boundaries and limited influence; hence, the answers supplied are 'so silly that we are not inclined to take them seriously' as Schrödinger observed. This matter has been dealt with at length in Volume II, Chapter 7 with

---

iii The exceptions shine out, almost in relief, against the flat background of the materialist. All such men and women necessarily embrace a spiritual perspective. We name Peter Fenwick, the neuropsychiatrist, neurophysiologist, and President Emeritus of the Scientific and Medical Network from 1986 to 2020, as one such exception.

iv The melody to 'Home, Sweet Home' was by the English composer Sir Henry Bishop (1786–1855) with lyrics by the American poet and playwright John Howard Payne (1791–1852).

reference to the work of Iain McGilchrist, the neuropsychiatrist and author of the best-selling book *The Master and his Emissary*. McGilchrist further pronounces:

> The science establishment makes unscientific assumptions, an inconsistency ignored by the mainstream who assume that they make no assumptions. To take one example, there is no single shred of evidence that matter gives rise to consciousness, and some reason from contemporary physics to believe that consciousness is prior to matter.[61]

To take another example of 'unscientific assumptions', reductionism is an essential methodological technique to understand and learn about the components of systems; but the assumption that it is entirely sufficient for a complete understanding is untenable.

Bracketed with the above, Martin Rees, who previously held positions of President of the Royal Society and Master of Trinity College, Cambridge, declares in his aptly titled article 'Beyond the Laboratory':

> [A] common perception of scientists is that they all follow a distinctive procedure, which is described as the 'scientific method'. This belief should be downplayed. It would be truer to say that scientists follow the same rational style of reasoning as (for instance) lawyers or detectives in categorising phenomena, forming hypotheses and testing evidence. A related and damaging misperception is the mindset that supposes that there is something especially 'elite' about the quality of their thought. Academic ability is one facet of the far wider concept of intellectual ability possessed in equal measure by the best journalists, lawyers, engineers and politicians.[62]

The prognosis, alluded to by Martin Rees, lies in the simple realization that a misuse or an over-canalized application of intellect starves intuition, deserts human values, and abandons plain common sense.

'The truth is not against intellect but above it, not opposed to thought but beyond it.'[63]

This does mean that the confirmed materialist who investigates innumerable natural processes empirically does not marvel at the seeming intelligence and order that seem to underlie these processes; but he stops short at this point and desists from asking the next logical question: why? Hence, he is unable to comprehend the inner significance of the process and so pronounces the universe to be intrinsically pointless and purposeless. By contrast, occultism throws light on the inner driving and guiding forces and intelligence which underlie all natural processes and phenomena and thus makes our conception much more meaningful and richer, albeit sometimes lacking the detailed and technical information forming part of scientific knowledge. Therefore, establishment scientists may strain every nerve and muscle and invest vast sums of research money in their efforts to wrest the secrets of consciousness from Nature. But they will never achieve their intended goal until they learn that Nature will never divulge her innermost secrets to those who bang loudly at the door that bars the sacred arcana of truth from the profane.

No scientist worth his salt would disagree that in order to learn about science one must first qualify oneself to receive due instruction. Using exactly the same reasoning we affirm that the secrets of life, mind, and consciousness will become an open book whose letters can be read without effort, only to those who qualify themselves in terms of joyful self-sacrifice, deep humility, a spotless morality, reverence for nature, and a philanthropic outlook. And all that allied to a profound study of the perennial wisdom balanced with experiments, not in a laboratory with hapless, suffering creatures, but in the 'laboratory of the mind', by reading the 'Book of his own life'. With rare exceptions, this is undeniably a tall order for most people; however, those who measure up to it are the sages and adepts and they are indeed a rare breed since they epitomize the efflorescence of the finest attributes of humanity. Nonetheless, there is no law that forbids anyone sincerely aspiring towards such an ideal. Therefore, we say that those scientists, still much in the minority, who strive very sensibly to enlarge the domain of physical science by trespassing on the forbidden grounds of mysticism and metaphysics—still so unacceptable to the majority of materialists—are the pioneers of our generation because, having studied physical nature in depth and detail, these enlightened scientists have sensed that their wonderful discoveries will remain largely misused and ungoverned unless they cross into the domain of occult science and lift the veil of physical matter to see beyond and search for its noumenon.[64]

Metaphysically minded scientists are the torch bearers of science

Such scientific pioneers represent the bright face of science as their work is in complete alignment with the oft quoted occult maxim:

> Modern science is our best ally,

whilst those scientists whose work unwittingly, or otherwise, represents the dark face of science typify the rarely mentioned, and equally significant, phrase which follows:

> Yet it is generally that same science which is made the weapon to break our heads with;[65]

the word 'our' referring of course to those sages and adepts who strive to enlighten humanity by disseminating relevant portions of the perennial philosophy and occult science furnished, where appropriate, with evidence from its best ally, modern science.

Science through the Looking-Glass – A Wide-Ranging Perspective on Science

Occult science attaches great importance and value to the methods and discoveries of modern science. This much should be clear by now. But given the current scientific imperative over virtually all other ways of acquiring knowledge of the world, nature, and human beings, allied to its role invariably taken as the universal panacea for all kinds of problems, it may not be disrespectful at this stage to point out a few things that seem to be taken for granted without further questioning.

The True Business of Science

'Promissory materialism' is a form of philosophical monism espoused by many scientists, including the more high profile ones, such as Richard Dawkins and Peter Atkins. It holds that matter is the fundamental substance in nature and that scientific materialism will therefore eventually explain everything, literally everything—including consciousness, mind, subjective feelings, and all human experience—purely in terms of physics and chemistry. Does science, even now, *explain* anything, even in the physical world?

Science neither creates nor explains anything: it only observes, discovers, and then describes physical nature, formulating the laws governing the latter. Science is not the invention or creation of scientists and as Schrödinger pointed out, 'we do not belong to this material world that science constructs for us' (see the full quote in the Introductory to Volume I, page lxi). Truly staggering as are its discoveries, they are just that—discoveries—and their applications. Scientists have neither designed, nor created, nor produced anything original in the universe—definitely not the human body, the elements, or the stars—and not even the universe. Nor have they invented or created or explained the laws of physics and chemistry—only discovered them and then applied them in what is known as applied science, or technology. For example the Swiss mathematician and physicist Daniel Bernoulli FRS (1700–1782) discovered that the pressure of a fluid (liquid or gas) decreases at those locations where the speed of the fluid increases. This discovery (together with Newton's third law of motion) was applied by future scientists to glorious effect as in aerofoil design to provide lift to the wings of an aeroplane. The fluid law was not created, or even explained, only formulated, by Bernoulli in 1738 (Bernoulli's equation[66]), notwithstanding the marvellous technological applications of the *discovery* of the law and its formulation. Likewise, neither did Darwin create his much-vaunted natural selection; it existed before Darwin (and Wallace) discovered it. Likewise, gravity existed before Newton discovered its action; nor did he create the laws of gravity whose cause he openly and humbly professed not to know:

Science has neither created nor explained anything

> You sometimes speak of gravity as essential and inherent to matter. Pray do not ascribe that notion to me, for the cause of gravity is what I do not pretend to know, and therefore would take more time to consider of it.[67]

The fluid law, natural selection, gravity, etc. did not suddenly materialize or become operative all of a sudden upon their discovery. They have existed and been in operation by nature for aeons. Birds were flying before Benoulli formulated his equation.

In *Introduction to Science*, the Scottish naturalist Sir John Arthur Thomson, Fellow of the Royal Society of Edinburgh (1861–1933), who sought to reconcile science and religion does not mince his words. He says: 'The vulgar belief that Science has "explained everything" is a hopeless misunderstanding', and that 'it would be nearer the truth to say that Science has explained nothing.' Nearly a century after Thomson penned those words in an age of extreme materialism, we could rephrase his observations less forcefully by remarking that, in a limited sense, science explains things by reducing complex systems to simpler units and by relating the observed facts to a general formula or equation. But as Thomson again observes, 'in this sense only does science explain things, and it does not really get beyond a description.'[68] In his Gifford Lectures, and in a number of books written with his friend, the British biologist and philanthropist Sir Patrick Geddes FRSE (1854–1932), *he argued for a form of holistic biology in which the activity of the living organism could transcend the physical laws governing its component parts.*[69] The same approach could be applied to the activity of the living Earth, and the living universe.

Distinguishing observation and discovery from actual creation

Such open and humble acknowledgement of the role of the scientist as observer and discoverer, rather than explainer of nature, comes from no less a mathematician than G. H. Hardy, who discovered, and then nurtured, the young mathematical genius Srinivasa Ramanujan—see Chapter 9. What does Hardy, a man of rare humility confess?

> I believe that mathematical reality lies outside us, that our function is to discover or observe it, and that the theorems which we prove, and which we describe grandiloquently as our 'creations', are simply the notes of our observations.[70]

Regarding life and consciousness—our central theme—scientists may know a great deal *about* the body and brain, but no scientist ever designed, created or produced such an entity from scratch—nor has natural selection. Discovering the neurological mechanisms of the brain is only a limited explanation of how the brain works *in toto*. Scientific knowledge about the brain is, like all else in science, a discovery of what Nature, the handmaiden of Divine Consciousness has bestowed. Even the smallest atomic particle artificially created in particle accelerators (like the Large Hadron Collider at CERN) is not an original creation on the part of scientists—it relies on laws and forces within objective nature herself. Genetic modifications in the laboratory to create new life forms rely on pre-existing life forms and the laws of physical nature.

But what of the importance of scepticism in science?

The Role of Doubt and Scepticism in Scientific Enquiry

> I have studied these things—you have not.

In the *Life of Isaac Newton*[71] the British scientist and academic administrator Sir David Brewster FRS (1781–1868) refers to Newton's simple retort above. Purportedly, this was levelled at the English Astronomer Royal Edmond Halley FRS (1656–1742) whenever he ventured to say anything disrespectful about religion and, arguably, astrology. Brewster attributes the anecdote to the English astronomer Nevil Maskelyne FRS FRSE (1732–1811) who passed it on to the English Savilian Professor of Astronomy at Oxford, Stephen Peter Rigaud FRAS (1774–1839).

One must study in order to know

Many scientists condemn any notion of belief, claiming that scepticism is one of the greatest strengths of science. Is it so?

There is a quaint tale about a village fool who complained bitterly to an itinerant mystic that his folk had decided that he was a complete idiot, so they all laughed at him. If he said something right, they laughed; if he remained silent, they still laughed at him. The mystic's advice to the fool was simple. 'For seven days, I advise you just to condemn whatever anyone says, demanding proof from everyone, and always staying in negation. For example if someone speaks of the beauty of the sunrise, immediately demand proof of what is so beautiful about a globe of fire that has been burning for billions of years. You must demand proof of beauty. You must swiftly counter any mention of the eloquence of scriptures by demanding proof of what is so eloquent about a mere repetition, borrowed from other books.' After seven days the idiot went again to the mystic, this time not alone, but at the head of many villagers who had become his disciples. They hung garlands of flowers around his neck and wherever he went he was revered and feted.[72]

Misuse of scepticism

What is the message? It is almost impossible to disprove a negative statement but difficult to prove a positive one. The psychology of scepticism and condemnation is a cheap way out. For example nothing is essential to deny divinity but a great sensitivity, an open heart, and purified consciousness are needed to affirm divinity. This is why scientists, in their droves, much prefer to condemn. (Refer to Volume I, Chapter 4, page 119–21 about the various syndromes used by scientism to justify their many sceptical standpoints.)

But in order to preclude obfuscation, it is important to consider two things. First, 'staying in negation', as related in the tale above, is not in any way synonymous with the *via negativa*, or the negative apophatic theology— a philosophical approach to theology which asserts that no finite concepts or attributes can adequately describe God. Indeed, God cannot be adequately 'de-scribed' as that would mean we had somehow 'written Him down', effectively reducing Him to our own understanding. However, we can certainly 'point to the Moon' by affirming His Aspects (the cataphatic or *via positiva* theology). The value of the *via negativa* method lies in positing all that God *is not* which has the miraculous effect of revealing all that He *is*. But even this 'isness' cannot adequately speak of the One beyond all Names.

Second, it is essential to point out that 'staying in negation' bears no relation to 'negative thinking' as expounded by the sage and philosopher Jiddu Krishnamurti. Similar to, but not the same as, the *via negativa*, Krishnamurti holds negative thinking 'as the highest form of thinking', namely, without a starting point, concept, proposition or conclusion, all of which constrain the mind to move in well-worn grooves of thought, which is 'positive thinking' in Krishnamurti's words.[73] Propositions and clear definitions are indispensable in science and to abjure is a mark of mental indolence. But the danger here is that we mistakenly accept our definition of reality as fact, whereas it is no more than a particular hypothesis or theory. Is the only way to truth through the intellectual tools of logic, reason, and mathematics, along with detached observation, i.e. objectifying reality unemotionally? Would it not be true to say that our conclusions are dependent upon our exclusions? Does not the way we frame our questions determine the answers? Along these lines, does refining, even to the 'nth' degree, our definition of terms like consciousness, love, God, etc. lead to deeper understanding or more frustration? At such times the insecurity of indefiniteness must be welcomed. In fact, negative thinking is a very positive course of action when pondering abstruse subjects of high metaphysical or philosophical import. It is interesting to reflect on how a mere eight-letter word 'negative' can assume a variety of meanings depending on the context and teacher.

In summary, then, doubt and scepticism are indeed the humble servants of truth—but only in the hands of genuine truth seekers. Otherwise they are merely the counterfeit coin of belief and gullibility—what scientists delight in laughing at. It requires great discrimination to understand the role of scepticism in science. With great humility and insight, Schrödinger enunciates this in 'The Competition, Reason v. Senses', quoted in the epigraph and repeated below due to its seminal importance for science:

> Scepticism alone is a cheap and barren affair. Scepticism in a man who has come nearer to the truth than anyone before, and yet clearly recognises the narrow limits of his own mental construction, is great and fruitful, and does not reduce but doubles the value of the discoveries.

So also does intellect on its own—the handmaiden of 'scepticism alone'—when unwatered by feeling and untempered by intuition, become a barren affair. This is evinced by several scientists who express their frustration at attempting to define God as a purely intellectual concept, as exampled earlier by Steven Weinberg.

Is it possible to think without being a slave to thought?

The 'negative' can sometimes be very 'positive'

Much easier to criticize than to understand

An open mind is not a credulous mind. It is a mind of utter clarity free from all conditioning: neither believing, nor disbelieving—purely observing in search of truth.

The Scientific Spirit – A Rare Quality

> If we cannot disprove Bohm, then we must agree to ignore him.[74]

The above directive to his fellow scientists was issued by the American physicist Robert Oppenheimer (1904–1967) upon finding that there was no mathematical flaw in his student David Bohm's novel interpretation of quantum mechanics. Bohm's paper proposed that the behaviours of quantum particles are not chance events, but are guided by what he called 'pilot waves', which cannot be observed, but nevertheless control the trajectory of particles and can be mathematically expressed in terms of hidden variables.[75] Oppenheimer was one of the most powerful figures in the world of physics in the 1940s, having co-ordinated the Manhattan Project, the war-time atomic bomb project at the Los Alamos Laboratory in New Mexico. The outcome of his directive was that Bohm was effectively ostracized by major sections of the physics community for the rest of his life.

To what extent is science dedicated to discovering truth?

This incident, amongst several others that could be cited (see Volume I, especially Chapters 3 to 5), should serve to shatter the myth that science is an open-ended exploration of reality, concerned with facts and not beliefs.

With extreme care, we therefore need to distinguish between science as generally understood in the West, namely, natural science in its two principal branches of physical science and life science, and the term 'Science', in its fullest and truest sense. To reiterate what was explained in Chapter 7 of Volume I, the word

Establishment science, supposedly fact-based, is as faith-ridden as orthodox religion.

derives from the Latin *scientia*, meaning 'knowledge', 'a knowing', a noun from the present participle of *scīre*, (to) 'know'. The vital point is this: 'knowledge' and 'to know' mean knowledge about *everything*, to know *everything* about reality—not an arbitrarily Occam's razor-truncated version of the latter restricted just to the physical plane whilst ignoring the subtler dimensions of existence. On this matter, readers should consult the Annex to the Definitions in Volume IV on the genesis of natural science.

Science, in its true sense is, like all else, an Idea in Divine Mind and hidden within the bosom of Nature (Nature yearns to know Herself, or there would never be evolution); and its appearance on the world stage in the present epoch signifies a momentous stage in the evolutionary cycle of nature. The great scientists are the chosen instrumentality for the discovery, or uncovering (revelation), of a few of nature's secrets. Legendary scientists, like Newton and Einstein, Schrödinger and Bohm, have sensed their role as instruments in Higher Hands and therefore shown a knee-bending reverence and awe towards nature. A similar dose of humility would not go amiss amongst some of the most famous contemporary mainstream scientists who possess tremendous scientific knowledge, but display none of the spirit of Science, nor evince an understanding of scientific principles. In other words, they may have amassed a great deal of scientific facts but show little by way of scientific training or education in the philosophy of Science and its metaphysical basis.

Distinguishing scientific training from scientific facts and details

The ideal of Science bears no relation to the ideology of scientism.

That is precisely why they talk nonsense when venturing an opinion in fields that lie outside the strict confines of their chosen discipline: astrology, religion, and dowsing are the classic *bête noir* of the uninformed. It is a scientific principle that in order to judge, one must first understand; to understand one first has to know, and knowing must be preceded by

Physical science is
valid only within
its legitimate
boundaries

unremitting study. He who is trained in science applies such a principle. Have those scientists who dismiss, say, religion out of hand devoted the same time, energy, and effort towards its study over decades in the same way that they have given to science? Does it make sense for doctors, who dedicate several years of study and training in medical schools, to dismiss near-death and out-of-body experiences without sacrificing an equal amount of time studying the evidence? Then take water divining. It is an age old practice and water companies to this day use dowsers. Unable to explain dowsing on the basis of existing physical science, instead of asking deeper questions about the subtle psycho-physical phenomena that might possibly be at work to account for phenomena that are plainly visible, the practice and the practitioners are jeered on the basis that dowsing is not scientific and so must be a form of mediæval witchcraft (the default reaction from scientists unable to explain phenomena in their terms).[76, 77]

It is a common fatal error, and totally unscientific, to presume that knowledge and authority in one field can automatically be grafted on to, and hence used, to evaluate the worth of another, totally different, field. We find an obvious example of this in medical science where doctors trained exclusively in conventional (i.e., allopathic) medicine will denigrate outright therapies, like acupuncture and homœopathy, on the basis of their concepts about mainstream medicine without bothering to understand the different standpoints and methodologies of these complementary therapies which are essentially holistic and not reductionist, as in allopathy. Paraphrasing the satirical quip of the Lebanese–American poet and artist Kahlil Gibran:

> The man who denies or criticizes what he never bothers to understand is no better than an ass loaded up with erudite, scientific books.[78]

Krishnamurti (whose regard for David Bohm, mentioned above, was equally reciprocated) gave out exactly the same message, rather more tactfully:

Statistics and
opinions
ultimately prove
nothing

> Remember that though a thousand men agree upon a subject, if they know nothing about that subject their opinion is of no value.[79]

In other words, as that outstanding scholar Seyyed Hossein Nasr remarks:

> It is as if an audience of deaf people testified together that they did not hear any music from musicians playing before them and considered the unanimity of their opinion as a proof of its objectivity.[80]

The difference between facts and opinions is well illustrated in the above quotes by Krishnamurti and Nasr. The latter shows that solely on the basis of statistics, there is total, one hundred per cent proof that no music was being played; after all, not one single person claimed to have heard anything. But is the lack of music the actual fact or is it just the unanimous opinion of deaf persons? Therefore, the fact is that even 'though a thousand men agree upon a subject'—no music heard—'their opinion is of no value', despite 'the unanimity of their opinion as [statistical] proof of its objectivity'—because they were all deaf. *Herein lies the immense danger of using statistics to prove or disprove a phenomena (especially in the paranormal field) without due cognisance of the underlying assumptions.*[81]

That is why we affirm that the scientific spirit is a rare quality to find and a pearl beyond all price. It involves ruthless self-honesty, an understanding of the extent and the limits of one's own understanding, and its sphere of application. This is something that Einstein must have been painfully aware of when in 1924 he wrote to his great friend and colleague, the German Nobel physicist Max Born FRS (1882–1970):

> Of all the communities available to us, there is not one I would want to devote myself to except for the society of the true seekers, which has very few living members at any one time.[82]

That these two legendary scientists of the quantum era disagreed strongly over many issues in quantum theory, but maintained a close friendship of some forty years (playing Beethoven's violin sonatas whenever they met) is a glowing example that disagreements, handled impersonally and with mutual respect, far from undermining, in fact strengthen close ties.

He who delights in the tension between *apparently* opposing points of view is the mark of a true searcher and a man who has attained to wisdom.

The upshot of all this is that science is not restricted to just natural science. The scientific spirit and attitude applies to all departments of human enquiry and endeavour. There is a Science behind everything: yoga, breathing, meditation, love, healing, and all else. All these call forth the scientific attitude and use appropriate methods and instruments in their legitimate fields of enquiry. In this wise, it has to be admitted that physical science is a subset of Science, as this writer has previously argued,[83] whereas *occult science* is Science in the truest sense. That is why occult science has been referred to as the *Royal Science* because it encompasses all dimensions of reality in its scope. Occult science displays the finest attributes of SCIENCE in that every theory or proposition is tested and checked for evidence, obviously not in a physical laboratory, but in the realm of consciousness. Whereas physical science uses instruments, like microscopes and telescopes, as extensions of the physical senses, occult science uses the instruments of unfolded inner faculties of consciousness to transcend the senses, for example, the *Samyama* technique of *aṇimā* (micro-psi), which is the consciousness equivalent of the microscope—see Chapter 9, page 191, and also Chapter 8 of Volume I, pages 254–5. Both methods are needed in their rightful contexts; one is not a substitute for the other.

The spirit of Science is ubiquitous

It is the writer's hope that these Volumes will have made plain, and self-evident, what was advocated earlier in Volume I, Chapter 7: that such is the stature of the *philosophia perennis* as the source of all true traditions—the Mysteries—that it contains within itself the overarching solution to the problems of any epoch. This does not mean that the Mystery Teachings—disseminated through the legendary sages and philosophers—have anticipated and analysed every complexity of this or any other generation, but rather that the reasoning faculties were organized by a simple process of mental culture—based on Eternal Verities—whereby it was asserted that where reason reigns supreme, conflict or confusion cannot exist. It was realized that problems, individual and societal, stem mainly from man's character and disposition, and only secondarily from economic and material factors. Likewise, the health of the body depends primarily on the health of the mind— a truth that, sadly, our world leaders and their scientific and medical advisors have failed to appreciate fully as they grapple with the 2021 COVID-19 pandemic at the time of writing this Volume.

With that in mind, let us now summarize the precepts of the *philosophia perennis* and see how it embodies the highest principles of SCIENCE.

The Perennial Philosophy – The Sacred Thread that Binds

> The body comes from the elements, the soul from the stars, and the spirit from God. All
> that the intellect can conceive of comes from the stars [the spirits of the stars, rather than
> the material constellations].
>
> Paracelsus[84]

These words by the legendary sixteenth century philosopher, physician, and alchemist
Paracelsus encapsulate, in a single sentence, the teaching of occult science on the origin
and genesis of man's compound nature: mortal and immortal. What follows is an
explication of its essential meaning constituting, in effect, a summary of the detailed
expositions given in this work on Consciousness and man.

Principal Attributes of the Perennial Philosophy

The pre-eminence of the *philosophia perennis* (by whatever name) lies in its self-
consistency at all levels: from the physical to the spiritual, from the microcosm as to the
macrocosm. There are no fundamental conflicts or anomalies between the great esoteric
traditions, *once the dogmatic interpretations and outer forms of expression are stripped out to
reveal the bare inner meaning*. In Chapter 7 of Volume I the distinction between exoteric
and esoteric teachings was carefully explained. It was pointed out that the distinction lies
between the description and the described, the outer covering concealing the inner
meaning, the word, and that for which the word stands, as a label. Accordingly, throughout
this work we have attempted to show, in H. P. Blavatsky's words, that:

> The narratives of the Doctrine [the *philosophia perennis*, by whatever name] are its cloak.
> The simple look only at the garment—that is, upon the narrative of the Doctrine; more
> they know not. The instructed, however, see not merely the cloak, but what the cloak
> covers.[85]

All sages who have dipped their pens into the inkwell of universal wisdom have written in
their individual handwriting but with the same ink on the universal esoteric wisdom. As
expounded earlier, this is why the esoteric philosophy is known as the 'thread doctrine'
since, 'like *Sutrātman*, in the Vedānta philosophy, it passes through and strings together
all the ancient philosophical religious systems, and reconciles and explains them all.'[86]
But as Blavatsky continues, it does even more: 'It not only reconciles the various and apparently conflicting systems, but it checks the discoveries of modern exact science, and shows
some of them to be necessarily correct, since they are found corroborated in ancient
records [the tenets of the Eternal Wisdom, or *philosophia perennis*]. All this will, no doubt,
be regarded as terribly impertinent and disrespectful, a veritable crime of *lèse-science*;
nevertheless, it is a fact,'[87] the truth of which, or otherwise, is left to readers to research
for themselves drawing upon some of the material in this work. Nonetheless, we may
adduce the example of Isaac Newton.

Priest of Nature by Rob Iliffe, the contemporary British Professor of History of Science at
Oxford, is a work of immense scholarship which highlights an important fact, namely, that
'Newton considered his Bible to be a sort of divine hypertext in which various texts in
different parts of Scripture were related to, or "interpreted", one another. Learning which
passages from the New Testament shed light on one another or on sections of the Old
Testament was a key part in the education of a Christian. On these grounds, Newton

argued that there was "no better way of interpreting scripture than by comparing the parts of it & reconciling all the synchronall & all the analogous parts of prophesy wch can be reconciled without force".'88 See an example of Newton's approach from the General Scholium cited in Volume I, Chapter 8, page 231. Both Blavatsky and Newton thus stress the *reconciling characteristic* of divine texts. Coming from persons of such pre-eminence, our case about the *philosophia perennis* as the thread doctrine (whether expressed through the sacred scriptures of the East or the West) is made.

Be that as it may, we have also made a strong case for the study of the occult sciences as a complement to mainstream natural science. In the latter we study discrete particulars, otherwise known as specialization, which of course has its advantages, but also disadvantages in engendering a narrow-minded and lopsided attitude, pejoratively referred to as 'knowing more and more about less and less'. But the occult sciences present a far greater hurdle. The prime difficulty here is not so much the understanding of particular doctrines of the occult philosophy, as much as acquiring a total appreciation and unified understanding. This is because all these doctrines are intimately related, and interlock, to form an organic unity—but they are all based upon just a few fundamental edicts. The equivalent in science would be to study physics, chemistry, biology, evolution, cosmology, etc., not piecemeal but as an integrated whole. So, the challenge to the serious occult student is twofold: first, to acquire a clear idea about the fundamental doctrines in general terms; and then to comprehend their relation to one another as an integrated whole. This is a far cry from the popular conception of knowledge as a linear stockpiling of fact upon fact by accumulating a great weight of data. Ironically, it is the very simplicity of the fundamental occult doctrines that causes the difficulty! And that is because our minds nowadays are so trammelled by detail and complexity that we have difficulty is assimilating doctrines of simplicity that are in direct proportion to their depth and profundity. Simplicity is not always simple or easy to comprehend!

Contrast organic comprehension with detailed knowledge

A Matter of Proof and the Methodology of the Perennial Philosophy

In dealing with the common origin of world religions, or the origin and genesis of cosmos and man, it is not quite as easy to deal with the subject matter in the same manner that the various disciplines of mainstream science explore a particular topic, for example the philosophy of one particular race, its traditions and beliefs, and its evolution. This is especially so regarding the evolution of the human race involving the secret annals and traditions of so many nations, whose very origins have never been ascertained by mainstream science and geology on more secure grounds than inferential suppositions. The Secret Doctrine, or *philosophia perennis*, is the common property of the countless millions of men and women born under various climes, in times with which mainstream history refuses to deal, and to which esoteric teachings assign dates incompatible with the theories of the conventional sciences of geology, anthropology, and evolution. It is true to say that such incompatibility is, in almost every case, attributed by modern criticism to lack of observation in the ancient writers, or to superstition born out of the ignorance of antiquity. It therefore bears emphasizing that it is impossible to treat arcane subjects as one would the ordinary evolution of an art or science in some well-known historical nation or age. *It is only by adopting a holistic approach, by amassing an abundance of proofs from diverse sources all tending to show that in every age, under every condition of civilization*

Proof by consilience

and knowledge, the learned classes of every nation made themselves the more or less faithful echoes of one identical system and its fundamental traditions—that readers can be made to see that so many streams of the same water must have had a common source from which they started.[89] What was this source? If it is true that 'coming events cast their shadows before', past events cannot fail to leave their impress behind them. It is, then, by those shadows of the hoary past, and their silhouettes on the external screen of every religion, science, and philosophy, that we can, by checking them as we go along, and comparing them, trace out finally the body that produced them. There must be truth and fact in that which the wisdom teachings of every nation of every age and culture accepted and made the foundation of its religions and its faith. Moreover, as the Canadian politician and judge Thomas Chandler Haliburton (1796–1865) said, 'Hear one side, and you will be in the dark; hear both sides, and all will be clear.'[90] This clearly points to the need for a holistic methodology of investigation for the serious enquirer. Newton was one such enquirer and we cited the example of how he researched theology in Volume I, Chapter 8, pages 230–2.

Testimony through Divine Revelation

But for the great sages it is different. These saviours and elevators of mankind did not come to their wisdom merely by a historical, 'horizontal' interchange of ideas by virtue of, for example, the Greek initiates deriving their wisdom by travelling to Egypt to learn from the hierophants of that country. Undoubtedly such cross fertilization of ideas did occur (and we cited the case of the great Pythagoras taught by the ancient Brahmins— see Volume I, Chapter 7, page 216). But more significantly, their wisdom was acquired by a 'vertical' accessing of the divine Omniscience. The mythology of all nations speaks with one voice albeit in many tongues conditioned by the culture. This is why we find a common meaning assigned to, for example, the after-death state known as *Devachan*, the Sanskrit-Tibetan term for 'dwelling of the gods', known by various other names like *Sukhavati* in Mahayana Buddhism, *Elysium* by the Greeks, *Sekhet-Aaru* for the Egyptians, and *Valhalla* of the Scandinavians—see Volume II, Chapter 5, page 70.

Perennial teaching is always disseminated from the universal standpoint

In light of the above, the diverse expositions of the *philosophia perennis* were written from the Platonic standpoint, rather than the Aristotelian (see Volume I, Chapter 8 for more details about their contrasting approaches). There is a sound reason for this. Difficulties are invariably experienced in understanding perennial teachings when attempting to access them 'from below', that is, from the individual viewpoint, rather than 'from above', from a general, or cosmic standpoint (from the standpoint of mathematics, as an algebraic formula rather than an arithmetical series). Therefore, the effort must be made to look down from above as though a panoramic scene were being unfolded. That is why we have entitled Volume I: 'A Panoramic Survey'. At first glance, there is a great danger in becoming enmeshed in details rather than attempting to understand the overall doctrine. For example, if the Physical body is considered first and then the other six principles super-imposed upon it, it becomes difficult to comprehend the significance of man's Divine Self (*Ātma*) from below (see Volume II, Chapter 2, Table II-3, page 21). However, when viewed from above, the Divine Self is a universal principle, united with its Originating Source, and sending its radiance through the six emanated principles of man's constitution, which are all linked with the Self. Thus man, from the standpoint of the Esoteric Philosophy, is an *unfolding of consciousness*, not an entity consisting of seven separate principles which may be peeled apart like the skins of an onion (as explained in more detail in Volume II, Chapter 1, page 10).[91]

An immense aid to the method of study of the perennial teachings, as counselled by Colonel Henry Steel Olcott (1832–1907), the American military officer, journalist, lawyer and the co-founder and first President of the Theosophical Society, is a deep appreciation of the Three Fundamental Propositions/Axioms in the Proem of *The Secret Doctrine*[92] (and elucidated also in Volume I, Chapter 8, page 237 f. and Chapter 9, page 279).

For its fuller understanding, any teaching of the *philosophia perennis* must be brought into a universal setting.

General Precepts of the Perennial Philosophy

Accordingly, with simplicity in mind, Table III-7 on page 292 presents the fundamental precepts of the *philosophia perennis* which have been cast in three ways: according to the idiom of occultism, science, and esoteric philosophy in columns one, two, and three, respectively. They are all broadly comparable and point to the same essential truth differently expressed. The fourth column shows how these universal principles can be refocused according to the Hermetic Axiom to highlight the primacy of consciousness. Let us take in the wide-ranging meaning encapsulated in the first three columns, before we deal with consciousness.

Complete understanding must be holistic

Readers may recall one of the main reasons given earlier (in Chapter 1 of Volume II) for the confusion prevailing over the complicated and vexed subject of the composition of man. This is the tendency to divide, for the purposes of analysis, that which is essentially whole, then to regard the various parts in isolation, ascribe unique labels to them, and finally mistake the several labels—the descriptions—for the reality they represent—the described; i.e., to confuse the several 'anatomical and physiological maps' with the 'human territory'. Cosmos is 'one integrated whole and functions as such, not as a magnified layer-cake with a sponge base, a filling of cream and jam and a topping of chocolate and nuts.'[93] Similarly, man, the microcosm, must be viewed as one multifaceted organic entity.

It is precisely because of the innate, organic unity of cosmos and man that the fundamental principles of the *philosophia perennis* are few in number, but so far-reaching in their import. However, being metaphysical, or 'para-physical' in character, they need to be understood in a wider context, *which includes the importance of the conscious point of view of the human.* This is in radical contrast to the predominant scientific model of reality which, despite the discoveries of quantum physics, is still steeped in the concept of the human being as a detached observer. With rare exceptions, this entrenched attitude is especially prevalent in biology and by implication, neurobiology, neuroscience, and the mainstream philosophy of mind.

Scientific understanding from purely detached observation without the human element is always incomplete

The orthodox scientific world-view is that the matter of the universe is basically inanimate, hence what is known as life, including human life, is a secondary phenomenon (epiphenomenon) of the interactions of the forces between matter. But who says so? The answer is, of course, the viewpoint of the scientists who tell us so. But does that make it a fact? As the well known English Theosophical author and speaker Adam Warcup (1945–2019) perspicaciously observes:

> We need to see that the scientific world-view is just that—a view—no more and no less.[94]

The rejoinder from the scientific camp that their viewpoint is upheld by the facts from theory and experiment neither holds water nor cuts ice. As McGilchrist has stated: current mainstream science makes unscientific assumptions, even while assuming that they make no assumptions (see page 276). This is because it is the same consciousness that devised the theory and designed the experiment that also formulated the viewpoint based on the results of the theory so devised and the experiment so designed. It is a circular argument. There are not two separate 'consciousnesses': one for the theory and experiment, and another for the overall viewpoint based on the latter.

By contrast, the *philosophia perennis* affirms that the entire Cosmos—the macrocosm in its totality—is an organic, living process and a living Being or 'cosmic Gaia'. Humankind—the microcosm—displays, rather mirrors, the same characteristics and so is not uniquely, or intrinsically, different. Is this far-reaching proposition viable, or is it just a convenient assumption?

By experiment or experience?

In addressing this question, could not the same arguments about the scientific viewpoint also be aimed at the viewpoint of the *philosophia perennis*, namely, that its tenets are also the world-view of those who propound it? What is the acid test: experiment or experience or both? In science it is, of course, experiment, but ultimately, experience must gain the upper hand. Can the world-view of the *philosophia perennis* be borne out in experience?

Consciousness is an ELEMENT

> An idea is a *being* incorporeal, which has no subsistence by itself, but gives figure and form unto shapeless matter, and *becomes the cause of the manifestation*.
>
> Plutarch[95]

It is crucial, therefore, to acknowledge the primacy of consciousness. Because every idea that we may have, all our dreams and aspirations, joys and sorrows, in fact, all that we know, is experienced by, in, and through consciousness. It is only from this starting point that we can make sense of the riddle of life and resolve the problem of subjective and objective reality.

Having established—*through our own experience*—that we humans are conscious, let us move first down the scale, initially to animals and then to plants. Are they conscious? There is every evidence that they respond to human feelings and thoughts, but would that constitute consciousness? If so, then what about birds, reptiles, insects, jellyfish, molluscs, and amoebas? Are they conscious? If not, then where in the vast spectrum of life does consciousness begin and end? Which of the following two arguments seems the more reasonable:

1. That there is some arbitrary line or point of origin that demarcates the starting point of consciousness;

Is consciousness arbitrary or universal?

2. Or that there is a graduated scale of consciousness, such that:
   i. the lower down the scale, the lesser is the degree of awakened consciousness;
   ii. conversely, the higher up the scale, the more complex are the evolved vehicles through which consciousness can express its potentiality, as encapsulated in the Qabbalistic proverb in the third column of Table III-7, page 292?

As mentioned in Chapter 2 of Volume I, page 9, a few scientists and philosophers of mind, like Galen Strawson[96] and Christof Koch,[97] who was Francis Crick's collaborator, are now moving towards panpsychism because it offers an attractive middle way between physicalism on the one hand and dualism on the other. Nonetheless, the vast majority of scientists would in fact make the case for the first argument above on the basis that the biological cell constitutes the basis of all life on Earth (and possibly even elsewhere in the universe) and therefore constitutes the dividing line between consciousness and non-consciousness, i.e., the animate and the inanimate. If that be the case, we must ask what is so special about a cell? Is the cell therefore conscious? The DNA at the heart of a cell is, after all, only a chemical in the final analysis. Then what is so special about a chemical? After all, a chemical is made up of molecules, atoms, and subatomic particles. It only requires an extension of this line of argument to reason that consciousness is present in the cell, in its chemical constituents, in the molecules, atoms, atomic particles, subatomic particles, and so on, until we find that what we call 'matter' is *mental in essence* (see the Mathematical Codicil, page 349). This idea is of course a complete anathema to confirmed materialists and reductionists such as Nobel physicists Philip Anderson[98] and Steven Weinberg who maintains that, 'there is nothing like intelligence [consciousness] on the level of individual living cells, and nothing like life on the level of atoms and molecules.'[99]

<aside>Panpsychism: a promising, recent trend in science</aside>

Moving up the scale, the obverse argument is equally valid. Why should the Earth not be conscious, as also the Sun and all the celestial bodies in the solar system? Rupert Sheldrake recently gave a thought-provoking lecture asking us to look beyond the strict confines of scientific materialism and consider how the consciousness of stellar bodies (such as our sun) is not only of anthropological or cultural interest but a valid field of enquiry in modern philosophy, psychology, cosmology, and neuroscience.[100] But why stop there arbitrarily? Are not also the Milky Way, the distant galaxies and indeed, the whole universe, seen and unseen, conscious?

<aside>Where is the animate/ inanimate borderline?</aside>

There is, therefore, no boundary between the animate and the inanimate and there is no arbitrary cut-off point in the scale of life from which we can declare that consciousness operates from here onwards in biological life, but not in so-called inanimate, mineral life. The concept of dead matter is a total oxymoron. As the Qabbalistic proverb again affirms, there is nothing but life, in various stages of being, and becoming. 'There is no such thing as either "dead" or "blind" matter, as there is no "Blind" or "Unconscious" Law. We men must remember that because *we* do not perceive any signs—which we can recognise—of consciousness, say in stones, we have no right to say that *no consciousness exists there*.'[101] The whole universe is teeming with life in infinite shades of being and becoming at all levels from the spiritual to the physical.

Therefore, we state that CONSCIOUSNESS CAME FIRST, or in other words, that CONSCIOUSNESS IS AN ELEMENT. But strictly speaking, what is an 'element'? In physical chemistry, the meaning is of course well known: a chemical element is a substance that cannot be broken down by chemical means. But the modern sense of the word in chemistry (from around 1813) is not essentially different from the philosophical one. The etymology of the term is revealing. It derives from Middle English, via Old French *element*, from Latin *elementum* 'rudiment, first principle, matter in its most basic form', translating in Greek as *stoikheion*, 'a first principle'. In this truest sense, Consciousness is the quintessential principle: it is irreducible; it is not the product of anything else; it is not a plurality. As hydrogen is the most abundant chemical substance in the universe and the lightest element in the periodic table, Consciousness may be seen as the ever-present primary ('lightest') Element of all manifestation.

<aside>What is an element?</aside>

Clearly, alluding to the role of *māyā* (explained in detail in Chapter 7), Schrödinger's thoughts on the subject are apposite. He declared unequivocally:

> The plurality that we perceive is only an *appearance; it is not real* [italics by Schrödinger].[102]

Furthermore, much in line with our argument that any concept of dead matter is a contradiction in terms, he continues:

> We cannot but attribute *some kind of consciousness*, however dim and undifferentiated, to our primitive little cousin on the ladder of life. [...]. This cannot be logically proved, but we can *feel* that any other notion would be meaningless. To divide or multiply consciousness is something meaningless. In all the world, there is no kind of framework within which we can find consciousness in the plural; this is simply something we construct because of the spatio-temporal plurality of individuals, but it is a false construction. Because of it, all philosophy succumbs again and again to the hopeless conflict between the theoretically unavoidable acceptance of Berkeleian idealism[v] and its complete uselessness for understanding the real world [realism]. The only solution to this conflict, in so far as any is available to us at all, lies in the ancient wisdom of the Upaniṣads.[103]

Schrödinger, like Blavatsky, underscores shortcomings of intellect

Why is this? Echoing Blavatsky's famous apothegm in *The Voice of the Silence* that 'The Mind is the great Slayer of the Real' (quoted earlier in Volume I, Recapitulation, page 323) Schrödinger explains:

> We intellectuals of today are not accustomed to admit a pictorial analogy as a philosophical insight; we insist on logical deduction. [...]. In a considerable number of cases logical thinking brings us up to a certain point and then leaves us in the lurch.[104]

A 'definition' of Consciousness

Given that Schrödinger also said that 'the unity and continuity of Vedānta are reflected in the unity and continuity of wave mechanics,'[105] in that same spirit we propose a definition of Consciousness—insofar as this ineffable term can be expressed adequately in words: *Consciousness is an* ELEMENT—*an all pervading primal and divine organizing field of intelligent energy-substance, the collapse of the 'spiritual wave function' of which precipitates manifested universes and their contents.*

Thus, the hierarchy from consciousness to matter can be unfolded in two ways, from the viewpoints of 'spirit' and 'matter'; the former in the vocabulary of the *philosophia perennis* and the latter in the terminology of modern science:

The unfolding of Consciousness

> ❖ *REALITY as* PURE CONSCIOUSNESS *is the primary* ELEMENT ⟱➡
> > *Mind its form* ⟱➡
> > > *Energy–Matter the appearance, or form, taken by Mind.*

> ❖ *REALITY as* PRIMAL INTELLIGENT ENERGY-SUBSTANCE *is the basic*
> > CONSCIOUSNESS-ELEMENT ⟱➡
> > > *Mind its expression as Energy* ⟱➡
> > > > *Matter as Energy imprisoned in form.*

---

v Subjective idealism, or empirical idealism, was the metaphysical doctrine of the Irish philosopher George Berkeley (1685–1753), also known as Bishop Berkeley, that denies the existence of material substance and instead contends that objects are only ideas in the minds of perceivers and, as a result, cannot exist without being perceived.

Thus, from either viewpoint:

❖ Consciousness takes the form of (presents) as Mind which takes the form of (appears) as Energy–Matter.

❖ Matter–Energy is subsumed in Mind as Mind is subsumed in Consciousness.

With the primacy of consciousness firmly established, it is axiomatic that every human enquiry and endeavour must fall within this fact. So our understanding of religion, philosophy, science, indeed the whole spectrum of human experience, is known by, in, and through Consciousness—the primary ELEMENT.

Why, then, does mainstream science experience such immense difficulties in understanding a fact so simple and self-evident and instead claim that it has not discovered consciousness, other than relegating it to a by-product of matter? Because as Schrödinger points out, we cannot evict consciousness from the scientific arena and then claim triumphantly that we haven't found it by applying the scientific method! You cannot find what you are not disposed (or able) to look for, and a very important step will have been taken by scientists when they begin to incorporate this realization into their work.[106]

The scientific method applies strictly to its self-limiting field of discourse

By contrast, the world-view of the *philosophia perennis* has inverted the materialistic scientific viewpoint. Instead of saying that there is no such thing as life *per se* but only the complex interactions of inorganic components that give an appearance of life and an *illusion* of consciousness—and who, incidentally, is the perceiver of the illusion?—we have started at the opposite end with the one thing that none of us can dispute: the primacy and fact of our own consciousness and our inability to find any point in the whole scale of being from which life and consciousness are excluded. Clearly, we are not detached third person spectators, but participate in an organic life and not in a mechanical universe, although its physical characteristics and outward behaviour can of course be modelled *like* a mechanism, which science does to such perfection, and to our tremendous benefit, *when applied in the right context*. The importance of a first-person participatory perspective has been declared in unequivocal terms by many scientists, notably by the American physicist John Wheeler. It bears repeating his quote from Volume I, Chapter 3, that: '"Participator" is the incontrovertible new concept given by quantum mechanics. It strikes down the "observer" of classical theory, the man who stands safely behind the thick glass wall and watches what goes on without taking part.'[107] But it is regrettable that the wider philosophical implications of such seminal remarks have remained with enlightened quantum physicists and not pervaded other areas of science, especially mainstream biology and psychology, and even particle physics when bereft of the metaphysical implications of quantum physics (see the Epilogue).

Participation over detachment should now be on the scientific watch

With Consciousness firmly established as an ELEMENT, we find overwhelming evidence that the complex has evolved from the simple, with no cessation of evolution at some arbitrary stage after a successful species has been evolved. However, in pointing to evolution from the simple to the complex, this is not meant in the limited sense of emergentism or complexity theory (see Volume I, Chapter 3, pages 30 and 44, respectively) but in the sense of Consciousness (technically, the Monad—see Volume II, Chapter 3, page 41) evolving more complex vehicles for its self-expression—again, as encapsulated in the Qabbalistic proverb cited in Table III-7 overleaf. Furthermore, the

Table III-7 Fundamental Propositions of the Perennial Philosophy

The *Philosophia Perennis* expressed through the idiom of:			
Occultism	Science	Esotericism	The Hermetic Axiom and the Primacy of Consciousness
There is an eternal, ever active Law: I. Whatever happens is a result of that Law; II. The Laws of Nature are sub-laws of this boundless, immutable Law; and III. This Law acts on all planes: unmanifest and manifest. Nature is threefold: i. Spirit, the source of all forces, indestructible and eternal; and Matter—visible and invisible Nature—its medium of expression, in its objective aspect being transitory in form, hence impermanent and temporal; ii. A subjective (invisible), indwelling and energizing nature, being the exact model of the objective aspect, and its vital principle; iii. An objective (visible and invisible) nature. Corollary As is nature, so is man threefold in composition: 1. the immortal SPIRIT; 2. the Astral body or Soul; 3. the Physical body.	1. The Universe, seen and unseen, unmanifest and manifest, is based upon, emanated from and derived from, an Ultimate Reality which is of the quintessential nature of pure Consciousness; 2. Therefore the Universe is, in essence, a mental phenomenon; 3. What science refers to as matter ('bottled-up waves' or crystallized energy) is the appearance taken by mind. *Note*: the terms 'mental phenomenon', 'matter', and 'mind' are used in a generic and wide sense. Corollary As mind, at any level, is the modification or derivative of consciousness, there is consistency and no contradiction between the three ideas above.	1. Cosmos as a whole, the macrocosm, is an organic entity, a living process; and — humanity, the microcosm, is subsumed under the same laws and processes that operate in the macrocosm; 2. The hylozoic principle that there is absolutely nothing in the universe such as dead matter; that everything from below the mineral kingdom to beyond the human kingdom is conscious and interacts and responds to its environment with intelligence and purpose; however 3. What varies as we progress from sub-mineral to superhuman is the *degree*, but not the fact, of consciousness. The higher on the evolutionary ascent, the more awakened (evolved) is the consciousness; the lower down the scale the more it is dormant. Corollary The Qabbalistic proverb: *I slept in the stone; I stirred in the plant; I dreamt in the animal; and I awoke in the man.***	Cosmos—the macrocosm—is a living organic entity; and – Man—the microcosm—is subsumed under the same laws that operate in the macrocosm – hence – Nothing in the cosmos is dead or inert – but – The higher an entity is on the evolutionary ascent, the more awakened is its consciousness; – so extending the argument … Consciousness is in the human being → in his organs → the cells in his organs → the chemicals in the cells → the atomic particles in the chemicals → → with no cut off, or cut in point from which consciousness ends or begins – therefore – Consciousness came *first* – and so – Consciousness is an ELEMENT. Corollary The whole spectrum of human experience is known by, in, and through Consciousness, the primary Element.

** This refers to the Qabbalistic doctrine that man becomes a stone, a plant, an animal, a man, a spirit, and finally like a god, thus accomplishing his obligatory cycle and returning fully self-conscious to the point from which he started 'unconscious'. By 'man' of course we mean the enduring spiritual entity—the Monad—not its physical vestures.

question of destiny, meaning, and purpose in the universe is resolved. Before dealing with this, it is important to outline the obstacles on the spiritual path.

We close this section with another peerless insight from, arguably, the greatest modern mystic-scientist who saw the urgency of marrying Eastern wisdom with Western knowledge.

> *Vedānta teaches that consciousness is singular, all happenings are played out in one universal consciousness, and there is no multiplicity of selves.*
>
> ERWIN SCHRÖDINGER[108]

Problems and Challenges of the Spiritual Aspirant – The Dark Janus Face of Spirituality

Earlier, we did not mince our words about the dark 'Janus face' of science, due to its failure to learn from the past and move forwards into the future. In the same vein we need to be equally forthright about the delusions and confusion caused by those professing spirituality as this too sinks into the quagmire of materialistic ideologies when severed from its ancient roots.

In the world of science and technology the peer review system, along with professional institutions, exist to vet the qualifications and views of the scientist. However imperfect or politically dominated it may be, the peer review system does, at the very least, restrain wacky ideas from gaining a foothold in science. Unfortunately, in the spiritual realm there are no professional or academic qualifications to endorse the spiritual attainment and status of an individual. There is nothing like quality management, as in engineering projects, to prevent product defects (quality assurance) and to identify any defects (quality control). A title like 'Fellow of the Royal Society of Spirit' would defy the imagination or 'Diploma of the Wisdom of the Gods' would be an affront to both wisdom and the gods. But this is not in any way to deny the enormous value of academic qualifications on the historical and cultural aspects of Hermeticism, and related subjects, at accredited institutions like the University of Exeter, the University of Amsterdam, and Sorbonne University; or the crucial importance of training and accreditation in areas of consciousness, transpersonal and spiritual psychology by global leaders in transformative education like the Alef Trust.[109] Hence, in the realm of subjectivity and the Spirit, the only trustworthy 'peer reviewer' is the guiding hand of the *Spiritual* Ego (see Volume II, Table II-5, page 40) over the thoughts and actions of the individual concerned. When that guidance is firm the individual behaves ethically and directs his actions impersonally towards engendering universal goodwill; but when weak, the lower, or Personal ego, thus undisciplined, can give rise to a whole spectrum of defects ranging from self-importance, then to delusion, and finally to megalomania. This is why, as periodically stressed throughout this work, the qualifications for occult instruction are 'qualifications of the spirit'—compassion and altruism, over and above (but never excluding) 'qualifications of the brain'—intellect, the latter, being useless and dangerous when unbridled by the higher nature.

Spiritual qualities must overrule intellectual qualifications

On this theme, refer also to Volume II, Coda, pages 202–3, explaining why an aspirant who pledges to dedicate his life to the spiritual path invariably faces immense trials and tribulations that test his resolve.

Warning Signs of Evil Motives and Influences

It is, therefore, a colossal mistake to believe that members, or leaders, of spiritual or esoteric societies, are all 'bringers of light' and so, by definition, spiritually a 'cut above' so-called materialistic or ordinary folk. New Age and esoteric societies can also be (and several are) shark-infested with highly self-serving and ruthlessly ambitious people—in many ways the more dangerous than the career-goaded politicians or the financial heads of industry—because the motives of the latter are clear, whereas those of the former are veiled by a mask of spirituality. Blavatsky makes this very clear in the following passage:

Intellectual masks of depraved spirituality

> There are thoroughly wicked and depraved men, but yet as highly intellectual and acutely *spiritual* [*sic*] for evil, as those who are spiritual for good. […] In such men, cunning develops to an enormous degree.[110]

At first sight, the term '*spiritual* for evil' might seem like a contradiction in terms—a complete oxymoron—for surely, 'spiritual' connotes an attitude of benevolence and philanthropy as opposed to self-gratification. In the vast majority of instances that would, hopefully, be so. However, that is not automatically the case. Being 'spiritual' (using the term in the widest sense) simply means mastering, the 'laws of Spirit', namely, controlling nature's hidden laws, resulting in the acquisition of psychic and occult powers. The manner in which such powers, acquired through self-effort, are used will determine whether a man is '*spiritual* for evil' or 'spiritual for good'.

A classic account of the contrast between '*spiritual* for evil' and 'spiritual for good', and the ultimate victory of the latter, is to be found in the narrative allegory of the great Indian epic poem *Rāmāyaṇa*.[111] In that poem Rāvana, the demon-king of Lanka, was granted tremendous psychic powers by the gods, having earned them through great penance and ascetic practice. But these powers were abused to abduct Sīta, the wife of the Lord Rāma, who then waged a colossal battle to rescue his consort. Having superior command over the Cosmic and celestial powers, Rāma was inevitably victorious.

What are the warning signs of a man whose bent is 'acutely *spiritual* for evil'? The clue lies in the preceding words from the quote: 'highly intellectual'. This is obviously not saying that a high intellect *per se* implies a propensity for evil. It means that a high intellect, when unbridled by ethical and moral restraints, can all too easily degenerate into *cunning*, which is certainly a step in the direction towards evil leading to perdition as Blavatsky clearly asserts. Likewise, Paul Brunton warns us that:

Tests in life come at crucial moments

> Deep down in the lowest layers of the subconscious nature there lurk evil tendencies and evil memories [which] rise to the surface layers and challenge us at crucial moments when we seek initiation into the Higher Self [and] whose character is marked by extreme sensuality or extreme cunning or extreme brutality, or even by a combination of two or three of these.[112]

Absolute sincerity and purity of motive are thus the sole attributes and shields of the spiritual aspirant and occult scientist.

Brutality and sensuality are relatively easy to recognize: not so, cunning, because it invariably wears a 'spiritual mask' perfumed with much glamour. Bear in mind the Apostle Paul's warning that, ultimately, our battle is spiritual, not physical:

> For we wrestle not against flesh and blood, but against principalities, against powers, against the rulers of the darkness of this world, against spiritual wickedness in high places.'[113]

Destiny, Meaning, and Purpose

> *Der schwer gefaßte Entschluß* (The Difficult Decision)

The epigram shows Beethoven's heading to the final movement of his last String Quartet No. 16 in F major, Op. 135. Then, under the introductory slow chords, Beethoven wrote in the manuscript:

> *'Muß es sein?'* ('Must it be?')

to which, with the faster main theme of the movement, he responds,

> *'Es muß sein!'* ('It must be!').

The problem in dealing with such topics as destiny, meaning, and purpose is the misconceived idea, especially in the *orthodox* interpretation of Western religions, of a God who is supposed to have created the universe and then endowed it with meaning. It is this outworn 'God-as-designer' notion which scientists still struggle with, and some, like Richard Dawkins, fulminate against, without bothering to probe the esoteric dimension of Christianity and its derivation from Judaism—let alone research other religions of the East. However, the *philosophia perennis* affirms that destiny, meaning, and purpose are not externally injected into, or superimposed upon, the process but are intrinsic to the very process itself. This was realized by David Bohm when he proposed an implicate order in the very 'substance' out of which the universe emerged and became explicate. (This, incidentally, would provide a sounder basis for understanding the concept of *emergentism* in science—see Volume I, Chapter 3, page 30.) So to understand purpose, we have to look at the underlying consciousness that seeks ever newer and more complex forms. Merely looking to the outer forms draws a blank. And this explains why Weinberg, and the majority of establishment scientists, see no innate purpose in the universe: they are merely looking to the changes in outer appearance—the 'shell of cosmos', or the 'fabric of the universe' the current term in vogue—and wondering what is the point of it all. A simple analogy with the microcosm, the human being, should make this clearer.

As an illustrative example, take the case of the outer form of the human body as it changes from infancy to old age, via adulthood. Let us consider the case of a sportsman. Looking with detachment, purely at the outward and visible appearance and nothing else, we would see the suppleness of the infant body changing to the virile muscularity of the adult and finally to the stiffness and wrinkles of old age. We know in minute detail all about the anatomy and physiological functions and mechanisms within the body that enable such changes to occur, but we would be entitled to observe, paraphrasing Weinberg's words (see page 268), 'The more the human body seems comprehensible, the more it also seems pointless in that what was once so youthful and virile should now look so decrepit.'

Consider now the same changes from the standpoint of the indwelling consciousness that uses the body as its vehicle of expression at different stages of growth. During the infant stage the suppleness of the body is needed for the indwelling consciousness to fulfil its life's purpose; during adulthood the inner purpose of the man to be a sportsman needs an appropriate body geared to high physical output; then old age signals the fact that the physical vesture, *which is temporal*, no longer fulfils the requirements of the evolving consciousness and so the body withers away and ultimately dies in order that

Teleology pertains to consciousness, not to its outer vehicles of expression

The 'I', as the sleeper-stirrer-dreamer-awakener, is *consciousness in different modes of operation working through progressively more complex vehicles of manifestation that allow it increasingly more sophisticated functions and refined forms of Self-expression.*

a new life of a new incarnation may inhabit a new form, just as the same man changes his outworn sports gear for new garments.

Meaning and purpose are therefore to be found in the consciousness of the man evolving towards his goal and destiny—not in the outer form which is the vehicle of the inner purpose. Just so in the case of the universe. This is the whole meaning of the Qabbalistic proverb cited in Table III-7, page 292, which again needs to be emphasized.

We have highlighted the inestimable boons to humanity that ensue from a wise and ethical use of both science and spirituality, each within its proper context. And whereas we have not minced our words about the iniquities and suffering caused by the exploitation and misapplication of science and technology, we have been equally forthright in criticizing all forms of sham spirituality and its abuse of nature's secret powers. However, the main thrust of this Chapter has been to show that only by acknowledging the primacy of Consciousness can there be a resolution of innumerable problems that have beset scientific materialism, especially in its current frenetic pursuit of 'how consciousness arises'.

So it would seem appropriate to close this Chapter with two quotes: the first on the oft overlooked distinction between scientific knowledge and scientific principles; the second, which we encountered in Volumes I and II, and which bears underlining, because it encapsulates the entire teaching of the *philosophia perennis* on the relation between consciousness and its vehicles of expression:

> *The colleges have produced many science graduates who possess much scientific knowledge, but little scientific training. They have assimilated a fair amount of scientific knowledge through the use of memory and other faculties, but they have not organized their reason and sharpened their intelligence by the assimilation of scientific principles. The study of philosophy demands a certain mental equipment, a preliminary expansion of the intellectual faculties, before it can become really fruitful and actually effective. The knowledge of a number of facts contained in a number of books is not sufficient to make a scientist; such a knowledge is sterile from the viewpoint of [the spiritual] quest, however valuable it be from the viewpoint of commercial and industrial development.*
>
> PAUL BRUNTON[114]

> *That which makes one mortal a great man and another a vulgar, silly person is [...] the quality and makeup of the physical shell or casing, and the adequacy or inadequacy of brain and body to transmit and give expression to the light of the real,* **Inner** *man; and this aptness or inaptness is, in its turn, the result of Karma. Or, to use another simile, physical man is the musical instrument, and the Ego, the performing artist. The potentiality of perfect melody of sound, is in the former—the instrument—and no skill of the latter can awaken a faultless harmony out of a broken or badly made instrument. This harmony depends on the fidelity of*

transmission, by word or act, to the objective plane, of the unspoken divine thought in the very depths of man's subjective or inner nature. Physical man may—to follow our simile—be a priceless Stradivarius, or a cheap and cracked fiddle, or again a mediocrity between the two, in the hands of the Paganini who ensouls him.

H. P. BLAVATSKY[115]

NOTES

1   'The Theosophical Society and Its Work', *Letters from the Masters of the Wisdom: First Series*, Letter 1 from the Mahâ-Chohan (Adyar: Madras, Theosophical Publishing House, 1919).

2   Erwin Schrödinger, 'Nature and the Greeks' from the Shearman Lectures delivered at University College, London, 1948, in *Nature and the Greeks* and *Science and Humanism*, foreword by Roger Penrose (Cambridge: Cambridge University Press, 1961), 33.

3   Plotinus, *The Enneads*, trans. Lloyd P. Gerson, et al. (Cambridge: Cambridge University Press; repr. edn 2019), 'On Beauty', Ennead 1.6.9, 102.

4   Letter to Johann Nepomuk Kanka of 6 April 1814, in *The Letters of Beethoven*, ed. Emily Anderson (New York: W. W. Norton & Co, 1986), Letter No. 540.

5   Lisa Grossman, 'Ripples of the Multiverse', *New Scientist* (1 March 2014).

6   —— 'Multiverse Gets Real with Glimpse of Big Bang Ripples', *New Scientist* (18 March 2014).

7   John M. Kovac and Clement L. Pryke, 'Collaborative Research: BICEP2 and SPUD – A Search for Inflation with Degree-Scale Polarimetry from the South Pole', *National Science Foundation*, Award Number 1044978 (18 July 2011).

8   *SD*-I, 'Gods, Monads, and Atoms', 610.

9   Revd Professor Stephen Wright, 'Making (Sacred) Space for Staff Renewal and Transformation', *Journal of the Scientific and Medical Network*, 125 (2018), 21.

10 Johannes Kepler, *Tertius Interveniens* (Third-party Interventions) (Germany: Verlag C. H. Beck, 1941).

11 Patrick J. Boner, 'Book Review: *Tertius Interveniens* in Translation, Kepler's Astrology: The Baby, the Bath Water, and the Third Man in the Middle', *Journal for the History of Astronomy* (1 February 2009).

12 'Albert Einstein in Brief', *American Institute of Physics* <https://history.aip.org/exhibits/einstein/inbrief.htm> accessed 22 December 2020. Quoted also in 'I Visit Professor Einstein', *Ojai Valley News* (Ojai, California, 28 September 1983).

13 Burndy MS, Sotheby lot no. 66; now Dibner Collection MS 1031 B, Dibner Library of the History of Science and Technology of the Smithsonian Institution Libraries, Washington, DC, Appendix A, f. 3v. See also: Alain Bauer, *Isaac Newton's Freemasonry: The alchemy of science and mysticism* (Rochester, Vermont: Inner Traditions, 2003); Ayval Leshem Ramati, *Newton on the Secrets of Creation Hidden in the Jewish Temple*, Hebrew University, Jerusalem, Israel, *circa* 2010.

14 Rupert Sheldrake, *Science and Spiritual Practices: Reconnecting through direct experience* (UK: Coronet, 2018).

15 —— *Ways to Go Beyond and Why They Work: Spiritual practices in a scientific age* (UK: Coronet, 2019).

16 'Using Brain Signals to Drive Prosthetic Devices', *National Eye Institute* (February 2011) <https://nei.nih.gov/news/scienceadvances/discovery/brain_devices> accessed 24 June 2020.

17 *New York Times*, 20 May 2015.

18 Jordon Pearson, 'Scientists Found a Way to Email Brain Waves', *Motherboard* (August 2014). <https://motherboard.vice.com/en_us/article/539548/scientists-found-a-way-to-email-brainwaves> accessed 4 April 2020.

19 Ellie Zolfagharifard, 'Could We Soon Send Emails "Telepathically"? Scientist transmits message into the mind of a colleague 5,000 miles away using brain waves', *Mail Online* (August 2014) <http://www.dailymail.co.uk/sciencetech/article-2737532/Could-soon-send-emails-telepathically-Scientist-transmits-message-mind-colleague-5-000-miles-away-using-brain-waves.html> accessed 4 April 2020.

20 Steven Weinberg, *The First Three Minutes: A modern view of the origin of the universe* (UK: Flamingo, Fontana Paperbacks, 1977), 149.

21 Erwin Schrödinger, 'Nature and the Greeks' from the Shearman Lectures delivered at University College, London, 1948, in *Nature and the Greeks* and *Science and Humanism*, foreword by Roger Penrose (Cambridge: Cambridge University Press, 1961), 95.

22 Steven Weinberg, *Dreams of a Final Theory: The search for the fundamental laws of nature* (London: Hutchinson Radius, 1993), 204.

23 Psalm 19:1, 21st Century King James Version.

24 Steven Weinberg, *Dreams of a Final Theory*, 193.

25 Romans 8.5, King James Version.

26 Romans 11.8, New International Version.

27 Peter Atkins, *On Being: A scientist's exploration of the great questions of existence* (New York: Oxford University Press, 2011), 100.

28 Vasileios Basios, in foreword to Emilios Bouratinos, *Science, Objectivity and Consciousness*, ed. Richard Grant (Princeton, New Jersey: ICRL Press, 2018), 11.

29 Vasileios Basios, in 'Endorsements for the Galileo Commission Report', *The Scientific and Medical Network* <https://archive.galileocommission.org/category/people/roland-benedikter> accessed 5 April 2020.

30 Steven Weinberg, Address at the Conference on Cosmic Design, *American Association for the Advancement of Science* (Washington, DC, April 1999).

31 Steven Weinberg, 'A Designer Universe?' *Physics & Astronomy Online* <https://www.physlink.com/Education/essay_weinberg.cfm> accessed 12 June 2020.

32 Steven Weinberg, *Dreams of a Final Theory*, 204.

33 —— *op. cit.*, 205.

34 —— *op. cit.*, 132–151.

35 —— *op. cit.*, 133.

36 —— *op. cit.*, 134.

37 —— *op. cit.*, 135, 136.

38 —— *op. cit.*, 205.

39 A slight rephrasing of the 'First Fundamental Proposition' in *SD*-I, 'Proem', 14.

40 Errol Morris, *A Brief History of Time*, Anglia Television (1992) <http://www.errolmorris.com/film/bhot.html> accessed 5 July 2020.

41 Cited and elaborated from *STA*, 'Ceremonial Magic and Sorcery', CI–CII.

42 Deidre McPhillips, 'On Thanksgiving, Who Wants Second(s)?' *U.S.News* (23 November 2016) <https://www.usnews.com/news/best-countries/articles/2016-11-23/thanksgiving-meals-not-enough-to-make-us-no-1-in-turkey-consumption> accessed 8 April 2020.

43 Rod Addy, 'Thanksgiving Turkeys to Raise $1.05bn in US', *GlobalMeatnews.com* (9 November 2016) <https://www.globalmeatnews.com/Article/2016/11/09/Thanksgiving-turkeys-to-raise-1.05bn-in-US> accessed 8 April 2020.

44 Peter Singer, *Ethics in the Real World: 82 Brief Essays on Things That Matter* (US: Princeton University Press, 2017).

45 Henry Bodkin, 'First Mammal with Two Mothers is Born as Gene-Editing Breakthrough Creates Mouse with No Father', *The Telegraph*, 11 October 2018 <https://www.telegraph.co.uk/science/2018/10/11/needs-men-first-mammal-born-same-sex-female-parents-gene-editing> accessed 8 April 2020.

46 Jennifer Leman, 'Baboons Survive 6 Months after Getting a Pig Heart Transplant', *Science News* (5 December 2018) <https://www.sciencenews.org/article/baboons-survive-6-months-after-getting-pig-heart-transplant> accessed 8 April 2020.

47 Sarah Knapton, 'World's First Human Head Transplant a Success, Controversial Scientist Claims', *The Telegraph*, 17 November 2017 <https://www.telegraph.co.uk/science/2017/11/17/worlds-first-human-head-transplant-successfully-carried> accessed 8 April 2020.

48 Sam Shead, 'Elon Musk Says his Start-up Neuralink has Wired up a Monkey to Play Video Games using its Mind', CNBC (2 Febrauary 20021) <https://www.cnbc.com/2021/02/01/elon-musk-neuralink-wires-up-monkey-to-play-video-games-using-mind.html> accessed 27 March 2021.

49 BBC News, 'Patient Plays Violin during her Brain Surgery' [video] (19 February 2020) <https://www.bbc.co.uk/news/av/uk-england-london-51557044/patient-plays-violin-during-her-brain-surgery> accessed 20 February 2020.

50 Nicholas Maxwell, *How Universities Can Help Create a Wiser World: The urgent need for an academic revolution* (UK: Imprint Academic; USA: Ingram Book Company, 2014).

51 HRH The Prince of Wales, Tony Juniper, and Ian Skelly, *Harmony: A new way of looking at our world* (London: HarperCollins*Publishers*, 2010). See also Edi Bilimoria, 'The Quest for Harmony: A Unifying Principle in Spirituality, Science, Sustainability and Healthcare', review of conference for the 70th birthday celebration for HRH the Prince of Wales, in *Journal of the Scientific and Medical Network*, 129 (2019), 26–8.

52 *National Review*, 9 December 2016 <http://www.nationalreview.com/article/442901/white-american-death-rates-rising-life-expectancy-declining> accessed 24 June 2020. See also *The Week*, 7 January 2017, 14.

53 Kim A. Jobst, Daniel Shostak, and Peter J. Whitehouse, 'Diseases of Meaning, Manifestations of Health, and Metaphor', *The Journal of Alternative and Complementary Medicine*, 5/6 (September 2007).

54 BBC News, 'Steep Rise in A&E Psychiatric Patients', 10 January 2017.

55 *Daily Telegraph*, excerpted in *The Week*, 14 October 2017, 16.

56 *Guardian*, Editorial, 29 August 2018.

57 Dean Burnett, 'Psycho-Logical: Why mental health goes wrong – and how to make sense of it' [podcast], Lecture (4 February 2021), Royal Institution <https://www.rigb.org/whats-on/events-2021/february/public-psycho-logical?utm> accessed 4 February 2021.

58 Carl Jung, *Letters Vol. 2: 1951–1961*, ed. Gerhard Adler, trans. Jeffrey Hulen (Princeton: Princeton University Press, 1976), 503–4, cited in <https://carljungdepthpsychologysite.blog/2019/09/27/carl-jung-on-homesickness/#.XqSwYWhKg5s> accessed 25 April 2020.

59 Carl Jung, *Modern Man in Search of a Soul* (1933; Oxford and New York: Routledge, 2001).

60 Paul Brunton, *The Spiritual Crisis of Man: An examination of the concept and experience of God* (London: Rider and Co., 1970).

61 Iain McGilchrist, 'Foreword – Science needs to be more scientific', in *Galileo Commission Summary Report: Beyond a Materialist Worldview – Towards an Expanded Scienc*e (The Scientific and Medical Network, 2019), 5.

62 Professor Martin Rees, 'Beyond the Laboratory', *RSA Journal*, 1 (2019), 20.

63 *NPB-5, Part 2: The Intellect*, 'The Place of Intellect', ¶ 15, 4.

64 Paraphrased from *SD-I*, 'Gods, Monads, and Atoms', 610.

65 *ML*, Letter No. 65.

66 Daniel Bernoulli and Johann Bernoulli, *Hydrodynamics & Hydraulics* (US: Dover Publications, 1968).

67 Four Letter from Sir Isaac Newton to Doctor Bentley Containing Some Arguments in Proof of a DEITY (London: Printed for R. and J. Dodsley, 1756). See also <https://www.sophiararebooks.com/pages/books/3537/sir-isaac-newton/four-letters-to-doctor-bentley> accessed 24 June 2020.

68 J. Arthur Thomson, *Introduction to Science* (New York: Leopold Classic Library, 2016).

69 Peter J. Bowler, *Reconciling Science and Religion: The debate in early-twentieth-century Britain* (Chicago, Illinois: The University of Chicago Press Books, 2001).

70 G. H. Hardy, *A Mathematician's Apology*, foreword by C. P. Snow (1940; Cambridge: Cambridge University Press, 1967).

71 Sir David Brewster, *The Life of Sir Isaac Newton* (1st edn, London: John Murray, 1831).

72 Reworded from Osho, *Die Yogi Die – Talks on the Great Tantra Master, Gorak*h (Pune, India: Tao Publishing PVT), 276–7.

73 J. Krishnamurti, *The Importance of Negative Thinking* (India: Krishnamurti Foundation, 1992), 3.

74 Paul Howard, 'Infinite Potential: The life & ideas of David Bohm', 16, *Beshara Magazine* (Summer 2020), 4 <https://besharamagazine.org/wp-content/uploads/2020/08/16-1-Paul-Howard.pdf> accessed 6 December 2020.

75 David Bohm, 'A Suggested Interpretation of the Quantum Theory in Terms of "Hidden" Variables', *Phys. Rev.*, 85/2 (January 1952), 166–79.

76   BBC News, 'Scientist Finds UK Water Companies use "Magic" to Find Leaks', 21 November 2017
     <http://www.bbc.co.uk/news/uk-england-oxfordshire-42070719> accessed 5 April 2020.

77   Matthew Weaver, 'UK Water Firms Admit Using Divining Rods to Find Leaks and Pipes', *The
     Guardian*, 21 November 2017 <https://www.theguardian.com/business/2017/nov/21/uk-water-
     firms-admit-using-divining-rods-to-find-leaks-and-pipes> accessed 5 April 2020.

78   Kahlil Gibran, *goodreads* <http://www.goodreads.com/quotes/969368-learn-the-words-of-
     wisdom-uttered-by-the-wise-and> accessed 5 April 2020.

79   Alcyone [J. Krishnamurti], *At the Feet of the Master*, preface by Annie Besant (1910; 12th edn,
     Adyar, Madras: Theosophical Publishing House, 1968), 11

80   Seyyed Hossein Nasr, 'Contemporary Man, between the Rim and the Axis', in Mehrdad M. Zarandi
     (ed.), *Science and the Myth of Progress* (Bloomington, Indiana: World Wisdom, 2003), 100. Quoted
     also in Avinash Chandra, *The Scientist and the Saint: The limits of science and the testimony of sages*
     (Cambridge, UK: ArcheType Books, 2018), 292–3.

81   Edi D. Bilimoria, *The Snake and the Rope: Problems in Western science resolved by occult science* (Adyar,
     Madras: Theosophical Publishing House, 2006), 76–80.

82   Letter from Albert Einstein to Max and Hedwig Born, 29 April 1924, in A. Einstein and M. Born,
     The Born–Einstein Letters: Friendship, politics and physics in uncertain times 1916–1955, introd.
     Werner Heisenberg, foreword by Bertrand Russell (US: Palgrave Macmillan, 2004).

83   Edi D. Bilimoria, *The Snake and the Rope*, 56, 57–9 *passim*.

84   Franz Hartmann, *Life of Paracelsus and the Substance of His Teachings 1896* (2nd edn, rev. and enl.,
     London: Kegan Paul, Trench, Trübner & Co., 1896), quoted in *STA*, 'The Zodiac and Its Signs', LIV.

85   Zohar, iii, 152, in Adolph Franck, *La Kaballe ou la philosophie religieuse des Hébreux* [The Kabbalah
     or the Religious Philosophy of the Hebrews] (Paris: Librairie Hachette et co., 1843), 119, quoted
     also in *SD*-II, 'Esoteric Tenets Corroborated in Every Scripture', 447.

86   *SD*-I, 'Gods, Monads, and Atoms', 610.

87   *ibid.*

88   Rob Iliffe, *Priest of Nature: The religious worlds of Isaac Newton* (New York: Oxford University Press,
     2017), 246. The book was reviewed by Edi Bilimoria in *Journal of the Scientific and Medical Network*,
     125 (2018), 37–40.

89   Paraphrased from *SD*-II, 'Conclusion', 794.

90   *ibid.*

91   Rephrased from Geoffrey Barborka, *The Divine Plan* (2nd edn, rev. and enl., Adyar, Madras:
     Theosophical Publishing House, 1964; repr. 1980), vii–viii.

92   Foreword by H. S. Olcott to the Bowen Notes, being extracts from the notes of personal teachings
     given by H. P. Blavatsky to private pupils during the years 1888 to 1891, in *Madame Blavatsky on
     How to Study Theosophy* (London: Theosophical Publishing House, 1960), 4.

93   Geoffrey A. Farthing, *Deity, Cosmos & Man: An outline of esoteric science* (US: Point Loma
     Publications, 1993), 26.

94   Adam Warcup, 'A Theosophical Worldview', *The Quest* (Summer 1996), 12.

95   Plutarch, *De placitis philosophorum*, Bk I, ch. x. Quoted also in *SD*-I, 'Gods, Monads, and Atoms', 622.

96   Galen Strawson, 'Physicalist Panpsychism' (draft 2017) <http://www.academia.edu/25420435/
     Physicalist_panpsychism_2017_draft> accessed 6 April 2020.

97   Christof Koch, 'Is Consciousness Universal? Panpsychism, the ancient doctrine that consciousness
     is universal, offers some lessons in how to think about subjective experience today', *Scientific
     American* (January 2014).

98   P. Anderson, 'More is Different', *Science*, 177 (1972), 393.

99   Steven Weinberg, *Dreams of a Final Theory* (New York: Pantheon Books, 1992), 39.

100 Rupert Sheldrake, 'Is the Sun Conscious?' [video], *Renegade Tribune*, 7 July 2018
     <http://www.renegadetribune.com/rupert-sheldrake-is-the-sun-conscious> accessed 6 April 2020.

101 *SD*-I, 'Summing Up – The Pith and Marrow of Occultism', 274.

102 Erwin Schrödinger, *My View of the World*, trans. Cecily Hastings (New York: Cambridge University
     Press, 1964), 18. Quoted extracts from this book are in Walter Moore, *Schrödinger: Life and thought*
     (Cambridge: Cambridge University Press, 1989).

103 ——*op. cit.*, 31.

104 ——*op. cit.*, 19.

105   Walter Moore, *op. cit.*, 173.

106   Emilios Bouratinos, Richard Grant, and Vasileios Basios, 'A Galileo Moment', *Journal of the Scientific and Medical Network*, 128 (2018), 18.

107   J. A. Wheeler, K. S. Thorne, and C. Misner, *Gravitation* (San Francisco: W. H. Freeman and Co., 1973), quoted in Yvonna S. Lincoln and Egon G. Guba, *Naturalistic Inquiry* (US, UK, India: Sage Publications, 1985), 87.

108   Walter Moore, *A Life of Erwin Schrödinger* (Cambridge: Cambridge University Press, 1994), 125.

109   The Alef Trust <https://www.aleftrust.org> accessed 11 December 2019.

110   *CW*-XII, 'E. S. Instruction No. III', 638.

111   *Adhyātma Rāmāyaṇa: The Spiritual Version of the Rama Saga* (original Sanskrit with English translation by Swami Tapasyananda) (Madras: India, Sri Ramakrishna Math, 1985). A highly readable version of the epic is by Channing Arnold, simplified by Marjorie Sykes, *The Story of the Ramayana* (Calcutta, Bombay, Madras: Orient Longmans, 1951).

112   *NPB*-7, Part 2: *The Negatives: Understanding the Powers of Darkness*, 'Their Roots in Ego – Special Tests for Questers', ¶ 52, 21.

113   Ephesians 6:12, King James Version.

114   *NPB*-5, Part 2: *The Intellect*, 'Influence of Science', ¶ 22, 17.

115   *CW*-XII, 'Genius', 15.

Epilogue:
Towards Immortality

Truth can never be reached by just listening to the voice of an authority.

FRANCIS BACON[1]

The bee makes its honey from many flowers.

J. KRISHNAMURTI[2]

Que veux-je? que suis-je? que demander à la nature? ...
Toute cause est invisible, tout fin trompeuse; toute forme change, toute durée s'épuise ...

(What do I want? What am I? What should I ask of nature? ...
Every cause is invisible, every end is deceptive; all forms change, all duration is
exhausted ...)

ÉTIENNE DE SÉNANCOUR[3]

SYNOPSIS

The final Epilogue brings our ever-onward and upward journey temporarily to rest. Here we touch upon the subject of man's yearning for immortality. Drawing together the cardinal themes of the complete work, we review the whole question of the inroads of spirituality into the contemporary predominating materialistic paradigm. We explain that mankind is faced with a choice of just two paths regarding the unfolding of consciousness. He must choose one path exclusively: he cannot journey on both, or a part of each contemporaneously, or sequentially. The two paths have a major bearing on the question of immortality: either the scientific endeavour of enhancement and preservation of the body through transhumanism and cryonics, or the spiritual way of constant renewal and refinement of the vestures of consciousness.

KEY WORDS: symbolism, materialism, science and scientism, science industry, logical positivism, neurology, Templeton Foundation $20 million neuroscience project, Large Hadron Collider, colonizing Mars, scientific hubris, paranormal debunkers, religious ossification, philosophical sterility, ethics and economics, global COVID-19 challenges, Galileo Commission Report, insights from poetry, complementarity model, transhumanism, cryonics, choice of two life paths, significance of death, immortality, Eben Alexander, H. P. Blavatsky, Brian Cox, Kahlil Gibran, William Harvey, Julian Huxley, J. Krishnamurti, Iain McGilchrist, Wolfgang Amadeus Mozart, Harald Walach, Alfred Russel Wallace

The Proem to the three Volumes of this work opened with essentially the same question as in the third epigraph. Having arrived at the Epilogue, are we any closer to even an approximate understanding of 'Who, or What Am I?' in the course of our transitory existence on Earth? Be that as it may, it should be obvious by now that approaching these sorts of questions merely intellectually or academically inevitably leads to a dead end. So let us resort to a favourite theme that has run the course of this work, especially in

302

Volume III—universal sacred symbolic teaching, the neglect of, and contempt for which has led to serious errors on the part of conventional science and the orthodox religions of the world in their understanding of the true and inner meaning of scripture and mythology, arcane philosophy and occult science. Accordingly, we illustrate the symbolic meaning of the Boar and the Butterfly, and it is for good reason that we saved this for the Epilogue.

The Boar – Symbol of the Divine Messenger

What is so special about a boar that even today, there are pubs in England bearing the name 'The Boar's Head', as in the favoured tavern in Eastcheap of Sir John Falstaff in Henry IV? Let us cycle back to the hoary past, at a time when the gods walked the earth, so to say, and the spiritual truths enshrined in the Vedas were pronounced by those mighty Beings known in India as the *Rishis*. Written between the thirteenth and sixteenth centuries AD, the *Varāha Upaniṣad* is based on a portion of the Vedic truths. We are not going to delve into this sacred work, but what is the meaning and especial significance of the title? *Varāha* in Sanskrit means a Boar.

Now let us return again to England during the same period of the sixteenth century. This was the era of the English Renaissance and the Scientific Revolution, one of its principal luminaries being Sir Francis Bacon. And what was the crest of the Bacon family? A Boar's Head. Why then have both cultures, so geographically widely spaced, adopted the symbol of a boar?

The Boar, a universal symbol for the Divine Messenger

In Indian mythology, *Varāha* specifically refers to the incarnation of the Second Deity of the Hindu *Trimūrti*, *Viṣṇu*, as a Boar.[4] But what is so exceptional about a Boar? The Boar stands as a symbol for a Messenger, and the Boar Avatar signifies a messenger of divine truths—truths about such subjects as the nature and relationship between the individual soul and the Ultimate Reality, the seven stages of learning, the characteristics of a *Jīvanmukti* (inner sense of freedom while living), and the four types of *Jīvanmuktas* (liberated persons). The Varāha Upaniṣad also conveys the universal teaching about liberation from sorrow and fear.

The Boar Avatar of India is represented in the West as the Messenger carrying the 'Book of the Apocalypse'—the book containing the Secrets of God. This carrying of the Book of God appears to have been the reason why the Boar was held in high veneration. It seems that the custom of carrying the Boar's Head at Christmas time, when the Incarnation (the birth or revelation of Christ) was celebrated, arose from this symbolic custom. Then the purely symbolic meaning of Divine Messenger and Truth-bearer got taken more literally by degrees with the progress of time and became a near-meaningless ritual. This Truth-bearer, or Messenger, is the Holy Spirit, whose priests, the Kabiri (deities and very mysterious gods worshipped by the ancient nations) were styled 'Sues', or Swine. So in truth, the Pig is a figure of the Holy Spirit, a Celestial to be revered rather than a terrestrial to be scorned or served up on the dinner table. Both Greece and Rome consecrated the Sow to Ceres (the Greek Demeter as a symbol of fertility, or the productive principle), giving her the name of the 'mystical animal'—as the Boar was one of the forms of the Hindu Incarnation.[5]

The above instance of the same symbol used to convey the same meaning adopted by two such widely differing cultures during the same epoch (around the sixteenth century in this case), plus several other examples in this work (see especially Chapter 1 earlier), demonstrate the universality of sacred symbology and present sufficient evidence to confirm that this is not a capricious choice of interpretation.

Consequently, whether we consider the sacred books of the Orient or the Occident, what, in a nutshell, does the Divine Messenger teach? It is the evolution of consciousness: from the selfish, animal-man to the unselfed, liberated man—the transformed man. Why then is it that the butterfly is another universal symbol of the evolution of man from the crude and unregenerate to the refined and spiritualized; in other words, a symbol of transitions in his state of consciousness?

The Butterfly – Symbol of Transitions in Consciousness

Psyche (*Psyché* in French) is the generic Greek term for 'soul', or 'spirit' (ψυχή). The Butterfly, under the appropriate name of *Psyche*, a beautiful maiden with wings of opalescent light, symbolizes the (generic) human soul because of the stages it passes through in order to unfold its power of flight. The three divisions through which the butterfly passes in its unfoldment resemble, closely, the three degrees of the Mystery Schools (see Volume I, Chapter 7, page 179), which degrees are regarded as consummating the unfoldment of man by giving him emblematic wings by which he may rise above his material nature and soar to the skies. Unregenerate man, ignorant and helpless, is symbolized by the stage between ovum and larva; the disciple, seeking truth and wrapped in contemplation, by the second stage from larva to pupa, at which time the insect enters its chrysalis (the tomb of the Mysteries); the third stage, from pupa to imago (wherein the perfect butterfly comes forth) typifies the unfolded enlightened soul of the initiate rising from the tomb of his baser nature.[6]

The Butterfly symbolizes three phases of consciousness

Are the vast majority of scientists and neurobiologists who devote their lives, quite sincerely, to researching and probing the mystery of consciousness at all aware of evolutionary transitions in the stages and states of consciousness? With possibly rare exceptions, it is certainly to be doubted. Despite the wonderful work of a few enlightened scientists (see for example, Chapter 3 of Volume I) it seems that the foundation of mainstream scientific enquiry is still firmly underpinned and entrenched in glowering materialism.

Materialism Still Smoulders

> There will be a large rent made in the Veil of Nature, and materialistic science will receive a death-blow.
>
> H. P. Blavatsky[7]

> With the programme of explaining the structure of matter, physics had to transcend materialism.
>
> Karl Popper and John Eccles[8]

Why does mainstream science still adhere to its outworn paradigm?

In the previous Chapter we struck a cautiously optimistic note about the emerging outlook in science. It was explained that the physical sciences are based upon, and constrained by, assumptions that have hardened into dogmas so that the scientific paradigm, or what is popularly known as the 'scientific world-view', is becoming increasingly outworn and in need of a reformation. And that reformation comes from science itself. By its own methods and discoveries, spurred by its devotion to investigating truth, science is now transcending the materialist philosophy, and pointing towards a new sense of a living world whereby the universe is no longer regarded as a machine running down towards its 'heat death', but—rather like our own Earth, Gaia—as a living, evolving organism with an inherent memory. These new paradigm shifts in the sciences shed a fresh light on the whole question of spirituality and spiritual practices; also on paranormal phenomena, or *psi*, the generic term used by parapsychologists to refer to all kinds of psychic phenomena, experiences, or events that seem to be related to the psyche, or mind in general terms, and which cannot be explained by the established physical laws of nature. However, there is a long way to go. Despite the overt pronouncements by modern astronomers, philosophers, and neurophysiologists of such distinguished international standing as Sir James Jeans OM FRS and Sir Arthur Eddington OM FRS, Alfred North Whitehead OM FRS FBA, Sir Karl Popper CH FRS FBA, and Sir John Eccles AC FRS FRACP FRSNZ FAA that modern science has transcended materialism, which Blavatsky foretold over a century ago (see the quote opposite), the road ahead for science is steep and narrow, beset with thorns on every side, in its unavoidable ascent towards the summit of realizing that: (*a*) the origin of all life and existence is spiritual, not material; (*b*) the intrinsic nature of the universe and all beings is not material but mental in essence; and (*c*) consciousness in man is not generated by the brain. A few contemporary examples make the point about the territory that neuroscience still needs to traverse in its understanding of consciousness and mind.

The Current Neurological Imperative

The Brain: The story of you[9] by the American neuroscientist and professor at Stanford University, David Eagleman (*b*. 1971) is one of the latest in a long line of books that champion the current neurological imperative. The author states essentially the same position as his mentor, Francis Crick, but in terms of the modern hypothesis of emergentism (see Chapter 3 of Volume I, page 30) which adamantly maintains that the human mind is an emergent property of the co-ordinated, bioelectrical activity of several trillions of neurons and their interconnecting networks—hence the hypothesis of emergent mind-from-brain.

At this juncture the reader is asked to conduct a simple thought experiment. Connect and interconnect several billions upon trillions of the most powerful computers to a suitable electrical power source. Then, *without a human programmer*, see, even after zillions of years, whether this vast network of co-ordinated electrical activity would be just a gigantic storage and calculating machine or whether any kind of software, like Microsoft Word, would present itself as an emergent, software-from-computer property of the vast assembly; and, if somehow it did, whether the word-processing software would *self-write* a book like Newton's *Philosophiæ Naturalis Principia Mathematica* or, to wit, *The Brain: The story of you*, as a further emergent property. Moreover, could such a device self-decide to self-write its own anti-virus program (such as Norton™ Antivirus) in order to 'vaccinate' itself against electronic malware and 'viral infections'? Is all this beginning to sound mildly absurd?

Materialistic ideology still dominates mainstream neuroscience

Nonetheless, let us continue, briefly, with *The Story of You*, where it is admitted that it is not known how conscious awareness, or the experience of sensations, arises from physical brain processes—other than the fact that it does—an unsupportable presupposition, to put it mildly. (Readers should refer back to Volume I, Chapters 3 and 6 for academic references citing the lack of success in mainstream science about any understanding of *how* consciousness arises.) Therefore, it is tantamount to a dogma to declare that for every mental experience there is a corresponding correlate of brain activity. The neural correlate of mind (and consciousness) is the central plank in the hypothesis of the neurosciences, even to the extent of saying that the brain can generate (how, and why, we might ask) neural correlates of heightened conscious processing at near-death—which statement neatly ignores the robust evidence on NDEs showing the inactivity of the brain during the experience (see especially the experience of Eben Alexander summarized in Volume I, Chapter 2, page 15). But what is so special about a neural correlate? First though, what is *not* so special is that correlation is not the same as causation—a common error and a source of much confusion in science, as explained in Chapter 5.

Even a child would soon realize that a violinist needs a violin in order to produce a sound, and that the better the instrument, the better will be the *emergent* sound from it in the hands of the performer. Conscious intention must be linked to a corresponding medium and mechanism to carry it out. However, the instrument and the performer, although linked, are not on the same level: otherwise the violin could play itself or a computer could write its own software. Eagleman claims that 'our thoughts and our dreams, our memories and experiences all arise from this strange neural material' because 'who we are is found within its intricate firing patters of electrochemical impulses'. Therefore, 'when that activity stops, so do you' and 'when that activity changes character, due to injury or drugs, you change character in lockstep' because all incoming sensory impulses are translated by the brain's electrochemical processes to create an emergent mental reality.[10] But, other than further technicalities about neural mechanisms, this is just a variant on Crick's, '"You", your joys and your sorrows, your memories and your ambitions, your sense of personal identity and free will, are in fact no more than the behaviour of a vast assembly of nerve cells and their associated molecules'[11] (refer back to Chapter 2 of Volume I on page 8). The philosophical naïveté of such concepts is palpable, as was realized by the great neurologist Sir Francis Walshe who said that 'it would be quite childish to identify the instrument with its user, even though the user be dependent upon the instrument for operating' (see Chapter 7 of Volume II, page 127). It certainly appears, as Eben Alexander puts it, that 'mainstream neuroscience just hasn't been doing its homework' (see Chapter 8 earlier) ever since Crick's dictum over a quarter of a century ago in 1994.

This way of thinking about ourselves (and all animals) as just 'temporary brain activity leading to emergent mind organisms based upon sensory system input' has become common currency in society, at least in the Western world, but not according to the eternal verities enshrined in the *philosophia perennis*, where such a standpoint can be dismissed as neuroscientific hubris. The counterclaim, that the neuroscientific case is based on findings from ever increasing research confirming this inescapable brain-mind relationship, is as fallacious as the metaphysical underpinnings of such research are riddled with unsupportable presuppositions and assumptions—see Volume I, Chapters 4, 5, and 6 and the verdict of Ian McGilchrist later on page 322.

On precisely the same Crick-ian theme, scientists at Imperial College seem convinced that 'You Are Your Brain' and that 'it has long been understood [by whom, we ask] that the brain is the *storehouse* [emphasis added] of personhood—of emotion, thought, memory—of all the things that make us the individuals we are.'[12] But how does this fleshy,

Neuroscience still conflates the 'instrument' with its 'performer'

vulnerable looking organ actually do it? The short and simple answer is, of course, that it does not do it—long understood by the *philosophia perennis*, the world over, as also by enlightened science and psychology (see Volume I, Chapter 6). But not according to the contemporary British computational neuroscientist Dan Goodman of the Intelligent Systems and Networks Group at Imperial College, who is using cutting-edge technology to investigate '"spikes"—tiny bursts of electrical activity that occur when a neuron talks to another neuron' to find out 'how they might work together to process information in the brain more efficiently.'[13] Zillions of co-ordinated spikes are just zillions of co-ordinated spikes: they do not explain consciousness any more than zillions of computers intercon-nected (as in the thought-experiment earlier) will utter the words 'I Am Self-Conscious'—unless humanly-programmed to do so.

Others of similar mind, like Douglas Fields the contemporary American neuroscientist and international authority on brain development, seem to be in no doubt that it is in 'our cerebral cortex, where consciousness arises.' Moreover, from the standpoint of neuroanatomy, 'the human brain has not changed since the stone age, [and in fact] the neural circuits of rage[i] in our brain were forged in a survival-of-the-fittest struggle on the prehistoric open plains of Africa.'[14]

Crick's manifesto and Darwinism continue to dominate the dicta of neuroscience

And so mainstream neuroscience, still hitched to its twin guiding stars of Crick's mani-festo and a primitive version of Darwinism, has given us precious little in the way of fresh insights into consciousness, least of all into 'Who, or What Am I?' as it wearily grinds the same materialistic millstone over the past quarter of a century, dogmatizing on the basis of completely unsupportable assumptions that the answer lies in physical matter, proven by mechanistic concepts, Darwinian theories, cutting-edge technology, and the results of experiments inflicting untold suffering on innumerable rats and other animals. Volumes of learned papers are produced all in a desperate attempt to prove that we humans of body, soul, and spirit are nothing but our physical bodies and fleshy brains, hence our subjective sense of Self is an illusion, and self-realization, so-called, is demon-strated by electrodes attached to the brain and scanned on to a screen for objective assess-ment.[15] And all this despite the unassailable verdict of: legendary quantum physicists (like Max Planck, Erwin Schrödinger, and Arthur Eddington) about the primacy of consciousness, and mind as the matrix of matter; neurosurgeons like Wilder Penfield and Eben Alexander that the brain does not generate consciousness; psychologists and psychiatrists like William James and Iain McGilchrist that there is not a shred of evidence that matter gives rise to consciousness.

Thus it is a tragedy that whereas fundamental, non-local interconnectedness has been acknowl-edged in physics, and the undeniable irreducibility of consciousness starkly declared by Max Planck and Erwin Schrödinger, and more recently acknowledged by David Chalmers and, even now, by Christof Koch, Francis Crick's one time primary collaborator, these insights have barely penetrated biology, medicine, and neuroscience, which disciplines are still firmly wedded to an outmoded mechanistic paradigm.[16]

So in view of that, would it be of any use to remind mainstream scientists, and neurosci-entists, in particular, about Paul Brunton's remark (slightly paraphrased):

---

i Presumably, this means the neural circuits in the brain that are supposed to generate rage in a person.

> Are the scientists and neuroscientists not already worthy to be called dead who know so little of their own selves, and so much of the bodies and brains in which they are lodged?[17]

Or would this be the right time to implement Brunton's other searing comment?

> We are compelled to wither the preachers of a mad materialism with scathing scorn. Gentle words fall off their ears like water off a duck's back.[18]

Probably not just yet. Why? For several reasons that could, arguably, be considered in two parts: philosophical and psychological.

The Primacy of Matter as the Legacy of the Vienna School

First, we cited in Volume I, Chapter 7 the insights of the modern philosopher Renée Weber that the Grand Unified Theory (attempting to formulate a single theotetical framework) is, in a sense, pursued more aptly by mysticism, than by science, because the mystic leaves nothing out of his reckoning, whereas the scientist detaches himself, the observer, from his observations. Weber further states that 'now [in quantum mechanics] observer and observed are admitted to constitute a unit. But the full meaning of this has not yet caught up with most of the community of scientists who, despite quantum mechanics, believe they can stand aloof from what they work on.'[19] In other words, as stated above, the philosophical implications of the startling revelations of quantum physics (also the earlier influences of Goethean science) have not penetrated the corpus of mainstream science, still wedded to classical (materialistic) physics. Consequently, as David Lorimer remarks in the Foreword to this work: 'Culturally, we are dominated—especially in the West—by science and technology with its prevailing philosophy that mind is an emergent property of matter [consciousness an epiphenomenon of matter] and that everything can or will ultimately be explained in material terms [i.e., in terms of the known laws of physics and chemistry]. To doubt this proposition is to risk branding as a heretic and undermine one's reputation as a "serious scientist", as many have found to their cost, notably in our time […] [a] Nobel laureate […] among many others'—see Chapter 3 of Volume I and especially Volume II, Chapter 7. The principal source of error and confusion in the positivism of the Vienna School is their failure to perceive that their propositions were in fact based upon unsupportable presuppositions—see again Volume I, Chapter 7, page 203.

Quantum science has scarcely displaced logical positivism in mainstream science

> **It is important to distinguish the human being, his state, and his condition from the human body. Scientists and doctors know much about the detailed mechanisms of the latter, the material garment and conduit, but little about the former, its informing spirit, which is the province of mystics, artists, occultists, and that rare breed of modern mystical scientists like Arthur Eddington and Erwin Schrödinger.**

There are clear signs to read in support of the above assertions that, despite the magnificent findings of quantum physics over the past century, materialism is still the governing scientific world-view at large, especially in biology and medicine. At the heart of the matter is the underlying philosophy of the Vienna School of Logical Positivism (also known as the Vienna Circle of Logical Empiricism) of the 1920s, which has morphed into modern scientism that continues to deny, and refuses to acknowledge, its own status as a *belief system or presupposition*—refer to Chapter 3 of Volume I describing the philosophy and metaphysical basis of scientific materialism. The central thesis of the Vienna School is the principle of verification, championed by the likes of the British philosopher Sir Alfred Jules Ayer FBA usually cited as A. J. Ayer (1910–1989).[20, 21] This is the view that scientific knowledge is the only kind of factual knowledge—verifiable through empirical observation—that is cognitively meaningful; therefore, since religion and all traditional metaphysical doctrines cannot be verified as being either true or untrue, they are to be rejected as meaningless. This view, sometimes pejoratively referred to as 'see-touch realism', commits the blunder of mistaking suppositions for propositions and therefore inferring that logical efficacy belongs only to propositions. However, proof depends on presuppositions, not presuppositions on proof. Ironically, then, any attack on metaphysics in this true sense is taken as an attack on the foundations of science.[22] This legacy of the Vienna School about the confusion of presuppositions with propositions is primarily responsible for the materialistic world-view about the primacy of matter, from which follows the logical proposition that mind is an emergent property of matter but which is, in fact, *a mere presupposition about the primacy of physical matter taken at face value*. We can readily discern how this state of affairs plays out in mainstream science nowadays as over the past century.

Meaninglessness or meaning depend on the positivist's level of consciousness

What positivists regard as meaningless becomes meaningful when considered with higher understanding.

Earlier we cited *The Brain: The story of you* by the Stanford University neuroscientist purporting to show that the human mind, and all that we humans experience, is only an emergent property of the interconnecting networks of several trillions of neurons. We follow with a few more representative examples to reinforce our contention about the current domination of materialism in practically all departments of science, other than quantum physics.

First published in 1869, *Nature* is a world-class multidisciplinary, international journal publishing the finest peer-reviewed research in all fields of science and technology. Of all submissions published in the scientific field, forty two per cent are in biochemistry or molecular biology and only ten per cent are in physics.[23] The clear indication is that molecular biology—a mechanistic discipline (based on the physical sciences of chemistry, biology, genetics, and biochemistry)—is attracting more interest from the scientific community than physics, which has been nudged into non-physical realms of investigation and speculation by ideas of non-locality, besides reinstating the central role of consciousness (still so disdainful to most materialists), thus, in a sense, shifting the emphasis from the outer to the inner universe. Closely related to this is the vanquishing of vitalism in the 1920s by the central dogma in biology making the gene and DNA into the 'elementary particles' of biology and assuming a strictly one-way process from DNA to RNA to proteins to function. Although overtaken by complexity theory and epigenetics, this mindset still dominates the biological community pervaded by linear and mechanistic thinking.[24] Significantly, however, in 1933 the Danish Nobel physicist Niels Bohr addressed the question as to whether living processes could be described in terms of pure physics and chemistry in his article *Life and Light* published in *Nature*. He argued that mechanism and vitalism in fact represent a complementarity, which viewpoint the writer totally reinforces.[25]

Molecular biology currently dominates the scientific field

Next we may mention how the marvels of modern technology have mesmerized people into believing that modern science (underpinned by its philosophy of materialism taken at face value) is the only valid pathway to discovering the truth about ourselves, nature, and the universe.[26] Related to that, religion (whose language is symbolism and allegory) has been banished because of our symbolically illiterate culture characterized by an excess of quantitative measures over qualitative values and by literalism and fundamentalism in religion and also the sciences.[27]

New particle collider proposed at CERN

Finally, there is, arguably, no finer example of the primacy of matter in the mainstream scientific mind and its obsessive matter-centric world-view than the current project at the European Organization for Nuclear Research (CERN) to build the next gigantic particle collider. Known as the Future Circular Collider (FCC), it will be a 100-kilometre ring-shaped particle accelerator buried underground near Geneva.[28] It will be many times more powerful than the current largest scientific instrument in the world—the Large Hadron Collider (LHC) at CERN contained in a 26.7-kilometre diameter tunnel at a depth ranging from 50 metres to 175 metres underground. It was the LHC that discovered the Higgs boson, an elementary particle in the Standard Model of particle physics, but it appears that many questions about the universe still remain unanswered. Hence the justification for the FCC to probe ever deeper to find out what is the nature of our universe and what it is made of.[29] As stated in the abstract of the lecture on 7th March 2019 at the prestigious Royal Institution of Great Britain in London, 'This awesome machine [the FCC] will allow physicists to seek answers to some of the deepest questions it is possible to ask about our Universe, including the nature of dark matter, and the balance between matter and anti-matter […]'[30] regarding which the Big Bang should have produced equal amounts but this does not seem to have been the case. The writer attended this lecture and heard, 'We are still only scratching the surface in our understanding of what the Universe is made of.' Apparently, physicists know only five per cent about the total matter in the universe. The Standard Model of Big Bang cosmology is inadequate to explain the remaining ninety-five per cent thought to be made up of dark energy and dark matter—regarding which the FCC is postulated in order to discover new particles to seek answers to the kind of questions posed above about our Universe. In the same lecture it was openly admitted that whereas the science educational technological spin-offs from this project are tangible in the short term, the scientific outcome is uncertain and, in any case, lies in the long term. For example, the Higgs boson was discovered in 2012[31] almost half a century after its initial theoretical prediction in 1964 by the British physicist Peter Higgs FRS, FRSE (*b.* 1929) along with five other scientists. Higgs and the Belgian theoretical physicist François Englert (*b.* 1932) received the Nobel Prize in 2013 for their theoretical predictions several decades ago.

Discovering the 'ultimate' fundamental particle currently dominates particle physics

The total operating budget of the LHC runs to about US$1 billion per year; and taking all costs into consideration, the total cost of finding the Higgs boson ran to about US$13.25 billion.[32] By comparison, the international science journal *Nature* states that the cost of the FCC is expected to be €21 billion (US$23.8). Moreover, a similar project is also planned in China.[33]

All things considered, then, some US$23.8 billion (and presumably of the same order again for a Chinese machine) is being proposed to build a machine to discover the secrets of the universe by probing the heart of matter—and all this when legendary physicists and philosophers like Jeans, Eddington, Popper, and Eccles have pointed to the primacy of consciousness and pronounced the essential stuff of the universe as being, not matter, but of the nature of Mind—see Volume I, Chapter 3. A sombre prognosis, then, for science (and government funding agencies) in the years to come.

The Masks of Omniscience

The second reason why the current global culture (especially in the West) is not propitious 'to wither the preachers of a mad materialism with withering scorn' on a large scale is largely to do with the power-and-prestige-driven egos of scientists, to put it bluntly. In our age of modern science there has risen amongst the ranks of the so-called learned, especially the learned of philosophy, neurobiology, and science of mind, a new order of thinkers whom we may term an 'Academy of the Worldly Sapience', about whom Blavatsky would assuredly have assigned the moniker of 'the intellectual and moral murderers of [our age and] future generations', referring, in her time, to the likes of '[Ernst] Hæckel, Carl Vogt, or Ludwig Büchner, in Germany, or even of [Thomas] Huxley and his co-thinkers in materialism in England—the colossal erudition of the first named notwithstanding.'[34] After arriving at the astounding conclusion that being the intellectual salt of the earth, so representing the acme of human learning on everything, these gentlemen of letters have appointed themselves as the final arbiters of all knowledge. Here is just one of their many absolutely unequivocal pronouncements, curiously 'understated': it comes from a senior member of the 'Academy' and a world renowned 'authority' on religion:

> The God of the Old Testament is arguably the most unpleasant character in all fiction: jealous and proud of it; a petty, unjust, unforgiving control-freak; a vindictive, bloodthirsty ethnic cleanser; a misogynistic, homophobic, racist, infanticidal, genocidal, filicidal, pestilential, megalomaniacal, sadomasochistic, capriciously malevolent bully.[35]

Do rants display balanced reasoning?

One might be permitted to observe that anything worth saying is more effectively accomplished using sober language than through a glut of rants which only serve to camouflage sterility of thought. After all, it is far easier to attack than to discredit sound arguments. The English writer and literary critic Samuel Johnson, byname Dr Johnson (1709–1784), would surely have quipped in relation to Dawkins's outburst:

> You raise your voice [and use a plethora of expletives] when you should reinforce your argument.[36]

Likewise, an ordinary grievance in one's personal life, when unresolved, can all too easily metastasise into the sort of cancerous tirades just exampled. (The same principle also applies on the larger international scene—witness, for example, the aggressive rhetoric between the USA and North Korea in 2020).

Characteristically, then, this motley group declares Deity to be a fabrication of the gullibly superstitious, which God-delusion will all be explained, eventually, purely by brain neurology. And that neurology will eventually prove that the brain generates consciousness—despite the unequivocal pronouncement of sages, and numerous enlightened scientists and psychologists, to the contrary. Moreover, the universe has no particular purpose—notwithstanding the US\$23.8 billion required to construct the FCC to study the so-called fabric of the universe. Furthermore, the visions of all mystics and saints are the delusions of the neurotic or else explainable by perfectly sound physiological arguments. For example, the prophetic visions of Hildegard of Bingen OSB, also known as Saint Hildegard and Sibyl of the Rhine (1098–1179), the German Benedictine abbess, composer, philosopher, Christian mystic, visionary, considered to be the founder of scientific natural history in Germany—were due to migraines! Apparently, she was 'among the earliest migraine sufferers to record her experience in pictures as well as text.'[37] With mainstream science attempting to explain away phenomena completely beyond its legitimate field of discourse, we are unable to resist retorting again with Schrödinger's quip: 'Science sometimes pretends to answer questions in these domains, but the answers are very often so silly that we are not inclined to take them seriously.'

Examples of
unbridled
scientific hubris

Immortality of the soul and spirit is a figment of the naïve imagination, but extinction of consciousness upon death is a scientifically proven fact, since mind and consciousness are emergent properties of the matter of the brain. The authentic accounts from distinguished scientists (like the neurosurgeon Eben Alexander) of their own personal near-death experiences that provide robust 'proof of heaven' are just deluded perorations[38] that can all be explained perfectly adequately by materialist theories like 'continuous electroencephalography in rats during experimental cardiac arrest that show intense brain activity in the dying brain'[39]—which finding can, presumably, be extrapolated to dying human brains.

Moreover, for these cognoscenti, genius is but a fortuitous combination of genes, and legendary figures, like Paracelsus, were infamous quacks, with Blavatsky being the outstanding fraud of history. To cap it all, Newton's supposition of a capricious God interfering, occasionally, in the orbits of the planets and hence in the laws of nature is regarded as the most well supported interpretation, attributed to Hawking, of the famous statement in *Opticks* '[…] till this System wants a Reformation.' Furthermore, some famous scientists on the world stage like to 'enlighten' us that Newton resorted to the 'God of the gaps', an argument in the General Scholium of *Principia*, in an attempt to account for phenomena that he was unable to explain using mechanical principles. In other words, that God must be invoked to bridge the gap between what science can, and cannot, explain—the gap in scientific knowledge being the evidence for the existence of God.[40] The consensus among these scientists is that he was slightly unhinged at the time he dabbled in theology and alchemy—but never mind that Newton studied the Old and New Testaments assiduously, having thirty Bibles in his library in English, Latin, Greek, French, Hebrew, Syriac/Latin, and Greek/Latin; or that his alchemical researches, conducted over thirty years, were contemporaneous with his work in mechanics and optics.[41]

Is the public being
misled about the
real purpose of
science?

These savants of 'the public understanding of science' cherish a blind belief that they wish to impose upon society, namely that science deals only with proven facts and completely explains everything—or will do so in the near future (promissory materialism), except that, given that physicists currently openly acknowledge that they know only around five per cent about the total matter in the universe, and therefore are 'still only scratching the surface' in their understanding of what the universe is made of (see above), there seems to be an awfully long way to go to realize such a dream. Even so, any other claims to knowledge through religion and mysticism, for example, can summarily be dismissed as 'superstitious nonsense' or 'pseudoscience', stated condescendingly. They seem unaware that such historically demonstrable error, plus philosophical naïveté, has merely turned this kind of science into another brand of religious fundamentalism, otherwise known as scientism (having naught to do with the spirit of science), with materialist heavyweights like the Dawkins's, Shermers, Atkins's, Winstons, Wolperts, and Maddoxes as its popes and archbishops. Sadly, these intellectually stunted specimens, propped high on the stilts of media hype, are held in sycophantic esteem by a misguided public.

And how do these highly influential scientists wielding immense political power and control deal with dissenters? We have cited many examples in our work: in the same manner that the Cathars and the Occitanian culture were eradicated in the mid-thirteenth century by the Albigensian Crusade[ii] (which gave rise to the Inquisition in hunting down heresy), the same tendency undoubtedly exists within modern science and medicine in regard to mainstream and alternative, 'heretical' views.

It is for precisely this reason that we have stated periodically throughout this work that famous scientists are not always great scientists. Why? Because the usual trappings of arrogance and self-glorification that go hand in hand with fame can all too easily result in diminishing wisdom, as stated by none other than Einstein, in his typical manner of extreme modesty and self-effacing humbleness, with perhaps a touch of irony:

> With fame I become more and more stupid, which, of course, is a very common phenomenon. There is far too great a disproportion between what one is and what others think he is, or at least what they say they think one is. But one has to take it all with good humor. How wretchedly inadequate is the theoretical physicist as he stands before Nature.[42]

Apropos, it is the writer's judgement that by virtue of his religious convictions,[43] Einstein maintained his enduring humility—see the letters he wrote late in life to his old friends Maurice Solovine and Michael Besso quoted in Volume I, Chapter 5 on page 133. Why? The benefits conferred by a wise marriage of science and religion are numerous; but at the very least, the devotional aspect of religion serves to temper the not infrequent arrogant propensities of science. Wherefore? It is in the nature of science to work predominantly through the intellect, and arrogance is a common casualty of the latter, when in excess; by contrast, religion involves mainly the feelings, and, when exaggerated, gullibility is a predisposition of the latter. Thus, when science and religion or science and mysticism are in dynamic balance, the finest qualities of intellect and feelings, reason and reverence, facts and values are engendered by virtue of the one exerting a constructive counterbalacing influence on the other.

How religion can temper scientific pride

Denying or living in denial of religion and spirituality denies neither religion nor spirituality.

The Promise of Promissory Materialism

In *The Self and Its Brain* by Sir Karl Popper and Sir John Eccles, Eccles states, 'So I am constrained to believe that there is what we might call a supernatural origin of my unique self-conscious mind or my unique selfhood or soul; […]. By this kind of supernatural creation, I escape from the incredible improbability that the uniqueness of my own self is genetically determined (see Volume I, Chapter 4, page 77). In the same book, Popper explicitly states 'materialism has thus transcended itself'; therefore, promissory materialism is essentially an act of faith (see Volume I, Chapter 3, page 35).

Reminding ourselves of the meaning of promissory materialism given in Volume I, Chapter 3, page 35: it is the belief that anything that cannot be explained by materialist science, such as consciousness and the origin of life, will ultimately be explained in the near future by advances in materialist science. Certainly, the Templeton World Charity Foundation (TWCF),[44] seems to have such faith regarding the hard problem of consciousness: how does a physical thing, the brain, generate an internal subjective experience, such

TWCF's faith in promissory materialism

---

ii The 20-year military campaign initiated by Pope Innocent III to eliminate Catharism in Languedoc, in southern France.

as delighting in the colours of sunrise or being moved to tears by music? (This is precisely the Schrödinger mind–sensation problem posed in Volume I, Chapter 3, page 35 and explained at length in Chapter 8.) What is TWCF's solution to the problem that despite thousands of years of enquiry by philosophers and scientists, and notwithstanding such clues from disease, stroke or injury, and sophisticated techniques for mapping activation of brain regions during functions such as speech, decision-making, and sensation, the origins of consciousness have never been fully understood by mainstream neuroscience?

In October 2019, the *Financial Times* announced that 'now a $20 million effort will pit competing theories against each other.'[45] The project by the TWCF was announced at the Society for Neuroscience meeting in Illinois and reported in the journal *Science*, which states that 'the first phase of the $20 million project, launched this week at the Society for Neuroscience meeting in Chicago, Illinois, will compare two theories of consciousness by scanning the brains of participants during cleverly designed tests. Proponents of each theory have agreed to admit it is flawed if the outcomes go against them.'[46]

Are we then any closer to the final and decisive solution? Some scientists certainly think so. A couple of examples should suffice.

The title on the front cover of *New Scientist*, 21 September 2019, proudly announces: 'THE TRUE NATURE OF CONSCIOUSNESS: WE'RE FINALLY CRACKING THE GREATEST MYSTERY OF YOU'. This is in connection with *Rethinking Consciousness: A Scientific theory of subjective experience* by the American Michael Graziano (*b.* 1967), the professor of psychology and neuroscience at Princeton University. It is the latest in a series of learned papers and books offering the promise that the full and final materialistic solution to the hard problem of consciousness is just looming.[47] In keeping with previous books of such ilk this latest book is supposed to be 'eye-opening', offering 'groundbreaking' new theories.

Michael Graziano's imminent promise on how to know ourselves

Graziano's basic premise is that the brain *generates* consciousness which can be discovered through evolutionary theory and by analogy with machines. So by tracing evolution over millions of years we find examples from the natural world to show how neurons first allowed animals to develop simple forms of attention: taking in messages from the environment, prioritizing them, and responding as necessary. Focusing attention apparently helps an animal find food or flee a predator. It also may have led to consciousness. But in order to monitor and control this specialized attention, the brain evolved a simplified model of it—a cartoonish self-description depicting an internal essence with a capacity for knowledge and experience—in other words, consciousness.[48] ('The writer apparently considers it impolite to enquire into the identity of the cartoonist.)

In the related *New Scientist* article, Graziano states, 'In this account, consciousness isn't so much an illusion as a self-caricature.' He then suggests an engineering approach to the problem because 'sometimes, the best way to understand a thing is to try to build it'. Accordingly, 'to engineer human-like consciousness into a machine […] would require just four ingredients: artificial attention, a model of that attention, the right range of content […], and a sophisticated search engine to access the internal models and talk about them.'[49] In essence, this requires uploading the data structure of consciousness into machines.

There is nothing 'groundbreaking' about such ideas. They are merely a left-brain rehashing of outworn mechanistic concepts. His book is indeed a celebration of the machine paradigm of mainstream science wedded to a basic version of Darwinism offering the promise of the natural consciousness of a person uploaded into a machine for a digital afterlife. (But then, somewhat in contradiction, Graziano does state in his *New Scientist* article that he is not advocating conscious robots, whatever he means by that. Nor does he regard consciousness as an ill-defined epiphenomenon.) The same *New Scientist* also quotes Richard Dawkins as saying: 'I think we are all susceptible to a certain level of irrationality,' which must, then, by his own reckoning, include Dawkins himself.[50] But if self-caricature engenders irrationality, the irony will not be lost on our readers.

There seems to be an increasing number of books nowadays by famous neuroscientists offering radical breakthroughs and revolutionary ideas to inform us who we are and who we are supposed to be. The very latest in this genre is *Being You: The inside story of your inner universe*[51] by Anil Seth, Professor of Cognitive and Computational Neuroscience at the University of Sussex. His theory that our brain hallucinates our conscious reality was outlined in Chapter 7, page 115 in connection with the topic of *māyā* (freely translated as illusion, or appearance). Needless to say, his new book unequivocally continues the neuro-centric dogma that everything that makes us who and what we are is inscribed in the brain. Moreover, he purports to explain what happens in the brain to turn mere electrical impulses into the vast range of perceptions, thoughts, and emotions we feel from moment to moment. But how does the combined activity in our brain of billions of neurons, each one a tiny biological machine generating a conscious experience, generate our own unique conscious experience of the world around us and of ourselves within it? 'Once we start explaining its properties in terms of things happening inside brains and bodies, the apparently insoluble mystery of what consciousness is should start to fade away. At least that's the plan.' It certainly is an ambitious plan! But what is not in doubt is that we are constantly hallucinating (and that must include neuroscientists as well). To repeat from Chapter 7 Seth's novel 'definition' of reality: 'when we agree that we have hallucinations "we call that reality."'[52]

Anil Seth's promise to solve the 'insoluble' mystery of consciousness

When will the scientific tide turn towards the *philosophia perennis* so that a true SCIENCE may emerge from its sepulchre of brain-centric scientism? Alas, scientists of the humility and vision of Erwin Schrödinger and the Cambridge professor Julian Allwood (see later) are few and far between. We may have to stretch our patience to the limit and follow Max Planck's advice:

> A new scientific truth does not triumph by convincing its opponents and making them see the light, but rather because its opponents eventually die and a new generation grows up that is familiar with it. . . . An important scientific innovation rarely makes its way by gradually winning over and converting its opponents: it rarely happens that Saul becomes Paul. What does happen is that its opponents gradually die out, and that the growing generation is familiarized with the ideas from the beginning: another instance of the fact that the future lies with the youth.[53]

Insights from enlightened science have barely dented scientific othodoxy

On present reckoning, we may be waiting for an age before mainstream science comes to regard consciousness as *Ātma*, the Divine Self, rather than an illusion or the activity of tiny biological machines known as neurons or the latest 'groundbreaking' ideas—a cartoonish self-description or a self-caricature or a hallucination.

A Hippocratic Oath for Scientists

> 'A very interesting lecture, Barrett, but it's all tosh you know.'

The English physicist and parapsychologist Sir William Barrett FRS (1844–1925) was greeted with the above taunt from a scientific colleague when he had just given a lecture on telepathy. Barrett replied (very much in the spirit of Newton's rejoinder to Edmond Halley—see page 279):

> 'Well, you are a scientific man; when you have given as many weeks as I have given years [fifty years] to the investigation of these subjects I shall value your opinion.'

The quick and generous reply from his colleague was,

> 'You're quite right, I have no right to an opinion, but I will give some time to it myself.'

The result? A similar conviction from Barrett's colleague of the value of such research.[54]

The Hippocratic Oath is taken by physicians. So why not by scientists?

With rare exceptions, as exampled above, it seems that whenever establishment science is unable to explain something (like dowsing or paranormal powers exhibited by animals and humans) the evidence is either just ignored or airbrushed aside as pseudoscience or the stuff of mediæval black arts or witchcraft. Conversely, a true scientist would recall the wise words of both Sir William Crookes OM PRS quoted in Chapter 9: 'To stop short in any research that bids fair to widen the gates of knowledge, to recoil from fear of difficulty or adverse criticism, is to bring reproach on Science'; and Sir William Grove FRS, FRSE (first quoted in Chapter 3 of Volume I): 'Science should have neither desires nor prejudices. Truth should be her sole aim.' Based on these seminal injunctions and in line with the admission made by William Barrett's colleague, the writer proposes the following Hippocratic Oath for scientists:

> As a scientist I cannot deny phenomena that I have witnessed but on the basis of current science I cannot explain them. Maybe physical science must be extended; or perhaps there is a non-physical science of subtler realms of matter with its own laws. I do not know the answer, but I will enquire and try to find out without presuppositions or preconceptions.

Here is an example (first quoted in Appendix I-B to Volume I in the different context of the limitations of the theory of natural selection) of such an enquiry, without presuppositions or preconceptions, from an independent co-discoverer of the theory of natural selection—Alfred Russel Wallace:

> The present gigantic development of the mathematical faculty is wholly unexplained by the theory of natural selection, and must be due to some altogether distinct cause.[55]

Alfred Wallace shows the true spirit of science

It is worth pausing here to evaluate Wallace's thoughts further since they uphold the true spirit of scientific enquiry and allude to the tenets of esotericism about consciousness and mind at a time when materialistic theories were gaining a stranglehold on science due to the ascendency of Darwin's theories, or rather, by the commandments of Darwin's disciples who took up their Master's ideas with a zeal amounting to religious fanaticism. For example, responding to the extended criticism[56] of his statement that 'man consists essentially of a spiritual nature or mind intimately associated with a spiritual body or soul, both of which are developed in, and by means of, a material organism,' Wallace explains: 'There is, I conceive, no contradiction in believing that mind is at once the cause of matter and of the development of individualised human minds through the agency of matter. [And if I were asked,] "Does mortality give consciousness to spirit, or does spirit give consciousness for a limited period to mortality?" I would reply, "Neither the one nor the other; but, mortality is the means by which a permanent individuality is given to spirit." '57

Here, Wallace is pointing to the distinction between an immutable principle—'spirit'—and its vehicle of expression—'permanent individuality'—through forms that are ever changing and subject to decay—'mortality'. This is all perfectly consonant with esotericism.

Scientism Versus the True Spirit of Science

It is one of those tragic and ironic twists in the history of science that whereas Darwin rose to fame, Wallace, ultimately, faded into obscurity, albeit there are now signs of a welcome revival. Nowadays, to reiterate what we just said, mainstream evolutionary biology (championed by the likes of Richard Dawkins and Stephen Jay Gould) has effectively afforded Darwin's theory of natural selection the status of a faith-based religious dogma and completely failed to see its materialistic limitations, which were not lost on Darwin's more enlightened associate, as the above quotes unmistakably show.

But then as Wallace realized, and as we first pointed out in Chapter 4 of Volume I:

> Truth is born into this world only with pangs and tribulations, and every fresh truth is received unwillingly. To expect the world to receive a new truth, or even an old truth, without challenging it, is to look for one of those miracles which do not occur.[58]

A blatant example can be drawn from the researches of William Harvey (1578–1657), the English 'Physician Extraordinary' to King James I. In, or around 1623, Harvey discovered that the circulation of blood in the human body is caused by the pumping action of the heart.[59] This was not on the grounds of conjecture, but after vivisection experiments on dogs and other animals where he actually observed a beating heart. The prevailing physiology was that of Galen of Pergamon (129–210), the Greek physician and surgeon in the Roman Empire, who based his ideas mainly on Aristotle.[60] Galen held that the heart was a 'producer of heat' (convection heater). Thus, after cooling down by the brain the blood flowed to the lower parts of the body and was transported back to the heart by the temperature gradient.[61]

But Harvey's discovery invalidated the Aristotelian–Galenic orthodoxy and his ideas were born into the world 'with pangs and tribulations'. Sadly, his premonition[62] that his discovery would be met by the leading medical authorities with scepticism, then derision and, finally, abuse was entirely justified.[63] It created an outcry throughout Europe. Some doctors affirmed they would 'rather err with Galen than proclaim the truth with Harvey.'[64]

Emilio Parisano, (1567–1643), a leading Italian anatomist and physician quipped sarcastically in 1635:

Presuppositions dominate clear perceptions

> If a horse swallows water, a sound can be heard; we admit that … but that the transport of the blood … should produce a sound that can be heard, this we do not perceive, nor do we think that it should ever be possible, except Harvey borrows us his hearing aid … how should a pulse be felt in the breast? How a sound? … Harvey says from (the motion of the) blood a beat follows and (what he says in addition) a sound: That we deaf ones cannot hear, and there is no one in Venice who can. If he can hear it in London, he may be happy, blessed and lucky. We write in Venice.[65]

This story illustrates how deep-seated assumptions, can not merely distort, but literally block a person's observation of truth. The Aristotelian–Galenic paradigm blinded Parisano from following the obvious course of action—simply to place his ear on a living person's chest, unless of course, he, like his fellow Venetians, happened to be deaf!

It took some twenty years for Harvey's theory of the circulation of the blood to be generally, and grudgingly, accepted.

Devotion to truth
extracts a heavy
price

In principle, the situation these days is no different. For these reasons it is not difficult to appreciate why scientists (especially young researchers embarking upon a career path) feel compelled to 'toe the line' and submit to the authority of the scientific establishment for fear of being ostracized and losing their research grants, and possibly their job. But has this not always been the case, only worse nowadays? Take the case of the 2020 Coronavirus (COVID-19) pandemic. 'Keep washing your hands regularly' has virtually achieved the status of a government mantra for preventing the spread of the virus.[66] Who would argue with that now? But the first recorded discovery of the life-saving power of hand-washing was met with violent opposition (as Wallace would have predicted)—*from the medical profession*. The Hungarian doctor Ignaz Semmelweis (1818–1865), described as the 'saviour of mothers', provided clear evidence in the Vienna hospital where he was working that the mortality rate for new mothers had dropped from eighteen per cent to about one per cent after he ordered trainee doctors to wash their hands and their instruments in a chlorine solution following the dissection of corpses in the morgue before going to the maternity ward to deliver a baby. Alas, the egos of his medical colleagues counted for more than the evidence. Semmelweis met with a tragic end: he lost his job and died in a psychiatric institution.[67]

Neither does the Harvard neurosurgeon Eben Alexander evince much faith in 'look[ing] for one of those miracles which do not occur'. As he succinctly states in connection with his own near-death experience, which clearly demonstrated the survival of consciousness beyond the brain (see Volume I, Chapters 2, page 15):

When science
morphs into a
pseudo-religion of
scientism

> Materialist science has grown into scientism, the worship of science 'for its own sake', although I have come to see materialist science as more of a pseudo-science given its disregard for much of the empirical data and reasoned analysis concerning consciousness, the brain-mind relationship, and quantum physics (as the ultimate ground for the mind-brain question). Materialist science has become a faith-based religion, all based on assumptions taken at face value to be ultimate truth (i.e., 'the physical world is all that exists'). The deeper problem is truly a metaphysical one, involving those basic assumptions. [...] This emerging science of consciousness [is] a rich embodiment of science in its purest form of seeking wisdom about our interrelated universe, not just useful technological manipulations of scientific knowledge to support various human agendas, often aggressively denying the existence of the one thing any one of us truly knows to exist—our conscious awareness.[68]

The earlier phrase 'materialist science as more of a pseudo-science' and the final phrase, 'aggressively denying the existence of the one thing any one of us truly knows to exist—our conscious awareness' both chime strikingly with this warning by Paul Brunton well over three decades ago:

When science
becomes a
superstition

> The intellectuals, including the scientists, have substituted faith in intellectual processes for faith in religious ones. In the last case it is open belief; in the first one, it is masked, hidden, covered up, but still faith.[69]

> All of those who use the data of science to support their belief in intellectual materialism and to justify their scorn for religion and mysticism, deny the very source from which they ultimately draw their intellectual capacity to make their criticism. And to the extent that it lets them use it so, *science itself becomes superstition* [emphasis added].[70]

Furthermore, 'worship of science', the phrase also used by Alexander, finds its perfect echo in Brunton's insight that:

> The right use of science is the physical release of man. The worship of science leads to its wrong use and from there to the downfall of man.[71]

Is it not self-evident that science, meaning physical science, can only address the physical aspects of life, nature, and humanity?

But unfortunately it is not that self-evident to some of our modern feted scientists. Take, for example, Brian Cox FRS (*b.* 1968), the English professor in the School of Physics and Astronomy at the University of Manchester who announced that the year '2020 shows that science has the answers'. Admittedly, this remark was made in a popular magazine, and mainly with reference to the 'progress we've made on [the COVID-19] vaccines'.[72] But the covert message to the public appears to be that we should turn to science for all the answers, either now or in the near future (another case of promissory materialism). Erwin Schrödinger who lamented that 'Science sometimes pretends to answer questions in these [higher] domains' and Max Planck who understood why 'Science [unaided] cannot solve the ultimate mystery of nature' (see Volume I, Introductory, page lxi) would surely have preferred to hear Professor Cox inform us that: 'Mainstream science has many answers regarding our physical life but tells us little about our real nature—who, or what we truly are: religion, art, and philosophy provide the missing complement'. So also would Albert Einstein, who fully acknowledged the precious gifts of science, but realized that 'all our Sciences, measured against Reality, are primitive and child-like' (see Chapter 11).

Science has its priests no less than religion

The gaping hole in scientific knowledge

Thus we are obliged to point out to science that the Mysteries of every single nation are concerned not with the world *outside* but the universe *inside* man. With a few glorious exceptions, modern science and technology is mastering the physical universe and building huge industries, but it is completely unaware of that mysterious fount of *conscious* power within each living being. Without that power there would be no scientific research, no industries, no genome research, no COVID-19 vaccines, no Large Hadron Colliders, no rockets to Mars, no transhumanist attempts to attain immortality, and not even such passionate zeal by atheist scientists to write books about our ultimately purposeless life in a godless universe.

> **Scientific fundamentalism, or scientism, is simply the obverse face of the coin of religious fundamentalism. Both are based on blind faith and superstition. In fact, many scientists have first been devoutly religious (like Michael Shermer, initially staunchly Christian) and then swung to the opposite pole of 'scientific religion' when they entered academe.**

The Legacy of Materialism in Science, Religion, Philosophy, and Economics

What does the lofty wisdom of the world's illumined saviours and sages have in common with the dwarfed and distorted products of the 'physical realism' of our modern authorities and their twists and turns to explain all life and consciousness on a pseudo-materialistic basis ending up as just so much logical twaddle? Nothing at all. All over the world, men and women worn out by the numerous, soulless cultural systems of today are crying out for the return of a lost age of beauty and enlightenment—for something practical in the highest sense of the word. A few are beginning to realize that so-called civilization in its present form is certainly at a turning point, if not at its vanishing point; that heartless commercialism and material efficiency are impractical, and only that which offers opportunity for the expression of truth, love, and wisdom is truly worthwhile. Jean-Paul Sartre (1905–1980), the French existentialist philosopher, playwright, and Nobel laureate in literature wrote of the 'God shaped hole' in our consciousness—that void in our being longing to be filled, rather fulfilled, with the stuff of all that makes us feel truly human and gives our lives a sense of purpose.[73]

Why are people unable to find the happiness and purpose they desperately seek?

It may be a platitude to say that human beings the world over desire happiness and are seeking purpose and direction in their lives by any manner or means, but it is nonetheless true and no exaggeration. Instances regarding the latter are not hard to find. The column appropriately titled 'Spirit of the age' in the April 2021 edition of the British magazine *The Week* informs us that on the social media site TickTock, 'videos with the hashtag #witchtok—offering advice on, for instance, how to discern your future, divine with coins, or perform a hex [place a hurtful spell for revenge] on a cheating lover—have racked up more than 11.7 billion views. That is 2.3 billion more than #Biden.'[74] Concerning the former, new data released by NHS Digital in the UK shows that self-harming among the teenage population is rising at an alarming rate.[75] Not knowing where happiness truly lies, many are flailing around, lost in a miasma of despair caused by separation from their true natures. Hence, they become ready prey to the glitter of gain, duped in large measure by the leaders of nations preaching never-ending economic growth as the royal highway to Shangri-La. But not only this... tied into the vast economic and political systems, medical technology is feted as the 'magic bullet'—the cure all—for all the health problems that face mankind. Man gazes at the Medusa-like face of greed and, standing petrified, looks either to conventional science and medicine as his only salvation or seeks various forms of escape from himself.

Is sound health purely a matter of accidental genes or medical intervention? What has humanity learnt from the pandemic?

An example of the former is the range of vaccines that are being promoted for mass inoc- ulation against COVID-19. The unwritten and unspoken message, full of hope and promise seems to be: 'After vaccinating the population all will be well and we can revert to our former ways—"business as usual".' No one—least of all the writer—would wish to deny the benefits of vaccination to those who have carefully considered such a course of action, but how many are following the medical dictates blindly with little under- standing that physical medicine can do but little to alleviate problems that are the result of faulty thinking, unnatural lifestyle, and starvation of soul and spirit? Whether one chooses to be inoculated or not, there is no doubt that the 2020 pandemic was, and is, a resounding wake-up call to mankind to reorient his sense of values away from unbridled commercialism towards a more natural lifestyle with greater reverence towards his fellow beings, nature, and the planet he inhabits. Notwithstanding the judicious use of vaccines, or any other form of physical medicine, radiant health is no fortuitous concurrence of 'simply the right genetic makeup' or, merely, 'lucky personal circumstances'. In most cases, it is the result of the individual having worked for it, therefore having deserved, and earned it, in this and former incarnations. How? By living on all three levels of his being—spirit, soul, and body; more technically by the interaction of the seven principles of his consti- tution (see Table II-3 on page 21 in Volume II).

As regards escapism, this of course takes myriad forms, from illicit sexual encounters, alcohol, and drugs to vacuous or lewd entertainment on smartphones or similar such 'intelligent' devices—and ultimately, self-harm or suicide. The latest escape route is about the finest example of the panacea of scientific technology under the command of billionaires with galactic ambitions—namely, to colonize Mars. The South African born American engineer and business magnate Elon Musk FRS (*b.* 1971) has confirmed that the next flight test of SpaceX's Mars-bound Starship rocket is imminent.[76] The SpaceX spacecraft is designed to carry a cargo and up to one hundred people to the Moon, Mars, or anywhere else in the solar system, and land back on Earth standing on its base. His ultimate objective? Seeing human life on Mars.[77] Why? Well, having polluted, over-populated, and basically made a mess of living on our dear planet Earth, let's move on to another planet and do it all over again. It is important to extend consciousness beyond our planet—so we are told, but we might ask: 'what kind of "consciousness"'? But why just stop at that? Why not compete with another entrepreneur over such 'laudable' aims? Having stepped down after twenty-seven years as chief executive of Amazon, the American industrialist Jeff Bezos (*b.* 1964) has other ideas about how his wealth can save humanity. Blue Origin, his space Company, is currently focussing on space tourism 'but he is preparing for a future in which most humans will live in floating space colonies with Earth-like features (geo-engineered countryside and replicas of real cities); mining and heavy industry is conducted on other planets; *and Earth becomes a national park* [emphasis added]. It is the only way, he says, of ensuring rising living standards for an expanding human population without destroying Earth.'[78] Given that Bezos's fortune is estimated (in 2021) at around $200 billion (incidentally, double the figure mooted by the US military to develop a new intercontinental missile—see below) the writer might respectfully suggest that Blue Origin be renamed 'Blue Earth' to regenerate the ecosystems on our own planet, starting with, of course—the rainforest known as Amazon. And who, may we enquire, has granted Bezos divine rights to extract minerals from other planets and supposedly pollute their environments through 'heavy industry'?

Will colonizing Mars save the human race?

The sheer ignorance and naïveté of such super-egocentric thinking by supposedly intelligent people (especially plutocrats) beggars belief. The cardinal error is to think that by changing outer circumstances the inner life will improve. It is completely the other way round. The unequivocal teaching of sages since time immemorial is that only by a radical change in the inner structure of consciousness—an enrichment of the inner life which in turn is dependent upon the unfolding of the Higher mind with its accompanying higher faculties of true Reason and Intuition—can we change the outer conditions of our lives.

It is precisely because these faculties have not been adequately unfolded that in this increasingly commercial age, mainstream science is still largely concerned with the cold classification of physical facts and knowledge, technological progress, and the investigation of the temporal and illusionary parts of nature (with technical jargon occasionally invented to mask ignorance). That which concerns man's soul nature and the purpose of his life is supposed to be the stuff of idle dreams, unrelated to the practicalities and economics of daily life. Recall Schrödinger's plaintive observation, quoted in the epigraph to Volume I, Chapter 3, page 22 as to how science 'gives a lot of factual information, puts all our experience in a magnificently consistent order, but it is ghastly silent about all and sundry that is really near to our heart'—in other words, having naught to do with morality, virtue, philanthropy (notwithstanding the confident claim that such qualities will ultimately all be explained by science alone—refer to the section on the 'Church of Scientism' in Volume I, Chapter 4, page 119 et seq.). Why has this sorry state of affairs come about? Why have mainstream science and medicine not been pursued within an expanded world-view for decades? There are three strands to the contention as Iain McGilchrist's seminal insight lays bare:

> Nowadays science [and medicine] is an industry, practised factory-fashion, with huge empires, awards, egos at stake, and dependent on vastly expensive machinery [recall the US$23.8 billion needed to build the Future Hadron Collider at CERN described earlier]. No young scientist now dares step out of line if he or she wants a career, and the more established ones have everything to lose by doing so. As a result, *true science is practised less and less* [emphasis added]. It takes huge moral commitment and courage to think less narrowly, but without thinking differently no great discoveries are made. In the second place, broadcasters and journalists are afraid of appearing foolish by giving any credence to anything other than scientism (and are also now locked into huge, inflexible bureaucratic systems); and the humanities have lost their nerve, for a host of reasons, and just want to ape what they see as 'science', but which is in fact scientism.[79]

Science now virtually an industry

And the result? The so-called practical (meaning, predominantly utilitarian) discoveries of science invariably bind man but more tightly with the bonds of physical limitation by way of largely useless technology (like iphone apps) cunningly publicized and marketed as 'progress'. Certainly, science and technology have greatly alleviated physical suffering and improved material conditions in all manner of means, as we have been at pains to acknowledge, but have they added to the overall stock of human *happiness*? Schrödinger, for one, has his doubts. His slim volume *Science and Humanism* opens with 'The Spiritual Bearing of Science on Life' from which this passage stands out:

> I consider it extremely doubtful whether the happiness of the human race has been enhanced by the technical and industrial developments that followed in the wake of rapidly progressing natural science.[80]

Does peace between nations arise from a change in consciousness or more weapons of mass destruction?

And Schrödinger penned those words in 1951. What would he have written as we approach the third decade of the twenty-first century? How would he have responded upon hearing that in addition to America's current nuclear arsenal of 3,800 warheads, the US Air Force plans to order more than six hundred new weapons of mass destruction currently being developed in America: an intercontinental nuclear missile the length of a bowling lane, able to travel some six thousand miles, carrying a warhead more than twenty times more powerful than the atomic bomb dropped on Hiroshima, able to kill hundreds of thousands of people in a single shot—at a cost (2021) of $100 billion.[81] Would he have recommended maintaining peace by elevating our thinking or by keeping the military industrial complex going by upgrading weapons under the theory of deterrence? How would he have commented on the fragmented consciousness of current humanity spending, on the one hand, billions to develop a COVID-19 vaccine to save millions of lives, and on the other hand, billions to upgrade nuclear missiles potentially to destroy millions of lives? Would Schrödinger have qualified his doubts with Brunton's observation (see page 319) about the worship of science leading to its wrongful use and subsequently to the downfall of man; conversely, the rightful use of science furthering the physical release of man? But science is here to stay, therefore: 'It is no use denouncing science for the horrors of war, the miseries of industrialism, and the unbelief of materialism. The way to conquer the evils arising from the unethical abuse of science is to go right inside its camp and win it over to philosophy.'[82] This is the approach that the writer has been advocating throughout this work.

And what of religion? It too has, in the main, become materialistic, in a different sense. Having all but lost the truly life-affirming guidance imbued in the esoteric import of the scriptures, it remains stuck to outworn exoteric concepts of a bygone age, the beauty and dignity of faith measured by largely empty prattle and dogma from the pulpits of churches, mosques, and temples. That is the main reason why one frequently hears scientists making belittling remarks like: 'Religion is based on faith whereas science is based on facts.' In point of fact, RELIGION in the deepest sense, is more fact-based than science: it is based on the *facts of unassailable experience* (see Volume I, Chapter 7, page 190 et seq.) rather than, as in much of science, faith in intellectual processes, supposedly backed by the 'facts' of physical experiments.

Why have the orthodox religions become like empty vessels making a lot of noise?

Moreover, orthodox Christianity owes the Devil thanks and gratitude for 'His' existence. Having cunningly personified what is the impersonal, counteracting force in Nature, the tracts of real estate and overflowing coffers of the Church are due, in large measure, to its exercise of power and control over unthinking people. Such people, in good faith, believed—and still do believe— that allegiance and material donations to the Church will alone afford protection from Satan corrupting their souls. In short, they imagine that they can buy salvation. Recall the examples given in Volume I, Chapter 9, page 290 about prosperity preachers and televangelists in America having amassed huge personal fortunes, including private jets, thanks to donations from their followers who were merely being asked to follow the will of God.

How about philosophy: that which connects Heaven to Earth (akin to the Deductive Method of reasoning from universals to particulars) and Earth to Heaven (akin to the Inductive Method of reasoning from particulars to universals)—an immense ladder, up the rungs of which the illumined of all ages have ascended into the living presence of Reality? The majesty, dignity and transcendence of that Reality are no more in much of academe as it has mostly degenerated into a prosaic and heterogeneous mass of conflicting, cerebral concepts to be fought out in the gladiatorial halls of academia. Like other branches of human thought, philosophy has been made 'practical' and 'rational' (again mistaking the utilitarian for the practical and the cerebral for the rational) and its activities have become so denigrated that they have been prostituted to the material. In this sense they have undoubtedly contributed to the erection of this modern world of steel and concrete, robots and computers. However, on a positive note, the once taboo term 'consciousness' is slowly becoming acceptable currency in academic psychology. Nonetheless, any young researcher expressing an interest in parapsychology is sure to sound the death knell to his career advancement. And needless to say, to talk these days unguarded in public, let alone in the higher echelons of academia or prestigious scientific institutions,[iii] of the ever-invisible, benevolent hand of higher intelligences guiding the course of evolution is not just to risk, but to guarantee a derisory snort.

Why has much of academic philosophy become just a 'cerebral gymnasium'?

And what about the social science that studies the production, distribution, consumption of goods and services, and transfer of wealth—economics? In the main today, the vast majority of economists are concerned with the balance between capital and labour, with

---

iii For example, the Royal Institution of Great Britain and the Royal Society of London.

land and environmental concerns relegated to second place. Are economic and business models, then, based on entirely materialistic and fiscal considerations bereft of ethical values? With rare exceptions, it would seem so.[83] What better example than this quote, which speaks for itself, from Baron Kalms (b. 1931), life president and former chairman of Dixons Retail, which owns Currys, PC World, and various international electronics retailers:

Should ethics not figure in economics?

> Sir, Around 1991 I offered the London School of Economics a grant of £1 million to set up a Chair of Business Ethics. John Ashworth, at that time the Director of the LSE, encouraged the idea but he had to write to me to say, regretfully, that the faculty had rejected the offer as it saw no correlation between ethics and economics. Quite.
>
> Lord Kalms, House of Lords.
> *The Times* 8th March 2011[84]

The Disdain of Wisdom and Ethics

If, then, the economic institutions and scientific establishment think they have, or will soon acquire, all answers to all questions about life, existence, and consciousness, why are there diametrically opposed categorical statements about consciousness from Nobel laureates such as detailed in Chapter 2 of Volume I on page 8? Then, why all the hair-splitting hypotheses and internal inconsistencies in the various versions of physicalism as summarized in Chapter 3 of Volume I, page 29 f.—such as identity theory, behaviourism, functionalism, revisionary physicalism, anomalous monism, emergentism, eliminative materialism? And what about the plethora of pseudo-materialist theories scientists promulgate attempting to explain away near-death experiences which all seem to generate more confusion and heated debate on the nature of the phenomenon?

So it is deplorable to see the modern intellectualist profiling a flourish of post-nominal initials of scientific accreditation after his name, whilst assuming a contempt towards the sacred sciences proportionate to the honours he has received in the physical sciences. And he may not stop there, but seeks to impress upon the public two things: (*a*) that the infinite diversity of our mental life, our ambitions and aspirations, our loves and joys, our sorrows and struggles are all purely and simply the by-product of the 'jelly' in our brains, meaning the physical, nominal electrochemical, and biological cerebral processes—and absolutely nothing else; and (*b*) that we humans have evolved by descent from barbarians and apes. Regarding the first, mainstream science openly admits its bafflement, but still obdurately chooses not to look 'above and beyond', as exampled by Eagleman who admits that it is not known how conscious awareness, or the experience of sensations, arises from physical brain processes, other than the fact—according to him—that it does; and regarding the second, on the grounds of still uncertain fossil evidence and a theory of evolution that is increasingly cracking at the seams.

What drives science to discover human origins?

Amongst the latest revelations from these aficionados of materialism concerns our human origins. It now seems that the clue lies in the *Saccorhytus coronarius* discovered in China— a one millimetre sized invertebrate sea-dweller with a wrinkled sack-like body, an oversized mouth, and no anus, that lived some 540 million years ago. Discovered in 2017 by an international team of academics, including the English evolutionary palæobiologist Simon Conway Morris FRS (b. 1951) from Cambridge University and the Chinese palæontologist Degan Shu (b. 1946) of Northwest University in Xi'an City, China, this fossilized organism is thought to be our oldest evolutionary ancestor. According to Shu, 'Saccorhytus gives us remarkable insights into the very first stages of the evolution of a group that led to the fish, and ultimately, to us [humans].'[85] But the issue is far from being resolved. Less than a year later, researchers at the University of Bristol used statistical techniques to evaluate various evolutionary models used, and have now declared the 'sponge' to be the true 'sister' to all living species. This finding is supposed to be of crucial importance because it finally resolves the dispute about the origin of animals and sheds light on what our oldest common ancestor was like, namely, a simple, filter-feeding spongey organism.[86] However, we are not informed how the Saccorhytus or the sponge, itself came into being. An august pedigree indeed for mankind, with the 'final and definitive answer' periodically changing in the quicksand of scientific research severely crippled by its own materialistic preconceptions.

But simple, or even illiterate, folk who go about their ordinary lives, devoted to their families and tending to sick relatives, who spend their days toiling in the fields or the factories or working diligently for long hours in a monotonous job, glued to their computer screens at the office, are not so easily fooled by all this highfalutin intellectual froth. Being more in touch with the heartbeat and pulse of life, they inwardly sense that a theory or idea in vogue that attracts the highbrows of academia, or the media, does not necessarily make it the more valid or beneficial to life and society; and that hygiene applies as much to the world of physical matter as it does to the realm of mind, such that *some of the latest ideas and experiments in science (see especially below regarding transhumanism and cryonics) are the intellectual equivalent of utter filth.* These so called 'ordinary' people may not have any academic qualifications or scientific training, they may not have written erudite books or be able to express their thoughts in eloquent language, yet, they realize in their heart-of-hearts that there is more to life than the fortuitous concurrence of 'selfish' genes that make up a human being, especially his human qualities of love, compassion, and supernal genius. They instinctively feel and know that hidden influences, mystery, and magic cast their invisible spell over our lives, raising us from the rank of 'lumbering robots' to the dignity of the gods. No wonder, then, that the Harry Potter books and films have achieved such overwhelming popularity amongst the population at large. So also Wagner's *Ring Cycle* amongst music lovers, especially *Das Rheingold*, the first opera, with its theme of love versus power, set in a world of mythical giants and castles, scheming dwarves and magic potions, and the poisonous influence of the all-powerful Ring guarded by the Rhinemaidens.

Common folk sometimes show more wisdom and common sense than the intelligentsia

That the spiritual intimations of ordinary, humble people, as also the wisdom of enlightened scientists striving to elevate scientific endeavour and human thought out of the mire of selfish materialism, are still ousted by the last word of the intellectual literati regarded as the ultimate authority of the present age—the self-appointed debunkers of the mystical and paranormal, even the 'pseudoscientific', to wit—is a spectacle as old as the hills. As far back as the thirteenth century, the Persian Sūfī poet and mystic Saadi of Shiraz (1210–1291/1292) said it all in just four lines:

> So it has happened since the world began –
> The witless ape outstrips the learned man;
> A poet dies of hunger, grief, and cold;
> A fool among the ruins findeth gold.[87]

Similar sentiments were echoed in modern times by Einstein:

> Great spirits have always found violent opposition from mediocrities. The latter cannot
> understand it when a man does not thoughtlessly submit to hereditary prejudices, but
> honestly and courageously uses his intelligence and fulfils the duty to express the results
> of his thought in clear form.[88]

With rare exceptions, like Einstein, the world has ever been prone to heap plaudits upon its imposters and fools and calumny upon its profound thinkers and sages. Add to this the almost universal tendency of blind trust in the opinion of 'experts', surely one of the best examples being the 'amazing' James Randi (1928–2020), the Canadian–American stage magician and self-appointed scientific sceptic eulogized in science journals and the media as the arch-debunker of allegedly paranormal and pseudoscientific claims.[89] Alfred Russel Wallace issues this salutary warning in a short essay communicated to the Psychical Congress held in Chicago in August 1893:

> I thus learnt my first great lesson in the inquiry into these obscure fields of knowledge,
> never to accept the disbelief of great men or their accusations of imposture or of imbe-
> cility, as of any weight when opposed to the repeated observation of facts by other men,
> admittedly sane and honest. The whole history of science shows us that whenever the
> educated and scientific men of any age have denied the facts of other investigators *on a
> priori grounds of absurdity or impossibility* [emphasis added], the deniers have always been
> wrong.[90]

The denial of 'the repeated observation of facts' of *psi* and related phenomena on 'a priori grounds of absurdity' admirably proves the point—see especially Volume I, notably Chapter 4.

Be that as it may, is it possible to discern the hidden purpose in what appears at face value to be so dispiriting?

Nature's Hidden Purposes

We may still remind those who yet despise all that is spiritual, religious or mystical that such a day may come, in fact must come, when, as the visionary Lebanese mystic Kahlil Gibran eloquently puts it:

> But you do not [yet] see, nor [yet] do you hear, and it is well.
> The veil that clouds your eyes shall be lifted by the hands that wove it,
> And the clay that fills your ears shall be pierced by those fingers that kneaded it.
> And you shall see
> And you shall hear.
> Yet you shall not deplore having known blindness, nor regret having been deaf.
> For in that day you shall know the hidden purposes in all things,
> And you shall bless darkness as you would bless light.[91]

When that day shall come when man painfully and laboriously manages to unblock his ears and rent the veil covering his eyes to hear and see for himself 'the hidden purposes in all things' cannot be prophesied, as each man's destiny, linked to his own karma is uniquely different. But what we can be certain of is that his ignorance is but a temporary phase state in the transition to enlightenment: that is why the worldly man of flesh will 'bless darkness as [he] would bless light', for how would man be fully self-aware of enlightenment other than through a remembrance of his former state of spiritual blindness? The tides of evolution however are not at a scientist's behest as some transhumanists seem to imagine (see below) and the inexorable onward march of man's evolution of consciousness will bestow on humanity in the future that which a few have realized even now. Then mankind will realize that the hidden purposes are none other than what the Science of the Eternal and Ageless Secrets of Cosmos, Nature and Man—Occult Science—has imparted since the dawn of humanity. And, for those who care to observe and listen, this royal Science has taught the overriding influence of greater 'parental' Intelligences from planetary and solar schemes higher than our own ('gods', relatively speaking) watching over and guiding the spiritual evolution and consciousness of our humanity and supplying an impulse at rare, epochal moments to assist its limitless evolutionary progress and unlimited flowering of consciousness. The writer speculates that this general idea might be what Newton alluded to in guarded tones in Question 31 of *Opticks*, quoted earlier in Chapter 6, which bears repeating due to its tremendous import:

Newton's intuitions on planetary Guardianship

> Blind Fate could never make all the Planets move one and the same way in Orbs concen-trick, some inconsiderable Irregularities excepted, which may have risen from the mutual Actions of Comets and Planets upon one another, and which will be apt to increase, *till this System wants a Reformation* (emphasis added).[92]

So Why is it that 'Science is Our Best Ally'?

Whereas the above sections may have sounded a bleak note of pessimism in the interests of realism, it is necessary to provide a counterbalance of optimism, springing not from wishful thinking, but based on an objective appraisal of long term future trends and cycles in line with the prophetic remark of one of the Adept founders behind the modern Theosophical movement quoted in the subheading above.[93] The message is that the verities revealed by Occult Science will slowly find their rightful justification later through the ongoing march of modern science.

Our last example of a scientist who understood both the blessings and limitations of science and technology, and saw the need to look beyond, is Julian Allwood FREng, the contemporary British Professor of Engineering and the Environment at the University of Cambridge. In regard to the current climate crisis he cautioned that 'We cannot rely on technological innovation to solve the climate crisis'[94] because 'Our habits must change to deliver on PM's [Boris Johnson's] climate targets.'[95] Then, in a moving interview on 23 September 2020, part of BBC Radio 3's *Beethoven Unleashed* season marking the 250th anniversary of Beethoven's birth, Allwood drew our attention to the fact that when Galileo invited Claudio Monteverdi (1567–1643) to look through his telescope, the great Italian composer was inspired to write *Vespro della Beata Vergine* (Vespers for the Blessed Virgin), sometimes called Monteverdi's *Vespers of 1610*. Allwood told us that the fashionable idea that science has, or will have, the answer to all things (i.e., promissory materialism—see Volume I, Chapter 3, pages 35–6) is highly unsatisfactory. He pointed out that there is always the need for art, music, and poetry, drawing our attention to Percy Bysshe Shelley's claim in *A Defence of Poetry*, written in 1821, that poets are 'the unacknowledged legislators of the world'.[96] What did Shelley mean by this? Legislators, or lawmakers, manifest

Enlightened scientists draw inspiration from Art

ideas—that is, they actualise what is potential, much as a bud develops into a flower and sometimes a fruit. Moreover, like legislators, Shelley believed that poets and writers shape and lead society because they are able to reveal to men the inner nature of things and thus envision a brighter future, 'writ large' for lesser mortals to glimpse a finer order of things and express it. Shelley describes this well when he further wrote that the poet 'not only beholds intensely the present as it is, and discovers those laws according to which present things ought to be ordered, but he beholds the future in the present, and his thoughts are the germs of the flower and the fruit of latest time.'[iv]

Why are poets 'the unacknowledged legislators of the world'?

So too did Einstein, upon contemplating such lofty matters as the structure of the universe and the genesis of scientific laws, come to a conviction in his later years that science rests on mysteries unknowable to the human intellect. Therefore, scientific theories convey only part of reality; beyond them lie the immeasurable, the inexplicable, and even the miraculous.[97]

Scattered throughout these three Volumes, we have referred to the 'best ally' of Occult Science and have been at pains to point out how enlightened scientists have ever sought to expand the scope of scientific enquiry beyond the confines of strict materialism—the remit of the Galileo Commission outlined in Volume I, Chapter 5.

The front cover of the Galileo Commission Report is topped by the picture of a telescope. In the same spirit that Galileo invited the philosophers in Padua to look through his telescope rather than turning a blind eye and taking refuge in their preconceived theories, the Galileo Commission is an invitation to mainstream science to look through the telescope and to find ways in which to expand and deepen science beyond its materialistic preconceptions. In similar vein, Volume III of our work is subtitled *Gazing Through the Telescope – Man is the Measure of All Things*.

Looking with the eyes of flesh or through the eyes of Spirit?

But, as always in such matters, there are two diametrically opposed ways in which to look: using the eyes of flesh, we may look and find that the stars are mere spheres of glowing gas and then lament with Steven Weinberg that since David's day the heavens have lost their divine status (see Chapter 11); or else, whilst not belittling the physical discoveries of astronomy, we may also take inspiration from Monteverdi who looked through Galileo's telescope, using the eyes of spirit, and was inspired to write his sacred *Vespers*, which has uplifted generations of humanity for over four centuries.

Through what 'eyes', one wonders, would scientists of today look through that same telescope? The writer believes that there is good reason to be optimistic in that, driven by Science's unimpeachable quest for truth and its increasing dissatisfaction with purely materialistic approaches to the deeper issues of human existence, increasing numbers of scientists will follow in the footsteps of Plotinus who realised that Truth is revealed only to those who have become like it, viz:

> For the one who sees has a kinship with that which is seen, and he must make himself the same as it if he is to attain the sight. For no eye has ever seen the sun without becoming sun-like, nor could a soul ever see Beauty without becoming beautiful. You must first actually become wholly god-like and wholly beautiful if you intend to see god and Beauty.[98]

---

iv See Volume I, Chapter 6, pages 169–71 for the context in which William James drew upon Shelley's poem *Adonais* to illustrate the transmissive function of the human brain.

The principal aim of the Galileo Commission Report of the Scientific and Medical Network is to challenge the adequacy of the philosophy of scientific materialism (scientism) as an *exclusive* basis for knowledge and values.[99] Represented by a distinguished group of some one hundred scientific advisers affiliated to more than thirty universities worldwide, and supported by over six hundred and thirty references by eminent scientists, psychologists, and philosophers, the Galileo Commission Report breaks new ground in expounding the argument that materialism, on its own, does not have sufficient explanatory power over numerous phenomena, least of all regarding *psi* occurrences or the nature of consciousness.

Whilst fully acknowledging the immense contributions of science, the purpose of the Galileo Commission Report is to invite scientists and academics to 'look through the telescope' at such research evidence that has been ignored or dismissed because it is philosophically incompatible with materialism. This would be accomplished by identifying and addressing those factors that currently inhibit or vitiate scientific progress. It is well known that science is currently under attack, both from self interest groups trying to advance their own agendas and from others who are motivated by economic or political considerations. Understandably, there is public disenchantment about the trustworthiness of scientific findings, from even within the scientific community itself.

> The Galileo Commission seeks to expand science and raise it to a higher metaphysic

Thus the Galileo Commission Report invites scientists to question the existing implicit background philosophy and assumptions in science that are taken for granted, without demur, at face value. The main argument of the Report calls for a richer and better science—a science that has a wider perspective and a broader philosophy. This wider approach would take into consideration subjects currently considered taboo because they cannot be accommodated within the self limiting paradigm of contemporary science—for example, mysticism, religious experience, paranormal phenomena, and the whole issue of divinity. The Galileo Commission Report lays out a road map to a wider area of science and invites discourse so that scientific progress is not blocked by an outdated view of the nature of reality and consciousness. This significant step forward is needed urgently so that science can advance unencumbered by its outmoded mindset and address the challenges of the twenty-first century—challenges it has been unable to accomplish for philosophical reasons.

The arguments in the Galileo Commission Report take on an even deeper significance as the impact of COVID-19 continues to play out in the world. They highlight the conflict over the accuracy of science and political decisions along with a lack of public trust. More importantly, the Galileo Commission Report offers a practical solution.[100]

On the overarching subject of consciousness, the Galileo Commission Report advocates a complementarity model, that is, when consciousness and matter are seen as co-primaries, which is, arguably, the best scientific way of affirming the co-primacy (*not* a fundamental, or irresolvable duality) of: 'Spirit (or Consciousness) and Matter [which] are, however, to be regarded, not as independent realities, but as the two facets, or aspects, of the Absolute (Parabrahman), which constitute the basis of conditioned Being whether subjective or objective',[101] in terms of occultism; or in terms of Sāṃkhya philosophy, *Puruṣa* and its correlate, *Prakṛti*—see Chapter 8, page 155 et seq. This theme is developed in an academic journal entitled 'Inner Experience – Direct Access to Reality' by Harald Walach, psychologist, medical researcher, philosopher of science, and author of the Galileo Commission Report.[102]

> The Galileo Commission model of consciousness and matter

In physics, energy and matter are co-primary. So why not Consciousness and Matter?

To expand on what has been said above, a complementarity model is, in effect, a dual aspect, or minimum-consensus, model in which matter and mind, consciousness and its physical substrate, are two aspects of reality that are irreducible and simultaneously occurring perspectives of an underlying reality to which we would otherwise have no direct access. However, see the elucidation in Chapter 8 on pages 156, 161, and 168 about the occult doctrine on the perception of the whole manifested universe in its infinite states of subtlety, right down to the physical plane, being the result of the involution of Consciousness **as Matter**—not **in Matter**—thus, a phenomenon of pure Consciousness. By way of a simplistic illustration, no one would argue that ice *produces*, or *generates*, say, water vapour; rather that ice (visible and tangible) and water vapour (invisible and intangible) are different phase states of one substance—H_2O. Continuing this line of reasoning, when invoking $E = mc^2$, no physicist would ever declare that energy expresses *in*, or *through* matter, or for that matter (excusing the pun), that matter *generates* energy: rather, that energy expresses *as matter* ('bottled-up waves', as Sir James Jeans put it[103]); conversely, matter expresses *as energy* ('unbottled waves'). All physicists would agree upon the co-primacy of energy and matter, at the physical level—that matter is, in truth, a phenomenon of pure energy. Is it not then logical to suppose that the same line of reasoning also applies at the transcendent level? The writer is at a loss to understand why there is what amounts to an obsession in mainstream science to prove a *non sequitur*, namely, that consciousness is the *product* of physical matter, which means that the matter in the brain *generates*, or *produces* consciousness?

Shown below are journal articles, YouTube, and digital downloadable versions accessed on 20 January 2021 of the *Galileo Commission Report: Beyond a Materialist Worldview – Towards an Expanded Science*, given in hierarchical order according to the needs of enquirers ranging from serious scientists to laypersons:

Academic and simpler versions of the Galileo Commission Report

1   Harald Walach, *Galileo Commission Report* (The Scientific and Medical Network, 2019) <https://galileocommission.org/wp-content/uploads/2020/02/Science-Beyond-A-Materialist-World-View-Digital-18.02.20.pdf>

2   Harald Walach, *Galileo Commission Summary Report* <https://www.galileocommission.org/wp-content/uploads/2019/03/Galileo-Commission-Summary-Report-Digital.pdf>Summary of argument in English and ten foreign languages: 'Beyond a Materialist Worldview – Towards an Expanded Science' <https://galileocommission.org/report/#summary>

3   Harald Walach, 'Report of the Galileo Commission Project', *Paradigm Explorer – Journal of The Scientific and Medical Network*, 128 (2018) 5–10.

4   Tabitha Jayne and Harald Walach, *Galileo Commission – The Layman's Guide* <https://galileocommission.org/the-laymans-guide-to-the-galileo-commission-report-final-3-12-20>

5   David Lorimer, 'The Galileo Commission: towards a post-materialist science. An Invitation to Look Through the Telescope', *Journal for the Study of Spirituality*, 9/1 (2019).

6   YouTube video Harald Walach, 'Galileo Commission Report – Beyond a Materialistic Worldview', *Society for Scientific Exploration* [video], YouTube (recorded 18 December 2019, uploaded 20 January 2021) https://www.youtube.com/watch?v=ngFfYtf-Aok

Since its inauguration in 2019, the Galileo initiative has received considerable acclaim and its progress has accelerated. Unsurprisingly, the mainstream media have ignored, and virtually snubbed, its *raison d'être*. Nonetheless, some thirty learned societies dedicated to the advancement of human understanding and progress have forged partnerships with the Galileo Commission and seem to be gravitating towards the view that consciousness now occupies centre-stage and is not an epiphenomenon of brain neurochemistry. These societies are listed in Endnote III-7 and include the Institute of Noetic Sciences, the Academy for the Advancement of Postmaterialist Sciences, and the Society for Psychical Research. *Is Consciousness Primary?* is a multi-authored landmark volume where leading consciousness researchers describe how their studies and life experiences led them to the conclusion that mind and consciousness are fundamental, and not incidental, to our understanding of reality. This marks a revolution in our perception of consciousness.[104]

Learned societies and funding organizations recognizing value of the Galileo initiative

The Galileo Commission is generously supported by grants from a Charitable Foundation, one of whose principal objectives is 'to encourage studies on the phenomenon of consciousness and to support initiatives favouring the evolution of consciousness and a better understanding of personal and transpersonal psychology.' The grant for Phase 1 of the Galileo Commission Report was awarded in 2017 for the production of the Report, cited in point 1 opposite. The grant for Phase 2 of the Report was awarded in 2019 and this was mainly to promote outreach.

In continuing recognition of the seminal value of its work, the Galileo Commission was awarded another substantial grant in 2020 for Phase 3. This Phase comprises the development of two strands of work over the next three years in order to extend the reach of the Galileo Commission's initiative in relation to:

1. A group working on the elaboration of a self-reflective and interdisciplinary science of consciousness that takes into account the inseparability of the knower and the known. (Recall Max Planck's insight, stated in Volume I, Introductory on page lxii, that science, unaided by the likes of music and art, cannot solve the ultimate mystery of nature because, in the last analysis, we ourselves are part of nature and therefore part of the mystery that we are trying to solve.)

Ongoing Galileo initiatives

2. A group working towards a renaissance of the human element within the humanities so that these can be recontextualised as the study of consciousness within culture. This same group also encourages self-reflectively taking into account the nature of the knower, as above.

Both of these initiatives derive from the contention in the Galileo Commission Report, articulated with philosophical and scientific rigour, that *consciousness can give us direct access to the deeper structures of reality*. Obviously, this represents a radical departure from the mainstream neuroscientific dictate about consciousness being entirely a *productive* function of the brain (recall the Templeton World Charity Foundation $20 million project launched in 2019 to compare two competing theories of consciousness by scanning the brains of participants).

The two factors that mark out the uniqueness of the Galileo Commission compared to several other worthy initiatives with similar aims are:

1. the global dialogue about a science of consciousness;

2. the imperative of a self-reflective (experiential, first person perspective) approach allied to the conventional theoretical (detached, third person perspective) methods to consciousness studies.

The writer nonetheless foresees that this third phase will, in due course, help to promote a quantum leap in the understanding of the true nature of consciousness along with an appreciation of the value of post-materialist science by the mainstream scientific community, promoted by the media, and therefore appreciated by the public at large.

Humanity's Yearning for Illumination

Has there ever been a time when, in his moments of inward reflection, man does not yearn for an absolute and abiding truth in order to understand the meaning of life with its joys and sorrows; to seek a way to transcend suffering and death in search of immortality and bliss? The means that man employs in his search are as varied as there are human beings on earth, but the nature of the quest is still the same, whether this be for the so-called common man or philosopher, the scientist or mystic, the atheist or believer, the billionaire or beggar, even the criminal and wastrel. As we have constantly emphasized, the history of all lands has supplied ample proof about the existence of those few in number, variously known as the sages and philosophers, saints and prophets, mahātmās and rishis, who have discovered Truth which is Universal and Eternal and out of their love of humanity sought to lead man towards It, whilst suffering ingratitude and persecution at the hands of those who needed it the most. These luminous disseminators of the Perennial Wisdom always looked beyond and above the names and outward forms of the various religions and philosophies which have existed throughout history, and sought for a common, self-consistent core knowledge which reflects the Universal Truth and allows people of every generation to connect with It. Most significantly, they recognized what is universal in the different teachings of the world and discarded that which was parochial and time bound. The Universal cannot be fathomed in syncretistic fashion by validating the differences that exist at the surface: the stillness of the ocean exists at its depth, not on the surface.

Perennial wisdom is, by definition, eternal

Then there are others who want to create a universal tradition anew by discarding world religions altogether on the grounds that they are limited and have become obscured by accretions which are foreign to their true nature. Yet this would be like trying to create a new science by discarding all that science has previously discovered. We must take what is universal in the teachings of the world in any field, neither validating them at the level of their surface differences, nor discarding all that they have to offer. As eloquently articulated by the Austro-Bohemian composer Gustav Mahler (1860–1911): 'Tradition is not to preserve the ashes but to pass on the flame.'[105]

As such a Tradition always exists in Cosmic Mind (the 'Mind of God' in common terms), we only need to restore its outer functioning. To do this we must recognize the Tradition which has always existed and the forms it has created. And a profound aspect of the universal teaching enwrapped in time-bound outer forms is the fact of immortality. But immortality of whom or what, and how? This is touched on after explaining that in this matter, as in all others in relation to evolution and progress, man has a choice of two paths.

The Two Paths – Two Classes of Human Beings

> The Self of matter and the SELF of Spirit can never meet.
> One of the twain must disappear; there is no place for both.
>   H. P. Blavatsky: *The Voice of the Silence*, Fragment I[106]

What do the 'Self of matter' and the 'SELF of Spirit' mean?

A constant theme of this work has been the polarity between spirit—the active principle, and matter—its vehicular aspect, or garment of expression—at any level of manifestation. For this reason, matter is sometimes referred to in the esoteric schools in both the Orient and the Occident as the 'shadow' cast by the spiritual light of the divine side of nature; in other words, its negative, or nether pole, as spirit is the upper, or positive pole. (On the physical plane, this is the polarity between light and its 'shadow', i.e., matter as crystallized light as science has proven.)

Even though human beings are faced with, and must necessarily choose between a multitude of paths each calling for his attention at different times under varying circumstances, yet, without exception, the path that predominates over all others will be the one to which he is most strongly drawn.

For this reason, one path will always prevail and ultimately predominate. This much is obvious and needs no elucidation. Nonetheless, the above quotation from one of the most profound books of spiritual instruction tersely lays out the choice of one of two paths in life facing each person: the 'Path of Matter' or the 'Path of Spirit'. The implications of the choice are momentous.

Those who are instinctively of the nature of matter will choose the Path of Matter otherwise known as the 'Path of the Shadows'. When it is recollected that 'matter' is a generalizing term comprising a virtually infinite number of degrees of increasing refinement from gross physical substance up to the most ethereal, or spiritualized substance, then the subtle logic of the technical term 'Shadows', and more fully, the Path of the Shadows becomes apparent. Those who tread the Path of the Shadows are referred to in occultism by the quaint term 'Brothers of the Shadow'. Their motives are essentially self-seeking: any extraordinary powers and faculties attained are turned to personal gain for power and control. Hence, when taken to extremes, they can descend to the Left-Hand Path of sorcery or worse, black magic—refer to Volume I, Chapter 7, page 200 for a fuller meaning of these terms and their distinction.

The Path of Matter or the Path of Spirit?

Multitudes of human beings are unconsciously treading the Path of the Shadows, so we are informed, and only relatively few self-consciously follow the Right-Hand Path of self-renunciation and self-conquest, compassion and expansion of heart, mind, and consciousness towards philanthropic service. These few are known as the 'Sons of Light'. The divergence is clear-cut between the 'centripetal', or self-centred characteristic and the 'centrifugal', or expansive characteristic of those who tread the Path of Matter and the Path of Spirit, respectively. That is why the above quote states: 'One of the twain must disappear; there is no place for both.' There is a supreme logic to this. Attempting to walk both paths would be as absurd as trying to be both misanthropic and philanthropic at one and the same time or to attempt crossing a bridge leaving one foot behind on the former bank.

Distinguishing
characteristics of
two classes of
human beings

In the broadest sense, the two classes of human beings can be distinguished between the authoritarians and the liberals—and both would seem to be increasingly staunch in their views.[107] The extreme end of the first class is characterized by a secular, aggressively anti-religious attitude and a materialistic, even mechanistic, philosophy of life. Hence, they seek the security and authority of structured environments with rules and protocols, algorithms and artificial intelligence. Unsurprisingly, their outlook is one of imposing a global uniformity (philosophically, socially, politically, etc.). They prefer to be convinced by lots of data rather than personal experience. Progress is seen primarily in terms of technological advancement, material prosperity, and economic growth. By contrast, many extremists of the second class are religiously or spiritually inclined and those that are atheists are not vociferous about their views. Their individuality thrives in an environment of freedom and independence and they instinctively understand the implications of diversity within unity. A distinguishing hallmark of the two classes is their attitude towards science and technology: the first tends to use the latest scientific discoveries for personal gain and power along with dominance over others and nature and, when taken to extremes, to prolong life by artificial and synthetic means (see the section below on transhumanism and cryonics); the second seeks to liberate society and points towards the possibility of a higher world-view than materialism *per se*. But it must be stressed that most people are somewhere around the middle of these antithetical extremes.

Outward
characteristics
rarely betray inner
traits

It would, however, be a great mistake to suppose that the Brothers of the Shadow are unpleasant or repulsive persons. In fact, they are often men and women with personal charm, cultured—and intelligent, or rather, intellectual; and judging from their conversation and works, are fully able to quote from erudite books just as eloquently as do the Sons of Light. An equally erroneous assumption would be on the one hand, that the Path of the Shadows pertains to those who deal with matter in the course of their daily lives, such as material scientists, geologists, miners, and metallurgists or pathologists, embalmers, and undertakers; and on the other hand, that evangelists, ministers, and members of spiritual societies are all treading the Path of Spirit. Nothing could be further from the truth. The criterion that distinguishes the two Paths is the *inner nature and motive of the person, his actions and how he behaves and treats others—not* his relation with the external world in terms of his profession, or even whether or not he upholds a materialist or a spiritual ontology as an intellectual concept. For instance, a hard-nosed scientist whose quest for truth drives him to propound atheism and ontological materialism, if he be supportive of his colleagues and kind-hearted to his family and friends, such a person is a far better candidate for a Son of Light than a self-appointed messiah who infiltrates a spiritual or esoteric organization professing 'universal brotherhood and love of mankind'. In the latter case, it may well be that such an individual can discourse persuasively on occult and spiritual matters but his *inner motive*—whether conscious or, more often than not, unconscious—is self-glorification at the expense of others. This last point needs every emphasis. As stated at the close of the previous Chapter, numerous professedly spiritual, esoteric, and New Age groups are infected by self-serving imposters operating under an umbrella of spirituality, whereas there are more spritual and altruistically motivated individuals in the so-called materialistic scientific community than would otherwise appear to be the case at first sight.

Scientists who investigate matter and its properties are no more Brothers of the Shadow, by definition, than professedly spiritual people who denounce materialism are necessarily Sons of Light.

How then, does the contrast between the two Paths figure in man's never-ending quest for eternal youth and beauty, omnipotence, and, above all, immortality?

Man's Yearning for Immortality

> We are outwardly creatures of but a day; within we are eternal.
>
> H. P. Blavatsky[v]

Throughout all ages there has never been a time when man has not yearned for the secret of eternal youth and immortality; and atheists prove the rule as described below. We touched upon this question earlier, in Chapter 7, pointing out that the answer to eternal youth lies in the enduring quality of consciousness, in living in the Eternal, rather than resorting to facial creams and face-lifts. But the desire for immortality is even more deeply embedded within man's innermost nature and each man, including hardened materialists, feels that immortality is, or ought to be, his birthright. Some men have attained to immortality by creating works of such phenomenal genius that they live on through their works, so to say. Such are the likes of Leonardo and Newton, Shakespeare (Bacon?) and William Blake, Mozart and Chopin, Blavatsky and Brunton. Others seek immortality in different ways ranging from the ridiculous to the sublime. How do science and spirituality respond to the idea of immortality?

Men long for immortality, but why?

The Way of Eugenics, Transhumanism, and Cryonics

> For what is a man profited, if he shall gain the whole world, and lose his own soul?
>
> (Matthew 16:26, King James Version)

Transhumanism (allied to artificial intelligence) and cryonics are contemporary, twin avenues of investigation and research in the scientific quest for superhuman powers and immortality. *The Prospect of Immortality* was published in 1962 by the American atheist academic Robert Ettinger (1918–2001) who later founded the Cryonics Institute[108] and the related Immortalist Society. His book made quite an impact in the mid-1960s, since it gave birth to the idea of 'cryonics'—the process of freezing a human body after death in the hope that at some time in the future, scientific advances might restore life. After all, its author declared:

> Would you like to live forever and ever, here on earth? In the near future this may become a real possibility. The Prospect of Immortality is a sober, scientific, and logical argument founded on the undeniable fact: that a body deep-frozen stands a better chance of being revived than of one rotting in the ground; and that many people who died fifty or a hundred years ago of 'incurable' diseases would today be cured.[109]

That perishable foodstuff and organic produce would last longer in the domestic freezer than in the open air were evident even in the 1960s as an 'undeniable fact' plain enough to all and sundry—without resorting to 'sober, scientific, and logical argument'. Anyway, the cryonics procedure involves: packing the body in ice immediately after death; replacing the water in the cells of the body with a kind of human anti-freeze; finally, storing the

---

v Blavatsky's message to the fourth annual American Convention in 1890 at the Palmer House Hotel, Chicago, Illinois.

Is cryonics a
classic example of
promissory
materialism?

body, head down, in a tank full of liquid nitrogen at a temperature of minus 196 degrees Centigrade. Eventually, when the supposed cure were found for whatever caused the death (which, presumably, would also include plain old age), the body would be defrosted bringing the person back to 'life' when presumably they would regain their former 'consciousness'. After Ettinger formulated his theory, some two thousand 'cryomembers', including Ettinger himself, at age ninety-three, have paid considerable sums to be 'cryopreserved'; and some members cryopreserve their pets. The Alcor Life Extension Foundation offers two options: Whole Body preservation starting at a minimum policy (in 2020) of $200,000 and Neurocryopreservation which requires a minimum policy of $80,000. Surcharges for both options are $10,000 for cases outside the US and Canada other than China; and $50,000 for cases in China.[110]

Incidentally, cryonics is not the modern scientific equivalent of mummification practised by the ancient Egyptians, whose profound understanding of the life, death, and the after-death states bears no relation whatsoever to the assertions of 'cryoscience' on these subjects. There is no question of the Egyptians believing that a mummy could be brought back to life at a future date.

Closely related to cryonics is transhumanism—the international intellectual movement that aims to transform the human condition by developing, and making widely available, sophisticated technologies, supposed to be used ethically, to expand human intellect and physiology into different beings with abilities so greatly enhanced from the natural condition as to merit the label of 'posthuman beings'.[111]

Historical roots of
transhumanism

Fundamental ideas of transhumanism, itself closely related to eugenics, were first advanced in 1923 by the British geneticist J. B. S. Haldane (1892–1964) in his paper 'Daedalus, or, Science and the Future' read on 4th February 1923 to the Heretics Society, an intellectual club at Cambridge University.[112] He predicted that great benefits would come from applications of advanced sciences to human biology; and that every such advance would first meet with the objection of being unnatural or perverted. In particular, he was interested in the development of the science of eugenics (selective breeding), ectogenesis (creating and sustaining life in an artificial environment), and the application of genetics to improve human characteristics, such as health and intelligence. The biologist Sir Julian Huxley is generally regarded as the founder of transhumanism, after using the term for the title of an influential 1957 article,[113] although the term itself derives from an earlier 1940 paper by the Canadian lawyer, novelist, and philosopher W. D. Lighthall (1857–1954).[114] Huxley was a leading member of the Secular Humanist movement, arguing that humans should take control of their own evolution and enhance the human race by eugenics: the intention being to improve the human race and society by encouraging reproduction by people with 'desirable' traits and discouraging reproduction by people with 'undesirable' ones. Huxley's solution was a new breed of genetically advanced children fathered by artificial insemination from sperm donors who should be men of long scientific lineage and high achievements in science and public life. True to his word, Huxley put himself forward as the ideal sperm donor as his contribution to create this supposed uplift in humanity.[115] There is no arguing about the fact that the British Huxley family excelled in science, medicine, arts, literature, and senior positions in the public service of the United Kingdom. However, the fabled connection between genius and madness is not just anecdotal: several members of this illustrious family were also afflicted with serious mental health issues, breakdowns,

Is transhumanism
the finest
example of
promissory
materialism?

and suicide. Amongst several cases that could be cited, the scientist and humanist Thomas Henry Huxley (1825–1895) suffered from periodic clinical depression[116] which ultimately precipitated his resignation from the Presidency of the Royal Society in mid-term;[117] and his own father became 'sunk in worse than childish imbecility of mind'[118] and later died in Barming Asylum, founded in 1833 as the Kent County Lunatic Asylum. The problems continued sporadically into the third generation of the family and Julian Huxley himself suffered a number of breakdowns.[119]

Thus, the advocates of Julian Huxley's method to enhance the human race by eugenics should carefully note the words of the English eugenicist and polymath Sir Francis Galton FRS (1822–1911):

> The direct result of this enquiry [into hereditary genius] is [...] to prove that the laws of heredity are as applicable to the mental faculties as to the bodily faculties.[120]

Whereas Julian Huxley's basically mechanistic ideas on evolution were not entirely hidebound by the materialism of his time (see Volume I, Chapter 3, page 52), it is, nonetheless, deeply ironical that he had for a brother an advocate of the perennial wisdom and spiritual subjects such as parapsychology and philosophical mysticism—Aldous Huxley (see the Proem in Volume I, page xxxviii f.). That two such radically contrasting characters should appear in the same family further reinforces the occult teaching that parents provide only the physical vehicle (body and brain) and not the soul for the newly incarnated entity which has to expiate its own karma and work out its own destiny within the confines of the collective psycho-physical karma of the family into which it is born.

Anyhow, inspired by these sorts of mechanistic ideas about artificially enhancing the human race, common transhumanist themes ever since[121] comprise radical changes to human bodies and intelligence through bionic implants[vi] and cognitive enhancements.[122] Modern advocates include Anders Sandberg (b. 1972), the Swedish researcher, science debater, and currently (in 2020) a James Martin Research Fellow at the Future of Humanity Institute at Oxford University. Unsurprisingly, Sanders has also supported and advocated cryonics, and is an advisor to the UK Cryonics and Cryopreservation Research Network.[123] Another leading figure on the matter of biologically enhanced human capabilities is the Australian philosopher and bioethicist Professor Julian Savulescu (b. 1953), Director, Uehiro Chair in Practical Ethics at the University of Oxford. He coined the phrase 'procreative beneficence'—the presumed moral obligation of parents to select their children, for instance through preimplantation genetic diagnosis, to favour those expected to have the best life,[124] arguing that traits such as empathy and memory are 'all-purpose means' in the sense of being instrumental in realizing whatever life plans the child may come to have[125] (but never mind other factors like the hand of destiny related to the immutable Law of Karma).

Another enthusiast of transhumanist ideas is the former President of the Royal Society, Lord Martin Rees. His book *On the Future* spans the main scientific, technological, ecological, and planetary issues and challenges that humanity faces. Regarding artificial intelligence Rees is aware of its limitations when he writes that it is difficult to instil common sense and understanding into AI and that autonomous robots might have competence without comprehension: 'being able to compute something is not the same as having an

Oxford University's involvement in transhumanist movement

---

vi Bionic implants are robotic or semi-robotic biological implants that are electronic or electromechanical.

Lord Rees
guardedly
advocates
transhumanism

insightful comprehension of it'.[126] But then he obfuscates his own contention by straight-away going on to write about machines surpassing human intelligence in such a way that they could design and assemble a new generation of even more intelligent machines. He speculates as to whether a combination of genetic modification and cyborg technology (an organism with both biological and technological components) might mark a transition to 'fully inorganic intelligences'. He posits that it is likely that these 'inorganics' will eventually gain dominance. So although he does not use the actual terms, he envisages a 'post-human' or 'transhumanist' future with a long-term future life with electronic rather than organic 'life', which is not as we know it or humans as we define them.[127]

So a key question is, what exactly do transhumanists mean and understand by consciousness, intelligence, and artificial intelligence? Furthermore, can electronic rather than organic life and humans possess a soul? If the artificial intelligence courses at UCL[128] and Oxford[129], run by Google DeepMind,[vii] are anything to go by, 'their definition of "intelligence" is so impoverished that it doesn't extend beyond the abstract calculations that an algorithm can achieve, and completely fails to understand that human intelligence is embodied and distributed throughout our physical selves—and indeed between them, in the mirror neurons that fire in sympathy when we watch a dancer or help an injured friend. In short, it's not just depressing, it's bad science.'[130]

The scientific
roadmap to
immortality by
the year 2600

But what is 'bad science' today may become the fate of the science of the future—at least according to two Russian researchers who maintain 'there no evidence of an afterlife. But there's also no proof that medical death is the end of subjective experience, or that death is irreversible, or immortality impossible.'[131] Their ideas are expounded at length in a scholarly paper charting the 'roadmap to immortality'.[132] A key element involves super-intelligent AI systems powered by Dyson spheres (explained below) as the primary technology that might someday make resurrection possible. To ensure immortality, both conventional and future technologies of making humanity immortal are examined, ranging from 'cryonics to uploading brains onto the cloud [service] then transplanted into clone[d] bodies.' The researchers claim 'strong AI' will be the most critical technology to download the brain's contents, but that technology could be years away. One reason is 'the power supply behind the AI would have to be so powerful that it would need a "Dyson spheres," a megastructure of solar panels that encompasses a star and captures a large percentage of its power output.'[133]

Their immortality roadmap comprises a timeline with specific milestones up to the year 2100 (but '2600, to be sure') when immortality will supposedly have been attained—'with help of Strong AI'—to include not just 'Immortal body' but also 'Creation of immortal soul'. Also, we are promised the 'Revival from Cryogenic Storage', 'Reconstruction of the Identity of the Deceased', 'The colonisation of the solar system', 'Colonisation of the Galaxy', and 'Exploring the Universe, solving the question of the end of the Universe'.

Notwithstanding the confusion resulting from the blurring between human intelligence and artificial intelligence, in addition to the immense ethical issues posed by transhumanism and cryonics, this writer poses eight pressing questions to their advocates:

---

vii *DeepMind Technologies Limited* is a British artificial intelligence company founded in September 2010 and acquired by Google in 2014.

1. Are transhumanist and cryomembers caught up in a lurid phantasy world of science fiction or genuine scientific innovation?

2. Would transhumanism and cryonics qualify as just about the finest examples of scientific materialism taken to bizarre extremes, whereby the entirety of life is equated solely with the physical body, and consciousness regarded as generated solely by the physical material in the brain?

3. By way of background to this question, in the 1950s, dog head transplants were performed by the Soviet scientist and organ transplant pioneer Vladimir Demikhov (1916–1998) resulting in two-headed dogs, which achievement inspired the American neurosurgeon Robert White (1926–2010) to transplant one monkey head on to the body of another monkey, which creature could then hear, smell, taste, eat, and follow objects with its (presumably four) eyes.[134] During the 1990s, White planned the same operation on humans and practised on corpses at a mortuary, hoping that he could then perform head transplant surgery on Stephen Hawking and the actor Christopher Reeve.[135]

The continuation of White's work in head transplantation research, and supposed applications, has been enthusiastically taken up by the Italian neurosurgeon Sergio Canavero (b. 1964),[136] who has a Chinese volunteer for the first-ever human head transplant surgery, mooted for 2018 in Harbin, China, with assistance provided by the Harbin Institute of Technology and Harbin Medical University—at a cost (estimated in 2015) of some €15 million (£11 million), involving one hundred and fifty medics, including eighty surgeons, over seventy-two hours for the intricate neurological connections involving the gullet, windpipe, spinal cord, etc.[137] Incidentally, no such transplant on a living person took place in 2018. However, as a possible step in this direction, in an operation conducted in 2017 in the Harbin Medical University, China, 'the world's first human head transplant has allegedly been performed on a corpse in an 18 hour operation which successfully connected the spine, nerves and blood vessels of two people'.[138] Sergio Canavero 'said they would "imminently" move onto a living human who was paralysed from the neck down.'[139] As of 2020, no lasting successes have been achieved.[140]

Reasoning, then, along similar lines, given that some cryomembers, like the US baseball star Ted Williams (1918–2002), have decided on cryopreserving their head and body separately,[141] would scientific transplant surgery at its current rate of advancement enable a 'cryohead' to regain its memory and consciousness, either just on its own, or grafted on to its parent 'cryobody', or on to a different cryobody, or on to a recently deceased body?

4. After a 'cryoperson' or a cryohead and cryobody have been suitably defrosted, then united and brought back to 'life', does such a 'person' then live for ever, or does he eventually 'die' and then have to undergo a future cryonics procedure to prolong his 'immortality'?

5. Transhumanism and artificial intelligence are strongly coupled. Both would lead to a progressive blurring of the sense of self (see also Chapter 9) and an erosion of the unique distinction between a human being and a machine. How then do transhumanists respond to the dire warning recently given by Stephen Hawking that

Are we humans just sophisticated biochemical machines or computers?

Or are we humans beings, spiritual in essence and physical in form?

rampant artificial intelligence could be the 'worst event in the history of our civilization' (see the epigraph to Chapter 7 of Volume II on page 112)?

6. Following 'Reconstruction of the Identity of the Deceased' (see page 338) after thawing out a cryopreserved body of someone who died in old age, would that reconstruction also entail restoring the wrinkle free appearance and carefree outlook of the 'deceased' person when in his youth?

7. What is the driving force behind such frantic attempts to attain immortality? From where, and from what level, does it arise? Is it all purely a matter of gratifying egoistical desires, or is there something else besides? If transhumanists maintain that ageing and mortality may be transformed by future technology, then how and why is it that what they regard as a purely physical, biological machine—the human being—would want to be immortal? Do other pieces of machinery, even sophisticated computers to wit, yearn for eternity or immortality?

8. In reducing humans and mind to computers and algorithms, are transhumanists guilty of elementary category errors?[viii]

Currently, there seems to be a real battle being waged for our humanness. Thus, at this juncture, it is left to readers to decide which of the Two Paths, described above, the transhumanists and 'cryonicists' are following—and what would be the inescapable outcome of their choice. But whatever be the choice, the question to ask is: 'are transhumanism and artificial intelligence supposed to be the only ways to enhance human intelligence, and cryonics the only way allegedly to gain immortality?' Some people, fortunate enough to have a spare $200,000, might choose to preserve their dead body post-mortem. Others, more altruistically minded and hopefully in the majority, would, the writer believes, much prefer to donate such a sum towards their family or a charitable cause.

Materialistic and spiritual standpoints on immortality

In summary, from the standpoint of scientific materialism, the human being is a complex biological machine representing an intermediary stage in evolution towards a superior transhuman cyborg status and ultimate 'human-machine immortality'. Conversely, from the universal perspective of spirituality, the human spirit is already immortal and evolves through successive reincarnations in mortal bodies—through death as transition.

The Path of the Spirit

Krishnamurti spoke of dying to the past in order to live in the present

During the 1980s the writer personally attended several talks by Krishnamurti in which he often expounded, at length, on the subject of death. What did this most enigmatic sage of modern times mean by 'death'? The extinguishing of the discord of time as the psychological burden of the past; the shedding of outworn and lifeless thought forms that suffocate attentiveness to the living moment; release from the restricted known into the boundless unknown; out of limited being into infinite non-being…In short, psychologically dying wholly to the past in order to be fully awake and alive to the present.[ix]

---

viii Category errors are explained in Volume II, Chapter 1, page 8.

ix To reiterate, the 'death' referred to is 'psychological death', physical death being, of course, its culmination. This is not in the same context as, and so must not be confused with, the memory that is inherent in nature, the 'Presence of the Past' as per the title of Rupert Sheldrake's book (see Volume I, Chapter 4, page 71).

In not dissimilar vein, at thirty-one years of age, the immortal[x] composer Mozart had this to say about death in the famous letter of 4th April 1787, to his father Leopold:

> As death, when we come to consider it closely, is the true goal of our existence, I have formed during the last few years such close relationships with this best and truest friend of mankind that death's image is not only no longer terrifying to me, but is indeed very soothing and consoling, *and I thank my God for graciously granting me the opportunity (you know what I mean) of learning that death is the key which unlocks the door to our true happiness* [emphasis added]. I never lie down at night without reflecting that—young as I am—I may not live to see another day. Yet no one of all my acquaintances could say that in company I am morose or disgruntled.[142]

Mozart understood that death is transition

The British composer, musicologist, and esoteric author Joscelyn Godwin (*b.* 1945), has drawn our attention to the fact that since Mozart attained the third Masonic degree of a Master in 1785, the ritual would have included a symbolic enactment of the 'death' and 'resurrection' of the candidate. Furthermore, the degrees of initiation of the Mystery Teachings, or Mystery Religions of antiquity (see Volume I, Chapter 7, page 179 and, typically, Chapter 9, pages 271–272), from which much of Freemasonry is derived, involved not merely a simulation of death, but the actual temporary separation of the consciousness of the initiant[xi] from his physical body, thus engendering in him: (*a*) the sensation of mortal death; (*b*) the allied unshakable conviction that in his innermost and truest Self, he is incorporeal and immortal; and (*c*) that death is but the portal to higher planes of existence.[143] This is not at all far-fetched. Modern accounts of this experience can be examined in the autobiographical accounts of Paul Brunton[144] (see again Volume I, Chapter 9, page 309) and Carl Jung,[145] and similar experiences on the part of ordinary people collected by Raymond A. Moody.[146]

What, then, does the *philosophia perennis* say about how we can acquire superhuman powers and attain to immortality? A somewhat cheaper option with no need of 'strong AI' or 'Dyson spheres' and with the added guarantee of eventual triumph over either transhuman technology or cryonics, it affirms, to recapitulate, that terrestrial man is a compound tripartite being composed of a strictly mortal man of flesh, his impermanent physical body; an immortal principle, Spirit; and his Soul partaking of Spirit at the upper pole and matter at the lower pole. Man (including the transhumanists and cryonicists), therefore, in his innermost Self is immortal. However, when Soul consciously merges with Spirit, man then becomes a self-realized immortal being. The secret of immortality therefore lies in passing through the gateway of death—death as transition.

The *philosophia perennis* alone illuminates the Path to Immortality

For this reason the *Voice of the Silence* affirms:

> Give up thy life, if thou would'st live.[147]

Why? 'The whole course of evolution bears witness to the principle of dying for the sake of life.'[148]

---

x This is no exaggeration. Mozart's earthly body was buried first in a pauper's grave, but the true spirit of Mozart—his music—is immortal as the world of classical music bears ample witness for over two centuries and will ever continue to do so.

xi An 'initiant' is one who is beginning, or preparing for, initiation. An 'initiate' is one who has successfully passed at least one initiation—see G. de Purucker, *Occult Glossary: A compendium of oriental and theosophical terms* (1933; Pasadena, California: Theosophical University Press, 1972), 65.

The shedding of the outer temporary form is a divine imperative for the Immortal Dweller within to acquire newer and finer robes of consciousness–substance for Its unending evolution. That is why our physical bodies are called 'shadows' in the mystic schools. Such Truths are indeed ineffable, inherent in that great Silence of which Blavatsky wrote and yet, in essence, they may be voiced as in *Light on the Path*:

1. **The soul of man is immortal, and its future is the future of a thing whose growth and splendour has no limit.**
2. **The principle which gives life dwells in us, and without us, is undying and eternally beneficent, is not heard, or seen, or smelt, but is perceived by the man who desires perception.**
3. **Each man is his own absolute law-giver, the dispenser of glory, or gloom to himself; the decreer of his life, his reward, his punishment.**[149]

These truths of the *philosophia perennis* are as great as is life itself, yet, as simple as the simplest mind of man. But they cannot be imprisoned in words or nailed down by definitions. They may be glimpsed, or even experienced, by circumambulating in ever closer circles around the INEFFABLE.

Should this work elucidate, in however small a measure, where the 'white dove of truth' may find some room 'to rest her weary, unwelcome foot', the writer would be amply rewarded.

Superior Intelligences working through the agency of the Sages and Holy Ones of all cultures since time immemorial have taught us three things in order to quicken the divine Spirit in man to an awakening of his innermost and innate divine status:

1. The absolute fact of a benevolent Higher Power identical with unconditional Love

2. That It can never be touched through thought or intellect alone

3. That there is a Way of approaching and contacting the impersonal Nameless Higher Power of which each speck of cosmos, and each one of us, is both an aspect and Its instrument …

In the Proem to this work we started with:

'Man, Know Thyself'

Over three Volumes, our narrative has been entirely about the Unfolding of Consciousness. Along the Journey, over difficult terrain at times, we have showed how the whole world of science is feverishly seeking an answer to the mystery of Consciousness—to the essential nature of our being. In order to do this it is spending vast sums in research, producing acres of learned papers, inflicting untold suffering upon innumerable animals … yet all the while each of us—each single one of us without exception—is literally bearing that secret that he seeks.

A 'near-death' life 'review'

If we were privileged to examine the beauty of a pearl beyond price in our hand, would we knowingly throw it to swine to trample on; or else, go looking for it far and wide in the four corners of the Earth—or would we simply look at it in the very hand that holds it?

Where, then, does that 'pearl' lie for each one of us? In all that huffing and puffing to build another gigantic machine that will reveal 'the ultimate secrets of the universe'? In the innumerable concepts woven out of our brain fabric that will soon solve the mystery of 'the origin of consciousness'? Or have we finally come to realize, in the words of that illimitable sage from the East: 'your body is the Path, and Consciousness is the Traveller'.[150] There is never-ending joy in journeying the terrain of Consciousness approaching ever-closer to an always-receding destination.

We must close this trilogy by pointing to the answer to the age old enigma of where lies the Pearl of Wisdom that reveals our Divine Consciousness—Who We Truly Are:

> *Behold! thou hast become the light, thou hast become the Sound, thou art thy Master and thy God. Thou art THYSELF the object of thy search:*
>
> *The VOICE OF THE SILENCE.*

NOTES

1   See Michael Taylor, 'The Secret Bard' <http://www.sirbacon.org/links/thesecretbard.html> accessed 29 March 2021.
2   Stated during a public lecture at Brockwood Park, UK, in 1980.
3   OBERMANN, Lettre 53.
4   *Thirty Minor Upanishads*, trans. K. N. Aiyar (Madras: Vasanta Press, 1914), 220 n.1.
5   The writer is grateful to the Francis Bacon Society for this extract on the symbol of the Boar in English custom.
6   *STA*, 'Fishes, Insects, Animals, Reptiles, and Birds – Part One', LXXXVII.
7   *SD*-I, 'Gods, Monads, and Atoms', 612.
8   Karl R. Popper and John C. Eccles, *The Self and Its Brain: An Argument for interactionism* (London, New York: Springer International, 1977), 7.
9   David Eagleman, *The Brain: The story of you* (UK: Canongate Books, 2016).
10 —— *op. cit.*, 5.
11 Francis Crick, *The Astonishing Hypothesis: The scientific search for the soul* (New York: Charles Scribner's Sons, 1994), 3.
12 Lucy Jolin, 'You Are Your Brain: Which is why Imperial scientists want to understand how it works', *Imperial*, 42 (Spring 2017), 23.
13 *ibid.*
14 R. Douglas Fields, 'Brain Reactions', *RSA Journal*, 4 (2016–17), 34–7. See also Douglas Fields, *Why We Snap: Understanding the rage circuit in your brain* (US: Dutton, 2016).
15 See Kingsley L. Dennis, *The Sacred Revival: Magic, mind & meaning in a technological age* (New York: Select Books, 2017).
16 See Brenda Dunne and Robert Jahn (eds), *Being & Biology: Is consciousness the life force?* (Princeton, New Jersey: ICRL Press, 2017).
17 Rephrased from *NPB*-5, Part 2: *The Intellect*, 'When Science Stands Alone', ¶62, 123.
18 *NPB*-8, *Reflections on My Life and Writings*, 'A Warning Shared', ¶184, 160.
19 Dean Radin, *The Noetic Universe: The scientific evidence for psychic phenomena* (UK: Corgi Books, 2009), 305; quoted from Renée Weber, *Dialogues with Scientists and Sages: The search for unity* (New York: Routledge & Kegan Paul, 1986).
20 Alfred Jules Ayer, *Language, Truth and Logic* (US: Dover Publications, 2002).
21 Graham Macdonald and Nakul Krishna, 'Alfred Jules Ayer', *The Stanford Encyclopedia of Philosophy* (4 September 2018) <https://plato.stanford.edu/entries/ayer> accessed 6 April 2020.
22 See R. G. Collingwood, *An Essay on Metaphysics* (Oxford University Press,1940; US: Martino Fine Books, 2014).
23 Jeremy J. Baumberg, *The Secret Life of Science: How it really works and why it matters* (Princeton and Oxford: Princeton University Press, 2018).

24 —— *op. cit.*

25 Neils Bohr, 'Life and Light', *Nature*, 131 (1933), 421–3.

26 See Kingsley L. Dennis, *The Sacred Revival*.

27 See Avinash Chandra, *The Scientist and the Saint: The limits of science and the testimony of sages* (Cambridge, UK: ArcheType Books, 2018).

28 'Future Circular Collider', CERN <https://home.cern/science/accelerators/future-circular-collider> accessed 6 April 2020.

29 CERN <https://home.cern> accessed 6 April 2020.

30 The Royal Institution <http://www.rigb.org/whats-on/events-2019/march/public-the-next-super-collider> accessed 7 March 2019.

31 'The Higgs Boson', CERN <https://home.cern/science/physics/higgs-boson> accessed 6 April 2020.

32 Alex Knapp, 'How Much Does It Cost To Find A Higgs Boson?' *Forbes* (5 July 2012) <https://www.forbes.com/sites/alexknapp/2012/07/05/how-much-does-it-cost-to-find-a-higgs-boson/#188ddbcb3948> accessed 6 April 2020.

33 Davide Castelvecchi, 'Next-generation LHC: CERN lays out plans for €21-billion supercollider. The proposed facility would be the most powerful collider ever built', *Nature* (15 January 2019) <https://www.nature.com/articles/d41586-019-00173-2> accessed 6 April 2020.

34 *SD*-II, 'Archaic, or Modern Anthropology', 651.

35 Richard Dawkins, *The God Delusion* (Boston: Houghton Mifflin, 2006), 51.

36 Samuel Johnson, *goodreads* <https://www.goodreads.com/author/quotes/22191.Samuel_Johnson> accessed 8 April 2020.

37 Stephen D. Silberstein, 'A Perspective on the Migraine Mind', *American Scientist*, 102/3 (May–June 2014).

38 Donald Prothero, '"Proof of Heaven"?' *Skeptic Insight* (19 September 2014) <https://www.skeptic.com/insight/proof-of-heaven> accessed 8 April 2020.

39 Jimo Borjigina, UnCheol Lee, Tiecheng Liua, Dinesh Pald, Sean Huffa, Daniel Klarrd, Jennifer Slobodaa, Jason Hernandeza, Michael M. Wanga, and George A. Mashour, 'Surge of Neurophysiological Coherence and Connectivity in the Dying Brain', *Proceedings of the National Academy of Sciences of the United States of America*, 110/35 (2013), 14432–7.

40 See for example, how this argument is used by Michael Shermer, in 'Sheldrake–Shermer Dialogue on the Nature of Science: May–July 2015', *TheBestSchools.org* [video] <http://www.thebestschools.org/special/sheldrake-shermer-dialogue-nature-of-science> accessed 8 April 2020.

41 John Harrison, *The Library of Isaac Newton* (Cambridge: Cambridge University Press, 1978). See also Rob Iliffe, *Priest of Nature: The religious worlds of Isaac Newton* (New York: Oxford University Press, 2017).

42 Jack Brown, 'Reminiscences – I Visit Professor Einstein', *Ojai Valley News*, Ojai, California, 28 September 1983 <http://www.blavatskyarchives.com/brown/jackbrownoneinstein.htm> accessed 29 November 2019.

43 Albert Einstein, 'Science and Religion', address at Princeton Theological Seminary (19 May 1939) < https://www.panarchy.org/einstein/science.religion.1939.html> accessed 28 March 2021.

44 John Templeton Foundation <https://www.templeton.org> accessed 1 January 2020.

45 Anjana Ahuja, 'Consciousness is one of Science's Final Frontiers', *Financial Times* (23 October 2019) <https://www.ft.com/content/f40d2de4-f4c0-11e9-bbe1-4db3476c5ff0> accessed 1 January 2020.

46 Sara Reardon, '"Outlandish" Competition Seeks the Brain's Source of Consciousness', *Science* (16 October 2019) <https://www.sciencemag.org/news/2019/10/outlandish-competition-seeks-brain-s-source-consciousness> accessed 1 January 2020.

47 Michael Graziano, *Rethinking Consciousness – A scientific theory of subjective experience* (New York: W. W. Norton & Company, 2019).

48 Adapted from 'Description', in Michael Graziano, *Rethinking Consciousness: A scientific theory of subjective experience* <https://www.wwnorton.co.uk/books/9780393652611-rethinking-consciousness> accessed 8 April 2020.

49 Michael Graziano, 'What is Consciousness?', *New Scientist* (21 September 2019), 36, 37.

50 *New Scientist* (21 September 2019), 39.

51 Anil Seth, *Being You: The inside story of your inner universe* (London: Faber & Faber, February 2021). The promotional piece for this book is *Being You: The new science of consciousness*

<http://www.janklowandnesbit.co.uk/anil-seth/being-you-new-science-consciousness> accessed 10 October 2020.

52 Anil Seth, 'Your Brain Hallucinates Your Conscious Reality', TED conference, Vancouver, Canada, 2017 <https://www.ted.com/talks/anil_seth_your_brain_hallucinates_your_conscious_ reality?language=en> accessed 28 June 2020.

53 Max Planck, *Scientific Autobiography and Other Papers* (New York: Philosophical library, 1950), 33, 97.

54 The Galileo Commission [https://www.galileocommission.org/] *Newsletter* (April 2020).

55 Alfred Russel Wallace, *Darwinism: An exposition of the theory of natural selection with some of its applications* (London and New York: Macmillan and Company, 1889), Chapter 15; quoted also in Noam Chomsky, *Language and Mind* (3rd edn, New York: Cambridge University Press, 2006),184.

56 Fredk. F. Cook, 'A Rejoinder to Mr. Alfred Russel Wallace, LL.D.', *Light: A journal of psychical, occult and mystical research*, V/237 (18 July 1885) <https://people.wku.edu/charles.smith/wallace/ zCook1885aLight.pdf> accessed 8 April 2020.

57 Alfred Russel Wallace 'The Harmony of Spiritualism and Science' (S383: 1885) in response to Frederick F. Cook's criticism reproduced from *Light* (London, 25 July 1885), 352 in Alfred Russel Wallace Page <https://people.wku.edu/charles.smith/wallace/S383.htm> accessed 8 April 2020.

58 W. B. Northrop, 'Obituary Interview on Alfred Russel Wallace', *The Outlook* (New York), 22 November 1913 <https://www.spiritualismlink.com/t728-obiturary-interview-w-b-northrop-on-alfred-wallace> accessed 8 April 2020.

59 William Harvey, *Exercitatio Anatomica de Motu Cordis et Sanguinis in Animalibus* [An Anatomical Exercise on the Motion of the Heart and Blood in Living Beings] (Frankfurt: Warnock Library, 1628); trans. Robert Willis, 'On the Motion of the Heart and Blood in Animals', *Harvard Classics*, 38/3 (New York: P.F. Collier & Son Company, 1909–14).

60 Aristoteles, *Parts of Animals, Movement of Animals, Progression of Animals* (Cambridge, London: Cambridge University Press, 1968).

61 William Osler, *The Evolution of Modern Medicine* (UK: Kaplan Publishing, 2009).

62 B. Barber, 'Resistance by Scientists to Scientific Discovery', in B. Barber and W. Hirsch (eds) *The Sociology of Science* (New York: Free Press, 1962), 555.

63 W. I. B. Beveridge, *The Art of Scientific Investigation* (New York: W. W. Norton, 1950).

64 National Anti-Vivisection Society (Great Britain), *The Animal's Defender and Zoophilist*, 13 (London: The Victoria Street Society for the Protection of Animals from Vivisection, 1893–4), 297.

65 See: Emilio Parisano, *Recentiorum Disceptationes de Motu Cordis, Sanguinis et Chyli* [Recent Debates about the Circulation of Blood and Lymph] (Leiden: Ioannis Maire, 1647), 107, trans. Harald Walach: '*Psi* and the Limitations of Materialist Science', SPR Study Day No. 79, 12 December 2020 <https://www.spr.ac.uk/civicrm/event/info?id=142&reset=1> accessed 12 December 2020; *Beyond a Materialist Worldview – Towards an Expanded Science*, Galileo Commission Report (The Scientific and Medical Network, 2019), 24; J. H. van den Berg, *Het Menselijk Lichaam* [The Human Body] (Callenbach, Dutch ed., 1962).

66 'Coronavirus (COVID-19): What you need to do', *GOV.UK* <https://www.gov.uk/coronavirus> accessed 11 April 2020.

67 'A Brief History of Handwashing', *The Week*, 28 March 2020, 55. See also Leslie S. Leighton, 'Ignaz Semmelweis, the Doctor who Discovered the Disease-Fighting Power of Hand-Washing in 1847', *The Conversation*, 14 April 2020 < https://theconversation.com/ignaz-semmelweis-the-doctor-who-discovered-the-disease-fighting-power-of-hand-washing-in-1847-135528#:~:text= In%20fact%2C%20it%20was%2019th,prevent%20the%20spread%20of%20germs> accessed 10 December 2020.

68 E-mail correspondence from Eben Alexander to Harald Walach on *Beyond a Materialist Worldview – Towards an Expanded Science*, Galileo Commission Report (15 October 2018).

69 *NPB-5, Part 2: The Intellect*, 'When Science Stands Alone', ¶45, 121.

70 *NPB-5, op. cit.*, ¶46, 121.

71 *NPB-5, op. cit.*, ¶42, 121.

72 *Radio Times*, 19 December 2020 – 1 January 2021, 35.

73 Jean-Paul Sartre, *Being and Nothingness: An essay on phenomenological ontology* (US: Philosophical Library, 1956).

74 *The Week*, 10 April 2021, 6.

75 *The Week*, 13 February 2021, 21. See also Kat Lay, 'More Teenage Girls Admitted to English Hospitals for Self-harming', 1 February 2021, *The Times*.

76 Edward Browne, 'Elon Musk Hints next Starship Launch could happen in WEEKS amid Mars Mission Pledge', *Express*, 6 January 2021 <https://www.express.co.uk/news/science/1380237/ Elon-Musk-news-spacex-space-starship-launch-sn9-sn10-boca-chica-mars-mission-when-ont> accessed 12 April 2021.

77 Staff writer, 'Elon Musk Unveils SpaceX Rocket Designed to Get to Mars and Back, 30 September 2019, *news.com.au*.

78 'Jeff Bezos: The Amazon billionaire's galatic ambitions', *The Week*, 13 February 2021, 22.

79 'Galileo Commission Correspondence', *Journal of the Scientific and Medical Network*, 128 (2018), 22.

80 Erwin Schrödinger, 'Science and Humanism' from lectures delivered at University College Dublin in 1950, in *Nature and the Greeks* and *Science and Humanism*, foreword by Roger Penrose (Cambridge: Cambridge University Press, 1961), 107.

81 Elizabeth Eaves, 'Why is America getting a new $100 billion Nuclear Weapon?' *Bulletin of the Atomic Scientists* (8 February 20021) <https://thebulletin.org/2021/02/why-is-america-getting-a-new-100-billion-nuclear-weapon> accessed 15 February 2021. America's nuclear arsenal is currently made up of 3,800 warheads.

82 *NPB-5, Part 2: The Intellect*, 'Science', ¶ 105, 129.

83 Brian Hodgkinson, *How our Economy Really Works: A radical reappraisal* (London: Shepheard-Walwyn, 2019). Refer also to the books listed under <https://shepheard-walwyn.co.uk/ product-category/ethical-economics> accessed 24 June 2020.

84 E-mail correspondence from Anthony Werner of Shepheard-Walwyn (Publishers) Ltd., 11 October 2019.

85 New Scientist and Press Association, 'Ancestor of all Vertebrates was a Big Mouth with no Anus', *New Scientist* (30 January 2017).

86 Press release, 'Bristol Study Resolves Dispute about the Origin of Animals', *University of Bristol* (30 November 2017).

87 Saadi Shirazi, *Golestan Saadi: Volume 3 (The Treasures of Iranian Literature)* (US: CreateSpace Independent Publishing Platform, 2015).

88 'Albert Einstein', quoted in *New York Times*, 19 March 1940.

89 Christopher Reed, 'James Randi Obituary', *The Guardian*, 25 Oct 2020 <https://www.theguardian.com/stage/2020/oct/25/james-randi-obituary> accessed 3 February 2021.

90 Alfred Russel Wallace, 'Notes on the Growth of Opinion as to Obscure Psychical Phenomena During the Last Fifty Years (S478: 1893)', The Alfred Russel Wallace Page hosted by Western Kentucky University (retrieved 20 April 2007) <http://people.wku.edu/charles.smith/wallace/S478.htm> accessed 8 May 2020.

91 Kahlil Gibran, *The Prophet*, introd. John Baldock (London: Arcturus, 2018), 124–5.

92 Isaac Newton, *Opticks, Or, A Treatise of the Reflections, Refractions, Inflections & Colours of Light* (London 1730; 4th edn, New York: Dover Publications, 1979), 402.

93 *ML*, Letter No. 65.

94 *Varsity*, 'Professor Julian Allwood: "We cannot rely on technological innovation to solve the climate crisis"' <https://www.varsity.co.uk/interviews/19117> accessed 19 January 2021.

95 Professor Julian Allwood, 'Letter: Our habits must change to deliver on PM's [Boris Johnson's] climate targets', *Financial Times*, 8 December 2020 <https://www.ft.com/content/ dc7ecd2b-0a6d-4d5c-9386-2fb7de50584a> accessed 19 January 2021.

96 Shelley, *A Defense Of Poetry*, ed. Albert S. Cook (Montana, US: Kessinger Publishing Co, 2010).

97 Rephrased from Oliver Robinson, *Pathways between Head and Heart: Exploring the harmonies of science and spirituality* (UK and US: O-Books, 2018), 6, citing Albert Einstein: 'Physik und Realität' ['Physics and Reality'], trans. Jean Piccard, *Journal of the Franklin Institute*, 221 (1936), 348–82; repr. *Ideas and Opinions* (New York: Bonanza Books, 1954), 290–323.

98 Plotinus, *The Enneads*, 'On Beauty', Ennead 1.6.9, 102.

99 Harald Walach, *Galileo Commission Report* (The Scientific and Medical Network, 2019).

100 Rephrased from Tabitha Jayne and Harald Walach, *Galileo Commission – The Layman's Guide* <https://galileocommission.org/the-laymans-guide-to-the-galileo-commission-report-final-3-12-20> accessed 21 January 2021.

101 *SD*-1, 'Proem', 15.

102 Harald Walach, 'Inner Experience – Direct Access to Reality: A complementarist ontology and dual aspect monism support a broader epistemology', *Frontiers in Psychology*, 11/640 (23 April 2020) <https://pdfs.semanticscholar.org/eab0/61fd99281c37a2cf530cba2263f719060ae1.pdf?_ga= 2.216721494.1183445481.1611227102-556072577.1604773707> accessed 21 January 2021.

103 James Jeans, *The Mysterious Universe* (Cambridge: Cambridge University Press, 1930), 37–8. The book opens with a full-page citation of the famous passage in Plato's *Republic*, Book VII, laying out the allegory of the cave.

104 *Is Consciousness Primary?* ed. Stephan A. Schwartz, Marjorie H. Woollacott, and Gary E. Schwartz (Battle Ground, Washington, US: AAPS Press, 2020).

105 'Gentleman's Quotations', *Gentleman's Gazette* (June 2012) <https://www.gentlemansgazette.com/gentlemens-quotations> accessed 9 April 2020.

106 *VS*, Fragment I: The Voice of the Silence, 12.

107 There is an insightful discussion on this in, 'Polarised: Exploring divisions', *RSA Journal*, 2 (2018), 6.

108 Articles of Incorporation of the Cryonics Institute', *Cryonics Institute* (28 April 1976) <https://www.cryonics.org/resources/articles-of-incorporation> accessed 9 April 2020.

109 Robert C. W. Ettinger, *The Prospect of Immortality* (UK: Sidgwick & Jackson, 1965), from dust jacket of British hard cover edition.

110 'Alcor Cryopreservation Agreement – Schedule A: Required costs and cryopreservation fund minimums', *Alcor Life Extension Foundation* (1 January 2020) <https://alcor.org/BecomeMember/scheduleA.html> accessed 9 April 2020.

111 Nick Bostrom, 'A History of Transhumanist Thought', *Journal of Evolution and Technology*, 14/1 (April 2005).

112 J. B. S. Haldane, 'Daedalus, or, Science and the Future' (London: Kegan Paul, Trench, Trübner & Co., 1925).

113 Julian Huxley, 'Transhumanism', in *New Bottles for New Wine* (London, Chatto & Windus, 1957), 13–17.

114 'Notes and Queries', in Peter Harrison and Joseph Wolyniak, *The History of 'Transhumanism*, 62/3 (Oxford: Oxford University Press, 1 September 2015), 465–7.

115 Rupert Sheldrake, *Science and Spiritual Practices* (UK: Coronet, 2017), 2.

116 Cyril Bibby, *T. H. Huxley: Scientist, humanist and educator* (London: Watts, 1959), 7.

117 Adrian Desmond, *Huxley: Evolution's high priest* (London: Michael Joseph, 1997), ii, 151 et seq.

118 Letter from T. H. Huxley to eldest sister Lizzie 1853, in 'Huxley Papers' at Imperial College: 31.21.

119 Ronald William Clark, *The Huxleys* (New York: Heinemann, 1968).

120 Francis Galton, *Hereditary Genius* (London: Macmillan, 1892), xix.

121 Nick Bostrom. 'A History of Transhumanist Thought'.

122 Arthur C. Clarke, *Greetings, Carbon-Based Bipeds!: Collected Essays, 1934–1998* (New York: St. Martin's Press, 1999).

123 UK Cryonics and Cryopreservation Research Network <http://www.cryonics-research.org.uk/about-us.html> accessed 10 April 2020.

124 Julian Savulescu, 'Procreative Beneficence: Why we should select the best children', *Bioethics*, 15/5-6 (October 2001), 413–26.

125 K. Hens, W. Dondorp, A. H. Handyside, J. Harper, A. J. Newson, G. Pennings, C. Rehmann-Sutter, and G. De Wert, 'Dynamics and Ethics of Comprehensive Preimplantation Genetic Testing: A review of the challenges', *Human Reproduction Update*, 19/4 (2013), 366.

126 Martin Rees, *On the Future: Prospects for humanity* (Princeton and Oxford: Princeton University Press), 192.

127 The above section is a reworded extract from the book review of Martin Rees, *On the Future* by David Lorimer in *Journal of the Scientific and Medical Network*, 128 (2018), 55–6.

128 'UCL Students Learn State-of-the-art AI in DeepMind Partnership', *UCL News* (20 January 2017) <http://www.ucl.ac.uk/news/students/012017/012017-200117-ucl-students-learn-state-of-the-art-AI-in-DeepMind-partnership> accessed 10 April 2020.

129 'University of Oxford teams up with Google DeepMind on Artificial Intelligence', Department of Computer Science, University of Oxford (1 November 2014) <https://www.cs.ox.ac.uk/news/847-full.html> accessed 10 April 2020.

130 Sheila Hayman [Director's Fellow of the MIT Media Lab], *The Guardian*, 3 November 2017 <https://www.theguardian.com/technology/2017/nov/03/google-deepmind-is-making-artificial-intelligence-a-slave-to-the-algorithm> accessed 10 April 2020.

131 Tyler Durden, 'Researchers Believe It's Possible To Become Immortal', Qresearch (20 March 2021) <https://www.zerohedge.com/technology/researchers-believe-its-possible-become-immortal> accessed 09 April 2021.

132 Alexey Turchin and Chernyakov Maxim, 'Classification of Approaches to Technological Resurrection', *PhilArchive copy v3* (5 October 2021) <https://philarchive.org/archive/TURCOA-3v3> accessed 28 March 2021.

133 Tyler Durden, *art. cit.*

134 John McCrone, 'Monkey Business', *Lancet Neurology*, 2/12 (December 2003), 772.

135 *ibid.*

136 Sergio Canavero, 'HEAVEN: The head anastomosis venture Project outline for the first human head transplantation with spinal linkage (GEMINI)', *Surgical Neurology International*, 4 (13 June, 2013), 335–42.

137 Sergio Canavero, '"I'll do the first human head transplant"' [interview] *The Guardian – Medical Research*, 3 October 2015 <https://www.theguardian.com/science/2015/oct/03/will-first-human-head-transplant-happen-in-2017> accessed 10 April 2020. See also *New Scientist*, Newsletter: Health (25 February 2015).

138 Sarah Knapton, 'World's First Human Head Transplant a Success, Controversial Scientist Claims', *The Telegraph*, 17 November 2017 <https://www.telegraph.co.uk/science/2017/11/17/worlds-first-human-head-transplant-successfully-carried> accessed 12 April 2021. See also Wang Xiaodong, 'Surgeons Transplant a Human Head', *China Daily* (21 November 2017) <https://www.chinadaily.com.cn/china/2017-11/21/content_34797003.htm> accessed 12 April 2021.

139 'Experts Weigh In on Head "Transplant"', *China Daily* (20 November 2017) <https://www.chinadaily.com.cn/china/2017-11/20/content_34777823.htm> accessed 12 April 2021.

140 'Head transplant', Wikipedia (last modified 3 June 2020) <https://en.wikipedia.org/wiki/Head_transplant> accessed 10 June 2020.

141 'Ted Williams Frozen in Two Pieces', *CBS News*, 20 December 2002 <https://www.cbsnews.com/news/ted-williams-frozen-in-two-pieces> accessed 10 April 2020.

142 'Letter to Leopold Mozart (4 April 1787)', in Andrew Steptoe, *The Mozart–Da Ponte Operas* (New York: Oxford University Press, 1988), 84. It is a tragedy that other than this letter which provides a strong clue regarding Mozart's intimations of immortality, all of Mozart's Freemasonic correspondence has disappeared.

143 Jocelyn Godwin, 'Layers of Meaning in "The Magic Flute"', *The Musical Quarterly*, 65/4 (October 1979), 471–492.

144 Paul Brunton, *In Search of Secret Egypt* (London: Rider, 1954), Chapter IV, 'A Night Inside the Great Pyramid' and Chapter XI, 'The Innermost Rite of Egyptian Temples'.

145 C. G. Jung, *Memories, Dreams, Reflections*, recorded and ed. Aniela Jaffé (New York: Vintage Books, 1961), 289–95.

146 Raymond A. Moody, Jr., *Life After Life: The bestselling original investigation that revealed 'near-death experiences'* (New York, HarperOne, 2015).

147 *VS*, Fragment I: The Voice of the Silence, 5.

148 Dr Massoud Homayouni, *The Origins of Persian Gnosis*, trans. F. J. Stone (London: Mawlana Centre, 1992), 24, quoted from Reynold A. Nicholson (trans. and ed.), *The Mathnawi* [*Masnavi*] *of Jalaluddin Rumi* (Lahore, Pakistan: Suhail Academy, 2011), 24.

149 'The Three Truths', in Mabel Collins: *The Idyll of the White Lotus* (BiblioLife, 2009), Chapter VIII; *Light on the Path* (London: Theosophical Publishing House, 1972), 11.

150 P. D. Mehta, *Zarathushtra: The transcendental vision*, foreword by Professor Noel King (UK: Element Books, 1985), 104–5.

A Mathematical Codicil: Mathematics Alludes to the World as Mind, the Matrix of all Matter

How can it be that mathematics, being after all a product of human thought which is independent of experience, is so admirably appropriate to the objects of reality?

ALBERT EINSTEIN[1]

I consider the ambition of overcoming opposites, including also a synthesis embracing both rational understanding and the mystical experience of unity, to be the mythos, spoken or unspoken, of our present day and age.

WOLFGANG PAULI[2]

The first epigraph was quoted by the Polish physicist and Rockefeller fellow at Cambridge University Leopold Infeld (1898–1968), who was none other than Albert Einstein's close colleague at the University of Berlin. It hits the proverbial nail on the head when Einstein muses about how it can be that a purely mental subject, like mathematics, 'being after all a product of human thought', can so admirably model the world of physical matter, 'the objects of reality'?

The second epigraph by Wolfgang Pauli, one of Einstein's highly esteemed colleagues, indicates how the question posed by Einstein might be addressed.

This Mathematical Codicil considerably extends these ideas in three parts: the first comprises a general appreciation for non-technical readers; the second will appeal to those who comprehend the eloquence of mathematical equations; and the third comprises reflective ideas from legendary mathematicians and sages.

A General Appreciation

Throughout these Volumes we have made the point, in various ways, that what appears to the normal physical senses as physical matter—and what mainstream science holds to be the primacy of matter (see Volume I, Chapter 4)—is quintessentially mental, that is, of the nature of the mind. A simplistic example of this distinction was given earlier in Chapter 8, page 150.

Staying for the moment with Einstein, the following two quotes, both by Einstein, supplement and amplify the first epigraph:

> Matter is conceived as being only space in a peculiar form.[3]

> We may therefore regard matter as being constituted by the regions of space in which the field is extremely intense…. There is no place in this new kind of physics both for the field and matter, for the field is the only reality.[4]

What are mind, force, and matter?

The British philosopher of science Karl Popper FRS famously declared: 'Materialism has thus transcended itself' (see Volume I, Chapter 4, page 35), thus echoing the above discoveries from modern physics by Einstein and his colleagues and further back to the pronouncement from the founding father of quantum physics Max Planck in his Nobel acceptance speech quoted. Quoted in Volume I, Proem, page xlv it bears repeating:

> As a man who has devoted his whole life to the most clearheaded science, to the study of matter, I can tell you as a result of my research about the atoms this much: There is no matter as such! All matter originates and exists only by virtue of a force which brings the particles of an atom to vibration and holds this most minute solar system of the atom together. We must assume behind this force the existence of a conscious and intelligent mind. This mind is the matrix of all matter.

What then is matter; and how is it that, 'All matter originates and exists only by virtue of a force', which therefore precludes the possibility of conceiving matter as an objective substance? The next section is an attempt to elucidate this theme.

How Does Matter Originate and Exist by Virtue of a Force?

We address this topic first by way of a simplistic geometrical illustration and then a brief outline on the contribution of quantum physics.

Figure III-41 shows a series of straight lines crossing at a central point. Let us suppose that each line represents an active force. We see that the locus of convergence approximates to the shape of a curve indicated by the black arc. If an infinite number of lines so converged, the curve would be perfectly smooth. The contention, however, is that the curve was not drawn, as such. It represents the 'outer skin', or appearance, as the aggregate resultant of the converging straight lines representing active forces as its originant.

Thus, pertaining to the esoteric philosophy, if we substitute 'spirit' for 'force', we see that spirit (the active, force-principle) and matter are correlated at any level of emantional descent from divine realms to the physical plane—see Chapter 8, Figure III-30, page 157.

Turning to quantum physics, Chapter 4 of Volume I, page 95 et seq. explained how it has broken down, not only the entrenched concepts of classical (materialistic) physics, but the philosophical implications of the latter. An intrinsic unity has been postulated to exist

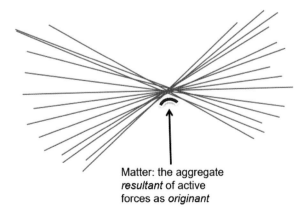

Matter: the aggregate
resultant of active
forces as *originant*

Figure III-41   A Geometrical Illustration of Matter as the Resultant of Force

at a deep level of the universe, that what we call matter is but a conglomeration of forces (as Max Planck affirmed—see above), and the interconnection of all parts of the universe has been shown by rigorous theory and punctilious, repeated experiments. It can only be a matter of time (excusing the pun) before the philosophical implications of such rarefied ideas of the latest physics pervade the collective consciousness of mainstream science, which is still firmly wedded to the classical paradigm, especially in biology and neuro-science. Regarding the latter, neuroscientists can generally be divided into two camps regarding their beliefs about consciousness: those who maintain that what we call consciousness is just another backstage output (epiphenomenon) generated by neural machinery; and those who challenge this, believing that consciousness is like a ghost in the machinery of the brain, meriting special attention and study in its own right.

Divided theories of consciousness from neuroscientists

Notwithstanding, the Harvard neurosurgeon Eben Alexander[i] observes that neuroscientists still believe the machine is real enough, and see the ghost as, well, just a ghost. It is hard for them to make the leap to realizing the ghost absolutely exists, but not the machine, at least, as they perceive it. The machine (physical brain, body, and world) exists within the realm of perception. They fail to realize the importance of acknowledging perceptions as just that, following Bishop Berkeley's famous principle, '*esse* is *percipi*' ('to be is to be perceived'),[ii] which the physicist John Wheeler echoed in his Participatory Anthropic Principle. Furthermore, there is Heisenberg's uncertainty principle (see below) pertaining to quantum physics.[iii] Alexander further pronounces that mainstream neuroscientists should realize that all aspects and properties of perceptions are filtered through the mechanism of ion channels and synaptic clefts on neurons in the physical brain. Such ion channels and synaptic clefts operate entirely within the quantum domain of the atomic and molecular level of existence, and are thus completely beholden to Heisenberg's uncertainty principle. Given this tight spatial confinement of such ions and neurotransmitters, the momentum vector[iv] becomes crucial in determining 'fire–no fire', the fundamental bit of neuronal communication. This is where the 'top-down' causal role of the mental realm of the universe comes into play, such that mind-over-matter becomes possible, enabling such things as the still imperfectly understood placebo effect[v] and spontaneous remission of

Neuroscience needs insights from quantum physics and philosophical idealism

---

i See the several references to Eben Alexander's ideas and referenced books, based on his personal near-death experiences, in this Volume in Chapter 8, page 162 and the Epilogue, page 318; Volume I: Chapter 2, page 15; Chapter 4, page 88; and Chapter 7, page 203 footnote.

ii George Berkeley (1685–1753) was an Anglo–Irish philosopher and an idealist. He held that ordinary objects are only collections of ideas, which are mind-dependent. He was also an immaterialist, maintaining that there are no material substances per se—only finite mental substances and an infinite mental substance, which he termed God, for which we have used the preferred term Divine Consciousness throughout these Volumes.

iii The anthropic principle is described in Chapter 10, pages 240 –242, and Wheeler's emphasis on the importance of a first person participatory anthropic perspective is outlined in Chapter 11, page 291. The uncertainty principle is explained in Volume I, Chapter 4, page 109.

iv Momentum is the product of mass and velocity. It is a vector quantity in that it possesses both magnitude and direction.

v The placebo effect is defined as a phenomenon in which some people experience a benefit after the administration of an inactive look-alike substance or treatment. The placebo effect (and its converse, the nocebo effect) represents the connection between mind and body. It is still imperfectly understood in mainstream science and psychology, albeit, often used as a prophylactic to explain away phenomena for which medical science can provide no satisfactory answers.

cancers and severe infections through the power of belief. Ultimately, idealism is the best explanation for this broad explanation of reality, though these materialist-thinking neuro-scientists are a very long way from appreciating the explanatory power of idealism.5

It is of profound significance that Carl Jung believed that the door to understanding the unity of spirit and matter would be found in the world of quantum physics and for many years he worked with the Nobel physicist Wolfgang Pauli trying to find it, as adumbrated in the section below on the predictive power of mathematics. (Apropos, the writer maintains that the deep friendship and collaboration between Wolfgang Pauli and Carl Jung, and David Bohm and Jiddu Krishnamurti clearly demonstrates that science, psychology, and philosophy are in perfect harmony and can engage in productive dialogue.)

Philosophical Propositions

As the Austrian–American logician, mathematician, and philosopher of mathematics Kurt Gödel (1906–1978) and Gregory Chaitin (*b.*1947), the Argentine–American mathematician and computer scientist have demonstrated, and have proved mathematically, truth cannot be entirely enclosed in any formal axiomatic system, no matter how complex this system is; which therefore points to there being always an inner, experiential aspect to mathematics.6

To expand on the above, the following extract from *Shadows of the Mind: A search for the missing science of consciousness* by the Nobel physicist Roger Penrose is especially noteworthy:

> Gödel's argument [in his incompleteness theorem] does not argue in favour of there being inaccessible mathematical truths. What it *does* argue for, on the other hand, is that human insight lies beyond formal argument and beyond computable procedures. Moreover, it argues powerfully for the very existence of the Platonic mathematical world.[7] Mathematical truth is not determined arbitrarily by the rules of some 'man-made' formal system, but has an absolute nature, and lies beyond any such system of specifiable rules. Support for the Platonic viewpoint (as opposed to the formalist one) was an important part of Gödel's initial motivations. On the other hand, the arguments from Gödel's theorem serve to illustrate the deeply mysterious nature of our mathematical perceptions. We do not just 'calculate', in order to form these perceptions, but something else is profoundly involved—something that would be impossible without the very conscious awareness that is, after all, what the world of perceptions is all about.8

Kurt Gödel and Roger Penrose argue that mathematical truths transcend formalism and mere calculation

Roger Penrose has, in effect, reinstated the Leibniz–Mill argument concerning the relationship between mentality and machines, by contending that 'human mathematicians are not using a knowably sound algorithm in order to ascertain mathematical truth;'9 and that 'intelligence cannot be present without understanding. No computer has any awareness of what it does.'10 The natural corollary, as stated by the contemporary American doctor and philanthropist, John Swanson is that 'the mind must employ indeterminate effects that can be described only by quantum mechanics or some new physical theory. Implicit in these speculations [by Penrose] is the concept that free choice is part of the microstructure of reality.'11

The 'absolute nature' of 'mathematical truth' to which Penrose refers might convey the impression that once mathematics has settled any issue, there is no further argument about it, which is not correct. *It is important to realize that a conclusion based on a mathematical solution can be correct only if it takes into account all factors involved in the enquiry*; if some factors are incorrect or omitted, or arbitrary assumptions are made, then the conclusions may be wrong or partially correct. A good example is Einstein's theory of general relativity which many physicists tacitly regard as the final verdict on the nature of space and time.[12] Monumental as this theory was at the time, and still is, it most certainly is not the last word on the nature of space and time as Einstein himself would surely have admitted—recall his own misgivings about his theories stated at the opening of Chapter 5, Volume I on page 133. Now Einstein based his theory only on the facts of the physical world (the shell of cosmos as occultists would say) and since subtler worlds do exist, then his theory cannot automatically be extrapolated to those realms. So relativity theory cannot be regarded as elucidating the nature of space–time in general, but only as they appear to the human mind working under the limitations of the human brain in the ordinary world of three dimensions of space and one dimension of time. For a more complete understanding of space–time, *the nature of mind must crucially be invoked* because mind is not only what finds its expression through the physical brain, but has innumerable overtones of subtlety and expression. Therefore, a total understanding of the nature of space and time must involve the whole of man at all levels.

Mathematical truths depend on completeness of all relevant factors

From Mathematics to Consciousness

As a natural corollary to the above, if undifferentiated Consciousness is the only Reality—underpinning the Universe in its subjective and objective aspects, unseen and seen, superphysical and physical, and all phenomena are modifications of Consciousness, or in Consciousness—then it follows, logically, that all phenomena and their underlying noumena are nothing other than *relations* in that underlying field of Consciousness. This is the reason why: (*a*) mathematics, being, in essence, the *mental science of pure relations*, must underlie the truth of all existence and, so also, must reflect that truth in every sphere of life and existence; and (*b*) why the entire manifested universe—physical and superphysical—must ultimately be based upon mathematics, when all factors are taken into account—a major proviso, as just stated.

Modern physics is pointing to the mentalizing of space and spatializing of time

Science is slowly converging towards acknowledging the role of mind. For example, string theory posits many higher dimensions above the familiar four dimensional space–time. Such higher dimensions must be in 'mental space' so to speak, otherwise the concept of higher order dimensions, mathematically formulated, is meaningless. On this subject, the most recent and comprehensive account on higher dimensions and mind is a book chapter by the mathematical physicist Bernard Carr.[13] A shorter and more accessible account proposing a new paradigm of matter, mind, and spirit can be found in the *Journal of the Scientific and Medical Network*.[14] How the gulf between matter and mind might be bridged by psychical research is contained in the *Proceedings of the Society for Psychical Research*.[15]

Further Examples on the Power of Mathematics, with Technical Details

This section is intended to provide no more than a foretaste of the power of mathematics in support of the thrust of this Codicil, and as a restrained response, so to say, to Einstein's question quoted in the first epigraph. It cannot be sufficiently stressed that the treatment is in no way comprehensive or definitive, which would require a detailed book of its own. Given this proviso, three further examples, supplemented with technical details, are provided in support of the theme of this Codicil—to demonstrate the power of mathematics in alluding to the physical word as mental in essence. They are intended primarily in the manner of the proverbial finger pointing at the moon—to evoke intuition.

Our first example is a purely mathematical derivation (that is, without any recourse to experimental data) of the physical constants in nature, and the human gestation period. The following two examples are written in the style of an opening exposition, then posing open-ended queries, followed by supporting arguments or inferences, which lead to ensuing propositions, and further musings.

Accordingly, our next example comprises a mathematical demonstration of what was stated earlier, namely, that a mathematical concept can only be fully complete and correct if all factors involved in the enquiry are taken into account; but when all factors have not been considered and checked for completeness the results will be different, incomplete or conflicting. This principle is then extended in relation to consciousness and the limits of the human brain expressed in terms of existing mathematical theories.

Our final example is a graphic demonstration of how, and why, mathematics—an entirely mind-based subject, it bears repeating—can simulate and predict phenomena in the physical and objective world.

The Predictive Power of Mathematics – Examples of Physical Constants of Nature and Human Gestation Period

Earlier in Chapter 10 on page 239, we stated the discovery by modern cosmology that numbers representing the fundamental physical constants and ratios of natural forces appear to be finely tuned for the existence of the universe and for life on Earth, citing the remark by the astrophysicist and cosmologist Lord Martin Rees in his book *Just Six Numbers*: 'These six numbers constitute a "recipe" for a universe. Moreover, the outcome is sensitive to their values: if any one of them were to be "untuned", there would be no stars and no life.'

Physical constants are numbers used by scientists in their calculations but unlike the constants of mathematics, such as Pi (π), mainstream science has not been able to establish the values of the constants of nature purely from first principles; their derivation depends on sophisticated laboratory measurements supported, in some cases, by theoretical relationships.

We now show, uniquely, it is claimed, how some fundamental constants can be deduced from first principles by mathematics alone. The two fundamental quantities chosen are:

❖ *Planck time*, which is the shortest time measurement that is possible due to the indeterminacy expressed in Werner Heisenberg's uncertainty principle. It is calculated from the Planck constant (Planck's constant), which relates the frequency of a radiation with its quantum of energy, strictly, the increase in energy of a photon (elementary particle transmitting light) when the frequency of its electromagnetic wave increases by unity (in Système International d'unités).

❖ *Fine structure constant*, which is derived from the charge on the electron, the velocity of light, and Planck's constant.

The human gestation period can also be so derived mathematically from first principles. This may not seem that surprising when we invoke the Hermetic Axiom and apprehend that the human being is a child of nature. The mathematical solution this applies to is the psychophysical problem. This is expounded in further detail below, but in summary, it is the problem which arises when an attempt is made to frame a complete description of an experience. Prima facie, the psychophysical problem seems fairly trivial, especially so when a description be framed in terms of an object and a subject. Closer consideration of the problem reveals, however, that it goes far deeper than this. As the Nobel physicist Erwin Schrödinger realized, using music as an example, science can describe the detailed acoustical mechanisms and neurological processes but is completely ignorant of the feelings of delight and sorrow, i.e., the experience, that accompanies the process. This is the Schrödinger Mind–Sensation problem fully referenced and described in detail in Chapter 8. The mathematical complement to the occult explanations provided in that Chapter is now described.

At face value, what follows may seem to make astounding claims. They are fully backed up with detailed evidence by the British mathematician and chemist Dr Ray Walder (*b.*1945) in *Experience and Essence*, a book of some 700 pages and over 200,000 words.[16] Walder qualified from the universities of London and Oxford, held a University Fellowship in mass spectrometry from Rice University in the USA, and pursued a professional career in industrial radio-chemistry. He took early retirement in order to devote all of his time to his book comprising the fruits of some twenty-five years continuous, detailed research. A technical paper in collaboration with the writer titled 'A Mathematical Solution of the Psychophysical Problem' presents the mathematical essence of the book.[17] An article co-authored with the writer written for the general reader, 'Confirmation of the Existence of an Ancient Worldwide Wisdom Religion' provides a qualitative justification for the assertions in the technical paper and book.[18]

The book, associated paper, and article take their principal inspiration from the intuitions of one of the most eminent scientists of the twentieth century golden era of quantum physics— Wolfgang Pauli. Quoted in the epigraph, it bears repeating: 'I consider the ambition of overcoming opposites, including also a synthesis embracing both rational understanding and the mystical experience of unity, to be the mythos, spoken or unspoken, of our present day and age.'[19] Not only a Nobel laureate held in the highest esteem by his peers, such as Heisenberg and Einstein, Pauli was also a mystic and a friend and collaborator of Carl Jung (see Volume I, Chapter 3 on Synchronicity, page 45). Pauli fathomed (spurred, undoubtedly, by his long discourses with Jung) that the psychophysical problem is the problem which arises when an attempt is made to frame a complete description of an experience. In the conventional view, experience is that which mediates between an object and a subject. A view based upon object and subject is, however, insufficient for finding a solution of the psychophysical problem and, in Walder's exposition, object and subject are put aside. Rather than consider the nature of the world in the third-person objective sense as does science, or the nature of the self in a first-person subjective sense as do many spiritual teachings, *experience* is considered as an entity in itself, an 'entity' which can be shown to possess its own structure.

Wolfgang Pauli's intuitions fully developed by Ray Walder

A possible structure for experience was indeed suggested by Pauli. It was the finest product of his intuition but now a structure for experience has been *derived* with mathematical rigour and shown to be just that structure which Pauli proposed.

How a structure for experience can be obtained and how it reveals that the mathematical form of the structure is precisely that suggested by Pauli, is outlined in the above mentioned technical paper (and expounded in meticulous detail in the foundational book on which it is based). This structure makes possible predictions of (qualitative) claims made within philosophical, religious, and esoteric texts—predictions that are often astonishingly accurate. It also allows the recovery of subject and object (the 'I' and the 'real world', as they might be termed) in forms that can be handled both semantically and mathematically.

The mathematical form and details of the structure of experience having thus been established, a good value of the fine-structure constant (of atomic spectra) can be derived from it: 7.291×10^{-3}, against the accepted value of 7.297×10^{-3}, CODATA[vi] 2021 (rounded). The fine-structure constant is, as explained above, the measure of photon–particle coupling—in other words, the measure of what it takes to decouple a photon from a particle, or, in the words of *Genesis* 1:4 (King James Version), that 'God divided the light from the darkness'. This 'measure' appears in the structure for experience—and at just the right point.

It can be seen that the value of the fine-structure constant derived from the Body of Experience is in agreement with the experimentally-determined value—suggesting that the statement in *Genesis* 1:4, that the first step of Creation (i.e., the process of experience arising) being the division of 'the light from the darkness', is apposite. Indeed, a similar statement has been made by the American Nobel physicist Richard Feynman (1918–1988): 'You might say the "hand of God" wrote that number [the fine-structure constant].'[20] It seems, then, that Moses, the claimed author of the *Book of Genesis*, had already arrived at this thought.

Mathematical underpinnings of theological precepts

Having yielded predictions of qualitative claims, the structure shows that the input of a key number (indicating a duration[vii]) from a Buddhist text[21] leads to a good prediction: first, for the human gestation period of 267.39 days, against the generally-accepted period of 266 or 267 days; and then for the smallest possible increment of time, the Planck time, 5.397×10^{-44} seconds, against the accepted value within science of 5.391×10^{-44} seconds, CODATA 2021 (rounded).

The quantitative investigation of the structure for experience, or 'Body of Experience' therefore proceeds from science to Buddhism, from Buddhism back to science, and from science to Judaeo-Christianity   all with numerical rigour. This numerical rigour arises from the mathematical basis of the work, but it must be emphasised that the mathematical basis does not imply that a thinking, feeling person can be reduced to a number or a mathematical equation. Far from it. However, as humanity's most fundamental understanding of All-That-Is is a mathematical understanding, it is to be expected that the ultimate nature of All-That-Is will be of a mathematical *form*.

---

vi Every four years, the Committee on Data for Science and Technology (CODATA) issues recommended values of the fundamental physical constants. The values are based on all the available theoretical and experimental information, determined by a least-squares adjustment (a statistical technique to estimate the most likely values in series of related data). The selection and assessment of data is done under the auspices of the CODATA Task Group on Fundamental Constants.

vii The number is 49 and it is of profound significance that it is a multiple of the number 7. See Volume II, Chapter 3, page 18 explaining the algebraic basis of 7, which number is anything but arbitrary.

The method demonstrates that consciousness is fundamental; it also shows that the real world is 'contained within' experience, rather than experience being acquired from the world. It may be noted that these demonstrations are outcomes of the internal self-consistency and mathematical formalism of the method itself and are wholly free of the requirement for any preconceptions. Readers who are uncomfortable with associating science with religion, via mathematics, would have all fears allayed from a careful perusal of another *magnum opus* on this subject—*The Mathematical Connection Between Religion and Science.*[22]

Structure of the Body of Experience – The Complex Unit Circle

This section outlines the mathematical aspects of the structure of the Body of Experience through, *inter alia*, exploration of the unit circle in the complex plane (centred on the origin). Wolfgang Pauli suggested (from intuition) that this circle—henceforth referred to as the 'complex unit circle'—will solve the psychophysical problem. As the contemporary Dutch physicist Herbert van Erkelens points out, Pauli regarded the complex unit circle as just that mathematical entity which 'may bring a new orientation to the world of science'.[23] The following quotation, in which Pauli is referring to the complex unit circle (translated as 'the ring with the *i*'), shows that he saw in such a circle the possibility of the 'grand unification' of psychological elements ('the instinctive or impulsive'), scientific elements ('the intellectual or rational'), and spiritual elements:

> It makes the instinctive or impulsive, the intellectual or rational, the spiritual or supernatural … into the unified or monadic whole that the numbers without the *i* cannot represent. … The ring with the *i* is the unity beyond particle and wave, and at the same time the operation that generates either of these.[24]

In 'Dr. Herbert van Erkelens: Wolfgang Pauli and the ring i', the contemporary consultant and IT Due Diligence practitioner Richard Irwin writes:

> Wolfgang Pauli discovered through his dreams and his active imagination 'The Piano Lesson' a dimension beyond quantum physics and depth psychology connected with love and synchronicity. A Chinese lady offered him in the Piano Lesson a ring that would enable to stay in contact with that dimension. Inside the ring there was an energy present, personified as an inner teacher and turned from lead into gold.[viii] The ring is known in mathematics as the complex unit circle and in physics as the heart of quantum physics. It is the ring *i* where *i* stands for the imaginary unit. The energy inside the ring represents a consciousness still unknown either to quantum physics or depth psychology, the sacred consciousness of the inner Christ.[25]

The form of the Body of Experience as the complex unit circle (centred on the origin)—i.e., the function $z = e^{i\theta}$ (in which θ is measured anticlockwise from the point marked I_1)—is shown in Figure III-42 overleaf. It should be noted that the orientation of the axes conventionally employed within mathematics has been reversed in order to maintain the representation of the flow of (developmental) time as 'upwards'.

---

viii Intriguingly in Richard Wagner's *Ring of the Nibelung*, the ring, created from gold, is the 'symbol of omnipotence, endowing its possessor with supernatural strength, with superhuman power over his fellows'—Alan Blyth, *Wagner's Ring: An introduction* (London: Hutchinson, 1980), 15–16.

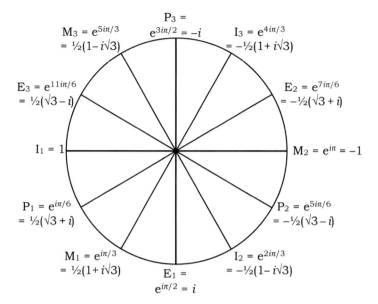

Ray Walder's
mathematical
formalization of
Pauli's intuition

Figure III-42   The Complex Unit Circle

Although description of the manner in which the symbols marking the points corresponding to stages in the development of experience were obtained is beyond the scope of this Codicil, it is fully detailed in Reference 16. It can be said that experience has been analysed in terms of four 'states'—designated 'I', 'P', 'M', and 'E', each of which appears in three 'modes' as indicated by the subscripts.

Consciousness and the Human Brain Mathematically Formulated

In this section we develop what was stated above, namely, a mathematical concept can be correct only if it takes into account all factors involved in an enquiry; but when all factors have not been considered and checked for completeness the results will be different, incomplete or conflicting. This theme is then extended in relation to consciousness and the limits of the human brain expressed in terms of existing mathematical theories.

The Exposition

Consider the scenario when taking limits for integration, not all functions are integrable over a given domain, for instance, if the area for that given domain is infinite. In general, a definite integral is integrated over an interval $[a, b]$ but there are no defined limits for an indefinite integral. The mental science of truth can be regarded as being analogous to the subconscious mind,[ix] which is a powerful influence that has no limits. It is unbounded and when the soul departs from its physical chrysalis, it is akin to an endless

---

ix For simplicity, the term 'subconscious mind' is used here in the conventional psychological sense of that which exists and/or operates outside of, and so not generally accessible to, ordinary, everyday consciousness (occult by speaking, the Lower mind, or *Kāma-manas*—see Volume II, Chapter 2, page 21). Broadly speaking, the subconscious mind may be related to the philosophical concept of 'extended mind' in that the mind is not exclusively restricted to the brain or even the body, but extends into the physical world and beyond.

hyperbolic function, over positive domain values $(0, \infty)$ in the case of $coshx$. In terms of the holographic universe concept, the hyperbola curve depicts the symmetry to the self and projected self. Mathematically, the concept of bounds and limits can be expressed in terms of *integration*. Integration is more than just the converse of differentiation (anti-differentiation, so to say). However, 'integration arose as a limiting case of a sum, where the individual summands [quantities to be added to another] tend to zero and the number of summands tends to infinity, and it is this aspect that is fundamental.'[26] *The Riemann Integral*—the first definition of an integral of a function—satisfied this philosophy that a bounded function f on a closed interval $[a, b]$ is bounded above and below. The question is what constitutes a function f to be defined as Riemann integrable on a bounded set $[a, b]$, $\int_a^b f$, defined as a definite integral? Conversely, when is a function not defined as Riemann integrable? If there is no upper limit for a function x on $[a, x]$, the result would be a function of x, referred to as an indefinite integral.

Consider a non-empty subset of S of a set $\mathbb{R}$.[x] If it is bounded above, it will consist of a least upper bound, referred to as the *supremum* and conversely if it is bounded below, it will have a greatest lower bound, known as the *infimum*.

Let f be a bounded function on a closed interval $[a, b]$, where $\{x_0, x_1, x_2, \ldots x_n\}$ denotes the set with the properties that

$$n > 1, \ a = x_0 \text{ and } b = x_n.$$

Denote the set $S(a, b)$, where f is bounded above and below on the interval $[a, b]$, for which the supremum and infimum can be defined as below:

$$\operatorname*{Sup}_{(x_{i-1}, x_i)} f = M_i, \quad \operatorname*{Inf}_{(x_{i-1}, x_i)} f = m_i$$

Where the supremum is the least upper bound, it is the least element that is greater than, or equal to, all the defined set elements; and where the infimum is the greatest lower bound, it the greatest element that is less than, or equal to, all the defined set elements.

From the axiom of completeness, a non-empty subset S of $\mathbb{R}$ is bounded above if $\exists b \in \mathbb{R}$, such that $\forall b \in \mathbb{R}$, $b \geq s \ \forall s \in S$. Therefore, S has a least upper bound (the supremum). Similarly, if S is bounded below, then $\exists c \in \mathbb{R}$, such that $\forall c \in \mathbb{R}$, $c \leq s \ \forall s \in S$. Take the set $-S = \{-s: s \in \mathbb{R}\}$, then $-c \geq -s$ and is therefore an upper bound for the set $-S$. Therefore, $-S$ has a least upper bound a and S therefore has a greatest lower bound $-a$ (the infimum).

Based on the supremum and infimum concepts, the area under the curve can therefore be defined and approximated by small summations as shown below:[27]

For the upper sum: $U(f, S) = \sum_{i=1}^{n} M_i(x_{i-1}, x_i)$

For the lower sum: $L(f, S) = \sum_{i=1}^{n} m_i(x_{i-1}, x_i)$

Mathematical insights into zero and infinity, limits and bounds

---

x   In mathematics, a 'set' is a collection of distinct elements which can be any kind of things, such as people, letters of the alphabet, numbers, points in space, lines, other geometrical shapes, variables, or even other sets.

Therefore, it is clear to see that the lower sum is less than the upper sum and the following result is shown below:

$L(f, S) < U(f, S)$ and thus $U(f, S) <= \sum_{i=1}^{n} M_i(x_{i-1}, x_i) = M \sum_{i=1}^{n} (x_{i-1}, x_i) = M(b-a)$

and $L(f, S) >= m(b-a)$.

Hence, $L(f) = \sup_{s \in \Pi} L(f, S)$ and $U(f) = \inf_{s \in \Pi} U(f, S)$

The upper integral of the function f is defined by the following:

$$\int_a^{\overline{b}} f = \inf \{U(f, S): S \in S[a, b]\}$$

The lower integral is defined by the following:

$$\int_{\underline{a}}^b f = \sup \{U(f, S): S \in S[a, b]\}$$

Hence the set of all the lower Riemann sums is bounded from above by $M(b-a)$ and similarly the set of the upper Riemann sums is bounded from below by $m(b-a)$, as depicted in the diagram below.[28]

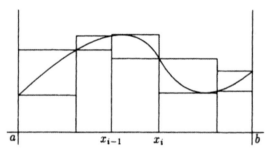

To emphasize this concept of partitioning the summations into small intervals and to illustrate the diagram above, a comparison to *The Trapezium Rule* used in Numerical Analysis for definite integrals can be made. The idea is that the area under a curve is approximated by dividing the area into small trapeziums under the curve and then the area of these trapeziums can be computed. The computation involves taking the difference between the upper and lower limits, in the interval $[a, b]$ and dividing this difference by the total number of trapeziums to achieve the perpendicular height h, required for the Trapezium area. The sum of the parallel sides is computed by evaluating the function at these incremental x values.

Mathematically, expressed as $\frac{h}{2}[y_0 + 2(y_1 + y_2 + y_3 + \cdots + y_{n-1}) + y_n]$,

where $h = \dfrac{b-a}{n}$, n = the number of trapeziums.

This is an example of how approximations can be used to evaluate integrals using numerical method techniques. A Riemann sum partitions the area under the curve with shapes, like trapeziums, and uses the end values of each subinterval but introduces the supremum and infimum methods evaluated at these subintervals and subsequently totals all the subintervals. These values then converge. The errors involved with this computation are reduced by dividing the areas into smaller intervals. This gives rise to smaller shapes, similar to the approach of partitioning the area into smaller but significantly more trapeziums in the Trapezium Rule defined earlier.

The upper sum represents the approximations above the curve and the lower sum the approximations below the curve.

It therefore follows that a function *f* is Riemann integrable if the infimum of the upper sums and the supremum of the lower sums are equivalent.

Mathematically expressed as $\int_{\underline{a}}^{b} f = \int_{a}^{\overline{b}} f$, where $L(f) = \int_{\underline{a}}^{b} f, \quad U(f) = \int_{a}^{\overline{b}} f$.

Hence Riemann integrable is defined as $L(f) \leq U(f)$.

To comprehend this, we need to consider limits, such that if a limit exists, then a function is bounded above and has a least upper bound, the supremum; and equally bounded below with a greatest lower bound, the infimum.

To check if a limit exists, then a function evaluated at its domain, $f(a)$, must be defined, the limit evaluated as *x* approaches *a* $\underset{x \to a}{lim} f(x)$ must exist and the value of the function at *a* must be equivalent to the limit as *x* tends to *a*. If the limit evaluated yields an indeterminate form, such as, $\frac{0}{0}$ or $\frac{\infty}{\infty}$, such that the limit is not clear, l'Hôpital's rule can be applied until a limit is found.[xi] This can involve differentiating a significant number of times until a limit is reached.

However, the Riemann Integral does not exist for those functions with high oscillations that, in some cases, are non-continuous, as discontinuous functions could be evaluated between intervals where the functions are continuous and unbounded, for example, and therefore cannot be applied in some cases. *This is an example which demonstrates the significance of taking all factors into consideration to ensure a function can be integrated and to identify criteria of when it can be used.*

Therefore, for completeness, all functions need to be considered for an application of a Riemann Integral. Considering the piecewise function, Riemann sums can be applied to these types of functions, where although the function is not continuous, if the function can be divided into subintervals that are continuous on finite domains, then Riemann Integrals can be implemented.

Conversely, if taken over positive infinity and negative infinity bounds, a function could either converge to a limit or diverge. In the case of the former, this would be *mathematically analogous to the soul 'returning' to Earth*; and in the case of the latter, the function tends to infinity, which is *mathematically synonymous to the limitless, or extended mind and the soul exitus from the body.*

Polarity, non-duality, and extended mind viewed through a mathematical lens

For example, the special type of Riemann Integrals, known as *improper Riemann integrals*, where if the domain includes negative or positive infinity a limit still exists. If the function is improper, then the following case holds:

$$\int_{-\infty}^{\infty} f(x)\,dx = \underset{b \to -\infty}{lim} \int_{b}^{a} f(x)\,dx + \underset{b \to \infty}{lim} \int_{a}^{b} f(x)\,dx,$$

for some value of *a* that is defined.

---

xi L'Hôpital's Rule provides a technique to evaluate limits of indeterminate forms by converting the latter to an expression that can be evaluated by substitution.

Query I

If a function, when taken over positive infinity and negative infinity bounds, either: (*a*) converges to a limit, or (*b*) if it diverges, in which case the function tends to infinity, is this the mathematical equivalent for the soul exitus from its material limitations in the former, and in the latter, to the limitless, or extended mind?

In that case, does the human mind behave in a manner analogous to Riemann Integrals, in that a function defined on a closed and bounded interval is Riemann-integrable if, and only if, it is continuous on that defined interval? By the same token, does this apply to the human mind which uses only a small proportion of its brain power which is closed and bounded by this mathematically expressed limitation or restriction?[xii]

However, if the domain of the integral is unbounded and the function is discontinuous then the Riemann Integral is not defined; analogously, does the subconscious mind (as defined in footnote ix earlier) behave analogously like an unbounded function that 'contains', or 'stores' everything and is interpreted as existing outside of, or rather, as an extension of, the normal, everyday consciousness, which is limited?

Argument I

In the above exposition, particularly regarding the supremum and infimum, this is derived from the axiom of completeness itself (see page 359). To comprehend the reality of limits and boundaries in the projected world, once parameters are considered, then intervals will exist between these parameters and thus be limited and/or restricted to these boundaries, etc. A parameter could be a deadline, which may or may not be realistic and therefore this activity, event, mental concept, etc. is closed and bounded by this deadline. Generally speaking, therefore, human minds in reality impose limits due to constraints which, in an ever-changing world that is evolving as humans evolve, is conceptually justified. The expectations and reality of the current manifested world was 'envisaged' as Divine Thought in Divine Mind subsumed in Supreme Consciousness, and has subsequently been externalized, or brought into manifestation (see the emanational process depicted in Chapter 7, Figure III-25, page 128).

Proposition I

It would seem reasonable to propose that normal consciousness may be mathematically represented by closed and bounded intervals of continuous functions; and the subconscious by those functions not Riemann-integrable, or by improper Riemann Integrals, if a limit is defined as approaching infinity, but never quite reaching it (i.e., asymptotically), hence 'subconsciousness' which is limitless.

Mathematically, only when all factors are taken into consideration (i.e., all mathematical arguments in all mathematical disciplines are applied) will completeness and accuracy be achieved. Likewise, the perception of all things seen and in existence, namely, mental states

xii Refer to the releasing, or permissive, function of the brain expounded by William James, outlined in Volume I, Chapter 6, page 168.

of mind (perceptions and concepts) will be limited and bounded unless a condition of utter inner clarity is achieved whereby subtle factors not normally accessible are brought into focus. This is the state of *pure observation*—a rare attainment indeed.

Query II

Can the mathematical formulation of dissection (outlined below) be applied to dissect meaning, here, to penetrate the deeper layers of the human brain into subintervals to reveal the subconscious?

Argument II

Riemann Integrals can be implemented on unbounded intervals if the function converges, hence if a limit exists, when as the function tends to infinity the integral approaches its real value. Conversely, the function $f = \frac{1}{x}$ is not Riemann integrable $\int_0^1 \frac{1}{x}\,dx$, as it is not defined at 0; in fact it has a vertical asymptote at $x = 0$ and a horizontal asymptote evaluated at $f(0)$. Therefore, the supremum is infinity and thus the upper Riemann summands are not well defined. Similarly, if on an unbounded interval, where the dissection into subintervals comprises an unbounded interval, then the function is not Riemann integrable.

Proposition II

Consciousness *per se* and the subconscious mind are unbounded, and those dimensions of the brain that are not used are 'seen' or experienced by the subconscious mind, for example, in dreams or mystical vision when the limitation imposed by the ego is held in abeyance. Hence, mathematically speaking, in this state there are no real limits, no closed or bounded set and therefore no supremum or infimum, only infinity which is larger than any real number. However, the function converges, symbolizing how all minds unite to one Over Mind.

Query III

Considering the transformation from everyday consciousness to the Supreme Consciousness and the eternal Divine Knowledge present in that transformation, is this a mathematical concept, derived mathematically or do the mathematics behind this transformation cease upon a particular transformation?

Argument III

Take the transformation from Cartesian to polar coordinates to solve the *Gaussian integral* named after the German mathematician Carl Friedrich Gauss (1777–1855), in the integration below that has no known antiderivative:

$$\int_{-\infty}^{\infty} e^{-x^2}\,dx,$$

How can this be solved? Without Divine Knowledge how can a concept first begin to manifest itself in the mind? Invoking the following mathematical techniques:

❖ squaring the above yields

$$\left(\int_{-\infty}^{\infty} e^{-x^2}\, dx\right)^2 = \left(\int_{-\infty}^{\infty} e^{-x^2}\, dx\right)\left(\int_{-\infty}^{\infty} e^{-x^2}\, dx\right)$$

❖ changing the variable gives

$$\left(\int_{-\infty}^{\infty} e^{-x^2}\, dx\right)\left(\int_{-\infty}^{\infty} e^{-y^2}\, dy\right)$$

❖ factorising

$$\iint e^{-x^2} e^{-y^2}\, dxdy = \iint e^{-(x^2+y^2)}\, dxdy$$

❖ transforming to polar coordinates gives

$$x = r\cos\varnothing, \quad y = r\sin\varnothing$$

❖ using the Jacobian to transform to polar, the *Jacobian Determinant* yields

$$\begin{vmatrix} \dfrac{dx}{dr} & \dfrac{dx}{d\varnothing} \\[2mm] \dfrac{dy}{dx} & \dfrac{dy}{d\varnothing} \\[2mm] \dfrac{dx}{d\varnothing} \end{vmatrix} = \begin{bmatrix} \cos\varnothing & -r\sin\varnothing \\ \sin\varnothing & r\cos\varnothing \end{bmatrix} = r$$

❖ using the range for the radius from 0 to ∞ and the range for ø from 0 to 2π, the solution to the integral is shown below:

$$\iint_{0}^{\infty} re^{-r^2}\, drd\varnothing = \left[-\frac{1}{2} e^{-r^2}\right]_{0}^{\infty} = 0 - -\frac{1}{2}$$

$$\int_{0}^{2\pi} \frac{1}{2}\, d\varnothing = \pi$$

we arrive at one of the most significant and astonishing of all numbers that has inspired countless mathematicians and philosophers for centuries, namely:

$$\left(\int_{-\infty}^{\infty} e^{-x^2}\, dx\right)^2 = \pi, \text{ so } \int_{-\infty}^{\infty} e^{-x^2}\, dx = \sqrt{\pi}$$

The transformation of the integration yields an irrational number that is approximately 3.141592653589793238 to 18 decimal places. In March 2019, π was computed to 31.4 trillion decimal places. Historically, the Babylonians and Egyptians recognised the importance of the circumference to diameter ratio around 2000 BC when multiplying the radius squared by 3 to compute the area of a circle; and later the Greek mathematician Archimedes (*circa* 287 – *circa* 212 BC) approximated π in his discovery that the circumference to diameter ratio approximated to less than $3\frac{1}{7}$, and greater than $3\frac{10}{71}$. The Pi symbol was introduced in 1706 by the Welsh mathematician William Jones FRS (1675–1749), a close friend of Isaac Newton and Edmund Halley; and later in 1737 by Leonhard Euler (1707–1783), the Swiss mathematician.

Do equations represent the thoughts of God?

Proposition III

The above analysis shows that *π can be expressed as the result of the infinite sum series that tends to, i.e. converges to, π!*

Fundamentally, then, this irrational, infinite number, π, that is derived from a transformation of Cartesian to polar coordinates, to solve an integration with unbounded limits, may be thought to represent, in mathematical terms, Divine Knowledge accessed from consciousness to the Supreme Consciousness. Stated otherwise, this irrational number is proposed as being the result of the movement, or transfer of everyday consciousness—when rendered quiescent—from the normal four-dimensional physical world towards the unknown multi-dimensions of Divine, or Supreme Consciousness—the incandescent spiritual world.

If the above seems reasonable then we should not be surprised by Srinivasa Ramanujan's famous remark that unless an equation represents a thought of God, it would have no meaning for him (see Chapter 9, page 207).

Reflections

We must bear in mind, constantly, that 'Mathematical truth is not determined arbitrarily by the rules of some 'man-made' formal system, but has an absolute nature, and lies beyond any such system of [arbitrary or] specifiable rules,' as affirmed by no less an authority than Roger Penrose (see page 352 above). An equation is emphatically not the same as an algorithm which is a set of 'specifiable rules' or a series of instructions for computation. Our exposition has attempted to show how the 'absolute nature' of the mathematical equations presented, 'being after all a product of human thought which is independent of experience' as Einstein stated (see the epigraph), have pointed to the primacy of Mind and Consciousness. Thus, *mind (rather, thought, the product of mind), has pointed to its own origins in Mind subsumed in Supreme Consciousness.*

The next section attempts to elaborate further Einstein's question about how 'the objects of reality' can be so well explained and understood by what is purely 'a product of human thought which is independent of experience.'

An Example of Mathematics Used to Solve Problems in the Objective, Physical World

Computational fluid dynamics is a branch of fluid mechanics that uses numerical analysis and data structures to analyse and solve fluid flow problems. Computers are used to perform the calculations required to simulate the free-stream flow of the fluid, and the interaction of the fluid (liquids and gases) with surfaces, defined by boundary conditions and starting conditions. The fundamental basis of almost all computational fluid dynamics problems is the *Navier–Stokes equations*, in their complete or simplified version depending on the complexity of the problem. The details do not concern us here. What is of note is that the Navier–Stokes equations are a set of partial differential equations which mathematically express the conservation of momentum and conservation of mass for Newtonian fluids,[xiii] thus describing the motion of viscous fluid substances. The equations comprise a time-dependent continuity equation for conservation of mass, three time-dependent conservation of momentum equations, and a time-dependent conservation of energy equation.

One form of the Navier–Stokes equations for compressible Newtonian fluids is:[29]

---

xiii Newtonian fluids are characterized by a linear relation between the fluid shear stress and the shear rate.

$$\rho \left(\frac{\partial \mathbf{u}}{\partial t} + \mathbf{u} \cdot \nabla \mathbf{u} \right) = \underbrace{-\nabla p}_{2} + \underbrace{\nabla \cdot (\mu (\nabla \mathbf{u} + (\nabla \mathbf{u})\mathrm{T}) - \frac{2}{3} \mu (\nabla \cdot \mathbf{u}) \mathbf{I})}_{3} + \underbrace{\mathbf{F}}_{4}$$

$$\underbrace{\phantom{\rho \left(\frac{\partial \mathbf{u}}{\partial t} + \mathbf{u} \cdot \nabla \mathbf{u} \right)}}_{1}$$

The fundamental laws of fluid dynamics

where u is the fluid velocity, p is the fluid pressure, ρ is the fluid density, and μ is the fluid dynamic viscosity. The different terms correspond to the inertial forces (1), pressure forces (2), viscous forces (3), and the external forces applied to the fluid (4). The equations were derived in the early 1800's by the French engineer and physicist Claude-Louis Navier (1785–1836) and Anglo–Irish physicist and mathematician Sir George Gabriel Stokes PRS (1819–1903).

How Do the Fluid Dynamics Equations Apply to Simulation and Modelling?

These equations are at the heart of fluid flow modelling. The equations, bare and abstract in themselves, are *unsolvable*. They can only be solved by limiting their application to a specific scenario. Thus, solving them, for a particular set of boundary conditions (i.e., defining the spatial boundaries of the field of application), and initial conditions (i.e., specifying the starting time and duration), and fluid properties (such as density and viscosity) predicts the fluid dynamic behaviour in a given geometry for a specific application. Because of their complexity, these equations only admit a limited number of analytical solutions as, for instance, flow in a circular pipe where a greatly simplified version of the equations can be used. For more complex geometries, however, the equations need to be solved using computational numerical techniques.

The essence of fluid dynamics modelling

Three fundamental factors are needed for the simulation: (1) defining the field of interest by enveloping it in a mathematical mesh, or web of intersecting grid lines; (2) inputting the fluid dynamics equations, i.e., Navier–Stokes equations and fluid physical parameters at each intersection of the grid lines, i.e. at each grid point; and (3) setting the 'starting' conditions, i.e. boundary and initial conditions. An example of this procedure is shown in Figure III-43. It shows a computational simulation of the evolvement of smoke from a fire to a train at the London Paddington North Pole deport, a centre for train maintenance.

Referring to Figure III-43, the top picture shows the London Paddington North Pole depot.

How smoke evolvement from a fire to a train is simulated

Seen in the middle is a schematic representation of the depot with six trains. Note the roof trusses with two vents. This establishes the boundaries of the field of interest.

The bottom diagram shows a mathematical simulation of the evolvement of smoke through the two roof vents resulting from a fire to one of the trains. (Animation software was used to highlight the light and dark regions corresponding to different concentrations of smoke.) This simulation was achieved by imposing a mathematical grid over the field of interest, and then inputting the Navier–Stokes equations to each grid cell. Running the simulation over several minutes entailed the iterative transfer of mathematical information from cell to cell. This transient phenomena could be regarded, imaginatively, as the 'firing' of 'mathematical neurons', covering the entire domain; thus, as an analogue, to the firing of neurons in the brain producing phenomena, objective to our senses.

It is stressed that the resulting smoke pattern is not a photograph of smoke from an actual fire on a train. It simulates, mathematically, the evolvement of smoke from a fire that *would*

Picture of the London Paddington North Pole Depot

Image Credit: Wikimedia Commons/Hitachi Europe/North Pole Train Maintenance Centre 2015.jpg

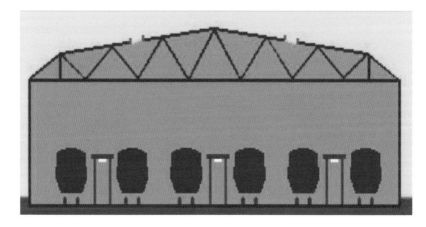

A Schematic Representation of the Depot, Showing Six Trains
and Two Vents in the Roof Trusses

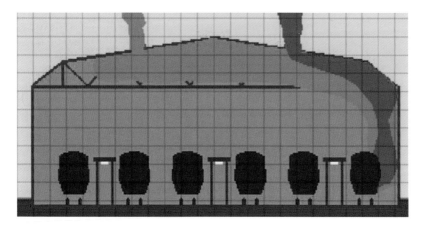

Mathematical Simulated Pattern of Smoke Evolvement from a Fire to One Train

Figure III-43   A Mathematical Simulation of Smoke Evolvement from
a Train on Fire

happen, in practice, in a real-life situation, should the physical conditions correspond to those applied to the mathematical simulation. The greater the refinement of the grid, the more closely would the simulation follow the contours of the actual (hypothetical) smoke movement. (The actual simulation had over 30,000 cells; obviously, only a few are shown in Figure III-43 for clarity.)

Leaving aside further technicalities, what can we intuit about the principal thrust of this simulation and indeed, this Mathematical Codicil as a whole—that mathematics shows that the world, apparently physical, is in fact mental, or mind-based in essence? Let us drive ourselves to ask some searching questions.

Queries

1. Let us terminate the simulation by switching off the computer. What would happen? The simulated smoke pattern would obviously be 'extinguished'.

   But does that mean that the laws of fluid dynamics, mathematically represented by the Navier–Stokes equations, and computer software coded, would be extinguished as well?

2. So when this particular *form* in which the fluid laws are expressed (i.e. smoke evolvement) has been terminated, do the underlying laws *themselves* become annihilated? If so, then aeroplanes which also rely on the *self-same laws* would not be flying at this moment, 'as we speak'.

   [margin note: Distinguishing between the form (phenomenon) and its animating principle (noumenon)]

3. Does the death of the form mean the annihilation of the animating principle behind the form?

4. Are the laws of fluid dynamics an epiphenomenon of the mathematics and software coding? Stated otherwise, does the firing of the 'mathematical neurons' around the field of enquiry (the mathematical grid) produce the fluid laws as a by-product, or is the 'firing' the means whereby the fluid laws—ubiquitous, invisible, and intangible in themselves—are rendered visible and tangible when constrained to a particular form of expression in space and time?

5. When the physically manifest form (smoke patterns in the simulation) changes and dies, do the Unmanifest laws (the fluid dynamics laws mathematicized as the Navier–Stokes equations) themselves die with the form?

Phenomena (in this case, the manifestation of smoke patterns) are dependent on their noumena, i.e., their causative ideas on a higher level (in this case, the laws of fluid dynamics), and ultimately, on Ideas in Universal Mind. However, the reverse is not true, i.e. an idea is not dependent upon its vehicle of expression except insofar as the vehicle is the means of its expression and that its *manifestation* is limited by the 'fit for purpose' aspect of the vehicle. As a simplistic example, if the lip of a water jug is chipped, it will still pour water, but not in the neat way that a pristine jug would do.

Inferences

1. Mathematics is a purely mental subject. We cannot use mental scaffolding to frame a physical edifice. So if the physical world can be modelled, or represented, by mathematics, then is not the so-called physical world really mental in essence—intrinsically of the nature of Mind? The so-called physical is thus a phenomenal appearance to our five senses of Mind as Noumenon.

2. Before the Channel Tunnel, the Paddington North Pole depot, or whatever, were physically constructed, where did they exist? Obviously, in Mind. And where will they exist after their transitory life-cycle has run their useful course and they are abandoned or crumble to dust? Arguably, still in Mind.

Forms are transitory; their noumena ever subsist

Can the paradox of quantum superposition be applied to this fire scenario in one of the trains, which implies that although the simulation has stopped, the states of fire and no-fire are in existence simultaneously? Can we argue that the quantum physics branch of mathematics prevails and continues even after the simulation has stopped but the fire has not been extinguished? (This is, of course, invoking the 'Schrödinger's cat' thought experiment that illustrates a paradox of quantum super-position, such that a hypothetical cat may be considered simultaneously both alive and dead as a result of its fate being linked to a random subatomic event that may or may not occur.[30])

4. If we were to take a scalpel to dissect the computer and scrutinize each component under a microscope, would we discover the computer code, or the mathematics or the laws of fluid dynamics—the *fluidic consciousness*, so to say? For that, surely we need to look beyond physical mechanisms because scalpels and microscopes will reveal the component hardware, but they can never cut a window to reveal the soft-ware code, let alone the mathematical equations so coded or the laws of fluid dynamics themselves.[xiv]

5. By analogous reasoning, if our mind=brain is no more than an electro-chemical mechanism—just biological computers 'made out of meat', as the majority of scien-tists would assert, then, can Consciousness *per se*—not its expression and behav-iour—ever be discovered by dissecting the brain? Can Consciousness be an epiphenomenon of brain neurons as mainstream neuroscientists would dogmatize, any more than the fluid laws might be a by-product of their mathematical representa-tion? Therefore, when the brain dies, the manifestation of consciousness using the brain is indeed extinguished at death, but Consciousness in itself never 'dies' and seeks newer forms of Self-expression.

Propositions

The physical world, man-made or natural, is an appearance to our senses of the activity of Mind—a deeply occult tenet promulgated by sages and legendary scientists since time immemorial, as also by the greatest of modern scientists like Arthur Eddington, James Jeans, Werner Heisenberg, and Wolfgang Pauli.

We propose the following esoteric analogies following directly from the mathematical simulation exampled.

---

xiv Would quantum computing in the coming era be able to invoke the *superposition principle* to solve multiple states simultaneously? With traditional computers, each problem is solved and tested individually, in terms of binary operations; is it 0 or 1? However, the principle of *quantum computing* is that both 0 and 1 are repre-sented simultaneously, even if a state is not observed, hence, instead of looping through all possible scenarios, and testing until criteria are met and then outputting the desired result, all combinations are considered all at once.

Mathematical Situation	Esoteric Analogue
The Navier–Stokes equations *in themselves* are *unsolvable*.	CONSCIOUSNESS *per se* is unbounded and unlimited.
The equations can only be solved by limiting their application to a specific scenario, as in the mathematical simulation of smoke evolvement.	The *manifestation* of CONSCIOUSNESS is dependent on, limited by, and conditioned by, its vehicles of expression.

Let us expand on the above by invoking the subtle distinction between *Brahman* and *Iśvara*.

1. As used in the Vedas and Upaniṣads, Brahman refers to the ultimate reality of the universe, in other words, the unmanifest Primordial Reality underlying the universe. Iśvara means the presiding Deity of a *manifested* solar system. Brahman is not transformed into the world. Chapters 7 and 8 have explained in detail that what we call 'creation' or 'manifestation' is, in reality, a process of explication, or emanation. The One Brahman appears as the manifold entities of the world—an illusory appearance, a *māyā*. Analogously, the Navier–Stokes equations are not themselves transformed into solutions. The One set of equations presents innumerable solutions as manifold aspects of 'itself', depending on the field of application.

2. The Navier–Stokes equations, thus, represent the pure 'consciousness' of all fluid phenomena, and that consciousness is reflected into each and every aspect of its solutions. Analogously, REALITY—the Supreme Consciousness—is mirrored and reflected in all manifestation. In man, our consciousness exists by virtue of the fundamental Deific Consciousness 'sparked' into us. So when our ignorance presents us with an appearance of manifold vision and multiplicity of disconnected events, and when we fail to appreciate the One Reality as their substratum, then perhaps we should remember that the many separate manifestations of fluid flow are all rooted in the One Reality of the Navier–Stokes equations.

Discerning the unmanifest from the manifest

3. Brahman is attributeless. Iśvara is with attributes; it is the God of the phenomenal Universe (or the presiding Deity of a manifested solar system as stated above), as it is 'the personal God—*divine Spirit in man*',[31] the latter, perhaps in one sense, akin to *Ātma*.

4. Where do we sense the analogy with Iśvara in our simulation? Iśvara is, analogously, the case of the Navier–Stokes equations particularized for a specific fluid scenario—smoke evolvement from a train fire in the simulation above. Whereas the Navier–Stokes equations, unsolvable in themselves, apply in an abstract sense to all fluid phenomena, their limited applications pertain to specific scenarios. So, for example, the Navier–Stokes equations particularized for the simulation just described would not apply to, say, smoke evolvement from an oil tanker fire, which would need the *same* equations limited with different boundary conditions and fluid properties. *For 'unsolvable', substitute 'unmanifest'; for 'particular application' substitute 'manifestation', or 'universe'; for 'different boundary conditions and fluid properties' substitute 'different conditions in space and time'—and our point is made*: the appearance, the description, bears a relation to, but must not be

Mathematics reveals the distinction between the unmanifest and the manifest

confused with the described, as the map is related to, but is not the same as the territory.

Reflections – Drawing the Threads Together

The mental logic applied to generate proofs derived from this logic and to form equations so that mathematics can be applied to physical problems, provides the evidence required that the physical world is archetypally mental. The human mind identifies the problem and then subsequently creates a methodology to solve the problem with a thought process, not yet brought into existence. This thought process then yields incredible results such as Newton's law of gravitation, which began with an enquiring mind, followed by an action to seek answers, and finally the solutions, based on evidence and proof. Consider the above simulation on the evolvement of smoke using the mathematical formulation of the laws of fluid dynamics. This problem fundamentally involves the laws of conservation, one of which is the conservation of mass, which concept arose from a *thought process* in the *mind* of Leonhard Euler in 1757, albeit disputed as to whether the concept (referred to as 'The Continuity Equation for fluids') was actually derived by either the Swiss mathematician Johann Bernoulli (1667–1748) or his son, Daniel Bernoulli FRS (1700–1782). Be that as it may, the solution is based on the mathematical calculus[xv] with the application of differential equations. *The result is the 'bringing into existence', the materialization of such enquiring thoughts, that is, the formation of ideas into reality with the application of mathematics, hence the physical world is manifested through mathematics, a purely mental subject*—'a product of human thought which is independent of experience'.

Mind expressed as matter via mathematics

Did mathematics manifest the physical world or is it an application that provides the foundations that the physical world can be modelled or represented thereby? Is the physical world the externalization of the mental world expressed through a mental subject—mathematics?

In which case, are mathematical numbers the *upādhis*,[xvi] or vehicles of expression for Ideal Numbers (abstract Ideas and Archetypes) which, in turn, are upādhis for Divine Numbers—the Powers and Attributes of the One? Thus, to give an example, there is the figure 2 (mathematical number) which is the upādhi for the *idea* of two-ness (the duad). This in turn might be the upādhi for the Divine Number, the Duad as God's reflection of Himself—the Transcendental Immanence. The numbers 1 to 10 are of course fundamental and called the Tetractys by Pythagoras.

Numbers in their common, abstract, and transcendental meaning

Is Divine Consciousness the mathematical equivalent of integration from $-\infty$ (infinity) to $+\infty$; and normal, everyday consciousness, integration over defined limits? *Pondering long and hard over these questions we do perhaps come to realize that mathematics characterizes Consciousness and thereby encompasses the unseen, noumenal origin of the objective world.*

---

xv The differential calculus may be regarded as the process whereby the One becomes the Many—the Many being the derivatives of the One. Conversely, the integral calculus may be viewed as the synthesis of the Many Derivatives to the One—an aspect of the One pervading, or reflected into all its constituents, the Many.

xvi See Volume II, Chapter 3, pages 35–7 for a fuller exposition on the meaning and significance of upādhi.

Finale

Thus we see that there exists an eternal wisdom–religion known to the sages of all cultures since time immemorial. For, as this Codicil has attempted to show, there is an *essence*— CONSCIOUSNESS, if you will—which can be discovered simply through the investigation of *experience* as an 'entity' in itself.

The following three quotes have figured prominently in these Volumes but are seminal to the subject of this Codicil and bear repeating.

The non-primacy of what mainstream physicists take to be the primal stuff of the universe was uttered to his student Carl Friedrich Freiherr von Weizsäcker by Werner Heisenberg, when close to death:

> I see now that physics is of no importance, that the world [of physical matter] is illusion.[32]

In that case, what *is* the fundamental stuff of the universe?

As Friedrich von Schiller put it:

> The Universe is a thought of the Deity. Since this ideal thought-form has overflowed into actuality, and the world born thereof has realized the plan of its creator.[33]

Schiller's cosmic vision perfectly affirmed by that supreme mathematician, the young Srinivasa Ramanujan, who, as mentioned on page 365, saw in his mind's eye the harmony between mathematics and mind:

> An equation has no meaning for me unless it represents a thought of God.[34]

The Voices of Great Souls echo down the Ages—their words enshrining and bearing that which is ineffable—Truth. We close with three verses from the Vedas—the timeless, and oldest, sacred texts of India. So poetically expressed in Edwin Arnold's *Light of Asia*, the words of the wise live in our hearts forever—each a dewdrop which brings us closer to the Shining Sea of Truth.[35]

> *Universal Order and Truth.*
> *were born of blazing spiritual fire,*
> *and thence night was born, and thence*
> *the billowy ocean of space.*
>
> *From the billowy ocean of space*
> *was born Time—the year*
> *ordaining days and nights,*
> *the ruler of every moment.*
>
> *In the beginning as before,*
> *the Creator made the sun,*
> *the moon, the heaven and the earth,*
> *the firmament and the realm of light.*

ṚG-VEDA X. 190. 1–3

NOTES

1   'Albert Einstein', quoted by Leopold Infeld, *Today in Science History* <https://todayinsci.com/E/Einstein_Albert/EinsteinAlbert-MathematicsHumanQuote800px.htm> accessed 12 May 2021.

2   Wolfgang Pauli, *Writings on Physics and Philosophy*, ed. Charles P. Enz and Karl von Meyenn, trans. Robert Schlapp (Berlin, Heidelberg, New York: Springer-Verlag, 1994). See also: *Gnostic Science and Literalist Science (2/2)* <https://www.scienceandnonduality.com/article/gnostic-science-and-literalist-science-22> accessed 23 July 2021; *goodreads* <https://www.goodreads.com/quotes/1064831-a-synthesis-embracing-both-rational-understanding-and-the-mystical-experience> accessed 14 May 2021.

3   A. Einstein, B. Podolsky, and N. Rosen, *The Physical Review*, 48/1 (1 July 1935).

4   Albert Einstein quoted in: Dr K. N. Prasanna Kumar, Prof B. S. Kiranagi, and Prof C. S. Bagewadi, 'Of Void (Vacuum) Energy and Quantum Field – A Abstraction–subtraction Model', *IOSR Journal of Applied Physics*, 1/1 (May–June 2012), 9; Milič Čapek, *The Philosophical Impact of Contemporary Physics* (Princeton: Van Nostrand, 1961).

5   Reworded e-mail correspondence from Eben Alexander to selected members of Galileo Commission of the Scientific and Medical Network, 9 June 2021.

6   Gegory Chaitin, 'The Limits of Reason', *Scientific American*, 294/3 (2006), 74–81.

7   Platonic mathematics is any metaphysical account of mathematics that implies mathematical entities exist, that they are abstract, and that they are independent of all our rational activities. See Julian C. Cole, 'Mathematical Platonism', Internet Encyclopedia of Philosophy <https://iep.utm.edu/math-plat> accessed 13 May 2021.

8   Roger Penrose, *Shadows of the Mind: A search for the missing science of consciousness* (London: Vintage, 2005), 418–9.

9   —— *op. cit.*, 76.

10   Quoted in John Swanson, *God, Science and the Universe: The integration of religion and science* (Durham, Connecticut: Eloquent Books, 2010), 260.

11   —— *loc. cit.*

12   A popular exposition is by Albert Einstein, *Relativity: The special and general theory*, trans. Robert W. Lawson (London: Routledge, 1993).

13   B. J. Carr, 'Hyperspatial models of matter and mind', in *Beyond Physicalism: Toward reconciliation of science and spirituality*, ed. E. Kelly, et al. (US and UK: Rowman & Littlefield Publishers, 2015), 227–73.

14   B. J. Carr, 'A Proposed New Paradigm of Matter, Mind and Spirit', *Journal of the Scientific and Medical Network*, 103 (2010), 3–8.

15   B. J. Carr, 'Worlds Apart? Can Psychical Research Bridge the Gulf Between Matter and Mind?' *Proceedings of the Society for Psychical Research*, 59 (2008), 1–96.

16   Ray Walder, *Experience and Essence* encompassing *Natura Naturans: Unification of the Material and the Spiritual*, and *De Anima et Spiritu* (Unpublished manuscript for private circulation, 2007).

17   Ray Walder in collaboration with Edi Bilimoria, 'A Mathematical Solution of the Psychophysical Problem Substantiated by the Prediction of the Human Gestation Period, the Planck Time, and the Fine-Structure Constant', cited with abstract in *Journal of the Scientific and Medical Network*, 110 (2012), 40.

18   Ray Walder and Edi Bilimoria, 'Confirmation of the Existence of an Ancient Worldwide Wisdom Religion – Transforming Belief into Knowledge', *The Theosophist*, 134/7 (April 2013), 14–19.

19   Wolfgang Pauli, 'Writings on Physics and Philosophy'.

20   Richard Feynman, *QED: The strange theory of light and matter* (London: Penguin Books, 1985), 129.

21   See W. Y. Evans-Wentz, *The Tibetan Book of the Dead* (Oxford: Oxford University Press, 1960).

22   Stephen Phillips, *The Mathematical Connection Between Religion and Science* (Eastbourne, UK: Anthony Rowe Publishing, 2009).

23   See H. van Erkelens, 'Wolfgang Pauli and the Spirit of Matter', in *Proceedings of the Symposium on the Foundations of Modern Physics 1990 – Quantum Theory Measurement and Related Philosophical Problems, Joensuu, Finland*, ed. Pekka Lahti and Peter Mittelstaedt (Singapore, New Jersey, London, Hong Kong: World Scientific, 1990), 425–39.

24 The quotation is, according to H. van Erkelens, from Pauli's very personal essay *Die Klavierstunde –
    Eine aktive Phantasie über das Unbewusste* [The Piano Lesson – An Active Fantasy About The
    Unconscious] and is given as translated by van Erkelens (in the previous reference). The original
    work is, again according to van Erkelens, held in the archives of the public research university ETH
    Zürich (where Pauli worked for most of his life) in the section *Wissenschafthistorische Sammlungen*
    [Science History Collections], Hs 176:85.

25 Richard Irwin, 'Dr. Herbert van Erkelens: Wolfgang Pauli and the ring *i*', *The Scientific and Medical
    Network*, 31 July 2016 <https://scientificandmedical.net/herbert-van-erkelens-wolfgang-pauli-and-
    the-ring-i> accessed 23 July 2021.

26 John M. Howie, *Real Analysis* (London: Springer-Verlag, 2001), 119.

27 —— *op. cit.*, 119–20.

28 —— *op.cit.*, 120.

29 There are several formulations of the Navier–Stokes equations. The one cited is taken from
    'Navier–Stokes Equations', *Multiphysics Cyclopedia*, cited in Wikipedia (last modified 22 February
    2017) <https://www.comsol.com/multiphysics/navier-stokes-equations> accessed 17 May 2021.

30 Erwin Schrödinger, '*Die gegenwärtige Situation in der Quantenmechanik*' ['The present Situation in
    Quantum Mechanics'], *Naturwissenschaften*, 23/48 (November 1935), 807–12.

31 *TSGLOSS*, 158.

32 *NPB-6, Part 2: From Birth to Rebirth*, 'The Event of Death', ¶ 104, 16.

33 *Theosophie des Julius* [Theosophy of Julius] © 2015 www.werkvermächtnisse.de <http://
    www.archiv-swv.de/pdf-bank/Theosophie%20des%20JuliusSchillerOriginal.pdf> accessed 7 July
    2021.

34 Shiyali Ramamrita Ranganathan, *Ramanujan, the Man and the Mathematician* (Bombay, NewYork:
    Asia Publishing. House, 1967), 88.

35 Edwin Arnold, *The Light of Asia Or, The Great Renunciation (MAHÂBHINISHKRAMANA) being The Life
    And Teaching Of Gautama, Prince of India and Founder of Buddhism (as told in verse by an Indian
    Buddhist)* (Boston: J. R. Osgood & Co., 1885). See also Inspiration Series, p. 132
    <https://universaltheosophy.com/pdf-library/Light%20of%20Asia.pdf> accessed 23 August 2021.

Endnotes to Volume III

Endnote III-1 Evidence possibly in Support of Cellular Memory

This extract concerns an eight-year-old girl who received the heart of a ten-year-old girl who was murdered. Shortly after receiving her new heart, the girl began having recurring nightmares about the man who had murdered her donor. She believed she knew who the murderer was. Her mother finally brought her to a psychiatrist and after several sessions, the psychiatrist 'could not deny the reality of what the child was telling her'. They decided to call the police and, using the descriptions from the little girl, the murderer was found. According to the psychiatrist, 'the time, the weapon, the place, the clothes he wore, what the little girl he killed had said to him … everything the little heart transplant recipient reported was completely accurate.'[1]

Psychological insights from heart transplants?

Some physicians and scientists have tried to gain an understanding of cellular memory through psychological, metaphysical, and even supernatural means, whilst others have disputed the veracity of the alleged claims. One can see why they would go to these unconventional lengths in order to try and explain, or disprove, cellular memory when faced with such disturbing incidents as just described (disturbing, that is, to a scientific orthodoxy still immersed, to a great degree, in crudely materialistic theories about memory and consciousness).

Endnote III-2 Bibliography on the Chakras

C. W. Leadbeater, *The Chakras: A monograph*, Theosophical Publishing House, 1947.
David V. Tansley, *Subtle Body: Essence and shadow*, Thames and Hudson, 1988.
Alice Bailey, *Esoteric Psychology*, Vol. II, Lucis Press, 1972.
H. P. Blavatsky, *The Secret Doctrine*, Theosophical Publishing House, 1993.

Endnote III-3 Root Races and Prehistoric Continents

Occult science teaches that the consciousness of humanity *in toto* passes through seven main developmental stages, each such stage called a Root Race. If we bring to mind the analogous process of seven stages that occur in the life of each human being, this is not as far-fetched as it sounds. Through each stage the consciousness of the same person uses vehicles of greater complexity that enable the innate potentiality greater degrees of self-expression. The developmental stages of a human being are the same for every racial type. Just so, the developmental stages of the Root Races that have nothing to do with ethnicity but apply to humankind. This is another example of the Hermetic Axiom: what applies on the small scale—to the human individual—applies on the large scale—to humanity.

As each human being, so the human races show distinct phases

Each Root Race is divided into seven minor Races which are in turn subdivided into subraces, etc. This division is not arbitrary. Each subrace displays its unique characteristics within the overall traits of the parent Root Race, just as an individual teenager would display different kinds of behaviour that are all characterized by adolescent traits. In the human being there is considerable overlapping of behaviours, for example between adolescence and maturity (as every parent would testify). Similarly, Root Races do not follow each other in sequential order with a definite cross-over point, but overlap each other and this overlapping likewise occurs within minor and 'branchlet' Races.

The subject of Root Races is inextricably connected with that of Racial Cataclysms as in the biblical flood narrative (Book of Genesis, Chapters 6 to 9) and similar accounts from other religions and cultures worldwide.

The whole question of Root Races and Racial Cataclysms is ever fascinating in its enormity and complexity. For serious enquiry into the matter of tracing the evolutionary history of the Root Races on Earth the reader is referred to:

- ❖ H. P. Blavatsky, *The Secret Doctrine*, Theosophical Publishing House, 1993.
- ❖ G. de Purucker, *Fundamentals of the Esoteric Philosophy*, Theosophical University Press, 1979.
- ❖ J. S. Gordon, *The Path of Initiation: Spiritual evolution and the restoration of the Western mystery tradition*, Inner Traditions, 2013.
- ❖ Geoffrey Barborka, *The Peopling of the Earth: A commentary on archaic records in* The Secret Doctrine, Theosophical Publishing House, 1975.
- ❖ Geoffrey A. Barborka, *The Story of Human Evolution: Written in the form of a commentary on the Stanzas of Dzyan*, The Theosophical Publishing House, 1980.
- ❖ Basil Crump, *Evolution: As Outlined in the Archaic Eastern Records*, Luzac & Co., 1930.
- ❖ An extremely simplified outline is given in Geoffrey A. Farthing, *Deity, Cosmos & Man: An outline of esoteric science*, Point Loma Publications, 1993.

Endnote III-4 Scientific Evidence about Rays from the Human Eye

1. Extract from the journal *The New York American*, dated 30 March 1933, about an instrument for detection of 'Life Waves' from a photograph of a person:

> It [the instrument] detects the movement of 'life waves' or 'Z waves' on a photographic plate, and the stillness of these waves after the death of the subject was reported to-day [i.e., in 1933] by E. S. Shrapnell-Smith, one of Britain's noted scientists. Shrapnell-Smith, an authority on chemistry, said, 'Life, like a radio station emits a distinct type of wave. These human life waves are transmitted to and fixed in a photographic plate. When the subject of the photograph is alive, movement of the waves is lively. The moment the person dies, no matter how far distant from the photograph, the life waves cease to emanate from the plate. I am unable to reveal at present just what the instrument consists of. But it is based and depends on first, radiation; second, magnetism; third, static electricity; and fourth, current electricity. There is nothing psychic or mysterious about it. It is a result of a new application of the laws of science.

The eye is also an organ of projection

2. Further scientific evidence about the rays from the human brain and eye was provided by:

❖ The Italian psychiatrist Professor Ferdinando Cazzamali (1887–1958) of the University of Milan who invented an apparatus for demonstrating electromagnetic waves sent out by the brain and affecting sensitive instruments in the room. He describes them as cerebral radio waves of short wavelength.[2]

❖ The late English scientist and doctor Charles Russ (MB Lond., MRCS Eng., &c) who invented an instrument (British Patent # 124,288, 24 March 1919) which can be set in motion by the mere impact of human vision. He had reflected on the fact that the direct gaze of one person soon becomes intolerable to another person, and this suggested to him that there might be a ray or radiation emanating from the human eye. Dr Russ gave demonstrations with his apparatus before various scientific societies.[3, 4] A full description of the apparatus, methodology, checks, data, and results is provided in http://www.rexresearch.com/russ/russ.htm (accessed 31 March 2020).

Commenting on the above,[5] Rupert Sheldrake states that the results are remarkably consistent with his findings published in his book *The Sense of Being Stared At*.[6] Typically, about 55% of the guesses are right, as opposed to 50% expected by chance. Repeated over tens of thousands of trials this result becomes astronomically significant statistically. In experiments in which the same subjects were tested repeatedly and given trial-by-trial feedback, there was a striking learning effect, with a significant improvement in scores with practice. In a German school, with repeated testing, some 8 to 9 year-old children achieved accuracies as high as 90%.[7]

The 'sense of being stared at effect' is widely replicable, with many studies yielding positive results. In Russia the phenomenon has been known for decades.[8]

Endnote III-5 Planetary Rounds, Kosmic Planes, and Human Principles

The phrase 'Planetary Rounds' is used in occultism in a specific way to denote the passage of the 'life wave' once round all the seven globes of a Planetary Chain. A Planetary Chain is a series of seven globes, six subjective and one objective (physical); for example, our Earth, which has six companion globes, three preceding it and three succeeding it in evolutionary development. The Chain preceding the Earth Chain is said to have been the Lunar Chain.

Planets, like the human body, are subject to cyclic evolution

The subject of Rounds is inextricably linked to Root Races and in fact is often referred to in occult literature as 'Rounds and Races'.

For serious enquiry into the doctrine of Planetary Rounds, as riveting as it is a massive and complex subject, the reader is referred to:

❖ H. P. Blavatsky, *The Secret Doctrine*, Theosophical Publishing House, 1993.
❖ G. de Purucker, *Fundamentals of the Esoteric Philosophy*, Theosophical University Press, 1979.
❖ Geoffrey A Barborka, *The Divine Plan: Written in the form of a commentary on H. P. Blavatsky's* The Secret Doctrine, Theosophical Publishing House, 1980.

❖ J. S. Gordon, *Self-Consistent Kosmos*, Orpheus Publishing House, 1995.
❖ An extremely simplified outline is given in Geoffrey A. Farthing, *Deity, Cosmos & Man: An outline of esoteric science*, Point Loma Publications, 1993.

Endnote III-6 The Allegory of Plato's Cave

The 'Allegory of the Cave' is featured in Book VII of Plato's *The Republic*.[9] It depicts a group of prisoners who have lived their entire lives chained to the wall of a gloomy cave. So they mistake the shadows cast on the cave walls—appearances—for realities. Only when one of the prisoners breaks free and walks outside does he realize that the shadows are ephemeral and their source is the light from outside the cave entrance thrown on to the walls.

Plato's cave allegory illustrates tunnel vision and intellectual myopia

The profound import of this allegory (similar to the underwater marine allegory in Chapter 10) is that knowledge, or rather, information, acquired through the senses and constrained by their viewpoint—*is no more than opinion*; and that real knowledge can be gained only by a wider outlook and through philosophical reasoning that transcends the limitations of the physical senses.

There is no shortage of examples of the cave allegory: doctors trained exclusively in Western medicine disparaging homœopathy without ever bothering to step outside their own allopathic cave; astronomers despising astrologers without realizing that the paradigms of astronomy and astrology are quite dissimilar; atheist scientists despising religious people without bothering to understand the different metaphysical standpoints of science and religion; persons of one religion attacking those of another without seeking out the unifying thread that binds all great religions. Readers will have little difficulty in adding substantially to this list of cerebral myopia!

Endnote III-7 Partners and Links with the Galileo Commission

Shown below are the Partners and links with the Galileo Commission as of January 2021 and their websites accessed on 22 January 2021.

Science, Spirituality, and Esotericism

Academy for the Advancement of Post-Materialist Sciences
> To inspire scientists to investigate mind and consciousness as core elements of reality.
> *https://www.aapsglobal.com/*

The Laszlo Institute of New Paradigm Research
> New Paradigm Research is a transdisciplinary inquiry into humanly and socially relevant ideas and conceptions emerging above all in the sciences, but also in social media and other areas of contemporary culture.
> *https://laszloinstitute.com/*

The Society for Scientific Exploration
> Since 1982, the SSE has provided a critical forum for sharing original research into conventional and unconventional topics.

https://www.scientificexploration.org/

The Study Society

Promotes moral and spiritual welfare by encouraging individuals to pursue a journey towards Self-realisation—realisation of their full potential—through experience of the true nature of Consciousness and its deep level of stillness, truth and love.
https://www.studysociety.org/

Université Interdisciplinaire de Paris

The objective of the UIP is to disseminate and compare knowledge, based on the study of contemporary scientific paradigms—mainly in the fields of astrophysics, quantum physics, theories of Evolution , neurosciences and philosophies of the mind.
http://www.uip.edu/

Institute of Noetic Sciences

A nonprofit organization dedicated to supporting individual and collective transformation through consciousness research, transformative learning, and engaging a global community in the realization of our human potential.
https://noetic.org/

Science And Nonduality

SAND is a community inspired by timeless wisdom, informed by cutting-edge science, and grounded in direct experience. We come together to explore the big questions of life while celebrating the mystery of being. SAND is a place for an open-hearted, authentic connection with people who are drawn together to explore what it means to be a human being, standing at the intersection of spiritual inquiry, science, social healing, and the arts.
https://www.scienceandnonduality.com/

Psychiatry, Psychology, and Parapsychology

British Psychological Association – Transpersonal Psychology Section

Transpersonal Psychology addresses the spiritual nature of humankind. Unlike religion and theology, its interest centres on the mind and behaviour; hence it is a branch of Psychology.
https://www.bps.org.uk/member-microsites/transpersonal-psychology-section/

British Psychological Society – Consciousness and Experiential Psychology Section

Consciousness was the original focus of psychological research and is once more a central topic of inquiry.
https://www.bps.org.uk/member-microsites/consciousness-and-experiential-psychology-section/

Royal College of Psychiatrists Spirituality and Psychiatry SIG

The Spirituality and Psychiatry Special Interest Group (SPSIG) was founded in 1999 to provide a forum for psychiatrists to explore the spiritual challenges presented by psychiatric illness, and how best to respond to patients' spiritual concerns.
https://www.rcpsych.ac.uk/members/special-interest-groups/spirituality/

The Parapsychological Association

The PA is the international professional body for the scientific and scholarly study of 'psi' (or 'psychic') experiences, such as telepathy, clairvoyance, remote viewing, psychokinesis, psychic healing, and precognition.

https://www.parapsych.org/

Religious Experience and Paranormal Phenomena

Alister Hardy Society for the Study of Spiritual Experience

Supports the work of the Alister Hardy Trust and Religious Experience Research Centre (RERC), and provides a focal point for people interested in the nature and study of spiritual, religious, and psychic experiences.

https://www.studyspiritualexperiences.org/

The Society for Psychical Research

Set up in London in 1882, the first scientific organisation ever to examine claims of psychic and paranormal phenomena.

https://www.spr.ac.uk/

Science and Religion Forum

The SRF had its inception in a series of discussions involving scientists, theologians, and clergy which took place in Oxford in the early 1970s.

https://www.srforum.org/

Holistic Medicine and Healing

Anthroposophic Medicine

An international, integrative medical movement celebrating nearly a century of caring for the whole human being, at the levels of body, soul, and spirit.

https://anthroposophicmedicine.org/

British Holistic Medical Association

A grassroots membership organisation of mainstream healthcare professionals, complementary and alternative medicine (CAM) practitioners, and members of the public.

https://bhma.org/?sfw=pass1611316886/

EUROTAS

The European Transpersonal Association developed from a group of practitioners of health and healing and researchers in sciences and spirituality. It was founded in 1984 during the first European Transpersonal Conference in Brussels, organized by the Belgian team.

https://eurotas.org/

The Pari Center

Conceived as a haven of peace and gentle action in a world increasingly gripped by turmoil. In adopting Carlo Levi's maxim that 'the future has an ancient heart' we look to the future while bearing in mind the wisdom of the past.

https://paricenter.com/

Consciousness and Near-Death Studies

Center for Consciousness Studies, University of Arizona
A unique institution whose aim is to bring together the perspectives of philosophy, the cognitive sciences, neuroscience, the social sciences, medicine, and the physical sciences, the arts and humanities, to move toward an integrated understanding of human consciousness.
  https://consciousness.arizona.edu/

Division of Perceptual Studies (DOPS), University of Virginia
Founded in 1967 by Dr. Ian Stevenson, DOPS is a highly productive university-based research group devoted to the investigation of phenomena that challenge mainstream scientific paradigms regarding the nature of the mind/brain relationship. Researchers at DOPS are particularly interested in studying phenomena related to consciousness functioning beyond the confines of the physical body, and phenomena that suggest continuation of consciousness after physical death.
  https://med.virginia.edu/perceptual-studies/

Existential Consciousness Research Institute
Unites and connects scientists, researchers, thinkers, authors, and pioneers from different disciplines. Questions around the research and development of consciousness are not only theoretical but focus concretely on the human being and being human in a constantly changing world. We are convinced that the social and ecological challenges of our time require new perspectives and solutions, which begin with a new way of creating consciousness for oneself and the world.
  https://www.ecr-inst.com/en/

International Association for Near-Death Studies (IANDS)
Founded in 1980 and is the oldest organisation dedicated to the Near Death and related experiences.
  https://www.iands.org/

International Consciousness Research Laboratories
ICRL is a consortium of individuals from all walks of life, united within a shared passion: understanding consciousness for a better tomorrow.
  http://icrl.org/

The Foundation for Mind-Being Research (FMBR)
Established in 1980 to assist in the creation of integrated models of human consciousness, models that encompass the physical, mental and spiritual aspects of the human experience. The objective was to bring the then-new field of consciousness studies into wider recognition as a bona fide field of science, and to explore whether consciousness arises out of physical matter (i.e., the brain) or whether it is a state of matter unto itself.
  https://fmbr.org/

Educational Institutes and Colleges

Alef Trust

A not-for-profit community-interest organization offering online transformational Graduate Programmes and Open Learning Courses for academic, professional, and personal development.

https://www.aleftrust.org/

Schumacher College

Attracts students from over 90 different countries, of all ages and backgrounds, drawn by its reputation for cutting-edge learning relating to ecology and sustainability.

https://www.schumachercollege.org.uk/

The Philosophy, Cosmology, and Consciousness program at California Institute of Integral Studies

The Philosophy, Cosmology, and Consciousness program at California Institute of Integral Studies is dedicated to re-imagining the human species as a mutually enhancing member of the Earth community. Our program attracts intellectually engaged individuals who are in varying degrees dismayed by what they see happening in modern societies and who are striving to find meaningful ways to develop their gifts to serve the future of the world. The program supports those called to meet the earth community's unprecedented evolutionary challenge by offering a rigorous and supportive learning community in which students find their voice and vision as leaders.

https://www.ciis.edu/academics/graduate-programs/philosophy-cosmology-and-consciousness/

Worldwide Indigenous Science Network (WISN)

Founded in 1989 as a result of meetings between indigenous women, elders, and Western scientists. Today our membership includes tribal elders, scientists, conservationists, scholars, and women's organizations from cultures around the world. All share a common vision of rediscovering and applying ancient wisdom for today's time. We coordinate a global network of indigenous Elders and are advocates for at-risk indigenous practitioners and traditional knowledge.We conduct research, host international conferences, and cultural exchanges and with academic partners offer advanced degree programs in Indigenous Mind.

https://wisn.org/

The Centre for Myth, Cosmology and the Sacred

This unique and ground-breaking project in transformative learning combines creative expression, personal reflection, and study of esoteric wisdom and contemporary exploration of the sacred. Our academic programme is formally ending in 2021, and our new web platform provides an archive of our work and publications, whilst also moving forward with new courses, lectures, podcasts, community building, and much more.

https://mythcosmologysacred.com/

Manifesto for a Post-Materialist Science

Signatories of the manifest for post-materialist science believe that the sciences are being constricted by dogmatism, and in particular by a subservience to the philosophy of materialism, the doctrine that matter is the only reality and that the mind is nothing but the physical activity of the brain. They also believe that the sciences would be more scientific if they were free to investigate the natural world in a truly open way—without the constraints of materialism and the prejudice of dogma—while adhering to the scientific methods of data collecting, hypothesis testing, and critical discussion. If you wish to show your support, you are invited to become a signatory and have your name added to the growing list.

https://opensciences.org/about/manifesto-for-a-post-materialist-science/

Skeptical About Skeptics

Dedicated to countering dogmatic, ill-informed attacks leveled by dogmatic skeptics on pioneering scientists and their research. Healthy skepticism is an important part of science, as in all walks of life, but some skeptics use it as a weapon to defend their dearly held ideology. Naturally, this inhibits free inquiry as certain ideas and lines of research are denigrated and the careers of scientists who pursue them anyway are threatened. They believe in a purely material world, a clock-work universe filled with machine-like creatures. They believe living minds are nothing more than brain chemistry, that consciousness is an illusion and automatically dismiss any evidence to the contrary.

https://www.skepticalaboutskeptics.org/

NOTES

1   Paul Pearsall, *The Heart's Code* (New York: Broadway Books, 1998).
2   *Zeitschrift für Parapsychologie* [Journal of Parapsychology], Leipsic; cited also in: *Popular Science Monthly* (February 1928); Bernard Hollander, *Methods and Uses of Hypnosis and Self-Hypnosis (Psychology Revivals): A treatise on the powers of the subconscious mind* (UK and US: Routledge, 2015).
3   Charles Russ, 'An Instrument which is Set in Motion by Vision or by Proximity of the Human Body', *Lancet*, 198/5109 (30 July 1921), 222–4.
4   Arthur Grahame, 'The Power that Lies in Your Eyes', *Popular Science*, 107/3 (September 1925), 24.
5   Brendan D. Murphy, 'How we Sense When We Are Being Stared At' (2012) <https://blog.world-mysteries.com/science/how-we-sense-when-we-are-being-stared-at> accessed 2 March 2020.
6   Rupert Sheldrake, *The Sense of Being Stared At and Other Aspects of the Extended Mind* (UK: Arrow Books, 2004).
7   R. Sheldrake, 'The Sense of Being Stared At, Part 1', *Journal of Consciousness Studies*, 12/6 (2005), 10–31.
8   Sheila Ostrander and Lynn Schroeder, *Psychic Discoveries Behind the Iron Curtain* (New York: Bantam Books, 1971), 121–2, 139.
9   Plato, *The Allegory of the Cave*, trans. Benjamin Jowett (US: CreateSpace Independent Publishing Platform, 2017).